Cognitive Psychology

Cognitive Psychology

John B. Best

Eastern Illinois University

WEST PUBLISHING COMPANY

ST. PAUL   NEW YORK   LOS ANGELES   SAN FRANCISCO

Copyeditor: Joan Torkildson
Composition: Graphic World Inc.
Cover design: Delor Erickson

Library of Congress Cataloging-in-Publication Data

Best, John B.
    Cognitive psychology.

    Bibliography: p.
    Includes index.
    1. Cognition. I. Title.
BF311.B485 1986   153   85-22708
ISBN 0-314-93154-6

In memory of my daughter Adrienne

CONTENTS

PREFACE   xiii

PART I   INTRODUCTION   1

**CHAPTER 1   Cognitive Psychology: Definition   2
                and Problems**

OVERVIEW   3

INTRODUCTION TO COGNITIVE PSYCHOLOGY   4
Neisser's Definition of Cognition   4
Kinds of Knowledge and Types of Processing   6
Topics of Cognitive Psychology   10

THE ROOTS OF COGNITIVE PSYCHOLOGY   13
Human Factors at Work during   16
   World War II
Broadbent's Studies   16
Computing Machinery   17
Linguistics   19
Skinner's Book and Chomsky's Rebuttal   20

THE FACE OF CONTEMPORARY COGNITIVE   23
PSYCHOLOGY
The Information-Processing Approach   23
   An Abstract Analysis   23
   Methods in Cognitive Psychology   28
Ecological Validity   29

CONCLUDING COMMENTS AND SUGGESTIONS   30
FOR FURTHER READING
FOCUS ON RESEARCH   30
KEY TERMS   31

PART II   PERCEPTION   33

**CHAPTER 2   Attention and Pattern   34
                Recognition**

OVERVIEW   35

THE NATURE OF ATTENTION   36
Definition   36
Problems with Definitions of Attention   36
Studies of Selective Attention   37

BOTTLENECK THEORIES OF ATTENTION   38
Filter Theory   38
Attenuation Theory   41
Late Selection Theories   43
Conclusions from the First Phase of Theory   46
   Building

ALTERNATIVES TO FILTER THEORIES: 47
CAPACITY MODELS
Some Questions Concerning Capacity   51
   Models

The Relationship between Practice and Attention ... 52

AUTOMATICITY ... 53
Conclusions from the Second Phase of Theory Building ... 56

PATTERN RECOGNITION ... 57
Template-Matching Theory ... 57
Feature Detection Theory ... 59
Independent Confirmation of Feature Analysis ... 61
 Biological Contributions ... 63
Context ... 66

CONCLUDING COMMENTS AND SUGGESTIONS FOR FURTHER READING ... 68
FOCUS ON RESEARCH ... 70
KEY TERMS ... 71

CHAPTER 3   Constructivist and Direct Theories of Perception ... 72

OVERVIEW ... 73

THE CONSTRUCTIVIST POSITION ... 74
The Höffding Step ... 74
The Constructive Nature of Perception ... 75
 Illusions ... 76
 Initial Summary of the Constructivist Position ... 78
Prototypes ... 79
 Abstraction of Prototypes ... 80
 Prototypes and Schemata ... 83
 Accounts of Prototype Formation ... 84
 Implications for Other Areas of Psychology ... 84
Summary and Evaluation of the Constructivist Position ... 88

DIRECT THEORIES OF PERCEPTION ... 90
The Ecological Approach to Visual Perception ... 90
What the Environment Affords Us ... 95
Evaluation of the Direct Theory ... 97

A SYNTHESIS ... 98

REPRESENTATIONAL THOUGHT AND PERCEPTION: COGNITIVE MAPS ... 101
Varieties of Spatial Cognition ... 102
Expertise in Cognitive Mapping ... 106

CONCLUDING COMMENTS AND SUGGESTIONS FOR FURTHER READING ... 108
FOCUS ON APPLICATIONS ... 109
KEY TERMS ... 110

PART III   MEMORY   111

CHAPTER 4   Basic Theories and Issues in Memory Research ... 112

OVERVIEW ... 113

THE INFORMATION-PROCESSING POSITION ... 114
Sensory Storage ... 116
 The Nature of the Icon ... 117
 "Reading" the Icon ... 118
Short-Term Storage ... 119
 Basic Findings ... 121
 The Nature of the Code in STS ... 124
 The Capacity of STS ... 125
Long-Term Storage ... 126
 Semantic Codes in LTS ... 126
 Neuropsychological Findings ... 126
Summary of the Information-Processing Position ... 127

EXTENDING AND MODIFYING THE INFORMATION-PROCESSING POSITION ... 127
The Existence and Importance of a Sensory Register ... 128
The Distinction between Short- and Long-Term Storage ... 131
 Semantic Codes in STS ... 132
 The Mechanism of Forgetting ... 133
 The Capacity of STS ... 134
 Neuropsychological Evidence ... 134
Modifying the Information-Processing Theory: A Summary ... 135

LEVELS OF PROCESSING ... 136
Maintenance and Elaborative Rehearsal ... 138
Other Complications for Levels of Processing ... 140

CONCLUDING COMMENTS AND SUGGESTIONS FOR FURTHER READING ... 141
FOCUS ON RESEARCH ... 142
KEY TERMS ... 143

CHAPTER 5   Encoding, Storing, and   144
                Retrieving

OVERVIEW   145

ENCODING   146
Context   146
Effort and Encoding   148
Encoding Specificity   150
   When Recall Beats Recognition   151
Encoding Text   153
   The Title as an Aid in Encoding   154
   The Influence of Scripts on Encoding   156
Encoding Events   157

STORAGE   159
The Work of Karl Lashley   160
H. M. and Anterograde Amnesia   161
   Studies of Amnesia   162
What About Storage?   164

RETRIEVAL   165
Retrieval from Working Memory   165
   Some Difficulties with the Serial   168
      Exhaustive Model
Retrieval from Permanent Memory   169
The Bartlett Tradition   170
Retrieval of Meaning and Retrieval   173
   of Wording

CONCLUDING COMMENTS AND SUGGESTIONS   177
FOR FURTHER READING
FOCUS ON APPLICATIONS   178
KEY TERMS   178

CHAPTER 6   Organization of Knowledge in   180
                Permanent Memory

OVERVIEW   181

EPISODIC AND SEMANTIC MEMORY   182

NETWORK MODELS OF SEMANTIC MEMORY   185
Assumptions of Network Models   186
Teachable Language Comprehender   188
   Assumptions of TLC   188
   Empirical Findings of TLC   190
Spreading Activation Model   193
   Semantic Priming   195
   ACT Theory   196
   Propositional Analysis   196

Representation of Semantic and Episodic   199
   Memory
Assumptions of ACT   202
Empirical Support   204
The Fan Effect   207
Comments about ACT and Network Models   210
   in General

REPRESENTATIONAL THOUGHT AND MEMORY   213
Metamemory   213
   Development of Metamemory   214

CONCLUDING COMMENTS AND SUGGESTIONS   217
FOR FURTHER READING
FOCUS ON APPLICATIONS   218
KEY TERMS   220

CHAPTER 7   Imagery   222
OVERVIEW   223

REBIRTH OF IMAGERY   224

DOING OPERATIONS OF MENTAL IMAGES   225
Mental Rotation of Abstract Shapes   225
Mental Rotation of Letters   229

LOOKING AT MENTAL IMAGES   233
Folding Mental Paper   233
Comparing the Size of Mental Objects   235
Mental Psychophysics   240
Mental Travel   242
Summary   247

FUNCTIONAL PROPERTIES OF IMAGES   247
Storage of Images   248
Functional Significance of Images   249
   Interference in Scanning Images   251

THE NATURE OF THE IMAGE   254

CONCLUDING COMMENTS AND SUGGESTIONS   257
FOR FURTHER READING
FOCUS ON RESEARCH   258
KEY TERMS   259

PART IV   LANGUAGE   261

CHAPTER 8   Linguistic Knowledge and Its   262
                Acquisition

OVERVIEW   263

WHAT IS LANGUAGE?   264
Design Features   265

GRAMMAR AND LINGUISTICS   270
Early Views on Grammar   271
  Objections to Finite State Grammars   274
Phrase Structure Grammars   275
Transformational Grammar   279
Origins of Grammatical Knowledge   281
Implications of Chomsky's Theory   282
Empirical Support for the Deep-Surface   282
  Structure Distinction
  Click Studies   282
  Phoneme Detection Studies   286
  Summary   287

ASPECTS OF LANGUAGE ACQUISITION: IS   287
KNOWLEDGE INNATE?
Skinner's Position   288
  Extensions of the Operant Analysis   289
  Criticisms of the Behavioral Approach   290
Arguments for Innate Knowledge   291
  Anatomical and Breathing Specializations 291
  Specializations of the Brain   292
  Categorical Perception of Speech Sounds   293

CONCLUDING COMMENTS AND SUGGESTIONS   295
FOR FURTHER READING
FOCUS ON RESEARCH   296
KEY TERMS   297

CHAPTER 9   Considerations of Language   298
             Development
OVERVIEW   299

COMPREHENSION AND PRODUCTION   300

STAGES OF LANGUAGE DEVELOPMENT   303
Crying and Cooing   304
Babbling and Single Words   305
Two-Word Stage   307
  Word Order and Inflections   310
Later Developments   313
Implications of the Developmental   313
  Sequence
Criticisms of the Stage Position   315
  Caretaker Speech   316
ACQUISITION OF LANGUAGE AMONG THE   317
DEAF
The Critical Period   319

LANGUAGE ACQUISITION IN ANIMALS   320
Washoe   321
Sarah   322
Nim Chimpsky   323

CONCLUDING COMMENTS AND SUGGESTIONS   326
FOR FURTHER READING
FOCUS ON RESEARCH   327
KEY TERMS   328

CHAPTER 10   Language in Use   330

OVERVIEW   331

PERCEPTION AND COMPREHENSION OF SPEECH   332
Why Speech Perception Is Such a Problem: 332
  The Stream of Speech
How Speech Sounds are Categorized: 333
  Phonetics and Phonology
  Articulatory Phonetics   334
  Distinctive Features in Speech   337
  Comprehension of Isolated Speech   339
    Sounds
  The Need for a Phonological Level   341
Stages of Speech Perception: From the   343
  Bottom Up
Perception of Continuous Speech: From the   345
  Top Down
Analysis by Synthesis: Interaction of   346
  Top-Down and Bottom-Up Processing

PRODUCTION OF SPEECH   347
Analysis of Speech Errors   348
Analysis of Hesitations and Pauses   350
A Model of Speech Production   351

READING   353
Mechanics of Reading   354
Recoding in Reading   356
Direct Access Hypothesis   357
Summary   361

LANGUAGE AND THOUGHT   362
Bilingualism   362
  Definitions   362
  Acquisition   363

CONCLUDING COMMENTS AND SUGGESTIONS   365
FOR FURTHER READING
FOCUS ON RESEARCH   367
KEY TERMS   368

PART V THINKING 369

CHAPTER 11 Reasoning and Concept 370
Attainment

OVERVIEW 371

LOGIC AND FORMAL REASONING 372
Human Thought and the Rules of Logic 372
Validity, Truth, and Soundness 372
  Cross-cultural Studies 374
Conditional Reasoning 375
Summary of Formal Reasoning 383

NATURAL REASONING 385
Representativeness 386
Availability 387
Framing Decisions 388
Summary of Natural Reasoning 389

CONCEPT ATTAINMENT 390
Artificial Concepts 391
  Strategies in Concept Attainment Tasks 395
Natural Categories 399
  Formation of Natural Categories 402

CONCLUDING COMMENTS AND SUGGESTIONS 405
FOR FURTHER READING
FOCUS ON APPLICATIONS 407
KEY TERMS 408

CHAPTER 12 Problem Solving 410

OVERVIEW 411

THE GESTALT HERITAGE 412
Stages of Thinking 412
  Incubation 413
  Insight and Creativity 415
The Importance of the Correct 418
  Representation
Summary of the Gestalt Position 422

DOMAIN-FREE PROBLEMS AND GENERAL 422
STRATEGIES
Well-Defined and Ill-Defined Problems 423
Typologies of Problems 425
  Problems of Inducing Structure 426
  Problems of Transformation 427
  Problems of Arrangement 431
Tactics for Solving Problems 432

Newell and Simon's Research 433
Subgoal Analysis 436
Working Backward 439
GPS 441
Summary and Comments on the Newell 441
  and Simon Theory

PROBLEM SOLVING IN A DOMAIN OF 442
KNOWLEDGE
How Knowledge Guides Search 442
Expertise 447

CONCLUDING COMMENTS AND SUGGESTIONS 453
FOR FURTHER READING
FOCUS ON APPLICATIONS 454
KEY TERMS 456
APPENDIX 456

CHAPTER 13 Artificial Intelligence 458

OVERVIEW 459

BACKGROUND AND ORIENTATION OF AI 460
A Small Amount of History 460
Orientation of AI 461
  Theory Development 461
  Metatheory 462
  Empirical Research 462
  Model Building 463

MACHINE VISION 464
A Computational Model of Vision 464
Evaluation of the Model 467

MEMORY AND ACTION FROM AN AI 467
PERSPECTIVE
Scripts 467
  Conceptual Dependency Theory 468
The Restaurant Script 470
  Psychological Validity of the Script 472
  Concept
Summary of the Script Concept 473
LANGUAGE PERCEPTION BY MACHINE 475
Speech Perception by Machine 475
Natural Language Recognition 477
  ELIZA 478
  SHRDLU 482
Implications for Cognitive Psychology 486

PROBLEM SOLVING 487
Chess 487

PARADISE   489
Expertise   490
  MYCIN   491

AI'S CONTRIBUTION TO THE STUDY OF   493
COGNITION
Questions about the Nature of Thought   493
Minds and Programs   495

CONCLUDING COMMENTS AND SUGGESTIONS   498
FOR FURTHER READING
FOCUS ON APPLICATIONS   500
KEY TERMS   501

REFERENCES   502
GLOSSARY   526
NAME INDEX   537
SUBJECT INDEX   543

What, do you imagine that I would take so much trouble and so much pleasure in writing, do you think that I would keep so persistently to my task, if I were not preparing—with a rather shaky hand—a labyrinth into which I can venture, in which I can move my discourse, opening up underground passages, forcing it to go far from itself, finding overhangs that reduce and deform its itinerary, in which I can lose myself and appear at last to eyes that I will never have to meet again. I am no doubt not the only one who writes in order to have no face. (Foucault, 1972)

This is a chilly passage, but it's a good depiction of what might be called the textbook author's dilemma. Like every other text writer, I'm interested in giving you an accurate and objective account of a particular field—in this case, cognitive psychology. And I've tried hard to produce such an account—in a metaphorical sense, writing as if I had no opinions of my own, as if I had no face. On the other hand, I recognize that all authorship requires interpretation. That is, I've chosen for you the studies, the terms, and the theories that are about to be described. In some cases, I've simplified the findings to make them easier to understand. Further, I've tried to present the material so that its underlying logic seems clear. This is an undisguised attempt to persuade you of cognitive psychology's plausibility and helpfulness in explaining some human actions. In other words, the "labyrinth" you're about to explore has been deliberately designed to lead you deeper and deeper within it. And like a real labyrinth, much in this book has been designed to challenge and puzzle you.

Under the circumstances, you're entitled to ask what you've gotten yourself into. I've intended the book to be read by upper-division students taking their first course in cognitive psychology. The book can be comfortably read in a course that is either a quarter or a semester long. The book should be understandable to those who have not had much background in psychology, but the introductory course would be helpful. Also, I've used some statistical and experimental design terms, such as *independent variable*. Students who have not had a statistics or research methods course should review these terms in their intro books. Although I think the book's chapters should be read in order from cover to cover, the enterprising teacher will no doubt think of other valid ways to cover the material. For example, Chapter 13 can be left out without significantly affecting the rest of the book. Similarly, in a course that emphasizes the constructive aspects of cognition, the teacher might wish to combine some elements of Chapter 3 with some of the material in Chapter 11. Reading Chapter 7 "Imagery" in the context of perception rather than memory gives a completely different slant to that material. However, the chapters are not completely independent of each other. Almost every chapter contains references both back and ahead to other chapters. If you read the chapters in a different order, some of these signposts may seem incongruous, but I don't think that you will find them too disorienting.

Cognitive psychologists are becoming increasingly allied with researchers in other fields such as neuropsychology and computer science. This interdisciplinary effort, known as cognitive science, has already begun to make its influences felt, and I've tried to address its issues in various chapters. For example, where biological or neuropsychological findings seem to contribute to our understanding of the cognitive processes involved in language, perception, or memory, I brought such findings into play. Similarly, cognitive psychology has become strongly allied with workers in the field of artificial intelligence—and for good reasons. Workers in both fields are concerned with the underlying nature of intelligence, and they tend to believe that our mental lives are "decomposable." By this term, they mean that our mental lives can be compared to the activities of computers. That is, the cognitive psychologist might speak of the memory system as a collection and of routines with inputs, buffers, outputs, and so on. This doesn't mean that your mind is just like a computer—far from it. But the comparison is appropriate because it helps us to better understand some mental events. This trend— that of incorporating cognitive psychology into a broader context called cognitive science—has begun only in the last few years, but it's a development that is sure to accelerate.

The book has some features that are designed to help you deal with the material. Each section begins with a part opener that provides you with a brief orientation to the important questions that I'll describe in the next several chapters. Each chapter opens with an overview. Here, an anecdote illustrates some phenomenon and serves as a springboard into the questions and issues of that chapter. Each chapter contains summary sections at various points. Each chapter also contains a focus section. These focuses deal with real-world phenomena in which the principles of cognitive psychology have been applied or in which cognitive research has shed some light. At the end of each chapter is a list of key terms. I suggest that you learn these terms completely. Finally, each chapter closes with some concluding comments and suggestions for further reading. The concluding comments are in part a summary of the chapter, but they also describe that chapter's implications, both for other areas of cognition and for future research. In the suggested readings, I've listed some books and articles that truly devoted students might consider as sources for paper topics or perhaps might use to satisfy their intellectual curiosity. If you use these features actively, you'll learn substantially more in the course.

All books are team efforts, and I was fortunate to play on a great team. My editors at West, Clark G. Baxter and Nancy Hill-Whilton, were extremely helpful. Like all good editors, they've obviously studied theories of motivation (principally the carrot and stick theory, which they've raised to a high art). Bill Gabler, the production editor at West, did a wonderful job in producing the beautifully designed book you're holding.

I benefited from the knowledge of my reviewers, all of whom made quite a contribution to whatever good qualities the book now has. Of course, I'm responsible for whatever errors of fact or interpretation may remain in the book. I've listed the reviewers in alphabetical order:

James I. Chumbley, University of Massachusetts, Amherst
Joseph H. Danks, Kent State University
Peter Derks, College of William and Mary
Robert Gregory, University of Idaho, Moscow

Edward Johnson, University of North Carolina, Chapel Hill
Connie Juel, University of Texas, Austin
Michael W. O'Boyle, Iowa State University
Fred Schwantes, Northern Illinois University
Steven Smith, Texas A & M University
Richard Wagner, Florida State University, Tallahassee

An awesome amount of clerical work is involved in making a book. I had several terrific helpers. Jeanne Hartmann proofed, typed, worked on permissions from publishers, photocopied, and did other tasks—all of them well. Janet Ryner and Rhonda Wolfe helped track down the references. The secretarial staff at Eastern—Julia Robinson, Pam Gutowski, and Opal Kelly—typed much of the earlier drafts before I started using a word processor. My colleagues at Eastern kept nudging me (in a nice way) to complete the book. My chairman, Paul Panek, released me from some of my teaching duties so that I could finish writing. My wife, Lorraine, was very supportive, as were my parents, Jack and Marie Best. Finally, I thank my stepson, Frankie Dominic Tarantino, who helped me relax by playing Stratego with me. Thanks to all of you.

For me, so much trouble and so much pleasure have come to an end. For you, I hope your troubles with this book are minimal and your pleasure great.

> John B. Best
> Charleston, Illinois
> 27 May 1985
> Memorial Day

PART ONE

INTRODUCTION

Preceding each section of this book is a part opener that describes some of the issues that are dealt with in each section. These part openers also provide an orientation to the material by giving some key phrases or concepts that will help students organize the material as they read.

While reading this chapter, students might facilitate their understanding of cognitive psychology by comparing the human mind to the operation of a computer. Some of the points of comparison are obvious: Both humans and computers have memories that are organized in particular ways, and both are capable of following directions on a line-by-line basis. But people and computers are similar in other ways that are not as obvious. Both humans and computers *represent* information internally. In other words, they take in information from the world in one form, and they store it in some other form. Once stored, this information can be altered repeatedly by the computer's program or, in humans, by cognitive processes. Cognitive processes are like mental programs. They operate on the information we have stored, modifying it to suit our current purposes. Cognitive psychologists have found this comparison between the human mind and the computer very persuasive. The opening chapter that follows discusses some of the reasons why.

CHAPTER 1

Cognitive Psychology: Definitions and Problems

OVERVIEW

INTRODUCTION TO COGNITIVE PSYCHOLOGY
Neisser's Definition of Cognition
Kinds of Knowledge and Types of Processing
Topics of Cognitive Psychology

THE ROOTS OF COGNITIVE PSYCHOLOGY
Human Factors at Work during World War II
  Broadbent's Studies
Computing Machinery
Linguistics
Skinner's Book and Chomsky's Rebuttal

THE FACE OF CONTEMPORARY COGNITIVE PSYCHOLOGY
The Information-Processing Approach
  An Abstract Analysis
  Methods in Cognitive Psychology
Ecological Validity

CONCLUDING COMMENTS AND SUGGESTIONS
FOR FURTHER READING
FOCUS ON RESEARCH
KEY TERMS

Many cognitive psychologists believe that we learn material better when we have some idea of what is going to be presented rather than when we have no idea of what is forthcoming. Consequently, I begin each chapter with a short orientation to the forthcoming material. These overviews will usually include a brief anecdote or episode that illustrates the cognitive processes described in each chapter.

This chapter begins with a definition of cognitive psychology. This definition focuses on two of cognitive psychology's chief problems: the problem of understanding and explaining human knowledge, and the problem of finding the relationship between this knowledge and human action. Some of the topics studied by cognitive psychologists seem to be at the core of our humanity. For example, we use our stored knowledge and reasoning to solve problems. Such reasoning ability is one characteristic that makes us distinctively human. Also, in reasoning, we see a relationship between thought and action. The complexity of human reasoning suggests that much activity must have taken place in people's minds prior to their acting. Consequently, the cognitive psychologist poses several questions about reasoning—questions about both the process of reasoning (What information did the subject seek? What facts were compared?) as well as the reasoning's outcome (What decision was made?). However, cognitive psychologists are usually not satisfied with a description of the subject's actions. In addition, they seek to understand the nature of the knowledge that permitted and enabled such actions to occur. In a sense, cognitive psychologists use human behavior as a pointer, or indicator that says something about what was going on in the subject's mind while the person acted.

The previous sentence might give you the impression that cognitive psychologists are principally concerned with our mental lives, or knowledge of which we are aware. Actually, many cognitive psychologists believe that some cognitive processes typically take place without leaving any trace of their activity in our awareness. This chapter considers the relationship between conscious knowledge and other forms of cognitive activity. We'll see that many cognitive psychologists maintain that humans are not necessarily aware of all the knowledge that they possess.

This chapter also considers some of the many origins of cognitive psychology. Its roots are to be found (among other places) in linguistics, computer science, and human factors research. You may be somewhat surprised to find out that cognitive psychology has a relatively short history and that many of its practitioners consider themselves revolutionary in their outlook on the field of psychology. All cognitive psychologists share a common interest in the problem of human knowledge. In addition, they frequently share a common theoretical approach to this problem: the information-processing theory.

Strictly speaking, the information-processing theory is not a single, unified theory, but rather is a broad approach to the problems of understanding human knowledge and action. Although not every cognitive psychologist would claim to be an adherent, many of them would nevertheless subscribe to one of the approach's most basic beliefs, namely that cognitive processes can frequently be thought of as a series of sequential transformations of some abstract code. The chapter concludes with a description of some of the research methods that cognitive psychologists use.

INTRODUCTION TO COGNITIVE PSYCHOLOGY

By the time you reach the period at the end of this sentence, you will have engaged in several distinct cognitive processes. Without any particularly strenuous effort on your part, you're grasping the meaning of this sentence right now, even as (perhaps) your attention has already begun to wander to an upcoming rendezvous, a test tomorrow, hunger pangs, or whatever. However, the ease with which we engage in cognitive processes shouldn't blind us to their complexity. The remaining 125,000 words of this text are spent in an effort to foster your appreciation of just how great that complexity is.

Neisser's Definition of Cognition

In 1967, Ulric Neisser published the now-classic text, *Cognitive Psychology,* which offers the following definition.

Cognitive psychology refers to all processes by which the sensory input is transformed, reduced, elaborated, stored, recovered, and used. The definition is worth elaborating. As Neisser states, cognition begins with sensory input. Our cognitive processes are perhaps most useful in responding to information that is present in the world and which is capable of being picked up by our sensory apparatus. Next, the sensory input is transformed—that is, altered. Our sensory apparatus is finely attuned to certain kinds of energy present in the world. This sensory apparatus converts physical energy into neural energy, or as a cognitive psychologist might say, physical stimulation is encoded into neural events.

The notion of a code is an important idea in cognitive psychology and so deserves at least a brief description. To what does the process of encoding refer? Literally, a code is a system of signals used to represent letters or numbers in transmitting messages. For example, children make up secret alphabets and use them to send messages to their closest friends in school. These messages are coded; the symbols used are the result of some (presumably) systematic transformation of the alphabet, and the squiggles that children make up bear the same relationship to one another that characters in the alphabet do. If *e* is the most commonly occurring letter in English text, then the character representing *e* in the code would also be the most frequently occurring symbol.

Apparently, our nervous systems are capable of a similar coding procedure. That is, physical stimulation is represented by the activity of the nervous system in a way that preserves many of the characteristics of the original stimuli. The transformation of the physical stimulation produces more than just a neural code, however. The transformation also results in the creation of a **cognitive code.** The creation of this cognitive code can be demonstrated quite simply. Look out the window or across the room for a few seconds, then look back at your book. Can you now imagine the scene outside the window without looking back out? You can probably do so without difficulty. The image thus created demonstrates the existence of a cognitive code—in this case, a mental event that seems to preserve many of the characteristics of the original physical stimulation. Cognitive codes are created by the activity of our nervous systems. For our purposes, the term refers to transformations of physical energy that are potentially capable of entering our awareness (i.e., mental events), or those transformations that form the basis of such an event.

The distinction between these two kinds of cognitions is necessary because our awareness of our cognitive codes is not complete. Some cognitive codes enter our awareness, but others don't. To see this, think about the process of reading. If you set out to read a word, the meaning of this word almost certainly enters your awareness. The experience of "meaning entering your awareness" is hard to describe, but you know the experience you're having was produced by reading that particular word. However, other transformations of the physical energy were certainly involved, and probably none of these entered your awareness. For example, the light reflected from the page had to be converted into a code that preserved the lines of the letters; these lines had to be assembled in some meaningful way; the resulting pattern of lines had to be recognized as letters; and presumably, at least some of the letters had to be identified. In each case, a cognitive code was created, although the results of such processing almost certainly did not enter your awareness.

Neisser describes the fate of the cognitive code in the next part of the definition. Once created, the cognitive code can be reduced or elaborated. The reduction of a cognitive code refers to the fact that neither the neural code nor the cognitive code preserves and retains *all* the characteristics of the original physical stimulation. This reduction isn't bad, because most of the physical energy in the environment isn't very informative and therefore isn't worth keeping. Even now, if you try to remember the exact words that began this chapter, you'll find it difficult to recall them, and you probably won't remember them accurately. Even when you read the words the first time, you probably recognized that the exact phrasing was not particularly important. What was important was the meaning of the introduction. Consequently, details like the exact phrasing, the style of the typeface, and so on, which may have been in the cognitive code for a short period of time, have now been reduced; they're no longer retrievable.

Elaboration of a cognitive code refers to the relating of specific mental events to one another. If, when you looked out the window, you noticed a tree and began to consider what characteristics of this particular tree resembled other trees in the area, you were elaborating a cognitive code.

In many cases, cognitive codes can be stored and recovered, and in addition, highly reduced cognitive codes can be fleshed out, or reconstructed. Reconstructions of cognitive codes occur quite commonly, and this ability seems to be based on our general knowledge of the world. Consider an example. Suppose you tell an acquaintance about the key volleyball game your intramural team won two weeks ago. Your account is almost certain to involve some reconstruction. Although some aspects of the game are sure to stand out vividly, some details have been reduced. To give a complete rendition of the game, however, these details must be filled in. How is this filling in accomplished? Knowledge of athletic contests in general, volleyball in particular, and chronological knowledge are probably all used. If you remember an incredible play you made to boost the score to 12–8 in favor of your team, and then you remember that your opponents came surging back to knot the score at 12 all, you may start to infer, and report, that they got the serve back on the next point and proceeded to reel off four straight points. To support this inference, you may try to recall where you were standing on the court when the opponents tied the score. If you believe you were still standing in the same place that you were in when you made the incredible play, then your belief about the order of the scoring is probably accurate: No rotation of players had apparently occurred in the meantime. But if you realize that you were standing in two different places when you made the play and later when the score became tied, then you know that the serve must have seesawed with no scoring, at least once, resulting in your rotating to a different spot on the floor. As this example hints, the processes involved in storing, recovering, and reconstructing cognitive codes are an aspect of our mental lives that we usually refer to as memory.

Perhaps the most important word of Neisser's definition of cognitive psychology is its last word: Cognitive processes create codes that are *used* by people. That is, the cognitive codes developed by individuals are the basis of their knowledge of the world. Such codes enable people to work, make decisions, study, play tennis, and so on.

Kinds of Knowledge and Types of Processing

Although the term *knowledge* encompasses a vast amount of territory, we can get some idea of the lay of the land by considering a few examples of knowledge in use. Consider the knowledge that Barbara has of her car's carburetor. She knows that this device measures out a tiny amount of gasoline, mixes it with air, and sprays the mixture into the engine's cylinders at just the right time. This knowledge can be quite useful to her sometimes, because she can use it to diagnose particular difficulties that her car is having. Like many people, however, Barbara doesn't know how to fix the carburetor; that requires a specialist. In contrast with her knowledge of carburetion, consider Barbara's knowledge of bicycle riding. She knows how to ride her own ten-speed bike, and she thinks she could ride just about any other ten-speed also. Barbara is certain that she would retain this knowledge even if several years elapsed without her riding a bicycle. Although she has knowledge of how to ride a bicycle, she can't explain what she does to keep her balance, how she makes a turn without falling over, and so on. In the case of the carburetor, Barbara has a certain amount of knowledge that she can describe verbally, but she has little practical knowledge. In the case of the bicycle, the situation is reversed. Barbara rides the bicycle well, but she can't describe what she does very completely.

Cognitive psychologists use two terms to describe these two seemingly different kinds of knowledge: **declarative knowledge** and **procedural knowledge.** Declarative knowledge refers to factual information that is somewhat static (i.e., unchanging) in nature, whose organization is often apparent to us, and which is usually describable. Let's take these items one at a time. Declarative knowledge often takes the form of a series of related facts. For example, the description of Barbara's carburetor knowledge mentioned a series of facts that are agreed upon by others who are familiar with carburetors. Even when our declarative knowledge is wrong, it's still expressible in this factual format, as would be true for someone who said, for example, that *Apollo 11* was the first Apollo spacecraft to land on the moon. In this definition, static means stationary or unchanging. I know that Abraham Lincoln was the sixteenth president of the United States. An excellent chance exists that I'll retain this knowledge to the end of my life, and I can't think of anything that would improve my grasp of this fact. We can control the organization of declarative knowledge in a very real sense.

To see this, suppose I were to ask you to develop a system that we might use to categorize sports. How would you go about it?

You might start by dividing all sporting activities into two categories: those that involve a ball and those that don't. Then, you might proceed to further divide each of those categories into team versus individual sports. However, if you wanted to, you could adopt a completely different scheme. You might begin by dividing all sports into two categories: those that involve animals and those that don't. Next, you might divide those categories into two further categories: sports in which the human participants are not athletes and those in which the human participants are.

Declarative knowledge is flexible and can oftentimes be reorganized to suit our purposes. The first categorization system might seem more natural to you, but both systems are arbitrary and could be combined. Thus, you could probably come up with an example of a team sport involving animals and a ball, in which the human participants were athletes. Finally, declarative knowledge is usually describable. No matter what categorization system you used, you would probably be able to tell someone what factors were involved in placing a particular sport in one or another category.

In contrast with declarative knowledge, procedural knowledge refers to the knowledge underlying skillful actions, and its nature tends to be dynamic (i.e., changing). The organization of procedural knowledge is not very clear to us, nor is procedural knowledge usually very describable. It is more easily *shown* to someone than it is *told*. Using the bicycle example again, biking is an action that is best understood as a skill. When Barbara was six, she acquired this skill by falling off her bike numerous times. The acquisition of a skill often seems to involve making and detecting errors. Unlike my knowledge of Lincoln's presidency, Barbara's skill at bicycle riding continues to improve, as does her typing ability and her tennis serve. If Barbara were to stop doing any of these things for an extended period, her knowledge of how to do them would apparently decline. The knowledge probably wouldn't disappear altogether, but nevertheless, procedural knowledge is dynamic in the sense that with additional experience, we continue to improve; without it, the knowledge begins to decline.

Procedural knowledge is not as flexible as declarative knowledge. We can't control it in the same way as we can declarative knowledge. For example, it's often difficult to specify in advance what skills will be helpful in acquiring new skills. The relationship between skills sometimes seems orderly; for example, people who are good at basketball are apparently good at volleyball. However, the relationship between skills is sometimes mysterious; for example, people who play racquetball frequently report that it has a negative influence on their tennis skill. Finally, procedural knowledge resists a verbal description. You can read a book on racquetball, but you could never learn how to play well simply by reading such a book.

The distinction between these two kinds of knowledge might best be summed up in the phrases "knowing how" and "knowing that." "Knowing how" refers to nonverbal knowledge of particular procedures that a person engages in to accomplish some objective. Whenever we hit a backhand, ride our bicycles, or make pancakes, we're using procedural knowledge to achieve some objective. "Knowing that" refers to knowledge that can be described more or less completely in a series of declarative sentences. When we describe how to program a computer or explain the workings of a camera, we're expressing declarative knowledge.

Cognitive psychologists have wondered about the relationship between declarative and procedural knowledge. Many—perhaps most—of our daily activities involve both kinds of knowledge. Nevertheless, a question that a cognitive psychologist might entertain concerns the cognitive codes in which procedural and declarative knowledge are represented: Are these codes fundamentally different from one another? If they are, then how does the brain know (in advance) what sorts of knowledge it will represent as a procedural knowledge code and what sorts as a declarative knowledge code?

Although a complete answer to these questions doesn't yet exist, there are some indications that, at least for adults, some knowledge is initially encoded in a declarative format and later transformed into a procedural format as we become familiar with the information. For example, consider what happens when you try to acquire a skill such as hitting a forehand in tennis. If you have an instructional book, it will probably depict a person hitting a forehand in a series of pictures with accompanying advisory text. The first drawing or photograph might be a sort of double exposure, showing the model in the ready stance and also in the preparatory stance, with the racquet prepared (i.e., out and behind the body). The text will advise you that adequately preparing the racquet is important and will probably give you some guidelines concerning the timing of this move. Significantly, the book will probably also provide a brief reminder that you can say to yourself when you prepare to hit a forehand, such as "Racquet back!" Notice that this type of presentation invites—even necessitates—a declarative encoding of the information. Also, breaking down the stroke into a series of numbered steps encourages the rote memorization of the text. And since we'll be able to tell somebody else these steps once we memorize what they are, declarative knowledge occurs once again. Similarly, the verbal reminders provided at each step foster an apparently verbal self-talk as we run around the court.

Hitting a forehand, however, doesn't really consist of a series of steps; it's one continuous, fluid motion. The business of enumerating the steps is simply a teaching convenience. What happens to the declarative knowledge as you improve? As you stroke the shot a number of times, you make and detect errors, which you can then begin to eliminate. Thus, the experience you acquire in hitting the shot begins to form the basis for procedural knowledge. This procedural knowledge eventually supplants the declarative code. Finding fragments of both codes coexisting in an intermediate-level tennis player is not unusual. As the player improves, the fragments of procedural knowledge get greater, and the declarative knowledge parts diminish until little declarative knowledge is left. For example, Billie Jean King apparently has only one bit of self-talk left; when she hits a ground stroke, she mentally recites the phrase "up and out" to remind herself to put top spin on the ball.

The declarative-procedural distinction is not the only signpost we can use to find our way in the land of mental events. Consider the role our awareness plays as we organize and assimilate sensory input. Many components, or facets, of awareness exist, but one striking aspect is the phenomenon of attention. A complete discussion of attention is reserved for later, but right now, attention can briefly be defined as the concentration and focusing of mental activity (Matlin, 1983). In the dim light of morning, I must pay attention to the pair of socks that I get out of the drawer, lest I select a pair that doesn't go with the rest of my clothes. Paying attention seems to accentuate, or enhance, the sensory input that has been focused on. Thus, when I pay attention to eating my Black Forest torte, the flavor seems much more intense than it does when I pay attention instead to what my dinner companion is saying.

Attention is such a hallmark of our mental lives that it would be tempting to conclude that allocating attention is necessary to initiate any other cognitive processing. Such a conclusion would be erroneous, however. Evidence from our daily lives, which has been supported by experimental findings, suggests that cognitive processes can sometimes be initiated and sustained with little or no selective attention paid to them. Have you ever driven on an interstate highway while daydreaming about the events in your life, only to realize an hour later that you're not sure if you've already passed your exit? During the hour that you spent daydreaming, your cognitive processes continued to work because you made an untold number of decisions about passing other cars, maintaining speed, and so on. Yet, these decisions did not seem to require any conscious effort.

Effortful cognitive processes that seem to require attention to initiate and sustain them are referred to as **controlled processes.** Processes that seem to be initiated and run without any conscious allocation of attention are referred to as **automatic.** Like the procedural-declarative knowledge distinction we have already examined, the automatic-controlled distinction allows cognitive psychologists to describe the type of cognitive processing that is taking place.

The topics that a cognitive psychologist might investigate are discussed in the next section. In the meantime, let's summarize what has been discussed so far. Cognitive psychologists are concerned with questions about the representation of human knowledge and its use as seen in human action. They have developed some terminology to describe both the nature of the knowledge being used (declarative and procedural) and the role of attention in the representation and use of knowledge (automatic and controlled processes). Table 1.1 depicts some examples of each type of knowledge and processing.

The entry in the upper left-hand corner of Table 1.1 is only half joking. During my lectures to first-year students, I sometimes find that Dr. Pavlov's high jinks with his dogs and meat power remind me that I may have forgotten to take the ground meat out of the freezer at home. Consequently, I begin to worry whether I did, and how I'm going to make the barbecued hamburgers if I didn't. I've discovered that such musings seldom interrupt my lectures. The students seem completely unaware that although I'm walking around and talking to them, I'm not really "there."

Topics of Cognitive Psychology

You may have gotten the impression that cognitive psychologists might study anything they pleased, because practically every human activity requires some sort of knowledge. Technically, you would be right. In practice, however, cognitive psychologists are more likely to investigate some specific sorts of mental events rather than others. Complete agreement will never be reached about which specific mental events should be studied, but at least some consensus exists about those subject matters that are truly cognitive. This section provides an annotated listing of some cognitive topics, along with the questions that cognitive psychologists might ask about those topics. Neither the list of topics nor the questions associated with them should be regarded as complete, but both can be regarded as typical.

1. **Attention.** We've already looked briefly at the phenomenon of mental focusing. The issue of attention is loaded with practical significance. For example, you've no doubt heard people say that a person can pay attention to only one thing at a time. Yet, various situations commonly demand that we attend to more than one thing simultaneously. For

TABLE 1.1

Relationship between Cognitive Codes and Cognitive Processing

		TYPE OF COGNITIVE CODE	
	Processing	Declarative	Procedural
	Automatic	Some of my lectures	Driving on the interstate
	Controlled	Solving simultaneous equations by hand	Driving downtown in rush-hour traffic

example, in class, I expect my students to listen to me. Yet, at the same time, I expect them to take accurate notes. If the "one thing at a time" theory is correct, I'm doing my students a disservice that compromises their ability to learn the material. On the other hand, maybe the students are so practiced that these two tasks—listening and writing—no longer require attention. The cognitive psychologist is often interested in the attentional demands that a task makes on a person. If a task is sufficiently demanding, do we pay attention to that task alone, or can we always divide our attention among a variety of tasks?

2. **Pattern recognition.** Survival often depends upon our ability to correctly interpret ambiguous sensory input. While driving home in the fog, we have to pay attention to the road so that we can correctly categorize, and evade, anything that suddenly looms out. However, this process of making sense out of sensory input goes on even when the situation is not life threatening. For example, while writing this book, I made numerous typing errors. In my case, detecting typing errors involves looking at my computer's screen and determining whether the patterns of pixels (points of light) are the appropriate ones. In other words, I have to determine, from the sensory input, whether the pixels have been organized in the right way.

Cognitive psychologists are interested in how this pattern recognition is done. What information do the letters have that can be preserved in a neural and cognitive code? As discussed, pattern recognition of letters is simply a specific example of a far more general problem. What information must be present in the world to enable our sensory and cognitive systems to detect and categorize it? Perhaps, as some cognitive psychologists reason, the problem should be turned around. What sort of cognitive programs exist in our minds that enable the detection and categorization of information in the world?

Somewhat related to the question of pattern recognition is the issue of concept attainment. Not every pattern that we're called upon to recognize is unique. In some cases, we judge that a recognized pattern is similar to patterns we have previously recognized. We might go on to say that names can be assigned to patterns of sensory input that have been judged as similar. For example, if Peter looks out his window and sees an object with four wheels, doors, headlights, a steering wheel, and seats, he's inclined to judge this pattern of sensory input as similar to others he's recognized in the past, and he'll also judge that it can be placed in the category *car*. You can probably guess some of the problems that cognitive psychologists have tackled here. What aspects of a pattern are sufficient or necessary to enable a person to include it in one category rather than another? Are some aspects of the pattern more important than others for this purpose? Also, how many experiences with certain stimuli must we have before we're able to make reliable judgments about their membership in certain categories?

3. **Memory.** We observe regularities in our own behavior as a function of the experiences that we have had. This simple fact implies that we (and others in whom we observe similar regularities) must possess a means of keeping copies of those experiences; otherwise, our experiences would be of no benefit to us. Many questions about memory fascinate cognitive psychologists, and so the list of questions here is by no means complete. Cognitive psychologists are interested in the nature of the organization of knowledge in memory. How does the memory of our personal experiences fit in with what we have learned about the world in general? Are procedural and declarative knowledge organized similarly in our memories? Are some memories verbal while others are primarily visual in nature? What has happened to forgotten memories? Are they still present somewhere in our minds, or have they truly been lost?

4. **Imagery.** We take for granted our ability to visualize things, but cognitive psychologists have been especially interested in imagery for a variety of reasons. First, some have claimed that the image is a cognitive code that preserves many of the stimulus's original characteristics in close to their original form. That is, in some sense, the image is thought to have color, length, and so on. Second, other cognitive psychologists have maintained that the undeniable existence of images suggests that some memories must be primarily visual in nature.

5. **Language.** As will be discussed, the phenomenon of language is one of cognitive psychology's most important initial bases. Like the topic of memory, there are enough questions about language to keep cognitive psychologists busy forever. How do children acquire language? We have a great deal of linguistic knowledge, and some of this knowledge (e.g., knowledge of pronunciation, knowledge of word order) seems to be expressible in the form of rules. Does this mean that the linguistically competent adult possesses a set of rules that governs pronunciation and word order? Some linguists have argued that this is so. In addition, some have claimed that the organization of such rules is itself subject to certain inherent limitations of our mental capabilities. According to such a view, therefore, a discovery of the rules of language is equivalent to a discovery of the rules of thought itself.

6. **Reasoning.** You may have taken a course in logic only to find that the principles of correct reasoning were often not intuitively obvious, and in some cases were downright confusing. To the extent that your experience is a common one, what does this say about naturally occurring human reasoning? Are people inherently illogical? This state of affairs would be unsatisfying, and such a proposition seems illogical itself. If it couldn't put two and two together, what would be the good of having a great cognitive system capable of accurate pattern recognition, vivid imagery, and amazingly complex verbal reports? Our experience with logic tells us that people are not necessarily intuitively logical, but our experience in the real world tells us that people are not inaccurate reasoners either. This evidence

suggests that people are perhaps using some other (nonlogical) system of reasoning that produces the correct outcome frequently enough to be useful in the real world. This leads to a question: If naturally occurring human reasoning is illogical, then what is its nature?

7. **Problem solving.** Playing chess and changing a car tire have some elements in common. In both cases, we recognize that the existing situation needs modification (the opposing king hasn't been checkmated; the tire is flat). Also, in both situations, we have an idea of the pattern that we seek. We are capable of forming a plan, that is, a mental event that seems to specify a sequence of actions, which if done correctly, might produce the desired outcome. How might we describe the knowledge that enables us to generate such a plan? The whole question of strategy use in problem solving is interesting. What are strategies? If I were to show you a problem that you've never seen before, your solution attempts wouldn't be unorganized for long. We would quickly see the emergence of some actions that indicated you had some plan in mind. How are people able to generate plans and strategies for problems they have never encountered before?

Mental events can be viewed in many other ways, too. For example, one could look at the roles that others play in the formation of one's own mind. Similarly, an investigator could study dreams and other phenomena that seem to have a strong mental component. However, cognitive psychologists usually don't take social factors into account in their study of cognition, nor do they usually study dreams. Further, cognitive psychologists have tended to de-emphasize individual differences in mental events. Of all the variables that might be considered cognitive, cognitive psychologists usually consider only a small part. This raises a question: What factors were responsible for molding the field into its existing shape? Answering this question requires delving into psychology's history.

THE ROOTS OF COGNITIVE PSYCHOLOGY

Speculation about the nature of mental events has been going on for some time. For example, Plato believed that the contents of our minds were merely copies of objects that we had just perceived. These copies, or *eidola,* were recognized and known because they matched with knowledge we already possessed but had "forgotten." In other words, Plato believed that we possessed at birth all the knowledge we would ever have. All "learning" was really "remembering." This doctrine, known as *amnesis,* has never been empirically disproved, yet few cognitive psychologists adhere to it now.

Aristotle's contribution to the study of mental events specified three laws, or principles, of association that are still with us. These three principles are contiguity, similarity, and contrast. According to the doctrine of contiguity, when mental events occur together, they will be remembered together. When these events are similar to or different from one another, the association between them will be particularly strong.

In 1879, with the founding of a psychological laboratory in Leipzig, appreciation of the complexity of mental events increased greatly. Wilhelm Wundt (1832–1920), the lab's founder, was determined to carry out a program of research designed to substantiate the associationist claims first proposed by Aristotle. Wundt's theoretical orientation was called **structuralism.**

Describing mental events as having structure implies that mentality or awareness could be viewed as a set of organized elements; Wundt was an adherent of this position. He believed that mentality could be decomposed into its constituent parts in the same way that a chemist could break down a complex molecule into its component atoms. These "mental atoms" were not simply strewn haphazardly throughout our minds, but rather they were all related to one another in systematic ways. That is, our mentality had the property of wholeness because all of its elements were systematically correlated. Wundt hoped to observe and measure these processes of mental analysis and recombination.

Accordingly, Wundt trained his human subjects in an exacting technique known as *introspection,* which literally means "looking into." The introspectionist was supposed to look into her own mind. In practice, the introspectionist was to report verbally the first associations that entered her awareness when a stimulus word or image was presented. Ideally, these reports were to be expressed in words that were as close to the raw sensory input as possible. Wundt hoped that by analyzing the subjects' reports, the laws of mental operation could be discovered.

What happened? When asked to introspect about the idea *dog,* Wundt's subjects reported generalized doglike images, accompanied by reports of kinesthetic sensations such as the feel of holding a dog on a leash, running away from a ferocious dog, or even being bitten by a dog. From a series of such reports, Wundt became convinced that the technique of introspection could be used to indicate the associationistic laws governing simple reflexive acts or physiological reactions. According to Wundt, the mental atom always consisted of an image of some sort, which could be combined, or synthesized, with other previously constructed images. Consequently, Wundt believed that imagery would be mentioned in the report of any introspectionist, regardless of the concept that was being introspected upon. Not surprisingly, Wundt's subjects produced images even when asked to introspect on ideas such as *triangularity.* One aspect of Wundt's work that was to have fateful implications for cognitive psychology was his decision to divide the subject matter of psychology into two classes. Reflexes and sensations could be studied with the experimental technique of introspection. However, the higher mental processes such as thinking could not be studied in this fashion. Why not?

Wundt believed that the higher mental processes produced imagery that was qualitatively different from the imagery that simpler mental events produced. Assessing this kind of imagery could not be done effectively on an individual basis; rather, Wundt believed that the higher mental processes could best be studied by looking at the mental products of an entire culture or society. Wundt argued that a historical rather than an experimental approach would be more fruitful in understanding this "folk soul," as he called it. Incidentally, Wundt undertook such an enterprise in his *Volkerpsychologie* (Wundt, 1912).

Although Wundt's influence on the new science of psychology was considered strong, a group of researchers in the university town of Würzburg soon began to chafe under the constraints imposed by the Leipzig school. The Würzburgers, led by Oswald Kulpe, began to apply the experimental technique to the problem of thought. Consider the following "problem" and introspectionist report:

Poem. In what larger category does it belong?
Once again, immediately a full understanding of the [question]. Then again an intensive glance, the symbolic fixation of that which is sought: then at once, the flitting memory of art, poetry, and so on appeared. The word "art," I think, in auditory-motor terms. Then the thought that I cannot subsume poetry under art but only under artistic production. With this, I am certain, no words and images: then I said, "work of art." (Humphrey, 1963, 137)

Although the style of the report and its terminology are somewhat old-fashioned, the introspectionist seems to be using controlled processes ("an intensive glance") to describe some knowledge that many of us would regard as procedural rather than declarative. That is, most of us would have a hard time telling somebody what exactly had been going in our minds when we categorized a stimulus. Regarding Wundt's structural position, the important implication of this report is that its author is certain that no images were involved in its production. From reports such as this one, Kulpe and his circle went on to develop the doctrine of *imageless thought*. This position refers to the idea that some mental events could not be classified according to any accompanying sensory content. The issue of the underlying form of thought is still very much with us, as we shall see in the chapters on memory.

From this brief description of Wundt's work, and the response it drew, it's hard to see how such reports could form the basis of modern cognitive psychology. Yet, although Wundt focused on certain topics and ignored others, much of the work of contemporary cognitive psychologists is clearly related to Wundt's ideas. For example, Wundt realized that attention was an important component of cognition. He also recognized that mental events could be described as concepts that were formed through experience. Studies in concept formation have been one of the foundations of modern cognitive psychology. Wundt's notion that mental events were related to one another also foreshadows modern work in an area known as *semantic memory*. Perhaps most striking is Wundt's idea that mentality was analyzable. Philosophers had long held the notion that mentality was examinable, but Wundt was among the first to maintain and demonstrate that mental events could be decomposed into simpler, more basic mental events. Moreover, these basic mental events seemed to be strung together sequentially. Although his introspectionists sometimes described mental events as occurring simultaneously, reporting a string of associations was more common for them. The belief that basic mental events can be strung together to form a composite mental life is still held by a number of modern cognitive psychologists.

Therefore, one could say that the first experimental psychologists were cognitive psychologists, in that they were concerned with describing and explaining mental events.

The train of thought that Wundt initiated jumped the track in this country, however. American psychologists were dismayed that Wundt's methods produced findings that were neither reproducible nor observable—two characteristics that seemed necessary for any science of psychology. American psychologists soon turned to behaviorism as their principal theory. For the first fifty to sixty years of this century, many—perhaps most—American psychologists strongly believed that this theory was essentially the only correct approach to erecting a science of behavior. Renewed interest in mental events began to take place in the United States around 1960. The next sections describe some of the events that led American psychologists to question their behavioristic beliefs.

Human Factors at Work during World War II

The field of **human factors research** deals with the problems of human-machine interactions, particularly with regard to improving human skills and performance. This field emerged during World War II when it became clear that the advanced technology then being developed required improvements in the layout and design of instrumentation. Nowhere was the problem of human use of instrumentation more critical than in the area of aviation.

Broadbent's Studies

In his work at the Applied Psychology Research Unit, Donald Broadbent noted that human workers were guided by the information, or "feedback" as it was called, given to them by machines. In the case of pilots, Broadbent observed that not all of the information being displayed was used by the pilot to fly the aircraft. Rather, certain instruments were monitored more diligently than were others. Broadbent also found that oftentimes, too much information was displayed; the pilots were unable to attend to all of it at once. Instead, the pilots had to focus their attention on successive gauges—a process that required a substantial amount of time.

Broadbent's work has several implications. First, he countered the idea that humans wait passively for stimuli to impinge upon them. Rather, the pilots and other technical personnel actively sought out information, a finding that was somewhat troublesome for the then-popular behaviorist theories. Second, human information processing seemed quite similar to the *servomechanisms* (automatic devices) controlling the complex machines. That is, as each servomechanism responds to a particular kind of information and in a particular way, so can the human information-processing system be thought of as a collection of such mechanisms. For the individual human operator, one key problem then became the allocation of attention to direct the information processing of such mental servomechanisms. The title of one of Broadbent's postwar papers, "A Mechanical Model for Human Attention and Immediate Memory" (1954), is indicative of how far this new approach to human performance could be taken.

Computing Machinery

The discussion of Broadbent's work alluded to the concept of **information.** Broadbent's interest in this term was typical given the spirit of the times. Shortly before World War II, several thinkers—notably Shannon—attempted to define the concept of information mathematically. Shannon reasoned that the function of information was to reduce the uncertainty of particular future events. Specifically, if we imagine future possible events as occupying a range, or space, and then find out that this range has been constrained by exactly half (that is, half of the future events are no longer possible), then our uncertainty about these future events has been reduced. We know that half of them cannot take place, so we have to worry only about the remaining half. How much information have we received? Shannon defined a bit of information as the amount needed to reduce the number of possible outcomes by exactly half. Let's consider an illustration. Suppose Maria tells Bill that she's thinking of a particular square on a chessboard, and Bill's task is to determine which particular square Maria has in mind. To determine which square Maria is thinking of, Bill is allowed to ask her questions about the chessboard that can be answered with a yes or a no. Further suppose that Bill is trying to figure out the correct square with the minimum number of questions. How would he proceed? A chessboard has sixty-four squares, so to get one bit of information, Bill needs to ask a question that eliminates thirty-two squares from further consideration. One way for Bill to do this is to ask if the square is in the top half of the board. If Maria said yes, Bill would restrict his search to the top half of the board. If she said no, Bill would know that the square was in the bottom half of the board, and he would begin to search there. Subsequent searches would consist of dividing the appropriate half of the board into halves again, and so on. If Bill did this efficiently, determining the square Maria had in mind would require that Bill ask six questions.

As Shannon phrased it, representing a particular square on a chessboard requires six bits of information. Phrased in a slightly different way, a string of six *Y*'s or *N*'s like this—*YYNYYN*—represents a particular square on a chessboard. Moreover, every square on the chessboard could be represented by some such string. Shortly after World War II, it became clear to a number of thinkers, including John von Neuman, that a machine capable of creating and storing such strings would also be capable of symbolically representing a wide variety of phenomena. With the publication of *Cybernetics* by Wiener in 1948, the information theory of Shannon was formally melded with the servomechanism theory of Broadbent, and the development of general-purpose computers was just around the corner. Some computing hardware was developed in the late 1930s, although the real power of the digital computer was not exploited until the development of programming languages such as FORTRAN, which took place in the early 1950s.

Psychologists were fascinated with the digital computer for several reasons. First, computers showed that complex actions could be broken down into a series of yes or no decisions. This capability was important because it indicated that theoretically, no matter how complex a human's knowledge or information, it could be represented by a code that was simply **binary.** When used as an adjective, *binary* refers to information that is expressible in two elements. If a computer could be given correct feedback as it worked its way through each step of a binary code, then a computing machine could (again, theoretically) duplicate the behavior of a person, no matter how complex that behavior. This led psychologists to develop models of behavior based on the ideas of feedback and binary operations. One of these systems was developed by Miller, Galanter, and Pribram (1960) in their famous book *Plans and the Structure of Behavior.* They conceived of human action as being represented by components they called TOTE units. TOTE is an acronym that stands for Test Operate Test Exit.

Figure 1-1 shows the workings of a famous TOTE unit; this one is designed to drive nails. In the first stage of the process, the nail is *tested.* If it sticks up, then the process must *operate* by swinging the hammer down on the nail. After the operate stage, the process must again *test* the nail. If the nail head is now flush with the surface, then the process may *exit,* going on to something else.

The beauty of this system is that TOTE units can be built upon one another in a hierarchical fashion, with increasingly general TOTE units near the top of the hierarchy. For example, a building contractor might be endowed with an extremely general TOTE unit for house construction, which might consist of several more specific TOTE units for wall construction, each of which might contain a nail-driving TOTE unit like the one just described. Imagining that humans are governed by such TOTE units does not furnish proof that humans *are* made up of them. Nevertheless, *Plans and the Structure of Behavior* was extremely persuasive because it demonstrated that the feedback and mechanism approach to human actions could have tremendous explanatory power—power that was strong enough to challenge the behavioristic account.

Psychologists became fascinated with computers for another reason, too—one that you may have already guessed. From a certain perspective,

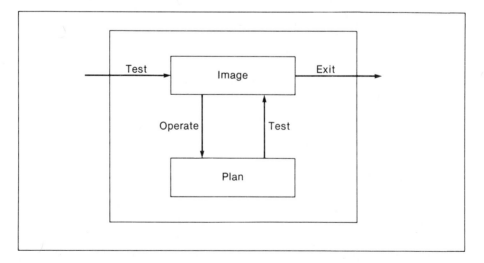

Figure 1.1.

A TOTE unit. (From Miller, Galanter & Pribram, 1960.)

computers could be thought of as nothing more than gigantic collections of vacuum tubes. The computer's power was awesome, but each vacuum tube couldn't do much: It was either on or off. The machine's power was derived from its speed in altering the on-off pattern of the vacuum tubes and from the fact that it had so many of them. Given what was known about neurology at that time, it seemed reasonable to compare the activity of the vacuum tube with the *action potential,* or firing of the individual neuron. If the analogy were continued, it seemed clear that the complexity of human action depended upon the speed of neural events (the action potential could take place one thousand times per second) and the fact that humans were endowed with billions of such neurons. In retrospect, it's not surprising that early computers were often referred to as "giant electronic brains." This name reflects the fond hope of many early computer scientists that the machines would do more than simply mimic the action of the nervous system; they would duplicate it.

For psychologists, this analogy was seductive. Behaviorism had treated the insides of people and animals as black boxes whose mysterious workings could be approached only through the defective technique of introspection. The behavioristic emphasis on stimulus and response led to a de-emphasis of the role played by biology and neurology in human and animal action. However, the arrival of computers suggested a way that neural events could be brought back into play. In the computer, many psychologists saw a model nervous system whose operation could be systematically and empirically altered. The hope was that investigations of this sort would produce programs representing neurological events and showing how such events were involved in classic psychological problems such as learning or perception. Although such attempts still surface occasionally (e.g., Albus, 1981), most cognitive psychologists have given up on the literal brain-computer comparison, for a variety of reasons.

The development of computing machines has had a profound influence on psychology nevertheless. Psychologists began to realize that although the human mind represents and organizes knowledge in particular and idiosyncratic ways, computers don't suffer any such liability. That is, in the computing machine, we see a device that is capable of representing knowledge in a wide variety of ways. Psychologists began using the computer to try out alternative forms of knowledge representation, not with the expectation of duplicating the neural events of the brain, but rather in an attempt to simulate or mimic cognitive events. Chapter 13 will try to show how advanced some of these simulation techniques have become.

Linguistics

Almost all of our utterances have a purpose: to communicate something. For thousands of years, scholars have been interested in both what people say as well as when they say it. In the past century or so, the study of speaking and listening has become decidedly psychological in tone. That is, many thinkers have realized that speech and hearing acts are closely intertwined and that both acts are influenced by the distinctly psychological process of perception. However, language is not always studied from a psychological perspective. Linguistics is the discipline that studies the structure of language. **Psycholinguistics** is the study of language from a psychological rather than from a linguistic perspective. Rather than focusing on the processes of speech and hearing per se, the linguist attempts to understand the *organization* of language, its regularities that seem more or less universal. Language seems intimately bound together with thought. The linguist hopes that by discovering the organizing principles of language, the laws of thought will also be revealed.

Skinner's Book and Chomsky's Rebuttal

One classic problem in the study of language is its acquisition. How do children learn to comprehend speech and produce grammatically correct utterances? The behavioristic perspective in psychology was firmly established by the time B. F. Skinner undertook a behavioristic analysis of language acquisition in 1936. Skinner created a phonograph record consisting of random groupings of sounds. The record had been made by recording natural speech and then editing the utterances so that the placement and ordering of the sounds were no longer typical. Skinner played this record—known as a verbal summator—for his subjects, and he noted that people read into the sounds, interpreting them as actual words. This phenomenon impressed Skinner. The verbal summator demonstrated that there was nothing inherently special about linguistic sounds and, Skinner argued, that meant language sounds could be studied as examples of operant behavior. Skinner reasoned that the same laws that governed the learning of other operant behaviors should govern the learning of language as well.

Consider the case of a child who makes a request of a parent, which is followed by the parent's response. A behavioristic theory of language would state that this particular verbal behavior was learned, because the parent reinforced the child for producing the utterance by complying with it. If a one-year-old holds up his cup and says "More!" the parent is reinforcing the child's utterance by providing him with more apple juice. Skinner called this function of language the **mand function.** Manded utterances are reinforced through compliance. Children must learn when to make the appropriate mands and what particular mands will be followed by a reward. According to Skinner, this latter problem boiled down to a case of discrimination learning. That is, the child plays a sort of naming game with the parent, during which words gradually become restricted to their appropriate referents. For example, the child might point to a red book and say "Red?" to which the parent might respond affirmatively. If the child then points to a blue book and says "Red?" the parent will respond with a no, and presumably, the child will learn that the operant *red* does not apply to the shape of the object but rather to some other feature. Proceeding in this way, the child eventually learns what cues must be present before the operant *red* will be rewarded, namely that *red* refers to the color of an object. The child is in a position similar to that of Skinner's pigeons, who would be reinforced for doing a particular behavior under some conditions but not under others. For the child as well as for the pigeon, the task consisted of discriminating the relevant features that signaled when a particular be-havior would be reinforced. Skinner referred to this recognition of the ap-propriate discriminative cues as the **tact function** of language.

As Skinner understood the problem of language acquisition, children go on tacting and manding their way through the first several years of their lives, gradually improving in emitting linguistic utterances. The publication of these ideas in Skinner's book *Verbal Behavior* (1957) was not well received by linguists, however. Noam Chomsky (1959) published a detailed and re-lentlessly critical review that seemed to devastate Skinner's claims.

First, Chomsky noted the problem of creativity in language. Some people have estimated that the number of humans that have ever lived is 40 to 50 billion. This number being so large, you might think that everything you could say has already been uttered by somebody, somewhere, sometime. This assumption is wrong. Constructing a completely novel remark is easy:

> Sophomores are limiculous.

Limiculous is an adjective referring to creatures whose habitat is mud. I'm sure that no one has ever applied that adjective to sophomores before. The problem for the behaviorist is explaining what enabled me to construct the remark. Because I've never created that remark before, no reinforcement could have existed for my constructing it. Simply put, the mand function of language does not appear powerful enough to explain novel remarks.

Chomsky also noted problems with the tact function. Skinner uses the tact function to explain particular responses to particular stimuli, such as when we respond to a piece of music by saying "Beethoven" or respond to a building by saying "Wright." In such situations, we have learned to discriminate when to emit particular verbal behaviors, namely in the pres-ence of particular stimulus characteristics of the music or of the building. For example, when we see a painting and respond "Dutch," we are re-sponding to particular characteristics of that painting—that is, particular stimuli that presumably exist in the world. But Chomsky maintains:

> Suppose instead of saying "Dutch" we said "Clashes with the wallpaper, I thought you liked abstract work, never saw it before, tilted, hanging too low, beautiful, hideous, remember our camping trip last summer?" or whatever else might come into our minds when looking at a picture. . . . Skinner could only say that each of these responses is under the control of some other stimulus property of the physical object. . . . But the word *stimulus* has lost all objectivity in this usage. Stimuli are no longer part of the outside physical world: they are driven back into the organism. We identify the stimulus when we hear the response. It is clear from such examples, which abound, that the talk of *stimulus control* simply disguises a complete retreat to mentalistic psychology. (Chomsky, 1959) (Emphasis in original.)

In this instance, Chomsky points out that the behavioristic account of language is no more scientific that the mentalistic accounts it had sup-planted a half century earlier. The behaviorist's frustrating problem is that the tact function is not powerful enough to explain why particular utterances are produced at particular times. The notion of stimulus control is no help because, as Chomsky points out, it's not possible to specify what the stimulus is until we hear the subject's response. In other words, the idea that characteristics of the world signal us to produce specific remarks seems false, because it's not possible to specify in advance what characteristics of the world did the signaling.

Another difficulty for the behavioristic position concerns the learning of grammar. One aspect of grammar whose learning seems particularly hard to explain is syntax. Syntax refers to the rules that specify the ordering of words. To understand the complexity of this learning, suppose we assembled a group of adults and told them that someone was going to utter a sentence and they were to repeat the sentence, one person at a time. The repetition must, however, include a word or phrase that has been inserted into the sentence in a grammatically correct way, and each subsequent repetition must include all of the previous insertions. The sentence might be "The boy went to the store," the first repetition might be "The boy went quickly to the store," the second repetition might be "The boy whose parents were physicians went quickly to the store," and so on. What's the longest sentence that could be constructed in theory?

No theoretical maximum length exists for any sentence in English, so the game could go on forever. Notice, however, that no simple rule governs the expansions. Not only could the game go on forever, but also each linguistically competent adult could make insertions of different grammatical *types* if he or she chose to. Therefore, given that each insertion seems to be governed by its own rule, the conclusion we can draw from this game is that each participating adult must be in possession of an infinite number of expansion rules. The question is, How did we learn all these rules? We've never heard all the possible sentences in English; in some sense, we've heard only a small sample of them. Yet, from direct exposure to a finite number of word orderings, we find ourselves the possessors of an infinite number of rules regarding word order. The criticism of the behavioristic account of syntax is similar to the criticism of the mand function: We seem to know much more than we have ever been reinforced for knowing. As Chomsky put it in his review of *Verbal Behavior:*

> The child who learns a language has in some sense constructed the grammar for himself on the basis of his observation of sentences and nonsentences (i.e., corrections by the verbal community). Study of the actual observed ability of a speaker to distinguish sentences from nonsentences, detect ambiguities, etc., apparently forces us to the conclusion that this grammar is of an extremely complex and abstract character, and that the young child has succeeded in carrying out what from the formal point of view, at least, seems to be a remarkable type of theory construction. Furthermore, this task is accomplished in an astonishingly short time, to a large extent independently of intelligence, and in a comparable way by all children. Any theory of learning must cope with these facts. (Chomsky, 1959)

Paraphrasing somewhat, competent adult speakers have in effect built a reliable theory of sentence construction that allows them to communicate with other members of the verbal community. That we can communicate with others is at least a superficial indication that others' theories of sentence construction strongly resemble ours, even though the number of identical utterances that both speaker and listener have heard is surely small. This means that the grammatical knowledge we have is both complex and abstract, and cannot be accounted for by a simple listing of stimulus-response relationships, no matter how lengthy such a list we make.

Chomsky's criticism of Skinner's book was extremely influential and initiated a relationship between psychology and linguistics that grew to be close throughout the sixties and early seventies. Whereas the literature on computers and feedback systems could be seen as an alternative account to behavioristic explanations of human performance, the evidence from linguistics was seen as a successful attack on a behavioristic position. One of Chomsky's main points was that the mental events of the speaker and listener must play a central role in their performances, and consequently, a theory of language must account for them. This point seemed to strike a responsive chord in the minds of many psychologists. Although many psychologists at the time were studying cognitive topics such as memory and concept formation, they began to realize how sterile the behavioral approach was to such problems. In looking for an alternative approach, it seemed natural to borrow some of the terminology of the human factors and computer fields, a viewpoint that soon emerged as the **information-processing approach.** In 1967, Ulric Neisser published the eagerly awaited book *Cognitive Psychology;* and in 1970 the journal *Cognitive Psychology* began publication. With these occurrences, interest in and research on mental events were reestablished as fixtures of the American psychological landscape.

THE FACE OF CONTEMPORARY COGNITIVE PSYCHOLOGY

The Information-Processing Approach

The phrase "information processing" has been used throughout this chapter, relying to a certain extent on your intuitions regarding its meaning. Information processing has a technical meaning for cognitive psychologists, however, and this section describes its use more explicitly.

An Abstract Analysis

When cognitive psychologists describe the information-processing approach as an abstract analysis, they mean that neural events are not described explicitly. Mental or cognitive events are abstract in the sense that while they depend upon neural events, they are not neural events, nor are they necessarily ever reducible to neural events. For example, suppose I ask you to imagine the house in which you grew up. I'm sure that you would be capable of scanning your mental picture of the house in response to questions such as "How many windows did the house have in front?" Are your actions (imagining, scanning, answering) accompanied by some activity in your brain? The answer to that question is almost certainly yes. But are these actions themselves neural events? No, because I can describe any of these events without ever using the word *neuron* or *synapse* in my description.

In a way, the cognitive psychologist who wants to describe mental events has something in common with a computer programmer. The programmer's task is to come up with a recipe (essentially) that will get the machine to carry out a particular series of computations. In writing the program, the programmer is not concerned about electron flow within the machine nor with many other aspects about the machine as a piece of *hardware*. Rather, the programmer thinks perhaps of data structures and operations upon them. The recipe, or program, that is eventually concocted is a piece of *software* that generally speaking, is more or less independent of the machine. Cognitive psychologists are in the same boat. They are not too interested in specifying the neural activity underlying a mental event—that's a hardware problem and one that may be unsolvable in principle. Instead, cognitive psychologists want to produce a description of the mental events in mental terms—those that are more or less independent of neurology.

In each of the abstract actions (scanning, imagining, and so on) we engage in, the cognitive psychologist is likely to say that some information has been processed. What sort of information is this? This chapter earlier described Neisser's definition of cognitive psychology, and we saw that in his definition, cognition begins with sensory input. This sensory input is what forms the basis of the information studied by the cognitive psychologist. Thus, when we look at something, our first cognitive act results from the transformation of physical energy into neural events. That is, just as information from the world is retained in the nervous system (in a coded way), so does the cognitive system swing into action at the same time to produce a cognitive event that is also a coded version of the sensory input. As the nervous system systematically continues to transform the original sensory input, so does the information in the cognitive code continue to undergo a series of transformations. As we think, the information we have represented within ourselves is continually modified and altered. We shouldn't be too surprised to find that the cognitive code doesn't bear much resemblance to the information outside our bodies in its physical form.

A very direct and I hope meaningful comparison is to be made here: Processed information is much like processed food. For example, you can buy the carcass of a fish, which has many of the properties of the living fish: size, color, face, and teeth. If you go to the supermarket, however, you can't buy unprocessed hot dogs, the carcasses of hot dog animals whose legs and tails have been chopped off so their torsos can be stuffed into a vinyl package. Hot dogs are made by curing, cooking, and grinding up the remnants of animals. The end result of these operations is still food; in that regard, a hot dog is just like a fish. The hot dog, however, is processed food. As a result of the transformations that have been carried out upon it, the hot dog no longer resembles the animals that comprise it. The same can be said of the information within us: Following all its transformations, neither the neural codes nor the cognitive codes have much in common with the physical stimulation from which they were constructed.

Like the hot dog maker, the cognitive psychologist would assert that the necessary operations often occur serially, one step at a time. **Serial processing** can be contrasted with **parallel processing,** which refers to simultaneously transforming more than one cognitive code. Although cases clearly exist in which the human information-processing system proceeds in parallel, many cognitive psychologists find it convenient to describe the fate of specific cognitive codes as the result of serial processing (Simon, 1978). This simplifying convenience is necessitated in part because of the extraordinary difficulty in modeling and researching parallel systems.

Cognitive psychologists usually divide the human information-processing system into components as shown in Figure 1.2. This differentiation is based in part on the supposition that some cognitive acts seem quite different from others.

The first component of the information-processing system is the sensory system, where the cognitive code is created. In this system, specific aspects of the environment are detected and their organization is begun. After the cognitive code is created by the sensory system, it is passed on to the memory. As Figure 1.2 shows, cognitive psychologists make a distinction between the permanent memory, sometimes referred to as the inactive memory, and the working memory. The permanent memory can be considered as a vast depository of both declarative and procedural knowledge. The permanent memory is a storehouse not only of facts but also of skills and motor programs that enable us to move and speak. Under some conditions, the central processor allocates attention to the working memory. When this is done, elements that have been passed into the permanent memory become activated, and at this juncture the cognitive code can be elaborated and modified.

Working memory is a kind of workbench for cognitive codes. As Figure 1.2 shows, working memory is the site where goals can be established. These goals will sometimes include the modification of a cognitive code. For example, in problem solving, the cognitive code might consist of representations of both possible solutions and possible operations that might be done to produce a solution. When solving problems, the central processor might use the working memory as a site to systematically match up possible solutions with possible operations to see if a fit can be achieved and the problem solved. The task of the central processor is to formulate goals. Once the goal is formulated, the central processor must develop a plan to accomplish the goal. In situations in which the central processor is dealing with multiple goals (which is probably the case for most real-life situations), a priority listing of goals must be established. When this has been done, the central processor must allocate attention to the cognitive processes involved to monitor their progress. The central processor uses working, or active, memory to keep track of its place in the plan, and from this site in the working memory, the response system is controlled.

Earlier, I mentioned the reminder Billie Jean King uses to help her put top spin on the ball. Let's see how the entire forehand drive would be described using an information-processing approach. First, the environment would offer Billie Jean information about the flight of the ball—information that would be picked up primarily by the visual and auditory systems (tennis pros listen to the sound of the ball as it leaves the racquet's strings). Presumably, Billie Jean's central processor has allocated attention to processes that recognize and categorize her opponent's shot. This categorization is

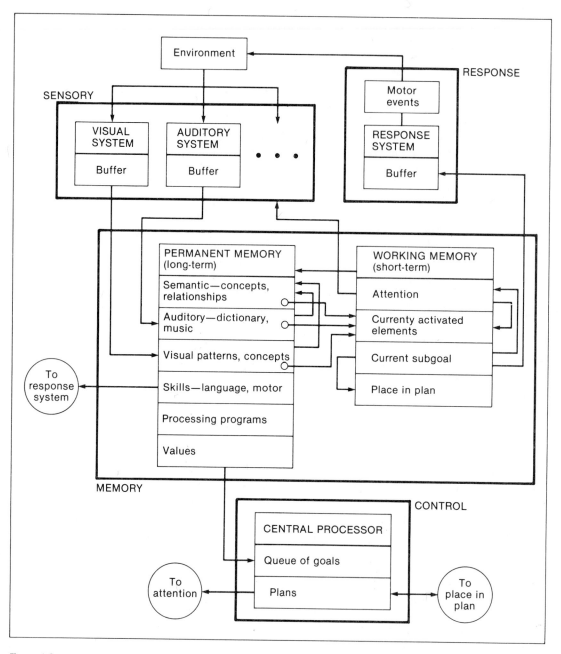

Figure 1.2.
A general working model of the human information-processing system. (From Dodd & White, 1980.)

important; it lets the tennis pro know where to go to be in position for the return. A second function of the categorization is that it affords the pro an opportunity to determine what kind of point is being played. If the ball is hit short, the pro has knowledge of the various patterns of play (a dropshot return, a crosscourt volley, and so on) that can be attempted from a short ball. Following the categorization, the central processor begins to allocate attention to the opponent's movements. Here, the goal is to determine an effective placement for the return shot: Is the opponent coming to the net? If that's the case, then a passing shot down the line could be the right response. While this has been going on, several automatic processes have been initiated. Billie Jean uses automatic and procedural running programs stored in her permanent memory to move quickly from her present position to the desired position on the court. Once there, Billie Jean attempts to hit the forehand drive, and for this she uses the procedural knowledge program that was described in the beginning of this chapter.

Not every cognitive psychologist would agree with every aspect of this account or with every aspect of Figure 1.2. As we'll see in Chapter 5, several theorists have wondered about the relationship between permanent and working memory; not all of them would agree that his distinction is valid. Similarly, the role of the central processor in the allocation of attention has been questioned. You should be aware that just as the theories in cognitive psychology are fluid and developing, there are no rigid boundaries around any of the boxes that make up our information-processing systems. With that proviso in mind, consider some of the points that most cognitive psychologists would probably agree on:

1. Mentality can be divided into a group of interrelated cognitive processes.
2. Our mental lives show many features predicted by the structuralism of Wundt and his colleagues. Perhaps the most striking of these features is the degree of organization involved in human knowledge.
3. Although much of our information processing takes place simultaneously, the fate of many cognitive codes can be traced in a serial fashion. This means that it is possible to build reasonable models of mental events in which the events are assumed to occur sequentially, that is, in particular orders. As will be discussed shortly, the fact that certain mental events occur chronologically before others suggests that the cognitive processes underlying those mental events must also occur in some specifiable order, at least in some situations.
4. Human mental events are abstract and so are often best comprehended by using an abstract analysis. Although information from biology and neurology may be helpful in understanding cognitive processes, this information is not essential. When cognitive psychologists try to build an abstract analysis of mental events, they are striving for an analysis that is not dependent on neurological terms. Rather, the analysis focuses on abstract or cognitive terms, such as "searching" your memory, "scanning" a mental image, or "analyzing" a problem.

5. We know a lot more than we think we know. Here, I'm referring to the fact that much of our knowledge is stored in a procedural format. We know how to use this knowledge to accomplish things, but because this knowledge doesn't enter our awareness, we're inclined to overlook its importance.

Methods in Cognitive Psychology

We've seen something of the topics discussed in cognitive psychology, and we've received an orientation to the terms and background of the field. One more task remains for us to accomplish in this chapter: to understand something of the methods and techniques used by cognitive psychologists.

Throughout the textbook are cited studies from which cognitive psychologists infer the characteristics of our cognitive functioning. Cognitive psychologists often use an experimental approach to their subject matter, which involves the manipulation of some independent variable and observations of changes produced in a dependent variable. The listing of things that have served as dependent variables in psychological studies is endless, but cognitive psychologists have become fond of two classes of events for this purpose: patterns of errors and reaction times to complex stimuli.

Consider the case of a person who wishes to say the phrase "a current argument" as part of an utterance but says instead "an arrent curgument." This error, which is authentic (Fromkin, 1971; Garrett, 1982), tells us a great deal about the cognitive processes involved in speech. How would we describe what has taken place? First, we would say that a syllable switch has taken place. The first syllable of "current" has been switched with the first syllable of "argument." From this observation, we might conclude that the human mind builds words by assembling them on a syllable-by-syllable basis. We might go on to theorize that prior to being completely assembled, each planned word is held in a group of slots marked First Syllable, Second Syllable, and so on. To assemble the word, a cognitive program draws the contents of the first slot and follows it with the contents of the second slot, and so on. If a mistake is going to occur, presumably it's because this particular program can't recognize which slots go with which other slots. Consequently, this particular program can't tell if an error is being made in the assembly process, because it apparently doesn't know the meaning of the words. This is what seems to be happening here, because there's no such thing as a "curgument."

In English, we use the indefinite article *a* prior to consonants and *an* prior to vowels. Although the person in our example intended to use *a*, the assembly error has resulted in a vowel sound being placed where the consonant sound had been intended. We notice that this error has been rectified in the actual utterance: The *a* has been changed to *an*. What can we conclude from this switch? Apparently, the program that determines the sounds of our utterances must operate after the program that assembles the syllables. If the program that determined the sound of utterances went first, then the person would have said "a arrent curgument"; but such errors do not occur. Chapter 10 takes a closer look at speech errors; for now, we should be aware that the analysis of errors is one of the cognitive psychologist's most powerful techniques for making inferences about mental events.

TABLE 1.2

Examples of the Pairs Used to Demonstrate Associative Pairing

Positive Pairs		Negative Pairs		
Unrelated	Related	First Nonword	Second Nonword	Both Nonwords
Nurse	Bread	Plame	Wine	Plame
Butter	Butter	Wine	Plame	Reab
940 msec	855 msec	904 msec	1,087 msec	884 msec

Source: Meyer and Schvaneveldt, 1971.

A second common approach consists of measuring reaction times to the presentation of stimuli. The work of Meyer and Schvaneveldt (1971) offers a good illustration of this approach. They hypothesized that conceptually related words would be recognized as words faster than unrelated words would be recognized. To test this assertion, they presented their subjects with pairs of related and unrelated words. They also presented their subjects with pairs of nonwords. The subjects' task was to decide as quickly as possible if both elements of a pair were words, and if so, they were to say yes. If one or neither element of the pair was a nonword, subjects were instructed to say no. Table 1.2 shows the findings. The positive pairs (those in which the subject was to respond yes) are of particular interest. When the words were related, subjects responded 85 msec faster than they did when the words were unrelated. Although this difference may not seem like much (and we would probably not be *aware* of such a difference), a 10 percent difference in processing time is usually accepted as substantial by many cognitive psychologists. If one group requires about 1,500 msec to carry out a particular task, and a second group requires about 1,550 msec to carry out some variation of the task, such a difference wouldn't pique our curiosity. If the 50 msec difference between the groups occurred against a base rate of 500 msec, however, then we would be curious.

What can we gather from the Meyer and Schvaneveldt findings? From the substantial difference in processing time, we might state that recognition of a word seems to facilitate the recognition and reading of a related word. Such a finding tells us that words are probably recognized at least in part by their *context*.

Ecological Validity

Although cognitive psychologists usually bring their subjects into the laboratory for study, during the 1970s a movement was afoot to increase the **ecological validity** of research in cognition. This term, which was popularized by Neisser (1976), refers to the quest for theories of cognition that describe people's use of knowledge in real, everyday, culturally significant situations. Although this quest doesn't restrict the researcher's use of the laboratory, the emphasis on ecological validity does mean that the contemporary cognitive psychologist feels a burden to explain cognition in a way that makes sense in everyday language. Further, cognitive psychologists are often interested in commonly experienced problems. Although the approach is theoretical, cognitive psychologists frequently hope for some possibility of applying their findings to day-to-day life.

The emphasis on ecological validity has a special implication for you, the nonspecialist reader. It means that much of what you are about to read should be useful to you. I can't promise that you'll be able to use everything that you read in this book, or that the applications will be obvious. But my hope is that after you study human reasoning, for example, (Chapter 11), your reasoning will improve. Perhaps after you study the material on problem solving (Chapter 12), you'll become more successful at detecting and avoiding some of the pitfalls that hinder creative thinking. Similarly, after you study memory (Chapters 4, 5, 6, and 7), I'm optimistic that you'll be able to use the material to improve your retention and retrieval. As long as you keep in mind that the theories presented are the current best guess about their respective phenomena and are not absolute truths, I'm confident that your studies in this book will be rewarded with both practical skills and a deeper appreciation of your mind's complexity.

CONCLUDING COMMENTS AND SUGGESTIONS FOR FURTHER READING

The end of each chapter presents titles of books and articles you might want to read if you're interested in the topics that were covered in that chapter. Students who want to find out about cognitive research in real-life situations could read Rogoff and Lave's (1984) book, *Everyday Cognition.* One of the chapters is an analysis of the cognitive processes that go on during grocery shopping. Students who want to know more about the methodology of cognitive psychology might try the book edited by Kintsch, Miller, and Polson (1984), *Methods and Tactics in Cognitive Science.*

FOCUS ON RESEARCH:
What Is the Subject Matter of Cognitive Psychology?

Asking that cognitive psychologists agree on the appropriate subject matter of their field is not an unreasonable request. After all, how can cognitive psychology exist unless the researchers agree on what it is? The issue, however, is far more complicated than this. Understanding the problem is easier if you have some background in the philosophy of science.

Some cognitive psychologists believe that their field has entered a period of *normal science*—one

that is governed by the information-processing approach (Lachman, Lachman, & Butterfield, 1979). Normal science refers to the idea that scientific findings are supposed to build on one another. In this way, knowledge accumulates. For example, suppose researcher A does a study on the retention of digits in memory, and then researcher B finds that the number of digits retained depends in part on which digits the subjects are asked to retain. This is normal science. The second study modifies the general conclusion of the first, but its conclusion is nevertheless an elaboration of the earlier finding. Moreover, the methods used in both cases are the same. Science doesn't always proceed normally. For a variety of reasons, researchers sometimes go off in new directions, and the findings produced by such studies do not build upon previous work. Indeed, a fundamental dissatisfaction with previous work is what often propels researchers into new areas. Kuhn (1962) has described this phenomenon as a *paradigm shift*. A paradigm shift is a radical change in a field's approach to its subject matter, its methods, and its interpretation of findings. In looking at the history of science, Kuhn argues that a given field is characterized by cyclical periods of revolutionary paradigm shifting, followed by more stable periods of normal science. The recent history of psychology is sometimes characterized this way. The change from a behavioristic to a cognitively oriented viewpoint represents a shift in paradigms. Since the revolution, psychology has settled down into a new period of accumulating findings.

If this is true, then some consensus should exist among researchers concerning the appropriate topics for a cognitive psychologist to investigate. White (1985) explored this question in an interesting way. He examined the reference lists of seven introductory cognitive psychology textbooks, all of which were published in 1979 or 1980. He reasoned that if cognitive psychologists are in agreement about the topics of their field, then they should describe and cite the same studies in their introductory textbooks. The seven texts cited over 3,200 references. Of these, just 19 publications were cited in all seven texts, and only 144 were cited in at least four of the seven books. Of the 3,200 references, 2,620 appeared in only one book. These findings strongly suggest that the writers of these books were not in basic agreement about the important findings of the field. Has cognitive psychology assumed the status of a normal science? The answer seems to be no. White's findings suggest that the revolutionary period is not yet over.

KEY TERMS

Cognitive codes
Declarative knowledge
Procedural knowledge
Controlled processes
Automatic processes
Structuralism
Human factors research
Information

Binary code
Psycholinguistics
Mand function
Tact function
Information-processing approach
Serial processing
Parallel processing
Ecological validity

PART TWO

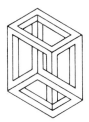

PERCEPTION

Cognitive psychologists refer to a large number of cognitive processes as "perceptual," and many of them are basic to your understanding of the rest of this book. Perceptual processes are those that take sensory input and transform it into a more abstract code. We know that our senses respond to particular forms of physical energy. In our nervous systems, a code is created in which aspects of the physical energy are preserved. For example, you probably remember from your introductory psychology class that the rods and cones in our retinae preserve certain aspects of electromagnetic radiation. But I'm not aware of what my rods and cones are doing; in describing the visual world, I use terms like *light* and *color*. These are psychological terms that correspond to, but are not equivalent with, the sensory information. What does this mean? It means that some other intervening processes have taken the sensory code—the neurological information being relayed by the rods and cones—and converted it into another code that gives rise to my awareness of the psychological experiences of light and color. These intervening processes are perceptual.

Cataloguing all such processes would be incredibly lengthy, but we know about some of them intuitively. For example, we know that we can direct our sensory capabilities, which is referred to as the phenomenon of attention. To a certain extent, all our senses can be aimed at sensory stimulation by turning our heads to look or by reaching out and touching. We can even get ready to hear something. Whenever we aim our senses, perception seems to occur faster. We also recognize that per-

ceptual processes sometimes seem to occur in a sequential order. This implies a sort of hierarchy of processing. For example, in order to read, groups of lines must be organized into letters, groups of letters into words, and groups of words into meaning. This kind of hierarchy suggests that some perceptual processes occur earlier than others in the processing of information. After all, how can the meaning of a sentence be known before we know what the letters are?

As important as sensory information is for perception, it can't be the whole story. If I look out into the parking lot on a bright day, my rods and cones nicely pick up reflected radiation from an object, which my perceptual processes elaborate until I recognize the pattern as a car. But I can still recognize the car on a foggy day or at night, when my rods and cones are not providing my perceptual processes with the same quality of information. How can this be? You may have already guessed the answer. In addition to using sensory information to perceive, I also use my knowledge of the world to make inferences about what sensory information I can expect to encounter. What else would be in the parking lot, if not a car?

We see, then, that perception involves two distinct types of cognitive operations. Perception is achieved by a combination of cognitive processes—some that begin by elaborating the sensory code and others that are inferential and begin with our knowledge of the world. Keep this interplay in mind as you read the next two chapters.

CHAPTER 2

Attention and Pattern Recognition

OVERVIEW

THE NATURE OF ATTENTION
Definition
Problems with Definitions of Attention
Studies of Selective Attention

BOTTLENECK THEORIES OF ATTENTION
Filter Theory
Attenuation Theory
Late Selection Theories
Conclusions from the First Phase of Theory
   Building

**ALTERNATIVES TO FILTER THEORIES: CAPACITY
MODELS**
Some Questions Concerning Capacity Models

The Relationship between Practice and
   Attention

AUTOMATICITY
Conclusions from the Second Phase of Theory
   Building

PATTERN RECOGNITION
Template-Matching Theory
Feature Detection Theory
Independent Confirmation of Feature Analysis
   Biological Contributions
Context

**CONCLUDING COMMENTS AND SUGGESTIONS
FOR FURTHER READING
FOCUS ON RESEARCH
KEY TERMS**

You've probably had an experience similar to the following. One morning I was intently reading a book while eating breakfast. It had snowed the night before, and my wife had filled the bird feeder on the deck behind our house. Something caught my eye as I read, and I looked up to see a cheering sight on a midwinter day: A red-bellied woodpecker had come to eat at the feeder. These magnificent birds, with their black and white zebra backs and vivid red-striped heads, are not commonly seen in my part of the country.

Although the bird may not be common, the episode is. We can concentrate our senses on particular sources of stimulation to gather information about them, but this concentration is always partial. Consequently, when other sources of stimulation present themselves, our concentration may shift to these new stimuli and leave the old ones behind. Not every new stimulus provokes this shift of concentration, however. Numerous sparrows came to the feeder that morning while I read. If you were to ask me how many sparrows there were, I would have no idea because I was reading my book and not concentrating on the sparrows. Perhaps you now see the problem the episode with the woodpecker creates: What do some stimuli have that enables them to provoke the shift of concentration that other stimuli don't have? This question is not adequately answered by responding that familiar stimuli don't provoke the shift, whereas rare or unusual stimuli do. This answer is unacceptable because presumably, I didn't know the woodpecker *was* a woodpecker and therefore rare until *after* I shifted my concentration to look at him. Although the episode with the wood-pecker may be common, it is not simple.

This chapter examines the concept of attention—a mental phenomenon that cognitive psychologists have used to describe and explain concentration and its shifts. We'll review several studies of **selective attention,** and we'll consider several theoretical models that have been erected to explain the findings of such studies. Generally speaking, we can divide the research into two phases. In the first phase of theory building, which took place in the 1950s, attention was commonly thought of as a bottleneck in the information-processing system. That is, stimuli could not be fully processed unless they were attended to, and our attentional mechanisms were limited to processing only a small amount of all the stimulation bombarding us. In the second phase of theory building, which has taken place in the last fifteen years, this conception has been supplemented with a view of attention as the allocation of resources. We'll consider this position and examine one of its implications—namely, that highly overlearned tasks require the allocation of few cognitive resources. When such a state of affairs exists, cognitive processes can take place without conscious guidance; this is referred to as automatic processing.

The function of attention is to bring cognitive processes to bear on external stimuli so that information can be gathered about them. In gathering information about the stimuli, one of our first tasks seems to be a determination of what sort or what kind of stimuli we're dealing with. Broadly speaking, we do this by discerning what *patterns* might be present in the stimulation. The perception of certain patterns in stimulation is used as the basis for recognizing and categorizing it. Going back to the woodpecker once again: Once my attention was focused, I detected characteristics in the stimuli (the vivid red-striped head) that enabled me to first recognize and then categorize the animal. This chapter considers what aspects of the stimuli are used as a basis for categorization. The chapter closes with a discussion of the role of context, or surrounding stimulation, as it influences the process of pattern recognition.

THE NATURE OF ATTENTION

Definition

Providing a concise definition of attention is difficult because the term has been used in so many ways. For example, when you take a test you have to attend to it, which implies that you have an ability to focus your mental effort on specific stimuli while excluding other stimuli from consideration. One important aspect of attention, therefore, is its *selectivity*. If a professor advises you to pay particular attention to a certain question and you do, your actions indicate that you have an ability to shift the focus of mental effort from one stimulus to another. In this case, you were able to change the focus of your efforts from one question on the test to another, and this ability seems to be under your control. That is, the shift in attention doesn't seem to be demanded by the stimulus alone (because you could choose to ignore your professor's instructions). Such facts tell us that not only is the focus of mental effort shiftable, but also some cognitive process must decide the timing and direction of the shift. If you go to a bar after the test to debrief with your friends, you may pay attention to their conversation and watch an episode of your favorite soap opera at the same time. This ability indicates that we can apparently maintain more than one focus of mental effort simultaneously. The focus of mental effort not only is selective and shiftable but also can be divided into parts. As a general definition, therefore, attention refers to the concentration and focusing of mental effort (Matlin, 1983)—a focus that is selective, shiftable, and divisible.

Problems with Definitions of Attention

When we focus mental effort on a task, the action seems to be under our conscious control. That is, we consciously decide which stimuli will be selectively focused upon and which will be excluded. Understanding attention would be much easier if all such selection decisions were made consciously, but unfortunately that doesn't seem to be the case. For example, if a friend takes a long car trip with you, you will pay attention to your friend's speech. This effort is a conscious decision to focus mental effort on particular stimuli. At the same time, you will continue to drive the car appropriately, which involves focusing mental effort selectively on continually changing highway conditions. But this sort of focusing, although ongoing, is probably not done with any awareness of the many decisions that are being made.

The role of awareness seemingly creates problems for the definition of attention. Why is this so? If awareness is not required for selection and shifts of mental effort, then attention is not under conscious control, because such shifts and selections would take place without any decision making that we were aware of. On the other hand, if awareness *is* required for attention, then attention is not selective, because in order to shift attention under those circumstances, we would already had to have been aware of all the stimuli around us.

A couple of difficult questions can now be formulated. Under what circumstances is attention truly under conscious control, and under what circumstances is it truly selective? To arrive at a preliminary answer to these questions, we'll explore the results of several **dichotic listening** studies that made up the first wave of research in this area.

Studies of Selective Attention

Early studies of selective attention often involved the dichotic presentation of material. The subject wore stereo headphones, and into each ear a different message was transmitted. The subject was told to attend to only one ear and to make sure this instruction was carried out; the subject was requested to *shadow* the attended ear. **Shadowing** involves listening to the message in the attended ear and repeating it aloud as soon as possible after hearing it. Assuming the subject makes no errors in shadowing the attended ear, the technique seems to be a good way of ensuring selective focusing on a particular message.

Using the dichotic listening procedure, Cherry (1953) found that subjects had remarkably little difficulty with the shadowing technique. They made few errors in shadowing the attended ear. Cherry was also interested in what the subjects remembered about the message in the *unattended* ear. He found that the subjects could accurately report whether the unattended message had been a human voice or a noise, and they could also report whether the voice had been a man's or a woman's, apparently on the basis of pitch. In other words, the subjects seemed to have some knowledge of the physical or acoustic properties of the unattended message. However, they seemed to have little knowledge of the *meaning* of the unattended message. For example, the subjects were unable to detect the language used by the voice in the unattended ear, nor were they able to recognize words that had been presented in the unshadowed ear thirty-five times (Moray, 1959).

Thirty years ago, such studies were widely interpreted as indicating the highly selective nature of attention. We became conscious of what was attended to. Moreover, the focus of attention was thought to be consciously directed so that little unattended information could enter our consciousness. According to such a viewpoint, subjects would have difficulty doing two demanding tasks simultaneously because as they focused on one task, they were no longer conscious of the events taking place in the second task. Consequently, some information would be lost no matter how quickly the

subjects attempted to alternate between the two tasks, and so their performance on both tasks would inevitably decline.

Mowbray's (1953) study supports this position. Mowbray instructed his
subjects to attend to two messages simultaneously. The subjects heard one
story while silently reading a second story whose content was unrelated to
the story presented aurally. Subjects then took a test measuring comprehension of both stories. The subjects almost always comprehended one of
the stories substantially better than the other; the subject's poorer score
was usually at the chance, or guessing, level.

BOTTLENECK THEORIES OF ATTENTION

Filter Theory

Broadbent (1958) developed a theory of attention that attempted to account
for the findings of Cherry and Mowbray. Broadbent proposed that the focus
of attention is determined by three components: a selective filter, which led
to a channel of limited capacity, which in turn led to a detection device.
These components are represented in Figure 2.1.

The sensory register, or sensory information store, is discussed more
fully in Chapter 4. Basically, this register is a memory of stimuli that have
recently been presented. Stimuli are stored in sensory memory in one of
several channels, each channel corresponding loosely to a different sensory
modality. Although the duration of this memory is brief, its contents are
thought to be exact representations of the original stimuli. While they are
stored in the sensory register, the stimuli are subjected to a **preattentive
analysis** (Neisser, 1967), which determines some of their physical characteristics, such as pitch, intensity, and so on. As a result of this preattentive
analysis, the selective filter determines which stimuli will undergo further
processing. Those stimuli that are not selected are essentially tuned out;
no further elaboration of them takes place.

Following their selection, the stimuli are shunted along a limited capacity channel to the detection device. The channel's relatively limited capacity has important implications for the human information processor. If
asked to pay attention to several demanding tasks simultaneously, the
shunting channel lacks the capacity to carry all of the incoming information
simultaneously to the detection device. Instead, the selection filter switches
as rapidly as possible among the channels in the sensory register, in each
case taking the information that has been loaded into that particular channel
and transferring it to the shunting channel. This process explains why
Broadbent's viewpoint is referred to as a *bottleneck* theory. A great deal of
information can be stored in the sensory channels simultaneously, but evac-
uating information from the sensory register is a laborious process that
must be done serially—that is, one channel at a time.

Information in the shunting channel is transferred to the detection device, where an analysis of the information's *meaning* is carried out. According to Broadbent's position, we "know" only about stimuli that make it

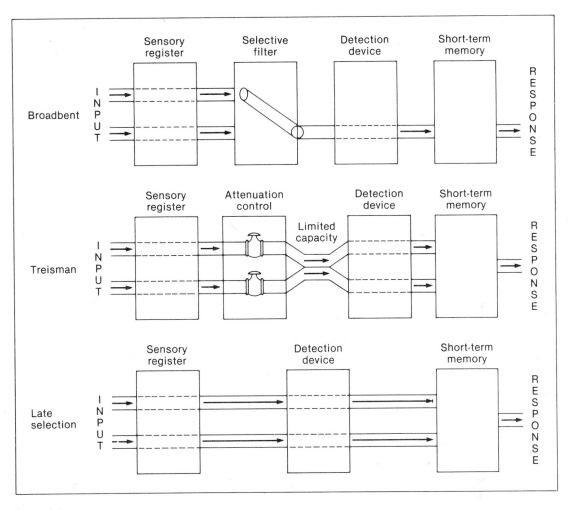

Figure 2.1.

Three models of attention and capacity in sensory processing.

past the selection filter. Information that was stopped at that stage is subjected only to a preattentive analysis, which is incapable of determining the stimuli's meaning.

This theory provides a reasonable account of Cherry's and Mowbray's findings. Recall that Mowbray (1953) found that subjects could apparently extract the meaning of only one story when two had been presented—one visually, the other aurally. In this case, the decrement in performance was produced by the selection filter's inability to switch between the auditory and visual channels rapidly enough. While information from one channel in the sensory register was extracted and loaded into the shunting channel, information in other channels of the sensory register could not be evacuated. As we'll see in Chapter 4, the sensory storage has a large capacity; however, material in sensory storage has an extremely short "shelf life." If the information stored there is not extracted within a short time, it begins to decay. This is why the subject could not answer questions about the information stored in the unselected channel. By the time the shunting channel was switched back to this information, it had decayed. Because information in the blocked channel was given only a preattentive analysis, the subjects were unable to answer questions about the passage's meaning.

Regarding Cherry's findings the filter is tuned to accept information from the shadowed ear; this information is loaded into the shunting channel and ultimately processed for meaning by the detection device. Material that is presented in the nonshadowed ear has a different fate. Because the filter is never opened to the nonshadowed ear, none of this material is transferred to the shunting channel and detection device. Consequently, the subjects in Cherry's study were able to report only the physical characteristics of the nonshadowed message. These characteristics were determined by the preattentive analysis.

However, it's possible to demonstrate that Broadbent's theory of attention, although convincing, cannot be completely correct. Moray (1959) found that subjects sometimes recognize that their name had been uttered in the nonshadowed message. According to Broadbent's theory, this recognition should not have happened. Names are meaningful to their owners, but the analysis of meaning is supposedly carried out by the detection device, which nonshadowed material never enters.

Similarly, Treisman (1960) reported that subjects could shadow the semantic content (i.e., the meaning) of a message even when the message was played into the nonshadowed ear. Treisman instructed her subjects to shadow a particular ear into which was played a meaningful message. The nonshadowed ear received a random string of words. At some point in the delivery, the semantic content switched ears, as shown in Figure 2.2. At the same time, the random words were switched into the shadowed ear.

Figure 2.2.

An illustration of Treisman's (1960) shadowing study.

Although the subjects had been instructed to shadow a particular ear, many of them ignored this instruction and shadowed the meaningful *message* instead. This finding indicated to Treisman that the subjects must have had some knowledge of the semantic content of the nonshadowed message.

In other studies, Treisman (1964a, 1964b) demonstrated that the analysis of a message's semantic content was accomplished fairly early on in the human information-processing system. Treisman used the dichotic listening procedure once again, telling her subjects to shadow a message. The message in the nonshadowed ear was to be ignored. Unknown (initially) to the subjects, the messages were identical. The nonshadowed message was started either slightly ahead of or slightly behind the shadowed message, and over the course of the presentation, the nonshadowed message was speeded up or slowed down to synchronize it with the shadowed message. The critical variables were whether the subjects detected that the two messages were the same, and if so, what the time interval between the two messages was when detection occurred.

Treisman found that all the subjects detected that the two messages were the same. When the shadowed message led the unshadowed message, detection occurred when the messages were still 4.5 seconds apart. When the unshadowed message led the shadowed message, detection did not typically take place until the messages were much closer, about 1.4 seconds apart. The difference in times probably reflects the extent to which the material has been processed. The shadowed message is processed by the detection device and is passed on to the short-term, or working, memory. Consequently, a fairly durable representation is created that enables the subject to compare and match the contents of the working memory with the nonshadowed ear even when the messages are 4.5 seconds apart. However, the nonshadowed message presumably never leaves the sensory register, and its representation is far less durable than that of the shadowed message. When the nonshadowed ear leads the shadowed ear, the subject probably won't be able to detect that the two messages are identical until the shadowed message is brought within the memory span of the auditory channel of the sensory register. This span has been estimated as being about 1 or 2 seconds long. This finding seems to indicate that a semantic analysis of the sensory register is carried out, which is contrary to the predictions of Broadbent's model.

Attenuation Theory

Accordingly, Treisman proposed a modification of the basic theory, which is known as the *attenuation model*. According to this theory, incoming stimuli might undergo three different kinds of analysis, or tests. The first test analyzes the physical properties of the stimuli. For auditory stimuli, the physical properties are equivalent to acoustic properties such as pitch and intensity. The second test determines whether the stimuli are linguistic and if so, groups the stimuli into syllables and words. The final test recognizes the words and assigns meaning to them. All three tests are not necessarily carried out on all incoming stimuli. Rather, the processing is continued until the competing stimuli can be disentangled from one another.

Disentangling competing stimuli sometimes requires little processing. If you're talking to a man at a party, and the people standing and talking nearby happen to be women, the stimuli can be sorted out on the basis of the first test. Under these circumstances, you would probably not become aware of the semantic content of the women's speech, because their conversation wasn't processed to that point. If the first test fails to disentangle the stimuli, then a second-level test must be carried out. For example, a friend called one day to tell me about the breakup of his latest romance. Unfortunately, he called in the middle of an exciting football game. Because the acoustic differences between the two messages were minimal, a second-level test based on syllables and words had to be carried out to separate the two messages. In this case, I *did* become aware of some of the words used in both messages. That is, my subjective report of the incoming stimuli was something like the following:

So then she says to me Washington, first and goal on the two!

According to Treisman, what takes place in such circumstances is not a complete tuning out of the nonshadowed message, a la Broadbent, but rather an attenuation (turning down) of some messages that have been sorted out following the results of the tests. Reference to Figure 2.1 shows a graphic comparison of Treisman's model with Broadbent's.

The attenuation model differs from the filter model in two ways. First, the filter model postulates that the basis of selective attention is a fairly crude analysis of the physical characteristics of the incoming stimuli. The attentuation model maintains that the preattentive analysis is much more complex and may even consist of semantic processing. Second, the filter in the filter theory is an all-or-none affair. What is not selected is tuned out completely. However, the attenuation model supposes that nonselected channels are not completely shut off but are simply turned down or dampened.

These distinctions are consistent with the findings of Cherry and Kruger (1983), who studied the selective attention abilities of learning disabled (LD) children. In their task, children age seven to nine years were required to point to the appropriate picture of a word that was presented in one channel of stereo headphones. In the other ear, the children were presented with one of three distractors: a nonlinguistic, nonsemantic sound called *white noise* (a hissing sound); backward speech, which is linguistic but nonsemantic; or forward speech, which is both linguistic and semantic. When subjected to a distractor, the performance of the LD children was substantially worse than the performance of normal-achieving children. The discrepancy in performance between the exceptional and normal children was greatest when the semantic distractor was used.

Treisman would argue that this finding indicates that the LD children's preattentive analysis includes a semantic analysis of the nonshadowed message. Also, such a finding suggests that LD children's problems stem at least in part from an apparent inability to control the attenuation of nonshadowed messages. The LD children apparently can't completely damp down the nonshadowed (and unwanted) competing stimuli. Incidentally, the Cherry and Kruger study is a good way to demonstrate how a cognitive analysis might help in understanding and possibly treating a practical problem.

Late Selection Theories

Although Treisman's theory provides a good account for many of the phenomena associated with selective attention, it has a serious shortcoming. Specifically, it seems too complicated. The theory postulates that the preattentive analysis is almost as complete as the attentive analysis. If that's so, then what's the point of doing the preattentive analysis in the first place? A simpler alternative to the Treisman position was originally proposed by Deutsch and Deutsch (1963).

These theorists argued that the bottleneck in selective attention occurred later in the processing of information than the Treisman theory proposed. Whereas Treisman maintained that the preattentive analysis determines what information is selected for further processing, Deutsch and Deutsch argued that almost all the incoming stimuli are sent on for further processing. When the information reaches working memory, selection for further processing takes place at that site. This viewpoint is referred to as the **late selection** position because the selection for further processing is made in working memory rather than earlier, in the channels of sensory memory. Figure 2.1 shows a comparison of the late selection position with the models of Broadbent and Treisman.

The late selection model predicts that all incoming stimuli are processed. Consequently, subjects should recognize information under almost any circumstances, even when information is presented to a nonshadowed ear. This assertion was tested in a study by Lewis (1970). In a dichotic listening task, subjects were told to shadow words that were presented in one ear and ignore anything presented in the nonshadowed ear. Words were also presented in the nonshadowed ear. These words were sometimes semantically unrelated to the words being shadowed, while on other occasions, the nonshadowed words were synonyms of the shadowed words. Lewis measured the latency between the presentation of the shadowed word and the subject's vocal response. He found that the presentation of a nonshadowed synonym produced a delay in the subject's response, which was not observed when the nonshadowed stimulus was an unrelated word.

This finding is not consistent with either model of early selection. If the filter theory was completely correct, the nature of the word should not have increased the latency of response, because the nonshadowed ear is supposedly completely tuned out. The attenuation model argues that nonshadowed words are turned down. Although the meaning of nonshadowed words might sometimes intrude on the shadowed message, semantic relationships such as synonymity should not. In Lewis's study, the subjects had recognized that a semantic relationship existed between the messages in the nonshadowed and shadowed ears.

As explained by Norman (1968), the late selection model operates in the following way. All information is transmitted to the working memory, but the nature of this transmission is different from that proposed by Broadbent or Treisman. Rather than describe the transmission as a serial (one step at a time) process, the transmission is thought to be in parallel (all at once, as shown in Figure 2.1). Since the capacity of the working memory is limited, parallel transmission strains the operation of working memory. Not all of the information sent there can be stored. In working memory, a judgment is made about the material's importance (this point is discussed later in the chapter). Material that has been judged important is elaborated more fully, which in turn creates a more durable representation of the information that may eventually enter permanent memory (Watanbe, 1980). What is not important is not elaborated or rehearsed, and is consequently forgotten. According to this view, the act of shadowing per se is not what determines what we attend to and consequently become aware of. Rather, the patterns that are formed and recognized in our working memory are what become the basis of our awareness.

A study by MacKay (1973) illustrates these points. The subjects were told to shadow sentences that were grammatically correct although semantically ambiguous. For example, the subjects might shadow the sentence "They were throwing stones at the bank." This sentence could refer to individuals who were standing beside a river throwing stones into it, or it could refer to individuals who were throwing stones at a financial institution. A word that might steer the subject toward a particular resolution of the ambiguity was presented at the appropriate time in the subject's nonshadowed ear. In this case, when the subject shadowed *bank,* either *money* or *river* was presented in the nonshadowed ear. After a series of such sentences, the subjects were given a memory task in which they were asked to recognize the sentences they had shadowed. In some cases, the subjects were given forms of the sentence that were congruent with the word that had been presented in the nonshadowed ear. In other cases, the forms of the sentences were not congruent with the word presented in the nonshadowed ear.

You can probably predict the findings of this study. Subjects tended to remember having shadowed sentences that were congruent with the word presented in the nonshadowed ear. In the previous sentence, for example, the subject might remember having shadowed the sentence "They were throwing stones at the financial institution" if the word *money* had been presented in the nonshadowed ear. But the subject would not remember this sentence as previously shadowed if *river* had been presented in the nonshadowed ear.

Another finding from the MacKay study might be more difficult to predict. When the subjects were asked to indicate which words had been presented in the nonshadowed ear, they could not remember which words they had heard. This finding is somewhat curious. The meaning of the nonshadowed words had been processed, although apparently only a fragile code had been created—so fragile that it no longer survived by the end of the presentation. The subjects therefore did not remember the nonshadowed words on the memory test.

Earlier I referred to the importance of the information entering the working memory. A major implication of the Deutsch and Deutsch (1963) and Norman (1968) position is that working memory can be preset to determine the value of incoming stimuli, and the evaluation of the incoming material can be consciously controlled even if unimportant information does not itself enter consciousness. These contentions were explored in a complex and provocative study by Johnston and Heinz (1979).

These researchers argued that humans could control the extent to which unattended stimuli are processed by carrying out different sorts of tests on the material in working memory. They also reasoned some tests should be carried out before others. Specifically, a sensible assumption is that a subject would carry out a sensory (or physical) analysis prior to carrying out a semantic analysis. Why? Because in many ways, a semantic analysis is much more effortful than a sensory analysis. A semantic analysis is more effortful because more knowledge is required to carry it out. If you think about this for a minute, you'll see what I mean. I can carry out some physical analyses of foreign languages, but I can't carry out a semantic analysis, because my knowledge is too limited. Johnston and Heinz argued that if the sensory tests provided enough information to disentangle the competing stimuli, the subjects would be unwilling to engage in the semantic test. So far, this reasoning should remind you of Treisman's theory. However, Treisman described these tests as ways of attenuating unwanted stimulation, whereas Johnston and Heinz had a different objective. They maintained that the processing capability of working memory is limited. Consequently, if the subject is required to carry out several tests to recognize and categorize incoming information, the subject would have little processing capability left over to deal with another ancillary task, and his performance on this secondary task should thus be poor. Remember, however, that the nature and extent of the evaluation are thought te be under conscious control. If the subject determines that incoming stimuli can be categorized without a complete semantic analysis, some of the working memory's processing capability should be available for executing the secondary task. In that case, performance on the ancillary task should be reasonable. To sum up, performance on some ancillary task should be poor if the primary task requires a semantic analysis. However, performance on the ancillary task might not be poor if the primary task does not require a semantic analysis. Let's see how this reasoning was enacted in the Johnston and Heinz (1979) study.

Subjects were asked to shadow messages that differed from the nonshadowed message in either physical characteristics, semantic aspects, or both. Messages of low physical discriminability were produced by having the same male voice recite both messages. Messages of high physical discriminability were created by using a male voice to recite one message and a female voice to recite the other. Semantic aspects varied in two ways. Messages of low semantic discriminability were created by reciting lists of items drawn from the same category. For example, two different lists of types of furniture might be played into the channels of stereo headphones. Messages of high semantic discriminability were formed by reciting lists of items drawn from different categories (such as a list of furniture types and a list of fruits). While subjects were shadowing one message in the familiar dichotic listening task, they were also required to detect and respond to changes in a light's brightness. This was the ancillary task.

The researchers were interested in whether changes in the nature of the shadowing task affect the subject's ability to detect and respond to changes in brightness. If the subject does not have control over the nature of the incoming stimuli's analysis, the differences in physical or semantic aspects of the messages should have no effect on the subject's ability to do the ancillary task. Why? Because if the subject has no control over the analysis, the entire analysis must be carried out regardless of whether the analysis is necessary. Whatever the processing demands of the full analysis are, they would be constant across all the different combinations of physical and semantic discriminability, and hence the subject would be left with a constant amount of processing ability to carry out the secondary task.

If the subject does have control over the analysis, however, a different prediction follows. For example, if the messages were discriminable on the basis of sensory characteristics, we might expect that the subject wouldn't bother carrying out the semantic analysis. If the semantic analysis were not carried out, the processing capabilities of working memory would not be as taxed, and the subject would be able to devote some of these capabilities to processing the ancillary task. If the messages were of low physical discriminability, the subject would be compelled to carry out the effortful semantic analysis to keep up with the to-be-shadowed message. In that case, we would look for a decrement in performance on the ancillary task.

The results of the study supported Johnston and Heinz's reasoning. Regardless of the messages' semantic discriminability, the subjects' reaction times on the ancillary task were much faster in the high physical discriminability condition than they were in the low physical discriminability condition. That is, when the messages had high physical discriminability, the subjects were able to rapidly detect and respond to changes in the light's brightness even when the messages were semantically similar. When the full (i.e., semantic) analysis had to be carried out, Johnston and Heinz found that the subjects had little processing capability left over to carry out the ancillary task. This decreased capability was reflected in their slower reaction times and reduced shadowing accuracy in that condition. In other words, when the messages were of low physical discriminability and the subjects had to engage in the semantic analysis, they became slower at detecting and responding to changes in the light's brightness.

Conclusions from the First Phase of Theory Building

The last several pages have dealt with several bottleneck theories of attention, each seeming to supplant its predecessor. Along the way, many findings have been mentioned. Now is the time for us to try to organize these findings into a coherent picture.

We have seen that Broadbent and Treisman thought of attention as a filter that operated in the earliest stages of human information processing to screen out stimuli. In particular, Treisman argued that a complex preattentive analysis was carried out early in the processing of information. Surviving information was sent serially along a limited capacity channel for recognition. Late selection theorists such as Deutsch and Deutsch postulated that all information is sent on in parallel to a recognition device. This change in viewpoint paved the way for another major change in our conceptualization of attention, namely that we can consciously control the nature of attentional analysis even though the results of such analysis might not enter our consciousness (MacKay, 1973; Johnston & Heinz, 1979). As these researchers have pointed out, the subject's intention can be critical in determining what material we become conscious of, which means that we have to consider what strategic factors might be involved in the subject's processing (Lowe & Mitterer, 1982). Paradoxically, however, the intention to process incoming information doesn't ensure that we will become aware of that material for any meaningful length of time. According to the late selection view, we will process to whatever extent necessary to disentangle the competing stimuli. When the stimuli have been sorted out, we'll elaborate the material we wish to keep, thus creating a more durable representation. What is not elaborated will be forgotten.

These findings superficially suggest that attention can be compared to a funnel—a constricted point in the information-processing system through which all incoming material must pass. More recent studies suggest, however, that such an analogy is somewhat misleading. Rather, we might think of attention as a spotlight that comes equipped with a controllable lens. Because this lens is under our control, we can narrow the beam to a pencil point of light, and in that case, the object of scrutiny comes under an intense and highly focused illumination. On the other hand, we can open up the lens and illuminate several objects at once, although less intensely than before. Notice that the wattage of the light does not change. What changes is the way in which we apply the light's power. The next section further explores this viewpoint.

ALTERNATIVES TO FILTER THEORIES: CAPACITY MODELS

The second phase of theory building in the area of attention began with a reconceptualization of the problem, which occurred with the publication of Kahneman's (1973) book *Attention and Effort*. Partly from everyday examples such as driving a car and carrying out a simultaneous conversation, Kahneman argued that the location of the bottleneck in selective attention tasks seemed less important than understanding what the task itself demanded of the person. For example, since driving and talking are usually not highly demanding tasks, we can do both of them simultaneously. However, driving in heavy traffic is more demanding than driving on the interstate, so we would expect that conversation might break down during heavy traffic conditions.

Rather than talk about funneling stimuli along some limited capacity channel, Kahneman maintained that attention could be understood as a set of cognitive processes for categorizing and recognizing stimuli. These processes, or **cognitive resources,** were limited. To fully recognize a stimulus, resources were required; and if the stimulus was complex, a large number of resources would be required. If several complex stimuli were presented simultaneously, the resources might be quickly used up; and if additional stimuli were presented to the person whose resources were used up, these newcomers would go unprocessed (and unnoticed). But the situation need not be so bleak. Kahneman postulated that incoming stimuli don't grab the resources all on their own. Instead, the cognitive system features a stage in which resources are allocated to process incoming stimuli. As Johnson and Heinz (1979) pointed out, the allocation of cognitive resources is flexible and under our control. Rather than being slaves to incoming stimuli, we are able to shift limited resources onto important stimuli.

Figure 2.3 is a depiction of Kahneman's model. Notice that Kahneman's model does not assume that the number of resources is completely fixed. Rather, the total pool of resources that are available at any one time is determined in part by the individual's arousal level. The greater the level of arousal, the greater the pool of resources, at least up to a certain point. Beyond that point, increases in arousal may result in a decrease in the number of available resources. Which incoming stimuli have resources devoted to them is determined by the system's **allocation policy.** The allo-

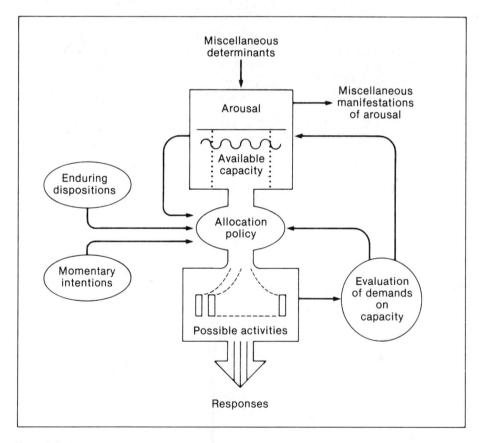

Figure 2.3.

A capacity model for attention. (From Daniel Kahneman, *Attention and Effort,* © 1973, p. 10. Reprinted by permission of Prentice-Hall, Inc., Englewood Cliffs, New Jersey.)

cation policy is set by enduring dispositions and momentary intentions. *Enduring dispositions* are tendencies that many creatures have to process loud noises, sudden motions, bright colors, and other unusual events. One enduring disposition of mature humans is the tendency to process our own names. *Momentary intentions* are situational dispositions to allocate cognitive resources to a particular source of incoming stimulation.

The **cognitive capacity** model makes several predictions, which we'll attempt to deal with. First, the capacity model assumes that the interference produced by competing sources of stimulation is nonspecific. That is, any problems that we might have in doing two things at once are not produced because the tasks interfere with one another, but rather because the tasks require more resources than we have available. Accordingly, the capacity model predicts that we will be able to do two things at once as long as these activities don't exceed the number of available resources. The second prediction follows from the first: Performance on one task will decline if we try to do a second task simultaneously when the sum total of the processing demands exceeds capacity. The third prediction states that the allocation policy is flexible and can be altered to suit the demands of the incoming stimuli. We have already looked at one study that bears on the third prediction. Recall that Johnston and Heinz (1979) demonstrated that their subjects would tailor their analyses of incoming information to the minimum depth necessary to shadow the message. If the subjects could shadow the message by using only a sensory analysis, which presumably requires fewer cognitive resources than the semantic analysis, then that's what they would do.

A study by Posner and Boies (1971) provides support for the first two predictions. Their subjects were required to do simultaneous tasks. The primary task (the one to which the subjects were told to devote their attention) was a letter-matching task. Following the visual presentation of a warning signal, the subject were shown a letter, such as a *T*, for a brief (50 msec) interval. After a 1-second delay, the subjects were shown a second letter, and their task was to indicate as quickly as possible whether the second letter was the same as or different from the first. The subjects indicated their responses by pressing one of two buttons. If the second letter was the same as the first, subjects were supposed to tap a button with their right index finger. If the second letter was different from the first, subjects used the right middle finger to tap.

The second task was an auditory detection task. On some trials, a tone was presented via stereo headphones. Here, the subjects were told to tap a key with their left index finger as quickly as possible when they heard a tone. I'm sure you've already figured out that the procedure leaves a little to be desired, because the handedness of the subjects influences their ability to respond quickly to the tone. Consequently, we'll have to be extra careful in interpreting the findings of this experiment.

Figure 2.4 shows the sequence of stimuli presentation and the results of the study. Point (1) shows the average response time on the tone detection task when the tone was presented prior to the warning signal. This point serves as a basis for comparison when the tone is presented later in the

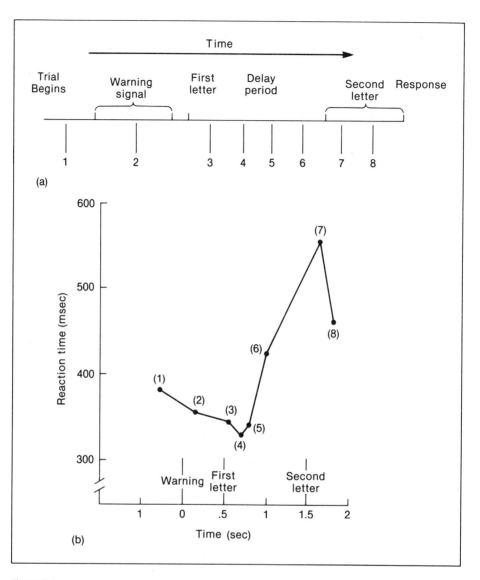

Figure 2.4.

The procedure and the results of the experiment on simultaneous letter matching and tone detection: *(a)*, the sequence of events in a single trial (the numbers designate the points at which tones were presented intermittently); *(b)*, the time required to detect the tones at various points during the trials. (From Posner & Boies, 1971. Copyright 1971 by the American Psychological Association. Reprinted by permission.)

sequence. If the tone is presented before any of the letters are shown to the subjects, a reasonable assumption is that the subjects can devote all of their resources to processing the tone. Consequently, any increases in response time to the tone when it is presented later are apparently the result of the subject's allocation of resources to the primary task. Notice from Figure 2.4 that the response time to the tone decreased somewhat during and immediately following the warning signal. One function of the warning signal is to increase the subject's alertness and arousal, which produces a corresponding increase in the available resources. At point (4), the graph of the response time is at its lowest point. However, this occurs immediately after the first letter has been presented and recognized.

This finding substantiates the first prediction of the Kahneman model: The subjects were able to process competing stimuli when the total demand did not exceed the available capacity. The arousal effects of the warning signal are not durable, and during the delay period, the subject must extract the first letter's code from sensory memory and develop a more durable representation in working memory. This accounts for the increase in reaction time seen at point (6). However, the greatest increases in reaction time are seen at points (7) and (8). At those points, the second letter has been presented, and the subject is occupied with categorizing, recognizing and judging it. These activities soak up most of the subject's available resources, leaving too few to process the tone quickly. This finding substantiates the second prediction of Kahneman's model: Performance of the auditory detection task declined when the processing demands exceeded capacity.

Some Questions Concerning Capacity Models

Kahneman's capacity model is designed to supplement rather than supplant the bottleneck position. Whereas the bottleneck position postulates that incoming stimuli always compete for space on the shunting channel and therefore always interfere with each other, the capacity model assumes that the demands made by stimuli do not compete. That is, as long as sufficient resources are available, all the incoming stimuli can be accommodated. One question that arises at the outset in comparing the two approaches concerns the interactions of incoming stimuli: Do they compete, or don't they? At this point, cognitive psychologists have hedged their bets on this matter. A reasonable assumption is that some stimuli do interfere with each other, meaning that some tasks are truly incompatible. In those cases, some version of the bottleneck viewpoint is necessary to explain the processing. However, as Posner and Boies (1971) demonstrated, simultaneous tasks can be comfortably handled in some situations. In those situations, the capacity model seems to be a reasonable explanation of events.

A second question is more problematic and concerns the nature of the resources: Exactly what are they? No one knows the answer to this question with any certainty. However, some researchers have maintained that the resources are basic and elemental operations of the nervous system. Several researchers have attempted to establish a link between these operations and cerebral architecture.

For example, Dawson and Schell (1982, 1983) had their subjects shadow a list of unrelated words presented via stereo headphones. A separate list of semantically unrelated words was presented over the nonshadowed channel. Occasionally presented in the nonshadowed ear was one of a series of words that had previously been paired with a painful electric shock. We would expect such words to be processed even when they were presented on the nonshadowed channel, because we have an enduring disposition to process events that may signal the onset of pain. Dawson and Schell found this to be the case. Certain skin responses known as **electrodermal responses** (or EDRs) were elicited by the presentation of shock-associated words in the nonshadowed channel. But now the plot thickens in an intriguing way. You probably know that the cortex of the brain is divided into two hemispheres. Each hemisphere controls one side of the body. However, hemispheric control over the body is *contralateral,* or opposite sided, meaning that the left hemisphere controls the right-hand side of the body and vice versa. In most people, one hemisphere—typically the left—is dominant.

Dawson and Schell found that when shock-associated words were presented to the right ear (whose neural pathway winds up in the left hemisphere), EDRs were observed only on those trials in which the subject showed independent indications of attentional shifts. These independent indications included errors in shadowing and increased latency in shadowing the attended word. However, when the shock-associated words were presented over the left ear, EDRs were observed even on trials in which no independent indications of attentional shifts were shown. What to make of this? The hemispheres apparently differ in the resources available to them, or differ in their allocation policies. For the dominant hemisphere, processing the significant word may require more of its resources, thus overloading capacity and producing increased latency in shadowing the attended channel. For the nondominant hemisphere, perhaps fewer or different resources are required to do the same thing. Indeed, Dawson and Schell (1983) have hypothesized that each hemisphere may have a partially independent pool of processing capabilities. This idea has not gone unchallenged (Walker & Ceci, 1983). To the idea that processing resources may be intimately linked with functional properties of the hemispheres, our best response is that it's a definite possibility.

The Relationship between Practice and Attention

Our first efforts at doing a complex task often seem clumsy and uncoordinated, regardless of the resources we allocate to them. When my tennis teacher first showed me the correct service grip, stance, and movement, my initial thought was, I'll never do it right. Indeed, my first attempts were not promising. Thousands of serves later, I still don't have it right, although I've improved dramatically and in some objective sense, my serve is reasonably decent. This little tale is more than another illustration of practice-makes-reasonably-decent, however. As I practiced this task, I became aware that I no longer had to allocate all of my attentional resources to monitoring kinesthetic sensations from my body and coordinating them with the toss of the ball. To use terms described in Chapter 1, my tennis serve has gradually become both procedural (I no longer remember the steps of serving that my teacher made me memorize) and somewhat automatic as well. That is, although I'm aware of when it's time to serve in a match, I'm not in conscious control of running off the service program in my brain.

This everyday example has some important implications for cognitive psychologists because it suggests that practice on a given task leads to a reduction in the number of resources needed to process the stimuli associated with doing the task. If practice were continued indefinitely, the performance not only would improve but also would become more automatic, requiring fewer and fewer cognitive resources. As fewer resources were allocated to the task, the subject's awareness would play a smaller and smaller role in the initiation and execution of the task. At the endpoint of such a process (which is probably only seldom reached in everyday life), performance on the task would become truly automatic, requiring virtually no resources and leaving no conscious trace of its execution. This point is important. Recall from our discussion of the capacity model of attention that several different sources of stimulation can be processed simultaneously as long as their demands do not exceed the supply of resources. Now we see that one way of solving the problem of attending to different sources of stimulation is to practice attending and doing one of the tasks involved, thus reducing the number of resources needed to process the task and leaving the remaining resources free to be allocated among the other tasks.

A second and perhaps controversial point is this: If practice reduces the number of resources needed to process incoming stimuli, then there are no demanding tasks, only unpracticed ones. In other words, if the attentional demands of a task can be reduced by practice, then what limits our ability to attend to different sources of stimulation is not our cognitive resources, but rather the time in which we have to practice the tasks. The next section considers the question of automatic processing.

AUTOMATICITY

As Hasher and Zacks (1979) have commented, two pathways lead to automatic processing. One is heredity, the other is learning. One implication of this position is striking: Hasher and Zacks argue that physical activities and mental events share the same pathway to **automaticity.** That is, mental actions, such as those involved in perception and memory, can be treated as though they were similar to motor skills. The same sort of repetition and drill that produce improvements in motor skills should produce improvement in cognitive skills as well.

Schneider and Shiffrin (1977; Shiffrin & Schneider, 1977) have shown that complex but highly practiced perceptual analyses can be done automatically. They have also demonstrated that such analyses will become automatic with practice even if they are not initially done that way. Schneider and Shiffrin (1977) gave their subjects a set of letters or numbers that they called a memory set, and instructed their subjects to determine if any of the elements of the memory set appeared on a set of slides that were presented for brief periods. This set of slides was varied in two ways. The slides might have one, two, or four characters printed on them—a factor called frame size. The relationship of the characters on the slides to the

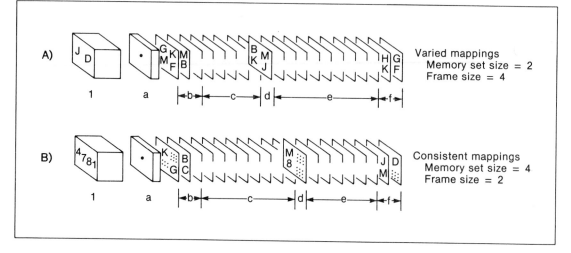

Figure 2.5.

The two detection conditions in Schneider and Shiffrin's experiments: the varied mapping condition and the consistent mapping condition. On each trial the sequence of events was: *1* presentation of the memory set; *a* a fixation point; *b* three dummy frames that never contain the target; *c* distractor frames; *d* frame containing the target; *e* more distractor frames; *f* dummy frames that never contain the target. (From Schneider & Shiffrin, 1977. Copyright 1977 by the American Psychological Association. Reprinted by permission of the publisher and the author.)

memory set characters was the second variable. In the varied mapping condition, the subject was given a memory set that consisted of one or more letters. All the to-be-searched characters were also letters. In the consistent mapping condition, the subject was given a memory set that consisted of numbers. However, the elements to be searched through were still all letters, unless the memory set number appeared on one of the slides. If one of the memory set numbers did appear, it was the only number present in the entire set of twenty slides. If after scanning the set of slides, the subjects had detected an element of the memory set, they were told to respond yes. If the subjects believed that no elements of the memory set were presented, they were instructed to respond no.

Figure 2.5 shows two examples of their trials. A good way to encode this study is to remember that in the varied mapping conditions, the subject is searching for a letter among other letters, and in the consistent mapping condition, the subject is searching for a number among letters. Schneider and Shiffrin were interested in how quickly subjects could scan this set of slides while maintaining 95% accuracy—that is, saying yes or no and being correct 95 percent of the time.

The findings of this study are shown in Figure 2.6. Examine them and make your own interpretation. Considering the hits (trials in which the subject correctly said yes), we see that subjects could quickly scan the slides in the consistent mapping condition and still maintain 95 percent accuracy. That is, when looking for a number among letters, subjects required only 80 msec per slide to accurately process the information. Indeed, apparently

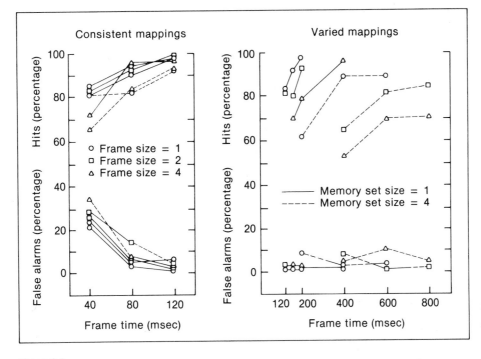

Figure 2.6.

Results of Shiffrin and Schneider's experiments. Subjects in the varied mapping condition showed the effects of frame time, frame size, and memory set size. In the consistent mapping condition, performance was affected only by frame time. (From Schneider & Shiffrin, 1977. Copyright 1977 by the American Psychological Association. Reprinted by permission of the publisher and the author.)

the only variable in the consistent mapping condition that affected the subjects was frame time—the time in which subjects were allowed to view each slide. However, in the varied mapping condition, such was not the case.

Let's compare the same presentation (memory set size = 1, frame size = 2) across the two mapping conditions. As we've seen, subjects could achieve the accuracy criterion when viewing the slides for only 80 msec in the consistent mapping condition. However, subjects required 200 msec to achieve the same accuracy in the varied mapping condition, that is, when they were looking for a letter among other letters. Schneider and Shiffrin reasoned that the processing of letters when searching for a number is automatic, requiring virtually no allocation of resources. However, searching for a letter among letters is not automatic. This process is controlled and requires attention. If this reasoning is accurate, we would expect that frame size should not affect processing speed in the consistent mapping condition. That is, if you're looking for a number among letters, how many letters there are on each slide doesn't matter, because the recognition processes are automatic and fast. But frame size should affect processing speed in the varied mapping condition. To maintain high accuracy levels, the subjects must scan each letter individually, and the more letters there are, the longer this process is going to take. This hypothesis was substantiated. Increases in the frame size had little effect on the subject's processing time in the consistent mapping condition, but similar changes produced substantial increases in processing speed in the varied mapping condition.

However, Shiffrin and Schneider (1977) demonstrated that the search for a target letter in an array of letters can be done automatically if this task is practiced. Subjects were given a target letter that was always drawn from a particular set (B, C, D, G, F, H, J, K, L) and they were asked to scan a series of slides in which the distractor elements were always letters drawn from a different set (R, S, T, V, W, X, Y, Z). Although it took over two thousand trials, the subjects nevertheless eventually performed as well on this varied mapping task as they did on the consistent mapping task in the previous experiment. This finding supports a point made earlier regarding the demands made by difficult tasks. As discussed, practice can tame difficult or time consuming recognition tasks. Practice not only smooths the performance of motor and cognitive tasks but also reduces the number of resources needed to be allocated to process the information.

A similar point was made by Hirst, Spelke, Reaves, Caharack, and Neisser (1980). Their two subjects attempted to read and take dictation simultaneously. During the reading-only trials, the subjects read short stories, which were followed by tests of reading comprehension. This procedure was done to establish a baseline for reading rate and ability. The dictation task consisted of writing down short sentences, such as "The dog got free," that were slowly (thirty words per minute) presented to the subjects. During the reading-dictation trials, the subjects simultaneously read and took dictation. In the initial trials, the dictation task interfered with reading, resulting in slower speeds and poorer comprehension. After approximately one hundred sessions, the subjects were able to take the dictation without its interfering with their reading. Their scores during the reading-dictation trials equaled the reading scores earned during the reading-only trials. Other evidence suggests that the subjects also comprehended the dictated sentences even though they had not been instructed to try to remember them. This second finding suggests that the two individuals in the study were carrying out two semantic analyses simultaneously.

Conclusions from the Second Phase of Theory Building

In the second phase of theory building, Kahneman and others have advanced the idea that attention consists of a group of cognitive processes that can be allocated systematically to deal with incoming information. Demanding tasks require a greater number of resources than do less demanding tasks, but this is true only for unpracticed demanding tasks. With practice, the mental effort required to do demanding tasks decreases, and if practice is continued, the processing of a task may become automatic.

Capacity models should be thought of as complementing the bottleneck theories. Although, as we have seen, in many instances humans seem to be able to process competing stimuli simultaneously, parallel processing cannot be done in some situations. An obvious example is that purely physical limitations, resulting from the way in which your body is constructed, make it impossible to simultaneously attend to visual stimulation in front of you and behind you.

At this point, it is simply not known to what extent incoming stimuli compete for allocation of resources. To the extent that they do compete, bottleneck theories seem to be good accounts of the fate of victorious stimuli—those that make it aboard the shunting channel. In the numerous cases in which competition seems to be absent, the capacity model seems to be a reasonable explanation. Another way of viewing this distinction was offered by Norman and Bobrow (1975). Certain difficult tasks were described as being data-limited. For example, we've all had the experience of trying to tune in a faraway radio station. Trying to catch the station's signal against the background of static tends to consume many of our resources as we try to make the fine discriminations necessary to tune in the station. Our processing of this auditory stimulus is limited by the poverty of the data: The signal is weak. We tend to become single-minded as we fiddle with the tuner. An appropriate description is that the signal passes through a bottleneck into a detection device, where we'll try to extract as much information as possible from it. **Data-limited processes** can be contrasted with **resource-limited processes.** As the name implies, tasks must have resources allocated to them before they can be processed, and when we're out of resources, we're out.

PATTERN RECOGNITION

The initial objective of our information-processing system is to recognize and categorize incoming stimuli. The result of this processing is the creation of a cognitive code that can be placed in some sort of context, or background. Against this background, the code can be elaborated and stored. This section describes two explanations of pattern recognition: the **template-matching theory** and the **feature detection theory.**

Template-Matching Theory

When I was a small child, one of my favorite playthings was a stencil that allowed me to trace various geometric objects and letters. To my juvenile eyes, the traced capital letters looked far better than the irregular letters I produced freehand. I was much impressed with the timelessness of such letters. The A that I traced one day was identical to the previous day's A, which could easily be verified by putting the stencil over the traced A and noting that only the correct A parts were visible.

Some researchers have proposed that human pattern recognition is achieved in a similar fashion. To recognize a particular pattern, such as the letter T, incoming information is compared with stored codes, called *templates,* until a good fit between the incoming information and the stored codes is found. Presumably, the best fit will be achieved when the incoming information matches the template for T. At that point, the incoming information will be recognized and labeled T.

Figure 2.7 shows a template-matching system engaged in a series of hits and misses for the letter *A*. Early proponents of this view were cheered by the news that such a system could recognize letters. For example, if you take out your checkbook and look at the computer digits printed at the bottom of each check, you'll notice that they have been made highly distinguishable from one another. These differences are apparently necessary to permit the digits' recognition by machine.

The template-matching theory has two strikes against it. First, such a system is inefficient. Banking firms care little if their recognition machines slap (figuratively) as many as ten different templates onto each digit before recognizing it, because only ten different digits exist, and the machines can rapidly compare the input with the templates. Humans, however, must be

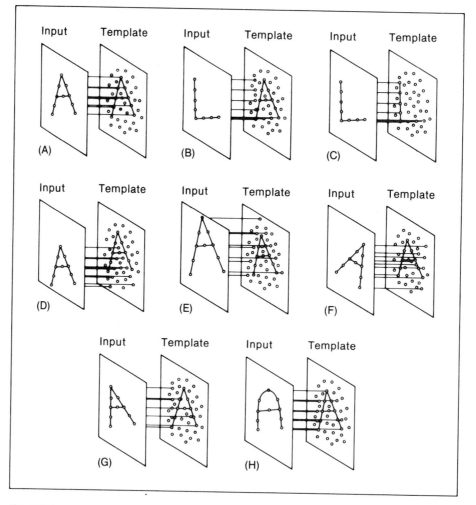

Figure 2.7.

Examples of template-matching attempts: *(A)* through *(C),* successful attempts; *(D)* through *(H),* failed attempts. (Adapted from Neisser, 1967.)

able to recognize an infinite variety of patterns, and they don't have the luxury of waiting until a match is achieved.

Second, template-matching systems are extremely inflexible, but human pattern recognition is successful in the face of great diversity of input. Notice from example *(H)* of Figure 2.7 that the input is clearly recognizable as an *A*, but the template system fails to recognize the stimulus because this particular *A* isn't the right kind of input. That is, strictly speaking, the template recognition device can recognize stimuli only when their size and orientation permit a match. This method of recognition has its limitations. If I showed you an upside-down *A*, you would no doubt recognize it as a perfectly good example of an *A* despite its being upside down. However, a recognition device endowed with only a template-matching analysis would draw a blank. These concerns have proved fatal for template-matching theories. Fortunately, a promising alternative exists.

Feature Detection Theory

Earlier I mentioned that as a child, I was never completely happy with the block letters that I drew freehand. I was dissatisfied with their irritating variability. Perhaps my annoyance was misplaced, because my ability to judge letters as being of one or another type indicates that I had detected that each example of a particular letter had something in common with all the other examples of that letter. The question is, What did each letter have in common with other examples of that letter?

Consider the letter *H*. It has two approximately vertical lines that are about the same length. Both of these vertical lines begin and end more or less in the same place, relative to the border of the page. An *H* has a horizontal line that intersects the two vertical lines, more or less at their midpoints. I have just provided a sort of checklist of things that an *H* must have. This list is not an exhaustive list; the relative lengths of the horizontal and vertical lines probably have additional stipulations. Nevertheless, a system endowed with the checklist just mentioned could scan a particular character, noting which items on the checklist the character had and which it did not. If a given character had all the items on the checklist, the system would conclude the character was an *H*. Thus, characters like these:

⊢ ⊣ ⋈ would not be called *H*'s.

Feature analysis is the name given to this approach to the problem of pattern recognition. The basic assumption is that all complex stimuli are composed of distinctive and separable parts known as *features*. Pattern recognition is accomplished by counting the presence or absence of the features, and comparing the count with a tabulation of the features associated with different labels. Naturally, the success of the approach hinges on the decomposability of stimuli. As Gibson (1969) has demonstrated, a tabulation of features can apparently be accomplished, at least for letters.

Figure 2.8 shows the listing of presumed critical features. Notice that letters similar in appearance, such as *E* and *F*, share many features. This leads to the expectation that when errors in letter recognition take place,

Features	A	E	F	H	I	L	T	K	M	N	V	W	X	Y	Z	B	C	D	G	J	O	P	R	Q	S	U
Straight																										
Horizontal	+	+	+	+		+	+								+			+								
Vertical		+	+	+	+	+	+	+	+	+				+		+		+				+	+			
Diagonal /	+						+	+			+	+	+	+	+											
Diagonal /	+						+	+	+	+	+	+	+										+	+		
Curve																										
Closed																+		+			+	+	+	+		
Open V																			+							+
Open H																	+		+	+					+	
Intersection	+	+	+	+			+	+							+		+					+	+	+		
Redundancy																										
Cyclic change		+						+			+					+								+		
Symmetry	+	+		+	+		+	+	+		+	+	+	+		+	+	+				+				+
Discontinuity																										
Vertical	+		+	+	+		+	+	+	+			+									+	+			
Horizontal		+	+		+	+								+												

Figure 2.8.

Critical features of letters. (Adapted from Gibson, 1969.)

letters should be mistaken for letters with which they share features. This hypothesis has been confirmed many times (Geyer & DeWald, 1973; Garner, 1979). Other support for the feature analysis model has been supplied by Neisser (1964). Neisser gave his subjects blocks of letters such as those shown in Figure 2.9. The subjects were told to scan the blocks as quickly as they could to find the target letter, *Z*. Try it. Like most of Neisser's subjects, you probably located the *Z* much more quickly in block (1) than you did in block (2). Let's consider the implications of this finding.

The basic premise of the feature analysis position is that cases of mistaken identity should occur among letters that share features. Thus, one might expect a greater number of such confusions when searching for *Z* in block (2), because the letters in block (2) share features with *Z*. Consequently, we should expect reductions in the accuracy of performance when subjects seek a target in feature-similar backgrounds as opposed to feature-dissimilar backgrounds. However, Neisser reported reductions in speed of performance when the subjects searched for the target located in a feature-dissimilar background.

The implications of this point have not been lost on cognitive psychologists, who contend that this distinction indicates that the analysis of features must take place in a series of steps, or stages. That is, in the first stage, the features are extracted from the stimulus and noted. After this

ODUGQR	IVMXEW
QCDUGO	EWVMIX
CQOGRD	EXWMVI
QUGCDR	IXEMWV
URDGQO	VXWEMI
GRUQDO	MXVEWI
DUZGRO	XVWZEI
UCGROD	MWXVIE
DQRCGU	VIMEXW
QDOCGU	EXVWIM
(1)	(2)

Figure 2.9.

Lists used to study feature analysis in a high-speed search task. (From "Visual Search" by U. Neisser. Copyright 1964 by Scientific American, Inc. All rights reserved.)

step is accomplished, the count, or comparison of the target letter with the background letter, is carried out. If the number of features in common is large, then the component of the system that is doing the counting will require more time, as Neisser noted. This is another reason why the feature analysis model is a more persuasive account of pattern recognition than the template-matching theory. Template matching is an all-or-none theory. If the incoming stimulus matches some template, recognition is accurate and complete. If the incoming stimulus does not match some template, then the recognizer would presumably be left completely in the dark. The power of the feature analysis point of view lies in its ability to explain both accuracy as well as latency of recognition. Incidentally, Neisser's subjects practiced tasks of this type for ten days. By now, you should be able to predict what changes had taken place in the subjects' performances by the tenth day.

A whimsical stage model of feature analysis was offered by Selfridge (1959). Called Pandemonium, his system described pattern recognition as taking place in a series of stages that were carried out by highly specialized cognitive processes. Each process was referred to as a demon. In the first stage, the image demons are responsible for converting the physical stimulus into some sort of cognitive representation acceptable to the other demons. Next, the feature demons analyze the representation, with each one looking for her particular feature (horizontal lines, intersections, and so on). Next, the results of the feature count are posted for the cognitive demons. Each cognitive demon looks for his particular array of features. With every appropriate feature that a cognitive demon sees posted, his noisemaking increases a notch. Finally, the decision demon listens to the resulting pandemonium and judges which demon is shouting the loudest; presumably, that is the incoming stimulus.

Independent Confirmation of Feature Analysis

Lines of evidence that are not purely behavioral also suggest that pattern recognition is frequently accomplished by feature analysis. Some of this evidence is biological (this is discussed later in the chapter). Other evidence has been produced from the field of artificial intelligence (AI). AI is concerned with the development of software that enables computing machines to act with intelligence. In this regard, several AI researchers have been concerned with computer vision. That is, they have attempted to determine what it takes to get a machine to "recognize" scenes such as the one shown in Figure 2.10. Waltz (1975) has argued that this simple task requires vast knowledge.

Some of what people do spontaneously, however, can be accomplished by a computer programmed to extract certain features from the array. First, the machine analyzes the bright and dark regions of the array. Although the variations in the intensity of reflected light are not shown in Figure 2.10, they are present in real life. After this analysis has been carried out, the machine computes locations that seem to border the various light and dark

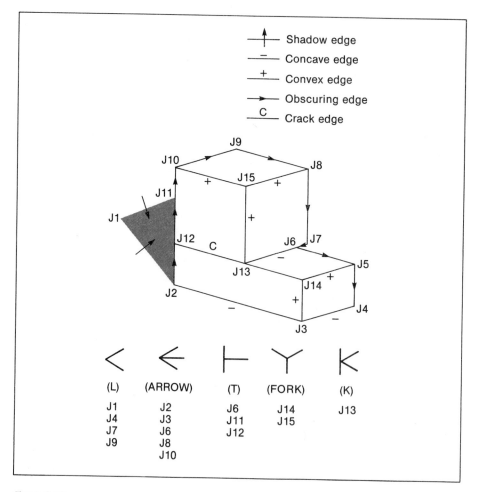

Figure 2.10.

A scene and the features that might be used to analyze it. (Adapted from Waltz, 1975.)

regions. In Figure 2.10, points J14 and J15 are examples of such points. From points such as J14 and J15, the machine goes on to recognize other types of intersections, such as *L's* and arrows. Finally, the program assembles the patterns of intersections. That is, much like the cognitive demons in Pandemonium, who added up the features they had observed and started shouting if they detected their pattern, Waltz's program adds up the pattern of intersections and attempts to determine what kind of shape it must be.

Waltz's program has been able to handle the scenes shown in Figure 2.11 in the times shown. That is, the machine can label the lines with names that are consistent with what humans see when they look at these drawings. The asterisked lines are segments that the machine was not sure of. This kind of analysis is important, not because it proves that human pattern recognition is accomplished by feature analysis, but rather because it demonstrates that a nonbiological information-processing system is nevertheless capable of feature analysis. Consequently, cognitive psychologists have been able to argue that information-processing systems, whether or not biological, seem to share certain characteristics, one of which is the ability to recognize patterns by abstracting features from an array.

Biological Contributions

Other researchers have demonstrated that although you don't have to be made out of cells to do feature analysis, your biology nevertheless plays a role in feature detection. You probably know that even when we gaze directly at an object, our eyes are not held perfectly still. Instead, the eye continues to move in a variety of actions known as *physiological nystagmus*. Some of these motions have small amplitudes but high frequencies. For example, the eye jiggles around in a visual angle of 20 seconds of arc (1/180 of a degree), thirty to seventy times per second (Lindsay & Norman, 1977). Other movements have lower frequencies but larger amplitudes. These motions are apparently necessary for visual perception. Their probable function is to give the retinal receptors adequate time to refresh themselves. Incoming visual stimuli can be stabilized on the retina using a system of mirrors (Riggs, Ratcliff, Cornsweet, & Cornsweet, 1953). The stimulus to be seen by the subject is first projected onto a small mirror, which has been cemented to a contact lens worn by the subject. This image is then picked up from this screen and bounced around a set of mirrors before finally being projected to the subject's eye. The result is that no matter how the subject's eye moves, the same set of receptors is stimulated by the incoming image.

Something interesting happens to the subjects in this situation: They become functionally blind within a few seconds. Perhaps even more interesting is that the stimuli don't disappear all at once. Rather, they fade away in pieces, and these pieces resemble the features described by Gibson and Selfridge. Figure 2.12 shows drawings of the stimuli that were used; these appear on the left. On the right are succeeding disintegrations of these stimuli as reported by the subjects (Pritchard, 1961). This finding suggests that feature analysis, which I have been describing as a cognitive process, has its basis in neurology. Implied here is that biological importance probably plays a role in determining what sorts of stimuli can serve as features.

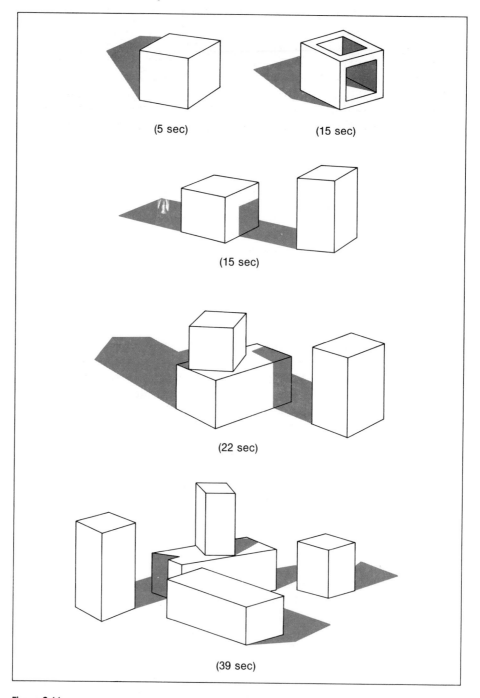

(5 sec)

(15 sec)

(15 sec)

(22 sec)

(39 sec)

Figure 2.11.
Some visual arrays and their processing times. (Adapted from Waltz, 1975.)

Figure 2.12.

Disintegration of stabilized retinal images. (From R. M. Pritchard, "Stabilized Images on the Retina."
Copyright 1961 by Scientific American, Inc. All rights reserved.)

This reasoning impelled Lettvin, Maturana, McCulloch, and Pitts (1959) to examine the retina of the frog. They argued the frog is a primitive animal who uses its visual system to achieve two important biological ends: acquiring food and avoiding turning into someone else's food. A sensible assumption was that the visual system would support biological needs by extracting those features of the visual array that seemed particularly important to meet those needs. Using advanced technology, Lettvin et al. were able to insert tiny wires known as *microelectrodes* into individual cells in the frog's retina. Lettvin et al. found that the eye of the frog had four kinds of feature detectors:

1. **Edge detectors,** which respond strongly to the border between light and dark regions
2. **Moving contrast detectors,** which respond when an edge moves
3. **Dimming detectors,** which react when the overall illumination is lowered
4. **Convex edge detectors,** which respond when a small, circular dark dot moves about in the frog's field of vision (Lindsay & Norman, 1977, 192).

The fourth detector is a highly specialized ability to detect features that are associated with flying insects—something that frogs like to eat. The other detectors are concerned with notifying the frog about the arrival of predators either on the ground (as dark shadows that move) or from the air (as shadows that would lower the overall illumination).

The physiological evidence for feature detectors offered by Pritchard and Lettvin et al. corroborates the account of Neisser and increases our confidence that this view is correct. The sensory system interprets visual tableaux (scenes) by first knocking them down into there constituent elements and then rebuilding them. The elements of the visual array (i.e., its features) seem to be determined in part by biological necessity. However, for two reasons, this account cannot completely explain human pattern recognition. First, if this viewpoint were completely true, you could not recognize anything unless you were endowed with some specialized neurons whose function enabled you to achieve some biological necessity. (For a while, cognitive psychologists flippantly announced that the search for the grandmother cell and the Volkswagen detector would commence shortly.) The second reason is that although the visual world of the frog is limited, the visual world of the human is not. Even if you were endowed with all the biological specifications you would ever need, they would be so numerous that they would defeat their own purpose. Remember, the essential attribute of human pattern recognition is its flexibility. This flexibility would be seriously compromised if all incoming stimuli had to be processed by a specialized feature detector. Put another way, the frog's system is efficient precisely because it has so few feature detectors.

Context

In addition to the biological constraints just described, considerations of processing time also appear to rule out a completely feature analytic theory of pattern recognition. For example, if we consider each letter as having five features, and a page of typed text as having about 300 words of five letters each, then reading each page requires about 7,500 features detections (an example modified from one appearing in Anderson, 1980). A typical reader can read at the rate of 250 words per minute, which would necessitate over 100 feature detections per second. When you recall the varied mapping condition of the Schneider and Shiffrin (1977) study, the notion that individual letters can be processed that fast seems unlikely. Then how can we read, and accomplish other sorts of pattern recognition, so quickly?

The best answer to this question is that we probably don't process each letter on a feature-by-feature basis. Rather, we use other surrounding letters as a basis for inferring what the intervening letter must be. An example of this use of **context** can be seen in Figure 2.13. Notice that the features of the ambiguous character are not as informative as those of the surrounding characters when making an interpretation. The contrast between feature analysis and contextual analysis is sometimes described by cognitive psychologists as data-driven versus conceptually driven processing (Lindsay &

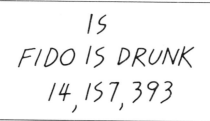

Figure 2.13.

The stimulus above the handwriting can be interpreted as either "15" or "is," depending on its context. The meaning of a stimulus is often determined in part by its context.

Norman, 1977). **Data-driven processes** operate from the bottom up, gathering and processing information in small pieces, which are later assembled in working memory. **Conceptually driven processes** operate from the top down and can be considered as expectations or plans. Conceptually driven processes gulp in large amounts of information while making deductions and filling in the gaps. In the case of letter recognition, conceptually driven processes are generated from our general knowledge of which letters are likely candidates to begin words, which combinations of letters are likely, and so on.

The effects of context on letter recognition have been known for some time (Reicher, 1969; Wheeler, 1970). The basic finding, known as the **word superiority effect,** is that subjects are more able to identify a letter accurately when it appears in the context of a word than when it appears by itself or in the context of a string of random letters. For example, Wheeler (1970) gave his subjects a brief presentation of a letter or a word. Following this, they were shown either two letters or two words, and were asked to determine which had been presented earlier. A letter trial consisted of showing a letter *(D)* and then two letters *(D, G)*. The word trial consisted of a word *(WIND)* and then two words *(WIND, WING)*. Wheeler found that recognition was about 10 percent better in the word condition, meaning that subjects were better able to discriminate *D* from *G* when these letters appeared in the context of a word.

This finding has been interpreted as showing the existence of some "higher-order unit" (Purcell, Stanovich & Spector, 1978)—a unit of knowledge in which conglomerations of individual features have been associated through repeated presentation. According to such a view, the recognition of some features permits the inference of associated features. Rumelhart and Siple (1974) have explained the word superiority effect in these terms. Suppose the subject in the word condition just described recognizes the letters *WIN*. The remaining letter is limited to few possibilities: *E, D, G, K, O,* or *S*. If the subject has detected even a single feature from the fourth letter (such as the vertical line), then enough information is present for the subject to guess *WIND* in the recognition task. However, the possession of only a single feature is not very helpful in the letter trials, because no letters can be recognized from a single feature alone.

This explanation, although appealing, has fallen on hard times. Solman, May, and Schwartz (1981) have stated that the word superiority effect has two possible sources. One of these sources is sensory memory. A possibility, they argued, is that some elements—particularly words—are retained in sensory storage longer than are nonwords. Because the words are stored longer, the subject could be "reading" them better on the recognition task. The second explanation is similar to that of Rumelhart and Siple (1974): The subjects could be using word knowledge to make sophisticated guesses on the recognition task.

Figure 2.14 shows the stimuli that Solman et al. used in their study and how they were presented to their subjects. Subjects were first shown fragments of words or nonwords. After a delay of 0 to 150 msec, subjects were

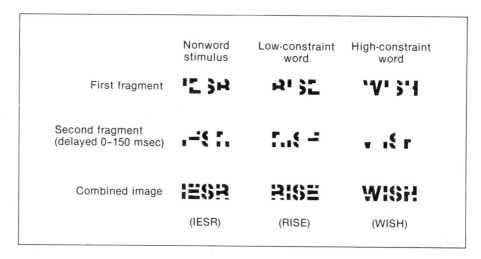

	Nonword stimulus	Low-constraint word	High-constraint word
First fragment			
Second fragment (delayed 0–150 msec)			
Combined image			
	(IESR)	(RISE)	(WISH)

Figure 2.14.

The word superiority effect: setup for Solman, May, and Schwartz (1981) study.

shown the second series of fragments. The two sets of fragments could be combined to form a nonword *(IESR)*, a low-constraint word *(RISE)* in which many letters could be substituted for the *S*, and a high-constraint word *(WISH)* in which only a few letters are acceptable in the third position. Following the presentation of the two fragments, the subjects were shown two letters (*S* and *T*), and were asked to determine which they had seen. The word superiority effect was again demonstrated: Recognition was better for the *S* when it appeared in a word as opposed to a nonword combination of letters. If the subjects were using word knowledge to guess about the *S*'s identity, we would expect that recognition would be better in the high-constraint condition. In the high-constraint condition, even the recognition of a single feature would allow the subject to pin down the *S*, whereas similar knowledge wouldn't be as helpful in the low-constraint condition. However, the performance of the subjects was the same in both word conditions. Similarly, the delay between the presentation of successive fragments had no effect on recognition.

Unquestionably, the effects of context on pattern recognition are powerful. Explaining exactly how these effects are produced has been troublesome for psychologists, at least as far as letter recognition is concerned. Subsequent chapters look again at data-driven and conceptually driven processes, and consider some of the cases in which these processes interact.

CONCLUDING COMMENTS AND SUGGESTIONS FOR FURTHER READING

I began this chapter by posing a question about the qualities that the stimulus must have to provoke a shift of attention. As you now know, phrasing the question this way was slightly misleading on my part. First, ascribing to the stimulus all of the power to provoke an attentional shift is incorrect, because in addition to data-driven processes, there are also conceptually driven processes. As the influence of context on the ambiguous figure showed us, pattern recognition is often propelled by our expectations. Things are seen or not seen, heard or not heard, depending upon whether they are congruent with the expectation in force. Second, to speak of shifts of attention is sometimes misleading. Over the last decade and a half, many cognitive psychologists have adopted the position that attention consists of resource allocation. It's unlikely that any action would be so engrossing that all processing resources would be allocated to it (strategically speaking, smart systems always keep a reserve). This means that some resources will be allocated to processing many of the stimuli surrounding us. Will we necessarily become aware of the stimuli we process? As we have seen, the answer to this question appears to be no. The processing of stimuli depends in part upon certain enduring dispositions of the cognitive system. Many of these dispositions are under conscious control in that the nature of the incoming information's analysis can be altered. The results of the analysis, however, may not necessarily enter awareness. As Shiffrin and Dumais (1981) have pointed out, the relationship between attention and awareness is problematic. The results of automatic processing frequently don't enter consciousness, and even the results of controlled processing may not enter consciousness under all circumstances.

Regarding pattern recognition, feature analysis is apparently a powerful method for detecting regularities in stimulation. The elements of stimulation that serve as features are at least partly constrained by biological need and neuronal architecture.

The student who wishes to pursue these topics further should read Kahneman's (1973) book, which contains an excellent review of the literature constituting the first phase of theory building. The original papers by Broadbent (1958) and Treisman (1960) are classics. A good outline of the second phase of theory construction can be found in Posner and Snyder (1975). Advanced state-of-the-art work in this area can be found in the series of monographs called *Attention and Performance*. A first-rate summary of the findings on automaticity can be found in Shiffrin and Dumais (1981). Lindsay and Norman (1977) provide a readable account of pattern recognition by humans; Waltz (1982) offers a good account of pattern recognition by machines.

This chapter mentioned that LD children may have attentional deficits of some sort. Recently, researchers have devoted some energy to understanding problems of attention. Attention deficit disorder (ADD) is apparently a component of the problems shared by LD, hyperactive, and brain-damaged children. Koppel (1979) is an examination of this problem. The relationship of conscious and unconscious perceptual processes and the role each plays in the development of awareness are fully treated in a challenging article by Marcel (1983).

FOCUS ON RESEARCH:

Automaticity, Skill, and Awareness

The distinction between automatic and controlled processes is a matter of degree. As we improve a skill, the process of automatization proceeds gradually, and the amount of control required gradually recedes.

The course of skill acquisition has been known to psychologists for a long time. Snoddy (1926) studied the acquisition of skill on a mirror-tracing task. This task usually involves subjects guiding a pencil through a geometric shape while watching the reflection of their hands in a mirror. The subjects improved, but the rate of improvement is what's particularly interesting. If we plot the time required to do the task as function of trials (holding errors constant), we would expect to see a decline. Snoddy plotted the *logarithm* of time as a function of the *logarithm* of the number of trials. When this log-log plot was created for individual subjects, Snoddy observed that the line of best fit was a perfectly straight line! Figure 2.15 shows how the log-log plot would look for a hypothetical subject.

You should note two important points here. First, the subject's improvement continued across the whole set of trials; there was no endpoint at which improvement ceased. Second, if you consider the amount of improvement (in time) from any one

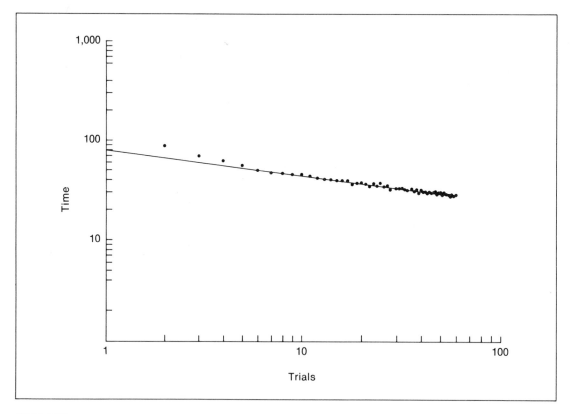

Figure 2.15.

Learning in a mirror-tracing task (log-log coordinates). (Redrawn from Snoddy, 1926.)

point on the X axis to any other point, you know that in the future, ten times as many trials will be required to produce a similar improvement.

Cognitive psychologists have since demonstrated that this log-log law holds not only for motor or perceptual skills but also for higher cognitive processes. For example, Newell and Rosenbloom (1981) studied the acquisition of skill in a solitaire card game called Stair. Here are the rules:

Stair involves laying out all 52 cards face up from a shuffled deck, in 8 *columns* (four with 7 rows, four with 6 rows). There are also four *spots* (initially empty), each of which can hold only a single card. The aim is to build four *stacks,* ace to king, one for each suit, by moving cards around under typical solitaire constraints. A card in a spot or at the bottom of a column may be moved: (1) to a spot, if it is empty; (2) to a stack, if the card is the next in order building up; or (3) to the bottom of another column, if the card is the next lower in the same suit (e.g., the six of spades appended to the seven of spades). (Newell & Rosenbloom, 1981)

You might wish to try playing this game a few times while charting your progress. Notice that this is a game of perfect information. Although a perceptual component is involved (a player might overlook a particular card) and a weak component of motor learning, this game is nevertheless primarily one of intellectual skill. That is, the subject's ability to analyze the initial layout is what determines victory. Newell and Rosenbloom's subject played five-hundred hands of Stair. He got better, winning about 28 percent of his initial hands and about 40 percent of his final hands. In addition, the log-log law held for the time involved in playing (regardless of whether the hand was won or lost). For winning hands, the subject started out requiring about 1,000 seconds. By the end, five-hundred hands later, this time had been reduced to about 550 seconds. All intermediate points fell close to the straight line established by the two endpoints, when the log of time was plotted as a function of the log of hand number.

Although playing this intellectual game had not become automatic, it was apparently on its way to becoming so. The implication of this finding is extremely interesting: With enough practice, the most challenging intellectual tasks could become automatic, requiring little or no awareness.

KEY TERMS

Selective attention
Dichotic listening
Shadowing
Filter theory
Preattentive analysis
Attenuation theory
Late selection
Cognitive resources
Allocation policy
Cognitive capacity

Electrodermal responses
Automaticity
Data-limited processes
Resource-limited processes
Template-matching theory
Feature detection theory
Context
Data-driven processes (bottom-up processes)
Conceptually driven processes (top-down processes)
Word superiority effect

CHAPTER 3

Constructivist and Direct Theories of Perception

OVERVIEW

THE CONSTRUCTIVIST POSITION
The Höffding Step
The Constructive Nature of Perception
  Illusions
  Initial Summary of the Constructivist
    Position
Prototypes
  Abstraction of Prototypes
  Prototypes and Schemata
  Accounts of Prototype Formation
  Implications for Other Areas of Psychology
Summary and Evaluation of the Constructivist
  Position

DIRECT THEORIES OF PERCEPTION
The Ecological Approach to Visual
  Perception
What the Environment Affords Us
Evaluation of the Direct Theory

A SYNTHESIS

REPRESENTATIONAL THOUGHT AND PERCEPTION:
COGNITIVE MAPS
Varieties of Spatial Cognition
Expertise in Cognitive Mapping

CONCLUDING COMMENTS AND SUGGESTIONS
FOR FURTHER READING
FOCUS ON APPLICATIONS
KEY TERMS

Most of us move easily through this world, seldom giving any thought to the problems inherent in locomotion, although these problems are substantial. In taking a step, you pitch your body forward by contracting the muscles of the leg and torso. For a split second, your body careens forward, out of control, until the stepping foot is swung into position to break the fall. This movement requires substantial musculature, because humans are large animals. Taken together, these facts suggest an unusual but accurate picture of pedestrial movement on downtown streets. During the noon hours on any given block in Manhattan, for example, thousands of densely packed people lurch forward in alternating periods of balance and falling. Because humans are large, at any given moment in time on that block will be tons of runaway mass, which could be disastrous if collisions were permitted. Although everyone moves at slightly different speeds and with slightly different gaits, collisions between pedestrians are relatively rare. Locomotion seems to require highly accurate, genuine information about the state of the immediate world, and the low rate of collisions among pedestrians suggests that humans must have this kind of information in their mental representations of the world.

Some situations exist, however, in which humans' representations of the world are highly *inaccurate*. For example, I'm always struck by the intensity of the ocean's coldness when I first enter the water. After a few minutes, though, the water feels warm. This change in mental representation might be explained in two ways. First, the ocean may really warm up, so my perceived change in warmth is based on a real physical change. This change seems unlikely, doesn't it? Alternatively, my body could be cooled by the ocean, so that the discrepancy between the two temperatures is reduced. This event is also unlikely. The human body comes equipped with certain features that are designed to forestall such a loss of heat. Two thermometers—one in my mouth and one in the ocean— would probably register almost constant temperatures during the entire time my perception of the ocean shifted from cold to warm. This means that I don't know what the ocean's exact temperature is. My mental representation of the ocean's temperature depends upon how long I've been standing in the water. My nervous system, which most of the time faithfully records worldly events, plays tricks when it comes to measuring the temperature of the ocean. The implications of this fact are slightly scary. If my nervous system can trick me into thinking the cold ocean is really warm, then how do I know *for sure* that my nervous system isn't tricking me at other times, too?

All of us recognize that our experiences are produced by some activity of our nervous systems. For cognitive psychologists, one question becomes, What exactly is the role of the central nervous system in producing these experiences? This chapter considers the two basic positions. The **constructivist theory of perception** (also called the transactional position, Ittelson & Cantril, 1954, and the computational position, Ullman, 1980) maintains that sensory stimulation is inadequate by itself to produce perception. Through experience, the brain learns how to interpret sensory cues, which themselves are inherently ambiguous. According to this view, the brain's interpretive activity is critical in perception. That is, the brain is not simply processing neural events that are straightforward alterations of physical energy. Rather, the brain is adding in information of its own based on knowledge that has been built up from previous perceptual activity.

The alternative position is referred to as the **direct theory of perception.** Simply put, direct theorists argue that, at least for vision, all the information we need to perceive is already contained and presented in the light that strikes our retinae. Also, this light is not random or chaotic, but instead is highly organized by the surfaces from which it has been reflected. Thus, the brain needn't add in or spruce up the incoming sensory stimulation. This stimulation is far from unorganized, according to the direct theorists. Instead, a highly accurate depiction of the world-as-it-is becomes available for us whenever we choose to bring our receptors to bear on it. Also implied by this position is the idea that our perceptual machinery has evolved to fit into, or mesh with, the types of information that are available on this planet.

This chapter considers the evidence favoring these two perspectives and offers a possible synthesis. The conclusion of this chapter ties some of the information in this and the previous chapter together with a discussion of cognitive maps—internal representations of geographical layouts.

THE CONSTRUCTIVIST POSITION

This section details the constructivist account of perception, starting with a historical problem in psychology and going on to see how the constructivist position deals with the phenomenon of illusions.

The Höffding Step

Having sensory mechanisms means that certain cells in our bodies respond to particular forms of physical energy. Some of these sensory mechanisms are quite sophisticated in that they are capable of creating a code in which many aspects of the physical stimulation are retained. We can do more than simply encode physical energy, however; we can *recognize* it as well. That is, a pattern of neural events can produce within us an awareness and an understanding of the physical object that has been neurally encoded. I can *see* in my wife as soon as the ambient light reflected from her strikes the receptors in my retinae. But I won't *recognize* her until something more than this happens. The creation of a neural code might eventually produce recognition, but only because that neural code leads to some other neural events that do the recognizing. How might this take place?

According to associationism, a doctrine that was popular during the 1870s (Weimer, 1977), the linkage between a physical object and the naming of a physical object was direct, meaning that the neural events representing some physical object could be equated with the neural events involved in saying the name of the object. Harald Höffding (1891) demonstrated that such a view could not be correct. Consider Figure 3.1. The left side of the

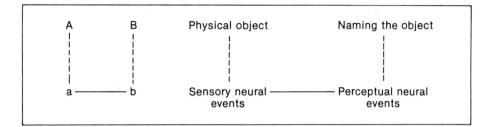

Figure 3.1.

The Höffding step in the process of pattern recognition or perception. (From Weimer, 1977.)

figure is a schematic representation of the activities shown on the right-hand side. Thus, *A* represents the physical object as it stands in the world. For recognition to take place, this object must be sensed, that is, represented neurally as in *a*. However, before the object can be named (either overtly or covertly) it must first be recognized, which requires additional neural activity of a different sort than that involved in sensation. The sensory code is just a neural representation of an object; it carries no information with it regarding categorization. This second kind of neural processing is represented in *b*—the perceptual neural events that categorize the object and allow us to name it. According to the associationists, the route from *A* to *B* was a straight line. Höffding showed that the path was not nearly so simple. The Höffding step is the step between sensation and perception, and with it, a question is produced. How do sensory neural events get changed over, that is, converted into perceptual neural events that give rise to our awarenesses and understandings?

Before examining the answer to this question, two points should be noted. First, the Höffding step is quite general. Although the previous example involved vision, each sense creates its own sensory code and consequently produces its own Höffding step. This means that enterprising psychologists who solved the Höffding step for vision might be at a loss to solve the analogous Höffding problem for audition. That is, they might be unable to specify how speech sounds are recognized so that meaning is extracted from them. Second, no psychologist, cognitively oriented or otherwise, has ever offered a solution to the Höffding problem that has proved satisfactory to everyone. At the risk of oversimplifying, the constructivist solution to the Höffding problem involves taking it head-on by specifying the laws that govern the transformation of retinal images into perceptual experiences. Against this, the direct position can be seen as a kind of end run. Rather than laboriously solve the Höffding step for each sense, direct theorists hope that by recasting the problem of perception altogether, the Höffding step will eventually be banished as a problem that lacks validity.

The Constructive Nature of Perception

The constructivist position begins with the premise that retinal events are inadequate to specify how objects are perceived. This proposition may seem unlikely to you, particularly if you believe that the retina transmits an amazingly detailed and accurate picture of the outside world to the brain. An abundance of information is probably surrounding you right now that might be persuasive in convincing you otherwise. In some situations, retinal signals can be ambiguous. First, although the retina has spatial extension, the space is only two-dimensional. It's not too hard to imagine how the retina might send the brain a code that specifies two of an object's three dimensions. But where does the third dimension come from? Our awareness includes knowledge of depth, and the constructivists argue that this awareness of depth could not have been produced at the retina. Rather, the brain must interpret aspects of the retinal code and, as a result of its interpretation, generate the third dimension. In other cases, the retinal code produces certain inaccuracies in our awareness of the external world.

For example, my office is in a wing that juts out at right angles to the main axis of a large building. The facade of the building is basically colum-nar, but the column effect has been softened by the placement of horizontal brick and concrete patterns. In architecture, such a horizontal effect is called a stringcourse. Viewed from the front of the building, the stringcourses are perfectly horizontal. But from my perspective, on the ground floor and looking across the face of the building, the second story stringcourse seems to be angled somewhat to the ground. The third story stringcourse is more sharply angled yet, and the fourth floor stringcourse appears very steeply angled. I know the stringcourses are horizontal; nevertheless, what I see is not what's out there. My awareness, which is presumably the result of retinal and central nervous system events, is of slanted stringcourses. If questioned, I would answer that they are not slanted, but only because I also have some other knowledge that dominates my awareness. I know the string courses are really not slanted; they just look that way.

According to the constructivists, this other knowledge must be added in to the retinal code to specify the object as it really is in the outside world. What is this other knowledge, and where did it come from? I've seen the building from a variety of perspectives, and in each case, my recognition of the building has been accompanied by an awarness of how the various parts of the building (including the stringcourses) look from that particular per-spective. Even if I remember only some of these views, eventually I'll acquire enough experience with the building to know how the building's appearance will change as a function of my perspective on it. According to the construc-tivist position, the other knowledge referred to previously is a memorized representation of the building produced by experience. This internal rep-resentation may or may not be imaginal. The internal representation doesn't necessarily have to be based on direct sensory experience. For example, if I were placed beside some building I had never seen before, I would still be able to answer questions accurately about it even though I had seen the building only from one perspective. This ability suggests that the internal representation that is added to the retinal code is abstract; it is generated by sensory experiences but is not limited to particular experiences.

Illusions

The constructivist position is cognitively oriented. This means that the con-structivists frequently try to specify the successive alterations of sensory stimulation in terms of an information-processing model. Moreover, they may attempt to describe that knowledge that results from this processing of information in terms that were used in Chapter 1. This sort of knowledge hinges on the *experiences* that we've had in the world. That is, the computational procedures used by the nervous system may be more or less independent of our experiences, but the knowledge produced by such procedures is strongly anchored on events that have happened to us. This connection is important for the constructivists because they argue that our perception of things is a function of our experience. Consequently, whenever we misperceive a stimulus, constructivists are interested in the nature of the misperception. If the misperception is congruent with our experiences, then the constructivist might feel more confident in saying that we don't necessarily perceive things as they are, but rather we perceive things according to the way we have previously experienced them. This is why the constructivists have historically been interested in the problem of illusions: What factors make us sometimes misinterpret sensory stimulation?

Psychologists have used a wide variety of illusions in their studies, but none are more famous than the **Müller-Lyer illusion** depicted in Figure 3.2. The horizontal bar between the fins-out segments is the same length as the horizontal bar between the fins-in segments. To most people, the fins-out bar looks longer than the fins-in bar. What factors produce the illusion?

Strictly speaking, the retina does not seem to play a large role in the creation of the illusion per se. For example, it has been known for some time that no eye movements are required to produce the illusion (Yarbus, 1967). But some more recent evidence (Petersik, 1982) has suggested that people do make inappropriate eye movements in scanning the Müller-Lyer illusion. Petersik asked his subjects to estimate the extent of their eye movements in scanning the fins-out horizontal bar, the fins-in bar, and a finless bar. Estimates for the finless and fins-in bar were similar and accurate. However, the subjects overestimated the extent of the eye movement necessary to scan the fins-out bar. Because eye movements are not required to produce the illusion, one way of interpreting Petersik's findings is that

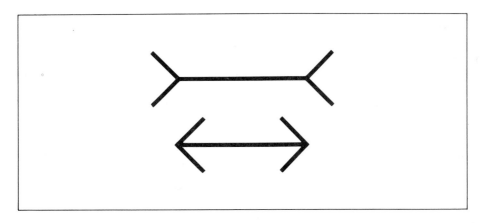

Figure 3.2.
The Müller-Lyer illusion.

the subjects were *misled*. That is, the faulty estimates were produced by the subjects' previous experiences. This interpretation suggests that it was the subject's brain, which directed the eye movements, that was the locus of the illusion.

This interpretation is strengthened by the findings of Gilliam (1980). In this research, the horizontal bars of the Müller-Lyer illusion were briefly presented to one of the subject's eyes while the fins were presented to the subject's other eye. The separate retinal signals were combined, or fused, by the central nervous system and when this took place, the subjects still showed the illusion's effects. The image of the fins-out bar looked longer to the subjects then did the image of the fins-in bar. This finding suggests that the previous experience of the Müller-Lyer illusion, represented in the subjects' memories, misguided their perceptual processing. But you're probably already aware of a potential snag in this reasoning. Surely some of the subjects had never seen the Müller-Lyer illusion before, so how could they have been misled by previous experience?

As Figure 3.3 shows, the world frequently presents us with stimulation in which some of the characteristics of the Müller-Lyer illusion are embedded. The vertical bar in each of the panels of Figure 3.3 is the same length. You know from your experience in the world that the vertical bar in the right-hand panel highlights the closest part of the doorway to you. Similarly, the vertical bar in the left-hand panels highlights the part of the doorway that is farthest from you. If these bars are the same size, then you know the doorway on the left must be bigger than the doorway on the right. When you look at the Müller-Lyer illusion, your experience in judging the sizes and distances in our highly angular world is what misleads you (Gregory, 1966).

Support for these contentions can be found in various cross-cultural studies of the Müller-Lyer illusion. For example, the Zulus of Africa live in a decidedly noncarpentered world. Although they build shelters, these are usually conical and windowless. If the Müller-Lyer illusion is produced by our experiences in a right-angled world, then it seems reasonable to expect that people such as the Zulus, who have little or no experience in such a world, would not fall prey to the illusion. This assumption seems to be accurate. Deregowski (1972) has reported findings showing that the Zulus don't perceive the Müller-Lyer illusion and other illusions that are thought to be based on experiences with right angles. As is the case with almost any cross-cultural study, some objections can be raised. First, pictorial representations could be among the things with which the Zulus are unfamiliar. Looking at and correctly interpreting pictures are skills that other cultures may not foster. Second, in this type of study, language problems are almost inevitable. That the Zulus understood what was being asked of them is not clear.

Initial Summary of the Constructivist Position

The constructivist position is an inherently cognitive one that can be clearly expressed as information-processing model. That is, it's easy to conceive of perceptual activity as involving the elaboration of a more or less primitive

Figure 3.3.
Müller-Lyer effects in everyday life.

retinal code by successive stages of processing within the central nervous system. In many ways, the processing of this code appears to be serial. Although it is beyond the scope of this book, a substantial body of physiological evidence supports the idea that cognitive events seem to be closely tied to neural events (at least for vision). Chapter 1 touched briefly on these matters.

What remains for us is specifying the outcome of this information processing. Our objective in the next section is to detail what sort of knowledge is built up from successive interactions with the world.

Prototypes

Many cognitivists argue that the perception of people, events, and objects proceeds by extracting from these stimuli their distinctive features. As we saw in Chapter 2, humans seem to have developed specialized neural and cognitive mechanisms whose purpose is to analyze complex worldly events by breaking them down into their constituent elements: their features. However, these features are not left in an unorganized state in the cognitive system. The features are in turn assembled into larger units of knowledge—larger in that the principle that organizes the features is extensive. Once developed, these large units of knowledge guide, or channel, subsequent feature extraction. One of the terms used to describe such large units of knowledge is the *prototype*.

Abstraction of Prototypes

Posner and Keele (1968, 1970) conducted a series of studies to show how such large units of knowledge are formed. First, they created a set of four random nine-dot patterns, three of which are shown in Figure 3.4. These patterns were called the prototypes. Next, for each prototype, Posner and Keele created distortions by moving some of the dots slightly, in different directions. Figure 3.4 shows four of the distorted dot patterns. The distortions are not as random as they might look. Although the rule used in producing the distortions is complicated, each dot in the distortion was moved, on the average, the same distance from its position in the prototype. In this way, the *average* position of each dot in the distortion was the same as the prototype.

Posner and Keele presented their subjects with four distortions of each prototype. The prototype was never presented, nor were the subjects told how the distortions were created. Subjects had to learn to associate each of the distorted dot patterns with a name. The subjects underwent a training period in which they learned how to categorize the sixteen distorted dot patterns into four piles reflecting the category names. After the subjects were able to do this perfectly, they were given a test in which they had to sort both old and new stimuli into piles. The old stimuli included the previously studied distortions. The new stimuli included the prototype as well as two previously unlearned distortions. The subjects made errors 20 percent of the

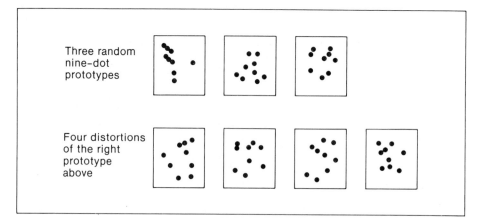

Figure 3.4.

Sample stimuli from Posner and Keele's (1968) study of the acquisition of prototypes. (After Posner, 1973. Reprinted by permission of the author.)

time in classifying previously studied distortions. Their error rate for the prototype was 32 percent even though they had never seen it before. The subjects made errors 50 percent of the time when categorizing previously unstudied distortions. If the subject had simply been guessing, the error rate would have been 75 percent (i.e., chance of guessing which stimulus belongs in which pile is only one in four). Notice that the error rate for the prototypes is low, and close to that of the previously studied distortions. Clearly, the subjects had learned about the prototypes even though they hadn't studied them explicitly. This implication was supported in another study by Posner (1969). Using a paradigm similar to the one just outlined, Posner gave his subjects a memory task in which they were asked to recognize various dot patterns as either old (previously studied) or new (never seen before). Even though the prototype had never been presented along with the other distortions, subjects were more likely to categorize it as an old stimulus than as a new one. This finding was not observed for other previously unstudied distortions.

Another interesting finding concerns the variability of the distortions. When the subjects are given only low-variability distortions during the training period (i.e., distortions that have been produced by only small movements of the dots), their ability to categorize or recognize previously unstudied high-variability distortions is impaired. However, if subjects are given only high-variability distortions during the training period, their ability to classify previously unstudied low-variability distortions is unimpaired. Although the presentation of high-variability distortions during the training period does not necessarily produce better recognition of the prototype, it does seem to produce better knowledge of the width or the boundaries of the category names (Homa, 1978; Homa & Vosburgh, 1976).

Other studies have focused on the spontaneity of prototype abstraction and the need for feedback in doing so. Fried and Holyoak (1984) presented their subjects with distortions of prototypical "artwork" created by two artists, "Smith" and "Jones." Figure 3.5 shows the prototypes and some of the distortions of each artist's work. The diagrams were shown one at a time to the subjects, who had to classify the designs into one of two piles by pressing a button. Subjects in one group were informed about the correctness or incorrectness of each guess as soon as the choice was made. The other half of the subjects were not given this information. Each subject continued sorting the designs until ten correct consecutive choices were made or until two hundred designs were presented. Although neither group of subjects was ever shown the prototype, and one group of subjects received no information concerning the correctness of this sorting, both groups did equally well on the sorting task. Although this fairly surprising finding has drawn fire (Homa & Cultice, 1984), this work nevertheless has an interesting implication. The Fried and Holyoak findings suggest that the corrective feedback given by adults to children who misclassify objects is probably not essential in enabling the children to form a prototype.

Bomba and Siqueland (1983) tested the validity of this assertion in a study involving the presentation of distorted dot patterns to babies age three to four months. The researchers made use of a habituation paradigm to

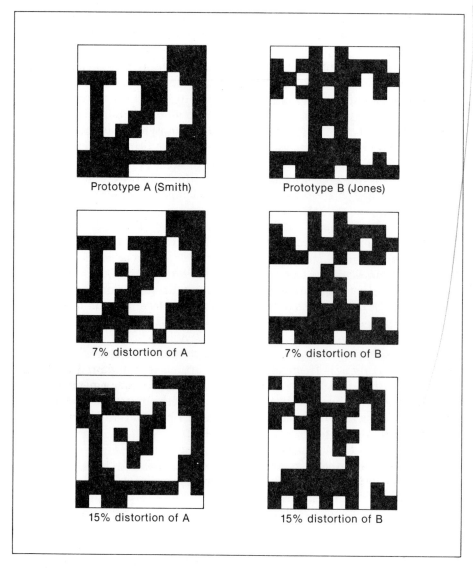

Figure 3.5.

Prototypes and distortions of designs by "Smith" and "Jones."

assess the formation of prototype knowledge of three geometric dot patterns: a square, a triangle, and a diamond. **Habituation** refers to our tendency to stop attending to, or noticing, stimuli as they become familiar. A variety of methods can be used to determine when habituation has taken place in infants. For example, the frequency and length of gazing, changes in heart and respiration rates, or even actions such as the intensity of sucking on a pacifier, have all been used to determine that an infant has lost interest in, and habituated to, a particular stimulus. Bomba and Siqueland found that the babies studied showed no initial preference for the prototypical geometric forms over their distortions. However, the babies did show habituation to the previously unseen prototype following the presentation of six distortions of each of the three prototypical forms. That is, the babies seemed to recognize that the prototype was similar to the six distortions that they had already seen, and therefore was not as interesting as a truly novel stimulus. Considered together, the Fried and Holyoak and Bomba and Siqueland studies suggest that the process of prototype abstraction emerges early in the life span and seems to operate independently of linguistic feedback. As discussed in Chapter 11, substantial evidence supports the idea that natural concept formation proceeds by stages, the first of which is formation of prototypical instances (Whitney and Kunen, 1983).

Prototypes and Schemata

From their experiences with stimuli that are judged to be similar, people abstract the distinctive features of those stimuli and assemble these features into a prototype. Over the last few years, cognitive psychologists (Anderson, 1980; Fiske & Taylor, 1984) have been likely to draw a distinction between the prototype and other terms that denote large or extensive units of knowledge. One such term is the **schema.**

The prototype has been defined as a hypothetical, "most typical" instance of a category (Anderson, 1980). Comprehending this definition might be easier if you think of membership in a category as involving the passage of a series of tests. The more tests that are passed, the closer a given instance is to becoming a central, or prototypical, member of that category. For example, consider the category *college professor.* Beyond certain formal qualifications for this role, what can we say about the informal characteristics of college professors? Some of the qualities that come to my mind are maleness, a slight obesity, being middle-aged, going bald, having a beard, and "tweediness." One could be a college professor without possessing any of these qualities, but with the possession of more of these qualities, a given professor becomes more typical and, with the possession of all of them, become prototypical.

The schema, on the other hand, is often used to denote what is *essential* about category membership rather than what is typical (Anderson, 1980; Fiske & Taylor, 1984). Whereas the prototypical college professor would have to possess all of the qualities just listed, the schematic college professor need not possess any of them. In addition to this denotative meaning, the term *schema* connotes a plan or procedure that could be useful in classifying people, objects, or events. In that sense, the schema is not an instance of a thing, but rather is a large cognitive structure that can be used to receive and organize information (Neisser, 1976). Hence, the term *schema* is a more general term than *prototype.* Schemas have been involved as organizing principles for some time in psychology (Bartlett, 1932). Apart from its historical use, the term has more recently been mentioned in attempts to synthesize (i.e., blend together) the constructivist with direct theories of perception (Neisser, 1976).

Accounts of Prototype Formation

We have seen that in successive encounters with the environment, people systematically build up organizational principles of knowledge that are used to help channel or categorize future transactions with the world. As we've seen, people seem to be able to do this from a very early point in their lives. Moreover, corrective feedback need not be given for the process of prototype formation to occur.

Cognitive psychologists have typically described the buildup of organized world knowledge as being dependent upon the abstraction of relevant stimuli from objects present in the world (Posner, 1969). According to this view, people are sensitive to perceived regularities among the stimuli in the world (Howard, 1983). Moreover, people are able to make use of the fact that certain stimuli seem to occur in the presence of certain other stimuli and from this they learn about the "correlational" structure of the world (Rosch, 1977)—the fact that certain qualities have a high probability of occurring together. Prototypes then can be thought of as simply one variety of cognitive structure—one that enables the owner to answer questions about the similarity among stimuli by comparing the stimuli to the most central members of varous categories.

This position on the influence of experience in perception is both common (Hull, 1920; Reber, 1967) and plausible. However, the position has not gone unchallenged. Brooks (1978) has argued that it is not feature abstraction per se that occurs during successive interactions with the environment. Instead, Brooks hypothesized that each object we encounter is stored intact in our memories, meaning that the object's features are not abstracted from it and stored separately. In dealing with new stimuli, the questions we ask ourselves concerns the similarity between the new stimulus and the memory of previously encountered stimuli. A person categorizes novel stimuli by constructing an analogy: What old stimulus is this new stimulus most like?

Although space precludes a complete detailing of his work, Brooks has found that people perform well on some sorting tasks that seem to require multiple prototype formation according to the feature abstraction viewpoint. The simultaneous formation of multiple prototypes should require greater cognitive effort than the formation of a single prototype, and consequently we should expect a greater number of classification errors on such a sorting task. However, Brooks (1978) observed that sorting performance under such conditions is not degraded, which suggests that the feature abstraction viewpoint may not be the whole story. As Brooks notes, the two viewpoints are not necessarily contradictory. Some situations may exist in which either method of prototype formation works effectively. Given that, what we may be seeing here is another example of a situation in which a person can exert some strategic control over the method of prototype formation, or perhaps the method of prototype formation is driven by certain characteristics of the environment.

Implications for Other Areas of Psychology

Until this point, the constructivist position has been described as though it were relevant only to the problem of interpreting information that is primarily visual. The constructivist argument is in reality far broader than that. This section provides a brief account of the ways in which the constructivist view of perception has affected other areas of psychology. The objective here is to show that the processes of **feature abstraction** and prototype formation are omnipresent aspects of our mental lives. These processes influence our knowledge of other people as well as our self-knowledge.

As Fiske and Taylor (1984) have pointed out, the concept of the schema has been fruitfully applied to social psychology, wherein the term denotes organized generic prior knowledge that enables us to function in a social world that would otherwise be of paralyzing complexity (Fiske & Taylor, 1984, p. 149). In other words, varieties of schemata allow us to organize incoming information about our social world in an efficient way. *Social cognition* describes this particular type of cognitive activity in which the psychological question of knowledge in human relationships is treated from the standpoint of the information-processing model. Table 3.1 shows several types of schemata that have been postulated as guides of human social interactions. For example, the **self-schema** is a complex cognitive structure into which information about the self is accepted and organized. As Markus (1977) has demonstrated, almost everyone is *schematic* regarding certain personal qualities, meaning that one's self is defined as possessing certain qualities, and information about these qualities presented by the world will be attended to. In that regard, schematic qualities are those that people have decided are important about themselves. Suppose, for example, I re-

TABLE 3.1

Types of Schemata in Social Cognition

A schema is a cognitive structure that contains knowledge about the attributes of a concept and the relationships among those attributes. All types of schemata guide perception, memory, and inference in similar ways, toward schema-relevant information, and often toward schema-consistent information. Disconfirming or incongruent information requires more effort to process than congruent information; if that effort is made, it may be well remembered.

Person schemata: People's understanding of the psychology of typical or specific individuals, composed of traits and goals, helps them to categorize others and to remember schema-relevant behavior.

Self-schemata: General information about one's own psychology makes up a complex, easily accessible verbal self-concept that guides information processing about the self.

Role schemata: Intergroup perception and stereotyping are affected by role schemata that describe the appropriate norms and behavior for broad social categories, based on age, race, sex, and occupation.

Event schemata: People's prior knowledge of the typical sequence of events on standard social occasions helps them to understand ambiguous information, to remember relevant information, and to infer consistent information where it is missing.

Content-free or procedural social schemata: A rather different kind of social schema consists entirely of rules for linking content but not much content; it guides information processing toward schema-relevant information.

Source: Fiske and Taylor, 1984.

gard myself as frugal. Assuming that this is one of my schematic qualities means that I will pay attention to how others describe my actions in financial matters, and I will likely respond if someone tries to assert that I am a spendthrift. In contrast with schematic qualities, the self has many other potential characteristics about which we care little and consequently, to which we pay little attention. On these dimensions of the self, we are *aschematic*. If asked whether I am political, I may not know how to respond; I don't think of myself in those terms. Consequently, I'm not inclined to think of this characteristic of myself as very important.

The possession of schematic qualities exerts a predictable effect on certain self-judgments. Bargh (1982) presented his subjects with a variety of adjectives; the subjects were told to respond, as quickly as possible, whether or not the adjectives were true about them. Subjects who were schematic on independence (referred to as independence schematics) responded quickly—almost automatically—to adjectives related to independence. However, they did not respond quickly to adjectives related to dependence. Independence aschematics, on the other hand, did not respond quickly to adjectives related to independence or dependence. Being schematic on a particular dimension confers an advantage to the person who is that way, because it allows that person to rapidly process particular kinds of information. Highly schematized individuals (those who are schematic on many dimensions and who consequently have a highly differentiated sense of self) might fare better in social situations than less schematized individuals, simply because they are more able to organize incoming information about the social setting. Thus, highly schematized individuals are more likely to know where they stand in a group.

Other evidence (Markus & Sentis, 1982) has suggested that people use their self-schemata to evaluate the characteristics and behavior of others. That is, we interpret the characteristics of others according to characteristics that we believe we possess. This find has at least two implications. First, a person who is schematic on a given dimension tends to group what appear to be isolated behaviors on the part of others into some coherent (schema-relevant) characteristic. Thus, if we imagine a person for whom body weight is a highly schematic dimension, then we would predict that such a person would group the idiosyncratic actions of others into a larger, schema-relevant picture. If the weight schematic observes another person having dry toast and grapefruit for breakfast, plain yogurt and fruit for lunch, swimming laps in the pool that afternoon, and drinking Perrier at a party that evening, then the weight schematic would assume that the other person is engaged in exercise and avoidance of high-calorie foods and beverages because the other person is dieting. Someone who was weight aschematic would not be inclined to link together all of these separate actions (Fong & Markus, 1982). However, someone who was weight aschematic but who *was* schematic on some other dimension might notice all the actions but assemble them into a different picture. Suppose a woman, having discovered she is pregnant with her first child, becomes quite concerned with nutrition and exercise. If the person whose behavior just described was a woman, the pregnant woman would assume that the person described was also pregnant.

The second implication is based on the origin of the self-schema. As we saw earlier, the prototype is apparently produced by abstracting the distinctive features from a set of stimuli. The self-schema is formed similarly. From the barrage of comments that are directed toward us and from those comments directed toward others that we overhear, we abstract those terms that are used in relation to us, either much more or much less frequently than they are used in relation to others. For example, we probably wouldn't abstract and building into our self-schemata the term *sloppy* unless we heard our actions described that way substantially more often than we heard the behavior of others described that way. Such terms denote characteristics that are thought by others to be distinctive features of our personality. As you are probably aware, this means that the abstraction and assignment of distinctive personality characteristics is highly dependent on the context in which such abstraction occurs.

Consider the case of a child who is told by others that he is bright. That kind of message is not given out randomly. To be described that way, the child must behave in some ways that are not characteristic of his peers. Under what sort of contexts are such performances likely? For the child who is able to do bright things against a background of normal children, such actions are distinctive and will be labeled so. If the development of the self-schema goes as expected, such a child would likely come to consider himself as being smart. However, if the same performances occur against a background of children who are all bright (i.e., capable of similar behaviors), then the child's actions would not be distinctive and the child would probably not be told that he is bright. Children raised under such circumstances would probably not incorporate the term *intelligent* into their self-schemata, even though in some objective sense they might be just as bright as the people who do regard themselves as intelligent.

Because the self-schema is so heavily dependent on context, using the self-schema as a predictor of one's actual personality is terribly problematic (Fiske & Taylor, 1984). As discussed previously, someone might be aschematic on some trait that is true about that person. Similarly, an individual might be schematic on some traits that are not accurate descriptions about her. People of moderate intellectual ability might think of themselves as bright if they were raised against a background of relatively low intellectual achievement. This means that no inherently obvious relationship exists between self-schemata and our "true" personality. Most people think they know themselves. But the research on self-schemata suggests that no necessary correlation is present between being schematic on a particular dimension and being correct about its authenticity as a component of one's personality (Fiske & Taylor, 1984).

According to the constructivist argument, the self-schema is a product of the same perceptual mechanisms that generate the rest of our mental lives. Consequently, to the extent that these other aspects of our mental lives are fabrications produced by our experiences, to that extent the self-schema is similarly fabricated. This type of reasoning is in opposition to traditional personality theories whose general objective is to uncover some enduring and stable characteristics of individuals that exist despite the apparent randomness of their behavior. Nevertheless, the cognitive standpoint on personality maintains that traditional approaches are not likely to bear fruit, because they overlook the fact that our dispositions are not necessarily anchored on reality, no matter how strongly we believe that to be the case.

Summary and Evaluation of the Constructivist Position

The constructivist position emphasizes the role of cognition in perception. That is, perception is thought to consist of a series of operations, beginning with a transformation of physical energy. The constructivist viewpoint takes a strong position with regard to the role played by the central nervous system in perception. Essentially, constructivists argue that perception would not be possible without the extensive computations performed by our brains. In other words, the position assumes that the events that are out there in the world aren't very informative *by themselves*. The various kinds of perception that we do (categorizing, for example—being a kind of perception) are possible only because the brain adds in some information to these stimuli.

In the position's strongest sense, the stimuli truly become informative only *after* the central nervous system has added its own processing into the recipe. In that sense, the categories we perceive as being out there in the world, aren't necessarily out there. This means that the categories we perceive as being real tell us far more about how our brains work than they do about the factual nature of the world. In this sense, too, the constructivist position strongly implies that our awareness of the world is not necessarily accurate. The stimuli in the world are inherently ambiguous and could be organized in any number of possible ways by the brain, with the result that how we look at the world and what we recognize would be markedly different. Awareness might be understood as a representation of worldly events, but it is almost certainly not a copy of them. According to the constructivists, learning plays an extremely important role in perception. Through our experiences with the world, large well-organized units of knowledge, called prototypes and schemata, are abstracted and assembled on the basis of distinctive features. Once assembled, these units of knowledge channel subsequent information processing; that is, their influence is top-down. If correct, the constructivist view of perception has strong implications for the areas of social psychology and personality theory.

It's possible to criticize the constructivist account on several grounds. The beginning of the chapter described the historical problem of the Höffding step and stated that the constructivist position tried to take this problem head-on by specifying how sensation was converted into perception. When I say that I perceive something, I'm really saying something about the contents of my mind. For example, if I tell you that I see my tennis racquet in the corner of the room, this is not true, strictly speaking. I can't "see" my tennis racquet because my retinae, which do the seeing, don't know anything about tennis racquets. At some point in time, presumably after my retinae did their work, other aspects of my cognitive system categorized the stimulus as a tennis racquet, and only then did these perceptual processes produce the term *tennis racquet* that finally entered my awareness as their output. The contents of my mind, then, seem to consist of categories into which stimuli can or cannot be fitted. The question for the constructivists is to specify how these contents got there in the first place. Saying that I abstracted the features of the tennis racquet and compared the abstracted list with a prototypical racquet won't do. After all, how many features does a tennis racquet have? Before I ever saw a tennis racquet, how did I know which features to abstract so that I'd be able to mentally build a prototype of one?

A second objection to the constructivist argument is grounded in evolutionary theory. The physical structures of animals and their actions often show adaptation to changing environmental circumstances. What advantage is conferred on an animal that constructs it world rather than responds to the real world? Although at times being able to perceive the world in a variety of ways is useful, a reasonable assumption is that being firmly anchored in the real world is generally *more* useful. Because our awareness of events and people is only one way of representing those things, and not necessarily the most faithful way either, the constructivist position implies that we may be divorced from the reality of the world in a fundamental way.

A related problem is that the constructivist approach to perception doesn't deal well with some basic empirical findings. For example, if I look at a book sitting on my desk, it's obvious to me that the book and the desk are two separate things. I can focus on the book, and the other objects in my visual field become the background against which the book is seen. Alternatively, I can turn the relationship around by focusing on the desk and letting the book recede into the background. The ability to make figure-ground distinctions of this sort does not seem to require any extensive experience with the world. This was shown in early experiments with congenitally blind individuals whose cataracts were removed during their adult years (von Senden, 1960). For the constructivists, the problem is to specify how events that are very close to one another in the retinal code become so distinct from one another in our awareness even when previous experience with the stimuli is ruled out as an explanation. Without elaborating this too much, a corresponding problem also exists. Sometimes events that are not nearby one another at the retinal level are nevertheless grouped together in our awareness.

For these and other reasons, not all cognitive psychologists have accepted the constructivist argument in its strictest sense. Some have moved to a modified constructivist position, and others have shifted to viewpoints that are radically different from the constructivist account. Some cognitive psychologists have disagreed with the fundamental belief of the constructivists, namely that physical energy in the world is inherently ambiguous. In other words, these cognitive psychologists have emphasized the basis from which feature abstraction takes place, rather than emphasize the process of abstraction itself. The next section describes such a viewpoint.

DIRECT THEORIES OF PERCEPTION

The direct approach to the problem of visual perception is typically associated with its originator, J. J. Gibson. Gibson's work is based on one central thesis: The light that strikes our retinae is highly organized and informative as is, and doesn't require extensive interpretation and elaboration by the central nervous system in order for it to become meaningful (Gibson, 1966, 1979). Our sensory systems are well matched with information that the environment offers us. Rather than discuss any sort of fundamental separation between awareness and reality, Gibson believes that because our sensory systems have developed to pick up information as it is from the environment, our awareness is not particularly tricky.

The Ecological Approach to Visual Perception

During World War II, Gibson worked as an officer in the Army Air Corps. One of his duties was to develop training films depicting the problems in taking off, landing, and navigating aircraft (Reed & Jones, 1982). Gibson quickly realized that what was known about such matters was inadequate for training purposes. He began to investigate the nature of the information that was available to the pilot, hoping that his investigation might prove useful in making teaching materials.

Consider the display in Figure 3.6 (A and B). What do the placement and length of the arrows tell you about the way these scenes might look to a pilot? According to Gibson, the arrows are a way of showing how information in the world unfolds to the eyes of a pilot in a moving plane. Specifically, information seems to emanate, or emerge, from the point toward which we are moving. In Figure 3.6 (A), if we focus our eyes on the imaginary spot from which the arrows seem to be emerging and imagine that the arrows are actually moving past us, then we might get some idea of what Gibson was driving at. The arrows are short near the point of emergence, indicating that as faraway objects come into view, their apparent motion toward us is at first slow. The arrows are progressively longer near the bottom of the scene.

This phenomenon corresponds to another we're familiar with. As we move toward objects, they seem to rush at us faster and faster until they become a blur as we finally move past them. If we were to keep track of the time involved in an object's emergence from the center of expansion at the top of the scene until its apparent disappearance at the bottom of the scene, then we would know something about our own velocity. That is, the shorter the time required for that process, the faster our velocity. Notice also that the information seems to expand radially outward from the point toward which one is moving. In Figure 3.6 (A), this fact tells us that we're moving toward the horizon and consequently, horizontal to the earth's plane.

Contrast this view with the one shown in Figure 3.6 (B). Here we see a radial expansion pattern similar to the one depicted in Figure 3.6 (A). However, in Figure 3.6 (B), the center of the expansion is not at the horizon but rather is located near the end of the runway. The arrows pointing back

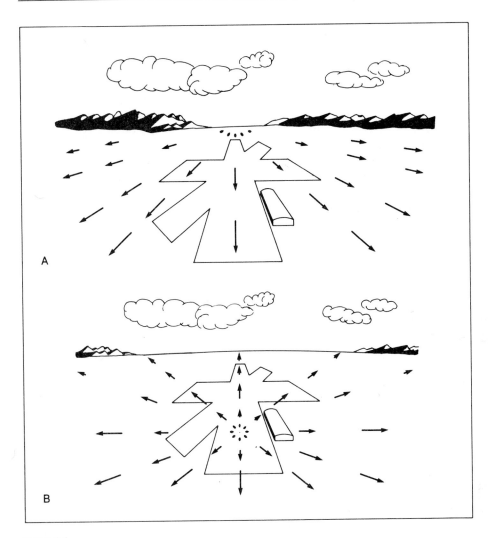

Figure 3.6.
Radial expansion patterns: *A,* retinal motion perspective looking ahead; *B,* retinal motion of gradients during a landing glide. (From Reed & Jones, 1982.)

to the horizon don't get progressively longer as they approach the top of the scene; indeed, they get shorter and shorter. But the arrows pointing to the bottom of the scene do get longer and longer as they approach the bottom.

To get an idea of what this phenomenon means, imagine that you are a pilot, bringing in a plane for a landing on this runway. As you approach the point of contact with the runway, the bottom of the runway will appear to stretch out under you as you get closer and closer. Moreover, the rate of such apparent stretching will increase as you get closer to the runway. The top of the runway will also appear to be stretching, too, but it will be stretching away from you, toward the horizon, and its rate of stretching will get slower and slower as you come in to land. Taken together, the arrows at the top and bottom of the runway are intended to show a pattern of emergent information that the pilot could use to gauge the rate and slope of descent during a landing attempt.

The arrows are simply a convenience but nevertheless indicate something important. As we move through the world, the visual field changes in highly predictable ways. At different points in time, as we move through space, some aspects of the visual array will change, while others will not. The aspects of the visual array that don't change are sometimes called its **invariant features.** For example, one of the invariant features of the visual array is the fact that the center of expansion is always the point toward which we're moving. This pattern of changing and invariant features of the visual array is referred to as the **optical flow pattern.** Optical flow patterns provide pilots with information about their direction, velocity, and altitude. But even those of us who are earthbound can use such patterns in navigation, as Figure 3.7 shows. Notice here that the pattern of radial expansion can still be observed even though terrestrial movement is in two rather than in three dimensions.

Also important is realizing that these patterns of change and invariance pointed out by Gibson were believed to be truly available to anybody who took the time to look for them. In other words, these invariances were not added in by the central nervous system, or inferred by our cognitive system on the basis of our experiences in the world. Instead, Gibson maintained that such invariances were truly seeable and seen. Gibson believed that the optical flow pattern was simply one type of invariance that was present in the world and immediately available to the perceiver. He also maintained that other sorts of invariances were similarly available. He called these *higher-order invariances* (i.e., the optical flow pattern is one type of higher-order invariance). Determining exactly how many higher-order invariances there are is impossible, although Gibson did describe various other kinds. For example, in Figure 3.8, the apparent distance between the successive ridges of the windblown sand decreases close to the horizon. Moreover, the detail in the drawing diminishes as you move your eyes from the bottom of the page to the top. The drawing seems to possess depth because it has retained elements of the world that are useful in judging depth. Gibson referred to such an invariance as a **texture gradient.** Certain details of the surface on which we stand diminish and become indistinct as their distance from us increases, and because the loss of clarity is progressive and orderly, we can use such facts about the surface to make judgments about depth and space. What is invariant about texture gradients is the fact that all surfaces display them. You can test the reality of this assertion for yourself using Figure 3.8. You most likely recognized right away what was depicted in the drawing because, in part, the texture gradient that was visible on the earth's surface when the drawing was made is still visible. But you can easily destroy the texture gradient by simply inverting the book. The drawing won't look like an upside-down desert but instead may look like an abstract painting of wavy lines. This effect means that the texture gradient is not a property of the drawing but rather a characteristic of the earth's surface. Consequently, as you move over the earth's surface,

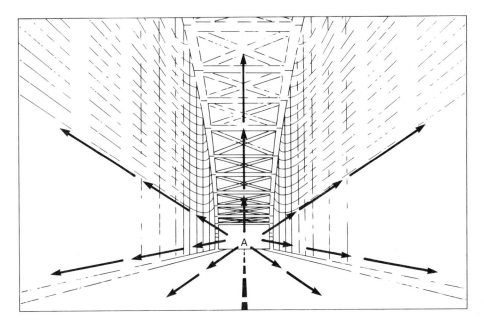

Figure 3.7.
The flow of the environment as seen from a car speeding across a bridge toward point A. The flow (shown by the arrows) is more rapid closer to the car (as indicated by the increased blur) but occurs everywhere except point A, the point toward which the car is moving.

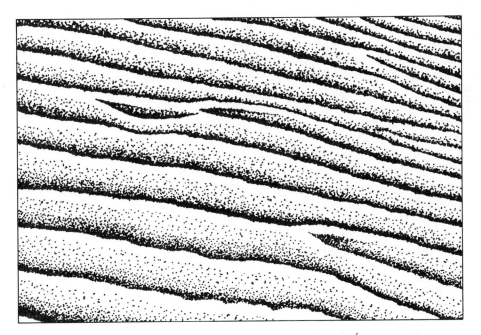

Figure 3.8.
A texture gradient made up of ridges in the sand. If viewed from above, the distance between each sand ridge appears approximately equal; however, when viewed from the ground, the ridges appear to be spaced closer and closer together as distance increases.

a continual presentation of information tells you about depth, that is, the distance between you and other objects or points on the surface. Like the information presented by the optical flow pattern, the information in the texture gradient is truly visible to the observer, rather than being constructed by the observer's brain.

In the 1950s, Gibson developed the notions of the texture gradient and optical flow pattern to counter the traditional idea that the product of retinal processing—the so-called **retinal image**—was inadequate by itself to produce perception. His attack focused on the retinal image, whose adequacy or inadequacy Gibson though was irrelevant. He argued that because we don't see retinal images anyway, debates about their functions weren't going to lead anywhere. Instead, Gibson maintained that the basis of visual perception was not the retinal image but rather a set of invariants such as those outlined previously. In so doing, Gibson completely reformulated the problem of perception (Mace, 1974, 1977). Whereas earlier, the problem of perception had consisted of specifying the cognitive mechanisms by which we process the inadequate stimulus, now the problem involved the development of a theory that specified, or described, all of the information that was already present in the visual array. Processing mechanisms were consequently de-emphasized.

Gibson's theory, therefore, is *not* an account of how retinal images are spruced up by the brain so they can become the basis of perception. Instead, his theory deals with accurately describing the pattern of information that is present in the world and directly available to the perceiver (Neisser, 1976). Perhaps you can now see why Gibson's theory is called a "direct" theory of perception. The perceiver is in direct contact with the real world. He is considered to be on intimate terms with the visual information in the world, rather than being separated or isolated from this information by several stages of cognitive processing. Rather, the information in the light is simply given to the perceiver (Gibson, 1960).

For Gibson's account to be correct, the light that strikes our retinae must be truly informative and complete; it cannot be chaotic or unorderly. This point leads to a question. Gibson assumes that the light that strikes our eyes is highly organized and well structured. How did the light acquire this organization? Gibson's answer is straightforward. The light that strikes our eyes has been reflected from objects on the ground, and the light carries information from these objects. In other words, the light is altered as it is reflected from objects. Some aspects of this alteration (i.e., changes in intensity and wavelength of the light) had long been known. However, Gibson believed that the nature of the alteration was more extensive than that. Because the objects on the ground were themselves organized and well-structured, and because the reflection of light was also orderly, then the light took on the organization properties of the objects from which it had been reflected.

To direct theorists, this answer meant that the role of learning in perception should be de-emphasized. According to them, we don't have to learn how to interpret the ambiguous information in the environment, because the information isn't ambiguous. Gibson's theory does not completely rule out the usefulness of experience in perception, but he and other direct theorists differ sharply from the constructivists in their beliefs about the role of experience. Whereas constructivist theory argues that the perceiver must learn how to see objects in the world by learning how to interpret retinal images, direct theorists maintain that the perceiver learns how the higher-order invariants are produced by motion through the world. In particular, such motion produces knowledge of the texture of geometrical surfaces such as edges, corners, convexities, and concavities (Gibson, 1960). This knowledge of geometrical shapes was referred to by Gibson as the **layout of perceivable space.**

All perceivable spaces had layouts, and knowledge of them was enhanced by attempts to move through them. This principle enabled Gibson to answer some of the criticism aimed at his theory for its apparent position on illusions. According to constructivist criticism, Gibson's theory could not explain illusions. If the perceiver is assumed to be in direct contact with the information in the light that is given, then why is the perceiver sometimes mistaken about that information? Why do we fall prey to illusions? The direct response to this criticism has two parts. First, Gibson notes that most illusions are static displays of information. However, the perceptual systems of most animals are designed to pick up visual information by movement through the world. Gibson argues that we shouldn't be too surprised if the invariants we usually detect are not picked up in this static and therefore artificial situation. In other situations, a person may misperceive because she has not yet learned to extract the invariants that specify the layout (Gibson, 1977). The information that is directly available to us is always in potential, but not necessarily actual, form. The person who approaches a glass door and, thinking it's open, tries to go through it may be doing a good job of perceiving some of the invariants of texture and optical flow. However, some of the other aspects of the layout, such as the highlights in the glass or dust on its surface, must also be detected if the collision is to be avoided.

To summarize, the **ecological approach to visual perception** is concerned with specifying the layout of perceivable space, with an emphasis on the word *layout*. Gibson's theory is not about the perception of space per se but rather how light is organized by its reflections from surface and objects on the ground.

What the Environment Affords Us

Gibson developed the notion of the **affordance** in an attempt to further specify the properties of the environment that are present in reflected light. An affordance of anything is a specific combination of the properties of its substance and its surfaces taken with reference to an animal (Gibson, 1977, 1979). Note that the definition refers to a combination of properties. Most objects, because they have a variety of properties that can be combined in a variety of ways, will also have a variety of affordances. Also, the affordance is uniquely related to the animal being considered (Gibson, 1977). For example, my cocktail table has a number of affordances. It affords support, its glass top affords transparency, and its chrome legs afford reflectance. Some of the affordances are related to particular animals. For me, the cocktail table has the affordance of color, but it doesn't have this affordance for my cat. On the other hand, the surface of the cocktail table affords walking for my cat but not for me.

Table 3.2 is a listing of affordances that Gibson (1976) described in a talk given to a meeting of architects. Some of the items in this listing provide a clue for getting a more intuitive understanding of the affordance. We might say that an affordance is a bundle of properties about some specific object that provides us with an opportunity to perceive something specific or to move through the world in a specific way. An affordance, then, is an opportunity to see something or to move in a characteristic way.

Saying that affordances are related to the perceptual system of an animal implies that the nature of an animal's awareness is highly dependent

TABLE 3.2

Some Natural and Artificial Affordances

1. A solid horizontal surface affords *support.* A water surface does not.
   —A surface of support affords *resting* (coming to rest).
2. An extended surface of support affords *locomotion,* for a terrestrial animal.
3. A *vertical* solid surface stops locomotion and affords *mechanical contact.* It is a *barrier.*
   —A rigid barrier surface affords injury by abrupt contacts, i.e., collision. It is an *obstacle.* Deceleration is necessary to achieve contact without collision.
   —A *nonrigid* barrier surface can avert injury by collision.
4. A *vertical double surface,* that is, a wall or screen, affords *hiding behind,* that is, being out of sight of observers on the other side. This is true if the double surface is *opaque.*
5. A double surface at sufficient height above the ground affords *getting under.* It is a *roof.*
6. Any layout of surfaces that encloses an appropriate volume of air affords *shelter* (from the wind, cold, rain, snow). A cave, burrow, or hut.
   —An enclosure affords being out of sight of observers in all directions ("privacy") and thus it affords protection from predators. (All animals sometimes need to *hide.*)
7. An aperture or gap in an enclosure affords *entry* and *exit.*
   —It also affords *vision* within the enclosure by admitting illumination (sunlight).
   —It also affords *looking through* (both looking *out* and looking *in*).
   —It also affords long-term *respiration* (breathing fresh air).
   —Note that all the complexities of doors, windows, shutters, grilles, and panes of glass, etc., get their utilities from these basic affordances. (E.g., the misperception of a glass door is a real danger in modern buildings.)
8. A horizontal surface at about knee height above the surface of support affords sitting, a *seat.*
9. A horizontal surface at about *waist height* above the ground affords support for objects and facilitates manipulation of objects, e.g., tools, and materials for writing and reading, a workbench, desk, table.
10. A large drop-off in the surface of support affords injury by falling off, a "brink." But a railing affords protection from falling off (like a fence, which is a barrier to locomotion).
    —A *small* drop-off in the surface of support affords stepping down without injury.
    —A series of "steps" in a *stairway* affords ascent or descent of a cliff by a pedestrian.
    —A *ladder* affords ascent or descent.
    —A *ramp* affords a different mode of ascent or descent.

Source: From Gibson, 1976. (Reprinted by permission of the Publisher.)

upon the match-up that is achieved between its sensory apparatus and the information available to be picked up. From all the invariants offered by reflected light, our sensory apparatus has become, over time, tuned to accept certain invariants but not others. The accepted invariants are the affordances. Because our sensory apparatus is unique, Gibson's theory raises the possibility that some affordances are uniquely human. To the extent that we are aware of these affordances, we can describe our mental lives as being channeled, or more accurately, canalized by our sensory system. Saying that our mental lives are canalized means that to a certain extent, the content of our minds is influenced and bounded by the nature of our perceptual systems (Turvey & Shaw, 1979).

Some evidence supports the idea of unique human affordances and hence the **canalization** of mentality. As you may know, a substantial body of literature demonstrates the universality of human facial expressions (Izard, 1971). Despite the variations in milieu, facial expressions are produced in similar ways, and photographs of them can be accurately recognized by people of different cultures. Bassili (1978) investigated this phenomenon using a somewhat unusual approach. Tiny lights were attached to the faces of professional actors who were instructed to portray certain emotions. These portrayals took place in a darkened room so that only the lights were visible. The resulting patterns of light movements were filmed, and subjects watching the films had no difficulty in correctly categorizing the expressions even though the actor's face was not visible.

A similar approach was used by Cutting and his colleagues (Barclay, Cutting, & Kozlowski, 1978; Cutting & Kozlowski, 1977; Cutting, Proffit, & Kozlowski, 1978). In these studies, lights were attached to various joints and body parts of a subject, who was then invited to walk through a darkened room. The pattern of light movement was once again filmed. Although individual slides and line tracings (similar to the pattern of lines created by head- and taillights of cars in a long-exposure photograph) were not recognizable to people viewing them, if the entire pattern was seen, it was recognizable. People were highly capable of classifying the pattern of movement as being produced by a walking person. Viewers were also able to accurately categorize the walkers as men or as women. They were even able to recognize the distinctive gaits of their friends.

Such studies exemplify the spirit of Gibson's work. Perceptual systems are designed to extract information from objects as those objects move about in the world, or from the nature of the changes in the world as we move through it. The human perceptual system appears to be particularly tuned in to certain kinds of motion, probably because the recognition of these motions is adaptive.

Evaluation of the Direct Theory

Perhaps Gibson's greatest contribution is that his work produced a radical departure in what psychologists thought of as the stimulus for visual perception. Prior to Gibson, psychologists had contented themselves with the description of retinal images, but now some consensus exists that the light reflected from objects must be organized in some way. Second, Gibson demonstrated that depth perception does not seem to require elaborate processing by the central nervous system. Instead, Gibson argued that depth can be picked up directly by a perceptual system that moves. Although Gibson's work has gained some currency among cognitive psychologists, this result is paradoxical because the theory is *not* cognitive. Gibson downplayed the role of information processing in perception, and he similarly de-emphasized physiological accounts of the brain's role in perception. From Gibson's perspective, the historical problem of the Höffding step simply fades away. Sensory neural events don't have to be converted into perceptual neural events, because perception is direct. The same neural machinery responsible for sensation also subserves perception.

Despite these solutions, some problems remain with Gibson's account. First, Gibson did not use the established vocabulary among psychologists of his era. Because he thought the standard vocabularly was incorrect, he decided to develop his own terminology. However, this special terminology makes his work hard to understand. More than one psychologist has made an earnest effort to come to grips with Gibson's work, only to wind up being somewhat baffled by it. In addition, Gibson's theory has not always been empirically supported. Although Gibson said that texture gradients are present at all times, in some situations they have been difficult to locate empirically (Goldstein, 1984). Also, Gibson's work is essentially a *sufficiency analysis*. This term refers to an analysis that shows how something *could* be accomplished, but not how it necessarily *is* accomplished. This means that, while texture gradients and optical flow may be available to the perceiver, it is another matter altogether to show that these invariants are really what the perceiver uses in moving. Similarly, the direct theory postulates that depth is directly visible through motion, but this doesn't deal adequately with the fact that depth is not lost when we are motionless. A good deal of consensus exists among cognitive psychologists that Gibson underrated the difficulty in detecting and using the invariants he proposed (Marr, 1982). Finally, some question has arisen concerning the role of the individual in his own perception: Learning about the layout of perceivable space must involve some sort of information processing (Heft, 1982; Heil, 1979).

A SYNTHESIS

We've considered two overarching perspectives on perception, and apparently neither the constructivist nor the direct account seems complete—a result that has led some theorists to develop treatments that emphasize the positive features of both theories. This section describes one such attempt (Neisser, 1976).

Neisser considers perception a cyclical activity that can be couched in an information-processing theory. Unlike most such theories, however, which assume a definite starting and concluding point, in Neisser's model, perception is never finished up because the components of the model are arranged in the form of a loop. Figure 3.9 shows the **perceptual cycle** as

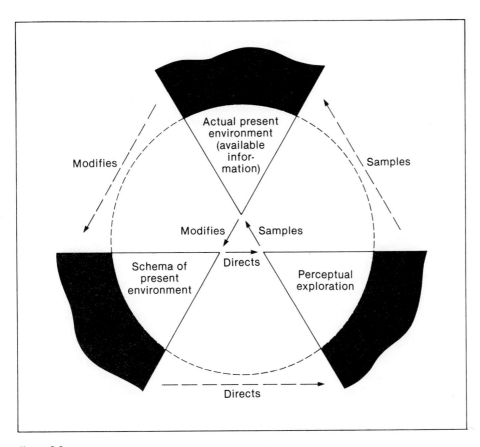

Figure 3.9.

Schemata as embedded in cognitive maps. (From Neisser, 1976.)

it is embedded in large units of knowledge shown as **cognitive maps.**
According to this model, perception is indeed a constructive process. For the
sake of convenience, we'll say that the process begins with certain schemata
of the present world. These schemata are similar to the ones discussed
earlier; they represent knowledge that has been assembled from previous
experience. The schemata have an important function: They act as plans or
expectations that guide subsequent information processing. In this way, the
schemata let the perceiver construct anticipations of what information is
about to become available.

Exploration refers to the application of our perceptual systems, as well
as any orienting movements of the head and eyes. As Figure 3.9 shows, the
perceptual exploration is rooted in the larger activity of locomotion and
action. This concept is consistent with Gibson's idea that the purpose of
direct perception is to allow the organism to move through the world efficiently. The function of such exploration is to sample, that is, pick up information from the world. This sampling is assumed to be direct. Notice
that information about the immediate object is embedded in knowledge of

the actual world that is potentially available. This means that the information picked up by the perceiver can be processed in several ways or, one might say, on several levels. If the perceptual system we are using is vision, then the information we pick up directly will be optical. But because the optical information has been picked up from an object that occurs in some context in the world, we can go beyond the merely optical pickup to analyze the information in other ways. We have to keep in mind, however, that such analyses won't be direct.

The example Neisser gives concerns a person's smile. Reflected light from the person's face can be picked up directly, affording us knowledge of the color and shapes of the person's teeth and the movement of her lips (Neisser, 1976). Because smiling occurs in certain contexts, we might use the optical information to infer something about the person's mood: Is she happy or just being polite? Making such evaluations will involve the use of different perceptual cycles. That is, determinations of a mood might require calling up different anticipatory schemata, which in turn would channel different sorts of explorations. Information picked up from the world modifies the schemata in use. The two aspects of this modification are *corrective* and *elaborative*. The corrective aspect refers to the fact that information from the world can be used to infer that the wrong anticipatory schemata have been called up initially. That is, the perceiver might realize that the pickup of information might be more efficient if guided by a different schema. The elaborative aspect refers to the fact that the coherency and depth of the schema are built up with use. In this sense, the nature of the schema is similar to that of the prototype. As we saw earlier, when people are given highly variable distortions during the training period of prototype acquisition, such training seems to improve their knowledge of the prototypes boundaries (Homa, 1978; Homa & Vosburgh, 1976). Neisser has suggested that experience can produce a similar improvement in schematic knowledge.

An example might help to show these components fit together. Before I moved to the Midwest, I didn't know that the county seats of rural areas in that part of the country were all so incredibly similar. Towns in other areas of the country have their distinctive features as well, but they tend to be somewhat different from those of midwestern towns. Almost invariably, the town is built around a central square fringed with shops forming the town's principal shopping location. On the lawn of the square is a reasonably imposing courthouse, and peppered around the lawn are monuments. Without fail, one of these monuments is dedicated to the townsmen who lost their lives in the Civil War.

When my travels take me through an unfamiliar county seat, I notice that Neisser's account of my perceptual process is persuasive. First, I look around and then call up certain anticipatory schemata. (Is there a square? A courthouse?) Then I pick up information in the world that confirms these expectations and suggests others. (Where's the monument?) When I see the monument and being to walk toward it, other schemata are brought into play. I begin to pick up information about the monument itself: its typical granite base, the weathered statue of the Civil War soldier standing on top. Even the status is characteristic: The soldier stands ready, holding his musket with its curiously long bayonet, wearing the typical slanted cap of the period, the kepi. As I detect these aspects of the object, still other anticipatory schemata will be used. I expect to see a plaque on the base of the monument that lists the names of the fallen. As I get closer and see the plaque, I expect some of the listings to conform to the naming practices of the period. That is, some of the men will have first names inspired by classical literature, such as Horace or Virgil.

So far, all my anticipations have been corroborated by my experiences in these towns. But suppose someday, in an as-yet-undiscovered town, I approach the plaque expecting to read "In honor of . . .", but instead find only the words

GENERIC
CIVIL WAR
MONUMENT

In that case, my schemes for monuments and county seats—even for the Midwest—must undergo dramatic revision. As long as my various schemata are accurate in guiding information pickup, there is no need to modify them. With new information, however, the horizon of my knowledge will be expanded. What was formerly only potential knowledge will become actual. In this case, future attempts to pick up knowledge in those situations must proceed much more cautiously. (After all, midwesterners may have introduced bogus monuments in other towns as well.)

Neisser's account of perception is an effective combination of the constructivist and direct points of view. It has a constructivist component in that the schema is a cognitive structure that guides information processing. But it also has a direct component that emphasizes that the visual array provides humans with some information with a minimum of cognitive processing. According to Neisser, each of the component accounts is incomplete because it fragments a normally fluid and ongoing activity. Perception is not a static and isolated event but rather a cyclical process.

REPRESENTATIONAL THOUGHT AND PERCEPTION: COGNITIVE MAPS

This and the previous chapter have dealt with findings in the areas of pattern recognition and perception. In this section, both of these topics come back into play because they have some implications for the kind of knowledge called a cognitive map. A cognitive map is a term that refers to knowledge of our own position in a spatial layout, and knowledge of the positions of objects and places relative to our location (Spoehr & Lehmkuhle, 1982). Such knowledge is usually visualizable, and for this reason, cognitive maps are often thought of as images that let us collect, organize, store, and manipulate information about the environment (Downs & Stea, 1977). The fact that cognitive maps seem so visual has suggested to several researchers that a record of someone's cognitive map can be obtained by simply asking the person to draw it.

Lynch (1960) carried out a classic study using this and other techniques. Residents of dissimilar cities, such as Boston and Los Angeles, were asked to describe their towns and imagine taking trips from one part of town to another. The participants also created sketch maps of the towns. Lynch found that city dwellers of dissimilar cities nevertheless seemed to organize their geographic knowledge of the city in similar ways. Their cognitive maps included **landmarks,** which were tall buildings easily seen from a distance, *paths,* which were frequently used routes (usually surface streets), and *nodes,* which were the intersections of two paths. Lynch also noted that city dwellers can name certain *districts,* which were regions bounded by cultural or ethnic limits as well as by geographic ones. Finally, the geographic, visible boundaries of districts were called *edges.* Although the terms used to describe the city were similar from person to person, Lynch nevertheless found that the location of a person's home within the city seemed to influence his perception of it. For example, a person's description of his own district was often elaborate and detailed, while descriptions of adjacent districts were often less complete. This was particularly true when the edge between the districts were something not easily crossed, such as a river or an expressway. The verbal distortions were accompanied by pictorial ones. When creating a sketch map of the city, respondents often exaggerated the size of familiar places within the city at the expense of less familiar places.

This effect has been replicated by other researchers. Saarinen (1973) asked students at the University of Arizona to draw maps of the campus. The student's major subject turned out to be a strong predictor of accuracy and detail in specific sketch maps. If, for example, a student's major was psychology, then it was likely that the psychology building was depicted as well as adjacent buildings and pathways leading to them. Other areas of the campus, however, were often fragmentary or even missing completely from the psychology major's map.

The map-drawing technique has certain limitations. The accuracy of the map is completely limited by the drawing skill of the subject. Regardless of the subject's drawing skill, motivation is a second concern. It's not clear how hard subjects try to make their maps as accurate as they can. The most common strategy in producing such a map is to start at a particular location and trace out particular routes. This strategy tends to result in cumulative rather than self-correcting errors in the final configuration. Finally, it has been shown that subjects are influenced by their knowledge of geometry in creating maps. Intersections that may not actually meet at right angles are sometimes deduced as "having" to meet that way—a fact that might limit the way other intersections are drawn. In short, the map-drawing technique doesn't simply *tap* a person's knowledge of the spatial layout; it also *alters* the person's internal representation (Byrne, 1982).

Varieties of Spatial Cognition

Another reason for going beyond the map-drawing technique is that it treats as similar various sorts of geographic knowledge that were probably acquired in dissimilar ways. For example, I could ask you to draw from memory a map of your town and a map of the United States. Although a superficial resemblance exists between the two tasks, I have ample reason to believe that the nature of your knowledge is different in each case. For example, knowledge of your town is acquired through personal experiences involving locomotion and visual contact. Geographic knowledge of the United States is not typically acquired that way but is learned instead from books, which means that talking about a continuum of spatial knowledge is probably appropriate. On one end of the continuum, we have knowledge of our body's location in space and knowledge of the location of objects in our immediate visual field. Farther along the continuum, we have spatial knowledge of the layout of large spaces that we have moved through and which are at least somewhat familiar to us.

For example, having been to New Orleans once, I have the typical tourist's cognitive map, which is limited to the central business district and the French Quarter. At the continuum's farthest extreme, I also have knowledge about the relative positions of places with which I've had no personal experience. As the physical distance between me and a given location increases, the less likely I am to have personally experienced that place, and consequently the nature of my knowledge is likely to be different from that of nearby locations. Whereas knowledge of my town is almost invariably accompanied by imagery that seems to unfold as I mentally move along the town's streets, knowledge of unvisited places can't be obtained that way. Instead, such knowledge is likely to be accompanied by verbal descriptors. Thus, if asked what states are south of Wyoming, I can consult a list of western states, each of which is stored with directional tags ("south of Wyoming," "west of Kansas") to come up with the answer: Utah and Colorado.

Although the term *cognitive map* is used to describe each of these types of spatial cognition, this term represents a substantial generalization of its original meaning. Tolman (1948) coined the term to describe rats' knowledge of the general direction to the goal box from specific points in a maze. Tolman demonstrated that rats seem to have such knowledge by letting them explore a maze in which a large number of exit paths radiated outward from a central area. Only one exit path led to the goal, however, and this path got there via an indirect, meandering route. When this correct path was blocked, a purely behavioristic explanation of the rats' learning would predict that the rats would take one of the paths adjacent to the original, now-blocked path. Stimulus generalization is the mechanism proposed to explain such behavior. However, Tolman's rats confounded the behaviorists by choosing an exit path that was not near the original path, but one that *did* seem to lead in the general direction of the goal box. Because the animals had never been reinforced for taking this path, the only plausible explanation for their choice would seem to involve the maze's spatial layout. An interesting note is that although rats seem to be good at getting and using this kind of spatial knowledge, humans aren't (Wilton & Pidcock, 1982).

Byrne (1979) asked his subjects, who were all long-time residents of a particular city, to draw maps of particular intersections. Byrne emphasized that the map was to be drawn as accurately as possible. In reality, all the roads met at angles of 60 to 70 or 110 to 120 degrees. Yet, even when the subjects were given a ruler, the subject's drawings showed the roads meeting at 90 degrees. As has been pointed out elsewhere (Byrne, 1982), an unlikely explanation is that the subjects knew that the roads met at 60 degrees but could not draw such an intersection with a ruler. Instead, Byrne's finding indicates that the subjects apparently thought the roads intersected at 90 degrees.

Moar (in Byrne, 1982) came to a similar conclusion using a different technique. He asked his subjects to imagine themselves at some well-known location within a city. Subjects were then told to point to the direction of another well-known location. By repeating this procedure for several points in the city, Moar was able to determine the person's cognitive map of the city without requiring the subject to draw anything. Moar found a number of inconsistencies in the person's map. For example, if a person imagines herself at location A and points to location B, the direction of her pointing can be expressed as some angular discrepancy increasing clockwise from due north. That is, due east would equal 90 degrees. If the person then imagines herself at location B and points back to location A, the angular discrepancy should always be equal to the original judgment plus 180 degrees. However, Moar found that this wasn't always the case in regard to judgments of personally experienced space. The subjects were influenced by the location from which they were pointing. Subjects' responses in pointing back to location B were not always predictable from their judgments at location A. Curiously, though, when Moar replicated his procedure on judgments involving large distances, these inconsistencies were not observed. In other words, when subjects were asked to imagine themselves in, let's say Boston, and point to Louisville, their performance was consistent and not influenced by the location from which they were pointing. Notice again that this type of task involves knowledge that is probably acquired by studying maps and atlases directly, and can be accomplished with nonimaginal reasoning. Thus, Moar's study supports the contention that there are varieties of spatial cognition.

A study by Evans and Pezdek (1980) explores this distinction further. Subjects were given trials in which they were presented with three labeled dots, which were called triads. In one condition, the dots were labeled with the names of states; in a second condition, the dots were labeled with the names of buildings on the campus with which the student-subjects were familiar. The subjects' task was to decide as quickly as possible whether the spatial arrangement of the dots was congruent with the spatial arrangement of their real-world referents, and their reaction times were recorded. Further complicating the subjects' decision was the fact that some of the triads had been rotated away from the standard north-at-the-top orientation shown in most atlases. Figure 3.10 shows the variations of one particular triad from their study.

Before going on to describe their findings, let's use our intuitions. If the spatial knowledge acquired by direct experience is truly different from the knowledge gathered by map reading, then we would expect that the rotation manipulation should have some influence on the reaction times of the subjects in the states condition but not in the campus condition. This is because maps of the United States are almost always presented in a typical orientation with north at the top of the page. If information about the states is presented

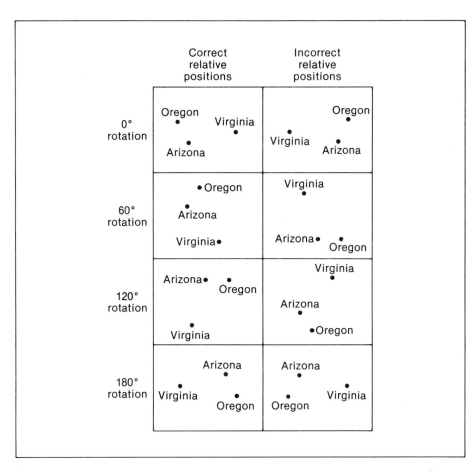

Figure 3.10.

A sample triad from Evans and Pezdek's experiment in its different orientations. Subjects were to decide if the relative positions in the triad were correct or reversed. Decision time varied with degree of rotation for these triads but not for triads of buildings on the subjects' college campus. (From Evans & Pezdek, 1980. Copyright 1980 by the American Psychological Association. Reprinted by permission of the publisher and the author.)

in some other way, then we would expect that the subjects would be disoriented. On campus, however, students approach buildings from a variety of directions, and so their ability to judge spatial layouts on campus should not be as dependent on receiving the information in a particular orientation.

Evans and Pezdek's findings were consistent with these intuitions. Reaction times in the states condition increased as a function of the states' rotation from the standard orientation. However, the manipulation had no effect on the reaction times in the campus condition. These findings suggest that spatial knowledge that is obtained by direct experience is represented in an orientation-free format, while spatial knowledge obtained from maps might have to undergo mental rotation to the standard orientation before it can be used to answer questions. Evans and Pezdek repeated their procedure with individuals who were not students and had learned about the campus from a map in the standard orientation. Under those circumstances, the rotation manipulation *did* produce an effect: Reaction times did increase as a function of angular discrepancy. This result demonstrates that the original effect was not produced by the relative differences in the size of United States versus the campus. Instead, Evans and Pezdek's finding argues that only some aspects of spatial relations can be learned from a map.

Expertise in Cognitive Mapping

Having personal experience with spatial relations encompassing large distances is possible. In his book *East Is a Big Bird,* Thomas Gladwin (1970) described the amazing cognitive maps of the Puluwatans, an island people of the South Pacific. Far from being stuck on their native island of Puluwat in the Caroline chain, the Puluwatans make voyages of up to 400 miles across the open sea in their sailing canoes. Navigation across open water is a tricky business. In the West, the minimum tool kit thought necessary has included a map and a placekeeper, that is, a way of keeping track of current position and heading. In addition, it seems essential to Westerners that a successful navigator have a compass, that is, a device for detecting orientation with regard to some external frame of reference (Byrne, 1982). In their initial contacts with the Puluwatans, Westerners, such as Captain Cook, were astonished to find that the Puluwatans would put to sea fairly spontaneously and apparently without the aid of any such devices. Also clear was that the Puluwatans were not sailing around haphazardly. Almost invariably, they arrived at their destination after having sailed a course that would be efficient by any standards of navigation. In the seventy or eighty years since regular contact has been established with the West, there have been only a few cases of Puluwatans getting lost at sea. How are the Puluwatans able to do this without the aid of technology thought necessary in the West?

Gladwin describes several kinds of information that the Puluwatans use in navigation. First, the Puluwatans are sensitive to certain aspects of the ocean's appearance. For example, changes in the ocean's color might signal the presence of a nearby reef. Similarly, the Puluwatans are adept at listening to the sounds made by the waves as they slap against the boat's hull. Apparently, several characteristic wave patterns are in that part of the South Pacific, and the Puluwatans are sensitive to the rhythms created by the combinations of different patterns. The Puluwatans also look for particular types of seabirds, some of which are indigenous to certain islands. These sources of information, which Gladwin calls *seamarks,* are picked up directly by the sailors and in that sense represent a group of affordances that went unnoticed by early Western visitors to the area. Guiding the pickup of such information, however, is a rather complex cognitive structure based on the Puluwatan system of navigation, which is called **etak.**

Life is not difficult in the Caroline chain, and taking care of life's essential needs occupies the Puluwatans for only a few hours each day. For the most part, the men of Puluwatan culture spend the day building and maintaining their sailing canoes and learning the etak system, a star-based set of navigational principles made possible by a peculiarity of the equatorial region.

In more northern or southern latitudes, when a star rises, it crosses the horizon and continues to rise at an angle relative to the horizon. Unless one knows the angle of ascent and descent, using the star's current position as an indicator of location is almost impossible. However, Puluwat is close to the equator, and there the stars rise and set perpendicularly to the horizon. Consequently, ascertaining where a particular star first appeared on the horizon is relatively easy, regardless of how much time has gone by since the star's rising.

To see how this feature helps the Puluwatans navigate, imagine that we are in a sailing canoe, sailing past an island on a starry night. We would imagine the island first in front of us, then beside us, then astern as we sailed on. For purposes of navigation, however, the Puluwatans have turned these events around. Rather than think of the canoe as moving, the islanders imagine instead that the canoe is stationary and the nearby island is moving. Because the stars rise and set vertically in that part of the world, describing this movement is easy. That is, the Puluwatans say that the nearby island is moving under a series of successive star positions. Thus, for every inter-island passage that the Puluwatans make, the navigator must learn a series of star locations under which the nearby island—called the reference island—will pass.

Figure 3.11 shows how the Puluwatans break up a long voyage into a series of segments; this is the literal meaning of etak. As the canoe leaves

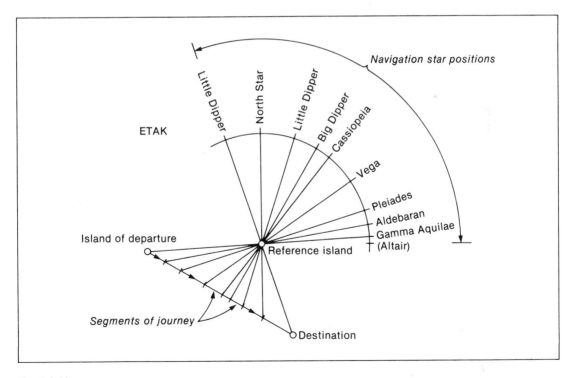

Figure 3.11.

Etak: the principle of navigation in Puluwat. (From *East Is a Big Bird* by T. Gladwin, 1970. Harvard University Press.)

an island, the navigator knows that the reference island for that particular passage is under the star Altair ("Big Bird" to the Puluwatans). As the trip proceeds, the reference island will slide backward—first under Gamma Aquilae, then under Aldebaran, and so on. The abstract nature of this cognitive map becomes clearer when we realize that the reference island is nearby only in relative terms. In most passages, the Puluwatans never get closer than 50 miles to the reference island, and in every case, it's always out of sight. Moreover, the etak system works on cloudy nights and during the daytime. If a Puluwatan navigator were asked his location, he would respond as if he sees the reference island and as if he sees the stars it is sliding under. In reality, neither source need be visible. Puluwatan navigation makes use of information that is picked up directly from the world in the form of seamarks. However, this information is interpreted against the background of a cognitive map consisting of an abstract mental structure. In considering the navigation of the Puluwatans, we see a good example of the cyclical nature of perception as described by Neisser (1976). In this case, direct visible information and abstract cognitive structures interact to enable accurate perception of the environment at sea.

CONCLUDING COMMENTS AND SUGGESTIONS FOR FURTHER READING

At this point, it's impossible to see how the issue of direct versus constructivist accounts is going to turn out. An interesting point is that cognitive psychologists who aren't particularly interested in the problem of vision almost always adopt some information-processing approach—that is, constructivist approach—to understand whatever problems they're working on. In the area of vision research, however, it seems that cognitive psychologists have been strongly influenced by Gibson's work, even though his theory is not inherently cognitive.

Those students who wish to get a good general introduction to the problems of perception could read Rock's (1983) book *The Logic of Perception*. The volume by Dodwell and Caelli (1984) is a good interdisciplinary approach to the problem of form perception. David Marr's (1982) book on vision is extremely challenging and excellent. The issues of perception, knowledge, and awareness have proved to be tough nuts for psychologists to crack. Dretske's (1981) book *Knowledge and the Flow of Information* represents the viewpoint of a philosopher (this book is not nearly as pro-Gibson as the title might lead you to believe). Dretske (1983) has written a synopsis of this book in the journal *Behavioral and Brain Sciences*. Those students who want to get a good introduction to Gibson's work should start with Goldstein (1984). Each of the volumes by Shaw and Bransford (1977) and Weimer and Palermo (1974, 1982) has several chapters with a Gibsonian influence. Reed and Jones (1982) have produced a collection of Gibson's essays with commentary. Those students who want to find out more about the opposition to Gibson's theory (of which there has been more than a little) should start with Ullman (1980). Neisser's attempt at reconciling the two perspectives can be found in *Cognition and Reality* (1976). Recently, Bruce and Green (1985) have written a comparison of the two views, which they refer to as "computational" and "ecological."

Social cognition is a growing field of research, and I recommend four books that will provide a solid foundation in this area. Fiske and Taylor (1984) have written an informative and lively account of the research. Sarah Hampson's (1982) book is also quite good, as is the book by Wegner and Vallacher (1977). The issue of person perception has been treated in a book by Mark Cook (1984).

The research on spatial cognition is also interesting. Readers who want to know more about it might start with Downs and Stea (1977). Kaplan and Kaplan (1982) is also a good source. Gladwin's (1970) book on the Puluwatans is a joy to read.

FOCUS ON APPLICATIONS:
Depth in Video Displays

The illusion of depth and motion in some video games such as Star Wars and I, Robot is convincing. The designer who produces these effects does so under stringent limitations. First, although these games give the appearance of looking through the screen into space, all depth must be created on the screen's surface. Second, although the illusion of motion is created, no substantial motion exists at all. The viewer's head remains more or less stationary throughout the game, as does the game itself. Again, the illusion of motion must be created on a two-dimensional surface. Strictly speaking, not even the figures on the two-dimensional surface are really moving. For example, in I, Robot, the birds who periodically try to gobble you up appear to be flying toward you. But no real motion is present here; the electron gun at the back of the screen is simply spraying a different pattern of electrons up against the phosphorescent screen. How are the illusions of depth and motion created?

If you've been reading this chapter closely, you can probably guess the answer. The illusions are created because the video display mimics the optical flow pattern and texture gradients that occur in real life. For example, radial expansions can be created by programming in the machine to move objects from the center of the screen to the corners and sides. When looked at, it affords the viewer the sensation of moving toward the center of the screen. When the time required for the apparent movement is decreased, this creates the illusion that our velocity toward the center of the screen has *increased.* This effect is used in a very telling way in the game Tempest.

The appearance of texture gradients can also be duplicated. I have a flight simulator program for my computer that creates the illusion of depth by laying out a square grid of white lines on the terrain below. When I look directly down from the plane, the grid looks square. But if I look directly out the plane's front window, the squares look like trapezoids extending out to the horizon, each one smaller than the one below it. In this way, an airfield that is three trapezoids distant seems much farther away than something located only one trapezoid away. The actual distance from my eye to different parts of the monitor's screen is more or less constant, so this appearance of distance is an illusion.

The fact that depth and motion can be created this way doesn't necessarily prove that Gibson's explanation of perception is correct. But it does suggest that the terms Gibson used do describe authentic events in the environment that can be used to pick up reliable information about the world.

KEY TERMS

Constructivist theory of perception
Direct theory of perception
Höffding step
Müller-Lyer illusion
Prototype
Habituation
Schema
Feature abstraction
Self-schema
Invariant features
Optical flow pattern

Higher-order invariances
Texture gradient
Retinal image
Layout of perceivable space
Ecological approach to visual perception
Affordance
Canalization
Perceptual cycle
Cognitive maps
Landmarks
Etak

PART THREE

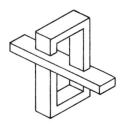

MEMORY

If we were to ask a sample of cognitive psychologists to list the core topics of their field, we would see substantial disagreements. But almost all cognitive psychologists would include the topic of memory, regardless of how short their lists might be. When academic experimental psychology began in Europe over a century ago, memory was one of the phenomena it began studying. And in this country, the study of memory has continued apace, regardless of what other theoretical doctrines dominated the psychological landscape.

You shouldn't conclude, however, that the study of memory has continued without any disruption, either from without or from within. In this country, research on memory was heavily influenced by the work of learning theorists and also by the findings of one of the original European investigators of the last century, Hermann Ebbinghaus. Ebbinghaus was preoccupied with finding out how much well-learned verbal material would be saved (i.e., retained) by his memory over various periods of time. The Ebbinghaus tradition in memory research thus approaches memory with the basic question, *How much* is retained? However, other European re-

searchers were more concerned with other issues. For example, Bartlett (1932) was interested in how memories *change* over time. The focus here is not necessarily on what has been lost, but rather on how the retained material has been altered. The Bartlett tradition in memory research thus begins with the question, *What kind* of material is retained? Over the next several chapters, we'll see elements of both of these traditions play their roles.

You should be aware of another distinction as you read the memory chapters: the distinction between structure and process. The structural approach to memory focuses on the organization of memories, their properties, and their relationships to one another. The process approach deals with the operations that can be used to transform memories, abbreviate them, or elaborate them. Both structure and process are (or should be) involved in every theory of memory, but the emphasis placed on these aspects differs from theory to theory. As you read, you might want to periodically ask yourself which of these components seems to be more important for the issues at hand.

CHAPTER 4

Basic Theories and Issues In Memory Research

OVERVIEW

THE INFORMATION-PROCESSING POSITION
Sensory Storage
  The Nature of the Icon
  "Reading" the Icon
Short-Term Storage
  Basic Findings
  The Nature of the Code in STS
  The Capacity of STS
Long-Term Storage
  Semantic Codes in LTS
  Neuropsychological Findings
Summary of the Information-Processing
  Position

EXTENDING AND MODIFYING THE INFORMATION-
PROCESSING POSITION
The Existence and Importance of a Sensory
  Register

The Distinction between Short- and Long-
  Term Storage
  Semantic Codes in STS
  The Mechanism of Forgetting
  The Capacity of STS
  Neuropsychological Evidence
Modifying the Information-Processing Theory:
  A Summary

LEVELS OF PROCESSING
Maintenance and Elaborative Rehearsal
Other Complications for Levels of
  Processing

CONCLUDING COMMENTS AND SUGGESTIONS
FOR FURTHER READING
FOCUS ON RESEARCH
KEY TERMS

All of us forget things. Sometimes we're irritated by our forgetfulness, but many other times, it doesn't seem to bother us. For example, I don't remember what I had for dinner last night, and I don't care a whit. Why am I not irritated with my memory failure?

I have no reason to be irritated, because I wasn't *trying* to remember my dinner. I'm irritated only when I forget things I want to remember. Forgetfulness is not what we mind so much; what we find frustrating is our occasional lack of control over our memories. This loss of control shows itself in at least two ways. First and most obvious, there are unintentional *losses* from memory. Second, there are unintentional *intrusions* into our memories. For example, as I typed the previous sentence, I had, without my calling for it, an astonishingly clear image of the boardwalk in Ocean City, New Jersey. I haven't been there in over twenty years, and during the times I was there, I can't recall ever having thought, "I must remember this." How did this image get into my memory, and what made it reappear? Have I been storing this image in my memory all these years? If I have been storing it, I should be able to recover the image from time to time. But my previous experience has been that such unasked-for images often make a one-time-only appearance.

Cognitive psychologists have been interested in these and other questions, and this chapter considers some of their answers. Much of the material in this chapter has been produced by using information-processing theories of memory. This viewpoint maintains that memory can be thought of as a system of components that have both structural and process aspects. By "structural aspects," we mean that memories seem to differ markedly in their nature and organization. For example, consider the *duration* of a memory. If I'm distracted while trying to memorize something unfamiliar to me, the memory will seem to evaporate. The memory is fragile. Other memories seem to be much more permanent. It's as if different memories are stored in different locations, and the properties of the memory seem to reflect the properties of the storage location in which the memory is housed. We can hang onto a memory stored in the permanent location, but it seems as if the memory has to go through a temporary location first. By "process aspects," we mean the cognitive operations that transferred and altered the memories stored in different locations.

The information-processing viewpoint has undergone a great deal of the-oretical development over the last 20 years, meaning that the emphasis on structural or process aspects of memory has shifted back and forth as new findings have come to light. This chapter examines some of this shifting and attempts to point out why cognitive psychologists have decided to modify some aspects of the basic theoretical account. A good grounding in the theoretical issues will help us to understand what some of the research battles have been fought over. As a result of the intense effort by many cognitive psychologists to refine and advance knowledge in the area of memory, our understanding of this complex topic has increased dramatically.

THE INFORMATION-PROCESSING POSITION

Approximately two decades ago, an information-processing theory of memory was developed (Atkinson & Shiffrin, 1968; Waugh & Norman, 1965), and this section provides an overview of its basic parts. The theory considers memory as a system of interrelated components. Each component, called a **storage,** is capable of processing particular types of **cognitive codes.** The theory also holds that cognitive codes can be transferred from storage to storage using **control processes.** One of the storages is known as the **sensory register,** where our feature detection and pattern recognition processes rapidly produce a cognitive code that can be stored for a brief period. The operation of the sensory register does not depend on resource allocation, meaning that person does not have to pay attention to incoming stimuli in order to have a cognitive code in sensory storage; it happens automatically. One implication of this position is that the sensory register's **capacity** must be large, because all incoming stimulation is assumed to be stored at least briefly. The sensory register is also thought to be **modality specific.** This term means that part of the storage is devoted to visual stimuli, part to auditory stimuli, and presumably, other parts devoted to each of the remaining senses. The duration of material in sensory storage is short. Visual stimuli remain there for about 250 to 300 msec, and auditory stimuli are kept for perhaps ten times that duration. Material stored in the sensory register is affected by the passage of time. Within the durations just mentioned, codes in sensory storage simply **decay.** *Decay* is a term that memory theorists use to refer to the loss of cognitive codes whose disappearance is produced strictly by the passage of time. To transfer the cognitive code from the sensory register, a person must allocate some resources to evacuate the information before it fades.

Information-processing theorists believe that cognitive codes are next transferred to a component called the **short-term storage.** Short-term storage (STS) differs from the sensory register in several ways. First, the capacity of STS is assumed to be quite limited (Miller, 1956). Second, information in STS is organized in a cognitive code that is acoustic, verbal, or linguistic. This organization is true even when the incoming information (i.e., the material evacuated from sensory storage) has been presented visually. Third, material can reside in STS much longer than it can in sensory storage. The duration of unrehearsed material in STS is about 30 seconds. STS and the sensory storage are similar in one aspect, however. In both cases, material that is not elaborated and transferred decays.

Codes stored in STS can be transferred to a **long-term storage** (LTS) whose capacity, like that of the sensory register, is extremely large. The control process that permits the transfer of coded material between these two storages is called **rehearsal.** *Rehearsal* is a term with many meanings in cognitive psychology, but for the time being, let's restrict its meaning to those cognitive operations that seem to have the following two functions. First, rehearsal refers to procedures that maintain the vitality of the code in STS. As long as the STS code is occasionally refreshed by rehearsal, it can apparently reside there for long periods. Second, rehearsal refers to operations that build up a corresponding code of the STS material in LTS.

In a sense, then, information in STS is not transferred intact to LTS. Instead, rehearsal operates by duplicating a representation of the STS material in LTS. We're familiar with the subjective experience that often accompanies rehearsal. When we try to retain an unfamiliar bit of knowledge, we often say it to ourselves over and over again. Whether rehearsal depends upon this kind of subvocal speech is currently controversial (Klatzky, 1980). Once stored in LTS, the code is believed to be permanent. Failures to retrieve information that has been transferred to LTS are the result of other codes that seem to have a blocking or inhibiting effect on the memory we're searching for. In other words, cognitive codes can sometimes interfere with one another. In STS, cognitive codes are organized on the basis of acoustic or verbal properties. In LTS, the organization is different. Once there, material is organized semantically—that is, by its meaning. Figure 4.1 summarizes the relationships between these storages.

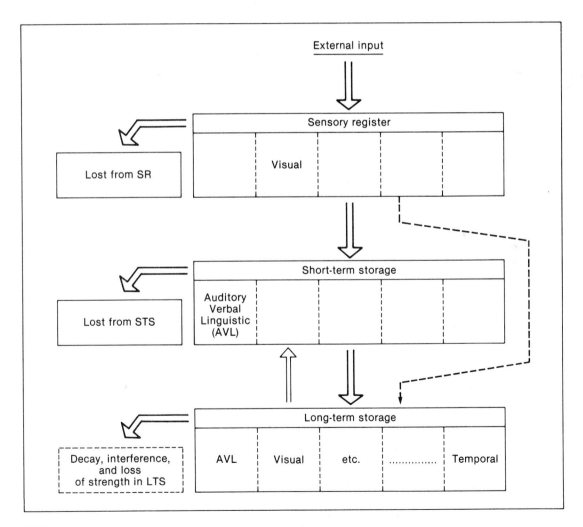

Figure 4.1.

Structure of the memory system. (From Atkinson & Shiffrin, 1968.)

This introduction to the information-processing theory has pointed out that the storages differ in their capacities, durations, and operating characteristics. The sections that follow describe each of these storages in greater depth and examine some of the evidence for the claims made in the introduction. Criticism is withheld until a later section so that we might appreciate the theory's strengths.

Sensory Storage

Sperling (1960) has conducted some of the classic studies in the area of sensory storage. These studies demonstrate that humans seem to have an extremely accurate and complete memory for visual stimulation, although this memory's duration is brief. Sperling found that if four or fewer letters were tachistoscopically presented to subjects for durations of 50 msec,[1] retrieval was good, often approaching 100 percent. Moreover, Sperling found that the way in which the stimuli were arranged on the tachistoscope slide didn't seem to have any effect on the subjects' retrieval. For example, it didn't matter if six elements were presented in a single row or in two rows of three elements. In either case, the subjects retrieved an average of four elements. Similarly, the number of elements in the array didn't seem to produce any effect on retrieval. When the array had nine or more elements, subjects still retrieved only about four of them. Finally, even when exposure time was increased dramatically, up to about five-tenths of a second, the number of elements retrieved stayed constant. This last finding indicates that the upper limit of retrieved items was not imposed by any difficulty in *seeing* the items—five-tenths of a second is plenty of time for that. Instead, the finding suggests that the difficulty in reporting elements from arrays of greater than four was produced by memory loss. This raises a question: What was the nature of memory deficit? Was it one of capacity (the initial storage being overloaded by more than four items) or one of duration (the items not remaining in the initial register long enough to get them out and into more durable storage)?

To settle these issues, Sperling abandoned the **whole-report technique,** in which he had asked the subjects to retrieve as much as they could from the array. In his next series of studies, Sperling substituted the **partial-report technique.** The subjects were now required to report only certain elements of the preceding display. The display consisted of an array of letters and digits arranged in three rows of four elements each. The subjects had to report only one row. However, unlike the whole-report technique, in which the subjects could begin responding as soon as the slide had been presented, in the partial-report technique, the subjects could not begin responding until they heard a musical tone, which signaled the row that was to be reported. A high-pitched tone was the signal for subjects to report the top row of the array, a medium-pitched tone was the signal for the middle row, and so on. Since the order of the tones was presented at random, the subject's could not know which of the three tones would be heard on any

---

1. A tachistoscope is an apparatus that is used to briefly expose visual stimuli.

particular trial. From a subject's perspective, the order of events went something like the following. First, the subject saw the array for 50 msec. Then the array was turned off, and the subject waited until the tone was heard. This interval—called the **inter-stimulus interval**—was originally set at 50 msec. During this time, the subjects relied upon their memories to hang onto as much of the original array as they could. Finally, at the end of the inter-stimulus interval, a tone was sounded and the subject began responding. Sperling found that the subjects' accuracy was good: Most could retrieve all four of the signaled elements. This finding may seem predictable for the results of the whole-report studies, but there is a difference. In the partial-report procedure, the subjects did not know in advance which row they would have to report. That subjects were accurate in reporting any signaled row strongly suggests that they had all twelve elements of the array stored in their memories across the inter-stimulus interval.

Sperling's next task was to determine how long the elements were stored. To determine this, he increased the inter-stimulus interval, and he found that retention was good until the interval was increased to about 250 msec. When the interval was increased to 300 msec, the subjects seemd to be guessing. If they correctly anticipated which row would be signaled, they were able to report it. However, if they misjudged the to-be-signaled row, they weren't able to say much about what had been presented. Sperling's interpretation of this finding was straightforward. The information-processing system seemingly held all incoming visual stimulation in a memory or buffer for an ultra-brief period. This memory was considered complete in that all the aspects of the original stimulation were present in the storage. In addition, the contents of the storage were considered *precategorical* (Crowder & Morton, 1969; Long, 1980), which means that the information had not yet been transformed into the acoustic or semantic codes that characterize the organization of STS and LTS. Sperling elaborated his original findings by developing a theory of visual perception. He argued that visual information is recognized, elaborated, and rehearsed after the sensory stage. The subjects could not report more than four or five letters from the inital array because subjects must recognize and transfer the contents of the sensory memory to a more durable location from which they can be reported. Clearly, some time is required for this process, and the transfer problem is made worse by the items being apparently transferred serially. By the time four items have been extracted from the sensory register, the remaining contents have decayed.

In 1967, Neisser developed a name for this brief visual memory: the **icon.** The sensory register is not restricted to visual events alone. The **echo** is the appropriate name given to auditory stimulation stored in the sensory register. Presumably, each sense contributes an accurate copy of the recent stimulation of sensory storage, although the icon and the echo have been investigated more than the other sensory memories.

The Nature of the Icon

One of Sperling's other studies addressed the precategorical nature of the icon. In this study, subjects were shown a typical matrix of letters and digits, but instead of signaling the subjects to report a row, Sperling cued the subjects to report one category (letter or digit) of the elements. Let's consider the implications of these instructions. If the icon is truly precategorical, its elements have not yet been encoded into any meaningful format, such as letters. Consequently, we would not expect this type of signaling to be very helpful. Sperling found that this expectation was confirmed. Using the partial-report technique, he discovered that if he gave his subjects a letter or a digit cue, they had no more of the array's elements available to them than if he had used the whole-report procedure. This finding seems to indicate that the material in the sensory register is stored without any attempt at pattern recognition.

Sperling found that icon's durability was strongly influenced by the adaptive state of the viewer's eye (Haber, 1983). When the presentation screen was illuminated at normal reading levels, so that the presentation of the stimulus didn't bring with it a change in the energy level of the visual field, then the icon lasted for about one-quarter of a second. However, if the viewer's eyes were dark adapted, and thus more sensitive to light, then the presentation of the stimulus was also accompanied by a change in the overall energy level in the visual field. The icon then might persist for as long as four or five seconds. Sperling observed something far different when the pre- and post stimulus fields were much brighter than the stimulus. The icon then became much harder to "see," and its durability was lessened substantially.

"Reading" the Icon

The nature of the cuing stimulus also seems to have an effect on the ease with which information can be "read" from sensory storage. Averbach and Coriell (1961) presented their subjects with a two-by-eight-letter array of letters for 50 msec. A typical array might look like this:

A   M   I   F   G   Y   J   K
L   Q   V   O   R   T   B   U

The subjects were required to extract only one letter from the array, which was signaled by the presentation of a bar just above one of the eight letters in the top row. When the bar was presented immediately after the array, the analysis indicated that subjects had about twelve letters, or 75 percent of the whole array, available. When the bar was presented 300 msec after the offset of the array, only about four or five letters still remained in sensory storage. This finding agrees closely with Sperling's work. But Averbach and Coriell found that particular letter positions seem to degrade earlier than others. In some cases, the chance of retrieval remained close to 100 percent, while other positions in the array had degraded to chance levels. They also found that if the physical locations of the bar and the target letter overlapped, decrements in performance occurred. These findings suggest several things about the icon. First, the capacity of sensory storage may not be infinite, although it seems to be extremely large. Second, extracting information from the visual store seems to be somewhat analogous to seeing: A cue that was close to the target stimulus in either time or location could cover the target and prevent it from being seen. The Focus section at the end of this chapter deals with the relationship between actual seeing and reading information from the icon.

This phenomenon seems to be involved in the erasure of material in sensory storage. Even though visual stimuli don't stay in the sensory register very long, there must be some way of erasing or terminating them, for reasons you may have already guessed. If we kept an accurate copy of all stimuli for one-quarter of a second, and such memories seemed to have some perceptual properties, then what would stop successive icons from piling up on top of one another? If this happened, then how could the cognitive system distinguish between information that was being picked up by our receptors and the highly accurate information stored in the sensory register?

These issues were explored in a study by Averbach and Coriell (1961). They showed their subjects the two-by-eight-letter matrix described earlier. In this study, the target letter was not signaled with a bar but rather with a circle that was presented after the offset of the matrix. The circle occurred in the same location where the target letter had been; that is, it would have surrounded the letter if the letter had still been present. The subjects were supposed to report the circled letter. Figure 4.2 shows the study's findings, which are somewhat surprising. At extremely short time intervals, the circle works as an effective cue. When the inter-stimulus interval approaches 300 msec, then neither the circle nor the bar are effective cues. After that length of time, the icon has decayed almost completely, and the partial-report technique is no longer superior to the whole-report technique. The surprising finding is the low level of performance when the circle is presented 100 msec or so after the matrix of letters. The circle seemingly blocks out or erases the letter it is supposed to cue. The subjects have a difficult time retrieving the letter; indeed, the subjects commonly report that they've seen only the circle, not the letter. This is an example of a more general phenomenon known as **backward masking**—a visual interference in which the recognition of visual stimuli is delayed or nullified by the later masking stimulus. Because 200 msec seems to be about the minimum time necessary to carry out pattern recognition on a visual stimulus (Ericksen & Ericksen, 1971), the relationship between pattern recognition and visual sensory storage seems straightforward. If a stimulus is presented for an extremely short time, then the sensory register obediently hangs onto the icon long enough to permit the pattern recognition routines ample time to extract the important information. However, if a stimulus is presented for a longer period, then other operations begin working to clear the decks in the sensory storage to prevent successive icons from building up and interfering with each other.

Short-Term Storage

The studies just reviewed have suggested that visual information that is presented for less that 200 msec is held until a more durable cognitive code can be made. Short-term storage (STS) is the name given to this more durable storage.

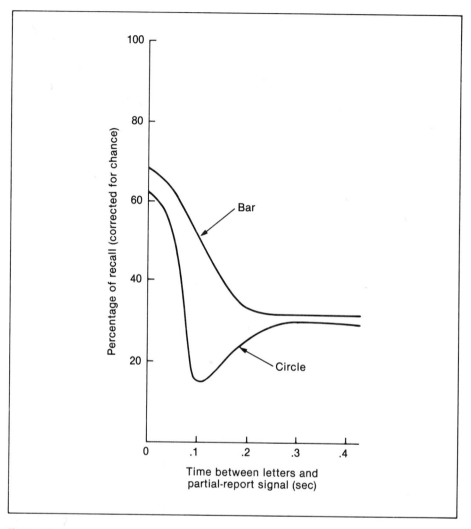

Figure 4.2.

Effects of two different partial-report signals: a circle and a bar. They yield similar results when the delay of the signal is either small or large, but performance with the circle is markedly inferior for intermediate delays. (After Averbach & Coriell, 1961. Reprinted with permission from *The Bell System Technical Journal.* Copyright 1961, The American Telephone and Telegraph Company.)

Our STS is often compared to a mental workbench (Klatzky, 1980). Items from other storages can be transferred onto this workbench, where they can be "worked on," meaning that the material can be elaborated or transformed in a variety of ways. The workbench analogy has other implications, too. Like a real workbench, our short-term memories have limited space, implying that we can work only on a few things simultaneously. Just as a real task on a workbench requires our concentration, working on material in STS also seems to require the allocation of cognitive resources (Atkinson & Shiffrin, 1968). For these and other reasons, the contents of the short-

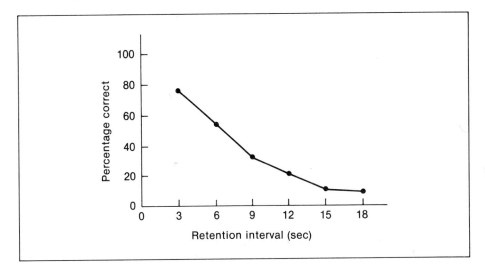

Figure 4.3.

Results of the experiment on forgetting in short-term memory, showing that recall decreases as a function of the retention interval. (From Peterson & Peterson, 1959. Copyright 1959 by the American Psychological Association. Reprinted by permission.)

term store have sometimes been equated with the boundaries of our consciousness.

Basic Findings

The classic study of short-term storage was conducted by Peterson and Peterson (1959). First, the Petersons demonstrated that subjects could retrieve a three-consonant trigram (e.g., MBN) after thirty seconds with no difficulty. Then the Petersons carried out the next phase of the study. Subjects were asked to recall only a single trigram, but during the retention interval, the subjects had to perform a distractor task. There are a variety of such tasks. The one used by the Petersons involved counting backward out loud by threes, starting from a three-digit number given to the subject right after the trigram. From the subject's perspective, each trial involved hearing the trigram, then hearing a three-digit number, let's say 987, then counting backward as quickly as possible, 987, 984, 981, 978. . . until a retrieval cue was given. At that point, the subject attempted to recall the trigram. Figure 4.3 shows the findings of this study. Note that the probability of retrieving the trigram decreases to about 10 percent after a period of only fifteen to eighteen seconds. This probability of retrieval is far less than that observed when the subjects were not given a distractor task. Clearly, the distractor task prevented the subjects from carrying out an important operation on their "workbenches"—namely, rehearsal.

As discussed earlier, rehearsal seems to refresh or regnerate the contents of STS, and without it, the material disappears. Because the distractor task seemed to prevent rehearsal, it was reasonable for the Petersons to interpret the retrieval failures as being produced by decay.

This finding was a landmark one, because cognitive psychologists had known for some time that decay was not necessarily a major reason for retrieval failure over long intervals (Jenkins & Dallenbach, 1924). Now, with the demonstration that simple decay was responsible for retrieval failures when the retention interval was short, the argument that two different storages must exist had a firm basis. The basis for this argument was the mechanism that produced forgetting. Decay produced forgetting from short-term storage, but forgetting fron long-term storage was caused by **interference.** Interference refers to the blocking effect that some memories can have on other memories. This line of reasoning also explained some aspects of the well-known **serial position effect.**

Suppose we present a list of forty common nouns to our subjects at the rate of one noun per second. Immediately after the presentation, we ask the subjects to recall as many of the nouns as they can. Would you expect the recall probability of each noun to be equal? As you may know, that's not what happens. When a lengthy list is presented using such a free-recall procedure, the subjects' responses are predictable. Nouns that were presented first and those that were presented last tend to be recalled with greater frequency than those that were presented in the middle (Deese & Kaufman, 1957; Murdock, 1962). A noun's position in the sequence of presentation affects the likelihood of its being recalled. The serial position effect has two components. The **primacy component** refers to the fact that the nouns presented first (and whose memory is therefore the oldest) are recalled better than items whose presentation occurred in the middle of the list. The **recency component** refers to the greater likelihood of an item's retrieval when its serial position is near the end of the list. These effects are observed because the subjects are retrieving the words from separate storages. When the subjects began seeing or hearing the list, their short-term storages were basically empty, and consequently, a great deal of rehearsal could be spent on each word as it entered the storage. Because the initial words were thoroughly rehearsed, we would expect that they would develop into a more permanent representation in long-term storage. However, as the short-term storage gradually became loaded to capacity, the subjects had less time to rehearse each new incoming word, and the probability of a permanent representation's being made was correspondingly diminished. Because material had to spend some time in the short-term storage before it could be transferred to LTS, the most recently presented nouns should be found in STS. This account suggests that subjects might not retrieve the material in the same chronological order in which it was presented. Instead, the subjects might spill the contents of their STS first, because it was prone to decay. Indeed, if you ever get a chance to observe the behavior of the subjects in a free-recall situation, you'll see that their response pattern is characteristic. When the list has been presented and the cue is given to recall as many words as possible, the subjects first write down the words that have just been presented, then they retrieve the words that were presented first, and finally, they jot down whatever else they can retrieve from the middle of the list.

If this retrieval pattern truly reflects storage in two different, independent locations, then apparently it should be possible to design an experiment that influences the retrieval from one, but not the other, location. Such a study was carried out by Postman and Phillips (1965). In one group of conditions, lists of ten, twenty, or thirty words were presented at the rate of one word per second. Recall was measured immediately after presentation. The top part of Figure 4.4 (labeled "0 sec") shows the findings from this phase of the study. Notice that the serial position effect is much stronger when the list is twenty or thirty words long than when it consists of only ten words. For the ten-word list, the probability of recalling the middle words approached 50 percent, which is a preliminary indication that the capacity of STS must be almost that size. The reasoning here is that if we made the list so short that all of it could be fit into STS, then we would expect the retrieval in the free-recall procedure to be good—in the 70 to 80 percent range. The observed retrieval probabilities for the middle words are close enough to those figures to enable us to infer that they've only recently been dropped from STS and begun their decay.

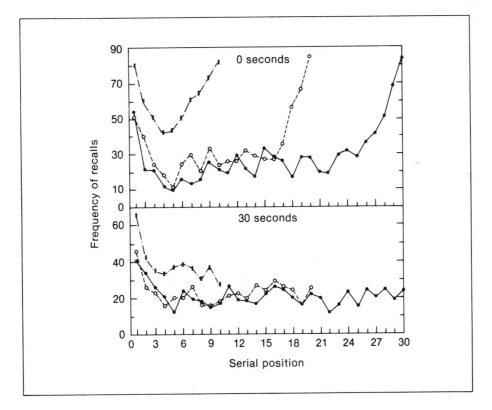

Figure 4.4.

Probability of correct recall as a function of serial position for free verbal recall with test following zero seconds and thirty seconds of intervening arithmetic. (After Postman & Phillips, 1965.)

In the second phase of the experiment, Postman and Phillips conducted a variation of the procedure used by Peterson and Peterson. The words were presented as before; however, the subjects were not permitted to recall the words immediately after the presentation. Instead, the subjects were given a three-digit number from which they had to count backward by threes. After thirty seconds of this process, the subjects were given the recall cue. What should we expect? The theory predicts that the distractor task should affect the contents of STS but not LTS. We would expect that the subjects would have some difficulty dumping the contents of their STSs, because after thirty seconds of decay, those contents should be long gone. However, the distractor task should not affect the contents or the retrieval of any words that had already been transferred to LTS. Consequently, if the subjects are truly retrieving the words from two separate storages, we should expect that the distractor task would affect the recency component but not the primacy component. As shown by the bottom half of Figure 4.4, this effect is exactly what Postman and Phillips found, and it has been replicated on several occasions (Atkinson & Shiffrin, 1968).

The Nature of the Code in STS

As discussed earlier, the contents of the sensory register have no real organization, meaning that they are more or less untransformed by the cognitive system. The sensory register is simply a copy of the stimuli in close to their raw form. The contents of short-term storage, however, are highly transformed, or coded, by the cognitive system. What is the nature of this code?

Wickelgren (1965) aurally presented his subjects with a series of letters, and the subjects' task was to remember as many letters as they could. When the errors were analyzed, Wickelgren found that the subjects tended to substitute letters that sounded like the letters they had forgotten. For example, a *D* might be subtituted for a *T,* and an *A* for a *K.* Notice that these substitution errors are not based on alphabetic proximity, nor are they visual confusions. This finding suggests that the nature of the code in STS is acoustic.

This finding was reinforced in a study by Conrad (1964), who wished to make a more explicit test of the acoustic code hypothesis. In this study, the letters were presented to the subjects visually as well as aurally. Conrad found that even when substitution errors were made for letters that had been presented visually, the nature of the error indicated the confusion had been acoustic. In other words, a *V* might be substituted for a *B* but not for a *U.*

This basic finding was complicated somewhat by the work of Hintzman (1965, 1967), who maintained that such errors were not acoustic per se, but rather were produced by the kinesthetic feedback the subjects got as they articulated the letters subvocally during the retention interval. His analysis of substitution errors, which were made against a background of white noise, indicated that such errors were explainable by the letter's voicing qualities (whether or not the vocal chords vibrate during the letter's production) and by place of articulation (where the tongue points during sounding). These qualities are closely related to the letter's sound, but Hintzman's findings suggest that the nature of the code in STS is verbal or linguistic rather than simply acoustic. Clearing up this issue has proved to be difficult (Atkinson & Shiffrin, 1968), which is why STS is sometimes referred to as the AVL storage. The nature of the code seems to be acoustic, verbal, or linguistic.

The Capacity of STS

Determining the capacity of STS has proved to be difficult. Before examining some of the studies bearing on this issue, we should note one point. Pinning down a storage's capacity has been a tricky task partially because different theorists mean different things by this term (Craik & Lockhart, 1972). For example, we can discuss the *storage* capacity of some memory location, which means we're trying to describe how much information that component of the system can *hold*. On the other hand, we can discuss the *attentional,* or processing, capacity of storage, in which case we're focusing on *how much can be done* on the information storage (Zechmeister & Nyberg, 1982). Going back to the workbench analogy, storage capacity refers to how many items can be physically placed on the workbench, whereas processing capacity refers to how many separate operations (like nailing things together or painting them) can be done on those items in some unit of time. Establishing which factor is dominant in limiting the capacity of STS is hard because we never see the "workbench" except in the form of the subject's verbal reports or other behaviors.

However, regardless of which definition of capacity we adopt, we know that the capacity of STS is limited. In his famous paper, Miller (1956) suggested that the capacity of the short-term store was seven, plus or minus two items. However, exactly what constitutes an "item" can be debated. For example, suppose you are given a list of unrelated digits at the rate of one per second, and you are asked to repeat the list in the original order. If you're like most college students, you'll show high accuracy in repeating a list of about seven or eight digits. This experiment is an easy way to demonstrate the so-called memory span and is the basis for Miller's "magic" number seven. However, suppose the list you're given is the following:

$$1, 4, 9, 2, 1, 7, 7, 6, 1, 9, 4, 1$$

Since this list has twelve digits, technically we shouldn't expect good retrieval. But, if you're an American, you'd probably have no trouble remembering all twelve digits, because they can be grouped into three clusters of four digits each. Each cluster represents a year in which a historical event significant to Americans occurred. The name of this processing is **chunking.** A chunk is a unit of information organized according to a rule or correspondence to some familiar pattern. A substantial body of evidence indicates that chunks are the items that fill up STS (Zechmeister & Nyberg, 1982).

Murdock (1961) demonstrated that three words would decay in STS about the same rate as three letters. But during the same time period, one word would show relatively little decay. If individual letters were the relevant items in short-term storage, then three letters should show more decay than one word. Similarly, three words should decay much more quickly than three letters. Murdock's findings indicate that the organizational unit in STS is the chunk. When three unrelated letters are entered in STS, they are stored as three chunks. When the letters are related because they constitute a word, then the word becomes the organizational unit and occupies one chunk.

Long-Term Storage

This section considers two lines of evidence that have traditionally been used to support the idea of a long-term storage, or LTS, which is the ultimate repository of our knowledge. First, we know that the nature of the memory code seems to change as a function of its time in the memory system. Second, evidence from the neuropsychological literature points to a distinction between STS and LTS.

Semantic Codes in LTS

If we show subjects a list of words and ask them to recall the words several hours later, we'll see that subjects typically make what are called intrusion errors—they recall words that were not on the list. These intrusions are interesting. The relationship between the intruding word and left-out word is almost always *semantic,* that is, based on shared meaning. In other words, if the original word on the list was *boat,* the intruder is much more likely to be *ship* than *bud* or *boar* (Baddely & Dale, 1966). These intrusions are far different than those that occur in STS, which tend to be acoustic.

Neuropsychological Findings

When a person suffers a painful shock induced by physical, electrical, or chemical stimuli, a common discovery is that after recovery, the person is unable to recall the events that took place immediately prior to the trauma (Russell & Nathan, 1946). In extreme cases, memory for events that happened up to an hour before the trauma occurred may be absent. From the time the person regains consciousness, his memory appears to function normally; events occurring after the accident are processed typically. The person usually regains the formerly wiped out memories, and this occurs in a characteristic fashion. The oldest wiped out memories (those that were farthest "in front" of the accident) are recovered first. Subsequently, the individual recovers memories that are closer and closer in time to the accident. The name for this type of memory loss is **retrograde amnesia.** What produces it?

If memories are transferred from STS to LTS, then we would expect the memory code to be particularly fragile at the time of transfer. Memories that had just been transferred, or were just about to be transferred, would be particularly likely to be disrupted. Those whose transfer had already occurred might be a little hardier and more able to survive the traumatic shock.

These concerns were addressed in an experiment by Chorover and Schiller (1965), who studied passive avoidance conditioning in rats. Their study was set up in the following way. The animal was placed on a small platform, which was raised several inches from the cage's floor. When the animal stepped onto the floor, it received an electroconvulsive shock (ECS). Chorover and Schiller varied the time delay between the animal's stepping down and the ECS. They reasoned that if the memories were truly being transferred, and were thus disruptible, then the rat should show poor avoidance learning when the time interval between stepping down and ECS was brief. This reasoning also implies that avoidance learning should improve if the delay between stepping down and ECS was increased, because the rat's memory system would have already transferred the memory into LTS and secured it. After exposing their animals to the ECS, Chorover and Schiller returned the rats to the experimental chamber twenty-four hours later for a memory trial. Their hypotheses were supported: If the ECS had been administered within ten seconds of the rat's stepping down on the learning trial, then the rat showed a significantly shorter step-down latency in the memory trial than rats who were shocked more than ten seconds after stepping down, or rats who hadn't been shocked at all. The interpretation seems to be that the rats who were shocked early (within ten seconds) were more likely to have the memory of stepping down wiped out by the ECS. Consequently, when they were placed in the experimental chamber twenty-four hours later, they duplicated their error and stepped down again. The rats who were shocked late knew better than to do this. They were more likely to remember what had happened to them twenty-four hours ago, and so they were cautious about stepping down from the platform. Chorover and Schiller concluded that the retrograde amnesia gradient was about ten seconds, during which the transfer of memories from STS to LTS could be disrupted.

Summary of the Information-Processing Position

Memory can be thought of as a system of interlocking but separate storages. Each of these storages has different capacities, each is organized differently, and the mechanism that produces forgetting also differs. The sensory register is a large-capacity storage that retains sensory stimulation in a raw form, meaning that no apparent code exists for material stored in the sensory register. Material stored here decays. For visual stimuli, the period of decay is about 250 msec. STS is a somewhat more durable storage capable of holding material for approximately thirty seconds. Material here is organized acoustically, and the capacity of STS is limited to about seven chunks. Unrehearsed material in STS decays. LTS contains our permanent memories. Its capacity is extremely large, and it can apparently hold material indefinitely. Material in LTS is organized semantically and is subject to interference by other memories.

EXTENDING AND MODIFYING THE INFORMATION-PROCESSING POSITION

During the 1970s and 1980s, cognitive psychologists continued to develop and modify their basic theoretical perspective on memory. First, a general attempt has been made to establish or refute the notion that the storages are truly distinct from one another. Second, cognitive psychologists have shown a sustained interest in memory processes, particularly those involving encoding and retrieving material. Those processes are examined in greater depth in Chapter 5. The next section considers some additional evidence bearing on the separability of the storages in memory.

The Existence and Importance of a Sensory Register

This section is somewhat misnamed. Although it refers to the sensory register, for reasons of space, the discussion is limited to visual sensory storage. Although nobody seriously questions the findings of the many studies dealing with sensory storage, some debate exists regarding the interpretation and implications of those findings (Haber, 1983; Kolers, 1983). This debate has focused on two issues. First, researchers have questioned certain technical matters such as the nature of iconic organization (Merikle, 1980), and its locus (Adelson, 1978; Banks & Barber, 1977, 1980). Second, some thinkers have expressed a more general concern with postulating the icon as the necessary first step in an information-processing theory of memory or perception (Coltheart, 1980; Neisser, 1967; Turvey, 1977).

To review briefly, Sperling and other researchers thought that the nervous system passively copied information, which it stored in a raw format in sensory storage. The sensory register was therefore said to be precategorical, meaning that the information there was uncoded. Consequently, cuing the subject to report a particular kind of stimulus (e.g., letters or numbers) was ineffective, because the material in the sensory register had not yet been transferred into STS, where the material is coded. However, Merikle (1980) questioned this interpretation, reasoning that the display used by Sperling and others was simply a random series of letters and digits. Because the display itself was unorganized, the subject had only one strategy available when asked to report letters or digits. Each element in the array had to be searched on a one-by-one basis. Under those circumstances, it should not be surprising that the partial-report technique shows no advantage over the whole-report procedure. In effect, the subject was being asked to carry out a full report. Merikle attempted to remedy this problem by varying the spacing and format of the display. Using these modified matrices, Merikle found that poststimulus cuing was as effective for categorical elements (such as letters or digits) as it was for purely physical elements (such as "elements in the top row"). On the basis of this evidence, Merikle argued against the notion of a sensory storage as a separate location in the memory system. Instead, Merikle suggested that different aspects of a stimulus are probably encoded and transformed at different rates by the nervous system. For example, information about a stimulus's location might be encoded first, perhaps followed by a code representing the element's identity. If these codes are assembled by the nervous system quickly enough, then iconic effects can be explained without the recourse to a separate storage.

Other researchers raised some questions concerning the locus of the icon; that is, what part of the nervous system was responsible for creating and preserving it? There are two obvious placed to begin looking for the icon's whereabouts: the retina and the brain (Haber, 1983).

That the icon can apparently be inspected, or looked at, gives it something in common with another perceptual experience, the *afterimage*. An afterimage is a visual experience in which a stimulus that is no longer present seems to persist. Lay people (who haven't studied cognitive psychology) apparently commonly mistake the icon for an afterimage (Loftus, Johnson, & Shimamura, 1985). Afterimages are produced and maintained by the photoreceptors; that is, they are retinal events. Demonstrating this experience is easy. If you cover one eye and stare with the other at a highly saturated patch of color for a minute or so, then look at a neutral surface, you'll see an afterimage in a complementary color. However, if you close the saturated eye, and look instead with the eye you originally had closed, the afterimage will disappear. In other words, the effect will not transfer from eye to eye, becuase it is a retinal rather than a central phenomenon.

Sakitt (1976) has argued that the icon represents a similar sort of discharge by the photoreceptors:

[A] significant part, or possibly all, of iconic storage is due to persistence of photoreceptor activity after a brief visual stimulus has been extinguished . . . icons are weak afterimages stored in the retina. (Sakitt, 1976, p. 273).

This claim was later modified to permit the existence of two kinds of icons: cone icons and rod icons. Cone icons had an ultra-brief duration that included color. They could be contrasted with the more durable icon maintained by the rods (Sakitt & Long, 1979).

Although this claim seems plausible, several reasons argue against accepting such a view wholesale. First, despite some superficial resemblances, icons are not very similar to afterimages. Typically, the icon decays in 300 msec, and under no circumstances can its life be extended beyond four or five seconds. However, afterimages usually endure far longer than that—as long as forty-five seconds to a minute. Also, the illumination required to produce afterimages is fairly intense. But the icon can be produced under fairly low levels of illumination (Zechmeister & Nyberg, 1982). These dissimilarities suggest that we look at the central nervous system to see if it might play a role in the icon's formation.

A study by McCloskey and Watkins (1978) bears on this issue. They examined a well-known illusion: If a visual stimulus is swung back and forth rapidly behind a narrow slit, subjects perceive the stimulus as being compressed in such a way that the whole stimulus is thought to be on view simultaneously through the slit. This effect is an illusion because the subject never sees the whole stimulus simultaneously. McCloskey and Watkins therefore named the effect the "seeing-more-than-is-there" phenomenon. In their study, fairly complex forms were oscillated behind a narrow slit at a rate of sixty-four cycles per minute. The subject's task was to draw the oscillating stimulus as accurately as possible. Figure 4.5 shows some examples of the target figures and subjects' subsequent attempts to draw them. Notice that the subjects saw the complete figure compressed in the narrow space of the aperture, even though at no point in the target figure's cycle was such a view available.

In their interpretation, McCloskey and Watkins commented that such findings seem to necessitate some type of iconic storage. The subject seems

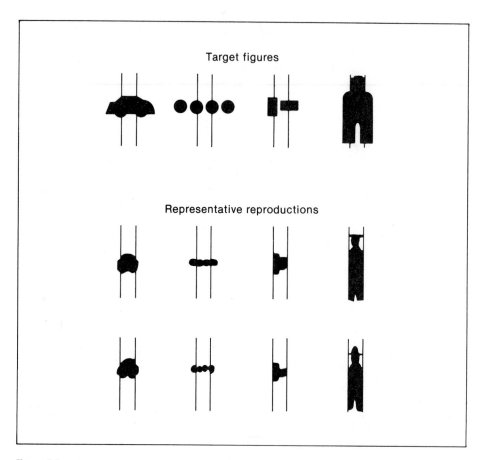

Figure 4.5.

Target figures actually presented and subjects' reproductions of what they saw. The size of the target figures is shown relative to the size of the slit behind which they oscillated. In the experiment, subjects could see only what is revealed in the space between the two lines. (From "The Seeing-More-Than-Is-There Phenomenon: Implications for the Locus of Iconic Storage," by M. McCloskey and M. J. Watkins. In *Journal of Experimental Psychology: Human Perception and Performance*, 1978, 4, 533–565. Copyright 1978 by the American Psychological Association. Reprinted by permission.)

to be holding one part of the target stimulus in the sensory register and incorporating additional information into her perception as it appears, as more of the target stimulus crosses the slit. For two reasons, such effects are not likely produced by the photoreceptors alone. First, it's hard to imagine how one set of photoreceptors could hold on to visual stimuli in some memorized format while simultaneously responding to additional incoming information. Second, the effect is produced even when the subject does not move her eyes. With eye movements, it's possible to conceive of a way in which the subjects might overcome the first objection mentioned. But without eye movements, it seems as if the subject is asking the photoreceptors to do two highly complex tasks (perceive and remember) simultaneously. McCloskey and Watkins argue that the illusion must be at least partially produced by the central nervous system, which suggests that the locus of the icon must be there, too.

Even if the definitive study were to appear that pinned down forever the icon's nature and its location in the nervous system, some thinkers have wondered how important the sensory storage would be in any case. Even Neisser, who bestowed the icon with its name in 1967, later felt that the icon must play only a small part in everyday vision and memory (Neisser, 1976). Other thinkers have echoed this belief. Turvey (1977) reasoned that theories of perception and memory that are initiated by pictures or picture-like entities such as the icon have been called into question by Gibson's account of perception (see Chapter 3), which postulates no such devices and yet is able to explain perception. The real problem here seems to be the nature of Sperling's task, which is highly artificial: In what sense does normal vision correspond to looking at something in a tachistoscope? The answer is, not much. Tachistoscopic viewing is heavily dependent upon our ability to detect highly discrete stimuli that have been presented for brief segments of time. Such viewing heavily weighs on our ability to differentiate the chronological order of visual events—something most people are not very good at doing. In everyday vision, such an ability doesn't seem to be necessary. This leads to a question: Why would our cognitive system depend on a component in whose use we weren't very skillful and which wasn't very useful anyway (Haber, 1983)?

All these findings suggest a modification of the basic position on sensory storage. The effects of sensory storage studies are reliable, so the nervous system clearly does have the capability to make highly accurate copies of sensory stimulation for short time periods. However, the copy made by the nervous system is not completely raw, or primitive, but rather has some code or organization. We know this because the central nervous system is implicated in the icon's formation. Also, the icon may be useful in some situations, but also clear is that the existence of the icon is not critical for accurate perception or memory. This evidence suggests that the boundaries around the sensory register—its limits—may be much fuzzier than was once thought.

The Distinction between Short- and Long-Term Storage

The distinction between separate storages beyond the sensory register is based on several lines of evidence (Wickelgren, 1973), only some of which are reviewed here. First, there is the coding issue. As we saw earlier, the information-processing theory describes short-term storage as acoustically organized, while long-term storage is semantically organized. Second, we have the mechanism of forgetting issue. Material in STS decays, while retrieval failures in LTS are produced by interference. This raises a question: Do situations exist in which material in working memory interferes with other material residing there? Third, there is the question of capacity. Is the capacity of STS much more limited than that of LTS? Finally, we have to contend with neuropsychological evidence. The following sections deal with each of these concerns.

Semantic Codes in STS

Shulman (1971, 1972) demonstrated that people do have semantic information about material being stored in STS. His subjects underwent a series of trials, each of which had the following format. First, the subjects saw a list of ten words that were presented for 500 msec each. The tenth word was followed by the probe word, and the subjects had to tell whether the probe matched a word on the ten-item list. However, the nature of the match varied from trial to trial. On some trials, the term *match* meant that the subject had to report if the probe was identical to one of the words appearing on the list. On the other trials, a match would be achieved if the probe word was a synonym of one of the words appearing on the list. The subject did not know in advance which trials would be synonym trials and which would be identity trials; the nature of the trial was signaled by flashing an *S* or an *I* just before the probe word appeared.

Before we go on to the findings of this study, let's review some of the implications of this procedure. If the subject has only acoustic information available in STS, then there should be no confusions about the probe word when it has only a semantic relationship to the words on the list. That is, we would not expect subjects to mistake the probe word as having been identical to a word on the list when it was a synonym of one of the words on the list. If such confusions are observed, they must be based on a semantic, not an acoustic, similarity, which means that the subjects must have some semantic knowledge available to them in STS. Figure 4.6 shows the findings of this study. When an identity match was signaled, and the probe was a word that was not semantically related to the words on the list, the proportion of errors was .11. However, when an identity match was signaled, and the probe was a word that was a synonym of one of the words on the list, the proportion of errors increased dramatically to .19 (this is the line on the graph labeled "IS"). Notice, too, that the proportion of such errors as a function of serial position in presentation remained constant. If an acoustic code dominated, or even existed alongside the semantic information, we would expect to see a reduction in errors when the probe was a synonym of the three or four most recently presented items. Presumably, these items would be the most likely to be coded acoustically and therefore the most resistant to confusion. The fact that such a reduction was not observed suggests that the semantic information was more than simply available to the subjects. Rather, it suggests that the subjects had coded the words on the list on the basis of their semantic properties.

It's important to note that Shulman's subjects were not left to their own devices in the formation of a code. The nature of the task must have encouraged the subjects to form a semantic representation of the list. Indeed, ample evidence suggests that when subjects are left to their own devices on a short-term task, the nature of their representation is likely to be acoustic to some extent (Drewnowski, 1980). Drewnowski and Murdock (1980) have presented findings showing that intrusion errors for monosyllabic words stored in STS are primarily acoustic (echoing Conrad, 1964). However, when disyllabic words were presented either visually or aurally, the intrusion errors could not be well explained on a purely acoustic basis. Instead, Drew-

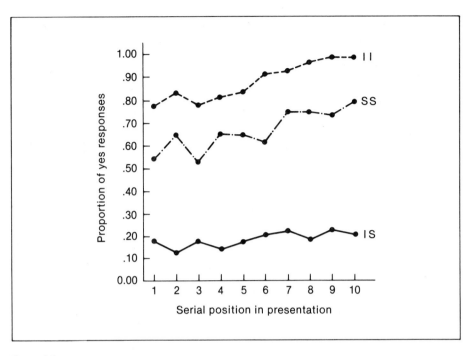

Figure 4.6.

Proportion of correct identity matches *(II)* and synonym matches *(SS)*, as well as proportion of times subjects mistakenly said yes to a synonym when an identity match was requested *(IS)* as a function of serial position. (From "Semantic Confusion Errors in Short-Term Memory," by H. G. Shulman. In *Journal of Verbal Learning and Verbal Behavior*, 1972, 11, 221–227. Copyright 1972 by Academic Press, Inc. Reprinted by permission.)

nowski and Murdock found that the intrusions were made on the basis of the syllabic stress pattern, the phonemic class of the initial and final syllables, and the identity of the stressed vowel. Recall Atkinson and Shiffrin's comment concerning the difficulty of separating acoustic from linguistic codes. The Drewnowski and Murdock findings seem to amplify the idea that a variety of codes are produced early on and perhaps nearly simultaneously by the cognitive system. Because of this, many cognitive psychologists are reluctant to use coding differences as a basis for establishing separate long- and short-term storages, and have taken instead to studying the emergence and transformation of these various codes (Horton & Mills, 1984).

The Mechanism of Forgetting

The difference in forgetting mechanisms—decay in STS, interference in LTS— has also been used as a basis for claiming that these storages are truly separate. Unfortunately, this distinction has been under a cloud for some time. Early critics of the original Peterson and Peterson finding noted that the possibility of interference from trial to trial had not been completely controlled for. According to this argument, the act of storing one trigram in STS may have interfered with the ability to store the trigrams that were presented on later trials. As more and more trigrams were presented on successive trials, a reasonable supposition was that the interference from one trial to the next might increase. If this putative explanation were correct, then the results observed by the Petersons were not produced by decay but rather by the interference of earlier trials on later trials. The Petersons defended themselves against this charge by saying that if this explanation were true, then the subjects' performance should get worse on successive trials of the counting backward task. But it didn't. Performance on the first trial and the Nth trial were essentially the same. This rebuttal seemed sound until Keppel and Underwood (1962) read the Peterson's procedure section closely and noticed that the Petersons' had given their subjects two practice trials. Keppel and Underwood wondered if interference might have been induced on those trials. When the study was replicated without the practice trials, they noticed that a buildup of interference occurred across trials. Retention was better on trial 1 than on trial 2, which was in turn better than retention on the third and subsequent trials. Keppel and Underwood's study concluded that at least some interference seems to be involved in forgetting from STS.

The Capacity of STS

The apparent difference in capacities between STS and LTS has long been used as a basis for inferring the existence of two different storages. However, the concept of chunking complicates the notion of a limited-capacity STS opposed to an infinite-capacity LTS. The material chunked in STS doesn't require an inherent, logical relationship between its elements. Indeed, as long as the material is presented slowly, almost any subjectively generated chunking strategy will succeed. This is why statements that announce the capacity of STS as seven or so chunks are hard to interpret. Because people can chunk together unrelated material, the size of a chunk is itself indeterminate (Anderson, 1980). The implications of this observation should be clear. If the size of a chunk is not specifiable, then we don't know much about the capacity of STS when we say that it can hold seven chunks.

Neuropsychological Evidence

Finally, we have considered the phenomenon of retrograde amnesia and its implications for the transfer of memories between STS and LTS. Recall that Chorover and Schiller (1965) demonstrated that in a passive avoidance procedure, ECS delivered within ten seconds of stepping down seemed to partially eradicate the memory of the punishment. This finding seems to indicate the existence of a ten-second retrograde amnesia gradient during which memories in STS are transferred to LTS, where they are consolidated. Unfortunately for proponents of the information-processing view, several other interpretations are consistent with the findings. First, the ECS may disrupt the storage of memories rather than their transfer. For example, memories may be transferred in an extremely brief time, let's say less than a second. ECS given within the ten-second interval following this transfer may simply scramble up the contents of the memory, making it hard to locate the memory at a later time. On the other hand, the ECS may disrupt the retrieval of a memory that has been successfully stored and transferred. The memory itself might be intact, but the ECS might disrupt the operation of certain retrieval processes whose job is to pull the appropriate file at a later time. Although space limitations preclude a complete discussion, another difficulty with the retrograde amnesia gradient stems from the fact that ECS sometimes does not completely prevent the formation of a memory (Miller & Springer, 1972; Quartermain, McEwen, & Azmitia, 1972; Schneider, Tyler, & Jinich, 1974).

Modifying the Information-Processing Theory: A Summary

Let's sum up the literature we've reviewed. First, we've seen that in the intervening twenty-five years since Sperling's initial studies of visual sensory memory, cognitive psychologists have learned a great deal about the icon. They now know that the icon does have some sort of organization; it is truly a cognitive code. The information is not simply stored in a raw, or precategorical, format. The capacity of visual sensory storage is not infinite. Cognitive psychologists have also discovered that information can be evacuated from sensory memory at different rates depending on the material and strategic choices by the person. Moreover, cognitive psychologists have realized that a sensory register or buffer may not be essential to an information-processing theory of memory.

Second, we've seen that researchers have gotten progressively more sophisticated concerning the contents of STS and LTS. Earlier, we believed that the structural aspects of the storage affected it contents. In other words, we would see acoustic errors when we asked people to retrieve material from STS, because STS organized material by sound. We now recognize that stimuli can be coded in a variety of ways at any point in their processing by the memory system. This means that the rigid division of the memory system into two separate locations is probably an overstatement of the situation. If people are left to their own devices, the sequence they go through in coding material apparently has some fairly reliable phases, including an acoustic and a semantic phase. This phenomenon does not necessarily mean that material is being transferred from one location to another—and we know that now.

The tone of the literature we have just reviewed may seem negative and perhaps has given you the impression that the information-processing approach is bad or wrong. This impression isn't accurate. True, most cognitive psychologists would probably be unwilling to endorse the notion of separate memory structures that correspond to either features of our brains or our cognitive systems. But despite its apparent retreat from its initial theoretical position, the information-processing approach validated the notion of memory processes that create and transform memory codes in ways that facilitate or inhibit their retrieval. As interest in debating the existence of single versus multiple storages subsided (Horton & Mills, 1984), cognitive psychologists turned to the notion of the code itself as a way of organizing the events in memory. The next section considers this perspective.

LEVELS OF PROCESSING

Craik and Lockhart (1972) rejected the idea that memory's location determined its characteristics. Rather than think of the to-be-remembered stimulus as a fixed object with distinct properties that were altered as it moved through a rigid system of storages and buffers, Craik and Lockhart maintained that the stimulus could be processed in a variety of ways. For example, an individual could bring sensory processes to bear on a stimulus and extract its physical characteristics from it. On the other hand, the person had control over other cognitive processes capable of extracting and encoding acoustic or semantic features of the stimulus. Craik and Lockhart viewed this as a continuum of progressively deeper cognitive processing—deeper in the sense that more background knowledge is required to carry out a semantic analysis of a word than to carry out an acoustic analysis. Material stored in memory—the memory code—acquired its semantic or acoustic properties not because it was being stored in certain locations but because it had been processed in particular ways that were under the person's control. The nature of the memory code is therefore a record of the cognitive processes that have been performed on it. In summary, each approach to processing produced a cognitive code that could be evaluated along a continuum of depth. Generally, the greater the semantic analysis (the more meaning extracted from the stimulus), the greater the **depth of processing.**

Craik (1979) has stated that the levels of processing model has two central postulates. First, a semantic analysis results in a deeper code, and thus a more meaningful one, than does a nonsemantic analysis. Second, the deeper the code, the more durable the memory. This means that forgetting is simply a function of depth of processing: We forget things that we have not processed semantically. To these central postulates I'll add some corollaries. First, you should be aware that we're not dealing with a multiple storage model. That is, there is no notion of the transfer of memories from one storage location to another. Second, and correspondingly, there are no capacity limitations. Evidence that seems to indicate the need for different storages with differing capacities (such as the phenomenon of memory span) can be interpreted in terms of processing limitations. Another implication is that the durability of a memory is somewhat independent of the time spent processing. A great deal of time spent processing material at a nonsemantic (shallow) level will probably not produce a more durable memory than would a short time processing at the semantic level (Craik & Watkins, 1973; Rundus, 1977).

A study by Parkin (1984) illustrates the basic depth of processing effect. His subjects were given a word, about which they had to make a semantic-orienting or nonsemantic-orienting decision. The orienting decision refers to a particular kind of judgment about the word. For example, a semantic-orienting decison might involve a category or synonym judgment. A nonsemantic task might involve making a judgment about how many vowels the word contained or whether it had been printed completely in capital letters. Following a series of such trials, the subjects were given a suprise free-recall test. The subjects who had been semantically oriented recalled significantly more of the target words than did subjects who were nonsemantically oriented. This result suggests that semantic processing produces a more durable memory code than does nonsemantic processing.

A study by Jacoby, Craik, and Begg (1979) supports this interpretation. Their subjects were given pairs of common nouns (e.g., *horse–goat*) and were told to evaluate the size of the difference between the objects on a 1 (not much difference) to 10 (vast difference) scale. In some cases, the difference between the named objects was relatively small, while in other situations, the difference in size was large. After the subjects had made these evaluations, they were given an unexpected memory test in which they were asked to recall as many of the objects as they could. Jacoby et al. found that an inverse relationship existed between the size of the difference between the objects and the likelihood of their recall. The subjects were more likely to recall the objects when the difference between them was small than when it was large. As Jacoby et al. explained, the task required a semantic analysis of the objects' properties. However, when the objects were approximately the same size, a deeper analysis was required, thus producing a more durable memory code. Notice that the subjects were not aware that a memory test was forthcoming when they made their evaluations of size differences. But the fact that they engaged in a semantic analysis of the words facilitated their retrieval. The implications of this finding are clear: Your chances of retrieving a memory depend on the type of processing you do to remember it, not on how *hard* you try to remember.

These effects were shown in a study by Hyde and Jenkins (1973). The subjects saw a list of twenty-four words, which was presented at the rate of three seconds per word. Each subject had one of two tasks. In one condition, the subjects simply had to check whether each word contained an *a* or a *q*. In the second condition, the subjects had to rate the pleasantness of the word, which presumably required a deeper level of processing than simply looking at the word's physical characteristics. This study had a second variable. Half of the subjects were told that a memory test would be given after the words were presented, and they were encouraged to learn the words. This group was called the intentional learning group. The other half of the subjects were uninformed about the subsequent memory test, and any knowledge they retained about the words was therefore incidental.

Table 4.1 shows the findings of this study. Notice that there is a strong depth of processing effect. When the subjects carried out the semantic anal-

TABLE 4.1

Percentage of Words Recalled as a Function of Orienting Task and Whether Subjects Were Aware of Learning Task

Learning Purpose Conditions	Orienting Task	
	Rate Pleasantness	Check Letters
Incidental	68	39
Intentional	69	43

Source: Hyde and Jenkins, 1973.

ysis, their recall was dramatically enhanced. Notice, too, that intentionality had only a small effect on the proportion of the words recalled. The levels of processing viewpoint is thus able to account for something that vexed multiple storage models. Our memories are not controlled as directly by our intentions (which makes the Atkinson and Shiffrin term *control processes* somewhat misleading) but rather by the type of processing we do.

Maintenance and Elaborative Rehearsal

To help make these processing effects clearer, Craik and Lockhart (1972) distinguished between two kinds of rehearsal. Type I rehearsal, sometimes called **maintenance rehearsal,** refers to the continual repetition of analyses that have already been carried out. It does not lead to stronger or more permanent memories; its principal function is to retain the availability of an item in memory. Maintenance rehearsal tends to emphasize the phonetic aspects of a stimulus (Wickens, 1984). Type II rehearsal, also known as **elaborative rehearsal,** refers to successively deeper processing of the stimulus and does produce more durable memories. It emphasizes the semantic aspects of a stimulus. Both types are under the person's control: They operate on material in working memory, and they compete for cognitive resources with other tasks.

Craik and Watkins (1973) demonstrated that the nature of rehearsal, not how much, is what determines a memory's durability. the subjects in their study were presented with a total of twelve lists, each containing twelve words. The subjects were told to rehearse these words consciously. Moreover, they were told that the last four words of each list were especially important, and these should be remembered at all costs. To emphasize this point, the last four words of each list were printed in block letters. The study had two retrieval conditions. Subjects were asked to recall the list either immediately or following a twenty-second delay. If recall was delayed, the subjects were told that active rehearsal of the list was permitted. When all twelve lists had been presented, Craik and Watkins sprang a surprise: They asked the subjects to recall as many of the entire set of 144 words as they could. The findings are shown in Figure 4.7.

As the top graph shows, the subjects took advantage of the opportunity to rehearse the last four items of the lists during the twenty-second delay. As the lower left graph shows, an expected recency effect occurred when the words were recalled immediately after presentation or after the twenty-second delay. The lower right graph shows the effects of the surprise. Even though the last four items of each list were rehearsed far more frequently than were the other items, and even though an immediate recency effect occurred, there was virtually no long-term effect. In the final recall test, words that had been presented in one of the last four serial postions were not recalled with any greater frequency than were words presented in other serial positions. Even though the last four words had been rehearsed more than the others, this was maintenance rehearsal, which did not necessarily lead to more durable memories (Craik & Watkins, 1973).

The distinction between elaborative and maintenance rehearsal sounds plausible, and the results obtained by Craik and Watkins make sense. How-

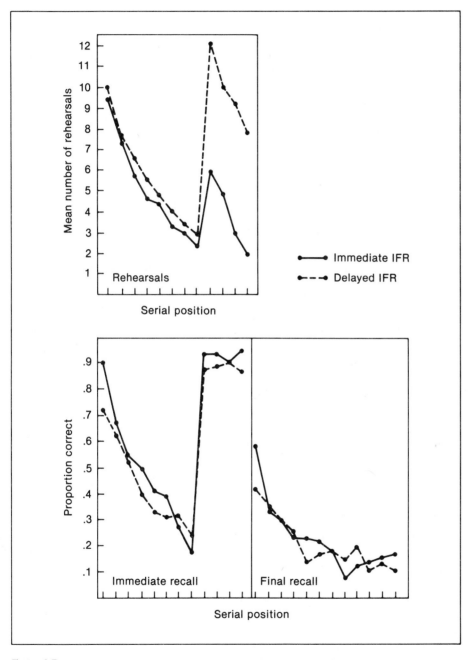

Figure 4.7.

Average number of rehearsals (top graph), proportion correct on the immediate free-recall test (lower left graph), and proportion correct on the final recall test (lower right graph) as a function of serial position. The two lines in the graphs show the results for groups that recalled after no delay or after a twenty-second delay in the immediate free-recall test. (From "The Role of Rehearsal in Short-Term Memory," by F. I. M. Craik and M. J. Watkins. In *Journal of Verbal Learning and Verbal Behavior,* 1973, 12, 599–607. Copyright 1973 by Academic Press, Inc. Reprinted by permission.)

ever, this position implies that *all* semantic processing is equal and thus should create memories of equal durability. But does it?

To answer this question, Craik and Tulving (1975) presented sentences and words tachistoscopically to their subjects. The words and sentences were shown concurrently, and the subject's task was to decide whether the word would meaningfully fit into a blank left in the sentence. The semantic complexity of the sentence was varied, too. The following three examples show the increasing semantic complexity of the sentences:

Simple: She cooked the _____.
Medium: The _____ frightened the children.
Complex: The great bird swooped down and carried off the struggling _____.

After making sixty judgments (twenty of each complexity level), Craik and Tulving sprang the by-now-familiar surprise: A memory test was given. A cued-recall format was used in this test. The subject was given the sentence and asked to recall the word that had been shown concurrently. This time the surprise was on Craik and Tulving: Subjects remembered more of the complex sentence fill-ins than the simple sentence fill-ins. Considering only yes responses, those in which the word could be meaningfully used in the sentence, the subjects recalled about twice as many from the complex sentences as they did for the simple sentences. But how could this have occurred? In all cases, semantic processing had been carried out, which is the deepest level according to the theory. Therefore, there should not have been any differences in retrieval as a function of the sentence's complexity. Why, then, did Craik and Tulving observe these differences? The answer must lie in the nature of the elaborative rehearsal *and* the larger cognitive structure into which the elaborated code was being fed. In other words, the semantic processing done by subjects on the complex sentences seem to have accessed other cognitive codes whose nature was richer or more elaborate than those accessed in the simple sentences.

Other Complications for Levels of Processing

Although the levels of processing account is persuasive, it has been dogged by a few problems. First, the approach has the problem we just touched on—that of contradictory findings. Nelson and McEvoy (1979) reasoned that if words have been processed at the semantic level, then providing a semantic cue should produce better retrieval than a nonsemantic cue. But as it turns out, presenting nonsemantic cues (such as the cue *IME* for the list word *DIME*) is just as effective as presenting semantic cues (such as "an American coin" for *DIME*). Further, Hunt and Elliot (1980) have demonstrated that words with an irregular and distinctive orthography (like *phlegm*) are retained better when they are processed as part of a list containing words with both regular and irregular orthographies than when a list is made up totally of such distinctive words. Even when the task requires a semantic analysis, some nonsemantic information—in this case orthographic distinctiveness—seems to be retained.

A second problem with this approach involves an independent definition of depth of processing. Usually, the level of processing is operationally defined by the nature of the orienting task that the subject is given to do. For example, if the subject is given a task involving checking letters or producing rhymes, this processing is considered nonsemantic. But if the subject is required to produce a synonym, then the subject must be processing the material at the semantic level. As many commentators have pointed out (Nelson, 1979; Postman, Thompkins, & Gray, 1978), this operational definition is barely adequate. It's hard to say exactly what the subject is doing when he is instructed to process the material in a particular way. Furthermore, it's hard to see a way around the problem of defining depth. Linking depth of processing to *time* spent processing is irrelevant by definition, and asking the subjects to self-report their own depth of processing is fraught with difficulties (Seamon & Virostek, 1978).

Yet another problem concerns the relationship between depth of processing and automaticity. As we saw earlier in the book, highly overlearned tasks become progressively more automatic; that is, they can be executed without heavy demands on cognitive processes. What if subjects become highly practiced at making semantic decisions? According to the levels of processing view, the subjects should show good retention of this material because it has been deeply processed. However, according to the automaticity viewpoint, the subjects should show little or no retention of such material. Fiske and Schneider (1984) pitted these viewpoints against one another. their subjects were extensively trained to categorize certain materials automatically. Categorization is an orienting task that is usually thought of as semantic. But Fiske and Schneider found that their subjects, who had done well at the categorization task, showed little recognition memory for the categorized materials. This find is contradictory to the levels of processing approach.

A problem can also be found in the concept of maintenance and elaborative rehearsal. For example, at least in some cases, maintenance rehearsal does improve memory (Glenberg & Adams, 1978). That kind of finding has suggested to many students of memory that a categorical view of rehearsal strategies is probably not correct (Craik, 1979; Jacoby & Craik, 1979). Rehearsal strategies can probably be graded along a continuum of elaboration. This formulation will almost certainly be assessed in future work.

CONCLUDING COMMENTS AND SUGGESTIONS FOR FURTHER READING

This chapter has examined the basic information-processing theory of memory, some of its modifications, and some alternative accounts. Along the way, we've received an introduction to some of the basic techniques and findings of the memory literature. What have we come up with so far?

First, what happened to the information-processing model could be approached as a case study of cognitive science in action. The original theory as erected by Atkinson and Shiffrin was a first-rate summary and interpretation of the huge memory literature that cognitive psychologists and their predecessors had painstakingly worked on. However, other findings accumulated, and the theory has had to undergo fairly extensive modifications over the last twenty or so years. These changes are to be expected and should be taken as a sign of vitality. A fair statement is that most cognitive psychologists would still endorse some version of the information-processing theory of memory, but perhaps not exactly as written by Atkinson and Shiffrin. What has changed? First, the operation of the sensory register has been downplayed in the past five or so years. In light of the recent findings, the evidence suggesting that sensory storage is necessary for further information processing no longer seems as compelling as it once did. If you read this chapter closely, you'll know the reasons for this.

Second, the distinction between STS and LTS has blurred over the last decade or so. Again, our intuitions tell us that we have both a working memory and a permanent memory, and countless reports in the literature indicate that these intuitions are essentially correct. What has changed over the years is the characteristics of these storages. I've used the words *distinct* and *separate* several times in the chapter to describe the border between STS and LTS. However, the recent findings have indicated that the characteristics of the memory code are not determined as it moves rather passively through our information-processing system. Instead, the evidence seems to indicate that people have great flexibility in how material is encoded, stored, and retrieved. Again, if you read this chapter closely, you'll know why cognitive psychologists are not likely to endorse the notion of completely separate short- and long-term storages.

Students who would like to find out more about these matters could probably start with the Atkinson and Shiffrin (1968) article. Two good technical reviews of iconic storage are Coltheart (1975) and Holding (1975). More recent (and more critical) reviews can be found in Kolers (1983) and Haber (1983). I didn't discuss echoic storage in any depth, but Crowder (1976) has written a first-rate review that points out the issues.

The development of the levels of processing viewpoint can be traced in a series by Craik and Lockhart (1972), Craik and Tulving (1975), and Jacoby and Craik (1979). For critical reviews of this approach, consult Nelson (1977), Baddely (1978), and Postman, Thompkins, and Gray (1978). A good review of the memory literature in general can be found in Horton and Mills (1984).

FOCUS ON RESEARCH:
How Much Is An Icon Worth?

The subjective experience of seeing an icon is powerful. Indeed, most people cannot tell precisely the point at which the physical stimulation stops and the icon's existence begins. This inability is what has led many researchers to wonder about the icon's perceptual properties. The same processes that are used to extract information from actual physical stimuli are apparently also used to extract information from the icon. But is this true? Is the information stored in the visual sensory register so raw that it can be accessed by perceptual processes? This question was addressed in a study by Loftus, Johnson, and Shimamura (1985). The reasoning and methodology used in this study were clever. Let's assume that looking at an icon is like looking at the physical stimulus. If the rate of information extraction is equal (and if the same processes are involved, it should be), then the subject who first sees a target stimulus and then sees an icon should have an advantage in recognizing the stimulus over a subject who sees only the target but no icon.

Loftus et al. formulated the problem in this way. Let's assume that a picture is presented to a subject for some base duration of *d* msec. Let's also assume that we let the subject have an icon. Finally, let's suppose that we later test the subject's recognition memory for the picture. We can formalize her performance as being helped by two components: the base duration and the icon, and we can let $p(d, i)$ stand for this performance. Contrast this approach with the stituation in which we let the subject have the actual physical stimulus for a period of *a* msec over and above the base duration. Suppose, however, that we use backward masking to prevent the formation of an icon. On the recognition task, we could symbolize the subject's performance with the term $p(d + a, i)$. That is, this individual has had access to more actual physical

stimulation but no icon, as opposed to the first hypothetical subject who had less physical stimulation but who also had the icon to look at. The question then becomes, How long does the *a* interval have to be before the two performances are even? In other words, what does *a* have to be to make the following equation hold: $p(d, i) = p(d + a, i)$?

The subjects saw 144 complex pictures, which were presented in durations ranging from 62 to 1,050 msec. The mask consisted of a jumble of black and gray lines. In some cases, the mask was presented immediately after the target picture; in other cases, a 300-msec delay occurred. Other subjects were not shown the mask at all. In the recognition test phase, the subjects were shown the pictures in a different order and were asked to indicate whether or not they had seen them before. The results indicated that *a* was about 100 msec. What does this mean? Suppose a picture had been presented for 270 msec. If this picture was not masked, the subjects formed an icon of it. In the recognition test, subjects correctly recognized pictures presented for that duration about 69 percent of the time. Their hit rate was therefore .69. However, if we compare this performance with subjects who were not permitted to form an icon, we find that a duration of 370 msec was required to achieve a hit rate of .69. In other words, having an icon was worth about 100 msec of additional physical stimulation.

KEY TERMS

Storage
Cognitive code
Control processes
Sensory register
Capacity
Decay
Short-term storage
Long-term storage
Rehearsal
Whole-report technique
Partial-report technique
Inter-stimulus interval

Icon
Echo
Backward masking
Interference
Serial position effect
Primacy component
Recency component
Chunking
Retrograde amnesia
Depth of processing
Maintenance rehearsal
Elaborative rehearsal

CHAPTER 5

Encoding, Storing, and Retrieving

OVERVIEW
ENCODING
Context
Effort and Encoding
Encoding Specificity
  When Recall Beats Recognition
Encoding Text
  The Title as an Aid in Encoding
  The Influence of Scripts on Encoding
Encoding Events

STORAGE
The Work of Karl Lashley
H. M. and Anterograde Amnesia
  Studies of Amnesia

What About Storage?

RETRIEVAL
Retrieval from Working Memory
  Some Difficulties with the Serial Exhaustive
    Model
Retrieval from Permanent Memory
The Bartlett Tradition
Retrieval of Meaning and Retrieval of Wording

CONCLUDING COMMENTS AND SUGGESTIONS
FOR FURTHER READING
FOCUS ON APPLICATIONS
KEY TERMS

When I was in college, a friend invited me to what turned out to be a large and incredibly raucous party. The beer was flowing freely, and as the evening wore on, I knew that I was as drunk as I had ever been in my life. I was seriously considering passing out when I met a gorgeous woman. She seemed to like me a lot, and we had a terrific time. By the end of the evening I had her phone number and promised to call the next day. She was sure that I wouldn't remember the number, because we found it impossible to locate any writing materials. I recall asking my buddy, who had driven to the party, to help me remember the number by repeating it in unison with me and by tracing it on the dashboard with our fingers.

When I woke up the next day, I remembered the number without any problem and eagerly dialed it. The number was the right one, but when the woman got on the phone, I discovered she had practically no idea of who I was.

A number of years have passed since that episode, but a least one aspect of it still surprises me: How did I manage to remember the number? From the standpoint of a cognitive psychologist, at least three separable operations were required. First, I had to **encode** the number. *Encoding* refers to a transformation of the stimulus into a format that can be retained by our cognitive systems. In this sense, encoding a stimulus means preparing it to be stored (Klatzky, 1980). This preparation in turn involves organizing the stimuli in some particular way. When we encode stimuli, we prepare them for our memories by organizing them in certain ways. After the number was encoded, it was **stored.** Like most people, you probably assume that when you store something in your memory, a change takes place in your brain; that is, your central nervous system is somehow phys- ically altered by the activities involved in storing things. This belief is valid to a certain extent. We know that the destruction of particular neural tissue produces disturbances in memory. Moreover, the relationship between the tissue de- stroyed and the memory deficit produced is often predictable. But nobody knows exactly what takes place in the brain when you store something in it.

No matter how good your storage system is, you have to be able to **retrieve** the material in your memory to use it. The final section of this chapter considers what happens when material is retrieved from short-term, or working, memory. We'll see that when people are asked to make a comparison involving the contents of their working memories, the ensuing memory scan seems to be exhaustive. That is, people seem to continue comparing the elements of their short-term memories even after they have apparently carried out the comparison that would enable them to answer the experimenter's question. People seem- ingly have a cognitive program called STM scan, which, once started, has to be run off completely. The last section of the chapter also considers retrieval from long-term, or permanent, memory. This matter is an important one, for obvious reasons. For example, what you get out of your education, and this course in particular, depends upon your ability to retrieve information that you have encoded and stored in your permanent memory. What do you suppose you will remember about this course? The specific studies? The entries in the tables and figures? Probably not. Long after the names Atkinson and Shiffrin have become irretrievable, I hope that you will be able to remember that our memories are highly organized and codified. Moreover, these codes are essentially distortions of the original stimulation. They are distortions in that not all of the original stimulation is encoded, and some material is encoded that was added by our cognitive systems; it was not part of the original stimulation. In other words, from this course you'll probably remember not the specific findings but rather the meaning, or the interpretation, of those findings. The myriad studies of retrieval from permanent memory seem to indicate that we usually don't remember words and events verbatim, but instead we remember the meaning underlying those words and actions.

One other point should be noted. This chapter is divided into three principal sections, and some passages imply that the three operations of encoding, storing, and retrieving are truly separable from each other. That implication is not completely true. The three processes almost always influence each other and are not to be understood as separate stages. Separating them here is a teaching convenience to provide some landmarks in what might otherwise be confusing terrain.

ENCODING

Chapter 3 described a debate that has arisen among cognitive psychologists concerning the organization of stimuli. Direct theorists believe that some stimulation—light in particular—is inherently organized as a result of its reflection from objects in the world. These theorists also typically believe that humans have evolved with a sensitivity to this type of organization. In other words, direct theorists believe that people are inherently tuned into the organization of stimuli in the world, and consequently, little cognitive work is required to encode much of the stimulation surrounding us.

Most memory theorists, however, would probably be reluctant to accept this position. Instead, they would argue that most of the stimulation impinging on us is ambiguous in that it can be encoded, or organized, in a variety of ways (Wickens, 1970). For example, consider the word *grounds*. What does it mean? "Meaning" implies "synonym" but *grounds* can be a synonym for *property,* for *reasons,* or for the sediment left in the coffeepot. The point here is that the word *grounds* doesn't have much meaning by itself. Yet, to remember this word, it must be encoded (i.e., organized), and for that purpose, some meaning must be assigned. This section considers some of the variables that influence encoding. We'll see that the nature of the encoding has a powerful influence on the ease or difficulty of retrieval.

Context

The **context** of a stimulus refers to the other stimuli that have been presented concurrently. As you might imagine, surrounding stimuli can exert a strong effect on the kind of encoding that is done. For example, *grounds* would probably be encoded as *property* in the context of *Country Homes* magazine, but an altogether different encoding would be carried out if the term *grounds* appeared in the *Amateur Electrician*. In the encoding of a stimulus, context sets the stage. Context is really another example of top-down, or conceptually driven, processing (Jenkins, 1974). The surrounding stimuli guide the interpretation of the to-be-encoded stimulus.

This issue was explored in a study by Light and Carter-Sobell (1970). Their subjects were presented with sentences in which a specific phrase had been emphasized (e.g., "The boy earned a GOOD GRADE on the test"). The subjects were told that following the entire presentation of sentences, a memory test would be given in which the subjects would be asked to recognize the emphasized noun but not the adjective. The recognition task had several conditions. In some cases, the noun was presented once again with the same adjective (i.e., "good grade"). In other conditions, the noun was presented with a different, but nevertheless meaningful, adjective. For example, the subject might see the phrase "steep grade." In either case, the subject's task was to report whether or not *grade* had been presented in a sentence.

This manipulation produced a dramatic effect. Subjects correctly recognized the nouns 64 percent of the time when they were presented in their original context. But the recognition accuracy was only 27 percent when the nouns were presented in a different context. Light and Carter-Sobell also found that recognition accuracy was superior even when the noun was presented with a never-before-seen adjective, as long as it established the same context as the original adjective. Recognition accuracy was not substantially diminished when the noun was shown in a context such as "bad grade."

This study is important for several reasons. First, it demonstrates that a stimulus such as a word is not a rigidly fixed thing that can be encoded in only one way (Hulse, Deese, & Egeth, 1975). Instead, almost every stimulus apparently has many properties, from which we choose the ones that will be used as a basis for the encoding. Second, the study demonstrates that the context produces its biasing effects, even though the context itself is apparently not encoded. In other words, the subjects were obviously influenced by the semantic content of the adjectives even though they were told that the adjectives weren't important and no apparent attempt was made to encode them.

One implication of this point is that the physical environment, which after all is the ultimate context in which all encoding takes place, influences the subject's representation even though aspects of the environment are not themselves encoded. These effects were explored in two studies. Smith, Glenberg, and Bjork (1978) had their subjects study lists of paired-associate words under different physical conditions. In the first condition, the subjects learned the lists in a large but windowless room, which was located off campus. The experimenter was dressed in a jacket and tie, and the lists were presented visually. In the second condition, the subjects learned the lists in a small room on campus. The experimenter (who was the same person in both conditions) was dressed informally, and the lists were presented on a tape recorder. The day after the subjects learned the lists, a memory test was administered in which the subjects were given one of the paired associates and were asked to recall its mate. Half of the subjects took the memory test in the same room where they learned the list; the other half of the subjects tried to recall the paired associates in the other room. The results were impressive. When the subjects were tested in the same room in which they had learned the list, they recalled 59 percent of the paired associates. When they were tested in the other room, however, their recall dropped to 46 percent.

We should be somewhat cautious in our interpretation of these findings, because further research by Glenberg indicates that while context can be an important factor in retention, its importance can be mitigated by the presence of other retrieval cues. In short, the situation is more complex than originally thought. The study nevertheless makes an important point: If the subjects had been graded on their performance, their drop-off would have meant the difference between an A and a B, which leads to another important and practical point: If teachers are serious about getting optimal performance from their students, then tests and finals should always be given in the same classroom in which the class meetings took place.

A study by Godden and Baddely (1975) makes a similar point. Their subjects were scuba divers who learned a list of forty words in one of two conditions: ashore or under water. The subjects then had to recall the list in one of two environments. Half of the subjects recalled the list in the learning environment (i.e., either ashore or under water). The other half of the subjects recalled the list in the other environment. Recalling words under water might seem difficult to you, but the subjects who learned and recalled the words under water performed about 50 percent better than subjects who learned under water and recalled on dry land.

The effects of context are not limited to the physical environment's influence. The mood of the subject who is learning some material is also part of the context, and the probability of retrieval is enhanced if the subject can reestablish the same mood at recall time (Bower 1981; Bower, Montiero, & Gilligan, 1978). This effect is related to a phenomenon known as **state-dependent learning.** For example, if people learn something while intoxicated with alcohol, they are somewhat more likely to retrieve the material if they are under the influence of alcohol (again) than if they are sober (Overton, 1972; Parker, Birnbaum, & Noble, 1976). Knowing what I do about state-dependent learning, it surprises me that I didn't have to get drunk again to remember the woman's phone number in my earlier example. Eich, Weingartner, Stillman, and Gillin (1975) have reported similar state dependent memory effects from marijuana smoking.

Effort and Encoding

Given the importance of encoding for retrieval, the person who makes a strong effort to organize material for memory apparently should be more likely to retrieve the material than the person whose efforts are haphazard. The issue here is not the nature of the encoding; the general assumption is that some encoding formats are better than others. Rather, the question we seek to answer here is this: Given a similarity in encoding format, is the person who puts more effort into the encoding better off at retrieval time than the person who doesn't try as hard?

Subjects in a study by Walker, Jones, Patrick, and Mar (1983) read a series of paragraphs and were later given a cue to recall the last sentence of each paragraph. Each of these last sentences expressed an *anaphoric* relationship with other material in that paragraph. An anaphoric relationship is one in which a particular word in a sentence refers to a word or phrase that occurred earlier in that sentence or in a previous one. For example, if I say, "I like to watch a short tennis match but not a long one," the word *one* refers back to the phrase "tennis match," and the relationship between these two terms in anaphoric. Determining the anaphoric relationship is sometimes difficult. This is especially true when the terms are somewhat ambiguously related or if the text distance between them is lengthy.

The difficulty in understanding the anaphoric relationship was the independent variable in the Walker et al. study. The researchers found that when the anaphoric relationship was hard to understand, recall of the final sentence was improved significantly. The implication is that the improvement in recall was produced by the greater processing effort required to comprehend the difficult anaphoric relationship. Looked at superficially, this finding might seem just another example of the depth of processing effect described in Chapter 4. But there's a difference. Walker et al. took some pains to make sure that the material was processed in similar ways, to similar depths, by all the subjects. Assuming that these measures were successful, their findings suggest that the effort involved in encoding material has an effect that is independent of the depth to which the material is processed.

Although this finding has been replicated by other researchers (Eysenck & Eysenck, 1979; Tyler, Hertel, McCallum, & Ellis, 1979), some questions have nevertheless arisen. First, if subjects are given a task that seems to require semantic, or deep, processing, and they are told to make as accurate an encoding as possible, then these subjects should put forth more effort and remember more than subjects who do the semantic processing without the instruction to encode accurately. Garrett and Langer (1983) tested this supposition and found that it wasn't true. They found that no consistent relationship existed between the instructions the subjects had been given and the accuracy of their encoding in a recognition task. This effect is similar to the findings of Hyde and Jenkins (1973), which were described in Chapter 4.

Zacks, Hasher, Sanft, and Rose (1983) had their subjects do a variety of tasks that seemed to require differing amounts of **cognitive effort.** In particular, in two of their experiments, subjects had to solve anagrams of varying difficulty. If the effort hypothesis is accurate, solving a difficult anagram should result in a stronger encoding than solving an easy anagram. However, that wasn't the case. None of the variables that were supposed to influence the effort involved in encoding had any effect on the retention of the material. Because Zacks et al. used several different tasks in their study (subjects also had to judge whether a word fit meaningfully into a sentence and had to name pictures under interfering conditions), and still found no effects on retention, the generality of the effort hypothesis has to be questioned.

Encoding Specificity

We've seen that context exerts a biasing influence on the encoding process in that the surrounding stimuli, which are used to organize a particular event in memory, also form a mental framework that helps in retrieval. If the same framework can be reestablished at retrieval time, then the ensuing memory search has a good chance of success. As stated earlier, the distinction between encoding and retrieval is somewhat artificial, and that point seems particularly valid here. The kind of encoding that is carried out almost always influences the ease of retrieval, and advance knowledge of the kind of retrieval that will be called for is almost sure to influence the nature of the encoding that the person will do. Another way of expressing this thought is to say that organization in memory is a process that encompasses both encoding and retrieval (Klatzky, 1980). This point is theoretical, but it has some practical implications as well.

For example, as a student you're subjected to a variety of tests. Some of these are probably essay tests or oral exams, while others consist of true-false or multiple-choice questions. Essay and oral exams measure a student's ability to recall material from memory, and multiple-choice questions tap the student's ability to recognize stored material. The distinction between recall and recognition often boils down to the number of cues or prompts provided. And as you probably well know, knowing which kind of test you have to face has a strong influence on the way you study. That is, knowledge of the retrieval task influences the nature of the encoding you do.

This point was well demonstrated in a study by Leonard and Whitten (1983). Half of their subjects studied a list of words with the expectation that they would be given a recognition task. The recognition task would be arranged like a multiple-choice test; the subjects would be required to pick out the listed word from among several alternatives. The other half of the subjects studied the list with the idea that they would be given a free-recall test. But these subjects were deceived. All the subjects were tested with the multiple-choice procedure. On some of the items, the previously studied word was presented in the context of semantically related words. On other items, the studied word appeared in the context of semantically unrelated words. Leonard and Whitten found that the performance of subjects who had studied for recognition showed a decrement when the words were presented in a semantically related context, but this effect was not observed in the subjects who had studied for recall.

This finding makes sense when you think about the task from the subject's point of view. Suppose one of the words on the list was *evil*. Subjects who expected a multiple-choice test may have prepared themselves to pick out a word that means "bad," "cruel," or "rotten." Subjects who expected a free-recall test had to do something different. They had to establish some sort of context for *evil* that they could reproduce from scratch at retrieval time. Consequently, when the alternatives were semantically related to the studied word, the subjects who had expected a recognition task apparently had trouble deciding what was the target word and what was the context.

The findings of the Leonard and Whitten (1983) study have several implications. First, they imply that subjects use different retrieval strategies depending on the nature of the memory task. Second, the findings suggest that the subjects know ahead of time that they will use different strategies to retrieve the material depending on the task. (A more complete discussion of this phenomenon will await us in Chapter 6.) Third, the findings suggest that the intended retrieval strategy affects the actual encoding.

Retrieval processes in recognition and recall have been thought to differ in the following way. In a recall test of a list of words, the subject generates candidate items and then makes a decision about each candidate's inclusion or exclusion from the studied list (Hulse, Deese, & Egeth, 1975). In a recognition task, this sort of process need not take place, because the candidates have already been provided by the experimenter. According to this view of retrieval, performance on recognition tasks should always be superior to performance on recall tasks. To recall something, a person has to do two things: generate the candidate and then recognize that it belongs on the list. But to recognize something, a person has to do only one thing: recognize it. The generation stage can be bypassed (Wessells, 1982).

When Recall Beats Recognition

A striking series of studies (Flexser & Tulving, 1978; Tulving & Thompson, 1973; Watkins, 1974; Watkins & Tulving, 1975) has demonstrated that under some conditions, recall is superior to recognition and that subjects are sometimes able to recall material that they cannot recognize.

Watkins (1974) gave his subjects lists of paired-associate nonsense words. The pairs consisted of a five-letter A part and a two-letter B part. Although the A and B parts were not meaningful by themselves, the combined seven-letter item was (as in SPANI–SH, or INVOL–VE). After a single presentation of the list, recognition memory was assessed by giving the subjects a list of the B parts they had just seen against the context of other two-letter nonsense syllables. In a later assessment of cued-recall memory, the subjects were prompted with the A part and had to recall the B part of the pair. Recognition accuracy was a dismal 9 percent, while cued-recall accuracy was 67 percent.

This effect was extended in a study by Watkins and Tulving (1975). Their subjects were given a list of paired associates such as HEAD–LIGHT, but they were told that they would be responsible only for the second word of the pair. This word was called the "to-be-remembered" word, or TBR. After the subjects had studied the list, they were given a word and were asked to generate the first four free associates that entered their minds. For example, the subject might be given the word *dark,* and the associates *light, night, shadow,* and *pitch* might be produced. The words given to the subjects were deliberately designed to elicit the TBR. If the subject spontaneously produced the TBR in response to this prompt, the experimenter then showed the subject the four free associates and asked which one was a TBR (subjects had to choose one of them). In this way, the recognition memory of the subjects was assessed. In the final phase of the experiment, the subjects were given the first word of the paired associates and were asked to recall the TBR. When the subjects gave the TBR as one of the free associates, they correctly recognized it 54 percent of the time. However, in the recall phase, accuracy improved to 61 percent. Perhaps even more startling was that 42 percent of the words that the subjects successfully recalled had not been recognized when the subjects had seen them a few minutes earlier.

These findings are usually explained in terms of the principle of **encoding specificity** (Flexser & Tulving, 1978, 1982). According to this principle, a cue will aid retrieval if it provides information that had been processed during the encoding of the to-be-remembered material (Tulving, 1979). When a prompt is presented that wasn't processed at encoding time, then such a prompt doesn't increase the probability of retrieval. In the Watkins and Tulving (1975) study, the prompts that were presented during the recognition task (i.e., the four free associates) weren't present during the initial encoding. However, since the prompt presented in the recall task was processed at encoding, the probability of successful recall was greater than the probability of successful recognition. We're accustomed to thinking of recall as a harder task than recognition. The Watkins and Tulving study, however, demonstrates that what really determines the difficulty of a memory task is the degree to which the encoding and retrieval contexts match.

More recent empirical and theoretical work in this area has dealt with the strength of the encoding specificity principle. To this end, a mathematical formulation predicting the degree of encoding specificity has been developed (Flexser & Tulving, 1978, 1982). But this formulation has been criticized on several grounds. Bower and Humphreys (1979; Humphreys & Bower, 1980) have maintained that the Flexser and Tulving model doesn't take into account the considerable priming effects of the recognition task on recall. The force of this criticism is that performance on the recall task is spuriously (i.e., artificially) high because, on many of the trials, the subjects had actually seen the TBR when they spontaneously generated it in the recognition phase, which gave the subjects an unfair advantage on some of the recall trials.

Other criticisms have focused on the generality of recognition failure among different types of verbal materials. Recognition failure is more likely to take place among some verbal materials than others, and this differential effect has some implications for encoding specificity (Horton & Mills, 1984). For example, Gardiner and Tulving (1980) performed two experiments in which the paired associated were either abstract nouns (Honor–Anxiety) or number-word pairs (47–Wet). When subjects were given "typical" instructions, performance on the cued-recall task was poor, and consequently, recognition failure of recallable items was also low. However, when the subjects were instructed to "elaborate" the pair so that the abstract terms became somehow related, then cued-recall improved and the number of recognition failures also increased.

This finding tells us that when the paired-associate terms are abstract or unrelated to one another, they don't provide much context for one another, and the effects of encoding specificity will be correspondingly weaker. However, when the paired-associate terms are strongly related, either inherently or by the subject's efforts, then the effects of encoding specificity become stronger. That is, if the encoding context can be reinstated at retrieval time, the probability of recalling the TBR is high.

Encoding Text

We've discussed the effects of encoding specificity as they apply to single words. These effects are persuasive but also artificial, because in real life we are seldom called upon to remember lists of paired associates. However, we are frequently called upon to retrieve as much as we can from passages of text that we have studied. Cognitive psychologists have tried to determine what encoding effects might be present in such situations.

Thorndyke (1977) had his subjects read different versions of stories such as the one shown in Table 5.1. This tale was manipulated in several ways. In one version of the story, the main point (getting the cow into the barn) was shifted to the paragraph's last sentence. Other versions had the main point eliminated altogether. In still other versions, the sentences were randomly strung together or had the cause-and-effect references deleted. Thorndyke found that these variations produced decrements in the subjects' recall of the passage. This finding is surprising because in some of the variations, material had been deleted that should have lightened the subjects' load. This finding suggests that subjects had some preexisting idea about how the story should go, which they used as a basis for encoding. The variations used in the Thorndyke study supply us with some hint about the contents of this preexisting idea. Prose passages are seemingly organized on the basis of the cause-and-effect relations among the actors. Chronological order is also an important variable. If a story conforms to certain conventions regarding the motivations of characters and chronological order, it fits into the subject's mental framework better and is consequently well encoded.

Thorndyke explored this idea in a second experiment. The subjects learned two stories. For half of the subjects, the second story repeated the structure of the first but featured new characters. For the other half of the subjects, the second story involved the same characters in a story with a different structure. If the subjects organized the stories on the basis of

TABLE 5.1

A Story Used in the Thorndyke Study

A farmer had a cow that he wanted to go into his barn. He tried to pull the cow, but it would not move. So the farmer asked his dog to bark and scare the cow into the barn. The dog refused to bark unless it had some food. So the farmer went to his house to get some food. He gave it to the dog. It barked and frightened the cow, which ran into the barn.

Source: Thorndyke, 1977. Reprinted by permission of the publisher.

certain characters, then we would expect recall of the second story to be better when the same characters reappeared. But if the subjects encoded the story on other bases, then this effect would not be observed.

Thorndyke found that the repetition of character names did not facilitate recall. In fact, recall of the second story was worse when the same characters were used in a story with a different structure than when the structure was repeated with different characters. The name for this sort of story structure is a **script** (Schank & Abelson, 1977). This notion is examined in more depth in Chapter 13. Basically, a script is a general, content-free, mental framework that can be used to organize particular sequences of common and familiar actions. The implication of the Thorndyke study is that adults can call up a fairly large number of general scripts into which incoming story information is fed.

The Title as an Aid in Encoding

Dooling and Lachman (1971) have investigated the effects of titles on text encoding and retrieval. Their subjects read the passage shown in Table 5.2.

How much of this passage do you think you would remember? What do you think would be a good title for this passage? How about "Columbus Discovers America"? If you review the passage, you can probably see why the subjects who were primed with the title recalled more than subjects who were not so informed. If you're an American, you probably know a lot about Columbus, and in this study, knowledge of Columbus was used to encode the details of the passage. When you hear about Columbus, you expect three ships to be mentioned, so the reference to the "three sturdy sisters," although metaphorical, fits in, as does the description of the stormy ocean ("turbulent peaks and valleys").

Other evidence has suggested the title must be presented before the text if it is to have a positive effect on encoding and retrieval. Bransford and Johnson (1972) presented their subjects with an ambiguous passage. In one case, the passage was preceded by the presentation of a cartoon that clarified the text. In other cases, the cartoon was withheld until after the subjects had completed their reading. On a subsequent recall test, subjects who had seen the cartoon first outperformed subjects who hadn't. In fact, no difference in recall was noted between subjects who had seen the cartoon

TABLE 5.2

The Passage Used in the Dooling and Lachman Study

With hocked gems financing him, our hero bravely defied all scornful laughter that tried to prevent his scheme. "Your eyes deceive," he had said. "An egg, not a table, correctly typifies this unexplored planet." Now three sturdy sisters sought proof. Forging along, sometimes through calm vastness, yet more often over turbulent peaks and valleys, days became weeks as many doubters spread fearful rumors about the edge. At last from nowhere welcome winged creatures appeared, signifying momentous success.

Source: Dooling and Lachman, 1971. Copyright 1971 by the American Psychological Association. Adapted by permission of the publisher.

after their reading and subjects who hadn't seen the clarifying cartoon at all (Bransford & Johnson, 1972).

The effects of encoding upon retrieval have been investigated by Sulin and Dooling (1974). Their subjects read the passage shown in Table 5.3. Another group of subjects read the same passage, except that the name Helen Keller was substituted for Carol Harris. One week later, all subjects took a memory test in which they were given a series of sentences and were asked to determine whether each sentence had been part of the passage. One of the critical sentences was "She was deaf, dumb, and blind." This sentence is not in the passage, and only 5 percent of the "Carol Harris" subjects claimed that it was. But a full 50 percent of the "Helen Keller" subjects falsely remembered reading the sentence.

This effect is an interesting one. We've seen that having some prior knowledge of the material seems to help in encoding and retrieval, but now we see that prior knowledge can have some unfortunate side effects on memory. In this case, the "Helen Keller" subjects had gotten something into their memories that didn't appear in the passage. One empirical question in this literature concerns the time at which this error was made: Did the subjects falsely encode the passage, or was the error committed at retrieval time? The distinction made here is between material that had been stored in the subjects' memories, which was perhaps retrievable, and inferences that the subjects made about the material when a scan of their memories had drawn a blank.

Several studies (Anderson & Pichert, 1978; Dooling & Christiaansen, 1977; Spiro, 1977) suggest that the latter interpretation is more correct. If the subjects are making inferences at retrieval time, we would expect that the likelihood of such inferences would increase with longer delays between encoding and retrieval. Since the actual encoding is likely to deteriorate with time, consequently, the subjects would be more likely to use their logic, or inference-making abilities, to determine whether the sentence had been part of the passage. This interpretation seems to be accurate. Dooling and Christiaansen (1977) and Spiro (1977) have found that **inferential intrusion errors** are more likely with increased delays between encoding and retrieval.

Dooling and Christiaansen also used an alternative procedure to substantiate this conclusion. Their subjects read the Carol Harris passage and reappeared one week later to take the memory test. At that point, the

TABLE 5.3

Carol Harris's Need for Professional Help

Carol Harris was a problem child from birth. She was wild, stubborn, and violent. By the time Carol turned eight, she was still unmanageable. Her parents were very concerned about her mental health. There was no good institution for her problem in her state. Her parents finally decided to take some action. They hired a private teacher for Carol.

Source: Sulin and Dooling, 1974. Copyright 1974 by the American Psychological Association. Adapted by permission of the publisher.

subjects were informed that Carol Harris was really Helen Keller. On the subsequent test, the subjects made inferential errors (such as falsely recognizing sentences that pertained to Helen Keller) at a rate comparable to the subjects who had read about Helen Keller in the first place. The "name switch" subjects had never seen any reference to Helen Keller until test time, and they would not have been likely to make such faulty encodings about Carol Harris.

The Influence of Scripts on Encoding

Other encoding effects were studied by Owens, Bower, and Black (1979). Their control subjects read a short story about a student's fairly routine day. The story consisted of five episodes, one of which follows:

Nancy arrived at the cocktail party. She looked around the room to see who was there. She went to talk with her professor. She felt she had to talk to him but was a little nervous about just what to say. A group of people started to play charades. Nancy went over and had some refreshments. The hors d'oeuvres were good but she wasn't interested in talking to the rest of the people at the party. After a while she decided she'd had enough and left the party. (Owens, Bower, & Black, 1979)

The other four episodes were also unremarkable. The experimental subjects read the same five episodes, but before they did so, they also read the following preamble:

Nancy woke up feeling sick again and she wondered if she really were pregnant. How would she tell the professor she had been seeing? And the money was another problem. (Owens, Bower, & Black, 1979)

We might expect that subjects who were primed with this knowledge of Nancy's problem might interpret her actions at the party and in other situations differently from those subjects who had not seen the preamble. Also, to the extent that the episodes described in the story matched scripts stored in the subjects' long-term memories, then we would also expect to see inferential intrusion errors. All subjects were given a free-recall test twenty-four hours after they had read the story. The subjects were encouraged to remember the sentences as precisely as they could. Table 5.4 shows the findings of the study.

TABLE 5.4

Things Remembered from the "Nancy" Story

Condition	Propositions Recalled from Text	Intrusions	Total
Problem	29.24	15.20	44.44
Control	20.24	3.76	24.00

Source: Owens, Bower, and Black, 1979. Reprinted by permission of the publisher.

Subjects who had been provided with knowledge of Nancy's problem were able to use this fact as an organizational device to aid encoding and retrieval. And it worked: Subjects in the problem condition recalled almost 50 percent more from the story than did the control subjects. However, the side effects were there as well. Subjects in the problem condition made almost five times as many intrusion errors than control subjects did. The nature of the intrusion errors is also interesting. Owens et al. characterized these errors as being of two types. *Script-based errors* resulted from subjects' recall of events that might typically occur in one of the episodes, even though that particular event was not mentioned. For example, in one episode Nancy makes some coffee for herself, and subjects typically recalled that she "turned on the stove to boil the water." Subjects also committed what were called *interpersonal theme errors,* which resulted from knowledge of Nancy's condition. For example, subjects sometimes recalled that Nancy didn't talk to the professor because she "was feeling miserable" or "felt depressed." The intrusion errors of control subjects were almost completely script-based. The intrusion errors of problem subjects were almost equally divided between the two categories.

Encoding Events

Loftus and her colleagues have carried out an important series of studies (1975, 1977, 1979b, 1979c; Loftus & Palmer, 1974) showing what sometimes happens when subjects encode and retrieve events they have witnessed. The typical paradigm for these studies consists of showing the subjects a film of some event (often a car accident), followed by a series of questions designed to influence the subject's encoding. In the final phase of the study, the subjects are asked to retrieve the event.

This procedure was used by Loftus and Palmer (1974). After seeing the film, the subjects were asked to fill out a questionnaire in which they made several judgments about what they had seen. One of the questions asked "How fast were the cars going when they   each other?" Subjects saw one of five verbs in the blank space: smashed, collided, bumped, hit, or contacted. Loftus and Palmer found that the verb definitely influenced the subject's judgment. Subjects who read the verb *smashed* estimated that the cars were traveling at 40.8 MPH. But subjects who read the less violent verb *contacted* estimated that the cars were only doing 31.8 MPH—a big difference! It's important to realize that Loftus and Palmer maintained that this sort of leading question truly changed the nature of the subjects' memories. That is, no matter how the subjects may have encoded the event when it was visible, after the researchers had biased the subjects with a particular verb, that original encoding was no longer available; it had been written over by the new encoding.

If the new encoding were really successful in **overwriting** the original encoding, then we would expect that the subjects would also "know" things about the event that were consistent with this new encoding. That is, we might expect the subjects to make intrusion errors similar to the ones observed by Owens et al. (1979).

In a second experiment, Loftus and Palmer (1974) tested this idea. Subjects saw a four-second film in which two cars collided. The subjects were then administered a questionnaire containing the critical item about the cars' velocities. One group read the verb *smashed,* a second group, *hit,* and for the third group, this item was deleted. All the subjects returned to the lab one week later to answer additional questions about the film. One of these additional questions was critical: "Did you see any broken glass in the film?" Although no broken glass had appeared in the film, 32 percent of the subject who had read the verb *smashed* said that they remembered seeing broken glass. Only 14 percent of the subjects who had read the verb *hit* responded that way, as did 12 percent of the subjects who had not made an estimate of the car's speed.

This demonstration that the subjects' memories have been overwritten seems convincing. Once subjects read the verb *smashed,* their memories were altered, and consequently at retrieval time, they were "accurately" retrieving something they believe to be true: If the cars were traveling at 40 MPH, then some broken glass would likely be visible.

Although the Loftus and Palmer paradigm seems convincing, critics argued that the subjects were not misled by the questions and that their memories were not altered. Instead, they argued, the subjects had simply figured out what the experimenters wanted them to say and were responding to these **demand characteristics** (Orne, 1962).

Loftus, Miller, and Burns (1978) developed what they hoped was a telling rebuttal to these criticisms. Their subjects viewed a sequence of thirty slides, which showed a red Datsun hitting a pedestrian after turning a corner. Half of the subjects saw a slide that showed the Datsun stopping at a stop sign before turning the corner. The other half of the subjects saw a slide that showed the Datsun stopping at a yield sign before proceeding. After viewing the slide set, the subjects were given a questionnaire. Half of the subjects saw a question that asked "Did another car pass the red Datsun while it was stopped at the stop sign?" For the other half of the subjects, the question was worded so that it mentioned a yield sign. These conditions were completely crossed. That is, half of the subjects who had seen the stop sign got a consistent question (it also mentioned the stop sign). The other half of the subjects who had seen the stop sign got an inconsistent question— one that mentioned a yield sign. Subjects who had seen the yield sign also got consistent and inconsistent questions.

Twenty minutes after the subjects saw the slide set, they were given a memory test. In this test, the subjects were shown a series of slides in pairs and were asked to pick out which slide of the pair had been presented earlier. All the pairs were of the same format. In each case, one slide had been presented earlier, and the other slide was designed to closely resemble an actual slide. The critical pair showed the red Datsun at a stop sign and at a yield sign.

Before I reveal the findings, let's think about the implications of this procedure. If the subjects are truly compliant, and they have an accurate memory of what was presented, then they should be able to pick out the slide that they had seen, because that's what they have been asked to do. If, however, the inconsistent question has produced a distortion in the subjects' memories, then no matter how compliant they are, the subjects will show some decrement in performance when asked to pick out the previously seen slide. This procedure seems to rule out whatever effects the demand characteristics may have had.

Now the results. When the subjects were asked a question that was consistent with what they had seen, they picked out the correct slide 75 percent of the time. However, when the subjects were given a question that was inconsistent with what they had seen, their performance was indeed lowered to 41 percent accuracy. This demonstration seems to effectively show that the earlier inconsistent question overwrote the encoding that was made when the subjects saw the slide. One further finding seems to anchor this interpretation. In a follow-up experiment, Loftus et al. asked the subjects point-blank if they had been given any misleading information in the questionnaire. They found that, of the subjects who had been misled—that is, given an inconsistent question—only 12 percent recognized that the misleading had been done. The overwhelming majority of the subjects did not detect the inconsistent question, which strongly suggests that their memories of the slide had been irretrievably altered.

STORAGE

A common tendency is to think of our memories as vast warehouses into which things have been put away. We recognize that this is a metaphor, but nevertheless it's a metaphor with a point. Most of us believe that our brains are able to make some kind of neurological copy of our experiences, and this copy is retained in some magical way. To complete the metaphor, many of us also believe that when we remember something, we direct some other part of our brain to look for the neurological copy and somehow reinstate it, which then reproduces the cognitive events, that is, the experiences that have been encoded.

Brain writing (Dennett, 1981) is a phrase that describes the idea that the brain makes and stores a physical trace of our experiences. Researchers who have looked for this physical trace (Babich, Jacobson, Bubash, & Jacobson, 1965; McConnell, 1962; Tate, Galvan, & Ungar, 1976; Ungar, Desiderio, & Parr, 1972) are apt to make a comparison between brain storage and computer storage.

For example, when I created this text on my computer monitor, my monitor "experienced" this text for the first time. Later, when I stored this writing on a diskette, a copy of the writing in some coded form was retained. Later, when I came back to resume writing, I retrieved this file, which means my computer got the code from the diskette, allowing my monitor to "reexperience' it.

The prior example implies that the memory code created by our experiences is somehow independent of the brain that has produced the code.

This is also true of my microcomputer. For example, I can store something on a diskette and send it to my brother, who has the same brand of computer that I do, and then his monitor can "reexperience" something that perhaps it's never projected before. But does the truth of disk writing really imply the truth of brain writing?

I'm not trying to imply that some relationship doesn't exist between the memory and the brain. The next section of the book describes some of the classic findings in this area. But for those of you who may be waiting for a pill in which all of the information in, say, this book is already encoded for you, the news from the front is disappointing.

The Work of Karl Lashley

Karl Lashley was born in 1890 and earned his Ph.D. in zoology from Johns Hopkins University in 1914. He had studied there with John B. Watson, whose research on learning had developed from the ideas of Ivan Pavlov. Pavlov had produced a fairly specific notion of the neurological changes underpinning learning. Specifically, Pavlov believed learning was accompanied by certain structural changes in the brain. Parts of the brain that had not communicated neurally prior to learning were associated during learning, and this association took the form of a physical, neural connection. Once formed, the association could not be uncoupled; however, the association did depend upon the continued integrity of the neural connection. If the connection were destroyed, whatever had been learned would be lost.

Lashley (1929, 1950) set out to prove this theory. His method was simplicity itself. A group of rats were trained to run one of a set of mazes varying in difficulty from easy to hard. After the rats were proficient at running the mazes, Lashley systematically cut the cortex of each rat; the cuts were made in a different location in each rat's brain. Lashley's thinking was that some of the cuts should interrupt the critical connections in the rats' brains, and the rats should show memory deficits on the mazes. But Lashley's expectation proved inaccurate. No matter where the cut was made, the rats still performed up to par, regardless of the maze's difficulty. Although Lashley may have missed the critical connection in every animal, this possibility is remote. Far more likely is Lashley's conclusion, namely that learning and memory don't seem to involve specific connections in the brain.

A second experiment underscored this point. Lashley once again trained his rats to run complicated mazes. Some of the rats had had various amounts of their cerebral cortexes removed prior to the training. The remainder of rats' brains were intact. The learning rate of the brain-damaged rats was indeed slower than that of the intact rats. Moreover, the extent of the performance decrement was more or less proportional to the amount of the brain tissue that had been removed. Again, the location from which the tissue had been taken was not relevant. When lesions were made in the brains of the intact rats, Lashley observed that their performance was similar to that of the original brain-damaged group.

From these and other studies, Lashley formulated two principles of brain organization:

1. **Mass action.** "The efficiency of performance of an entire complex function may be reduced in proportion to the extent of brain injury" (Lashley, 1929). *Mass action* means that the brain works en masse. If a small amount of brain tissue is removed, the brain can cope; but if a lot is removed, deficits will occur.
2. **Equipotentiality.** *Equipotentiality* means that all parts of the brain are created equal, at least as far as learning and memory are concerned. No one part of the brain seems to be more important than another for memory storage.

We can summarize Lashley's findings by saying that, regarding memory per se, the amount of brain tissue removed is far more important than the location of its removal. That is, if a small amount of tissue is removed, the location doesn't matter, and no apparent memory loss will probably result. If a large amount of tissue is removed, the location still doesn't matter, and memory loss will probably result.

Do not assume, however, that the location of damage in the brain is unimportant. A relatively small amount of damage to language or to vision centers can produce an irretrievable disability. In other words, the principle of equipotentiality may be true for humans up to a certain point. However, some areas of specialization within the human brain do exist. If these areas are destroyed in an adult, complete recovery is almost impossible.

H. M. and Anterograde Amnesia

Lashley approached the problem of memory storage from an experimental perspective. Although his efforts failed to find any trace of memories in specific cerebral locations, other experimental research (Mair, Warrington, & Weiskrantz, 1979; Mishkin, 1978) has determined that various subcerebral structures—in particular, the *hippocampus* and the amygdala—have been associated with memory loss in monkeys.

This finding substantiates a relationship that has long been suspected by clinical neuropsychologists who have observed a coincidence of memory deficits and hippocampal trauma in humans. One case is particularly well known (Milner, 1959; Penfield & Milner, 1958; Scoville & Milner, 1957). H. M. (referred to in this way to protect his privacy) is a man who developed an incapacitating form of epilepsy, which was intractable to all forms of treatment, including the anti-epileptic drugs then in use. His physicians decided that psychosurgery might be beneficial, and several brain structures, including his hippocampus, were removed. The operation was successful in some ways. The severity of the disorder was lessened, and H. M. showed no apparent disturbances of thought or mood. However, a severe impairment did result. H. M. showed an inability to remember anything that had happened since his hippocampus was removed. This form of memory loss is known as **anterograde amnesia** and can be distinguished from retrograde amnesia, which was discussed in Chapter 4. As it turned out, H. M. showed little or no memory loss for events that had taken place prior to the operation, nor was his working memory particularly impaired (Milner, 1959). However, if H. M. was distracted during any short-term memory task, his performance was poor. H. M. is institutionalized for good reason: His life has almost no continuity of events. As H. M. describes it, life seems as if he were constantly awakening from a dream.

Studies of Amnesia

H. M.'s deficits can be explained in a variety of ways. Each of the three memory operations we're considering (encoding, storing, and retrieving) has been implicated as the source of the amnesic's problem. One plausible argument is that H. M. and similar amnesics show memory deficits because they are no longer able to encode relevant information from stimuli (Butters & Cermak, 1975; Wilson et al., 1983).

Cermak and Butters (1972) gave their amnesic subjects a retrieval cue consisting of a category name (e.g., animals or fruits) for a mixed category list of items that had been learned shortly before. Although such a cue is known to aid retrieval among normal people, the amnesics were not helped by it. Also, amnesics are more likely than normal people to fall victim to a homophonic distractor (i.e., an alternative that sounds like or rhymes with the target) on a recognition memory task. In addition, other studies have shown that their amnesic patients were almost completely unable to engage in elaborative, Type II rehearsal, thus making semantic encoding extremely difficult. Apparently, amnesics find this type of rehearsal difficult in part because they have a hard time paying attention to the stimuli.

Research on animals (Hendrickson, Kimble, & Kimble, 1967) has shown that hippocampal lesions usually produce attentional deficits. These findings are typically interpreted as indicating a fairly shallow, acoustic encoding of verbal materials. In addition to these sorts of failures at effortful encoding, other findings (Huppert & Piercy, 1978) have indicated that amnesics show deficits at encoding events that normals seem to do automatically (Hasher & Zacks, 1979). Nevertheless, these findings can be explained in other ways (McDowall, 1979), and some findings have been contrary to the expectations of the encoding deficit position (Meudell & Mayes, 1980).

Retrieval processes have also been postulated as the source of the amnesic's difficulties. The leading proponents of this view are Warrington and Weiskrantz (1973; Weiskrantz & Warrington, 1975). They have argued that the amnesic's problems begin at retrieval time, when prior learning intrudes upon more recently encoded material. All of us have this problem from time to time, but this sort of response competition is unrelenting for the amnesic. This argument is based upon three principal findings, First, although the performance of amnesics is inferior to that of normals on free-recall or recognition tasks of verbal materials, their performance when given partial information (such as a word's initial letter) is not much worse than that of normals (Warrington & Weiskrantz, 1970). This finding is consistent with the response competition hypothesis. If the amnesics are given a little help sorting out the correct answer from the competing stimuli, then their performance is close to normal, indicating that they had successfully encoded the material but just couldn't get it back again.

Second, amnesics make more intrusion errors than do normals on a wide variety of memory tasks (Warrington and Weiskrantz, 1978). Specifically, Meudell, Butters, and Montgomery (1978) have demonstrated that amnesics made four times more prior list intrusions than did controls. In their study, 66 percent of all the amnesics' errors were prior list intrusions, whereas only 43 percent of the controls' errors were of this type. This demonstration of response competition is probably the clearest. The amnesics seem to be unable to sort out the current list from previous lists.

Third, amnesics are sometimes no worse than normals on tasks that require memory but which are also relatively uninfluenced by prior learning. For example, Brooks and Baddeley (1976) have demonstrated that amnesics are fairly good at learning and retaining knowledge of mazes and jigsaw puzzles.

As we saw for the encoding hypothesis, however, counterarguments can be mustered against the response competition theory. First, some of the spatial learning effects have been difficult to replicate. For example, H. M. can do the same jigsaw puzzle over and over again without any recognition that he has done it before (and without any improvement in performance). There is also a theoretical problem in sorting out the effects of response competition from other explanations. For example, it may be the case that contextual information decays more rapidly for amnesics than it does for normals. If this hypothesis is true, then the greater occurrence of intrusions among the amnesics may simply be a result of their "weaker" storage capabilities rather than a result of any specific retrieval deficits (Meudell & Mayes, 1982).

Given some of the difficulties we've encountered in explaining the amnesic's deficits on the basis of encoding or retrieval operations, it's worth considering the hypothesis that anterograde amnesia might be explainable as a storage deficit. That is, H. M.'s failures may be the result of an inability to keep information in permanent storage.

Mayes, Boddy, and Meudell (1980) have conducted an interesting study that bears on this question. They showed amnesics and normals lists of words under both intentional and incidental learning conditions. They recorded the electroencephalogram (EEG)[1] responses of the subjects during the three-second interval following the offset of the word list. Both amnesics and normals showed greater EEG power in the first second after offset than in the following two-second period, although the EEG strength of the amnesics was lower than that of the normals. During the next two seconds, EEG strength of the two groups was approximately equal. This result suggests that amnesics have an EEG power deficit for a brief period following the presentation of a stimulus. These EEG abnormalities suggest that am-

---

1. An electroencephalograph is a machine that measures and records slight electrical changes in the brain that occur as the result of neuronal activity.

nesics may suffer from a consolidation problem that is more or less independent of their encoding or retrieval strategies.

This evidence is no more convincing than the findings favoring encoding or retrieval deficits. But the point is that even though known memory effects result from hippocampal and other types of brain trauma, cognitivists and neuropsychologists have been thwarted for the most part in trying to pin down the exact nature of this relationship. Although no particularly strong reason exists for believing that amnesics have severe consolidation or storage problems, explanations based on encoding or retrieval deficits have also been muddied.

What About Storage?

Most memory losses seem to be the result of encoding failures or inadequate retrieval strategies, although some recovery failures are apparently the result of a "trace loss" (Begg, 1979). In some ways, this finding represents an embarrassment to cognitivists and neuropsychologists who have been at a loss to determine how the brain records a physical trace of experience. Beyond that, cognitivists have been unable to agree that such brain writing is even necessitated by their theories of memory. This ambiguity at both the empirical and conceptual levels partially explains why storage is the unwanted stepchild of the memory literature (as opposed to encoding and retrieval, which are hot topics).

Although cognitivists who have looked for storage locations in the brain largely come away empty-handed, a pervasive feeling nevertheless persists that some pure storage theory must be right. Loftus and Loftus (1980) surveyed the memory beliefs of 169 people, 75 of whom had advanced training in psychology. The others were occupied in a wide variety of other fields. They asked their respondents to indicate which of the following two statements came closer to expressing their opinion about memory:

1. Everything we learn is permanently stored in the mind, although sometimes particular details are not accessible. With hypnosis, or other special techniques, these inaccessible details could eventually be recovered.
2. Some details that we learn may be permanently lost from memory. Such details would never be able to be recovered by hypnosis, or any other special technique, because these details are simply no longer there. (Loftus & Loftus, 1980)

Eighty-four percent of the psychologists agreed with the first statement, 14 percent agreed with the second statement, and 2 percent were noncommittal. Of the nonpsychologists, 69 percent agreed with the first statement, 23 percent were in accord with the second statement, and 23 percent were undecided. A substantial majority of the people surveyed agreed with the proposition that memories last forever. The strange aspect of this finding is that psychologists were somewhat more likely than nonpsychologists to hold this belief. This aspect is strange because, presumably, psychologists should be more aware than nonpsychologists that such beliefs rest upon extremely shaky empirical ground.

RETRIEVAL

All the encoding and storage in the world are useless unless we are able to retrieve what is stored. Retrieval, in other words, is what makes a memory practical, and in a sense, the only time we use our memories is when we retrieve a stimulus that is no longer present. If we give subjects a list of words and ask them to retrieve the list after a rehearsal period, their performance will be different from that shown when we ask them to retrieve the same list twenty-four hours later. For this reason, this part of the chapter is divided into two sections. The first discusses retrieval from short-term, or working, memory. The second describes retrieval from long-term, or permanent, memory.

Retrieval from Working Memory

Sternberg (1966) has developed a procedure that illuminates the nature of retrieval from working memory. His subjects were given a series of digits referred to as the memory set. The memory set varied in size from one to six digits. Two seconds after the presentation of the memory set, the subjects were shown a single digit called the probe. The subjects were asked to indicate by pressing buttons whether or not the probe had been presented in the memory set. On some trials, referred to as positive trials, the probe had been presented. Negative trials were those in which the probe had not been presented. The correctness of the subjects' responses, however, was not the issue. The subjects were almost always accurate, because the memory set never overloaded either the capacity or the duration of working memory. Rather, the main dependent variable was the reaction time of the subjects. Figure 5.1 shows the findings of this study. The size of the memory set strongly influenced the latency of the subjects' responses, but the nature of the trial—positive or negative—did not. With each additional digit added to the memory set, subjects required more time to respond, and the increase was constant for each digit added—about 38 msec per digit.

Sternberg (1969, 1975) theorized that retrieval from working memory requires four operations. First, the probe must be encoded. Next, the probe must be compared with each of the items residing in working memory. After that, a decision must be made concerning a match between the probe and the digits in the memory set. Finally, an overt response must be commanded and enacted. Since the probe was presented in the same way in every trial, its contribution to the subjects' latency was effectively constant. Similarly, since the probe was always a single digit, the time required to encode it was also probably constant. Apparently, the only variables that should affect the subjects' latency are the nature of the trial (positive or negative) and the size of the memory set. Moreover, the effects of these variables should be limited to the second and third of the four operations.

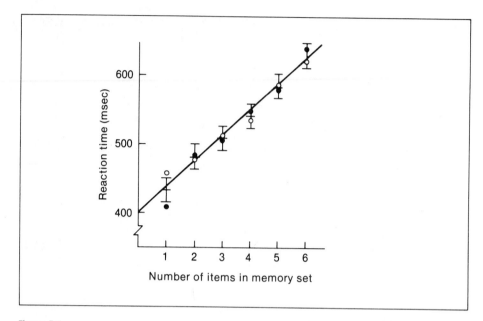

Figure 5.1.

Mean reaction time for memory sets of various sizes: *filled circles,* positive responses; *open circles,* negative responses. (Adapted from "High-Speed Scanning in Human Memory," by S. Sternberg. *Science, 153,* 5 August 1966, pp. 652–654. Copyright 1966 by the American Association for the Advancement of Science.)

If we apply this analysis to Sternberg's study, we can see that it sheds some light on the nature of the scanning that his subjects were apparently carrying out. The subjects could do Sternberg's task in several possible ways. Figure 5.2 is a graphic depiction of these possibilities.

1. **Parallel processing.** The subjects could compare the probe to more than one digit of the memory set simultaneously. Technically, the subjects could make the comparison between the probe and *all* the items in the memory set simultaneously. This type of comparison is called *parallel processing.* If the subjects were truly doing the task this way, then variations in the size of the memory set would have no effect on reaction times. That is, the subjects could compare the probe with six items as quickly as with one. As Figure 5.2 indicates, this line of reasoning is contradicted by the evidence.

2. **Serial self-terminating search.** In this case, the subjects compare the probe to the items in the memory set on a one-at-a-time (serial) basis. As soon as the probe is encountered, the subjects stop the comparison and answer yes, which is why this search is called *self-terminating.* If the trial is a negative one, then the subjects have to consider each of the items in the memory set before answering no. If this were the way the subjects carried out the task, then we would expect that the size of the memory set should produce differential effects on reaction

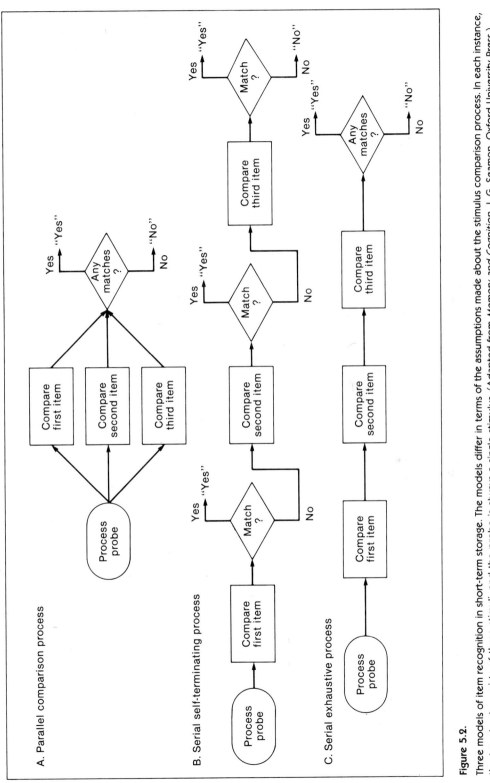

Figure 5.2.

Three models of item recognition in short-term storage. The models differ in terms of the assumptions made about the stimulus comparison process. In each instance, the target set consists of three stimuli, and the probe is always a single stimulus. (Adapted from *Memory and Cognition*, J. G. Seamon, Oxford University Press.)

time. However, the nature of these effects should differ in positive and negative trials. To see this, consider a memory set of four digits—8, 5, 2, 6—and imagine that the subjects were given the probe 6, making this a positive trial. Under these circumstances, since the subjects would have to make all the comparisons, we would expect the reaction time to be about 525 msec—the same as it would be if the probe weren't in the memory set. But now suppose that the probe were 5. In this case, we would expect the subjects to arrive at the yes conclusion sooner than if the trial were a negative one. In other words, if the search is self-terminating, the ordinal position of the probe in the memory set should have some influence on the reaction time of positive trials. How would this difference be reflected in the findings? The slope of the positive trial function should be less steep than the slope of the negative trial function. However, looking again at Figure 5.2, we see that the slopes of both functions were similiar.

3. **Serial exhaustive search.** An exhaustive search is one in which all comparisons are considered. For the negative trials, the search is necessarily exhaustive, because the subjects must look at all the comparisons before they know for sure that the probe wasn't in the memory set. Although it may seem hard to believe, the subjects apparently use the same scanning procedure for the positive trials as well. That is, the slopes of the positive and negative trial functions are the same in Figure 5.2, suggesting that whatever the subjects are doing on the negative trials, they're also doing it on the positive trials. That is, if the memory set is 4, 2, 3, 1, 5, 8, and the probe is 4, Sternberg's findings suggest that the subjects continue making all the comparisons anyway, even though the match between the probe and the memory set is encountered fairly early in the processing.

These findings are robust and have been replicated numerous times (Chase & Calfee, 1969; Wingfield, 1973). With a moment's thought, you might discover that the findings are plausible if considered in a certain light. Suppose the cognitive process that does the comparisons (Step 2, as outlined previously) can move much faster than the process that makes the decisions. In that case, a reasonable reaction is to wait until all the comparisons have been made before enacting the time-consuming decision process.

Some Difficulties with the Serial Exhaustive Model

Sternberg's findings indicate that retrieval from working memory is done in a serial exhaustive fashion for both positive and negative trials. However, there is some reason to believe that under some circumstances, retrieval can be self-terminating or even parallel.

For example, when we discussed automaticity (Schneider & Shiffrin, 1977), we saw that practiced subjects improved their ability to detect a target against a background of similar elements. Simpson (1972) observed an analogous effect in the Sternberg paradigm. His well-practiced subjects could scan their working memories for several probes automatically and in parallel. That is, for well-practiced subjects, the size of the memory set no longer seems to have a strong effect on reaction time (Lucariello, Toole, & Cauraugh, 1983). Also, serial position effects have been observed in the Sternberg paradigm (Burrows & Okada, 1971; Raeburn, 1974). For example, when the probe matches the last digit given in the memory set, reaction time is somewhat faster than if the probe matches an item located in the middle of the memory set. This finding is not concordant with a pure serial exhaustive search model. Further, Baddeley and Ecob (1973) demonstrated that reaction times were also influenced by repeating items in the memory set. For example, if the memory set were 4, 3, 6, 4, 5, followed by the probe 4, then reaction times were faster than in memory sets without repeaters. Again, if the subjects were truly engaged in a pure serial exhaustive search, these findings would not have been observed.

At one time, researchers hoped that a sort of catalog of short-term memory tasks would be assembled in which the principal scanning strategy (serial or parallel) could be listed. As time wore on, it became clear that such a catalog could not be created, because the subject's scanning operations were as dependent on practice and intralist factors as much as they were on the nature of the task.

Retrieval from Permanent Memory

One question marriage partners frequently ask each other is, "Did you see my [fill in the blank with familiar object]?" These everyday domestic disappearances are frustrating, because the owner usually knows that the object is around somewhere. If quizzed, people usually report experiences like this as prototypical instances of "forgetting." That is, you know you encoded it some time ago, and you know you can't retrieve it now

Retrieval failures from permanent memory actually occur in many varieties. First, you may not have encoded everything you believe that you have. Can you draw the face of a penny? I'm sure that you've seen it a million times. Yet, almost invariably, people make errors when asked to do this task. Why? Although some details of the environment may be encoded by mere exposure, in most cases, the depth of the processing determines the permanence of the memory. Although you've seen pennies almost every day of your life, unless you're a coin collector, you've probably never processed their appearance to any significant depth.

Even for material that has been successfully encoded, however, retrieval failures can be caused by several factors. For example, the failure to retrieve something may be the result of changes in the environment. You may have studied this material for the test, but if the final is given in a room you're unfamiliar with, contextual biasing may result in a retrieval failure. Physical factors such as those endured by H. M. or by individuals suffering from Korsakoff's syndrome[2] can also produce retrieval deficits. Also, some people believe that painful, wounding memories are deliberately made irretrievable by the defense mechanism of repression. Finally, all retrieval failures are

---

2. A disorder whose symptoms—lethargy, disorientation, and memory impairment—are produced by extended thiamine deficiency.

not necessarily deficits, in the sense of being a shortfall from the material originally encoded. In some cases, subjects retrieve more than the original information, or they distort what had been encoded. This latter observation has led many cognitivists to describe retrieval from permanent memory as a constructive process in which logical, or problem-solving, abilities are used.

The Bartlett Tradition

Modern accounts of retrieval have developed directly from the work of F. C. Bartlett who, in the early part of this century, approached the problem of memory in a pioneering way. Whereas most psychologists of the period asked *how much* learning was retained in memory, Bartlett asked *what kind* of learning had been retained (Hulse, Deese, & Egeth, 1975). An appropriate statement is that Bartlett was interested in qualitative changes in memory as well as quantitative ones.

In 1932, Bartlett published *Remembering,* which was an account of his findings using both his friends and Cambridge undergraduates as subjects. Since Bartlett was interested in studying the storage and retention of meaningful material, his subjects studied a potpourri of folktales, fables, American Indian hieroglyphics, and so on. The subjects were given a brief time to read or study the material, then after a fifteen-minute break, were asked to retrieve it. Bartlett often used the method of serial reproduction, which means that a subject might be asked to retrieve the same material over and over again. The retention intervals were often irregular depending upon when Bartlett was able to prevail on one of his friends to attempt another retrieval. Some of Bartlett's friends were long-suffering: In a few cases, his subjects tried to retrieve material that they had studied ten years earlier. With the method of serial reproduction, Bartlett hoped to measure the progressive nature of the deteriorations and distortions in the subject's memory. Bartlett's most famous story is entitled "The War of the Ghosts" and is reproduced in Table 5.5.

To get the same experience as one of Bartlett's subjects, read the story twice, take a fifteen-minute break, then try to write the story from memory as accurately as you can. Having done that, you might be interested in comparing your efforts with those of Bartlett's subjects. These results are shown in Table 5.6.

Bartlett was perhaps most interested in the subjects' errors. In this case, the subjects' errors offer strong evidence that they were reconstructing the story during their retrieval attempts. The effects of this reconstruction can be seen in many ways. The story is altered so that it becomes more consistent with knowledge that Cambridge undergraduates might have. For example, the canoe is remembered simply as a boat, and the natives were remembered as occupied with fishing. This second error is particularly telling. If one assumes that the activity was encoded it terms of abstract but related facts such as "requires a boat," "is done on a lake," and "is done to get food," and one asks an English student what activity this is, the student might well respond with what, in England, is easily the most plausible answer: fishing. Bartlett noted that many of the transformations and dis-

TABLE 5.5

The "War of the Ghosts" Story

Read the following American Indian folk tale, take a 15-minute break, and then attempt to reproduce the story by writing it down from memory.

One night two young men from Egulac went down to the river to hunt seals, and while they were there it became foggy and calm. Then they heard war-cries, and they thought: "Maybe this is a war-party." They escaped to the shore, and hid behind a log. Now canoes came up, and they heard the noise of paddles, and saw one canoe coming up to them. There were five men in the canoe, and they said:

"What do you think? We wish to take you along. We are going up the river to make war on the people."

One of the young men said: "I have no arrows."

"Arrows are in the canoe," they said.

"I will not go along. I might be killed. My relatives do not know where I have gone. But you," he said turning to the other, "may go with them."

So one of the young men went, but the other returned home.

And the warriors went on up the river to a town on the other side of Kalama. The people came down to the water, and they began to fight, and many were killed. But presently the young man heard one of the warriors say: "Quick, let us go home: that Indian has been hit." Now he thought: "Oh, they are ghosts." He did not feel sick, but they said he had been shot.

So the canoes went back to Egulac, and the young man went ashore to his house, and made a fire. And he told everybody and said: "Behold I accompanied the ghosts, and we went to fight. Many of our fellows were killed, and many of those who attacked us were killed. They said I was hit, and I did not feel sick."

He told it all, and then he became quiet. When the sun rose he fell down. Something black came out of his mouth. His face became contorted. The people jumped up and cried.

He was dead.

Source: Adapted from *Remembering,* F. C. Bartlett, Cambridge University Press.

TABLE 5.6

Attempts by One of Bartlett's (1932) Subjects to Reproduce the "War of the Ghosts" Story

First recall, attempted about 15 minutes after hearing the story:

Two young men from Egulac went out to hunt seals. The thought they heard war-cries, and a little later they heard the noise of the paddling of canoes. One of these canoes, in which there were five natives, came forward towards them. One of the natives shouted out: "Come with us: we are going to make war on some natives up the river." The two young men answered: "We have no arrows." "There are arrows in our canoes," came the reply. One of the young men then said: "My folk will not know where I have gone"; but, turning to the other, he said: "But you could go." So the one returned whilst the other joined the natives.

The party went up the river as far as a town opposite Kalam, where they got on land. The natives of that part came down to the river to meet them. There was some severe fighting, and many on both sides were slain. Then one of the natives that had made the expedition up the river shouted: "Let us return: the Indian has fallen." Then they endeavored to persuade the young man to return, telling him that he was sick, but he did not feel as if he were. Then he thought he saw ghosts all around him.

TABLE 5.6

**Attempts by One of Bartlett's (1932) Subjects to Reproduce
the "War of the Ghosts" Story—cont'd**

When they returned, the young man told all his friends of what had happened. He described how
many had been slain on both sides.

It was nearly dawn when the young man became very ill; and at sunrise a black substance rushed
out of his mouth, and the natives said one to another: "He is dead."

Second recall, attempted about 4 months later:

There were two men in a boat, sailing towards an island. When they approached the island, some
natives came running towards them, and informed them that there was fighting going on on the
island, and invited them to join. One said to the other: "You had better go. I cannot very well,
because I have relatives expecting me, and they will not know what has become of me. But you
have no one to expect you." So one accompanied the natives, but the other returned.

Here there is a part I can't remember. What I don't know is how the man got to the fight. However,
anyhow the man was in the midst of the fighting, and was wounded. The natives endeavored to
persuade the man to return, but he assured them that he had not been wounded.

I have an idea that his fighting won the admiration of the natives.

The wounded man ultimately fell unconscious. He was taken from the fighting by the natives.

Then, I think it is, the natives describe what happened, and they seem to have imagined seeing
a ghost coming out of his mouth. Really it was a kind of materialisation of his breath. I know
this phrase was not in the story, but that is the idea I have. Ultimately the man died at dawn the
next day."

Third recall, about 6½ years later.

1. Brothers.
2. Canoe.
3. Something black from mouth.
4. Totem.
5. One of the brothers died.
6. Cannot remember whether one slew the other or was helping the other.
7. Were going on a journey, but why I cannot remember.
8. Party in war canoe.
9. Was the journey a pilgrimage for filial or religious reasons?
10. Am now sure it was a pilgrimage.
11. Purpose had something to do with totem.
12. Was it on a pilgrimage that they met a hostile party and one brother was slain?
13. I think there was a reference to a dark forest.
14. Two brothers were on a pilgrimage, having something to do with a totem in a canoe, up a river
    flowing through a dark forest. While on their pilgrimage they met a hostile party of Indians in a
    war canoe. In the fight one brother was slain, and something black came from his mouth.
15. Am not confident about the way the brother died. May have been something sacrificial in the
    manner of his death.
16. The cause of the journey had both something to do with a totem, and with filial piety.
17. The totem was the patron god of the family and so was connected with filial piety.

Source: Adapted from *Remembering,* F. C. Bartlett, Cambridge University Press.

tortions the subjects made were attempts to make the story more coherent and rational—at least from the standpoint of British culture.

This kind of error is reminiscent of the script-based errors described earlier; certain similarities are present. The script is a unit of organized knowledge about actions and can be used to encode incoming information about actions. However, Bartlett invoked the notion of the **schema** to describe the subject's errors. For Bartlett, the schema was "an active organization of past reactions or past experiences" (Bartlett, 1932). The schema was used in learning about new material, in the same way that a script might be used, but it was also used in retrieving facts. As Bartlett understood it, the subject was more or less unable to separate encoded facts from the previously existing schema at retrieval time. Consequently, schema-based facts were "remembered" at retrieval time along with whatever was left of the actually encoded facts.

Retrieval of Meaning and Retrieval of Wording

Bartlett's work seems to indicate that the storage and retrieval of text is an "effort after meaning," implying that the subject is literally working hard to make some sense out of a passage. If Bartlett's main point is accurate, we would expect that people would have little memory for what was actually printed or spoken, as opposed to the passage's intended meaning. Bartlett's own work suggests that this expectation is true. His subjects seldom wrote down verbatim what they had read. This doesn't prove that they didn't have the material stored verbatim. In spite of Bartlett's instructions to write down what they remembered as accurately as possible, the subjects may have gotten fatigued or lost interest, and consequently, didn't transcribe all the details stored in their memories.

However, a study by Sachs (1967) examines this issue directly. Her subjects heard a recorded passage such as the one shown in Table 5.7. At some point, subjects were given a test sentence and were asked to determine

TABLE 5.7

The Galileo Story

There is an interesting story about the telescope. In Holland, a man named Lippershey was an eyeglass maker. One day his children were playing with some lenses. They discovered that things seemed very close if two lenses were about a foot apart. Lippershey began experiments and his "spyglass" attracted much attention. *He sent a letter about it to Galileo, the great Italian scientist* (0 syllable test here.) Galileo at once realized the importance of the discovery and set out to build an instrument of his own. He used an old organ pipe with one lens curved out and the other curved in. On the first clear night he pointed the glass towards the sky. He was amazed to find the empty dark spaces filled with brightly gleaming stars! (80 syllable test here.) Night after night Galileo climbed to a high tower, sweeping the sky with his telescope. One night he saw Jupiter, and to his great surprise discovered with it three bright stars, two to the east and one to the west. On the next night, however, all were to the west. A few nights later there were four little stars. (160 syllable test here.)

Source: Sachs, 1967. Reprinted by permission of the publisher.

whether or not the test sentence had been presented verbatim in the passage. If it had been, the subjects were to respond yes; if not, no. In one condition, the test sentence was presented immediately (0 syllables) after a particular sentence—called the base sentence—had occurred. In other conditions, the test sentence was presented either 80 or 160 syllables after the base sentence had been heard. The test sentence was presented to the subjects in one of several forms. In the *identical* condition, the test sentence was presented exactly as it had been heard in the passage. In our example, the identical form of the test sentence would be "He sent a letter about it to Galileo, the great Italian scientist." In the *formal* condition, the form of the test sentence was different from the base sentence, but the meaning was preserved: "He sent Galileo, the great Italian scientist, a letter about it." For the *voice* condition, the base sentence was changed from active to passive voice so that the test sentence became "A letter about it was sent to Galileo, the great Italian scientist." Finally, in the *semantic* condition, the meaning of the base sentence was altered so that the test sentence was phrased "Galileo, the great Italian scientist, sent him a letter about it."

This study has two independent variables. First, time has been manipulated, which allows us to make an inference about the duration of the subject's representation. Second, the test sentence conditions enable us to say something about the kind of representation that the subject had stored. The dependent measure was the percentage of correct responses, and the findings are given in Figure 5.3.

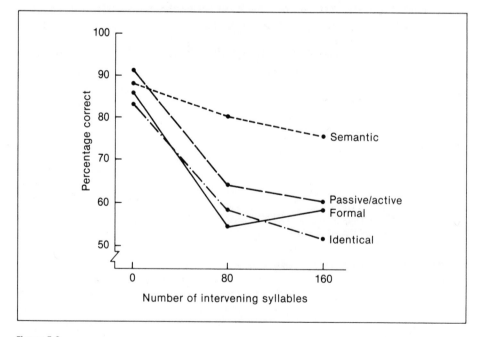

Figure 5.3.

The findings of the Sachs study. (From Sachs, 1967. Reprinted by permission of the publisher.)

When the test sentence was given immediately after the base sentence, the subjects were readily able to correctly respond yes to the identical form and no to all the other forms. The implication here is that the subjects had good memory for both meaning and wording for at least a brief period. However, the picture changed when 80 or 160 syllables had intervened between the test and base sentences. The subjects were still holding at about 80 percent correct responses in the semantic condition, but performance in the other conditions had fallen close to chance levels. Apparently, the subjects were able to retrieve the meaning of the base sentence after time, but the specific wording was gone.

We might expect, then, that as long as material can be held in working memory, the subject may have access to specific phrasings. However, as this material is elaborated and incorporated into permanent memory, larger cognitive structures are brought into play, which guide both encoding and retrieval. Support for this notion can be seen in a study by McKoon (1977). Subjects studied a passage that had a hierarchical organization; Its most general points appeared near the beginning, and the rest of the passage consisted of fleshing out the main argument. Subjects were tested either immediately after study or twenty-five minutes later. We might expect that subjects who were tested immediately would have more knowledge of specific phrasings than would subjects who were tested later. Those were the results. Subjects who were tested immediately didn't respond any faster to low-level statements from the passage than they did to high-level ones. But the subjects who were tested after twenty-five minutes answered high-level questions faster than they did low-level questions.

A practical point should be made here. Because professors usually test for main ideas rather than for specific facts, test performance might be enhanced if students could be induced to elaborate incoming material by associating it with material in permanent memory (Palmere, Benton, Glover, & Ronning, 1983). The findings also suggest that you're not necessarily helping yourself by keeping your textbook open until the last possible minute before a test—unless you're interested in retaining low-level facts.

Although retrieval from permanent memory generally recovers a highly schematized version of the meaning of a passage, some verbatim data is nevertheless retained. Anderson and Paulson (1977) used a Sachs-like procedure in their study. However, they developed an ingenious way to estimate the length of time the subject had access to verbatim knowledge of a sentence. First, they measured the time it took the subject to say "true" when the test sentence was identical to the base sentence. Next, they measured the time involved in saying "true" when the test sentence was a formal but not a semantic change of the base sentence. Then they subtracted the first measure from the second. Logically, no difference should occur in these times unless the subject has retained verbatim knowledge. In other words, if the subject has extracted only the meaning of the sentence and not the exact wording, then the response should be just as fast in either condition, as long as all we ask the subject to do is verify meaning. If the subject has retained verbatim knowledge, however, then we would expect the subject to respond faster to the identical sentence than to the formally changed sentence. In other words, the subject with verbatim knowledge should respond faster to a request to verify an identical sentence. If time differences are noted between these two conditions, they can be used as an estimate of the amount of verbatim knowledge remaining in the subject's memory.

A second variable in Anderson and Paulson's study was the effect of the time delay between the presentation of the base sentence and the test sentence. In their study, this variable was measured by the number of intervening sentences. Figure 5.4 shows their findings. Notice that the difference in response time declined steadily in the interval from zero to three intervening sentences, but no further decline occurred thereafter. More important, even with fifteen intervening sentences, the difference in response time is still present. This finding means that the subjects were still responding faster to the identical sentence than to the formally changed one, which indicates that some verbatim knowledge was still retained.

Other findings have suggested that verbatim knowledge of voice is retained in some circumstances. Anderson and Bower (1973) used Sachs' procedure and replicated one of her findings: Subjects did not retain verbatim knowledge of voice for very long. However, when Anderson and Bower repeated the procedure using unrelated sentences, they found that subjects were sensitive to that difference. Other researchers (Anisfeld & Klenbart, 1973) have pointed out that when grammatical form seems important to understanding the meaning of a sentence or utterance, then the grammatical form is often retrievable.

In summary, people are generally capable of retrieving verbatim material for only a fairly limited period. As information is elaborated in permanent memory, its meaning is abstracted and stored, which results in a

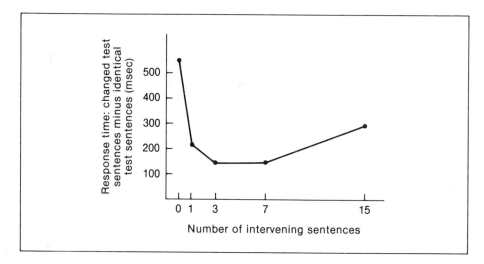

Figure 5.4.

Difference in response times to true test sentences that were identical or changed from original sentences. The measure is shown as a function of delay (in terms of intervening sentences. The measure declines with delay but does not reach zero. (After Anderson & Paulson, 1977.)

loss of ability to retrieve specific phrasings. However, people are neverthe-less capable of retaining specific phrasings, and they encode and store this information in situations in which the specific phrasing is important to understanding meaning.

CONCLUDING COMMENTS AND SUGGESTIONS FOR FURTHER READING

After reviewing this literature, three words came to mind: sensitivity, flexi-bility, and frustration. In looking at the work on encoding, I was struck by the incredible sensitivity of the cognitive system in its use of so many con-textual details as it prepares material to be stored. These contextual effects seem strong enough to warrant my statement that we really can't remember only one item. Efforts to store something necessarily store other things as well. Indeed, Alba and Hasher (1983) have commented that the final result of the encoding process in an event they call "integration," in which a holistic, unified, mental representation is created, incorporating aspects of the stimulus, its context, and previous knowledge.

I was also aware of the tremendous flexibility that the cognitive system possesses in retrieval. For example, the efforts to determine the nature of search in working memory were stalled when researchers discovered that their subjects had a great deal of latitude in how they searched. The nature of the task and the subject's level of practice constrained but did not deter-mine the strategy used in scanning. I have also been struck repeatedly by the great resourcefulness that people use in retrieving information from permanent memory. As time and experience go on, earlier memories appear to be overwritten. Also apparent is that the act of retrieval can, in some circumstances, alter the nature of the stored memory. This means that retrieval from permanent memory can't be compared to going into a nicely cataloged warehouse with a map of the contents and getting something that's been stored there. Indeed, retrieval is much like going into a reasonably well-organized warehouse whose goods are rearranged every once in awhile. You might find the object you're looking for, but you might instead find that some other, similar object has been stored in the original object's place, which you may have to use in place of the original.

I have often shared the frustration that my students experience when they are confronted with the tantalizing mystery of the central nervous sys-tem and its relation to the cognitive system. As closely allied as these two systems seem, some time will pass before cognitive psychologists will achieve a clear enough perspective on memory to suggest that the central nervous system must operate in certain ways. I also think that some substantial amount of time will elapse before neurologists inform psychologists of pre-cisely which theory of memory is mandated by neuropsychological findings.

Students who want to know more about these matters might start with Bartlett's (1932) book. The recent movement toward an ecologically based study of cognition is clearly reflected in Neisser's (1982) book *Memory Ob-served*. Loftus (1979a) summarizes her work quite well and provides food for thought. Scripts are examined closely in Mandler (1984). Klatzky (1984) has written a lucid and somewhat speculative account of the relation between memory and awareness, which covers many of the ideas dealt with in this chapter. Some of the implications of the memory literature for classroom performance are considered in Anderson, Spiro, and Montague (1977). A recent book by Gagne (1985) extends this analysis.

FOCUS ON APPLICATIONS:
A Cognitive Psychologist Goes To The Movies

In the fall of 1982, I saw a movie entitled *Blade Runner,* in which a corporation figures out a way to create artificial people who are almost indistinguishable from humans. These replicants, as they're called in the film, are used for dangerous or seedy off-world jobs and are not permitted to live on earth. If any of them do appear on earth, the government is allowed to shoot them on sight. Harrison Ford plays a legal hit man, or blade runner, and he meets (of course!) a gorgeous woman.

The woman turns out to be a replicant, but she's one of a new design and doesn't know she's a fake. Because she has childhood memories and a few blurry snapshots, she assumes that she arrived on earth in the normal fashion. Actually, the president of the corporation had made a copy of his niece's memories and had them inserted into the replicant's brain. Part of the movie's tension is built around the woman's discovery of her origins. When she finally makes the discovery, she plays the piano and then says something like, "I didn't know if I'd be able to play; I remember taking lessons."

I've seen the movie several times, and the audience invariably accepts this line at face value even though the memory theory it implies is so preposterous I have to stifle myself to keep from laughing out loud. If I could give you a copy of a memory of someone else's piano lessons, do you think you would be able to play the piano, even though you had never practiced? Do you see the problem here? If I had memories of taking piano lessons, then somewhere in my nervous system a code would likely exist that could guide my fingers and hands to play the piano. In humans, the memory of taking the lessons is intimately connected with actual practice. The woman replicant in *Blade Runner* had only the memory of taking lessons, which is not enough to enable someone to play the piano.

I like the movie anyway, which in its own strange way, provides a good illustration: A pure storage theory of memory sounds believable to most people, even when such theories are taken to their extreme—and ultimately silly—conclusions.

KEY TERMS

Encoding
Storing
Retrieving
Context
State-dependent learning
Cognitive effort
Encoding specificity
Scripts
Inferential intrusion errors
Overwriting

Demand characteristics
Brain writing
Mass action
Equipotentiality
Hippocampus
Anterograde amnesia
Serial exhaustive search
Bartlett tradition
Schema
Verbatim retrieval

CHAPTER 6

Organization of Knowledge in Permanent Memory

OVERVIEW

EPISODIC AND SEMANTIC MEMORY

NETWORK MODELS OF SEMANTIC MEMORY
Assumptions of Network Models
Teachable Language Comprehender
  Assumptions of TLC
  Empirical Findings of TLC
Spreading Activation Model
  Semantic Priming
ACT Theory
  Propositional Analysis
  Representation of Semantic and Episodic
    Memory

Assumptions of ACT
Empirical Support
The Fan Effect
Comments about ACT and Network Models in
  General

REPRESENTATIONAL THOUGHT AND MEMORY
Metamemory
  Development of Metamemory

**CONCLUDING COMMENTS AND SUGGESTIONS
FOR FURTHER READING**
FOCUS ON APPLICATIONS
KEY TERMS

Not long ago, my wife bought a fruit salad at the grocery and put it on the passenger side of the car on the way home. The container was defective, and some of the fruit juice leaked onto the upholstery. My wife didn't notice the accident until she got home. She was then concerned that the blueberry juice would stain the seat. A minor calamity ensued as we scrambled for something to clean the upholstery. A few days later at dinner, as I spooned some of the fruit salad onto my plate, I said to my wife, "This reminds me—the car seat looks OK." All I got from my wife was a blank look. "Remember," I said, "it leaked." "Oh! Right!" she said. She then told me that she hadn't associated the fruit salad with the car seat, but now she had a feeling that she would always associate the two. I always get a kick out of seeing mental processes at work, and this evidence of the apparent formation of an association in my wife's memory was a fine example.

We usually take for granted our cognitive system's ability to associate two apparently unrelated stimuli, but a moment's thought will show you how remarkable this ability is. For example, a principal technique of psychoanalysis is called *free association*. As practiced by Jung, the analyst supplies a word and the analysand produces the first thing that enters his mind. This technique relies upon the apparently associative nature of our minds, but there's more to it than that. Free association would hardly be a useful technique unless some associations were more or less expected and common, and others were unusual and perhaps deviant. In some sense, then, the success of free association depends upon the existence of some commonality of associations from person to person. If associations are produced by experiences (and the fruit salad episode strongly suggests that they are), then we must conclude that, even though you and I have had plenty of different experiences in our lives, we must have had enough similar experiences to generate the associations that we have in common. That people generate common associations also suggests that people have organized their different experiences in similar ways. In other words, the organization that seems to be inherent in most peoples' free associations could be indicative of the organization of their minds.

In its briefest form, this is the argument proposed by several memory theorists. They maintain that our knowledge of the world is highly organized and that this organization can be modeled. An adequate model of permanent memory would have several features:

1. The model would explain and predict the various retrieval phenomena that we saw in Chapter 5. That is, it would specify the conditions under which we would expect accuracy and memory loss.
2. The model would explain how associations (or some mechanism similar to associations) are formed and stored.
3. We would expect such a model to account for the constructive nature of retrieval from long-term storage, meaning that the model should pro-

vide a plausible account of both the insertions and the distortions that seem to occur when we retrieve permanent memories.

4. The model should account for the varieties of knowledge that we seem to have. For example, if I were to ask you to tell me your first free associate to *dog*, it might well be the same as mine: *cat*. But my next free associate to *cat* might be a word denoting some aspect of one of my own cats, whereas your next associate to *cat* might be something more general. We recognize that at any point in this chain of free associations, the words we produce may indicate knowledge that is idiosyncratic, or personal to us. The knowledge of the world stored in our permanent memories seems to be of at least two kinds. *General knowledge* of the world is presumably shared and organized in similar ways by all those who share a culture. Our intuitions tell us that mixed in with this general knowledge is *personal knowledge,* that is, knowledge of *our* world rather than *the* world. A fully developed account would explain this relationship.

5. Chapter 1 made a distinction between declarative (describable) knowledge and procedural knowledge, or skills that no longer have a verbal component. We would want a theory of permanent memory to account for both types of knowledge and to explain their relationship. That is, if we wish to argue that permanent memory is the repository of all knowledge, then the theory should explain skills as well as verbal knowledge.

Writing such an account is no easy feat, and no existing theory does it all. However, several cognitive psychologists have gamely advanced persuasive theories that at least have gotten the ball rolling. This chapter considers several attempts to model general, declarative world knowledge, or what cognitive psychologists frequently refer to as *semantic memory*. The conclusion of this chapter presents some of the findings on *metamemory*, that is, information we have learned and remembered about how our memories seem to work.

EPISODIC AND SEMANTIC MEMORY

Tulving (1972, 1983) proposed a distinction between two types of permanent memory. **Episodic memories** were autobiographical, personal, and sensitive to the effects of context. These memories were organized by time and place of occurrence and could frequently be described in terms of their perceptual characteristics. Episodic memories could be contrasted with **semantic memory,** which housed general, encyclopedic knowledge of the world and language. Semantic memory was organized on the basis of class membership and other abstract principles such as sub- or superordination. In other words, semantic memory seemed to consist of facts that could be organized hierarchically. For example, I know that dogs and cats are both mammals, but they can be grouped together in a superordinate category—chordates—along with other animals that are not mammals. Semantic memory was composed of knowledge that had no specific temporal or spatial referent, and was therefore not sensitive to the effects of context.

This distinction seems well founded, at least on an intuitive basis. Inevitably, however, cognitive psychologists have wondered whether these terms truly describe two functionally distinct memory systems. Researchers who have looked for empirical support for this distinction have usually taken one of two approaches (Horton & Mills, 1984). Some researchers have attempted to determine if the principles governing episodic memory are valid for semantic memory also. As an alternative, other researchers have tried to assess the influence of semantic on episodic memory and vice versa.

In some cases, an individual can apparently acquire semantic knowledge without any accompanying episodic memory. Cohen and Corkin (1982) gave their amnesic subjects a problem known as the Tower of Hanoi (we'll see more of this problem in Chapter 12). The subjects' task is to transfer a series of disks from one peg to another without violating the rules that govern the transfers. If normal subjects are repeatedly given different versions of this problem, they eventually learn a general procedure for solving all Towers of Hanoi, even those that they have not seen before. Cohen and Corkin found that their amnesic subjects behaved in a similar way, retaining a good bit of knowledge over long retention intervals. However, their amnesic subjects had no episodic memory of the problem. They didn't remember ever solving it or seeing it before, and were puzzled by their skill.

Kihlstrom (1980) reported episodic and semantic memory dissociation for normal subjects who were in a hypnotic state. The subjects were hypnotized and then memorized a list of unrelated words. Following the learning session, the subjects were given a posthypnotic suggestion, telling them that they would not be able to remember the memorized list until a specific retrieval cue was given. Following that, the subjects were told that they would now have to supply free associates to words given by the experimenter. These priming words were deliberately chosen because they had a high probability of eliciting the list words that the subjects had memorized. Subject performed well on this task, indicating that the hypnotic state had not affected their general (i.e., semantic) knowledge of the words' meanings. However, even after they had recited many of the words on the list, the subjects maintained that they were unable to retrieve the studied items. Yet, when the retrieval cue mentioned in the posthypnotic suggestion was finally given, the subjects' retrieval was close to perfect.

Numerous studies (Herrmann & Harwood, 1980; Shoben, Wescourt, & Smith, 1978) have also reported evidence favoring the episodic-semantic distinction, and with good reason: In numerous cases, we demonstrate some general knowledge of the world while simultaneously being unable to specify exactly how we came by this knowledge or without even being aware that we have demonstrated the general knowledge (Klatzky, 1984). Not all cognitivists, however, think that the distinction is valid (Anderson & Ross, 1980; McClosky & Santee, 1981; McKoon & Ratcliff, 1979). Hannigan, Shelton, Franks, and Bransford (1980) have concluded that both memories must affect performance on every task. Although it's theoretically possible to disentangle the contributions made by each memory to the final performance, practically speaking, this process has proved difficult.

In the Hannigan et al. research, subjects were presented with a long list of unrelated sentences. Some subjects were supplied with an organizing framework for these sentences, and other subjects were not. The memory task was slightly similar to the shadowing studies examined in Chapter 2. The subjects heard various sentences presented against a background of white noise, and their task was to repeat them out loud as accurately as they could. The performance of subjects who had been presented with the sentences was compared with a control group who had not. Subjects familiar with the sentences outperformed the control group.

This finding indicates an episodic memory effect. Even when the subjects had no organizing framework for the sentences, the fact that they had encoded and stored them conferred an advantage over subjects who didn't have that experience. The subjects who had been provided with a framework, however, outperformed all other subjects on the task. This finding demonstrates the effects of semantic memory. The subjects who had an organizing schema to guide the encoding process were apparently able to elaborate the sentences more completely, which in this case meant associating the sentences with previously stored general knowledge.

This effect was demonstrated in another way, too. During the white noise test, the subjects were also presented with new and unfamiliar sentences that were nevertheless appropriate to the framework. What might we predict about the subjects' performance on such sentences? Clearly, the control group should have no particular advantage in repeating such sentences, nor should the nonframework subjects, because their episodic encoding shouldn't contain much general knowledge that might be helpful in guiding the processing of sentences partially masked by the white noise. However, the framework subjects should have an advantage in processing these ambiguous stimuli. That is, the framework might help the processing of these sentences by at least constraining the range of guesses that the subjects might consider when they are forced to conjecture.

The Hannigan et al. study offers a good demonstration of the combined effects of semantic and episodic memory. Notice, though, what kind of inference we can't make from this study. When we looked at retrieval from working memory in Chapter 5, we saw that Sternberg was able to estimate time requirements both for scanning individual items in memory and for successive stages in the retrieval process. He made these estimates by comparing the time taken by the subjects to do different tasks and subtracting the times from one another in the appropriate way. Why can't we do something similar here? That is, why can't we make estimates of the relative contributions of semantic and episodic memory to the subjects' performance by subtracting the control group scores from those of the nonframework group and in turn subtracting that measure from the framework group scores?

One problem stems from Sternberg's reasonable assumption that the operations in scanning working memory were taking place serially. We have no way to assume that in the Hannigan et al. study. Also, Sternberg was able to assume that the various scanning and reporting operations were independent of one another; that is, the length of time required for, let's say, operation four was independent of whatever time had been required for the previous operations. We can't make that assumption here either. It's not known if accessing episodic memory does something to the semantic code. If accessing episodic memory does influence the semantic code, no prior theoretical grounds exist for assuming what the nature of that effect might be.

The Hannigan et al. study nicely points out a principal problem with the episodic-semantic distinction. Namely, in most everyday situations, both memory systems are apparently involved anyway. Further, although the distinction may be theoretically valid, on a practical level, researchers have had a difficult time teasing apart semantic from episodic effects. On an empirical level, distinguishing an episodic task from a semantic task has been difficult. In spite of these difficulties, Tulving's original point is well taken. As stated elsewhere (Howard, 1983; Klatzky, 1980), most memory research has focused on the effects of episodic memory, and Tulving's comments were a much-needed corrective to this trend. In the past fifteen years, researchers have expended a great deal of energy developing models of semantic memory. In studying this sort of enduring and context-free memory, cognitive psychologists have come closer than ever before to representing human knowledge.

NETWORK MODELS OF SEMANTIC MEMORY

The overview pointed out that world knowledge must surely be organized in our memories. One objective shared by all models of semantic memory is to capture or mimic this organization in a formal system. For example, we know that retrieval patterns from permanent memory are not unorganized. A good theory of semantic memory must clarify the factors that make certain retrieval patterns predictable. One frequently adopted tactic consists of developing a formal system (which, by definition, must be organized) and then arguing that the organizational principles of the formal system are analogous to, or even in some sense identical to, the organizational principles of permanent memory.

In looking for a philosophical basis for their theories, many cognitive psychologists have found appealing analogies between human and computer memory. In both cases, the processes of encoding, storing, and retrieval seem to take place. The successful storage of information in computers requires that the information be organized in some fashion. Moreover, the computer's retrieval of this organized information depends on a formal system called a *retrieval algorithm*. The questions posed by cognitive psychologists seem straightforward: What is the nature of the organization of human knowledge? Can this knowledge be represented by a formal system? Finally, is it possible to specify a formal retrieval procedure that seems to duplicate human retrieval processes?

One type of formal system that is often used is the so-called **network model.** Network models are so named because the associations among the elements of permanent memory are depicted as arrows. Figure 6.1 shows a tiny part of a generic model of semantic memory.

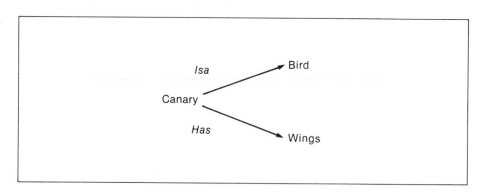

Figure 6.1.

A small part of a semantic memory model.

Although Figure 6.1 gives the impression that the elements of semantic memory are words, strictly speaking, that isn't the case. In Figure 6.1, the word *canary* stands for the concept of a canary, and this symbolism is true for the other elements of the figure, too. Concepts in semantic memory are generally referred to as *nodes*. Nodes are connected by arrows, but again, this is simply a convention for denoting a particular kind of relationship (or association) among the nodes. Figure 6.1 shows that *canary* and *bird* are ideas that are associated in particular ways, one of which is that a canary is a member of the superordinate, or higher, category *bird*. This association is denoted by the arrow labeled *"Isa."* Although Figure 6.1 specifies the canary node as having only one *Isa* relation, it could have others. Similarly, the *has* relationship is not the only one that could be specified. It's important to realize at the outset that the direction of the arrows sometimes has theoretical significance in these models. That is, the relationship between *canary* and *bird* can be expressed by *isa,* but that's not true for the relationship between *bird* and *canary.*

Assumptions of Network Models

One assumption generally made by network models is that the activity we call "searching our memories" is analogous to a search among the nodes of the model. In this instance, the search refers to a kind of metaphorical movement among the model's nodes, in the direction specified by the arrowhead. This search is considered to proceed node by node—that is, serially—as an unspecified cognitive process that accesses the node and reads out the knowledge contained there. If that knowledge enables the individual to answer a particular question, then the search stops. Otherwise, it continues until the person finds the answer or gives up. This is another way of stating that search in permanent memory is generally assumed to be self-terminating rather than exhaustive.

Typically, network models assume that the nature of the associations constrains the extent, or the scope, of the search. Although this point will be clearer when we look at some specific models, for right now we can say

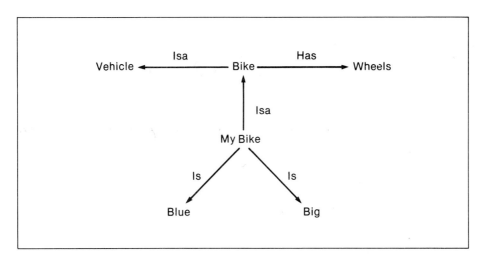

Figure 6.2.

Episodic and semantic knowledge in semantic memory.

that the nature of the associations is usually assumed to govern the nature of the search. It's also important to realize that these models consider themselves representations of knowledge that cannot be completely expressed verbally. Although all the models that we'll look at seem to consist of words and arrows, be aware that the nodes are supposed to represent concepts rather than words. The graphic depictions shown in these pages are just that: representations (not copies) of mental events that surely must be more complex than words alone.

Finally, most models of semantic memory make what is called a **type-token distinction.** Broadly speaking, this distinction refers to the differentiation we usually make between general categories (types) and particular, familiar examples drawn from that category (tokens). These relationships are expressed in Figure 6.2.

I know that bikes are two-wheeled vehicles, usually designed to carry only one or two people. This knowledge is semantic. Also, I know that my bike "isa" bike; it's blue and has a 27-inch frame to accommodate my long legs. You wouldn't have known this, because this knowledge of my particular bike is episodic. In other words, the type-token distinction affords the theorist a way of separating semantic from episodic knowledge. Stored at the type nodes are the facts that are true about that particular category. The facts define the category and are consequently context-free. Stored at the token nodes are facts that are true for that individual. This knowledge is context-dependent and can consequently be distorted, bypassed in the search, or even, as we saw in the Loftus and Palmer (1974) study in Chapter 5, overwritten by later episodic facts. If our objective is to develop a theory of semantic memory, why bother incorporating episodic knowledge into the model?

To answer this question, we need to remind ourselves of the findings of the Hannigan et al. (1980) study. You'll recall that they demonstrated that both episodic and semantic memory seem to be involved in almost every act of retrieval from permanent memory. This finding brings us to a related point. People typically use episodic memory as a basis for inference when semantic knowledge is lacking. An example might help clarify this. Suppose I were to ask you, "Could a car's battery fail on a hot summer day?" This question of battery failure involves technical knowledge of battery properties and their relationship to temperature changes. You could get this information from a book, and you might be able to answer without ever having any personal experience with car batteries. However, since most of us don't possess this knowledge, we think about all the car battery failures that we're familiar with. No doubt most, if not all, of them have taken place in the wintertime, so we're inclined to answer no to the original question. To answer the question, we've had to search among the token nodes dealing with battery failures to make a logical generalization about what must be true for the type nodes as well. Because such inferences occur routinely, any theory of semantic memory would have difficulty predicting certain responses if it failed to make provisions for episodic knowledge. Having examined these general considerations of semantic memory, let's turn to a specific model.

Teachable Language Comprehender

Teachable Language Comprehender **(TLC)** is one of the earliest modern models of semantic memory and is based on a doctoral dissertation by R. Quillian (1968). Quillian did not set out to build a static model of permanent memory. His objective was to demonstrate that language had certain formal properties that could be captured in a formal system—in this case, a computer program. Quillian designed the program to be able to demonstrate some rudimentary comprehension of language. Collins and Quillian (1969) made some modifications and simplifying assumptions, and produced a model of semantic memory that could be tested empirically.

Assumptions of TLC

Part of TLC's semantic network is shown in Figure 6.3. The concepts, or nodes, in TLC each have two kinds of relations. First, each node has a superordinate relationship to some other node, which determines category membership. Although it hasn't been shown in Figure 6.3, the superordinate characteristic expresses the *isa* relationship. For example, a canary is a kind of bird, which in turn is a kind of animal. Second, each node has one or more property characteristics, which express the *has* relation. A shark *has* the property *can bite*.

TLC also assumes that semantic knowledge can be captured in the sort of hierarchical display shown in Figure 6.3. That is, canaries and ostriches are organized by the more general and more inclusive category *bird*. Birds and fish are in turn characterized by the more general category *animal*. TLC also assumes that the cognitive system is characterized by what has been called *cognitive economy*. You know that nearly all animals have skin, but this fact is noted in TLC only once: at the highest—that is, the most general—level. Collins and Quillian designed this model to be stored in a

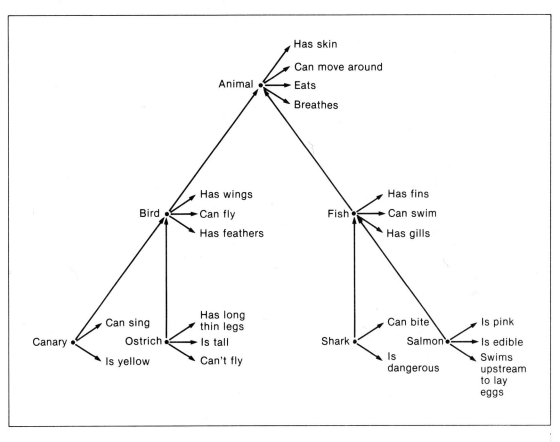

Figure 6.3.

An illustration of the memory structure assumed by TLC. One part of the semantic network for animals is depicted. (After Collins & Quillian, 1969. Copyright 1969 by Academic Press. Reprinted by permission.)

computer and were careful not to tie up too much of the computer's memory by repeatedly storing general animal facts with each specific animal. They reasoned, however, that the cognitive system must have similar storage constraints, and consequently, the assumption of cognitive economy seemed plausible.

TLC also assumes that scans of permanent memory are accomplished by **intersection searches.** This type of search specifies that the search process begins from particular nodes and fans out from them. The fanning out is in parallel, meaning that cognitive processes scan all the nodes associated with the entry nodes at the same time. The search is also assumed to have unlimited energy, meaning that the rate of search is not slowed by the number of associations emanating from any particular node. In other words, if the cognitive process fans out to three nodes from the entry node, it accomplishes this process in the same time that fanning out to only one node would take. With each node accessed in the search, the scanning processor leaves an indicator pointing to the node where the search originated.

This process is called *flagging*. If the search processes, which have begun their fanning out from different nodes, ever meet one another during the search, an intersection is then noted. When an intersection is discovered, cognitive processes check all the flagged nodes until they determine the pathway linking the nodes from which the search originally began. Once this pathway is determined, TLC can use its inference programs to determine if it indeed "knows" that particular fact.

Let's consider an example. Suppose we give TLC a statement—"A shark is an animal"—and ask it to verify whether this statement is true. The search begins from the *shark* and *animal* nodes and fans out from there. At *fish,* the search processes will intersect, and the nature of the pathway from *shark* to *animal* will then be evaluated. In this case, the pathway goes from one node to a superordinate node to another superordinate node, so TLC would say yes to the statement.

Empirical Findings of TLC

Although the intersection search is assumed to take place in parallel, it nevertheless requires time to move the search process from node to node. Consequently, the greater the semantic distance between the two originating nodes, the more time required by TLC to verify the sentence.

Consider the three following sentences from TLC's perspective:

S0: A canary is a canary.
S1: A canary is a bird.
S3: A canary is an animal.

In the case of S0, little time should be required to verify the sentence, because the search processes should intersect quickly, starting as they do from the same place. However, in the case of S3, the search processes have to fan out across two levels, and so we would predict that more time would be required to verify this sentence. These three sentences deal with superordinate relationships, but we would have the same expectation for property relationships. Consider the following three sentences:

P0: A canary is yellow.
P1: A canary can fly.
P2: A canary has skin.

In the case of P2, the search processes have to fan across two levels. If the mechanism proposed by Quillian and Collins is an accurate depiction of what goes on when permanent memory is searched, then subjects should require more time to verify P2 than P1 or P0.

These predictions were tested in a study in which a large group of subjects were given simple sentences whose truth or falsity had to be determined as quickly as possible. Subjects were given an equal number of true and false sentences. Figure 6.4 depicts the findings of this study. Note that humans performed in a way that was consistent with the theory, lending support to the notion that permanent memory is searched in the manner suggested by TLC.

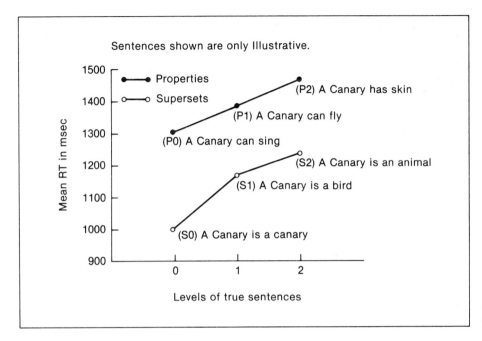

Sentences shown are only Illustrative.

Figure 6.4.

The results of Collins and Quillian's (1969) sentence verification experiment. The data depicted are for true responses only, showing mean RT as a function of the number of levels in the hierarchy that TLC assumes need to be searched. The sentences shown are only examples, since many sentences were used. Notice that RT increases systematically as the number of levels increases. (After Collins & Quillian, 1969. Copyright 1969 by Academic Press. Reprinted by permission.)

However, in the tidal wave of research generated by these findings, some problems were also washed ashore. First, Rips, Shoben, and Smith (1973) found that some superordinate relationships are verified faster than others. Consider the following two sentences:

A dog is a mammal.
A dog is an animal.

Collins and Quillian would predict that the first sentence should be verified faster than the second sentence. This prediction is based on their assumption that semantic knowledge is hierarchically organized. Since mammals are nested (subordinate) within the animal classification, the search processes should intersect sooner when verifying the first sentence. However, Rips et al. (1973) demonstrated that the second sentence is verified faster.

Now consider the following two sentences:

A peach is a fruit.
A watermelon is a fruit.

Each sentence mentions a perfectly good example of a fruit, and each example would be nested one level below *fruit* in TLC's semantic memory. On these grounds, we shouldn't expect any consistent differences in verification times for these two sentences. But there are consistent differences: People verify the first sentence faster than they do the second (Smith, Rips, & Shoben, 1974). Why is this so?

Each sentence does mention a perfectly good example of a fruit. However, although people recognize that all fruits are equal in some sense, some fruits are apparently considered more typical of the category than others. Knowledge of typical category members seemingly can be accessed and verified faster than knowledge of less typical members (Rips, et al., 1973). This concept of typicality is important and is related to the notion of the prototype examined in Chapter 3. That chapter stated that people seem to abstract relevant features from various stimuli in the world and then reassemble these feature lists to form higher-order (i.e., more general) units of knowledge, which can in turn be used to guide future perception. One such unit of higher-order knowledge is the prototype, the most central element of a category. What makes the prototype the most central element of a category? Many theorists believe that the prototype has more of the features that have been abstracted to form the category in the first place—more features than any other single element in the category. The implication of this view is that some fruit comes close to being the prototypical fruit (Chapter 11 will show that this is apparently true). The problem for TLC is that it's too simple to incorporate these effects, meaning that actual human knowledge has other, richer organizational principles than the limited hierarchical ones seen in TLC (McCloskey & Glucksberg, 1978).

Finally, the assumption of cognitive economy seems unwarranted. Recall that Collins and Quillian postulated that specific factual knowledge was stored only once—at the most general possible node. This was why the statement "A canary can sing" required more time to verify than the statement "A canary has skin." Because *skin* is stored only once—at the *animal* node—the search processes require time to fan out and note the intersection. Conrad (1972) questioned this claim, maintaining that the reason for the faster reaction times for the first sentence was simply because the concept *canary* is more strongly associated with the concept *can sing* than it is with the concept *has skin*.

Conrad tested this idea by asking her subjects to describe a series of common nouns, such as *canary, bird,* and *animal*. She found large differences in the properties that were ascribed to particular nouns. For example, canaries were often described as being yellow but hardly ever described as having skin. Conrad next computed a measure of the association strength based on the frequency-of-mention data she had collected. She then gave her subjects a sentence verification task similar to the kind used by Quillian and Collins. She found that the reaction times were predictable from the association strength measure, regardless of how many levels the subjects had apparently searched through. For example, subjects quickly verified statements such as "An orange is edible" even though these terms are separated by at least one level in the hierarchy. Also, subjects required a lengthy amount of time to verify statements whose terms were only weakly associated, even when those terms were adjacent in TLC's hierarchy. Conrad's work was influential in closing the door on a pure and simple hierarchical model.

Spreading Activation Model

As the shortcomings of TLC became more widely recognized, Collins and Loftus (1975) developed an alternative model for semantic memory, one that was not organized hierarchically. Instead, the notion of semantic distance, or semantic relatedness, was used as the organizing motif. Figure 6.5 shows a small part of their network. The lines connecting the nodes indicate that

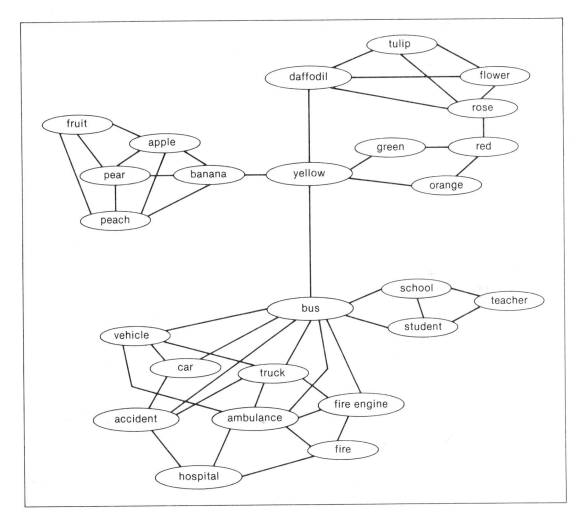

Figure 6.5.

A portion of the semantic memory network proposed by the spreading activation model. (From Collins & Loftus, 1975. Copyright 1975 by the American Psychological Association. Adapted by permission of the publisher and author.)

an association exists between those concepts. *Daffodils* are associated with *yellow,* which is in turn associated with *bananas.* However, *bananas* and *daffodils* are not associated.

The **spreading activation model** makes two other assumptions regarding structure. First, the length of the line connecting two concepts is intended to have theoretical meaning. The shorter the line, the more closely associated are the concepts. For example, *car* and *truck* are closely associated, but *yellow* and *bus* are only weakly associated. Second, like TLC, the spreading activation model assumes that superordinate relationships are labeled with an *isa* link. Thus, the linkage from bus to vehicle would be of this type. However, this model represents an advance over TLC in that it also includes some *isnota* links. This means that the model can quickly determine that some strongly associated concepts are nevertheless not superordinate. This point is an important one. Consider what might take place if subjects were given the following sentence:

A school is a bus.

TLC would begin by carrying out a search beginning from the *school* and *bus* nodes, eventually intersecting at some hypothetical *things in the world* node, and finally deciding that the terms were not on a superordinate path. If TLC were a completely accurate model of human semantic memory, we would predict that the subjects would take a lot of time before determining that this sentence was false. Although these terms are strongly associated, however, subjects are quick to refute the sentence, indicating that a complete search of memory is probably not carried out. Collins and Loftus developed the term **prestored knowledge** to describe such facts that do not require an extensive memory search. Some research (Smith, 1978) has indicated that at least some of our knowledge is like this. Knowledge of certain relations is stored directly in the network, thus obviating the need to scan our memories.

This notion of expert knowledge has important implications, although a fuller development of them is reserved for Chapters 12 and 13. Also, you probably already know that prestored knowledge wasn't always prestored: Small children don't know that a bat isn't a bird. The implication is that the organization of semantic memory—its structure—must be modifiable as people develop. The important point here is that some memory processes must exist that do more than simply search the structure of permanent memory in a somewhat passive way. Some processes must go to work on this structure, modifying it to incorporate new knowledge. That is, on a practical level, Collins and Loftus must shoulder the burden of specifying what experiences produce the *isnota* link in semantic memory. This objective hasn't been done very well in this model. This chapter later considers some proposals that accomplish this objective.

In addition to these assumptions regarding memory structure, the Collins and Loftus model also makes some assumptions about the search process, one of which is particularly important. As nodes are searched, the knowledge stored therein undergoes a change in status. Specifically, the activity of search is thought to activate searched nodes, meaning that the knowledge is brought into a state of heightened accessibility. Which nodes are activated depends upon several factors, including certain strategic decisions of the person searching her own memory. However, evidence suggests that highly associated nodes are activated more or less involuntarily. Having activated one node, the spread of activation radiates outward along strong associative lines to make other nodes more accessible. How far the activation spreads is determined by several factors. The strength of the initial activation, the amount of time since the initial activation, and of course, the degree of semantic distance between the nodes all play a role in influencing the resulting spread of activation. If an unusual, or remote, concept is the locus of the initial activation, then not many other nodes will be activated. If, however, a concept at the center of a richly interwoven network is stimulated, then many other nodes will be activated.

Semantic Priming

Collins and Loftus used the concept of spreading activation to account for the well-known **semantic priming** effect (Foss, 1982). A study by Meyer and Schvaneveldt (1971) illustrates this effect. (This study was also discussed in Chapter 1.) Their subjects were presented with pairs of elements, and their task was to judge as quickly as possible whether both elements of the pair were words. If both the elements were words, subjects were supposed to respond yes. If either of the elements was a nonword, subjects were told to respond no. Several kinds of trials were used. On positive trials, both elements were words, and in some cases these words were highly associated. On other positive trials, the words were unrelated. On negative trials, one or both of the elements were nonwords. Table 6.1 shows some examples of these trials and the subjects' reaction times.

The response times from the negative trials seem to indicate that the subjects read the top element and made a decision about it before reading the second element. The subjects' decisions were made faster when the nonword was the top element rather than the bottom element. The positive

TABLE 6.1

Examples of the Pairs Used to Demonstrate Associative Pairing

Positive Pairs		Negative Pairs		
Unrelated	Related	First Nonword	Second Nonword	Both Nonwords
Nurse	Bread	Plame	Wine	Plame
Butter	Butter	Wine	Plame	Reab
940 msec	855 msec	904 msec	1,087 msec	884 msec

Source: Meyer and Schvaneveldt, 1971. Copyright 1971 by the American Psychological Association. Adapted by permission of the publisher and author.

trials demonstrate the effects of semantic priming. When the words were strongly associated, the subjects were able to read and respond much more quickly than when the words were unrelated. This effect wasn't produced by any inherent quality of the words themselves—*nurse* isn't more difficult to read, nor is it more uncommon, than *bread*. The time difference was apparently produced by the relationship between *bread* and *butter*. Making a decision about *bread's* status as a word involved activating the node where *bread* was stored. The spread of activation to strongly associated nodes ensured that *butter* would be activated as well, thus reducing the time required to make a decision about it.

ACT Theory

The ideas contained in TLC and its extensions, along with several additional advances, have been systematized in a theory known as **ACT.** (ACT is not an acronym, but like most theories embodied in computer programs, it is usually written in capitals.) This approach was developed by Anderson (1976) and was derived from an earlier theory (Anderson & Bower, 1973).

Propositional Analysis

At the core of ACT is the notion that the elements of permanent memory are stored as *propositions*. A proposition has been defined as the smallest unit of knowledge that can possess a truth value (Anderson, 1980). Propositions are abstract, cognitive events, but for the sake of convenience, propositions are often depicted as short sentences. The remainder of this chapter adopts this convention, too, but don't be misled. What I'll be calling a proposition is really a sentence-form representation of a proposition.

According to Anderson's definition, then, "green" is not a proposition because it makes no assertion that can be proved true or false. On the other hand, "Green is a color" is a proposition because its truth can be verified. In ACT, complex units of knowledge are broken down into propositions. Consider the sentence "Joey kissed the beautiful girl, whom he had recently met." This sentence can be broken down into three propositions:

1. Joey kissed the girl.
2. The girl was beautiful.
3. Joey recently met the girl.

Once these propositions have been obtained, they are encoded into a notation originally developed for this purpose by Kintsch (1974). (A simplified version is presented here.) This notation specifies that all propositions must have at least two parts. The first of these parts is called the *relation*. The relation of a proposition can be determined by analyzing the parts of speech in the sentence. Verbs and adjectives typically make up the relations of a proposition. The second part of the proposition is called the *argument*, which is determined by the nouns in the proposition. In Kintsch's system, the prior list of sentences would be shown as a set of lists, each containing a relation, followed by a listing of arguments:

4. kiss, Joey, girl, past
5. beautiful, girl
6. meet, Joey, girl, recently, past

In ACT, such ordered lists are next converted into networks of propositions. The propositional network thus created bears a superficial resemblance to the semantic network of TLC. That is, the nodes of the propositional network stand for ideas, and the linkages among the nodes represent associations ammong those ideas (Anderson, 1980). In ACT, each node in the network represents a proposition and is designated by a numbered ellipse. Radiating outward from these ellipses are the relations and arguments, which are also labeled. Figure 6.6 shows propositions 1 through 3 represented individually and as a network.

Illustrating this analysis with the "Joey" sentence was easy, but some sentences present considerably greater difficulties. Understanding the rest of this chapter will be a lot easier for you if you know how to construct these networks. For this reason, I urge you to work a few sentences on your own. Table 6.2 is taken from Anderson (1980) and is useful as an aid in network construction.

If you developed a few representations on your own, you may have noticed that different sentences sometimes have an identical representation.

TABLE 6.2

Guidelines for the Construction of Propositional Representations

1. Identify all the relational terms. Mainly these will be verbs, adjectives, expressions such as *captain of* or *father of,* and some prepositions such as *above* or *on top of.*
2. Write simple sentences for each relation. These simple sentences will involve only the relation and its noun arguments. Each sentence will correspond to one of the sentence's propositions.
3. To begin constructing the network, draw an ellipse to represent the node for each proposition.
4. Write the relation for each proposition beside its node. Connect the proposition node to the relation via an arrow labeled *relation.*
5. Create nodes for each of the nounlike units in the propositions. Two kinds of nouns must be distinguished. If the noun refers to a specific object, such as *Nixon,* simply write this noun. If the noun refers to an instance of a class noun, such as a *man,* create a new node (call it something arbitrary such as *X*) and connect this new node to the class node by an *isa* label. In creating these nodes, be careful to avoid duplicating the same node. If *Nixon* appears in two or more propositions, it should be represented by only one node.
6. Draw arrows between each proposition node and the noun nodes it involves. Label these arrows with an appropriate semantic label such as *subject, agent, object, recipient, location, time,* and so on.
7. Rearrange the network to make it neat.

Source: From *Cognitive Psychology and Its Implications* (1st ed.), by J. R. Anderson. W. H. Freeman and Company. Copyright © 1980. All rights reserved.

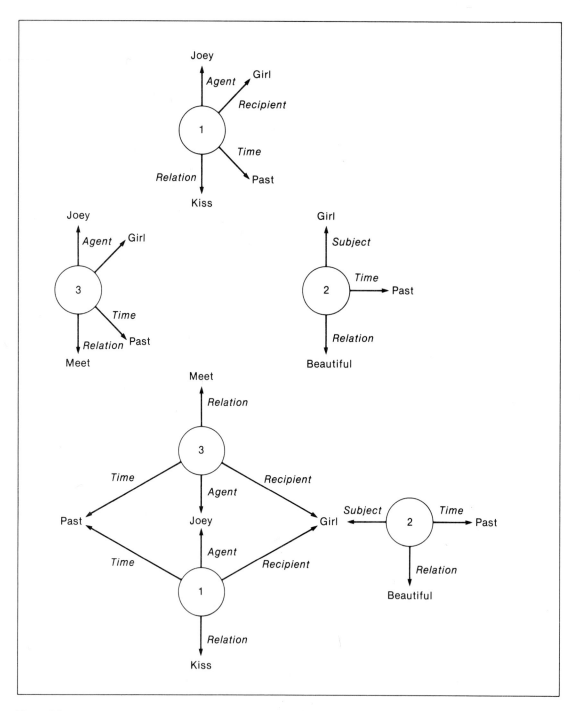

Figure 6.6.

A small propositional representation of the sentence "Joey kissed the beautiful girl, whom he had recently met."

For example, the sentences

Patrick is cooking supper for Cynthia.

and

Cynthia's supper is being cooked by Patrick.

both have the same propositional representation that is shown in Figure 6.7. This anomaly may at first seem unfortunate to you, but it is a good feature of ACT. Remember that these diagrammatic representations are not what is actually encoded and stored; they are simply vehicles for depicting the meaning of the sentence. The meaning of the sentence is what is actually stored. Recall from our discussion of Sachs's (1967) study in Chapter 5 that subjects are more or less unable to retrieve the actual wording of an utterance, although they retain a reasonable memory for its meaning. The structure of ACT implies a good explanation for this finding. Once the sentence has been represented propositionally, the subject is unable to translate it back into any specific phrasing, because the propositional representation doesn't possess the necessary instructions to do so.

Representation of Semantic and Episodic Memory

As discussed earlier, a good theory of semantic memory should show how episode knowledge is incorporated into its structure. In a real sense, the "Joey" sentence examined before is an example of episodic memory. We now need to discuss how such episodic knowledge would be couched in some

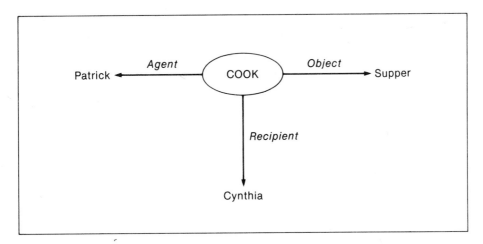

Figure 6.7.

Propositional representations don't preserve grammatical voice; that is, the model has no mechanism to distinguish active from passive voice. (From Lindsay & Norman, 1977. Reprinted by permission of the publisher.)

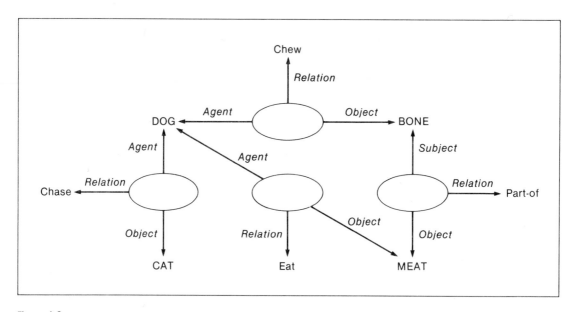

Figure 6.8.

A representation of *dog* in memory and some of its associated concepts. Presenting *dog* will prime these concepts. (From *Cognitive Psychology and Its Implications* (1st ed.), by J.R. Anderson. W.H. Freeman and Company. Copyright © 1980. All rights reserved.)

larger semantic structure. ACT has several ways of accomplishing this objective.

Figure 6.8 is a depiction of a possible propositional network for the concept *dog* and its associations. The knowledge represented here includes the idea that dogs chase cats. We can assume that the hypothetical person whose mind is depicted in Figure 6.8 has some other knowledge of cats that is not shown in the figure. We might speculate that the typical person's *cat* representation would include some nodes depicting cats' fondness for chasing helpless animals, their standoffish natures, and so forth. What if the hypothetical person were me, the not-so-proud owner of a bad cat who recently scratched the sofa? My representation would then have to include:

My cat scratched the sofa.

This sentence would be represented in the Kintsch system by the following ordered lists:

4. mine, cat
5. scratch, cat, sofa, past

Next, these lists would be converted into propositional representations of the sort shown in Figure 6.9. These representations would then be nested under the *cat* node in the semantic section of the propositional representation of Figure 6.8. This indicates that personal, idiosyncratic knowledge

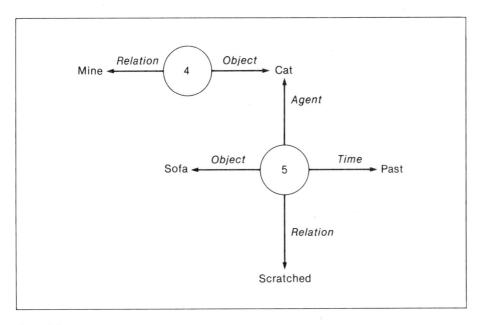

Figure 6.9.

Representation of episodic knowledge of *cat* in semantic memory.

can be depicted in propositional terms by taking advantage of the type-token distinction. Semantic knowledge is represented in the type nodes—those that actually define objects in more or less context-free terms. Episodic knowledge is represented by token nodes, which are situation-specific and enmeshed in some particular context. This distinction may seem only weakly made in a diagrammatic sense; that is, the two kinds of nodes don't seem particularly easy to distinguish from one another. Again, this apparent shortcoming serves us well: The boundary between episodic and semantic knowledge is not clear-cut. With a few more instances of sofa scratching by other cats encoded into the network, the knowledge would become less episodic and more semantic. That is, I would become more willing to say that sofa scratching is a general and context-free property of cats.

Anderson (1976) discusses a second aspect of episodic knowledge in ACT. Consider Figure 6.10, which shows part of a hypothetical propositional network for the concept *apple*. Notice that some of the expected type nodes are present, such as those that relate *apple* to its superordinate categories *fruit* and *food*. However, *apple* is also associated with certain primitive sensory and motor nodes. For example, apples come in various colors, and whatever meaning these colors might have is also stored propositionally. The meaning of these colors is stored in a location that is proximate to the kind of code that our nervous systems create when light of a certain wavelength (i.e., red or green) strikes our retinae. In other words, the meaning of the colors is stored adjacent to the code for the primitive sensory experience on which the meaning is based. Similarly, the term *eat* is stored adjacent to the code representing the motor behavior required in eating something. Most of the

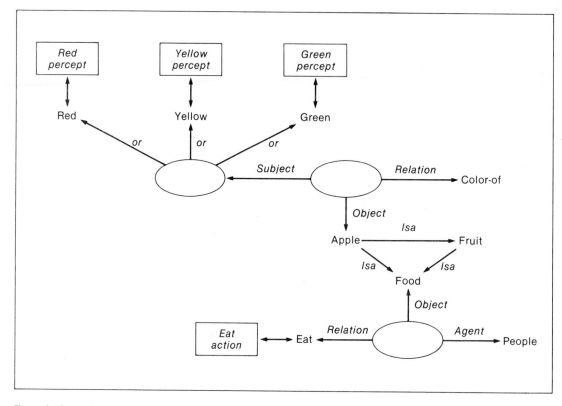

Figure 6.10.

A portion of a hypothetical propositional network structure for *apple*. (From *Cognitive Psychology and Its Implications* (1st ed.), by J.R. Anderson. W.H. Freeman and Company. Copright © 1980. All rights reserved.)

time, such nodes are not overtly depicted in the propositional representation, but their necessary reality is always implied.

My point in mentioning such nodes is to demonstrate Anderson's recognition that the meaning of a concept cannot be produced simply by embedding that concept in a network of other concepts. Aside from the obvious problem of circularity, such a view would run into other difficulties as well. The meaning of an object or person is always dependent upon some sort of event: an interaction of our cognitive systems with stimuli that are outside the system. Events, then, are necessarily mediated by our sensory and motor capabilities, meaning that at the edge of every propositional network must be nodes linking the propositional representations with the codes for primitive sensory and motor experiences upon which all knowledge is ultimately anchored and rooted.

Assumptions of ACT

We've seen how semantic knowledge can be represented propositionally and how episodic memory can be nested within larger semantic structures. Before detailing some of the empirical findings related to ACT, I'll list and

TABLE 6.3

Assumptions of Anderson's ACT Theory

Declarative Knowledge
1. Strength assumption: Each link has a specified strength, and the strength of a newly formed link is low but is incremented every time the link is used.
2. Activation assumption: At any instant, a small portion of the nodes in long-term memory are in an active state; all other nodes are not.
3. Spread of activation assumption: Activation spreads out from an active node to the passive nodes to which it is linked. The stronger the link between two nodes, the more likely it is that the activation will spread along that link. The spread of activation has a limited capacity, in that the more links that are being activated at once, the less activation will spread to any one.
4. Dampening assumption: Periodically, activation is dampened throughout the network (i.e., all nodes and links are deactivated).
5. Active list assumption: A maximum of ten nodes can be kept on the active list (ACT's working memory). Nodes on this active list are not dampened, so they remain active as long as they are kept on the list.

Source: Adapted with permission of Macmillan Publishing Company. From *Cognitive Psychology* by Darlene V. Howard. Copyright © 1983 by Darlene V. Howard.

describe some of its additional assumptions. ACT's five assumptions regarding the representation of declarative knowledge are enumerated in Table 6.3.

Assumption 1 (the strength assumption) indicates that the links radiating from a specific concept are not equally strong. Some nodes are highly associated, meaning that they share at least one linkage along which activation is likely to spread.

Assumption 2 (the activation assumption) is a statement about the distinction between working and permanent memory. What is activated is more accessible and more likely to enter consciousness. Most of our knowledge is inactive at any given point in time, and activating it requires a certain amount of time. This assumption is necessitated by a common and easily reproduced phenomenon of working memory: Bringing certain concepts into our consciousness usually lessens the time required to bring additional members of the same category into our awareness.

Assumption 3 (the spreading of activation assumption) is similar to the assumption made by Collins and Loftus (1975). An additional point is that the amount of activation energy is limited. If a large number of strongly associated links radiate outward from a particular node, then the strength of the activation spreading out along any particular link will be small. In other words, the total strength of the spreading activation energy is conserved. If only one strong link radiates from a node, then the strength of the activation on that link will be powerful. However, this strength is diluted if a large number of strong links radiate outward, because the activation energy is shared by all.

Assumption 4 (the dampening assumption) is an indirect way of making a theoretical statement about decay. Here, the assumption is that the spread of activation is periodically dampened, or toned down. The spread of activation won't necessarily go on forever. The inactive nodes in permanent memory seem inertial in that they offer some resistance to the spread of activation, gradually bringing it to a halt. The spread of activation is sometimes compared to the action of throwing a stone into a pool of water. The ripples radiate strongly at first, then weakly, and then the pool is calm again.

Assumption 5 (the active list assumption) states that ACT's working memory has a capacity of ten nodes. Chunking is not permitted; at least no theoretical way exists for grouping nodes together. Nodes that have been placed on the active list are not subject to the dampening assumption. This assumption is an attempt to deal with another well-known memory finding, namely, that items given maintenance rehearsal will not decay.

Empirical Support

One clear implication of ACT is that the retrieval of semantic knowledge should be facilitated if related semantic knowledge has been put into the active mode. The spread of activation assumption states that some energy should impinge upon related nodes, activating them and making them more accessible.

This implication was assessed in a study by Loftus (1974), who gave her subjects stimuli such as the following:

fruit—a

The stimulus mentioned both a category name and an initial letter. This stimulus cued the subjects to retrieve a fruit whose name began with (in this case) the letter *a*. When subjects were given this task, they required an average of 1.53 seconds to retrieve an appropriate fruit. After this task, the subjects were given another trial. The subjects were sometimes given another fruit trial immediately after the first. In this trial, the subjects might see

fruit—b

In other conditions, a one- or two-trial delay occurred before the subjects got another fruit trial. In these delay trials, the subjects got different category names such as *dogs—s* or *city—t*. When the subjects got the second fruit trial immediately after the first, they required 1.21 seconds to retrieve a second fruit name. When one trial intervened between the two fruit trials, subjects required 1.28 seconds to retrieve the second fruit name, and when two trials intervened, 1.33 seconds were required.

In this study, we see some support for the spread of activation assumption. Relative to the first time a category was activated, a large drop-off (from 1.53 seconds to 1.21 seconds) occurred in the time required to immediately retrieve a related node. However, the facilitating effect did not last long. With successive intervening trials in which nonrelated nodes were activated, retrieval time in the second fruit trial gradually increased. This finding is consistent with the dampening assumption. With time and activation of other nodes, the fruit nodes that were originally activated began to return to the inactive state.

These findings were amplified in a study by Anderson (1976). His subjects learned a series of sentences, all of which had the same format: A [specific type of person] is in [some specific location]. Subjects would therefore see sentences such as,

The sailor is in the park.
The lawyer is in the church.

The subjects were repeatedly drilled on these sentences until they knew them thoroughly. In the second phase of the study, the subjects were shown a sentence and then had to press one of two buttons indicating that the sentence was either one of those studied (a positive instance) or not studied (a negative instance). Negative instances were formed by combining elements of the positive sentences—for example,

The lawyer is in the park.

Because the subjects had studied the sentences intensively, they almost never made an error, and reaction time was therefore the variable of interest. The study had two independent variables. First, some of the sentences had been studied twice as much as the others. Second, like Loftus, Anderson was interested in seeing if a delay between presentations of a particular sentence would result in increased verification time. In some cases, the delay was short, meaning that from zero to two sentences intervened between presentations of a particular sentence. In other cases, the delay was long; three or more sentences intervened between presentations of the crucial sentence. Table 6.4 shows the findings of the study.

When the delay between presentations was short, the degree of study had little effect. In other words, in the short-delay conditions, the material was already activated and hadn't yet been completely dampened. Consequently, the strength of the original association was not a factor in facili-

TABLE 6.4

The Effects of Delay of Repetition and Frequency of Exposure on Recognition Time for Second Presentation of a Sentence

	Delay	
Degree of Study	Short (0 to 2 Intervening Items)	Long (3 or More Intervening Items)
Less study	1.11 sec	1.53 sec
More study	1.10 sec	1.38 sec

Source: Anderson, 1976. Copyright 1976 by Lawrence Erlbaum Associates, Inc. Adapted by permission of the publisher and author.

tating recognition of the sentence. However, when the delays were lengthy, then degree of study did have an effect. Subjects recognized the sentence faster when they had studied it more intensively. Assuming that in the long-delay condition, the sentence had been completely dampened and returned to an inactive state, we can compute how long it takes to activate a node in permanent memory by subtracting the time required to respond in the short-delay conditions from the time required to respond in the long-delay conditions. Carrying out this computation, activating a less-studied item takes .42 seconds (1.53 − 1.11 = .42). However, activating a well-studied item takes only .28 seconds (1.38 − 1.10 = .28). This study also has some implications for the strength assumption (assumption 1 in Table 6.3). When material is studied intensively, the associations between its nodes become progressively stronger. This increased strength could be manifested in any number of ways: improved accuracy, greater resistance to intrusion effects, or, as we have seen here, facility in recognition.

We looked at the effects of spreading activation in the Collins and Loftus (1975) model. Anderson and Perlmutter (in Anderson, 1980) have also duplicated these effects, using a technique derivative of that used in the Loftus (1974) study. Their subjects were presented with a series of words, each of which was followed by a single letter, as in

gambler—c
bone—m

The subjects were required to produce a free associate of the word, one that began with the indicated letter. This task was to be done as quickly as possible. The subject might therefore respond with "card" to *gambler* and "meat" to *bone*. In the control condition, each word in the series was unrelated. In the priming condition, the words were related to one another, as in

dog—c
bone—m

If you review the propositional network depicted in Figure 6.8, you'll get an understanding of why this series was of interest. Let's assume that Figure 6.8 is a good representation of peoples' semantic knowledge and that ACT is a good model of this knowledge. What takes place when a person is asked to generate a free associate to *dog?* First, the *dog* node is activated, and then this activation spreads outward along the strongly associated linkages to activate related concepts. In this case, the concepts *cat, bone,* and *meat* would all be activated. Because these concepts have been activated, they should be more accessible to consciousness. Consequently, we would expect faster reaction times to *bone—m* in the priming condition than we would in the control condition. This expectation was confirmed. Subjects required an average of 1.41 seconds to produce the second free associate in the priming condition, but they required 1.53 seconds to do the same thing in the control condition.

Regardless of how strongly associated specific nodes are, the spread of activation requires some time. Moreover, if the concept originally activated is at the center of an elaborate propositional network, then the amount of time required to activate one particular adjacent node might be longer than if the original node were associated only with the particular adjacent node. This is because the spread of activation is indiscriminate; it doesn't "know" which nodes should be activated next. Making an analogy between the spread of activation and a hydraulic system might be helpful. If a pumping station supplies water over a vast set of pipelines going in different directions, maintaining the water pressure will require more effort than if only a single pipeline exists. If the pumping capacity of the station is held constant, water in the large system is sure to move more sluggishly than in the single pipeline system, and the time it takes the water to reach a distant community will be correspondingly longer. The propositional representations we have been considering operate in a similar way. The activation of a node generates an amount of energy that is assumed to be more or less constant. If the node is central to a large group of nodes whose associative strength is also more or less equal, the spread of activation will require more time to reach any one of them than if the original node were not as completely enmeshed. This is referred to as the **fan effect** (Anderson, 1976).

These considerations were explored by Anderson (1974) in another study in which the person-location paradigm was used. Subjects memorized twenty-six such sentences, which had been varied in several ways. In some cases, a given person appeared in only one location. In other sentences, a person was mentioned who appeared in two locations, or sometimes a location was mentioned in which two people had appeared. Consider the following sentences:

1. The doctor is in the bank. (1-1)
2. The fireman is in the park. (1-2)
3. The lawyer is in the church. (2-1)
4. The lawyer is in the park. (2-2)

The numbers following the sentences indicate the number of facts associated with the subject of the sentence and the location in which the subject appears. Sentence 4 is labeled (2-2), meaning that the subject of the sentence—the lawyer—appears in two sentences (3 and 4), and the location mentioned in the sentence—the park—appears in two sentences (2 and 4). As previously, the subjects were drilled on these sentences until they could list all the places in which a given person appeared, or all the people who had ever shown up at a particular location. The subjects were then shown a series of sentences one at a time and were asked to determine as quickly as possible whether or not each had been part of the study set. Foil sentences were created by rearranging people and locations from the study set. The response times for the previously studied sentences (such as those just given) are shown in Table 6.5.

TABLE 6.5

Mean Recognition Time for Sentences as a Function of Number of Facts Learned about Person and Location

Number of Sentences Using a Specific Location	Number of Sentences about a Specific Person	
	One Sentence	Two Sentences
One sentence	1.11 sec	1.17 sec
Two sentences	1.17 sec	1.22 sec

Source: Anderson, 1974. Reprinted by permission of the publisher.

Table 6.5 is remarkably and beautifully symmetrical. Recognition time increased as a function of both the frequency with which a person appeared and the frequency with which a specific location was mentioned. Referring to sentences 1–4 just shown, we would expect sentence 1 to be recognized faster than either sentences 2 or 3, which in turn would be recognized faster than sentence 4.

To see how these findings are consistent with the assumptions of the fan effect, consider Figure 6.11, which is a simplified depiction of a hypothetical person's propositional network for the sentences used in Anderson's (1974) study.

To recognize a sentence such as "A lawyer is in the park," the subject would activate the nodes for *lawyer* and *park*. Activation would then spread out from *lawyer* to *park* and to *church*. Activation would also spread from *park* out to *lawyer* and to *fireman*. Because the rate at which activation spreads is inversely proportional to the number of links radiating from a particular node, the subject would require more time before the search processes noted an intersection for the nodes *lawyer* and *park*. That is, as the number of linkages radiating from a node increases, the size of the resulting activated fan that must be searched increases dramatically. However, to recognize the sentence "A doctor is in the bank," the search processes don't fan out nearly as much, with the result that the activation spreads quickly between the two nodes originally activated.

Other studies (Anderson, 1976) demonstrated that the size of the fan seemed to determine reaction time, rather than any specific characteristic of the subject or the locations involved. The same person-location procedure was used, but in this study, the size of the study set was somewhat larger, including sentences of the form 3-3. That is, some sentences mentioned people who appeared in three different locations and mentioned locations in which one of three different people could appear. A group of foils was generated by re-pairing the elements of the study set. The subjects' response times are shown in Table 6.6.

Looking first at the true sentences, we see that the response time indeed depends upon the size of the propositional fan. For example, sentences of the form 1-2 and 2-1 have similar response times, which is also true for some of the other pairs having the same size fans. Turning to the false sentences,

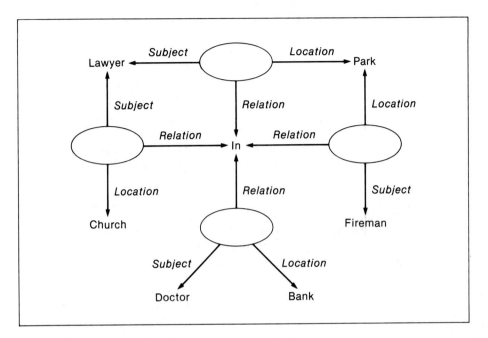

Figure 6.11.
A propositional representation of form sentences used by Anderson (1974).

TABLE 6.6

Results from Anderson's Fact Retrieval Study

	Propositional Fan	Reaction Time (msec)
True	1-1	1,111
	1-2	1,167
	1-3	1,153
	2-1	1,174
	2-2	1,198
	2-3	1,233
	3-1	1,222
	3-2	1,222
	3-3	1,357
False	1-1	1,197
	1-2	1,250
	1-3	1,262
	2-1	1,221
	2-2	1,356
	2-3	1,471
	3-1	1,264
	3-2	1,291
	3-3	1,465

Source: Anderson, 1976. Copyright 1976 by Lawrence Erlbaum Associates, Inc. Adapted by permission of the publisher and author.

we see that the average reaction times were longer than those for true sentences with the same size fan. For example, reaction time for the true sentences whose fan was 2-1 was 1,174 msec, but this time increased to 1,221 msec for a false sentence of the same format. Also, we see the fan effect in operation here, too. False sentences with large fans required more time to refute than false sentences with small fans. Why should this be so?

Anderson has theorized that ACT conducts an intersection search of the network, similar to the one carried out by TLC. When a false sentence is presented, the intersection search will be unsuccessful, because the network has no intersection in which both terms are associated. However, because the subject is essentially waiting for a negative event—that is, the absence of a report—then he must wait long enough to make sure that the search processes are not going to find an intersection. This attack on the problem will be successful only if the subject waits long enough to let the search processes do their work. Therefore, Anderson would expect that the false sentences would require more time than the positive sentences, because the decision to press the "false" button can be enacted only after the subject is fairly certain that the search processes aren't going to find an intersection. The fan effect is observed because, as Anderson theorizes, the subject knows that the larger fans require more time to search. Consequently, if the wait-to-respond strategy is to be successful, the subject must take the size of the fan into account before responding.

Comments about ACT and Network Models in General

ACT is a persuasive account of retrieval from permanent memory, and its persuasiveness is based on several findings. First, the semantic priming effects that we saw in the Meyer and Schvaneveldt (1971) study are most easily interpreted in the context of spreading activation. And incidentally, these priming effects have some clear implications for the use of free association in psychotherapeutic settings or in stream of consciousness writing. That is, we could argue—and fairly strongly, too—that the nature of the associations and their temporal relations do indicate something about their author's mental, or cognitive, organization of the world.

Second, as we saw in the last chapter, human retrieval from permanent memory is abstractive. What is stored is seldom what was actually heard or seen, but rather what meaning was drawn from those events. This finding dovetails nicely with the nature of propositional analysis and construction. You'll recall that specific phrasings are not built into the propositional representation—only the statement's underlying meaning. In other words, ACT has no mechanism for discriminating sentences such as "Dogs chase cats" from sentences such as "Cats are chased by dogs." This inability to detect changes in voice at retrieval time is consistent with actual findings (Sachs, 1967).

Third, retrieval from permanent memory is constructive. We saw these effects when we looked at Bartlett's work on "The War of the Ghosts" story in Chapter 5. His subjects altered the native American story to be consistent with the details of British life, and where the memory trace seemed to have evaporated completely, Bartlett's subjects inferred what must have taken place. ACT accounts for these findings by exploiting a feature of the type-token distinction. As various nodes are activated and associated, the distinction between type (semantic) nodes and token (episodic) nodes becomes increasingly blurry. This is the result of assumption 1 (the strength assumption). We saw that token nodes are initially nested under type nodes. As the type node is activated, activation spreads to the token nodes, which at first are only weakly associated with the type nodes. However, with every instance of activation, the strength of the association between the nodes increases. The result of this process is that the token nodes become assimilated into type nodes. These newly formed type nodes are then used as a basis for reasoning about, or inferring, what sorts of episodic knowledge should be nested below them.

Fourth, ACT seems to be an accurate portrayal of some of the difficulties involved in memory search. For example, so far we've thought of the propositional representation as a network along which activation energy flows. But this casts the would-be fact retriever as a passive spectator who simply awaits the results of a search process that seems to run more or less under its own control. Another way of viewing the search process is to look at the fact retriever as trying to get something back that is embedded in a tangled maze of associations. The more entangled a particular node, the greater the probability of its retrieval. The activation has so many channels along which to flow that sooner or later, the searched-for node is likely to become activated and accessible. However, the energy flowing along any particular linkage is weak under these circumstances, precisely because so many nodes are being searched (one of the consequences of assumption 3). The activation of any particular node adjacent to the searched-for node has only a small probability of in turn activating the desired node. This effect often produces the frustration we feel when we are unable to retrieve a well-known fact, regardless of how hard we search. Although we eventually get it, retrieval is often more time-consuming than what seems expected, because the search processes have encountered the resistance of densely populated sections of our semantic memories.

Although all of these phenomena are consistent with the postulates of ACT, a number of reasons call for leaving the door open for development of other approaches. First, as Anderson (1976) himself noted, not all empirical findings are as easily interpreted by his theory, and some findings (Foss & Harwood, 1975) are contradictory. Second, the ease with which ACT accounts for so many memory phenomena doesn't necessarily prove that it is correct. Although space limitations preclude discussing some of the alternatives to network models, rest assured that such models do exist (e.g., Smith, Shoben, & Rips, 1974). And these non-network models use a completely different formalism to account for the memory effects we have studied. In many cases, they are quite successful, too. The problem here is that the behavioral effects that we can observe, such as latency, accuracy, and so forth, are not necessarily powerful enough to let us determine the precise nature of the internal events underlying those responses. In the absence of such data, the alternative theories really aren't competing against one another. This is essentially the point made by (Johnson-Laird, Herrman, and Chaffin 1984), who criticized network models on several grounds. One of their objections was that these models specify only the connections between concepts, but the connections between concepts and the *world* are left unspecified. The theory of retrieval implied by such models is bound to be inadequate, because our retrieval processes are strongly based on our inference-making abilities—activities that are based on world knowledge. Some commentators (Wexler, 1978) have also discovered certain logical inconsistencies among ACT's postulates.

Perhaps the biggest stumbling block that network theories of semantic memory have faced is the unwillingness of some cognitive psychologists to accept what they view as serious drawbacks. (I'm in the debt of one of my reviewers, who suggested them to me.)

1. An assumption of sequential, as opposed to parallel, processing. You know that information-processing models of cognitive processes frequently assume that mental events occur serially. However, many cognitive psychologists have pointed out that this assumption of sequential processing is strictly for convenience' sake. Many cognitive processes involved in the encoding and retrieval of memories must occur in parallel.

2. No simulation of memory has ever come close to duplicating human performance. If we consider network models as a whole, we should become more impressed with our own semantic memories. This objection points out the tremendous amount of tacit knowledge that humans have. Formalizing this knowledge has proved to be extremely difficult. Part of the reason for this difficulty is that our retrieval processes are affected by our knowledge of linguistic discourse and practices in conversation. This kind of knowledge is called *pragmatics*. Our knowledge of pragmatics helps us interpret metaphors because we use pragmatics to determine when a conversationalist is speaking literally. In comments such as "I was shook up for a while after the accident" and "Shake up the orange juice before your pour it," the expression "shook up" is used in a metaphorical way in the first instance. Consequently, if we asked humans to retrieve the meaning of the sentences, different parts of their semantic networks would be searched. But a safe assumption is that none of the models we've reviewed could appreciate the difference in the two utterances.

3. Every model does at least one silly thing. This criticism is a corollary of the second objection. Because no network model has anything like the complete semantic network that humans possess, the models' retrieval processes can easily be made to look silly by asking them questions in which words cannot be interpreted literally.

4. The assumptions of the model are strange. Some cognitive psychologists are unhappy with assumptions such as those in Table 6.3. The logic is that these assumptions seem ad hoc in nature and are not based on any cognitive processes that we know about.

Chapter 13 also examines theories that attempt to model human organization and retrieval of knowledge. Some of these theories may have certain advantages over ACT, but to some extent, each of the prior criticisms could be leveled at those theories, too. For a variety of reasons, cognitive psychologists are still waiting for the ultimate theory of semantic memory.

REPRESENTATIONAL THOUGHT AND MEMORY

Chapter 3 contains a section similar to this one. That section attempted to discuss the relationship between awareness and perception, and suggested that in the literature on cognitive maps, this relationship could be clearly discerned. This section has a similar objective: to discuss the relationship between awareness and memory. We'll examine this relationship from the perspective of what has been called **metamemory** (Flavell & Wellman, 1977), which refers to the personal knowledge we have of how our memory systems operate. I'm sure you know that metamemory improves dramatically during the first part of a person's life. Children have significantly less knowledge than you have regarding the effective use of their memories. Accordingly, taking a developmental approach to this topic seems reasonable.

Metamemory

Flavell (1971) used *metamemory* to refer to any aspect of the relationship between awareness and memory. Later, Flavell and Wellman (1977) refined the term and described metamemory as being any one of several different kinds of knowledge that people might have about their storage or retrieval processes. Specifically, metamemory can be broken down into three different categories of memory knowledge (Wingfield & Byrnes, 1981):

1. *Knowledge of one's own characteristics* that are relevent to remembering. This kind of knowledge comprises our attitudes to our memories, as well as knowledge of our particular capacities and abilities. For example, you may know that you do better on essay tests than on multiple-choice tests because you find that retrieving information you've organized on your own is easier than making a judgment about the correctness of teacher-organized material. Similarly, you may know that remembering something that some has explained to you is easier than remembering something you've read about. On the other hand, you may know that the mode of input is not particularly important to you. In these cases, we remember what has worked for us in the past, and we retrieve this knowledge to guide the encoding of new material.
2. *Knowledge about differences among tasks* that are important in storage and retrieval. This category contains the knowledge we have concerning the memory demands of a task and how well our memories will be able to meet those demands. For example, you know what

happens when you are introduced to a large number of people at a party. As the introductions drone on, you probably become aware that you're not going to remember all the names you've just heard. The people being introduced sometimes challenge you to retrieve their names, which brings up a related point. If everyone knows that a long series of introductions imposes an almost impossible demand on someone's memory, then why do people persist in doing it? Most adults have a fairly large fund of such task knowledge. For example, you probably know that you will remember the meaning and tone of a conversation but not the exact wording. You probably also know that memorizing a list of related words is easier than memorizing unrelated words, and so on.

3. *Strategic knowledge,* which refers to our ability to direct encoding and search processes. For example, you probably know many retrieval strategies. If asked what you had for lunch yesterday, you might try to retrieve this information by thinking about what day of the week it was, who your companions may have been, where you went for lunch, and so on. The point is, if one of these approaches doesn't locate the information, you know that when you approach your propositional network from a different angle, you'll activate the nodes in a different order, which may activate the desired node.

Although I couched your knowledge of the search process in terms of activation in a propositional representation, you knew how to control retrieval long before you studied ACT. This point is important. Metamemory is implicit knowledge. Most people don't know where they learned about their memories or how they came by this knowledge, but they are nevertheless often fairly certain that their knowledge is accurate. This statement prompts two questions. First, can cognitivists outline the acquisition of metamemory? Second, is the assurance people have of their metamemorial knowledge well founded, or does peoples' knowledge of their memories contain some inaccuracies?

Development of Metamemory

Ample evidence indicates that small children don't have much knowledge in any of the three categories just mentioned. Flavell and Wellman (1977) found, for example, that their five-year-old subjects didn't rehearse a string of digits during a short-term retention task. This point is an interesting one. Children can easily be taught to rehearse strings of digits or lists of words, and when they do, their retention improves substantially. Even though children know the meaning of the phrase "Say these to yourself, over and over," and they have the ability to rehearse, they don't rehearse unless explicitly instructed. This type of failure is referred to as a **production deficiency**—a failure to use a strategy that one has the ability to execute. Production deficiencies can be constrasted with *process deficiencies* (Craik & Simon, 1980). The latter term is defined as an inability to execute some activity, because a memory process or capacity has not yet been fully developed.

Some findings suggest that during the early school years, childrens' knowledge of the memory demands imposed by different tasks increases significantly. Yussen and Levy (1975) asked their five- and eight-year-old subjects to estimate how many things from a list they could recall without a mistake—in essence, an estimate of their memory span. Both groups overestimated the number of elements they could recall. The subjects then heard strings of nine or ten elements and attempted to recall them immediately after the presentation. Working memory was clearly overburdened by these demands. After several trials, the experimenters again asked the subjects to estimate their memory spans. The eight-year-olds revised their estimates appropriately—that is, downward. But the preschoolers didn't revise their estimates and were optimistic that they'd get all of them right during the next trial. The preschoolers were apparently unable to tell that their working memories were being overburdened.

This finding has some implications for other memory processes. In a series of studies, Brown and Smiley (1977, 1978; Brown, Smiley, & Lawton, 1978) found that children learn to pick out important factors in a story and use them as a basis for retrieval. First, the experiments had a group of raters determine the structural importance of various idea units in a series of Japanese fairy tales that had been translated into English. The structural importance was a rating given to each of the passage's ideas and can be interpreted as an indicator of how necessary remembering that idea was to understanding the passage as a whole. Table 6.7 shows some of the idea units and their rated importance.

Next, Brown and Smiley gave the passage to third, fifth, and seventh graders, and to college students. After reading the story, the subjects were asked to recall as much as they could. When the proportion of recalled ideas was analyzed as a function of the idea's importance, the researchers found that all the subjects tended to recall the important ideas better than the less important ideas. Sixty-nine percent of all the subjects recalled the most important idea, but only 23 percent of all the subjects recalled the least important idea. Although this finding was true for all age levels, an age

TABLE 6.7

Idea Units and Their Rated Importance

Unit	Rated Importance
1. Once upon a time	162
2. there was a rich lord	356
3. who liked to collect carvings of animals	321
4. (those are like little wooden dolls)	106
5. He had many kinds	150
6. but he had no carved mouse	294
7. So he called two skilled carvers to him and said	341
8. "I want each of you to carve a mouse for me."	397

Source: Brown and Smiley, 1977. Copyright 1977 by the Society For Research in Child Development, Inc.

effect was nevertheless noted. Older subjects recalled more of the material regardless of its importance. That is, even of the less important material, the older subjects recalled more than the younger subjects did. Superficially, this finding suggests that the younger subjects had a process deficiency, meaning that they hadn't yet developed the ability to store large amounts of material.

Other findings have suggested a deeper interpretation. In an additional experiment, Brown and Smiley (1977) asked their subjects to make the structural importance ratings originally done by only the college students. The researchers discovered that the younger subjects were not very skilled at distinguishing the important ideas from the peripheral ones. Whereas the college students were able to distinguish four levels of importance in the passage, seventh graders were able to distinguish only three levels, fifth graders distinguished two levels, and third graders distinguished only one level. Table 6.8 shows the numerical evaluation made of the least important and most important ideas in the passage by third graders and college students. Note that there is no appreciable difference among the ratings made by the third graders. If the younger subjects indeed have a process deficiency, it is an inability to detect the important aspects of a story. This apparent inability is bound to affect the subjects' encoding and comprehension of the story, because the meaning of such a passage is largely dependent upon the readers' ability to abstract important or thematic ideas.

Smiley, Oakley, Worten, Campione, and Brown (1977) extended this idea in a study of retrieval among seventh graders. They found that recall patterns of good readers corresponded closely with ratings of idea importance: Important ideas were consistently recalled by good readers. However, this correspondence was not as good for poor readers. This finding suggests that the poor readers were not as sensitive to the structure of the story as were good readers. Perhaps more significant, it suggests that poor readers were not as sensitive to the importance of the story's structure as a vehicle, or medium, to aid memory.

Comparing the performance of college students with school age children might give the impression that metamemory is fully developed among young adults and that their knowledge is invariably accurate. These impressions are false, however. Shaughnessy (1981) asked college students to predict

TABLE 6.8

Ratings of Structural Importance by Subjects of Different Ages in the Brown and Smiley Study

Subjects	Importance Rating	
	Least Important Fact	Most Important Fact
Third graders	2.41	2.56
College students	1.61	3.52

Source: Brown and Smiley, 1977. Copyright 1977 by the Society for Research in Child Development, Inc.

which of two learning conditions would produce better performance on a memory test. In one case, a list of words was to be learned by simple rote repetition. In the second case, the list of words was to be learned using a procedure that prompted the subjects to elaborate the words' meanings. Subject predicted that the two techniques would produce equivalent learning, but they actually performed much better in the elaboration condition. The subjects' memory knowledge was obviously incomplete and inaccurate. They persisted in their belief that rote repetition was an effective rehearsal strategy even though their own behavior provided evidence to the contrary. Subjects who were given permission to learn the list any way they wanted frequently reported that they learned by rote repetition. This knowledge also seems inaccurate, because these subjects outperformed the group that had been instructed to memorize the list using rote repetition.

Earlier I phrased two questions about metamemory, and I'll now summarize my answers. First, cognitive psychologists have provided a reasonably detailed outline of the course of metamemory improvement. Specifically, improvement during the grade school years occurs in both the second and third categories of memory knowledge discussed earlier. That is, grade school children begin to get a better idea of the demands that various memory tasks impose, and they begin to develop more effective encoding strategies as their sensitivity to story structures increases. In response to the second question, adults are apparently not infallible about their metamemory. Some evidence (Klatzky, 1984) suggests that people are strongly influenced by certain folk beliefs about memory, some of which are incorrect.

CONCLUDING COMMENTS AND SUGGESTIONS FOR FURTHER READING

If you've read the last three chapters in order, you've seen a seesaw struggle between two important themes in cognitive psychology. The two themes are structure and process. When cognitive psychologists use the term *structure* to describe some psychological phenomenon, they mean to emphasize the organization that seems inherent in certain mental events. Structurally oriented psychologists frequently attempt to model mental events by developing a formal system whose organization seems to have the same properties as the mental events being studied. When cognitive psychologists use the term *process* to describe a mental event, they intend to emphasize the computations that the cognitive system engages in.

Chapter 4 examined the first information-processing model of memory. You'll recall that its structural components (the different storage locations) are no longer dogmatically endorsed by most theorists. In turn, Chapter 5 described the various processes of the cognitive system in memory. This chapter, however, showed that most of these processes have been invoked to explain the results of fairly artificial laboratory studies of memory that emphasized episodic knowledge. Current theories of semantic memory seem to have reclaimed the structural approach. The sequence of the chapters may give the impression that the star of the structural approach has once again risen, and to a certain extent, this seems to be true (Sternberg, 1984, p. 90ff.). However, any theory of memory will need both structure and process components. But still a problem remains. Some theorists (notably, Anderson, 1978) have wondered whether some basic indeterminacies exist that cannot be resolved by behavioral data. That is, behavioral data may not be powerful enough to either establish or rule out structure versus process descriptions of some memory phenomena.

Readers who wish to pursue these matters might be interested in examining a process-oriented model of semantic memory. A good place to begin is the work of Smith, Shoben, and Rips (1974). Their semantic features model was subsequently criticized by Hollan (1975), who pointed out that any non-network model of semantic memory could be modified into a network model with no loss of information or predictive power. Hollan's article was one of the first clear demonstrations of the indeterminacies just referred to. Some lucid commentary on the structure-process distinction can be found in Sternberg (1984).

Those interested in finding out more about ACT should try Anderson's (1976) book *Language, Memory and Thought*. Those who find the reading heavy going might try examining the somewhat more accessible *Human Associative Memory* (Anderson & Bower, 1973), in which HAM, the immediate predecessor of ACT, is described. For a thoughtful criticism of Anderson's work, read Wexler (1978) and then Anderson's (1980) rebuttal to the harsh words. Work on propositional analysis has continued apace, and people who want to read some of the latest findings might try Kolodner (1984).

Metamemory is sure to continue as a hot topic, and a good place to find out more about it is in Flavell and Wellman (1977). Readers who want further information (and a return to the structure-process distinction) should look at Flavell (1978). Cavanaugh and Perlmutter (1982) have offered a critical review of the metamemory literature.

FOCUS ON APPLICATIONS:
Making Your Own Semantic Networks

The material in this chapter is particularly abstract, and perhaps for this reason, getting a good intuitive feel for it is difficult for some students. Many of us consider our ideas as being either closely or loosely associated with one another, but some students have a hard time comprehending how this simple phenomenon can be translated into a representation that indicates something about the underlying mental structure.

This Focus section suggests an exercise that might help you understand how this translation can be done. You shouldn't view this technique as a scientifically legitimate way to formulate a semantic network, but it might yield some information about your mental organization. If nothing else, you might have some fun with it.

The exercise involves making a facsimile of a semantic network. You can start by first thinking of almost any term or concept that you have in your mental dictionary. But don't start yet. Before you think of a term or concept, get ready with paper and pencil and note the first free associate that

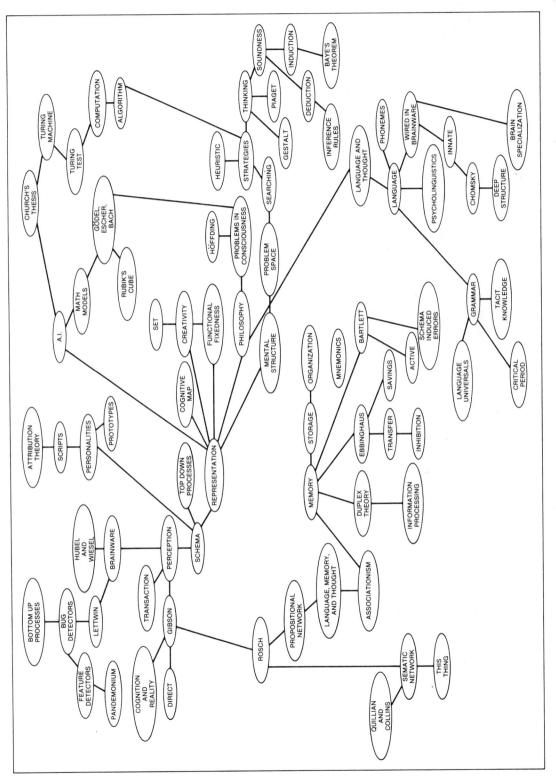

Figure 6.12. The author's semantic network for *mental structure*.

comes into your mind when you think of that term. Then note the second associate, and so on, until it seems to you that the words that you're writing are only loosely associated. Then arrange the initial term on a blank piece of paper and draw an ellipse around it. Next, make a subjective judgment about how closely related your first free associate was to this term. Write this term down (it can be above, below, or off to the side of the original term), draw an ellipse around it, and then connect the terms with a line. Then make a judgment about the degree of association between the second free associate and the original term. This degree of association will probably be less than that for the first free associate. Indicate this lessened degree on the page by increasing the distance between the original term and the second free associate. After you have all of your first-round associates depicted, pick one of them (in any order) and start free associating to it. After all these associations are drawn on the page, start free associating to another of the first-round associates. You can keep on going this way, probably forever, but don't do that. When you get to the point where all the concepts start to blur together (and they will—this is called semantic satiation), then stop. You may have to rearrange the ellipses to make them look neater on the page.

Just for fun, I tried this technique, starting with the term *mental structure*. So the structure wouldn't get too large, I held the association process to just one or two associates per term. I was thinking that I might get a view of my own semantic network for *cognitive psychology*. I think that it worked out fairly well. The resulting network is reproduced in Figure 6.12.

KEY TERMS

Episodic memory
Semantic memory
Network models
Type-token distinction
TLC
Intersection search
Spreading activation model

Prestored knowledge
Semantic priming
ACT theory
Propositional analysis
Fan effect
Metamemory
Production deficiency

CHAPTER 7

Imagery

OVERVIEW

REBIRTH OF IMAGERY

DOING OPERATIONS OF MENTAL IMAGES
Mental Rotation of Abstract Shapes
Mental Rotation of Letters

LOOKING AT MENTAL IMAGES
Folding Mental Paper
Comparing the Size of Mental Objects
Mental Psychophysics
Mental Travel

Summary

FUNCTIONAL PROPERTIES OF IMAGES
Storage of Images
Functional Significance of Images
    Interference in Scanning Images

THE NATURE OF THE IMAGE

CONCLUDING COMMENTS AND SUGGESTIONS
FOR FURTHER READING
FOCUS ON RESEARCH
KEY TERMS

The usefulness of imagery in answering certain types of questions can be demonstrated in many ways. For example, suppose a wooden cube, 3 centimeters on a side, is painted red. Then suppose the cube is sliced up in the following ways. First, two slices are made through the cube. These cuts are made parallel to the plane in which the cube is sitting, at heights of 1 centimeter and 2 centimeters from the surface plane. Then, two more cuts are made parallel to one of the vertical faces of the cube at distances of 1 centimeter and 2 centimeters from the vertical face. Finally, two more cuts are made that are parallel to one of the vertical faces and at right angles to each of the first two sets of cuts. These final two cuts also divide the faces they intersect into equal parts. What do we now have? If you say that we have twenty-seven wooden cubes, 1 centimeter on a side, your're correct. Suppose I persist: How many of the little cubes have three faces painted red? How many have two red faces? How many have one red face? How many have no red faces?

It might be possible to follow the description of cuts through the original block without constructing an image of the block. But is it possible to answer the second series of questions about the redness of the little cubes without inspecting a mental image? The responses of the people I've quizzed have shown no variation. Everyone says that they imagined the cube, imagined it being sawed up, "looked at" the cubes that were created, and counted how many red faces each cube had.

One striking characteristic of people's reports is their insistence that the image can be "watched." In this sense, the image is like a picture—a picture in the mind. Given this overwhelming agreement, can there be any doubt about the image's authenticity?

Unquestionably, the image is special. If we compare our abilities at image watching with other forms of sensory internal representation, the latter seem curiously shabby. To see I mean, imagine a popular tune with which you're familiar. Then try the following operations: Can you turn up the volume? How loud can you make it? Can you turn up just the bass? Can you imagine someone else singing the tune? People sometimes tell me they can do these things, but almost everyone agrees that the images thus created aren't nearly as vivid as visual images. Yet, when we're sitting in our living rooms, we're not aware of any differences in sensory stimulation. The Police album on our turntable seems just as vivid as the Mark Rothko print on our wall. Our ears seem to work as well as our eyes. Why, then, doesn't our mental stereo work as well as our mental VCR?

The past ten years have seen an enormous volume of research dealing with the many questions raised by mental imagery. This chapter describes some of the evidence dealing with the properties of images—in particular, their picture-like qualities. You may have already guessed that the image's similarity to a picture is one reason why cognitive psychologists find the *dual code position* so attractive. That is, because images seem to have picturelike properties that can't easily be converted into words, many cognitive psychologists have inferred that our cognitive system must have two formats for encoding and storing cognitive codes: a visual format and a verbal format. We've looked at the dual code issue in earlier chapters, and it reappears in this chapter. In addition to the reality of these picturelike properties, and its implications for encoding and storage, many cognitive psychologists have tried to answer other questions about images. When a person uses an image to solve a problem (as in the beginning of this Overview), is the creation of an image *necessary* to solve the problem? If it is, then we might argue that, yes, our cognitive system is apparently designed to process visual information in a special way. If, however, the creation of an image is *not* necessary (but simply convenient) to solve such problems, then questions arise about both the nature and the function (i.e., the purpose) of imagery. This chapter shows that such questions have indeed been raised. Although the chapter reviews a variety of studies that seem to be very convincing demonstrations of the necessity of imagery in doing certain tasks, a fair statement is that many of the claims made by the early researchers in this area have since come under heavy fire. The chapter later presents some of the reasons why many cognitive psychologists are no longer willing to believe that imagery is necessary to do certain tasks.

REBIRTH OF IMAGERY

Before going on to define and discuss imagery, putting this topic in its historical context might be helpful. Empirical knowledge of imagery was sadly lacking until about fifteen years ago. The lack of interest was the result of several factors. You'll recall from Chapter 1 that Oswald Kulpe and his Würzburgers formulated a doctrine of imageless thought near the beginning of this century. Although Kulpe was not opposed to studies of imagery, the focus of his work was nevertheless on alternatives to thinking in images. Later continental thinkers continued to deal with imagery as a sort of ancillary ability. Although the Gestaltists (of whom we'll see more in Chapter 12) argued that imagery is important in thinking, their objective was to demonstrate that perception is the common underpinning of all forms of mental activity. Consequently, Gestalt psychologists were more interested in the *function* of imagery (what role it played in thinking) than they were in imagery per se.

You may remember from Chapter 1 that when academic psychology took root in the United States, pragmatic Americans soon viewed behaviorism as sufficiently down-to-earth. As a result, large numbers of interesting psychological problems were purged because they were considered **mentalistic;** imagery was just one of the many casualties. Not until the late 1950s and early 1960s did psychologists rediscover something: The use of imagery could substantially enhance learning in some instances. As the 1960s progressed, psychologists became interested in what their subjects were doing when they used imagery to improve memory. As the findings from countless studies of imagery in verbal learning piled up, psychologists began to face up to an important problem: understanding the *nature* of the image as well as its function. When the 1970s dawned, cognitive psychologists girded and armed themselves for the hunt. The game has turned out to be very big indeed.

DOING OPERATIONS ON MENTAL IMAGES

The nature of the image seems pictorial to most people. That is, certain operations such as inverting, moving, or otherwise altering the image can be willfully initiated and carried out, and the effects of these operations can be subjectively viewed as if they were really happening to some physical stimulus. This common experience implies that the image must have at least some of the properties that the physical stimulus has. Indeed, the commonality between imagery and real perception has sometimes been used as a basis for defining images. Bower (1970, p. 502) writes: "A memory image . . . presents to the experiencing subject some of the same structural information as was presented in earlier perceptions." One implication of this viewpoint is that if images are like pictures in the mind, then the images should obey at least some of the laws of perception that physical objects obey. This implication leads to a question: Are at least some mental operations analogous to operations on physical stimuli? This section considers some of the findings in which subjects have been asked to carry out operations on images.

Mental Rotation of Abstract Shapes

Shepard and Metzler (1971) presented their subjects with pairs of abstract objects such as those shown in Figure 7.1. The subjects' task was to look at the pairs and, as quickly as possible, determine whether the drawings showed two different views of the same object or two different objects. Part A of Figure 7.1 shows two views of the same object: the right-hand view has been rotated 80 degrees from the left-hand view. Part B also shows two views of the same object. In this case, the right-hand view has also been rotated 80 degrees from the left-hand view, but the nature of the rotation is different from that in part A. In part A, the circles could be cut out from the page, placed on a surface, and physically rotated until they looked identical. This is referred to as a rotation in the picture plane. Part B shows a rotation in depth. The left-hand view has to be turned "into the page" to get it to match the right-hand view. Part C shows two views of two different objects. No rotation either in the picture plane or in depth will produce a congruence. If the two views were of the same object, the subjects were to respond "same"; if the objects shown were different from one another, the subjects were to respond "different." The time it took the subjects to make correct judgments was recorded.

One question Shepard and Metzler were concerned with was the *rate* at which these forms could be rotated. A moment's thought reveals why. If the subjects accomplish this task by "watching" one of the views mentally rotating, then this **mental rotation** would have to proceed slowly enough to permit the subjects time to see if the two views were going to match. If

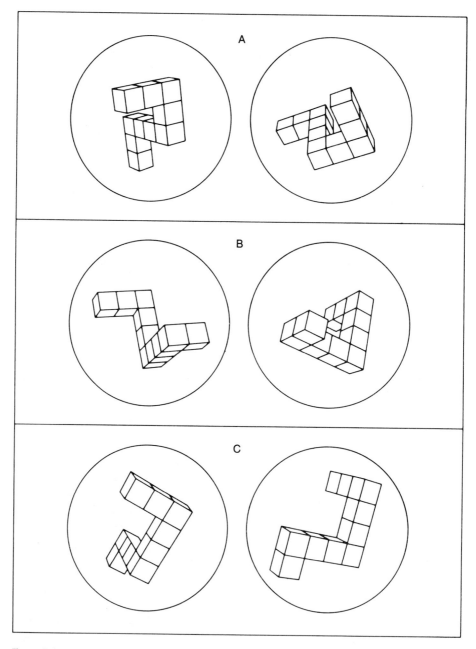

Figure 7.1.

Samples of the three-dimensional stimulus pairs that Shepard and Metzler used in their study of mental rotation: *A*, a pair differing by an 80-degree rotation in the picture plane; *B*, a pair differing by an 80-degree rotation in the depth plane; *C*, a pair that differs by a reflection as well as by a rotation. Subjects were to respond "same" to pairs like *A* and *B*, and "different" to pairs like *C*. (From "Mental Rotation of Three-dimensional Objects," by Shepard and Metzler. *Science* vol. 171, p. 701. Copyright 1971 by the American Association for the Advancement of Science.)

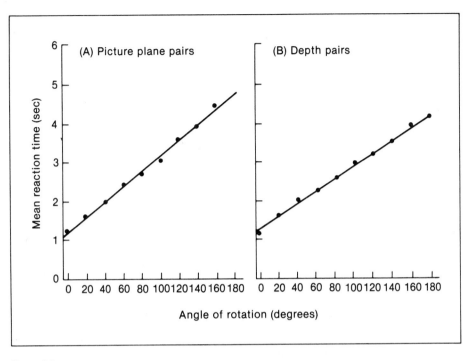

Figure 7.2.

Data from the Shepard and Metzler study of mental rotation. They depict the mean RT to determine that two objects have the same three-dimensional shape as a function of the angular difference in their portrayed orientations. Notice that the slopes for these two kinds of rotation are identical. (From "Mental Rotation of Three-dimensional Objects," by Shepard and Metzler. *Science* vol. 171, p. 702. Copyright 1971 by the American Association for the Advancement of Science.)

the two views of the objects were drawn so that there was a greater **angular disparity** between them, let's say 120 degrees instead of 80, then it should take the subjects a longer time to give the correct answer.

Figure 7.2 shows the study's findings. On trials in which the subject's correct response was "same," notice that the required time for response is linear as a function of initial angular disparity. Not only do the subjects require more time to make the correct decision as a function of angular disparity between the two views, but also the increased time is proportional to the increase in angular disparity. The subjects were apparently rotating the mental image at a fairly constant rate: about 50 to 60 degrees per second. Another remarkable fact about these data is that the slope of the line for picture plane pairs is virtually the same as that of the depth pairs. The depth pairs were no more difficult to rotate than were the picture plane pairs. From these findings, Shepard and Metzler concluded that the cognitive operations that are done of images are analogous to the operations that are done when viewing a physical stimulus. The subjects almost universally reported that they did the task by watching the mental rotation of an image, but Shepard and Metzler's conclusions go beyond simply verifying that the subjects were telling the truth. The findings, they argue, show that the subjects were not simply watching an image while other, perhaps nonvisual, cognitive operations or processes were "really" doing the computations that enabled the subjects to give the answer. Instead, they maintained their findings demonstrated that the real computational work was being done by the cognitive operations that rotated the images. All the subjects had to do was look at them.

This conclusion was extended in a study by Metzler (1973). One argument was that subjects in the original study were not getting the correct answer by watching a continuously rotating image. Perhaps the subjects were engaged in some other sort of computation that enabled them to get the correct answer. According to this view, the subjects required a greater amount of time to do the task when the angular disparity was greater because this task had greater computational difficulty, not because the image required more time to rotate. Metzler's (1973) study was designed to counter these criticisms.

If we give subjects a series of objects to be rotated mentally and compute the average latencies for a variety of angular disparities on a subject-by-subject basis, then we can determine an individual's average mental rotation velocity. For example, suppose a particular subject required three seconds more time to determine that two forms were the same when they were presented at 180 degrees difference than when they were presented with 0 degrees difference. We could then conclude that this subject was rotating the image at a rate of 180 degrees in three seconds, or 60 degrees per second.

Metzler used this information to determine the effects of the initial angular disparity on the subject's reaction time. She presented her subjects with an abstract form and instructed them to begin rotating it in a specified direction. After a time interval, Metzler presented the subjects with a second stimulus that had been rotated several degrees from the first stimulus. The subjects were told to judge whether the two stimuli were the same or different. The length of the time interval between the two presentations was determined by the degrees of rotation between the two stimuli and by the individual subject's velocity. For example, if the angular disparity between the stimuli was 180 degrees and the subject's rate of rotation was 60 degrees per second, then the stimuli were presented three seconds apart. The logic is that if the subject is continuously rotating a mental image throughout this three-second interval, then not much additional time should be required to make the judgment of "same," because the subject has already rotated the mental image to the point where it matches the second stimulus presentation fairly closely.

The stimuli's initial angular disparity had almost no effect on reaction time. That is, subjects required approximately one second to judge that the stimuli were the same regardless of whether they were initially presented with 45 degrees of angular disparity or with 270 degrees. This finding has some implications for the latencies observed by Shepard and Metzler (1971). For subjects who show consistency in speed of rotation (and not all subjects do), most of the time involved in making "same" judgments when the stimuli start out far apart is spent watching the stimulus rotate, and only about one second of the total time is spent making the "same" judgment.

These findings have since been confirmed by Cooper (1976). In this study, Metzler's procedure was again used. This time subjects were required to make judgments about irregular polygons. Like Metzler, Cooper found that the reaction time function was flat. The imagery effects we have examined are apparently not limited to the block figures used in the Shepard and Metzler studies.

Mental Rotation of Letters

We have considered the mental rotation of abstract shapes—those that have no obvious reference to real-world objects. As the literature on mental rotation accumulated, researchers began to wonder if people were also capable of rotating shapes that were meaningful to them. Such findings could be interesting for several reasons. First, familiar objects are usually meaningful. However, familiar objects acquire their familiarity in part because they usually occur in standard orientations. Consequently, meaningfulness could be a hindrance in mental rotation, especially if the subject does not know how to rotate objects that typically occur in some standard orientation. Finding that meaningfulness was a hindrance to mental rotation would be an embarassment to imagery theorists. After all, if the subject is doing the imagery tasks by watching a mental picture rotate, the subject should not have to know (in advance) what the object looks like upside down in order to carry out the task. The subject should simply be able to look at the mental picture and inspect it.

The second reason for interest in the mental rotation of familiar forms concerns the method that is used to extract information from the image. Chapter 2 described the process of feature extraction for letters and noted that this process seems to be basic in letter recognition. That is, the recognition of a letter is accomplished by noting the presence of certain features and assembling the pattern of noted features into a coherent form. What about imagined letters? Technically, some sort of similar process should take place. If the subject is "looking at" some mental array, the information gathered from that array should be accomplished in the same way that nonimagined information is gathered: by feature analysis. Phrased in a more concrete way, the "demons" that do our perceptual work should be able to "look at" all kinds of stimuli—real and imagined. One implication here is that confusions among imagined letters should be similar to those observed among actual letters.

Like Shepard and Metzler (1971), Cooper and Shepard (1973) argued that most of the time spent in making "same" judgments was taken up with rotating the mental image. They wondered if the preparation time could be reduced by supplying the subjects with certain kinds of information prior to their rotation. Three letters (R, J, and G) and three digits (2, 5, and 7) were used in their study. The stimuli appeared in one of two ways: normal or mirror image reversal. The stimuli were presented in one of six orientations: upright or 60, 120, 240, or 300 degrees from upright.

Part A of Figure 7.3 shows how R might be presented. The subjects' task was to determine if a stimulus had been presented in the normal or mirror image format. To accomplish this task, the subject would apparently have

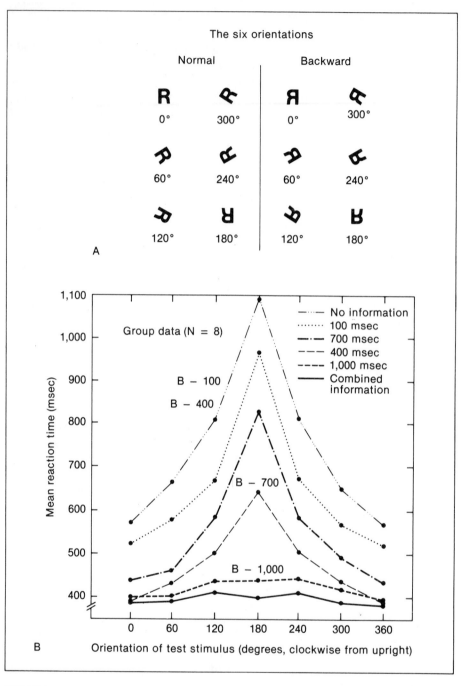

Figure 7.3.

A: Cooper and Shepard showed subjects characters and reversed characters in six orientations defined by their angle to upright. Subjects were to decide whether the characters were normal or backward. *B:* Reaction times were a function of stimulus orientation when subjects did not receive previous information that enabled them to prepare the image. They became uniform when subjects were given enough time to prepare an image of the correct stimulus at the correct orientation. (From Cooper & Shepard, 1973. Copyright 1973 by the Psychonomic Society, Inc. Adapted by permission of the publisher and authors.)

to rotate the letter to its upright orientation and then analyze its features. The farther away from upright that the letter was presented, presumbaly the longer the subject's reaction time. This expectation was confirmed. As Part *B* of Figure 7.3 shows, subjects in the "no information" condition required the greatest amount of time to make the "same" or mirror image judgment when the stimulus was presented 180 degrees from upright. Notice that the distribution of reaction times is almost perfectly symmetrical about 180 degrees. This means that the subjects did not rotate the stimuli in only one direction. The direction of rotation was determined by the subjects, who rotated the letters clockwise or counterclockwise depending upon which direction was closer to upright.

Other conditions of Cooper and Shepard's study were designed to assess the role played by prior information. In condition C, the "combined" condition, the subjects were informed simultaneously about both the identity and the orientation of the to-be-judged image. This was accomplished by showing the subjects an outline of the letter that would appear on the next trial. In addition, this outline was shown in the orientation (i.e., degrees of tilt) in which it would appear on the following trial. The outline was shown for two seconds, followed by a one-second blank interval. The subject was then shown the letter again and was asked to respond ("normal" or "mirror image") as quickly as possible. We would expect that the three seconds' preparation should be plenty of time to allow the subject to rotate and orient the letter. Consequently, reaction times should be brief and un-influenced by degrees of rotation required to make the letter upright. Notice from curve C in Figure 7.3 that this hypothesis was supported.

We have seen that if the subjects are given combined identity and orientation information and ample preparation time, the effects of angular disparity seen in the "no information" condition can be completely wiped out. What would happen if the subjects were given separate (rather than combined) identity and orientation information, and perhaps less than adequate preparation time? The B conditions were designed to answer this question. In these conditions, the subjects received the identity and orientation information sequentially, rather than simultaneously as they did in condition C. In these trials, the subjects saw an upright outline of the to-be-judged letter for two seconds. This was followed by an arrow showing the orientation of the soon-to-appear test stimulus. The directional arrow was shown for either 100, 400, 700, 1,000 msec. Next, the test stimulus appeared, and the subject responded as quickly as possible.

Figure 7.4 is a schematic representation of these events. The B-1,000 condition can be compared with condition C. Recall that in condition C, the subjects were given combined identity and orientation information, and the subjects essentially had three seconds to prepare for the test stimulus. The B-1,000 condition is similar: The subjects get identity information (they know what the test stimulus is going to be), and they get orientation information (in the form of the directional arrow). However, in the B-1,000 condition, the subjects get these facts sequentially, rather than simultaneously as they do in condition C. As Figure 7.3 shows, the B-1,000 findings are indistinguishable from the condition C findings. When the subjects know in advance what the

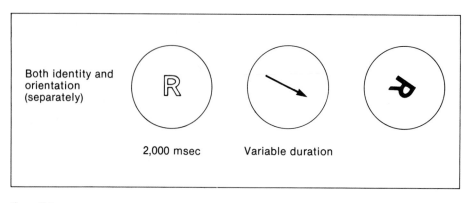

Figure 7.4.

In the B conditions, the information about the name and angle of rotation of the test character was presented sequentially before the presentation of the test character. (From Cooper & Shepard, 1973. Copyright 1973 by the Psychonomic Society, Inc. Adapted by permission of the publisher and authors.)

test stimulus is going to be, then 1,000 msec is enought time to rotate the letter into the same orientation as the test stimulus. In this sense, familiarity is no hindrance to mental rotation. Looking at the reaction time for the 180-degree stimulus in the B-1,000 condition, we see that subjects required only about 450 msec to respond. This finding indicates that the subjects were apparently rotating the letter at a rate far faster than the 50 to 60 degrees per second rate observed by Shepard and Metzler (1971). Knowing that 1,000 msec is apparently enough time to rotate the image, Cooper and Shepard next examined the other three B conditions.

In the B-700 condition, the subjects saw the directional arrow for 700 msec. As Figure 7.3 shows, this was almost enough time to enable the subjects to rotate the image. Except for the 180-degree point, most of the other reaction times are close to the B-1,000 curve. With 400 msec, there is an intermediate level of preparation; 100 msec offers hardly any advantage to the subjects. In that case, the reaction times are close to those observed in the "no information" condition.

The Cooper and Shepard study amplified an earlier conclusion from the Shepard and Metzler studies, namely that the subject seems to be engaged in a process of inspecting a continuously changing internal representation. Moreover, familiarity with the stimuli seemed to enhance the speed at which the rotation took place. Even though letters and numerals usually occur in a standard orientation (i.e., upright), the subjects were adept at mentally rotating them from a nonstandard position. From a cognitive perspective, these operations are surely complex. Consider the C condition once again. During the two-second interval, the subject has to rotate the image of the letter to an upright position and then engage in the process of feature extraction on the image itself in order to respond quickly when the test stimulus actually appears.

These findings seem to substantiate one of the claims made by pro-imagery theorists, namely that the cognitive processes active in the perception of physical objects are also involved in the perception of images. In this case, for example, the recognition of imagined letters is apparently accomplished in the same way that actual letters are recognized: by feature extraction.

LOOKING AT MENTAL IMAGES

The results of the rotation studies have strongly suggested that people can imagine familiar and unfamiliar objects rotating in space. The studies have also suggested that the rotation is continuous, meaning that once the rotation is started, the rate of rotation is constant and takes place without interruption until the subject gets the image to the desired point. One major implication of this work is that people can and apparently do "look at" the mental image as it rotates before their mind's eye. The subjects in these studies are clearly having some sort of visual experience, but its nature is hard to understand because the experience is not based on any visual stimulation per se. Yet, we've seen that operations on mental images indeed seem analogous to actual operations on physical stimuli.

These findings lead to several other questions that we'll attempt to deal with in this and subsequent sections. One question concerns the nature of the visual experience that the subjects seem to be having—that is, the nature of the image. Does the image actually "have" all of the information contained in the original physical stimulus? Second, what is the nature of the "looking" done by the subjects in these studies? When people gaze at a physical stimulus, we know that in many cases, such gazing is accompanied by eye movements, and some of the characteristics of these eye movements are known. What about the mind's eye? Are there some analogous types of **mind's eye movements** that take place when we ask subjects to gaze at, or scan, an image? This section considers some of the findings that are observed when people are asked to carry out operations that involve looking at and transforming their images.

Folding Mental Paper

Shepard and Feng (1972) devised an imagery task that, unlike rotation, consisted of imagining a series of discrete transformations. One of their objectives in doing so was to determine whether the ongoing motion of the image implied by the rotation studies was limited to mental rotation or whether subjects could execute ongoing movements when discrete steps were called for. Their subjects were shown drawings such as those in Figure 7.5. The subjects were told the shaded box represented the bottom of an unfolded cube and were asked to imagine that the other squares were other faces of the cube. Their task was to mentally fold the other sides to form a cube. If the arrowheads touched (or would touch) each other in the completed cube, the subjects were told to report yes. If the squares could not be folded so that the arrowheads met, the subjects were instructed to report no. The dependent variable was the subject's reaction time. As Figure 7.5 shows,

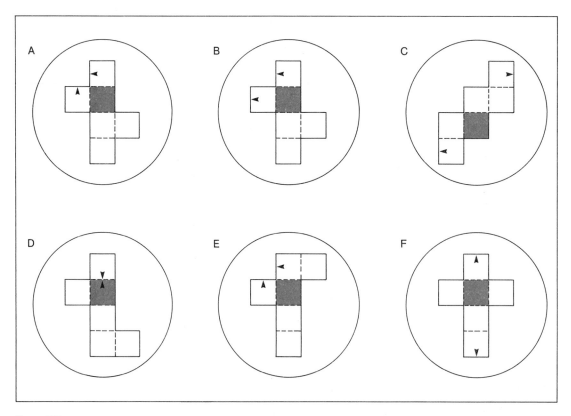

Figure 7.5.

Six illustrative mental paper-folding problems from the Shepard and Feng study. (From Shepard & Feng, 1972. Copyright 1972 by Academic Press, Inc. Adapted by permission of the publisher and authors.)

some of the cubes require more folding than others to determine if the arrowheads meet. For example, problem *A* can be solved in two folds, but problem *C* requires a complete construction (five folds) before the answer is known. Shepard and Feng reasoned that the greater the number of folds required, the longer the reaction time should be.

Their findings are shown in Figure 7.6. Notice that this task has substantially more intersubject variability than the rotation tasks. However, reaction times are a linear function of the number of folds required. Approximately one second was needed to make the yes or no decision, and in addition, about two seconds were required to make each mental fold. That is, even though the folds were made one at a time, the sequence of folding was nevertheless ongoing at a more or less constant rate. This point is important. Remember that in the rotation studies, the stimulus might start at an orientation of 180 degrees, and the subject knew that it had to be rotated to an upright position. Moreover, as the subject knew, this rotation task had no obvious intermediate stages. There was no reason for the subject to rotate the object to an orientation of 150 degrees, stop for an interval, then rotate the object to 120 degrees, and so forth. In other words, the rotation

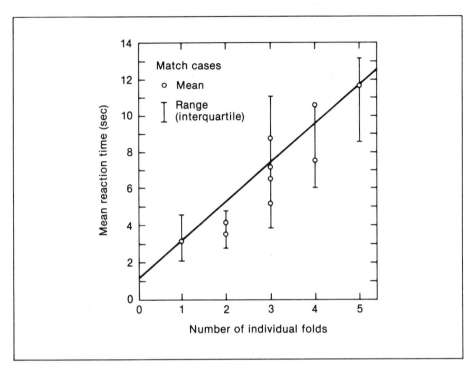

Figure 7.6.

Reaction times are a linear function of the number of folds necessary to make the decision. (From Shepard & Feng, 1972. Copyright 1972 by Academic Press, Inc. Adapted by permission of the publisher and authors.)

task invited the subject to engage in ongoing mental activity at a constant rate. But the paper-folding task doesn't invite the same procedure. Here, the nature of the task is far different. The subjects probably didn't know in advance how many folds would be required to complete the cube. Furthermore, this *was* a task that could be accomplished naturally in stages. Despite the inherent differences in the two tasks, the pattern of findings is similar. The Shepard and Feng study is therefore important because it shows that the findings of the rotation studies are not artifacts produced solely by the nature of the task (i.e., rotation). Rather, such findings are apparently generalizable to other tasks, including those involving discrete transformations.

Comparing the Size of Mental Objects

One important characteristic of visual perception is acuity, or resolution power. If we have normal vision, we can discern the details of the space surrounding us. I'm aware that I can discern the details of many images as well. For example, if I imagine my car, my image includes many of the car's details.

An important series of studies has been conducted by Kosslyn (1975, 1976, 1978) in an attempt to determine what details are characteristically included in people's images. Kosslyn reasoned that the details included in an image should be, at least in part, a function of the image's size. That is, large images should have more details than small images. Testing such a notion seems impossible, because there is no apparent way to control the size of a person's image. However, Kosslyn ingeniously devised a technique whereby some control could be achieved.

Kosslyn (1975) had his subjects imagine two different sized animals simultaneously. The logic here is that if we were asked to imagine a small animal, such as a rabbit, standing next to a large animal, such as an elephant, the image of the rabbit would be smaller than if we were asked to imagine a rabbit next to a tiny animal, such as a fly. If this technique were successful, Kosslyn could be reasonably sure of attaining some control over the size of the image. Recall that one central belief of the imagery theorists is that the subject is actually inspecting the image while answering questions about it. Assuming that the subjects are inspecting such an internal representation, Kosslyn reasoned that subjects should be able to answer questions about the details of the large image faster than they could about the small image. Why should this be? Presumably, the larger the image, the closer our mind's eye is to it. Consequently, the details of the large image are more visible and easier to "see" than the details of a small image. This prediction was supported. Kosslyn found that subjects answered questions such as "Does a rabbit have ears?" substantially faster when they inspected a large image rather than a small one. The difference in response times was 211 msec.

Before discussing how Kosslyn handled some of the possible objections to his study, let's briefly consider some of the themes that Kosslyn's work has in common with Shepard's. First, both researchers have presented findings that indicate that people can manipulate their mental images, and the transformations thus done appear to be orderly. Second, both researchers have presented evidence showing that people must watch the mental image to answer questions about it. In other words, Shepard's subjects apparently could not start the rotation of a mental object, then imagine something else, then refer to the original image to see if it had completed its rotation. Similarly, Kosslyn's subjects must have been looking at the image of a large or small rabbit if the difference in response times is to be accounted for. That is, if I approached people and asked them, "Is milk white?" I wouldn't expect any *systematic* variation in reaction times, because to answer such a question, a person doesn't have to imagine a large or small glass of milk or any glass of milk at all. Both researchers believe that the image has at least some of the characteristics of genuine percepts: Shepard argues that the image can move; Kosslyn maintains that the image has spatial properties.

Kosslyn anticipated some of the objections to his original findings. First, some critics might argue that people like rabbits more than flies, but not as much as they like elephants. Consequently, the rabbit-fly image is well developed in favor of the rabbit, but the elephant-rabbit image favors the elephant, perhaps because the better-liked animal is more detailed. Kosslyn countered this criticism by asking some of his subjects to imagine the rabbit next to an oversized fly—one that was as big as an elephant. Other subjects were asked to imagine that the rabbit was sitting next to a tiny elephant—one that was the size of a fly. In the first case, the rabbit image was presumably small; in the second situation, it was large. Subjects continued to answer questions about the rabbit faster when they inspected the large image rather than the small one. The mean difference in response times was 290 msec. This finding implies that the difference in response times cannot be atrributed to any inherent like or dislike for flies or elephants. Instead, the differences in latency seem to be produced by the size of image that the subject is inspecting.

Kosslyn also deflected a criticism involving the time required to construct the image. If your mental life is similar to mine, the construction of images of familar objects does not seem to require any time. We simply call for the image, and it's there. Our experiences are probably deceptive, though. Some time must be required for the construction of an image. You can get some subjective knowledge of this by imaging an animal such as a platypus; you might be aware that it takes slightly longer for this uncommon animal to come into your mental view. Kosslyn realized that instructions that constrain our natural imagery processes might produce delays in the construction of the image. Consequently we could argue that subjects might require more time to construct small images rather than natural size ones. The time factor has some implications for Kosslyn's previous studies. If subjects require more time to construct small images of objects, then critics of Kosslyn's original findings could argue that the findings were artifacts. The subjects could not answer questions about the small images, because such images had not been fully constructed at the time Kosslyn began his questioning.

The third phase of Kosslyn's (1975) study countered this objection in two ways. As a preliminary task, subjects were told to construct four mental squares of different sizes. Each of the squares was to have an area that was six times larger than the next smaller square. The smallest square might have an area of 1 mental square inch, the next would have an area of 6 mental square inches, and so on. Next, each of the squares was to be colored distinctively: brown for the largest square, then pink, green, and orange for the smaller squares. The subjects could do this task, although they apparently could not maintain all four images simultanously (this interesting point is developed later). Fortunately, the subjects were required to visualize only one square at a time. In one task, Kosslyn measured the amount of time required to construct mental images by asking his subjects to imagine animals that would fit into, but nevertheless fill up, different squares. For example, he might ask his subjects to imagine a brown fly (meaning a fly that was was as big as the brown square) or an orange fly. The subjects gave a signal when the image had been completely constructed. The time required to give the signal was the dependent variable in this study. By presenting his subjects with different combinations of animals and colors, Kosslyn was able to determine whether more time was required to construct small images of animals or images of small animals. Kosslyn found that the size of the animal had no effect on response latency. The only factor affecting such times was the size of the *image* that was being constructed. Specifically, more time was required to construct *large* (i.e., brown square) images of any animal than was required for small images. Referring to the original study, we can infer that the subjects did not require more time to construct the image of the rabbit next to the elephant than they did to construct the rabbit's image next to the fly.

Finally, Kosslyn (1975) went on to demonstrate that latencies in answering questions about images were not produced by the image's construction time but rather by the size and visibility of the constructed image. The subjects were trained to visualize the four different colored squares. When the subjects were proficient at this task, they were given an animal's name and a color (e.g., pink tiger) and were told to visualize the animal filling up the appropriate square. When the subject indicated that this had been accomplished, a statement about tigers was presented, and the subject's task was to answer "true" or "false" about the statement.

Figure 7.7 shows this sequence of events. Kosslyn found that the response time of the subject in this situation was a function of the size of the image used in answering the question. Figure 7.8 shows these findings. Once again, we see that looking at an image seems to be similar to looking

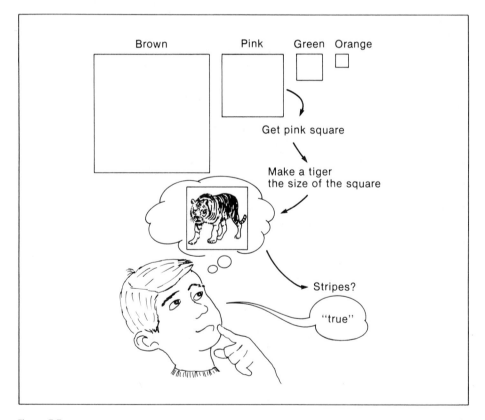

Figure 7.7.

Process in experiment in which subjects judged appropriateness of a property to an imagined animal paired with boxes of different sizes. (From Kosslyn, 1975. Copyright 1975 by Academic Press, Inc. Adapted by permission of the publisher and author.)

at a real object. Smaller objects, whether real or imagined, are difficult to inspect.

Later, Kosslyn (1976) found that the effects of imagery could be negated if people answered questions by consulting their general knowledge about animals rather than by looking at an image. Subjects were asked to verify, as quickly as possible, two kinds of attributes that an animal might possess. In the first case, subjects were given statements about large, easily seen common attributes and were asked to verify whether or not the animal in question had the attribute. For example, the subject might be given the statement "Cats have heads." In the second case, subjects were given statements about small, not easily seen but highly distinctive properties of animals, such as "Cats have claws." When subjects were told to construct an image of a cat before answering the questions, the results were predictable, given some of the other findings we've reviewed. That is, people verified the large, easily seen properties faster than they did the small but highly distinctive properties. However, when the subjects were specifically instructed *not* to construct an image, then older subjects (fourth graders and adults) verified the small, distinctive properties faster than the large, common properties. In this study, Kosslyn also noted that younger subjects (first graders) showed some indications of using imagery to answer the questions even when they were instructed not to.

This last finding probably doesn't mean that the first graders were being naughty or even that they had problems understanding the instructions

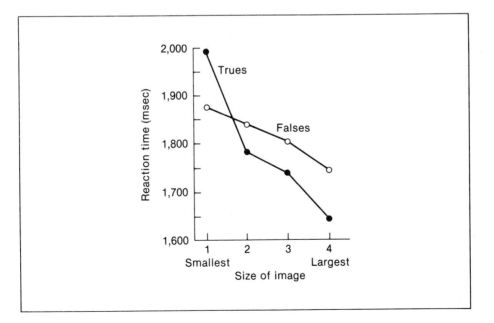

Figure 7.8.

Time required to determine appropriateness of a property to an animal in experiment depicted in Figure 7.8. (From Kosslyn, 1975. Copyright 1975 by Academic Press, Inc. Adapted by permsssion of the publisher and author.)

(although neither objection can be ruled out). The finding probably means that first graders have somewhat less world knowledge than do fourth graders or adults. In the absence of this explicit world knowledge, first graders do whatever they can do to answer questions about the world. Apparently, one way that graders answer questions about the world is by constructing a mental image and taking a look at it. If this reasoning is correct, the use of mental imagery might be considered a more primitive form of internal representation in that it is observed early in the human developmental sequence. As we age, we become more proficient at other forms of internal representation—ones that are no longer dependent upon our imaginal powers.

The studies done by Kosslyn in the early and mid-seventies are important for a variety of reasons, not the least of which is because they demonstrate that humans can apparently organize knowledge in at least two formats. One of these is an *imaginal format* in which the knowledge seems to retain many of the properties of the original sensory stimulation. That is, a visual image seems to have color, spatial characteristics, and clarity. The imaginal format can be contrasted with a format that we might call the *verbal format*. Knowledge organized in a verbal format, or code, is apparently no longer tied as directly to sensory properties. This type of code is useful, though, for answering questions about the *meaning* of certain stimuli. Recall that we've already seen this issue expressed as the **dual code position.** My main objective in bringing up this issue is to orient your thinking as we review some of the findings dealing with mental psychophysics and mental travel.

Mental Psychophysics

Psychophysics refers to the relationship between physical energy and its psychological effects. For example, you know that the cones in the retina are able to detect and discriminate the wavelengths of electromagnetic radiation within a small part of its complete spectrum. Neural events occurring after the initial detection preserve the information about wavelength and produce from it the psychological event, color. The psychophysicist is interested in how changes in physical stimulation are *experienced* by people. With careful investigation, it's possible to find out exactly what sorts of physical energy transformations the nervous system is capable of executing. The underlying assumption is that the relationship between stimulation and experience is orderly. The mental psychophysicist has exploited this argument by taking it, in a narrow sense, one step further. Hypothesizing that the image is a psychological event that preserves much of the information in the world in a direct way (i.e., the world has spatial characteristics, as does the image), the mental psychophysicist maintains that the properties of the image can be studied by applying various psychophysical techniques to it. Whereas the psychophysicist studies the relationship between stimulation and experience in the hopes of discovering how the nervous system transforms the world, the mental psychophysicist studies the relationship between two experiences (looking at an external stimulus and looking at an image) in the hopes of finding out how the cognitive system operates. The underlying assumption is that the relationship between mental events is orderly.

It is well known from psychophysical experiments that the relationship between size differences and decision times is inverse (Woodworth & Schlosberg, 1954). In other words, if subjects are shown two lines that are almost equally long and are asked to determine the longer line, their response times are greater than when the lines' lengths are markedly different from one another. Moyer (1973) hypothesized that the same finding would be observed if the subjects were asked to judge which of two nonpresent objects (in this case, animals) was larger. For example, a subject might be given a question such as "Which is larger, a bee or a rat?" A total of seven animals were compared with one another: ant, bee, rat, cat, hog, cow, and elk. Notice that the animals can be unambiguously ranked from largest to smallest. This feature of the study is important. If people maintain a simple verbal format for their knowledge of animals' sizes, we would not expect to observe a mental psychophysical effect. To see why, consider the following example. Suppose our knowledge of the size of animals was stored in the form of verbal tags such as these:

Rat: 6 inches, ⅔ pound
Cat: 15 inches, 10 pounds
Hog: 48 inches, 500 pounds

Under these circumstances verifying "A cat is larger than a rat" wouldn't take any longer than verifying "A hog is larger than a rat," because the computational procedure should not be influenced by the size of the difference between the animals. If, however, people's knowledge of animal sizes is represented in an imaginal format, the relative sizes of the animals being compared should make a difference in reaction times; namely, the less discrepancy between the animals' sizes, the longer the subjects should take to decide which animal is bigger.

Moyer (1973) confirmed this expectation. Subjects required more time to decide the larger of adjacent animals (in the prior list) than they did for nonadjacent animals. This finding means that the nature of the information stored in people's memories is affected by their knowledge of how big the animal looks. If we know that an animal is large, the image we produce is apparently also large. Notice too, that this effect is pure; information from the verbal, or tag, format cannot be contributing to the effect, because Moyer made sure that all the words were the same size (the word *ant* is the same size as the word *elk*). The inverse relationship between imaginal discrepancies and reaction time has been named the *symbolic distance effect* by Moyer and Bayer (1976, p. 230) and is defined as follows: "The time needed to compare two symbols varies inversely with the distance between their referents on the judged dimension."

An extreme application of psychophysical techniques to the problem of imagery was performed by Kosslyn (1978), who attempted to measure the **visual angle of the mind's eye.** We don't see everything around us; even objects directly to our sides are indistinct. Kosslyn reasoned that the size of the mental viewing space must be similarly restricted. In other words, because the images had spatial characteristics, they took up mental space. Paraphrasing Kosslyn, the question then becomes, Exactly how big is this mental space?

Subjects were required to construct a clear image of a particular animal. Next, the subjects were told to imagine that they were walking toward the animal. At the point where the animal's image began to overflow the size of the viewing space, the subjects stopped their mental walk. A variety of techniques, including self-report, were used to estimate the apparent distance between the mind's eye and the object. Estimates of the visual angle of the mind's eye thus made were not particularly stable. If a strict criterion were used to define the overflow phenomenon, the typical subject had a mind's eye with a visual angle of 20 degrees. The field of vision of our physical eyes is almost 180 degrees. The mind's eye therefore has a restricted field of vision—only about one-sixth the width of our real eyes. Thus, the size of the image space seems to be substantially smaller than our actual visual field (Weber & Malmstrom, 1979). However, the degree of intersubject variability was substantial; the visual angles computed ranged from 13 to 50 degrees. Kosslyn also determined that the boundary of the image space is not distinct but fuzzy (making it difficult for the subjects to report when the overflow had taken place). Once again, we see a similarity between actual perception and imagery. Visual acuity is greatest when the light falls on the fovea, located approximately in the center of each retina. In a follow-up study, Finke and Kosslyn (1980) found that mental visual acuity decreases rapidly at the periphery of the image space. The individual differences were again large but orderly. That is, people with good imagery ability had better mental acuity in the periphery of their image spaces than did people with poor imagery skills.

Mental Travel

One striking aspect of subjects' reports of overflowing images is their insistence that different parts of such an image can't be inspected simultaneously. For example, if a subject has constructed an overflowing image of an elephant, the tusks and the tail won't be in view simultaneously. If the tusks are in focus, and the subject is asked to mentally inspect the tail, some time will typically be required before the subject reports that the tail is in focus. This time is apparently spent shifting the mental gaze, much as we would have to turn to our heads and shift our gaze to see the parts of a real elephant if we were standing beside one.

This effect is apparently not limited to overflowing images. Kosslyn (1973) found that subjects who had memorized a group of line drawings of familiar objects would also demonstrate scanning effects even when the image was presumably kept well within the border of the image space. The subjects were told to generate an image of a speedboat whose picture they had memorized, holding the entire boat in view simultaneously. Next, the subjects were instructed to focus on one part of the boat (the stern). The subjects were then given a question about the original drawing and were asked to verify it. For example, a subject might be asked, "Was there a flag on the bow of the speedboat?" Kosslyn found that subjects took longer to answer this question when they started their scan from the stern of the boat rather than from someplace closer to the bow, such as the boat's cabin.

This scanning effect has also been observed in a series of studies (Kosslyn, Ball, & Reiser, 1978; Mitchell & Richman, 1980; Richman, Mitchell, & Reznick, 1979) in which subjects were asked to engage in **mental travel.** Kosslyn et al. (1978) had their subjects memorize the map of a fictitious island shown in Figure 7.9. Notice that the island has several landmarks: a beach, a rock, a well, a hut, a pond, and a thatch of grass. Subjects overlearned this map until they could draw it with high accuracy. After they achieved the accuracy criterion, the subjects were presented aurally with a landmark and were told to imagine the island and fixate on the named location. After five seconds, a second landmark was named, and the subjects were told to scan the map until the second landmark had been brought into view, which subjects signaled by pressing a button.

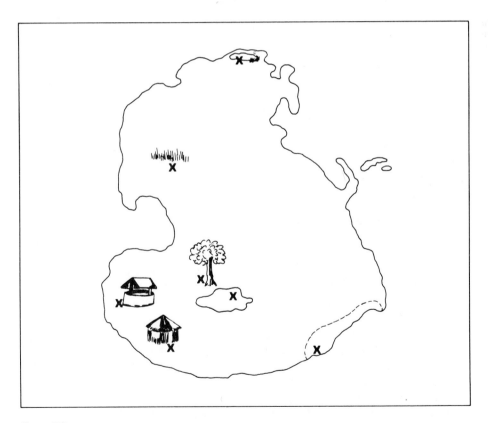

Figure 7.9.

The fictitious map used by Kosslyn, Ball, and Reiser (1978) to determine differences in processing time relative to the distance between images to be recalled. Subjects had to commit this map to memory and then mentally scan from point to point on the map. (Copyright 1978 by the American Psychological Association. Adapted by permission of the publisher and authors.)

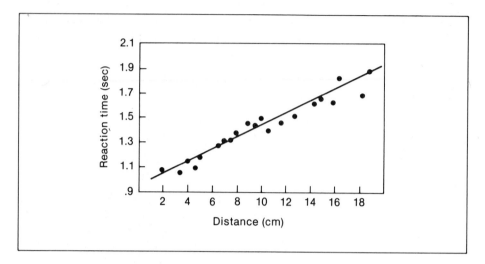

Figure 7.10.

Time to scan between two points in Figure 7.9 as a function of the distance betweeen the points. (From Kosslyn, Ball, & Reiser, 1978. Copyright 1978 by the American Psychological Association. Adapted by permission of the publisher and authors.)

The time required for the subjects to travel the twenty-one possible routes among the landmarks is graphed in Figure 7.10 as a function of the distance separating the landmarks on the original map. Notice that little variability exists among the points. The line of best fit indicates that this sort of image scanning is accomplished at a rate of about 20 centimenters per second. According to Kosslyn, subjects carry out this task by scanning the image of the island—that is, by moving the focus of their mind's eyes across the image that is assumed to have spatial properties.

However, this interpretation has been questioned by Richman, Mitchell, and Reznick (1979), who found that the spatial characteristics of images are influenced by nonspatial factors. Their subjects memorized an island map similar to the one used by Kosslyn et al. The Richman et al. island had five landmarks: a well, which was 13 centimeters from the hut, a tree, which was also 13 centimeters from the hut, a lake 12 centimeters from the hut, and a swamp 6 centimeters from the hut. Unlike the original map, however, the Richman et al. map had signposts placed between some of the landmarks. These signposts showed the mileages between the landmarks. Control groups saw signposts showing identical mileages (either 20 miles or 80 miles) between the well and the hut and between the tree and the hut. For the experimental groups, these mileages were altered somewhat. One experimental group saw signs that said the distance from the well to the hut was 80 miles, and the distance from the tree to the hut was 20 miles (remember, the actual distances were the same on the map). For a second experimental group, these mileages were reversed.

Figure 7.11 is a schematic representation of the Richman et al. island. All groups had excellent knowledge of the map and could draw it accurately

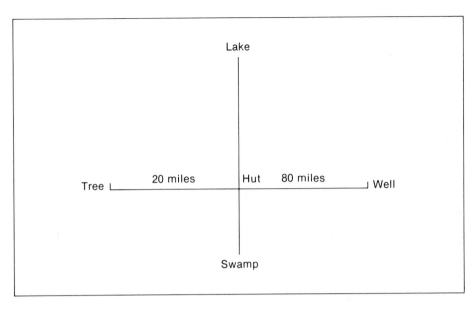

Figure 7.11.

Schematic representation of the map used in the Richman, Mitchell, and Reznick (1979) study.

from memory. The subjects were told to visualize the island and fixate on a specific landmark. When the subjects indicated that the image was achieved, a second landmark was presented, and the subjects were told to imagine a small speck traveling to the destination landmark. When the subjects arrived at the destination, they pressed a button stopping the trial.

Table 7.1 shows the findings of this study. The Richman et al. subjects traveled at a substantially slower pace than did the Kosslyn et al. subjects. Subjects who saw posted mileages of 80 required more time to respond than did subjects who saw 20 as the posted mileage. Notice, too, that the experimental subjects, who saw both 20 and 80 miles posted, required more time to travel the 80-mile distance than they did to travel the 20-mile distance, even though they could draw a highly accurate reproduction of the original map showing that both distances were the same. Because the subjects could make such a drawing, they must have known that the distances were equal. The subjects had been explicitly instructed to use imagery in calculating their arrival times, and given the almost constant scanning rates observed by Kosslyn et al. (1978), a reasonable expectation is that the experimental subjects should have required an identical amount of time to scan identical distances, regardless of their labeling.

Although the subjects seemed to be swayed somewhat by the verbal labeling of the mileages, the precise nature of the effect is hard to interpret. After all, the experimental subjects did not take four times longer to scan the 80-mile, as opposed to the 20-mile, distance. The findings suggest, then, that the response times of the experimental subjects may have resulted from the combination of at least two different cognitive processes. First, the sub-

TABLE 7.1

Mean Reaction Times (Sec) for Experimental and Control Groups in Experiment 1

	Posted Mileages	
Group	20 Miles	80 Miles
Experimental	3.118	3.496
Control	2.469	2.552

Source: Richman, Mitchell, and Reznick, 1979. Copyright by the American Psychological Association. Adapted by permission of the publisher and authors.

jects may have been trying their best to scan an internal representation according to the instructions. Second, the subjects apparently factored in the distances shown on the signposts when they computed their arrival times. This second process indicates that the experimental subjects might have had some implicit knowledge of what should happen when a mental image is scanned.

I can only speculate about the nature or origin of this knowledge. Still, almost all Americans are familiar with road maps that show the distances between various points in miles. On more than one occasion, I've looked at such a map thinking that two points, *X* and *Z,* were about equidistant from some third point, *A,* only to find that one of the distances was substantially greater than the other. When that happens, I tend to believe the map. That is, I recognize that making the drive will take longer than it looks on the map. The experimental subjects in the Richman et al. study may have been influenced by this kind of knowledge.

Subjects in psychological studies do not leave their knowledge of the world at the laboratory door. Moreover, such subjects are often compliant: They try to figure out what should happen in a study and act accordingly. Mitchell and Richman (1980) maintained that these so-called **demand characteristics** (Orne, 1962) had contributed to the stability of the findings observed by Kosslyn et al. (1978). That is, the subjects perceived certain aspects of the situation, which developed into an expectation of how they were supposed to act (Saslow, 1982).

Mitchell and Richman replicated Kosslyn et al.'s original experiment and added a verbal nonexperiment to it. Subjects in the nonexperiment were not shown the fictitious island map. Instead, they were given a verbal description of the island and its landmarks. When they were familiar with the island, these subjects were asked to predict the scanning times they would have reported if they had actually engaged in mental travel. Mitchell and Richman found that a high linear correlation existed between scanning distance and *predicted* scanning times. This finding was consistent with the demand characteristics explanation of mental travel. In other words, before subjects even begin to scan an image, they apparently already have a good idea of how long it should take to travel particular distances. This explanation casts some doubt on the findings of the Kosslyn et al. image-scanning study, because we can no longer be sure that the relationship between response time and distance was produced by the subject's effort to scan the image or by the demand characteristic of the experiment.

Summary

We've reviewed a number of representative studies of imagery. Before examining this research more critically, let's summarize. What have these studies apparently demonstrated? First, many cognitive psychologists were struck by the similarity between imagery processes and those involved in actual perception. Not only could the image be looked at, but also inspecting an image seemed *necessary* to performing some tasks—for example, mental rotation. When an image was inspected in this way, some of the principles derived from the perception of physical objects seemed to hold for the image as well. For example, we saw that the symbolic distance effect for images corresponds closely to what is observed when we ask subjects to make judgments about physically present stimuli. Also, the Kosslyn studies have suggested that the image has details,and the larger the image, the more details it has. The Kosslyn studies have also suggested that the image has spatial properties; that is, it takes up mental room. We've seen two other phenomena that seem to indicate spatial properties in imagery: the overflow phenomenon and mental travel. In the first case, as the subject mentally walked toward an imagined object, the image apparently got larger until it filled up the subject's entire mental viewing space, much as the light reflected from a real object would stimulate the cells over a larger and larger portion of our retinae if we actually walked toward it. The mental travel studies have suggested that just as some time is required to shift our gaze when looking at different parts of an external stimulus, some time is also required to shift the gaze of our mind's eye.

FUNCTIONAL PROPERTIES OF IMAGES

We've reviewed several of the basic studies upon which the rather vast imagery literature is based. The remainder of this chapter attempts to interpret these findings. We must deal with several issues. First, cognitive psychologists have been concerned with the storage and retrieval of images. One group of theorists, led by Paivio (1974), has contended that material can be stored in memory in one of two formats, or codes. Some knowledge (e.g., your mother's face, the street on which you grew up) is stored in an imaginal code—one in which the information is retained in a way that preserves much of the original sensory input, such as color and spatial properties. According to this view, other knowledge (your mother's name, the state in which your hometown is located) is stored in a verbal code. We have seen in earlier chapters that this position has not been accepted by all cognitive psychologists. Some believe that memories are not stored in either visual or verbal formats but instead are reduced to a code that is neither verbal nor visual. The imagery literature has been the central battleground for these two conflicting camps. The first group of theorists maintains that the imagery findings clearly demonstrate that some memories are stored in the form of images, and that some thinking is done in images. The second group argues that the imagery studies demonstrate no such thing.

The second issue dealt with in this section concerns the **functional significance** of the image (Kosslyn, 1975). Among cognitive psychologists, the phrase "functional significance" has become a shorthand expression for talking about the *necessity* of imagery for doing certain tasks. When cognitive psychologists say that the image has functional significance, they mean that a particular set of findings could not be observed if the subjects were not actively engaged in inspecting an image. Further, this process of image inspection wouldn't be going on if the subjects could do the task in some other way. Once again, there are two camps in regard to the functional significance issue. Adherents of one view maintain that certain results from the imagery studies could have been obtained only if the subjects were rotating, scanning, or otherwise watching a mental image. For these theorists, the image has functional significance. Contending thinkers maintain that the image is *epiphenomenal* in relation to the real operations in which the subject is engaged. For our purposes, **epiphenomena** are simply tagalong events, or by-products. For example, the noise of a motorcycle does not cause the motorcycle to go; the noise is simply a by-product of the forces that propel the motorcycle; which are consequently epiphenomenal to the motorcycle's propulsion. Regarding imagery, these theorists maintain that in imagery studies, the subject is actually engaged in some nonimaginal cognitive processes that simply produce an image as a by-product.

Both the storage and the functional significance issues are often thought of as bearing on what are called the *functional* properties of the image. When cognitive psychologists refer to the image's functional properties, they mean the factors relating to the image's operation: How do images *work?* In other words, cognitive psychologists are concerned with the operation of the image and with the cognitive processes that can or cannot be done on imagined information.

Storage of Images

Thinkers such as Paivio are often described as *dual code* theorists because they believe that the knowledge represented in memory is in one of two codes: a visual code or a verbal code. The alternative to this position is often called, somewhat unfortunately, *propositional* theory. Theorists of this stripe maintain that knowledge is organized in memory in the form of propositions—small, abstract units of knowledge that are neither verbal nor visual. At this point, it might be helpful for you to review some of the information on this issue in the previous chapters. You might want to make up your mind once again on this issue, because where you stand on this matter may influence your position on the functional significance question. For example, it's difficult to conceive of a propositional theorist who would also believe that the image is functionally significant. Why? Because if knowledge can be stored and retrieved from a **propositional format,** the cognitive system wouldn't bother converting the material into an imaginal format if it could carry out its computations on the propositional format directly.

Although many imagery findings seem easy to interpret within the dual code position, some are more easily understood from the propositional perspective. For example, Potter and Faulconer (1975) have determined that people can say "dog" more quickly if the eliciting stimulus is the printed word *DOG* rather than a picture of a dog. In the second phase of their study, Potter and Faulconer showed their subjects a category name such as *ANIMAL*. Following this, subjects were presented with a test stimulus that was one of two types. Subjects might be shown a word such as *DOG*, which was a member of the category, or a word such as *PEA*, which was not. The second type of test stimulus was pictorial. Subjects were presented with either a picture of an animal or a picture of a nonanimal. If the word or picture referred to a legitimate member of the category, the subjects were instructed to respond yes as quickly as possible. If the word or picture did not refer to a category member, subjects were supposed to respond no.

Dual code theorists would predict that response times in the word condition should be faster than the times in the pictorial condition, because category information is assumed to be stored in the verbal code. Consequently, when given a picture and asked to make a judgment about its membership in a category, the subject must first convert the pictorial representation into a verbal one and then verify its membership in the proper category. These operations require time. For the subject given a word, however, no conversion operations are required; the category membership can be verified straightaway. Somewhat surprisingly, though, Potter and Faulconer found that their subjects verified the category membership in 50 msec less time when they were given pictures and not words. Although this finding does not support the propositional position directly, a dual code theorist would have a difficult time explaining it.

Similarly, Anderson (1982) has shown that rehearsal rates for members of particular categories were not necessarily faster in the verbal rather than in the imaginal mode. Once again, the dual code theory would predict that the category membership should exert a helpful influence on rehearsal speed only when the to-be-rehearsed material is presented in the verbal manner. Anderson demonstrated that under some conditions, rehearsal of category members could proceed just as quickly using imagery instead of words.

Functional Significance of Images

Theorists who argue in favor of the functional significance of the image believe that the imaginal code is more than just a translation of some verbal code. Rather, the imaginal code is a form of internal representation that has some properties the verbal code doesn't have. Consequently, to carry out certain tasks, the imaginal code must be used. Theorists opposed to this position frequently maintain that images are epiphenomena. As Block (1981) has noted, this term is used differently by psychologists than it is by philosophers, who apply it to events that are always effects—and are never the causes—of any other event. Referring to the motorcycle example, the sound of the motorcycle's engine is always an effect and is never a cause of the motorcyle's motion. For the psychologist, the term carries some added baggage, implying that an event plays no causal role in the brain's processing (Block, 1981). Applied to the imagery question, the epiphenomenalist maintains that the image plays no causative role in the brain's work. That is, to do the task, the brain is engaged in some kind of computation that, as a by-product, produces the experience of having an image. The imagery theorist argues against epiphenomenalism by citing a wealth of data (such as the Shepard and Metzler 1971 mental rotation study) and posing a simple question: How else could any of this be done, if not by imagery?

One strategy that can be used to answer this question involves using blind people as subjects in tasks that are thought to require imagery. The success of sightless people on such tasks argues against the necessity of imaginal ability as being crucial.

Jonides, Kahn, and Rozin (1975) compared the performance of sighted and congenitally blind subjects on a variety of tasks. In some cases, the subjects were asked to use imagery to perform the tasks; in other cases, the subjects were not instructed to use imagery. The sighted subjects' performance improved under the imagery instructions, but the blind subjects' performance also improved when they were instructed to use mental imagery. The blind subjects were clearly doing something different when they were given imagery instructions (i.e., they were not just trying harder), although determining what that process might have been is difficult.

Marmor and Zaback (1976) carried out a haptic (i.e, information gathered by touch) version of the Shepard and Metzler study. Subjects felt two stationary objects and had to report whether the objects were identical or mirror images of one another. The amount of angular disparity between the objects was varied. Whereas Jonides et al. used only congenitally blind and normally sighted individuals, Marmor and Zaback made a distinction between people who were blinded early in life (at birth or before the age of five) as opposed to those blinded later in life (after the age of five). The response patterns of sighted, early blind, and late blind groups were similar: The greater the amount of initial angular disparity, the longer the response time needed to make the same or mirror image judgment. Substantial performance differences were noted, however. Normal subjects carried out the apparent rotation at a rapid rate of over 230 degress per second. Early blind subjects were slower (approximately 60 degrees per second), and late blind subjects performed at a level in between the two extremes. These findings suggest that visual experience is helpful in doing the Shepard and Metzler task, but it isn't critical.

Zimler and Keenan (1983) have supported this interpretation. Their study involved the use of an imagery task originally developed by Neisser and Kerr (1973; Kerr & Neisser, 1983). In this task, the subjects formed images of scenes containing certain *target objects*. In some cases, the target object was imagined as being in full view. Some subjects were required to imagine that the target objects were hidden, or occluded, by other objects in the scene and were not visible. After the subjects were given a series of imagery trials, they were asked to recall as many of the target objects as they could. All such memories were incidental, because the subjects were never given any explicit instructions to *remember* the targets. Zimler and Keenan (1983) found that both normally sighted *and* congenitally blind subjects recalled more of the pictorial (i.e., full view) targets than occluded targets. Zimler and Keenan interpreted their findings as indicating that the visual imagery used by sighted persons does not seem to enhance retrieval any more than whatever sort of nonvisual internal representation is used by the blind.

Interference in Scanning Images

A second strategy that can be used to assess the functional significance of the image involves investigating what sorts of ancillary tasks interfere with imagery. Some of these concerns were addressed in a provocative study by Brooks (1968). Each subject in the study was involved in one of two tasks: a visual task and a verbal task. In the visual tasks, subjects were shown a block letter such as the one pictured in Figure 7.12. The asterisk and arrow indicate the starting location and direction of mental scanning that the subjects would engage in. After the subjects had committed the letter to memory, a signal was given and the subjects were supposed to inspect the image, report the current location of the asterisk, and then move the asterisk to the next right angle of the block letter. If the asterisk was located at either the extreme top or bottom right angles of the letter, the subject reported yes, and if the asterisk was located anywhere else, the correct response was no. In scanning the letter shown, the subject encounters ten

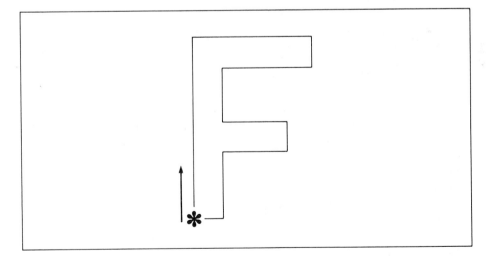

Figure 7.12.

An example of a simple block diagram used by Brooks (1968) to study the scanning of mental images. The asterisk and arrows showed the subject the starting point and the direction for scanning the image. (Copyright 1968 by the Canadian Psychological Association. Adapted by permission of the publisher and author.)

right angles; the pattern of correct responses is yes, yes, yes, no, no, no, no, no, no, yes. Subjects reported their response in three ways, or modes. In the *vocal* mode, subjects simply said aloud yes or no. In the *tapping* response mode, the subjects indicated yes by tapping with their left hands, and no by tapping with their right hands. The third response mode consisted of *pointing* to either a *Y* or an *N* from among those that appeared on the specially designed answer sheet depicted in Figure 7.13. The letters on the answer sheet were staggered so that the subject would have to scan it, reducing the possibility that the act of pointing would be routinized.

In the verbal task, the subjects were given a ten-word sentence such as "A bird in the hand is not in the bush." The subjects had to remember this sentence, and when signaled, scan it, classifying each word as a noun or not. Subjects who performed the verbal task reported yes or no in one of the three response modes just described. Brooks's reasoning is straightforward. If imagery requires the subject to scan some internal representation, the performance should be disrupted by forcing the subject to report in a manner that also requires scanning. Consequently, we would expect that subjects who scanned the block letter should be most negatively influenced when they have to point to their answers. The verbal task offers us a good way of assessing whether simply pointing per se is what produces the disruption. If that's the case, then the subjects in the verbal task should also be negatively influenced by pointing to their answers.

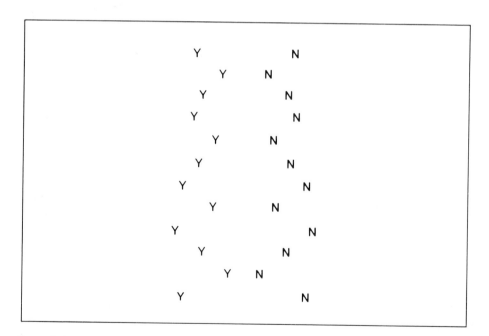

Figure 7.13.

An answer sheet for the pointing condition in Brooks (1968) for mental image scanning. The letters are staggered to force careful visual monitoring of pointing. (Copyright 1968 by the Canadian Psychological Association. Adapted by permission of the publisher and author.)

Table 7.2 shows the mean response times in seconds for both the verbal and visual task in each of the response modes. Notice that pointing did disrupt the scanning of the block letter. When subjects had to point to their answers, they required twice as much time to scan the letter as they did when they were able to tap out their responses. Yet, pointing one's response is apparently not difficult per se. On the verbal task, the subjects required the most time to respond when they called out their responses. Although this study may seem to support the notion that the image has functional significance, Brooks (1968) was careful to note that the problem with pointing was *spatial* rather than *visual*. In other words, the subjects had difficulty pointing because they had to make orienting decisions such as moving their hands left or right. Simultaneously, they had to remember which way the asterisk was supposed to be moving, which also involved left- and right-orienting decisions. Brooks argued that keeping track of these separate decisions made trouble for the subjects, rather than the fact that their mind's eyes were looking at an image while their physical eyes were looking at the printed page. The looking didn't slow down the subjects; they were slowed by the spatial decisions that had to be made at each right angle.

Baddeley and Lieberman (in Baddeley, 1976) supported Brooks's reasoning. The subjects in this study also scanned a block letter image a la Brooks. At the same time the block letter was being scanned, the subjects had to do one of two ancillary tasks. Half of the subjects monitored the brightness of a pulsating light, which periodically flashed with particular brilliance. The subjects pressed a key indicating they had observed the bright flash. This task required visual processing; however, no spatial decisions had to be made. The subjects were blindfolded for the second ancillary task. These subjects were given a flashlight and were told to aim the flashlight's beam at a swinging pendulum. The pendulum was equipped with a photo-electric cell that emitted a beeping noise when the light was trained on it. The subject's task was to keep the beam of light on target as much as possible. This second task required spatial processing but not visual processing. Of interest was which task would interfere more with the letter scanning. The findings were consistent with Brooks's reasoning. The flashlight task interfered more with letter scanning than did the light monitoring task.

TABLE 7.2

Mean Classification Times (Sec) in Brooks's Interference Study

Stimulus Material	Output		
	Pointing	Tapping	Vocal
Diagrams	28.2	14.1	11.3
Sentences	9.8	7.8	13.8

Source: Brooks, 1968. Copyright 1968 by the Canadian Psychological Association. Adapted by permission of the publisher and author.

Taken as a group, the studies we have reviewed in the last several pages do not add up to strong support for the notion that the image has functional significance. Neither have these studies provided strong support for the dual code position. Therefore, images are not likely stored in our memories in the form of pictures, nor is it likely that an image *must* be generated and inspected to carry out the instructions of many imagery experiments. My comments should *not* be interpreted as arguing that images are not real, however. I "have" and "use" images all day long, and I'm sure that you do, too. The question then becomes, What is the exact nature of the image's reality? The next section of this chapter deals with that question.

THE NATURE OF THE IMAGE

Although the image may seem like a picture in our minds, theorists don't believe that. Instead, they contend that the image is a sort of display that maintains certain aspects of the world, although in an abstract form. For example, Shepard (1978) has stated that the image should be understood as a **second-order isomorph.** *Isomorphic* means "having the same shape," and two events or objects are isomorphic if a simple one-to-one correspondence exists between their parts. For example, we might make a highly detailed model of a ship, perhaps out of the same materials as the real ship. If we did so, all the parts of the real ship could be found in miniature on the model. Since the only intentional difference between the two objects would be their size, the model would be a first-order isomorph of the ship. Now consider a highly detailed scale drawing of the same ship. The drawing corresponds to the ship in some ways, because we might recognize particular ships from their drawings. But the relationship between the drawing and the real ship is not simple. The real ship (and the model) are three-dimensional and have mass. The drawing is two-dimensional and has no mass. Although some properties of the ship are preserved in the drawing, many are not; therefore, the relationship between such a drawing and ship is *abstract* and a second-order isomorph. Shepard contends that the relationship between imagery and perception is similar. That is, having an image is not exactly like viewing a picture, but the experience of imagery is one that preserves some aspects of real perception in an abstract way. In addition to these isomorphic qualities, some evidence indicates that the image has certain holistic properties, at least for some people.

Cooper and Podgorny (1976) showed their subjects the nonsense forms shown in Figure 7.14. On each trial, the subject was shown one of the five stimuli called S (standard) stimuli. After the subject encoded the standard, a directional arrow appeared, and the subject rotated the standard stimulus to the instructed orientation. When this rotation was completed, the subject pressed a button, and the response time (RT_1) was recorded. Next, a test stimulus was presented. This stimulus was either S, R (the mirror reversal of S), of one of the different stimuli D1 through D6. As Figure 7.14 indicates, each D1 stimulus closely resembled its associated S stimulus, but the D6 stimuli were substantially different from their associated standards. The

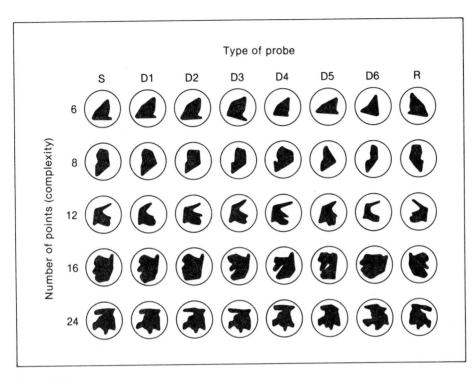

Figure 7.14.

Nonsense forms used by Cooper and Podgorny, 1976. (Copyright 1976 by the American Psychological Association. Adapted by permission of the publisher and authors.)

subject's task was to decide whether the test stimulus was the same as or different from the rotated standard. The time required to do this was recorded and is referred to as RT_2. Subjects who responded faster than the medians on both RT_1 and RT_2 were called fast subjects; all other subjects were called slow.

Interestingly, fast subjects were unaffected by the difference variable. They responded as quickly to D6 stimuli as they did to D1 stimuli, and in neither of these cases were their RT_2 times much slower than on S trials. Slow subjects showed a different response pattern. The difference variable produced changes in RT_2 times. The more similar the test stimulus was to the standard, the more time the slow subjects took to verify it. The fast subjects apparently were able to interpret the mental images all at once. This rapid detection has been interpreted as a sort of mental template analysis (Spoehr & Lehmkuhle, 1982), meaning that the *degree* of dissimilarity between the test stimulus and the rotated standard does not matter much to the fast subjects. As long as a difference is present, no matter how slight, the fast subject detects it. Slow subjects apparently compare the standard and test stimuli on a feature-by-feature (nonholistic) basis. If the test stimulus is similar to the standard (as in the D1 conditions), the subjects require more time to find the distinguishing characteristic. Robertson and Palmer (1983) have provided evidence showing that the nature of the mental rotation is also holistic, meaning that all the parts of a complex mental image rotate at the same speed at the same time.

However, other studies have questioned the notion that the image is a second-order isomorph with holistic properties. For example, Yuille and Steiger (1982) argued that subjects might actually be using the complexity of the shape as an aid in mental rotation. The found that when figural complexity was redundant (i.e., associated) with the direction in which mental rotation was to take place, complexity had no effect on the apparent speed of mental rotation. That is, the subjects were able to rotate complex forms at the same rate as simple forms. This finding is consistent with the holistic position, but Yuille and Steiger maintained that the holistic argument had not been put to a fair test, because the subjects could be using figural complexity as a good predictor for the intended direction of rotation.

In one experiment, Yuille and Steiger varied figural complexity by adding blocks to the ten-block arrays used in the original Shepard and Metzler (1971) study. In some conditions, the direction of angular rotation was restricted, meaning that certain patterns of blocks were to be rotated only in certain directions. In other conditions, this restriction was not in force; the patterns of blocks (and presumably their complexity) were of no use in predicting the direction of rotation. Under these conditions, figural complexity exerted a strong effect on the speed of mental rotation. The more complex the figure was (as determined by the number of blocks added to the original array), the longer the subjects' time required to carry out the mental rotation.

This finding can be interpreted in a number of ways, but none of them are consistent with the holistic argument. If the holistic position were correct, advance knowledge of the direction of mental rotation shouldn't have any effect on the *rate* of rotation of complex figures. This finding instead suggests that the holistic property of images may be an artifact of how imagery studies are conducted. Similarly, Cochran, Pick, and Pick (1983) found that facial patterns—a type of stimulus that has been assumed to have holistic properties—weren't rotated faster than comparable nonfacial patterns.

Further, the idea that the image has any isomorphic or analogue qualities has also been questioned (Anderson, 1978; Banks, 1981; Heil, 1982), perhaps most relentlessly by Pylyshyn (1973, 1979a, 1979b). Pylyshyn (1979b) has argued that many of the imagery phenomena we have discussed as demonstrations of isomorphism are instances of what he calls **cognitive penetration.** The findings of imagery studies are said to be cognitively penetrable, because such findings seem to be heavily influenced by cognitive factors such as the subjects' beliefs, expectations about the study, interpretations about how subjects should behave, and so on (Pylyshyn, 1979a). Recall that we saw evidence of these factors in the mental travel studies. The mileposts influenced the subjects' scanning rates, even though the subjects knew the physical distances were identical. Commenting on the idea that the image is an isomorph that preserves some aspects of the world, Pylyshyn (1979b) notes:

No one to my knowledge has suggested that the image must accelerate and decelerate or that the relation among torque, angular momentum, and angular velocity has an analogue in the mental rotation case. Of course, it may turn out that it takes subjects longer to rotate an object they imagine to be heavier. . . . But . . . in this case the explanation must appeal to the subject's knowledge of the behavior of heavier objects rather than to an intrinsic property of images. (Pylyshyn, 1979b, pp. 19–20)

If the subjects are told to mentally rotate heavy objects, and they require a greater amount of time to do so, the explanation cannot be based on any property of the image per se, because the image cannot have mass. Such a finding could be explainable only by recourse to subjects' knowledge of how they think such an image should operate.

Several other commentators (e.g., Block 1981) have noted that much of the confusion surrounding the nature of the image has been produced by sloppy use of terms on the part of cognitive psychologists. Saying, for example, that images "have" distance is different from saying they "preserve" distance, which is also different from saying that the image is an "isomorph" or "analogue" of perception. Cognitive psychologists need to be particularly careful when they use these terms, but another point should also be considered. Some theorists (Anderson, 1978; Palmer, 1978) have wondered if some of even the most precisely framed questions concerning imagery are answerable at this time. They have wondered if the behavioral data to which we have access are adequate to settle every question about the nature of the image. It's important here to realize that science is a technique for grappling with questions, and like all techniques, it has its limitations. Anderson and Palmer have speculated that in the imagery literature, we may have found some of the inherent limitations of our approach. Namely, no single observation may rule out one notion of the image's nature and support another notion.

CONCLUDING COMMENTS AND SUGGESTIONS FOR FURTHER READING

Cognitive psychologists were ecstatic over the first series of pro-imagery findings that emerged fifteen years ago. Since the late seventies, though, some of this happiness has diminished. Although nobody questions the authenticity of the imagery findings, their interpretation has created an uproar: People can't seem to agree on their meaning. Although fifteen years ago, the tendency was to accept the studies at face value, in the intervening time, many cognitive psychologists have developed strong reservations about face-value acceptance. Now, many of them are not as likely to believe that people think in images or that the image has functional significance in our mental lives. Although many mental tasks seem to be accompanied by imagery, many cognitive psychologists believe that the production of imagery is epiphenomenal to the cognitive processes that are actually doing the operations. The battle rages on. The pro-imagery theorists may have retreated somewhat from their earlier position, but the issue continues to be lively.

I think the volume edited by Block (1981) is the best single source for those wishing to understand the issues in mental imagery. In particular, the chapters by Dennett and Pylyshyn are clear expositions that go a long way toward defogging this cloudy area. Since Kosslyn has written one of the chapters and has contributed to another, this book is also a good place to find out about this important thinker's views. Those students who would like to read a fairly nontechnical introduction to the imagery literature might start with Kosslyn's (1983) book *Ghosts in the Mind's Machine*. The relationship between imagery and consciousness is addressed in a readable book by Morris and Hampson (1983). Like Block, these authors consider the philosophical implications of imagery.

For those wishing to take a historical perspective, I advise reading Pylyshyn's (1973) article entitled "What the mind's eye tells the mind's brain." Most commentators think of this article as the initial shot in the dual code versus propositional representation war. The responses of Anderson (1978), Kosslyn and Pomerantz (1977), Shepard and Podgorny (1978), and especially Palmer (1978) should be read next. Pylyshyn's later articles (1980, 1981) make a good rebuttal. By the time you've finished all this reading, you'll no doubt be tired of the whole issue. To perk you up, I advise reading Paul Kolers's brief review of imagery, in which the following marvelous comment appears: "The arguments [concerning imagery] sometimes seem like those of Medieval Scholastics debating the attributes of imagined Powers" (Kolers, 1983, p. 153).

Students are often interested in people whose imagery seems bizarre or exceptionally well developed. Luria's (1968) book describes an individual whose powers of imagery were so strong that in order to erase something from his memory, he had to imagine that the material had been written on a piece of paper that was then set afire, thus obliterating it! Readers who wish to know more about eidetic imagery are directed to Haber (1979) and Neisser (1982). Imagery is often used extensively in the field, and clinicians report that a wide variety of imagery techniques may have psychotherapeutic effects. Some of this literature is summarized in Sheikh (1983).

FOCUS ON RESEARCH:
Photographic Memory?

Our experiences with images tell us they're just like pictures, but scientific findings tell us otherwise. For most of us, the image's pictorial properties are something of an illusion; they are merely an analogue of a real picture.

However, some reports seem to point to the existence of something beyond normal imagery in a few people. For example, Stromeyer (1970) described a young woman who has an almost incomprehensible ability. Stromeyer sequentially presented the subject with what looked like two random dot patterns. Each pattern consisted of ten thousand dots, and if the patterns were superimposed, a letter or digit would emerge. The first pattern was presented to the woman's right eye for one minute. The first pattern was removed, and the second pattern was immediately presented to the woman's left eye. The woman successfully reported the item. How can this finding be interpreted?

The term *eidetic imagery* is used to describe such feats. Eidetic imagery can apparently be done only if the subject has access to an incredibly detailed, photographic memory. To be classified as an *eidetiker,* the subject should report that the image is truly in front of him. He should seem to be experiencing the picture rather than remembering it. The eidetiker should scan the image by moving her eyes around it, and the image should not move with her eyes. Finally, the subject's eye positions during reports from the image should match the eye positions that woould occur if the subject were looking at the original stimulus.

These criteria are stiff. Some people meet them, and almost all of them are children. Gray and Gummerman (1975) have found that about 5 percent of normal children can be classified as eidetikers. The reports of some of these children are fantastic. For example, when shown a complex picture, such as an illustration of the Cheshire cat from the original edition of *Alice in Wonderland,* the eidetiker can answer questions about details of the picture.

If eidetikers are asked to count the rings on the Cheshire cat's tail, they answer correctly. Since the eidetikers would not likely have anticipated this question, they apparently do have access to a photographic memory. This belief is bolstered by the even more incredible performance of some eidetikers who can mentally rotate the complex pictures! When this is done, the parts of the picture stay in the same spatial relationships with one another throughout and after the rotation.

Explaining such phenomena as the results of a photographic memory code is appealing. But if such a code exists, its operation is extremely complex. Not all eidetikers can do the Stromeyer task, but they should be able to if they were actually inspecting a highly accurate image. Furthermore, the eidetic ability seems to come and go. Subjects have sometimes been able to make extremely accurate and detailed reports of their imagery; at other time, they can't. Also, the eidetic image seems to be formed in parts, and it vanishes in parts. This evidence suggests that only a part of the image can be inspected at any one time. Finally, eidetikers usually can't retrieve the image, and their astounding imagery ability isn't related to any other aspects of normal memory. This pattern of observations is baffling and is sure to continue puzzling researchers for some time.

KEY TERMS

Mentalism
Mental rotation
Angular disparity
Mind's eye movements
Mental size
Dual code position
Mental psychophysics
Visual angle of the mind's eye

Mental travel
Demand characteristics
Functional significance
Epiphenomena
Propositional format
Second-order isomorphism
Cognitive penetration

PART FOUR

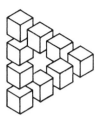

LANGUAGE

Understanding and producing language are fundamental aspects of our mental lives and our humanity. Without these abilities, we would be cut off from one another. Language enables us to erect complex social structures and to form intimate social bonds.

These claims may seem like overstatements to you. For example, you might point to colonies of insects, such as termites, who have elaborate social structure without having language. However, one striking finding to emerge from the studies of such creatures concerns the complexity of their communication systems, which seems out of proportion to the complexity of the creatures themselves. Termites, for example, signal one another by drumming their heads against the floor of their nest. This action produces a sound like that of sand falling on paper, but a close analysis of the drumming reveals that it is highly organized and complex. By varying the rhythmic phrasing and duration of the drumming, termites send complex codes throughout the whole colony.

In addition to being an apparently essential part of our social structure, language seems to be a crucial ingredient of our mental lives. Our intuitions support this assertion. When we think, we are often aware of some sort of internal speech that seems to accompany our thought processes.

For a variety of reasons, cognitive psychologists have turned their attention to the phenomenon of language. This part of the book considers some of their discoveries and deals with a number of issues. First, defining language is difficult. Second, expressing the essence of language in a set of formal rules has also proved undoable so far. Almost all linguists believe that our knowledge of linguistic sounds, of word order, and of meaning can be rewritten as a formal system of rules, and we'll examine some of the sound reasons for this belief. Not much is known about these rules, although psycholinguists have a good idea of some of the minimum elements that are required in any proposed theory of linguistic knowledge.

Another issue concerns the origin of language. The concern here is with the role of experience as both a necessary and a sufficient basis for language. The notion of innate predispositions in language acquisition and development is a recurring theme throughout the next three chapters. As you read, keep this idea in mind. We'll also consider some of the cognitive operations that are involved in the comprehension of speech, which involves both feature analysis and pattern recognition—bottom-up processes. The comprehension of speech also involves top-down processing: Our expectations about the speaker's intentions help guide feature analysis and pattern recognition.

CHAPTER 8

Linguistic Knowledge and Its Acquisition

OVERVIEW

WHAT IS LANGUAGE?
Design Features

GRAMMAR AND LINGUISTICS
Early Views on Grammar
  Objections to Finite State Grammars
Phrase Structure Grammars
Transformational Grammar
Origins of Grammatical Knowledge
Implications of Chomsky's Theory
Empirical Support for the Deep-Surface
  Structure Distinction
  Click Studies
  Phoneme Detection Studies

Summary

ASPECTS OF LANGUAGE ACQUISITION: IS KNOWLEDGE INNATE?
Skinner's Position
  Extensions of the Operant Analysis
  Criticisms of the Behavioral Approach
Arguments for Innate Knowledge
  Anatomical and Breathing Specializations
  Specializations of the Brain
  Categorical Perception of Speech Sounds

**CONCLUDING COMMENTS AND SUGGESTIONS
FOR FURTHER READING
FOCUS ON RESEARCH
KEY TERMS**

OVERVIEW

Consider the following passage:

Well, I will tell you. I got a little concern yesterday in the first three innings when I say the three players I had gotten rid of and I said when I lost nine what am I going to do and when I had a couple of my players. I thought so great of that did not do so good up to the sixth inning I was more confused but I finally had to go and call on a young man in Baltimore that we don't own and the Yankees don't own him, and he is doing pretty good, and I would actually have to tell you that I think we are more the Greta Garbo type now from success. (Quoted in Barrows, 1977.)

The great baseball manager Casey Stengel, who uttered these words, apparently used to talk that way all the time. Does the passage make sense to you? We recognize that a wide latitude must be given to individual speakers in matters of word choice and tone. But we would also assert that some commonality must exist among various speakers if any communication is to take place. Does Stengel's speech fall within these boundaries, or does it represent such a substantial departure from standard usage that it can hardly be considered language? Answering this question requires a definition of language, and so far, linguists haven't been entirely successful in coming up with one. This chapter examines some of the reasons why defining language is so difficult.

Perhaps you're thinking that I shouldn't be so hard on the old ballplayer. After all, if read closely, the passage is reasonable enough. Here's my translation: Stengel was worried that some players he had traded were doing pretty well against him, and he obtained the services of a young man who had not signed with any club. Consequently, the team had come out of its tailspin and was now playing pretty well; that is, they were now "the Greta Garbo type from success." I may seem to be stretching things a little, but this last part of my translation is based on several bits of knowledge stored in my propositional network:

1. Greta Garbo was a popular movie star during the 1930s.
2. Casey Stengel was old enough to have seen Garbo in the movies when she was popular.
3. Greta Garbo was widely regarded as beautiful.

Language comprehension inevitably requires vast knowledge. Moreover, several different types of knowledge are called for. First, speech comprehension requires knowledge of phonology, or linguistic sounds. Second, we must have some models or rules for generating and recognizing appropriate **syntax,** or word order. Finally, language requires semantic knowledge of the type examined in Chapter 7. Linguists refer to the conglomeration of all this linguistic knowledge as **grammar.**

For at least the past twenty-five years, syntax has probably been the most intensively studied component of grammatical knowledge. Many reasons account for this intensive study, not the least of which is that Noam Chomsky—perhaps the most important of contemporary theoretical linguists—believed that **semantics,** or meaning, was derived from and secondary to syntax. This chapter examines Chomsky's proposition.

Words and phrases can be put together in many different ways. Yet, all normal children seem to acquire the appropriate knowledge despite their immature intellectual abilities. How can this be? How can children learn language—an extremely complex ability—when they are still more or less incapable of other, similar intellectual feats? The realization of this paradox has led some theorists (Chomsky among them) to argue that children are helped in their linguistic quest by innate predispositions that make them sensitive to certain regularities in linguistic sounds and phrases. This chapter examines some of the evidence supporting that proposition and contrasts it with the alternative viewpoint—namely, that no innate abilities are required to learn language.

WHAT IS LANGUAGE?

Whenever I ask the question What is Language? in my classes, students usually seem content to let the following equation express their beliefs:

Language = Communication

Students who hold this opinion are (perhaps unwittingly) asserting that the *intention* of the gesturer determines whether language is being displayed. That is, if I make a gesture (broadly speaking, sounds should be considered gestures), and if the gesture is seemingly made in the context of a deliberate mental event, then my students are willing to say that this gesture is linguistic and that my other gestures are probably linguistic, too.

This view of language is sometimes called the **continuity theory** (Aitchison, 1983). According to this perspective, human language is a sophisticated calling system that is not fundamentally different from animal cries and calls. Proponents of this position often describe the work of Struhsaker (1967). Struhsaker studied the cries of vervet monkeys in the wild. Vervet monkeys use substantially different vocalizations for different dangerous animals. For example, a *chutter* is used to signal for the arrival of a cobra, but if an eagle appears, the monkeys produce the *rraup* sound. The argument that these sounds are one step removed from words doesn't seem too farfetched. That is, among our primitive ancestors, similar danger calls may have been used, and these calls gradually came to represent the animals themselves; they became the animals' names.

The continuity theory suffers from several problems. First, the vervet monkeys may simply be responding to the intensity of the danger rather than to anything specific about the stimulus. That is, the chutter may be used for something extremely dangerous, the rraup for a less frightening stimulus, and so on. This interpretation has been empirically supported; vervet monkeys sometimes chirp at the sight of an eagle. This call is usually given in response to a lion and suggests that the vervet monkey considers lions and eagles equally threatening. The implication is that the apparent specificity observed (heard?) in animal cries doesn't necessarily indicate that such animals have specific referents in mind.

A second problem with continuity theories is that the attribution of intentionality is often difficult to make in practice. Whale songs are one of the better-known illustrations of this problem. As you may know, certain species of whales produce sounds that have definite rhythm. These songs change in predictable ways. Over the course of a lengthy migration, certain themes are introduced, become dominant, and are eventually supplanted. Nobody knows why the whales produce these sounds; consequently, nobody knows whether these sounds are communicative.

Although my students might be willing to assume that regularity of gesture is an indication of both specificity of referent and intentionality (and therefore language), we might do well to modify the equation initially proposed: Language is communicative—at least potentially—but simple communications aren't necessarily linguistic. This statement suggests that to be considered truly linguistic, a set of gestures must have other properties besides the simple intent to communicate.

Design Features

Hockett (1963) has proposed a list of essential characteristics that seem to be required in any definition of language. Although many linguists believe that this approach is the only valid way to define language, we should first be aware that such an approach nevertheless has some problems. Even if Hockett had managed to isolate just those features of communication that determine the essence of language, such a listing wouldn't make clear how those features were *related* to one another. Yet, the relationship among such design characteristics may be the sine qua non of language: We are not necessarily interested in the parts that make up language; we are interested in how those parts have been put together.

Figure 8.1 is a pictorial representation of some of Hockett's **design features.** Some of these features are obviously more important than others. For example, use of the *vocal-auditory channel* is a desirable but not essential feature of language. Speaking and hearing are more or less nondirectional senses, which means that our eyes and limbs can be trained on other stimuli while we converse.

Broadcast transmission and *rapid fading* are also aspects of the physics of sound. We are amazingly able to locate the source of sounds, which can be an aid in communication. Typically, speech is an extremely transitory event. Although having linguistic codes that are more durable is sometimes advantageous, the transitory nature of speech can also be beneficial. Because this type of communication fades rapidly, privacy is enhanced. The rapid fading of speech also permits duplicity (telling different people different versions of something), but this isn't all bad, because at times, editing the content of certain messages is desirable. Rapid fading also implies a social function. To talk to someone, you have to get relatively close to him.

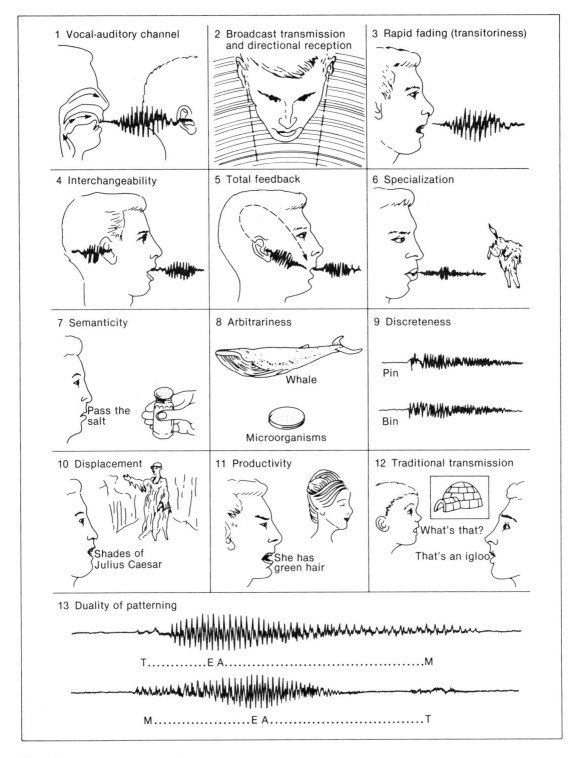

Figure 8.1.

A pictorial view of Hockett's design features. (From *The Origin of Speech,* by C.F. Hockett. Copyright © 1960 by Scientific American, Inc. All rights reserved.)

With *interchangeability,* we move closer to a characteristic of language that could be called essential. This design feature refers to a competent speaker's ability to reproduce any message that she can understand, and the content of that message is left undisturbed by this process. This ability isn't true for all animal communication systems. In some systems, particular gestures are sometimes strongly associated with sex roles and can't be reproduced by the opposite gender.

Total feedback refers to the fact that we hear everything we produce. *Specialization* is a term that linguists use in several ways. In this context, the term means that the usual purpose of human speech is to communicate. The sounds that we make are not simply incidental to some other purpose. In the case of some animal vocalizations, such as whale songs, this property is not obviously present. *Semanticity* and *arbitrariness* are related and refer to the fact that in language, no inherent relationship exists between the linguistic sounds and their referents, even though the linguistic sounds clearly mean something.

Discreteness refers to the idea that language consists of small, separable units of sound, called **phonemes,** each of which has an identity. Typically, only a small number of different phonemes are used in any given language. For example, the English language has about forty different phonemes. Standing alone, phonemes have no meaning. They can, however, be combined in a wide variety of ways. The combination of phonemes according to the rules of a particular language results in the creation of a **morpheme,** the basic unit of meaning. In the English language, morphemes are usually words, but not all morphemes are words. For example, the suffix *ly* is a morpheme.

Duality of patterning describes this process of creating an infinite number of meaningful words from a small set of phonemic building blocks. This ability is not unique to humans. For example, bird songs are made up of a series of notes, each of which is meaningless by itself. Whatever meaning the song might have is conveyed only by the entire sequence.

Traditional transmission refers to the idea that many (perhaps most) of the elements of language are handed down from one generation to the next; some sort of experience within a culture is necessary to acquire language. Children reared in isolation almost invariably seem to show deficits in linguistic ability, some of which seem permanent (Lenneberg, 1964). Traditional transmission is a hallmark of language; the role of experience doesn't seem nearly as clear in animal communication. For example, certain bird songs, such as that of the thrush, appear to be completely innate. For such animals, the presence or absence of other members of the same species has little or no effect on the acquisition or nature of the call. Incidentally, it's important to avoid thinking of these innate abilities in categorical—that is, either-or—terms. Other birds, such as the chaffinch, seem to hatch with the basic song pattern built in. Details of the song's pitch and rhythm, however, are acquired by experience (Thorpe, 1961, 1963).

Displacement refers to a feature of language that humans use and take for granted every day. We often refer to things that are far removed in time and place, but such talk seems acceptable to our listeners. Thus, a movie might begin with the narration "A long time ago, in a galaxy far,

far away"—which doesn't strike us as unreasonable. So common is this feature that we seldom stop to think about its implications. Although the cries of animals might be truly communicative, can they communicate about things that are no longer present? Your dog might bark at an intruder—perhaps might even emit a particular bark—but can the dog bark in the memory of last year's intruder?

Only a very few cases of bona fide displacement have been seen in animal communication, and even these are far more limited than human displacement. For example, von Frisch (1967) clearly demonstrated that bees have arbitrary communicative gestures, which have the property of displacement. When a bee discovers a source of nectar that is distant from the hive (i.e., at least 200 yards away), she returns to the hive and does a dance (von Frisch's term), which shows the appropriate direction of flight from the hive. Following that, the scout does either a "round dance" or a "waggle dance"—the former is the source is relatively close by, the latter if it is far away. The vigor of the scout bee's dance indicates something about the quality of the nectar. When the nectar is plentiful and good, the scout bee's dance is energetic. When the rest of the colony emerges from the hive to gather the nectar, they fly en masse to the indicated spot. This behavior is an impressive demonstration of displacement in animal communication. However, von Frisch (1954) also demonstrated the limitations of this system. A hive of bees was placed near the bottom of a radio tower. As the scout bees emerged, they were collected and taken to a container of sugar water, which had been placed on the top of the tower. Then the scouts were released, they dutifully returned to the hive and energetically reported (via the round dance) that a good source of nectar was nearby. When the rest of the colony emerged, they flew in all directions except up, because the communication system of the bees denotes only horizontal, not vertical, distance.

This failure on the part of bees highlights an extremely important aspect of human communication. We have the ability to use our language in novel, creative ways. If we were confronted with the bees' plight, making up a word (or, I should say, a dance) that communicated the idea of altitude would be relatively easy for us. This sort of creativity takes place every day. When actor Lee Marvin's live-in lover sued him a few years ago, the word *palimony* was created by an anonymous wag, and all of us knew exactly what it meant, even though we hadn't thought of it ourselves. This creativity in language is referred to as **productivity.** Unlike animals, whose vocalizations seem to be largely stimulus bound, we can decide what we want to say and when we wish to say it.

Figure 8.2 shows a comparison of language with several other phenomena in terms of the presence or absence of specific design features. As Figure 8.2 shows, only language has all the design features that have been described. Moreover, the least shared (and therefore the most essential) aspects of language seem to be displacement, productivity, and duality of patterning. This point is important, because these three features seem to be related. Duality of patterning and productivity in language indicate that the nature of linguistic rules must be general and abstract. For example, in the English language, the rules specifying the production of morphemes

	A Members of the Cricket Family	B Bee Dancing	C Stickleback Courtship	D Western Meadowlark Song	E Gibbon Calls	F Paralinguistic Phenomena	G Language	H Western Instrumental Music (since Bach)
1. Vocal-auditory channel	Auditory, not vocal	No	No	Yes	Yes	Yes	Yes	Auditory, not vocal
2. Broadcast transmission and directional recognition								Yes
3. Rapid fading (transitoriness)	Yes, repeated	?	?	Yes	Yes, repeated	Yes	Yes	Yes
4. Interchangeability	Limited	Limited	No	?	Yes	Largely yes	Yes	?
5. Total feedback	Yes	?	No	Yes	Yes	Yes	Yes	Yes
6. Specialization	Yes?	?	In part	Yes?	Yes	Yes?	Yes	Yes
7. Semanticity	No?	Yes	No	In part?	Yes	Yes?	Yes	No, in general
8. Arbitrariness	?	No		If semantic	Yes	In part	Yes, often	
9. Discreteness	Yes?	No	?	?	Yes	Largely no	Yes	In part
10. Displacement		Yes, always		?	No	In part	Yes, often	
11. Productivity	No	Yes	No	?	No	Yes	Yes	Yes
12. Traditional transmission	No?	Probably not	No?	?	?	Yes	Yes	Yes
13. Duality of patterning	?(Trivial)	No		?	No	No	Yes	

Figure 8.2.

Eight systems of communication that possess in varying degrees the thirteen design features of language proposed by Hockett. A question mark means that it is doubtful or not known whether the system has the particular feature. A blank space indicates that the feature cannot be determined because another feature is lacking or indefinite. (From *The Origin of Speech*, by C.F. Hockett. Copyright © 1960 by Scientific America, Inc. All Rights reserved.)

from phonemes are not dependent in any principled way on the nature of the phonemes themselves. Certain combinations are not permitted in the English language (no English word begins with *mg*), but most combinations are permitted, although the patterns thus created are far from random. Similarly, novelty in language is commonplace and is often comprehensible to our listeners. Recall that I demonstrated this by creating a novel sentence in Chapter 1. Demonstrations such as these show that patterns of morphemes we produce are not dependent in any rigid way on the morphemes that we may have already uttered. If they were rigidly dependent, we would never be capable of producing a creative utterance. Can you see why? Once we had picked a particular morpheme to begin our comment, that choice would rigidly constrain our subsequent choice, which in turn would rigidly constrain the next choice, and so on. The number of producible utterances would be large, but it would be finite. But we know this isn't true: The number of producible, and therefore creative, utterances is infinite.

Still, not all novel strings of morphemes are comprehensible to our listeners. Presumably, the reason why some novel strings of morphemes are comprehensible while others aren't has something to do with our adherence to some general rules in the former and our violation of them in the latter. Together, the features of duality of patterning and productivity combine to allow us to expand our ability to refer to objects that are remote. In the most extreme case, these features allow us to refer to things that are, strictly speaking, never present anywhere; here I'm referring to ideas such as truth or beauty.

Hockett's work suggests that the design features that are truly essential to language are those dealing with creativity and flexibility. For some time, a common tendency among linguists has been to think that peoples' grammatical knowledge can be expressed as a series of rules that are specific enough to permit the production of well-formed words and sentences but general enough to permit unlimited creativity.

GRAMMAR AND LINGUISTICS

Encountering the heading "Grammar and Linguistics" in a book about cognitive psychology may seem odd, but good reasons exist for discussing the theories and modus operandi of linguists.

First, as noted in Chapter 1, linguists were among the first to mount a successful attack on behavioristic psychology. In the 1950s, when this criticism first appeared, psychologists became highly interested in the work of theoretical linguists, and the discipline known as psycholinguistics was born. Psycholinguists and linguists have different but complementary ways of doing research. Whereas the psychologist is likely to design experiments that test fairly limited hypotheses about language comprehension in a fairly rigid way, the linguist is much more likely to study sentences that have actually been produced by speakers in a natural context. In some cases, the linguist may even compose sentences, which are then studied in light of the linguist's intuitions concerning the sentence's structure and what that structure might indicate about the nature of grammatical knowledge.

The second reason for studying theoretical linguistics is based on one of its stated objectives. Linguists are concerned with the discovery of **linguistic universals.** These universals are general principles of language that are thought to be embodied in every language. The evidence supporting linguistic universals is currently unclear; nevertheless, the linguist makes an interesting claim about them. You are no doubt aware that language and thought seem intimately bound together. For this reason, it is often thought that these linguistic universals reflect some underlying rules of thought. That is, linguists have maintained that by understanding fully the nature and organization of language, it will be possible to understand the nature and organization of the human mind.

Early Views on Grammar

Work in experimental linguistics began about thirty years ago when various thinkers realized that language has obvious regularities. For example, in the sentence

Would you please pass the _____?

the blank is more readily filled with "salt" than it is with "chilled monkey brains," and the entire sentence becomes somewhat ambiguous when the blank is filled with "skyscraper." This phenomenon occurs in many sentences and has suggested to some thinkers that the rules for syntax (word order) could be written in the form of a left-to-right grammar. Such grammars were governed by finite state rules, meaning that the next word choice at any point, or state, in the sentence was determined by consulting a finite number of candidates and picking one of them. In other words; the choice made at the left-most word in the sentence constrained the choice made at the next left-most word, and so on, until the sentence was completed.

What's implied by such a system of syntax? First, this view implies that human grammar consists of constraint rules that limit the word choices that can be made at any point in the production of a sentence. Second, this system implies that humans produce sentences on a word-by-word basis. That is, having chosen one word, the person consults some mental list of acceptable choices and produces one of them. Having made this choice, the person consults the mental list to see what choices are available for the next word, and so on, until the utterance is completed.

Early research with these types of grammars was impressive. Miller (1958) showed his subjects strings of letters, some of which were generated by the finite state system shown in Figure 8.3. The transition rules are indicated under the figure. For example, one of two paths can be taken from the node marked O. The system could move through N to node 1, or through S to node 3. From node 1, the system could move through N to node 3 or through G to O, the finish node. These pathways aren't the only ones through this network, but you can see how the strings were created. How many different strings could be created by this primitive system? Because the finite state rules permit a **recursion** at node 3, an infinite number of different

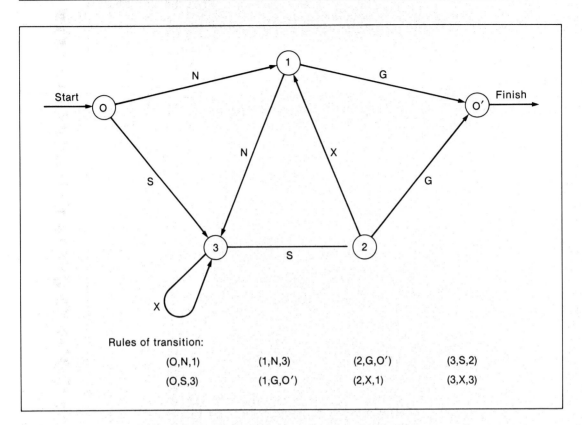

Figure 8.3.

Diagram of a finite state generator. A string is any sequence of letters generated by starting at state O and finishing at O'. A letter is added to the string by taking the path labeled by that letter from one state to another. (From Miller, 1958. Copyright 1958 © by the American Psychological Association. Adapted by permission of the publisher.)

strings could be generated. All strings produced by these finite state rules have some things in common: They all begin with either an *N* or an *S,* and they all end with a *G.*

Miller next used the same four letters to create another set of strings. This time, however, the strings were created by using a random numbers table to determine which letter should come next, the only constraint being that each of the random strings had to be of the same length as one of the grammar-generated strings. Table 8.1 shows the two sets of strings, which look similar. If you hadn't been reading the text up to this point, determining exactly what is different about the two sets of lists might be difficult for you.

The adult subjects attempted to learn all nine strings in two of the lists by looking at each string in the list one at a time. After looking at all nine strings, the subjects tried to write them down. Each such pass through the list constituted a trial. Subjects studied the list for ten trials or until they reproduced all nine strings without error. Figure 8.4 shows the findings of this study. Notice that the subjects learned the grammatical strings at a

TABLE 8.1

Lists of Redundant and Random Strings Used in an Experiment on the Learning of Structure

Structured (Redundant)		Random	
L₁	**L₂**	**R₁**	**R₂**
SSXG	NNSG	GNSX	NXGS
NNXSG	NNSXG	NSGXN	GNXSG
SXSXG	SXXSG	XGSSN	SXNGG
SSXNSG	NNXSXG	SXNNGN	GGSNXG
SXXXSG	NNXXSG	XGSXXS	NSGNGX
NNSXNSG	NNXXSXG	GSXXGNS	NGSXXNS
SXSXNSG	NNXXXSG	NSXXGSG	NGXXGGN
SXXXSXG	SSXNSXG	SGXGGNN	SXGXGNS
SXXXXSG	SSXNXSG	XXGNSGG	XGSNGXG

Source: Miller, 1958, p. 487. Copyright 1958 © by the American Psychological Association. Adapted by permission of the publisher.

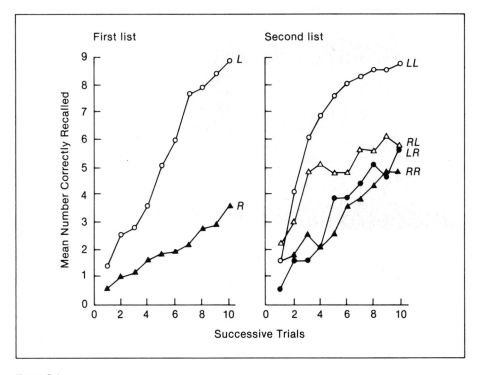

Figure 8.4.

The mean number of letters correctly recalled in free recall of random *(R)* and redundant *(L)* lists of letters. Notice that on the second list, those exposed to *L* lists at first performed better than those exposed to *R* lists. (From Miller, 1958. Copyright 1958 © by the American Psychological Association. Adapted by permission of the publisher.)

much faster rate than they learned the random strings. These effects carried over to the second list that the subjects learned. Having learned a grammatical list originally seemed to facilitate the learning of random strings. To see this, compare the performance of the *LR* subjects with the *RR* subjects. Those who had first learned a grammatical, or *L,* list tended to outperform the *RR* subjects (who had learned a random list previously) on each successive trial. Although the differences in the lists appear to be fairly subtle, the subjects were extremely sensitive to the regularities of the grammar-generated lists. At the time, psychologists were willing to interpret these findings as a demonstration that syntactical knowledge was formally equivalent to a **finite state grammar.**

Objections to Finite State Grammars

As theories of grammar acquisition, finite state systems fit in nicely with the general stimulus-response theories of learning then in vogue. The pronunciation of each word in a sentence is a response. But because we have total feedback and hear each word we say, the hearing of a word acts as a discriminative stimulus, which cues us to produce the next word in the sentence. At the end of the sentence, we are reinforced by our listeners' compliance. This approach reduces the learning of a sentence to a much simpler problem—that of learning a chain of stimulus-response associations. Because researchers had demonstrated many times in laboratories all over the world that animals could learn lengthy S-R chains, and because children must surely be capable of learning anything that a rat could learn, finite state grammars were thought to be the definite answer to the problem of syntax acquisition.

Finite state systems, however, suffer from a number of theoretical problems, some of which are worth reviewing. First, a competent speaker can embed any syntactic structure into an already formed sentence. We can do this with utterances, too, as demonstrated in Chapter 1. This ability means that the central premise of finite state systems—that a particular word choice is constrained by previous word choices—is false. Reviewing Figure 8.3, we see that we really don't have to move to any particular word in a sentence as a function of the words we have already uttered. We can move from any node to any other node if we wish to. Now we may *typically* produce utterances in accordance with finite state rules, but we are not obligated to follow them. Because we are not obligated to follow such rules means that our knowledge of syntax must consist of more than simple chaining rules. In other words, we apparently know how to do a lot more than we typically do when we speak. A complete theory of grammar should specify our capabilities as well as typical usage.

Second, according to finite state grammar, judgments of grammaticality would be dependent on the frequency with which individual words have been paired in the past. Grammatical sentences would be those that contained a large number of words that had been paired (that is, placed adjacent to each other in previous sentences, whereas ungrammatical sentences would not have this property. This idea is also wrong, however. Subjects sometimes judge sentences as grammatical, even though they contain words that probably have seldom been paired together. Consider one of Chomsky's most famous demonstration sentences:

Colorless green ideas sleep furiously.

Most respondents judge this sentence to be grammatical (although meaningless). Notice that the sentence is grammatical in spite of its violating the assumptions of finite state grammar. It's safe to say that not many of us have ever seen the pairs "colorless–green," "green–ideas," and so on, yet the sentence seems well formed. On the other hand, it's also possible to construct a sentence out of words that have frequently been paired together. Miller and Selfridge (1950) composed the following:

Was he went to the newspaper is in deep end.

Although the words of the sentence can be grouped together in a series of high-frequency pairs (e.g., "was–he," "he–went," and so on), the sentence has no meaning and isn't judged to be grammatical. This result demonstrates that people probably do not form sentences on a word-by-word basis. Instead, sentences are apparently composed and understood in units that are larger than pairs. This suggests that we look at such large units, called clauses, as the unit of grammatical knowledge. The contribution of finite state system, although negative, was nevertheless important because it pointed linguists and psychologists toward a path that has been much more productive.

Phrase Structure Grammars

Phrase structure grammars were originally developed by linguist Leonard Bloomfield near the turn of the century. Unlike finite state grammars, which operate on a left-to-right basis, phrase structure grammars are organized hierarchically—that is, from the top down. Probably the easiest way to show this hierarchical organization is by analyzing a particular sentence:

Joey kissed the girl.

In Chapter 6, we saw that a sentence like this one can be broken down into propositions. On an everyday basis, people are usually not aware of the propositional analyses that they perform. However, if asked, people are capable of breaking down a sentence like this one into parts that seem to have a kind of psychological unity—some of the words of the sentence seem to cluster together naturally. If people are asked to break down the "Joey" sentence into two parts, many speakers would do it this way:

Joey   kissed the girl.

Most speakers are capable of dividing the second part again:

kissed   the girl.

Finally, we recognize that the second of these two parts may be redivided:

the   girl.

These parts are referred to as constituents, and they can be arranged in a hierarchical pattern as shown in Figure 8.5. These treelike patterns are called **phrase structures.** Notice that each of the constituents can be matched up with a term called a *constituent symbol.* "Joey" has been labeled with the constituent symbol N (noun), whereas "kissed the girl" has been labeled VP (verb phrase) in Figure 8.5. We see that the grammatical knowledge of adults can be expressed as a set of constituent symbols and a set of rewrite rules of the form X and Y, which specifies when a particular constituent symbol, Y can be substituted for a constituent symbol X. To see how this works, consider the following sentence (Clark & Clark, 1977):

The likable general collapsed.

This sentence could be divided into two constituents: an NP (noun phrase) standing for "the likable general" and a V (verb) designating "collapsed." The NP can be represented with the following formula: $NP = ART + ADJ + N$. However, if you think about it for a minute, you might detect the limitations of such a formula. Although the formula is a perfectly good representation of some noun phrases, it does not represent all noun phrases. Some well-formed noun phrases could be cooked up with the following formula: $NP = ART + N$. And indeed, the phrase "The officer" could be substituted for the noun phrase in the "likable general" sentence (Clark & Clark, 1977). To fully represent the grammatical knowl-

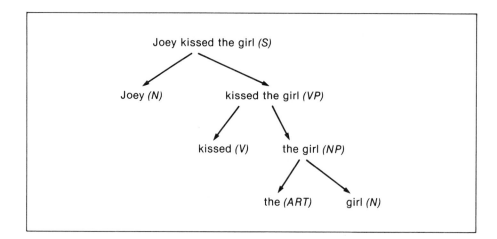

Figure 8.5.

The constituent structure of the "Joey" sentence.

edge on adults, then, we need a series of rewrite rules showing under what circumstances an *NP* of the *Y* type can be rewritten as an *NP* of the *X* type.

You may have noticed that I have been describing phrase structure grammars as representations of or as expressions of the grammatical knowledge of adults. This description is intentional on my part. Linguists don't necessarily claim that people actually use phrase structure grammars to produce or plan their utterances. Rather, they intend to state only that phrase structures are good ways to characterize the regularities observed in language and *describe* the features that grammatical sentences have in common. If this little proviso can be accepted, phrase structure grammars offer many powerful advantages over finite state grammars.

First, phrase structures account for judgments of grammaticality. If the phrase structures and rewrite rules are specified adequately, then all the sentences generated by the phrase structure grammar will be judged as grammatical, and none of the sentences thus produced will be judged as nongrammatical. Second, phrase structure grammars have a tidy explanation of ambiguity. What is the meaning of the following sentence?

They are cooking apples.

The interpretation of the phrase "cooking apples" is the problem. This sentence cannot be mapped onto just one phrase structure; rather it can be decomposed into two:

They   are cooking   apples.
They   are   cooking apples.

In the first case, "cooking" would be included in the *VP;* in the second, it would be an adjective in the final *NP*. When a sentence cannot be mapped successfully onto any phrase structure, it is judged to be nongrammatical. When it maps successfully onto just one phrase structure, the sentence is judged to be grammatical and meaningful. However, when the sentence maps onto two phrase structures, it is judged to be grammatical but not meaningful. In such cases, the explanation of ambiguity harmonizes nicely with the notions of constituent analysis and phrase structures.

A third advantage concerns the abstract nature of the phrase structures themselves. The possession of knowledge expressed as phrase structures allows its owner to do at least two things. First, he can accept as grammatical any sentence that maps onto a phrase structure, regardless of whether that sentence has been heard before. Second, the general nature of the phrase structure permits some creativity in utterances. For example, with the knowledge of the constituent symbols and rewrite rules shown in Figure 8.5, I can also generate the following sentences (assuming that all of the words are in my vocabulary):

Rainey parked the car.
Britain ruled the waves.

These sentences don't mean the same thing, but they can be mapped onto the same phrase structure. This has some implications for children, who are trying to learn appropriate syntax. According to finite state theories, children build up their knowledge of syntax on a pair-by-pair basis. That is, children learn to associate two words in a particular order. Once formed, this association could be used as a basis for learning successively longer strings. According to this viewpoint, the child acquires syntax in the same way that a tourist in a foreign country might operate, that is, by encoding and storing a series of stock phrases that could be helpful in a variety of situations. However, given what we know of children's memories, that children could acquire syntactical knowledge that way seems unlikely.

According to the phrase structure position, the task of the child is simplified somewhat. Phrase structure grammar proposes that, instead of a series of specific word orderings, children learn general rules that can be used as formulas to generate a wide variety of sentences. This simplifies the child's task because, presumably, there are fewer rules to learn than there are specific word orderings. In other words, while the number of sentences in the English language is infinite, the number of phrase structures probably isn't. However, this simplification is purchased at a price. Unlike specific phrasings, the phrase structures themselves are never heard directly. Instead, they must be inferred from all the utterances that the child hears. Given that the inference-making abilities of children are no better than their metamemories, phrase structure theory's explanation of syntax acquisition is far from complete.

Some other problems also prevent our adopting phrase structure theory wholesale. First, although not infinite, the number of different phrase structures is surely large. Is the expectation that children somehow infer this large number of rules a reasonable one? Other criticisms are founded on the idea that phrase structures don't tell us the whole story about a given sentence. According to the phrase structure position, sentences that have different phrase structures should be judged as dissimilar. The meaning of a sentence depends upon the constituent analysis that is carried out upon it. If this analysis points to two different phrase structures, the meaning of the sentence should be accordingly altered. But this phenomenon is not always observed, as the following trio of sentences shows:

1. Rainey parked the Renault.
2. It was the Renault that was parked by Rainey.
3. Americans won the gold.

Sentences 1 and 2 don't share the same phrase structure, but sentences 1 and 3 do. Yet, most of us would say that sentences 1 and 3 are more dissimilar than sentences 1 and 2, because the first two sentences share the same *meaning*. This response indicates that the meaning of a sentence is only partially dependent upon the results of a constituent analysis. The trio of sentences also shows that we must have some linguistic knowledge that is not expressed in the phrase structure rule.

A third problem with phrase structure grammars is their inability to explain some types of sentence ambiguity. For example, the sentence

Visiting relatives can be tiresome.

is ambiguous. What's tiresome—the visits from one's relatives or the act of visiting one's relatives? According to phrase structure grammars, ambiguity arises because a particular sentence can be mapped onto more than one phrase structure. However, both meanings of the prior sentence can be mapped onto the same phrase structure:

Visiting relatives   can be   tiresome.

Technically, this sentence should not be ambiguous, because its constituents can be divided up in one and only one way. The fact that the sentence is ambiguous amplifies one of our earlier conclusions. Namely, our linguistic knowledge must have more than what is expressed in phrase structure grammars.

Transformational Grammar

Transformational grammar is an extension of Bloomfield's ideas and is strongly associated with its originator, Noam Chomsky. In his (1957) book *Syntactic Structures,* Chomsky detailed the limitations of both finite state and phrase structure grammars, and proposed an alternative that attempted to represent more of the linguistic knowledge that we must have.

Chomsky reasoned that no single-level theory of grammar would ever account for all observed ambiguities in sentences, because these ambiguities were of at least two fundamentally different types. For example, the "cooking apples" sentence is ambiguous because it can be mapped onto more than one phrase structure. To resolve the ambiguity, all one has to do is ask whether the "cooking" goes with "apples" or with "are." However, the "visiting relatives" sentence is not ambiguous for that reason and can't be resolved by asking a question about which word "visiting" should be grouped with. The grouping is obvious, but the meaning isn't. Chomsky maintained that these two kinds of ambiguities were evidence that grammatical knowledge is organized in two levels. He referred to the first of these as **surface structure.** This term denotes a level of grammatical knowledge that is more or less captured by the phrase structure rules. Surface structure, then, refers to the words and phrases as they are produced in an actual sentence and as they are capable of being mapped onto a particular phrase structure. Chomsky referred to the second level of grammatical knowledge as **deep structure**—a more abstract syntactic organization that is closely related to the meaning of a sentence.

In producing a sentence, presumably, both levels of knowledge are involved. As Chomsky maintained, deep structure consists of a highly abstract set of linguistic rules, sometimes referred to as *phrase markers,* or *base markers.* Phrase markers are assumed to have syntactic aspects; that is, the elements of the phrase markers must be arranged in some sort of order. Chomsky's theory assumes that deep structure is converted to surface structure via transformational rules. Transformational rules are to deep structure what the rewrite rules are to surface structure. That is, transformational rules take as their input the phrase markers from deep structure and, after operating on such structures, produce a phrase structure that can then be used as a general formula to produce a specific sentence.

It's important to realize that the base markers are not purely and simply representations of meaning. Indeed, the semantic analysis is assumed to be performed only after a particular base marker has been selected. This means that the syntax of a sentence is selected before the sentence's meaning. You should recognize that Chomsky's proposal is radical and counterintuitive (at least as far as most cognitivists are concerned).

Prior to the publication of Chomsky's *Syntactic Structures,* most psychologists would probably have endorsed a view of language production that went something like this:

[meaning]⟼[deep structure, base markers]⟼[transformational rules]⟼[surface structure, phrase structure]⟼[sentence].

That is, an utterance begins with the speaker's intention to produce a meaningful comment. Following this, a base marker is selected, which is then converted by transformational rules into a phrase structure, which acts as a formula for developing a particular sentence. But Chomsky's theory puts meaning after the base markers are selected, and he offers two rebuttals to the commonsense point of view. First, he maintains that his theory is a description and explanation of grammatical knowledge. According to Chomsky, assuming that such a theory would imply a position on language production is incorrect. This point is worth elaborating. For Chomsky, **linguistic competence** refers to all the abstract linguistic knowledge that we possess. Linguistic competence is seen in the linguistic behavior that we actually undertake and execute. These linguistic actions are referred to as **linguistic performance.** Briefly put, Chomsky believes that linguistic competence does not equal linguistic performance. That is, linguistic performance tells us only about those competencies that a speaker possesses. But performance alone tells us nothing about what other linguistic competencies the person may possess. In other words, from linguistic performance we can infer something about the underlying competencies, but from the absence of linguistic performance, we cannot infer anything about linguistic competence. Since Chomsky believed that his was a theory of competence, not performance, the theory made no predictions about the cognitive processes that people use to produce sentences or comprehend them. He sought to describe and explain linguistic knowledge, not how that knowledge was enacted in specific performances.

Second, Chomsky argued that in only a few cases can a speaker proceed very far without extensive syntactic knowledge. This view is still firmly entrenched among linguists (Morgan, 1982). For these reasons, Chomsky's position is said to espouse what is called the *centrality of syntax*—the idea that syntax is the central ability underlying other grammatical competencies and can therefore be studied more or less in isolation. The rationale underlying this argument has been outlined by DeJong:

Native speakers have syntactic competence: they can judge the syntactic well-formedness of natural language utterances. Furthermore, their syntactic judgments seem to be purely recursive. That is, both membership and non-membership in the class of syntactically well-formed utterances is decidable. Or, put another way, there is an effective procedure that always halts and assigns an acceptable or unacceptable status to every finite input string of words. Such syntactic competence will necessarily be a part of any complete natural language competence. Thus, it may be studied more or less in isolation and later, after the other components have also been worked out, the various pieces can be connected together in whatever way then seems appropriate. (DeJong, 1982, p. 35)

Although DeJong admits that this statement is an oversimplification of the position, the tenor of the passage is crystal clear. According to transformational grammarians of whatever stripe, syntactic knowledge can be studied on its own. This has an important implication for psychologists: If Chomsky is correct, no syntax-free grammars could exist. The study of semantics would always be subordinate to the study of syntax.

Origins of Grammatical Knowledge

Where does grammatical knowledge come from? Clearly, experience must play a crucial role in its acquisition. We saw earlier in this chapter that traditional transmission seems one of the most essential of Hockett's design features. Nevertheless, Chomsky believes that much of our grammatical knowledge is based on innate predispositions that guide and channel experience, and which make us sensitive to the regularities of phonology, syntax, and discourse. Let's explore this idea further.

A child, states Chomsky, who is trying to acquire grammar is in a position similar to that of a scientist who is trying to understand a phenomenon. Like the scientist, the child observes the events around her and looks for orderly patterns. After observing, the child, like the scientist, makes a hypothesis about the rule or law presumed to be underlying those patterns and producing them. This hypothesis is almost certain to be incomplete. As the child continues to observe and record linguistic events, her next hypothesis will be more accurate, the succeeding hypothesis still more accurate, and so on. Ultimately, the child winds up with a hypothesis about language that is purely recursive and quite accurate.

But some substantial differences also exist between a child and a scientist. First, scientists are trained to formulate hypotheses; without that training, they aren't very good at it. Yet, even though the child doesn't receive any explicit training in syntax hypothesis formulation, he seems to do just fine. Second, the child accomplishes syntax acquisition in a short period of time. Third, a great deal of variation exists among the theories of scientists. Often (perhaps too often), a group of scientists can observe the same phenomenon and generate a large number of plausible and undisprovable hypotheses about it. But the opposite situation is true for children. They hear a wide variety of sentences and from it generate identical grammatical knowledge. This effect is astonishing: A theoretical linguist, working with exactly the same information a child has, can't duplicate that feat. Nobody has ever written a complete theory of grammar for any naturally occurring language, yet all children (and all of us) know what that grammatical knowledge is. How can children accomplish this?

Chomsky's answer is that the child is aided in the process of grammar acquisition because certain kinds of information about language is already built into the child's mind. That is, the child has innate knowledge about the general form that languages can and cannot take. These innate predispositions are called linguistic universals. Linguistic universals can be thought of in two ways. First, they are features that all languages have in common. Second, they act as boundaries or constraints around the permissable forms that specific languages can take on. These linguistic universals guide the hypothesis making of the child within fairly narrow boundaries, ensuring that the final hypothesis generated by the child is indeed equivalent to the grammar of that particular language. This state of affairs is shown in Figure 8.6.

Implications of Chomsky's Theory

Many ideas in Chomsky's work have implications for cognitive psychology, but space precludes our dealing with more than few of them. First, there is the notion of linguistic universals. If these truly exist and are discoverable, they might possibly represent a quantum leap in our understanding of the basic rules of language and thought. Second, Chomsky has argued that children cannot possibly acquire grammatical knowledge on their own—they must be helped by innate predispositions. The rest of this chapter and Chapter 9 detail some of the arguments supporting this claim.

The third implication concerns the basic premise of Chomsky's theory. Is our linguistic knowledge based fundamentally on syntax? If this is so, we should be able to find evidence for deep and surface structure in human judgments of grammaticality. In addition, the case for Chomsky's theory would be strengthened if some evidence could be marshaled in favor of transformational rules. These rules are assumed to differ from language to language, and they enable a person to translate the abstract knowledge contained in the base markers to the somewhat less abstract rules of the phrase structure. These issues are dealt with next.

Empirical Support for the Deep-Surface Structure Distinction

Click Studies

A classic and controversial study by Garrett, Bever, and Fodor (1966) seemed to demonstrate that the division of a sentence into constituents is based on its structure rather than on its sounds. The researchers composed two sentences:

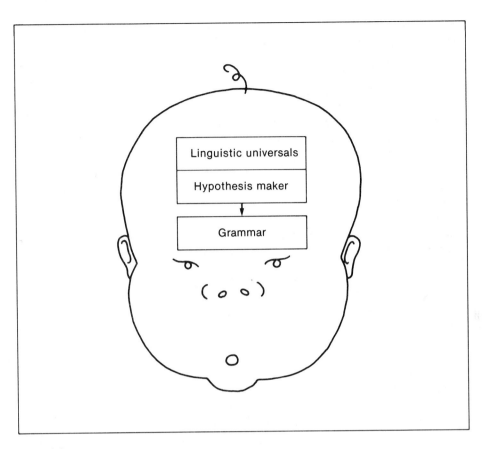

Figure 8.6.

The relationship of linguistic universals to grammar, as assumed in Chomsky's theory. (From *The Articulate Mammal: An Introduction to Psycholinguistics* (2d ed.), by Jean Aitchison. © 1976, 1983 by Jean Aitchison. Reprinted by permission of Universe Books, New York.)

1. In order to catch his train George drove furiously to the station.
2. The reporters assigned to George drove furiously to the station.

In each case, the sentence contains the words "George drove furiously to the station." However, in the first sentence, "George" is the subject of the sentence, and in the second sentence, the subject is "reporters." To understand the sentences, they must be parsed in the correct places:

1. In order to catch his train—George drove furiously to the station.
2. The reporters assigned to George—drove furiously to the station.

That is, in the first case, the break occurs before "George"; in the second case, right after it. Garrett et al. made recordings of these two sentences and devised an ingenious way to ensure that the utterance's sound would not cue subjects about the correct place to make the division. They cut each of the tapes right before "George" and then connected each "George" clause onto the *beginning* of the other tape:

1. In order to catch his train ⟋ George drove furiously to the station.
2. The reporters assigned to ⟍ George drove furiously to the station.

The spliced tapes were then played for the subjects, who heard them via stereo headphones. In one ear, the subjects heard one of the spliced sentences; in the other ear, the subjects heard a click. The click was timed to occur in the middle of "George." What was the purpose of the click? If the subjects were busy allocating cognitive processes to understand the sentence, they would not likely have enough processing capability left over to precisely determine the placement of the click. In that case, the subjects could misperceive the timing of the click. If the timing of the click was misperceived, the researchers were interested in knowing when the subjects thought it had occurred.

After hearing the sentence, the subjects were asked to indicate exactly where the click had occurred. Subjects tended to misperceive the location of the click, and their errors were predictable from an analysis of the constituents. In the first sentence, subjects tended to think the click had occurred earlier than it actually had. In the second sentence, they thought the click had occurred after it had actually been presented. These effects can be shown with arrows:

1. In order to catch his train $\overleftarrow{\text{George}}$ drove furiously to the station.
2. The reporters assigned to $\overrightarrow{\text{George}}$ drove furiously to the station.

Notice that in both cases, the click was moved closer to the border of the constituent in which "George" was included. Also, the basis for this movement could not have been the sounds of the sentences, because Garrett et al. had controlled for that effect by cutting and editing the tapes. The implication is that the constituent analysis is derived from the structure of a sentence, not from its sounds.

Other studies using the click displacement paradigm have also supported Chomsky's position. Bever, Lackner, and Kirk (1969) used sentences such as the following:

The corrupt police can't bear criminals to confess quickly.
The corrupt police can't force criminals to confess quickly.

These sentences have the same surface structures but different deep structures. Aitchison (1983) has suggested a good way to demonstrate that the two sentences have different deep structures (apart from simply realizing that they have different meanings). Try converting each sentence into the passive voice. You'll find that conversion is easy for the second sentence with no loss of meaning, but the first sentence cannot be converted without becoming ungrammatical:

Criminals cannot be borne by the police to confess quickly.
Criminals cannot be forced by the police to confess quickly.

If the two sentences had the same deep structure, they could both be converted into the passive voice with equal ease. Via a set of stereo headphones, the subjects heard the sentence in one ear and heard a click occurring at "criminals" in the other ear. The results were intriguing. For the first of the two sentences, the subjects displaced the click forward, congruent with Chomsky's theory that a deep structure break should occur after "bear":

The corrupt police can't bear   criminals to confess quickly.

But in the second sentence, the click was not displaced in either direction. The explanation of this lack of movement can be seen in Aitchison's representation of the deep structure of the second sentence, which is shown in Figure 8.7. As Figure 8.7 shows, the deep structure representation includes "criminals" in both clauses. This representation suggests that the click was not displaced because, in effect, it was being pulled in both directions by the occurrence of "criminals" in both clauses:

The corrupt police can't force criminals   criminals to confess quickly.

These findings are suggestive, but we must be cautious in our interpretation. On the one hand, these findings are consistent with some aspects of Chomsky's theory, namely that a sentence is parsed on the basis of its constituents, and that his parsing is apparently consistent with the rules

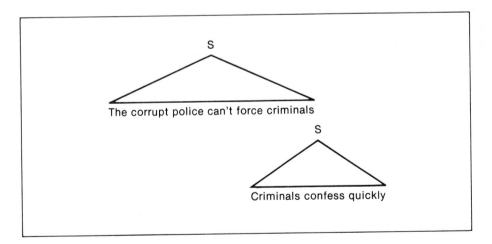

Figure 8.7.

A representation of deep structure. (From *The Articulate Mammal: An Introduction to Psycholinguistics* (2d ed.), by Jean Aitchison. © 1976, 1983 by Jean Aitchison. Reprinted by permission of Universe Books, New York.)

of surface and deep structure. However, although these findings are consistent with Chomsky's theory, they don't necessarily *substantiate* it, because other theories of grammar may make the same predictions. On the empirical level, there are several reasons for caution in interpreting the basic findings. First, Reber (1973) has pointed out that clausal boundaries are almost always confounded with other aspects of the sentence, such as serial position and intonation pattern. The tape cutting of Garrett et al. doesn't appear to control for all of these effects.

Second, the typical subject is not completely naive with regard to constituents. If she is in doubt about where a click occurred, she must have a strong temptation to push the click toward the direction of the nearest clause boundary. Reber and Anderson (1970) demonstrated this effect in a startling way. They used the standard click displacement procedure but added a twist. They also told their subjects that the experiment involved subliminal perception and that, in some cases, the click would be almost inaudible. In reality, no clicks of any kind were presented in some of the sentences. Yet, the subjects tended to say that they heard a click, and its location was usually at clause boundaries.

Phoneme Detection Studies

Other implications of the theory have also had a checkered history in the literature. For example, according to Chomsky, the meaning of a clause is not extracted until the clause boundary has been reached and the clause has been mapped onto a base marker in deep structure. If a word or part of a word has two meanings, this duality of meaning is thought to have an effect on the extraction process, because the ambiguous term cannot be clearly assigned to one particular deep structure. This type of ambiguity, known as *lexical ambiguity,* is not resolved until the clause boundary is reached (Olson & MacKay, 1974); and presumably, only the information from that particular clause is used to resolve the ambiguity. If all this is true, then both meanings of the lexically ambiguous term are activated, and they stay activated until the clause boundary is reached and one particular meaning can be assigned.

These theoretical points have studied using a so-called *phoneme detection* paradigm. Recall that a phoneme is a term referring to a basic unit of linguistic sound. In this paradigm, a subject first hears a phoneme in isolation, called the *target phoneme*. Next, the subject listens to a sentence in which the phoneme may or may not occur. If it occurs, the subject is supposed to respond as quickly as possible. When lexically ambiguous words occur right before the target phoneme, the detection latency is usually increased (Cairns & Kamerman, 1975; Danks & Glucksberg, 1980). This finding makes sense, given what we know about activation in permanent memory and the allocation of attention. Apparently, the subject waits until the clause boundary to disambiguate the troublesome lexical item, and consequently, substantial processing efforts are expended on that task at the clause boundary. When the target phoneme occurs there too, the subject doesn't have quite as many cognitive resources to allocate to processing the target phoneme, and the detection latency increases. Moreover, prior context—that is, information from previous clauses that could be used to resolve the ambiguity—typically does not eliminate this effect. These findings have been interpreted as supporting the idea that a lexical analysis is carried out on a clause-by-clause basis.

However, more recent studies have muddied the water in this area, too. Mehler, Segui, and Carey (1978) have argued that previous work did not control for all possible contaminating variables such as the phonemic composition of the words occurring immediately before the target phoneme. Blank and Foss (1978) and Swinney and Hakes (1976) did control for these and other variables, and found that information occurring before the clausal boundary could indeed reduce the phoneme detection latency. Such findings argue against a strict interpretation of Chomsky's theory.

Summary

On an intuitive basis, the distinction between surface and deep structure seems valid and necessary. Also, Chomsky has bolstered this intuititve argument by composing sentences demonstrating that rationally, we must have two levels of grammatical knowledge. Although Chomsky's theory has generated an impressive number of studies, the empirical findings are, however, mixed. If surface and deep structure are truly represented by different sets of abstract grammatical rules, these rules apparently don't behave in ways that are consistent with other aspects of the information-processing viewpoint. Similarly, regarding Chomsky's claims for transformational rules that bridge deep and surface structure, several researchers (Fodor, Bever, and Garrett, 1974) have noted the absence of any strong empirical reason for supporting a belief that Chomsky's position is the correct one.

This lack of empirical support has caused some cognitive psychologists to wonder if syntax-based grammars might not have run their course (Smith, 1982), which brings up the inevitable question, What's the alternative? In the last few years, psycholinguists have been likely to turn to semantically based grammars as possible solutions. For example, Charniak (1983) has proposed the beginning of a theory of grammar founded on a type of spreading activation model such as those considered in Chapter 6.

ASPECTS OF LANGUAGE ACQUISITION: IS KNOWLEDGE INNATE?

When we looked at Chomsky's theory, we saw that innate predispositions are assumed to play a major role in language acquisition. The main theoretical division is along these lines. On the one hand, we have a group of theorists who argue that language is learned—and learned in a way similar to other behaviors. According to this group, there is nothing particularly special about language; the same conditioning principles that seem to explain the acquisition of other behaviors can be fruitfully applied to language as well. On the other hand, we have a group of theorists who, although not exactly proposing a clear alternative, argue that theorists of the first group have simplified things dramatically. This second group maintains that language cannot be acquired simply by learning it. Consequently, the acquisition of language must at least be partially dependent on innate knowledge. This section of the chapter considers each of these two positions in turn.

Skinner's Position

Chapter 1 briefly discussed B. F. Skinner's views on language learning described in his book *Verbal Behavior* (1957). This section provides some of the details of Skinner's theory.

Skinner believed that overt actions can be divided into two broad categories. *Respondents* are reflexes that are largely unmodifiable by rewards or punishments. When a puff of air is shot into your eye, you will blink, and this blink is a respondent. Other actions are controlled by the skeletal nervous system and are modifiable by rewards and punishments; these actions are called *operants*. Linguistic behaviors (verbal operants) can be broken down into two main categories. First, *mands* are emitted when a person's body is in some sort of drive state. For example, if a person is deprived of water long enough, he will utter "water." *Tacts* are derived from the word contact and are verbal operants that are used to label physical objects or their properties.

Control is an important word in Skinner's theory and is used in a somewhat unusual way. When certain stimuli are present, and we have been rewarded for a particular behavior in the presence of those stimuli, the Skinner would say that the specific behavior is controlled by those stimuli. The behavior is controlled because we are likely to repeat that behavior if we again find ourselves in the presence of those stimuli. Tacts and mands can be controlled by either nonverbal or verbal stimuli. Skinner called this relationship between the controlling verbal stimuli and verbal operant emitted under those circumstances the *functional relationship*. He described several kinds of these relationships.

In some cases, we simply repeat something another person has said. In this case, our verbal operant is controlled by the previously heard speech and is called an *echoic*. When we read out loud, our speech is said to be under the control of the written materials, and such a verbal operant is called a *textual*. Certain stock phrases ("How are ya?") are emitted when other people around us emit them; these phrases and certain other terms denoting abstract entities are called *intraverbals*. The fourth and most important type of functional relationship is called the *autoclitic* relationship. There are two subtypes of these. The first is called the *descriptive autoclitic*. This term refers to strings of words or phrases that can be tacked on to other strings without changing their meaning, as in

It seems to me that the Cubs will fold in September.

Here, the first phrase doesn't alter the speaker's intention. Skinner maintained that people emit descriptive autoclitics for their own benefit; in most such cases, the behavior describes the speaker's own role (e.g., "I don't believe that . . . ," "I hesitate to say that . . . ") (Hilgard & Bower, 1981).

The second autoclitic subtype is called the **functional autoclitic,** which is the foundation of syntactic knowledge. Basically, Skinner argued that syntax is developed from the learning of what he called "partially conditioned autoclitic frames" (Skinner, 1957, p. 336). These autoclitic frames consist of word strings from which certain abstract concepts can be generalized. For example, the strings "The lady's car," "The lady's dog," and "The man's car" can all be treated as "possession frames" because they enable the hearer to abstract the appropriate form of the possessive. Notice, for example, that the possessor and the possessed object occupy identical slots in each of the strings. Once learned, these frames enable the listener to know what the "The man's dog" refers to. Phrased another way, the string can be tacted (discriminated) at first hearing. Skinner argued that the child might learn other word position frames, such as adjective-noun or actor-action relations, in the same way.

Extensions of the Operant Analysis

Braine (1963) and Staats (1968) have developed the notion of the autoclitic relationship into a theory of syntax. The fundamental idea is that syntactic structure boils down to knowledge of the grammatical properties that particular *locations* within a sentence produce. In other words, the structure of a sentence is not assumed to be the result of any truly abstract knowledge. Instead, the structure of a sentence is produced by regularities in the appearance of certain parts of speech in certain places in the sentence. For example, in English declarative sentences, the second word is usually a noun, a verb usually appears somewhere near the middle of the sentence, and so on. According to Braine, the mechanism underlying this learning is one similar to stimulus generalization; he calls it *context generalization:*

When a subject, who has experienced sentences in which a segment (morpheme, word, or phrase) occurs in a certain position and context, later tends to place this segment in the same position in other contexts, the context of the segment will be said to have generalized, and the subject to have shown contextual generalization. (Braine, 1963, p. 323)

To produce utterances longer than two words, the child first notices other regularities in word placements, particularly those that occur adjacent to the two-word segment. For example, the child who hears "The lady's car is" and "The man's dog is" learns that the verb *is* can be attached to the already learned possessive segment. These longer segments can be attached to still longer segments, and so on, with the result that the child acquires hierarchical knowledge of sentences. The child has learned that particular segments can be embedded or tacked on to other segments.

Probably the most persuasive aspect of Braine's approach is that it explains the acquisition of syntax that is dependent solely upon noticing regularities in word positions. This learning doesn't seem to be beyond the capabilities of a child. Second, this approach is based upon the mechanism of stimulus generalization, a well-known phenomenon whose validity has seldom been seriously questioned. Third, the child who acquires this kind of knowledge is capable of assembling the segments in a variety of ways, which permits creativity.

Criticisms of the Behavioral Approach

In addition to the criticism offered by Chomsky, other linguists (and psychologists) have maintained that behavioristic accounts of language are not powerful enough to explain all linguistic phenomena or even a large class of linguistic events. The first problem involves what have been called time and input conditions (Pinker, 1979). The child acquires grammar in a finite period of time and from a finite sample of sentences. Yet, from this finite sample, the child apparently acquires a grammar that enables him to comprehend and produce an infinite number of sentences. From a mathematical standpoint, determining how the child acquires the ability for infinite output from finite input is difficult. Time is another issue. Gold (1967) has estimated that for a finite state grammar with seven states, the person who tried to deduce its rules would have to consider over a *googol* candidates. (A googol is 10^{100}.) And surely, since our grammatical knowledge is more complex than a finite state grammar, that estimate is conservative. The child doesn't have all the time in the world to passively observe regularities in word locations, because a huge number of hypothetical grammars must be tested and disposed of—too many, it seems, for the child to accomplish this task in the time span within which childen usually acquire language.

A second problem with the contextual generalization theory concerns the phenomenon of recursion. Recall that Braine's approach was designed to handle these events, but some evidence suggests that it may not. McNeill (1968; and Chomsky, 1957) offers an example that shows schematically how sentences can be embedded within one another. Consider sentences in which a noun, *a,* is paired with a verb, *b.* Writing an infinite series of embedded sentences is possible by expanding a base sentence in the following way:

```
ab
aabb
aaabbb
aaaabbbb
```

When we repeat this process, we get a sentence that contains at least one different noun-predicate pair within it, such as "The mouse that the cat chased ate the cheese." Each *a* is paired with a *b*—the outermost *a* with the outermost *b,* and so on. A simple rule can be written to govern expansions like this. However, the rule must employ an abstract symbol, *X,* to indicate the insertions. Moreover, the *X* must be placed within parentheses to show that the embedding operation is both recursive—that is, capable of being executed repeatedly—and optional; the embedding doesn't have to be there. In its final form, the expansion rule looks like this:

$$X \rightarrow a(X)b$$

Notice that X represents a truly abstract repeating rule; the X never appears in any of the sentences. That is, none of the sentences have the form aXb. This rule presents substantial problems for contextual generalization positions, because these positions don't have a mechanism to explain how a sentence could be inserted between the elements of another sentence, particularly for indefinite lengths. Although we can see how the child might add tag-on questions and comments by observing the locations of parts of speech within sentences, not at all clear is how truly abstract rules could be inferred.

Arguments for Innate Knowledge

The difficulties of a purely behavioral approach have been compounded by a substantial body of literature suggesting that our linguistic knowledge is based on innate predispositions. Once again, Chomsky was among the recent protagonists in the controversy; he argued that the evidence in favor of this position was overwhelming. These claims have often been misunderstood. First, to argue that Chomsky espouses an innate position doesn't necessarily mean that all his opponents are non-innatists. Almost everybody agrees that most skills—even cognitive ones—are based in some way on innate predispositions. The question really is, Are there innate *linguistic* predispositions?

Second, what Chomsky means by *innate* has also been misunderstood. Aitchison has expressed his position quite well:

By innate, Chomsky simply means "genetically programmed". He does not literally think that children are born with language in their heads ready to be spoken. He merely claims that a "blueprint" is there, which is brought into use when the child reaches a certain point in her general development. With the help of this blueprint, she analyzes the language she hears around her more readily than she would if she were totally unprepared for the strange gabbling sounds which emerge from human mouths. (Aitchison, 1983, p. 31)

The evidence supporting this contention comes from diverse sources. First, we'll consider some of the biological adaptations of our bodies that seem to have no purpose other than to support language. Second, we'll consider some of the specializations in our brains. We'll also take a look at human infants' abilities to recognize speech sounds early in their lives.

Anatomical and Breathing Specializations

Aitchison (1983) has noted a number of characteristics of the human vocal tract that are somewhat unusual. For example, human teeth are different from those of other animals. The teeth are approximately the same height and typically have no spaces between them. The degree of overlap between the upper and bottom set is usually small. These features are not required for eating but are helpful—perhaps necessary—for speech. Certain sounds (e.g., *sh,* as in *shut,* or *th,* as in *thin*) are possible only because the flow of air can be controlled fairly precisely, which wouldn't be possible if air escaped through our teeth. The human tongue is relatively short, thick, and mobile compared with the tongues of monkeys. This characteristic is helpful in changing the size and shape of the vocal cavity, which is necessary to produce vowel sounds.

In all primates, the larynx contains the vocal cords, but the human larynx is different and, oddly, simpler than that of other primates. Such simplification is sometimes an indication of biological specialization. For example, birds don't have teeth, which enables them to consume their typical diet quickly because they don't have to chew it. In humans, the simplified larynx enables the air to flow through the vocal tract without impediment, permitting great control and flexibility. However, this simplication presents a disadvantage. Other primates can close off their mouths from their tracheas, which enables them to breathe while they eat. Humans can't duplicate this feat; and if they try, they risk getting a piece of food stuck in their tracheas. No self-respecting monkey would ever choke to death while eating, but for humans, that's an unfortunate possibility. This point is a telling one though. Evolution would not likely favor a dangerous development unless the advantage conferred were very great.

Breathing is a natural act, but in some cases, humans need breathing instructions. For example, in learning to play a wind instrument, such as the flute or oboe, the student needs to learn the proper breathing techniques. Similarly, in swimming, the usual impediment to going more than a lap or two is the oxygen debt that builds up from improper breathing. We don't think about it, but speech also imposes breathing demands. While speaking, the number of breaths per minute is reduced. Inhalation is accelerated, while exhalation is slowed (Aitchison, 1983). If we try to do other things that involve altering our natural breathing rhythm, we must be taught how to do them, or else we quickly get into trouble. Although speech also significantly alters our breathing rhythm, we can talk for hours without ever "coming up for air."

Specializations of the Brain

Pioneering work in brain specializations was done by the great French researcher Paul Broca in the 1860s. Broca discovered that if a certain area of the cortex was damaged by a stroke, an **aphasia,** or language disorder, was produced. This area is located in the frontal lobe and is now usually referred to as Broca's area. Broca also discovered that the aphasia appeared only if the stroke had taken place in the left hemisphere of the brain. Damage to the corresponding area in the right hemisphere did not produce language deficits. These findings confirmed what other researchers had suspected: that a specific location in the brain seems to be responsible for the production of speech. In most cases, this language center seems localized in the dominant (i.e., left) hemisphere. Broca's area is adjacent to the area of the brain that controls muscular movement in the face, and damage to Broca's area usually accompanied by partial paralysis of the right side of the face. However, Broca ingeniously demonstrated that the aphasia was not simply the result of this paralysis by asking his patients to sing. Surprisingly, singing ability was unimpaired. The muscles that wouldn't cooperate in order to speak, would work together to sing, suggesting that singing ability was controlled by another area of the brain.

People who suffer damage to Broca's area speak only with a great deal of difficulty. Their speech is slow and telegraphic, meaning that some words are left out. The pronunciation of verbs and pronouns is often impaired. Geschwind cites the following example of this aphasia. In this case, a person was asked about an upcoming dental appointment.

Yes . . . Monday . . . Dad and Dick . . . Wednesday nine o'clock . . . 10 o'clock . . . doctors . . . and . . . teeth. (Geschwind, 1980, p. 209)

This type of aphasia isn't the only kind. In 1874, Carl Wernicke identified another type of language disorder. This aphasia was the result of damage to a location in the temporal lobe of the left hemisphere, posterior to Broca's area. People with damage to this location (now known as Wernicke's area) produce speech that is fluent and often syntactically sound. However, the content of the utterance is often meaningless. The following is an example of this disorder. The patient was asked to describe a picture that showed two boys stealing cookies behind their mother's back.

Mother is away here working her work to get her better, but when she's looking the two boys looking in the other part. She's working another time. (Geschwind, 1980, p. 209)

Although not known to Broca and Wernicke, the two areas named after them are connected by a band of tissue called the *arcuate fasciculus*. This area has suggested a view of the brain's role in speech production that has gone more or less unchallenged in the past century. The meaning of an utterance, or its underlying structure, is first produced in Wernicke's area. This code is next transferred via the arcuate fasciculus to Broca's area, which is responsible for formulating a more detailed speech plan. This plan is next sent on to the motor area of the cortex, which activates the appropriate muscles of the lips, tongue, larynx, and so on.

These findings are easily interpretable as evidence that our linguistic ability is "wired into" our brains. We shouldn't be too hasty with that interpretation. In some cases, the hemispheric organization differs from the usual, and these people have no trouble speaking. Also, ample evidence suggests that Broca's and Wernicke's areas are simply centers for activity that can be taken up by other structures in the cortex. In most cases following a stroke, people make a substantial recovery of their language abilities. Neural tissue adjacent to that which was destroyed is apparently capable of taking on the functions of the original areas.

Categorical Perception of Speech Sounds

The human vocal tract is capable of making a wide variety of sounds, only some of which are linguistic. Moreover, babies are exposed to a wide variety of sounds, both linguistic and nonlinguistic. These facts put babies in somewhat of a bind. If babies are going to learn to speak, they must be able to distinguish linguistic sounds from nonlinguistic ones and must distinguish the linguistic sounds from each other. These are large problems, but babies seem to know the basis for distinguishing linguistic sounds from nonlinguistic ones. For example, babies imitate the sounds of human speakers, but they don't imitate other sounds (such as that of the refrigerator) that might be prersent at the same time. Similarly, they stop crying if someone speaks to them but not if someone rings a bell. The ability to make this discrimination appears to be present early—perhaps by two weeks of age (Wolff, 1966). Babies also seem to know how to distinguish linguistic sounds from one another. This ability has been demonstrated in a classic study of Eimas, Siqueland, Jusczyk, and Vigorito (1971).

Before discussing the study, some background information is necessary. The speech sounds *b* and *p* are produced by closing the lips, then opening them, releasing air. In producing *b,* the vocal cords begin vibrating as soon as the air is released. For *p,* a short latency occurs between the release of air and the slight vibration of the vocal cords. Speech sounds that involve vibrations of the vocal cords are called *voiced phonemes.* Listeners use the latency between the release of air and the beginning of the vibrations as a cue in determining whether the *b* or *p* sound has been produced. This cue is called *Voice Onset Time.*

Research with adults has demonstrated that Voice Onset Time has a major influence on how certain sounds will be heard. Lisker and Abramson (1970) were able to program a computer to produce acoustic information that corresponded to the *p* and *b* sounds. In this way, the buzzing sound associated with *b* could be produced separately from the acoustic information heard in *p.* Armed with this technology, they were able to systematically vary the timing of the voicing. The Voice Onset Time was varied from -150 msec (i.e., the voicing began 150 msec before the simulated release of air) to $+150$ msec (the voicing began 150 msec after the simulated air release). Lisker and Abramson found that subjects were unanimous in their judgment that the sound was a *b* unless the Voice Onset Time was 10 msec or greater, at which point a rapid shift in opinion occurred. At that point, the subjects began to hear the stimulus as *p,* and if the Voice Onset Time was extended to about 30 to 40 msec, the subjects were once again unanimous that the sound being produced was a *p.* The perception of speech sounds is called **categorical perception,** because subjects don't seem to be aware of any gradual fading away of the "*b*-ness" of the sound as the Voice Onset Time increases. Instead, the subjects seem to be fairly confident that the sound is a *b* until the critical Voice Onset Time is reached, at which point the subjects are sure that it's a *p.* Clearly, the subjects are imposing a fairly definite mental organization on the somewhat ambiguous speech sounds. This phenomenon is interesting enough, but researchers also wanted to know the age at which categorical perception of speech sounds begins.

To assess this, Eimas et al. used a procedure that relies on the infant's ability to become familiar with certain stimuli and to stop responding to them. In this procedure, the infant is given a pacifier that contains a device that measures the infant's rate of sucking. A sound is then played repeatedly for the infant until the sucking rate is constant. At that point, a new sound is played. If the baby notices anything different about the sound, this interest is translated into a heightened level of activity, which is expressed by a sudden increase in the rate of sucking for a short period of time. After the baby gets used to the new sound, the rate of sucking gradually declines.

Eimas and his colleagues presented one-month-old babies with a variety of synthetic speech sounds with differing Voice Onset Times. They found that the infants' perception of the speech sounds was indeed categorical. Moreover, the boundary between *b* and *p* was about the same for infants as it was for adults: approximately 20 msec. In other words, if the babies had gotten used to a sound in which the Voice Onset Time was 60 msec, and they heard a new sound in which the Voice Onset Time was 80 msec, the rate of sucking did not increase. Apparently, the infants did not consider these sounds to be different from one another. However, if the babies had gotten used to a sound in which Voice Onset Time was 0 msec, and then heard a sound in which Voice Onset Time was 20 msec, their rate of sucking increased. The infants seemed to regard these sounds as different from one another.

Infants don't know a *b* from a *p* in the sense that they can refer to these sounds with linguistic labels the way more mature humans do. For this reason, Eimas et al. (1971) maintains that humans must have some built-in system that is sensitive to the acoustic properties of speech (Clark & Clark, 1977).

CONCLUDING COMMENTS AND SUGGESTIONS FOR FURTHER READING

Two overarching points should be made about this chapter. The first point concerns the nature of linguistic knowledge, and the second has to do with its foundation in the human mind. Regarding the first point, we've seen that it's extraordinarily difficult to specify the knowledge that enables us to speak and comprehend the utterances of others. Nobody has written a complete account of the grammar of any naturally occurring language. Indeed, specifying any part of this knowledge is extremely difficult. For example, nobody has written an account of grammar that specifies how people make decisions about acceptable syntax. Yet, the cognitive processes involved operate reliably and quickly. We know this because we quickly make judgments about appropriate syntax, and the consensus about such judgments is good. Perhaps the main point of Chomsky's work is that such knowledge cannot be expressed by a set of rules that work on just one level. For the reasons that we reviewed in the chapter, grammatical knowledge must exist on at least two—perhaps more—levels. As we saw in the chapter, extracting the nature of this knowledge has proved extremely difficult for cognitive psychologists and linguists. This difficulty too, is puzzling. Over the last two decades, researchers have acquired more facts about mentality than they did in the entire previous history of psychology. Yet, despite the overall yielding of many bits of knowledge in many areas, the cognitive operations underlying language have proved frustratingly resistant to the research techniques that have been brought to bear upon them. Why?

Responding to this question brings me to the second of the chapter's main points. Many cognitive psychologists have come to believe that the mental operations underlying language will remain obscure precisely because they are not assembled from simpler information-processing routines, as are many of the other cognitive events we have studied. In other words, because the degree of innate knowledge involved in language seems greater than for other mental events, the operation of this knowledge is correspondingly more obscure. To a certain extent, how strongly you believe this is probably partially dependent upon on how persuasive you found the material on innate predispositions. If you found this evidence convincing, you are probably willing to believe that language will remain forever mysterious. On the other hand, some cognitive psychologists don't find this sort of evidence particularly convincing. They maintain that, while it's obvious that some sort of innate influences affect the course of language development, the application of the correct research technique, the correct angle on the existing findings, or whatever, will demonstrate that language is not necessarily different in kind than the other cognitive processes we have studied. This issue is sure to be surrounded by more debate in the years ahead.

Students who want to learn more about these topics must realize that they cannot be approached by any easy route. The literature in this area is difficult. Chomsky (1972) has written an introduction to his thinking, which is intended for an educated but nonprofessional audience. Some of his more recent work (1979) might also be a good starting point. Chomsky (1983) has contributed a chapter to a volume edited by Mehler and others, and other chapters in this book also make a contribution to Chomskyian theory. Students who want to tackle some of Chomsky's professional writing might try *Aspects of the Theory of Syntax* (1965). His (1959) review of Skinner's book is informative. Moore and Carling (1982) have written a book that extends rather than rebuts Chomsky's work, and a chapter by Fodor (1981) seems to suggest that some form of innate predispositions will be required in any theory of language and mind.

We discussed the neuropsychology of language, and students who want to find out more about this topic should read the appropriate sections in the clear and thorough book by Kolb and Whishaw (1985).

FOCUS ON RESEARCH:

Language Acquisition in Feral Children

This chapter discussed categorical perception of speech sounds by infants, and the research suggests that at least the basis for discriminating speech sound seems to be inborn. But this doesn't mean that children have speech sounds built into their brains. Clearly, some sort of experience with language is necessary to become fluent. But exactly what sort of experiences are necessary, and how

much of them are necessary? Perhaps this questions is what prompted many theorists to wonder what would happen to a child who wasn't talked to.

Over the years, many cases of so-called feral children have occurred. Feral children are abandoned children who have fended for themselves in the wild, and they invariably have linguistic deficits. Usually, it's not clear how long such children have been left on their own. Neither is it typically known to what extent they were cared for prior to their abandonment. For these reasons, it's difficult to know the extent to which the language deficits were produced by the social deprivation. For obvious ethical reasons, a controlled experiment cannot be done to answer this question, but sometimes the world offers illuminating cases.

Genie was born April 1957 and was reared under the most abject conditions:

"From the age of twenty months, Genie had been confined to a small room . . . She was physically punished by her father if she made any sounds. Most of the time she was kept harnessed into an infant's potty chair: Otherwise she was confined in a home-made sleeping bag in an infant's crib covered with wire mesh." (Curtiss, Fromkin, Krashen, Rigler, & Rigler, 1974, p. 529)

Genie was fed by her blind mother in a highly routinized way; little or no conversation took place between them. Apparently, her father and older brother never spoke to her. Genie was almost fourteen years old when she was discovered; at that time she could not speak at all. Since then, researchers have followed the course of her language acquisition with interest. Soon apparent was that in most areas, Genie's development proceeded at a pace much slower than that of other children.

For example, normal children begin expressing negatives by simply putting the word *no* in front of already established utterances ("No want go"). Genie also used this form. However, whereas normal children typically pass through this stage quickly, Genie used this primitive form of negation for two years. Normal children begin asking "Wh——" questions (Where mommy?) around two years of age. However, Genie never mastered this ability, and her attempts were ungrammatical. She did excel in the acquistion of vocabulary. Although her overall language competence seemed to be that of a three-year-old, her vocabulary was much larger than that of a typical three-year-old.

Curtiss (1977) later wrote a follow-up account of Genie, who by then was eighteen years old. Curtiss noted that Genie spoke in short sentences whose grammatical forms were fairly primitive. However, Genie's knowledge of speech, including her knowledge of English word order, seemed fine. Although her production of syntactically correct sentences is limited (and Curtiss apparently believes that these effects are permanent), Genie's comprehension is more or less unaffected by her years of deprivation.

Apparently, some innate linguistic predispositions can survive a traumatic and deprived upbringing. But other specializations, including those that enable people to acquire syntax, can apparently be destroyed if the individual doesn't have adequate opportunities to use them.

KEY TERMS

Syntax

Grammar

Semantics

Continuity theory

Design features

Phoneme

Morpheme

Displacement (as a design feature)

Productivity

Linguistic universals

Recursion

Finite state grammar

Constituents

Phrase structure

Deep-surface structure distinction

Competence-performance distinction

Functional autoclitic

Specializations for language

Aphasia

Categorical perception

CHAPTER 9

Considerations of Language Development

OVERVIEW

COMPREHENSION AND PRODUCTION

STAGES OF LANGUAGE DEVELOPMENT
Crying and Cooing
Babbling and Single Words
Two-Word Stage
  Word Order and Inflections
Later Developments
Implications of the Developmental Sequence
Criticisms of the Stage Position
  Caretaker Speech

ACQUISITION OF LANGUAGE AMONG THE DEAF
The Critical Period

LANGUAGE ACQUISITION IN ANIMALS
Washoe
Sarah
Nim Chimpsky

CONCLUDING COMMENTS AND SUGGESTIONS
FOR FURTHER READING
FOCUS ON RESEARCH
KEY TERMS

I have a friend whose daughter's birthday falls near Christmas. Almost invariably, children who are in that situation think that they're getting shortchanged on their birthday gifts, because holiday gifts are so widespread and plentiful. Kelly was no exception, and to make her feel better, her mother had invited several people to the house (including grown-ups) to have a little party and watch the just-turned-five Kelly open her birthday presents.

Kelly had acquired an amusing (to us) linguistic habit within the previous six months. After hearing people talk about clothes, as in, "Kelly, pick up your clothes," Kelly had concluded that any single garment could be referred to as a "clo." That is, a mitten was a clo, a boot was a clo, a shirt was a clo, and so on. Small children generally don't like to receive gifts of clothing (as opposed to toys), and I'll never forget how Kelly broke us up as she reluctantly opened an obvious garment and announced in an utterly woebegone voice, "I just know this is gonna be a clo."

Much of the charm that small children have is the result of their novel linguistic constructions. Kelly's use of the term *clo* is an example of **overregularization**. English has regular rules for pronunciation, pluralization, and indication of past tense. After learning that plurals could be created by adding an *s* sound to the end of the singular form, Kelly had apparently decided that the reverse procedure could also be done. The *s* could be taken off an apparently plural term to produce a singular. Kelly's use of the novel term *clo* shows that she had learned how to use the plural form of nouns and knew how to work backward to get the singular. She was mistaken in this particular case; *clothes* is an irregular term. Overregularization is an error, but it shows that some underlying rule has been learned.

Overregularization is a common error in children of Kelly's age but an interesting one nevertheless. It's common to think that children acquire language by listening to the speech of adults, then by analyzing this speech in ways that are currently mysterious, and finally, by producing utterances whose grammatical form is then corrected by adult speakers. According to such a viewpoint, language development is primarily an imitative act. But the existence of overregularization proves that imitation can't be the whole story. Who was Kelly imitating when she first used *clo*? Who had ever said that word in her presence? Kelly was not simply imitating an adult when she started using this term, because *clo* and other overregularizations (e.g., *goed* for *went*) are similarly uncommon among adults. Of course, saying that she wasn't imitating doesn't answer the most interesting question: Where did the word *clo* come from?

Chapter 8 considered the nature of language and the extent to which linguistic knowledge is built into our brains. This chapter again considers the nature of linguistic knowledge, but this time the focus is different. Regardless of whatever knowledge may be built into our brains, language does not simply emerge but is built up from successive early experiences with language. Certain experiences seem to produce linguistic knowledge, which in turn paves the way for a new and perhaps better interpretation of later linguistic experiences. In other words, a dynamic interplay exists between people's current levels of linguistic knowledge and their ability to process linguistic information. These components are generally in sync with one another, but we also recognize that over the course of people's lives, both components advance, not necessarily at the same rate. When cognitive psychologists take such a *developmental* perspective on language, they are attempting to map out the course of this interplay. Whereas Chapter 8 examined the nature of language and its origin—as though language were a seedling—this chapter examines the processes that turn the seedling into a tree.

The chapter first describes the linguistic knowledge that children seem to have and then discusses the difficulties in inferring the extent of this knowledge from what children say. The distinction between comprehension (what children understand) and production (what they say) is related to the distinction between competence and performance that Chapter 8 examined. Language development is commonly described as occurring in a series of stages. This chapter considers these stages. Also considered is atypical language development—for example, the extent to which a hearing impairment disrupts language development. Even animals have been called upon to help settle some of the mysteries of language development. In the last twenty years, psychologists have undertaken several investigations of language acquisition among chimpanzees. This chapter examines just a few of their numerous studies and attempts to assess what such studies have told us about our own mental processes.

COMPREHENSION AND PRODUCTION

The successful use of language requires the coordination of various abilities. This requirement makes language somewhat different from other skills. Let's compare language use with skills such as swimming or biking (an example taken from Clark & Hecht, 1983). Biking requires the coordination of various muscles. But we could learn to bike without explicit instruction from anyone and without seeing anyone else ride a bike. In other words, comprehending the purpose of bike riding is not necessary to being able to bike. The same is true of swimming. Successful swimming doesn't require that we coordinate any abilities other than those within us.

We should also be aware, however, that simple comprehension of the purpose of swimming or biking doesn't enable us to do these activities. In other words, we might watch the swimming of others and, through watching, comprehend the purpose of this activity. However, such observation by itself would not enable us to swim or to bike. Successful recognition of biking or swimming doesn't ensure successful production of these behaviors, although in some instances, it might be helpful. When I was fifteen, I thought that I knew how to drive a car (although I had never driven one) because I had watched other people drive. Within the year I found out how wrong this assumption was.

Unlike swimming or biking, language does require the coordination of at least two major abilities. To use language, we must first be able to comprehend it. **Comprehension** requires listeners to take in an utterance, analyze it, construct an interpretation, and use this interpretation in the way the speaker intended (Clark & Clark, 1977). The second major ability is **production.** To produce an utterance, speakers must plan what they want to say, choose the appropriate words, and then execute them correctly (Clark & Clark, 1977).

Demonstrating that comprehension and production are not always perfectly correlated, even for adults, is easy. For example, many of us can understand dialects and accents even though we can't duplicate them well enough to fool people who actually speak that way. For most of us, our recognition vocabulary (words we comprehend) is far larger than our working vocabulary (words we use in our own speech). In those cases, our comprehension has exceeded our production. In a few cases, the asymmetry works the other way. We can learn to sing songs phonetically, which enables us to sing in languages that we don't understand. In such cases, production has outstripped comprehension. In children, the gap between comprehension and production appears even greater than it is for adults.

Goldin-Meadow, Seligman, and Gelman (1976) found that one- to two-year-old children seem to have comprehension of the word *dog* as indicated by the children's ability to pick out a picture of a dog from among those of other animals. However, children of that age don't necessarily use the word *dog* in their own speech; instead they use a word like *wuf-wuf.* Presumably, since these children comprehend *wuf-wuf,* too, we see here an imbalance between comprehension and production. The children can comprehend and produce *wuf-wuf,* but they can only comprehend *dog.*

The asymmetry between comprehension and production is also seen in older children. Thompson and Chapman (1977) found that children age 1:9 to 2:3 (i.e., one year, nine months to two years, three months) overextended several words, such as *doggie* or *ball,* in production tasks. For example, when given a series of pictures of both familiar and unfamiliar animals, the children picked out several different four-legged animals, calling them all "doggie." However, this overextension was not observed on comprehension tasks. When the children were shown pairs of pictures, such as a picture of a dog and one of another animal, and were asked, "Which one is the doggie?" they picked out only the appropriate object. The performance difficulties on the production task might be interpreted as a retrieval problem. For example, suppose a child is able to correctly identify a picture of a cat but spontaneously calls the cat a doggie. The comprehension task—identifying the picture—involves recognition memory. But the production task—calling out the name of the creature—relies upon recall. We saw earlier that recognition memory tasks are generally easier than recall tasks. This may be why Thompson and Chapman's subjects showed better comprehension than production.

Generally, most studies have concluded that comprehension precedes production (Huttenlocher, 1974; Rescorla, 1980). In many ways, this conclusion seems reasonable, because production seems to include comprehension. People may often understand things they can't produce, but they seldom produce things they can't understand (Clark & Clark, 1977).

The distinction between comprehension and production also complicates the relationship between competence and performance. Recall that a speaker's performance (an actual utterance) generally allows us to infer something about the speaker's knowledge (i.e., linguistic competence). The distinction between comprehension and performance shows us that linguistic competence is multifaceted. Tested in certain ways, via comprehension tasks, a child might appear to have mastered the knowledge of, let's say, pluralization rules, and from such performances, we would infer competence. However, if assessed via production tasks, the same child may not manifest this competence. This is not to say that the distinction between competence and performance is invalid. Rather, we have to conclude one of two things. One possibility is that not every type of performance indicates linguistic competence equally well; some tests are better than others. On the other hand, linguistic competence might not be monolithic—that is, indivisible. A person may have some linguistic competencies (which are in turn performable) while not having others.

Unfortunately, the data have not been too helpful in resolving this matter. Although generally speaking, comprehension seems to precede production, in some situations it doesn't. Several studies (Slobin & Welsh, 1973; Bloom, Lightbown, & Hood, 1975) have demonstrated that children sometimes produce uterrances spontaneously that they are subsequently unable to imitate. If the children truly comprehend these utterances, it would be difficult to imagine why they wouldn't have been able to imitate them later. Here, we have to conclude that the children have produced something that they really haven't comprehended. This point is critical: Production tasks don't necessarily always indicate the speaker's intentions. When children produce complex utterances, they may not necessarily be manifesting any true linguistic competence; they may simple be imitating a well-learned routine that has been picked up in one chunk from an adult (Clark & Hecht, 1983).

For example, Clark (1974) observed one child who could copy lengthy phrases from adults and maintain them for several weeks. The child (age 2:9–3:0) apparently used certain stock phrases to string together smaller, less complex utterances into larger, fairly complex ones. One stock phrase was "let's go see," which could be inserted into other utterances to form strings, as in the following:

Baby Ivan have a bath, [let's go see] Baby Ivan have a bath.

The routine nature of these utterances has been demonstrated by Johnson (1981), who found that children use phrases like "what's that" to extend other utterances. The routine nature of the phrase is seen in utterances like "What's that the dog?" The expression was used to mean "What's the dog doing?"

Information about intentions can be used by the child in other ways, too. Children often rely on their knowledge of the world to understand utterances that they haven't really comprehended. For example, some general knowledge of the relationship between adults and babies lets three-year-olds understand the meaning of the sentence "The baby was fed by the girl," even though children of that age don't actually comprehend the use of passive voice. This lack of comprehension is indicated when children make mistakes in sentences, such as "The girl was fed by the baby" or "The baby fed the girl."

Indeed, tests that would be fair assessments of adults' linguistic competence may be unusable with children to certain ages. For example, Clark (1980) found that children of age two or less will consistently indicate the uppermost surface of an object when asked to touch the object's top. In an adult, we might take this action as good evidence for comprehension of the term. However, children of this age also touch the uppermost surface when asked to pick out the bottom, the side, the front, or the back. Only when children touch the uppermost surface for "top" and the lowest surface for "bottom" can the investigator be sure that the child is responding to purely linguistic cues (Chapman, 1978; Clark, 1983).

The distinction between comprehension and performance has several implications for cognitive psychologists wishing to record the development of language. First, the research must determine which linguistic ability (comprehension or production) is being assessed. This determination isn't easy, because linguistic performance may tap some competencies better than others, or the nature of the competence may be complex. Second, the clever cognitive psychologist has to be aware that although comprehension usually precedes production, children can sometimes use nonlinguistic strategies to produce utterances that aren't actually comprehended. Similarly, the child may use world knowledge to understand remarks that have not been comprehended on the basis of their linguistic content. Third, a person's ability to coordinate (i.e., match) comprehension and production is probably not constant across the life span. As we develop, we almost certainly achieve a closer fit between these two abilities. However, at any point in the life span, different linguistic tasks probably require differing degrees of coordination between comprehension and production. This puts the developmental cognitive psychologist in somewhat of a bind. Does a child's failure to perform on a given task mean that the child has not yet achieved the necessary coordination, or is the failure attributable to something about the task itself?

STAGES OF LANGUAGE DEVELOPMENT

Table 9.1 shows the "stages" of language development. The word *stages* is in quotes to provide a clue about its meaning. Usually, children are not completely in one stage or another. Since children's behaviors show substantial overlap, the table indicates the dominant linguistic behavior at each

TABLE 9.1

Milestones of Language Development

Language Stage	Beginning Age
Crying	Birth
Cooing	6 weeks
Babbling	6 months
Intonation patterns	8 months
One-word utterances	1 year
Two-word utterances	18 months
Word inflections	2 years
Questions, negatives	2¼ years
Rare or complex constructions	5 years
Mature speech	10 years

Source: From *The Articulate Mammal: An Introduction to Psycholinguistics* (2d edition), by Jean Aitchison. © 1976, 1983 by Jean Aitchison. Reprinted by permission of Universe Books, New York.

age. Also, the ages given in Table 9.1 are only approximations. Some children begin producing their first words before their first birthdays; other children's first words don't occur until much later. The range of individual differences is fairly great. Also, a child who "misses" the average onset age for any given stage may not necessarily be behind at the next milestone. Children sometimes speed through several stages, only to spend a longer than usual time at a later point. Other children might go slowly at first and spend less time at the later stages. The order of events listed on Table 9.1 is probably invariant. For example, once children enter the stage of two-word utterances, they will not likely revert to babbling.

Crying and Cooing

For the first four weeks of an infant's life, his cries are undifferentiated. This means that the same cry is used regardless of the stimulus. During the second month, some differentiation occurs, which may be universal. For example, Ricks (1975) found that English parents could detect various messages in the cries of both English and foreign babies. Despite this finding, however, thinking of crying as truly linguistic is probably incorrect. Even babies of several months' age don't appear able to use their cries productively, and their behavior seems largely reflexive. However, crying does help lay the foundation for language by strengthening the vocal cords and the lungs (Aitchison, 1983). Also, the baby's cries usually elicit a response. This point is important. Early on, the baby has an opportunity to find out that vocalization can be functional, and speech almost always has that property.

Anywhere from six weeks to three months of age, children begin to coo. Cooing is hard to describe. The sounds are apparently vowel-like. Yet, the acoustic properties usually associated with adult vowels are not present in the infant's coos. Cooing seems to be universal. The child seems to be playing with her articulatory apparatus. Generally, this is a time during which the child explores the world, and cooing is probably best understood in that sense. Like crying, cooing is not truly linguistic but also bolsters the development of language. Adults seldom cry when babies cry, but they coo (or try to) when babies coo. Also, babies seem to be able to imitate some adult gestures (such as protruding the tongue) from a very early age (Meltzoff & Moore, 1977). The combination of adults' willingness to coo and babies' ability to detect and mimic various gestures suggests that babies begin to learn about reciprocity in vocalization before they begin to speak. By about six months of age, the child also uses consonantal sounds in her vocalizations. At this point, the child is said to have begun babbling.

Babbling and Single Words

Babbling has been described as a period of advanced motor play and vocal experimentation for the prelinguistic child. The consonantal and verblike sounds are strung together in lengthy chains that sound like words. Probably for eons, parents have incorrectly assumed that their progeny were addressing them with "dadada" or "mamama," and maybe it's just as well they don't know the truth. No evidence is available to support the idea that babbling children attach any meaning to their utterances. It was once thought that during the babbling period, children make almost every sound possible by the human vocal apparatus (Jespersen, 1922). This assumption is now known to be untrue; the variety of babbling sounds is not particularly great. Another past belief was that babbling is universal, that is, done by children everywhere, regardless of the cultural forces impinging on the child. However, there have been reports of children who never babbled yet nevertheless managed to acquire language. Babbling, however, is widespread and common.

One question that researchers pose concerns the role of the linguistic culture as a modifier of the child's utterances. If the babbling sounds are uninfluenced by the language that the child hears, this supports the idea that babbling is programmatic—a more or less innate and rigid stage of development. This idea has been supported by findings (Lenneberg, 1967) showing that congenitally deaf children babble. If, on the other hand, children are affected by the language they are exposed to, this suggests that whatever the nature of the children's innate knowledge, it must be flexible.

Weir (1966) attempted to answer this question by examining the influence of tonality on children's babbling. Tonal languages are those in which variations in pitch can produce variations in meaning. For example, in Chinese, the same word may have different meanings when uttered at different pitches. Weir found that the longer babbling went on, the more likely Chinese babies were to produce monosyllabic utterances with a great deal of tonal variation. Nontonal babies (American, Arabian, and Russian) were more likely to show polysyllabic babbling. Interestingly, American mothers were often able to pick out American babies on the basis of their babbling sounds, as were Russian mothers able to pick out Russian babies, and Arabian mothers, Arabian babies. However, mothers of the three nontonal nationalities could not discriminate babies babbling in languages that were not the mothers' native tongues. This finding has been used to support the idea that between the ages of nine to fourteen months, children undergo a **babbling drift** during which they gradually restrict their productions to only those sounds occurring in the language they will eventually master. At this point, children's utterances sound particularly like well-formed speech.

At approximately one year of age, the child begins to produce single words. During the interval from twelve to eighteen months, the child may acquire up to fifty words, although fifteen seems closer to the average. Some children may use as few as four or five words during this period. Babbling may continue for a short period after the production of true words, but it tends to disappear fairly rapidly.

This period is also referred to as the **holophrastic stage** of language development because the child seems to use a single word to stand for an entire sentence. These words are typically nouns or adjectives (McNeill, 1970) and usually refer to concrete objects that are present or to motivational or emotional states. Nelson (1973) found that animals, toys, and food were the three categories most frequently referred to by children who had learned their first ten words. These utterances have a variety of meanings. For example, the child who says "shoe" may be indicating that the shoe in question is his, that he wants to have his shoes put on, that someone has been observed who's not wearing shoes, and so on. Only by analyzing the context in which the utterance occurs can the child's intentions be understood.

Greenfield and Smith (1976) have stated that the content of the child's message may not be as important as the context. When the context is analyzed, the child's utterances are seen to express several sorts of functional roles. Greenfield and Smith followed two children around and recorded their utterances. They found that the children's initial utterances usually named things that were movers, or instigators of actions. Later, the childrens'

TABLE 9.2

Roles and Actions Talked About in One-Word Utterances

Role or Action*	Utterance	Context
Agent	Dada	Hears *someone* come in
Action or state resulting from action	Down	When sits *down* or steps *down* from somewhere
Object affected by action	Ban	When wants *fan* turned off
State of object affected by action	Down	When *shuts* cabinet door
Object associated with another object or location	Poo	With hand on bottom while being changed, usually after bowel movement
Possessor	Lara	On seeing *Lauren's* empty bed
Location	Bap	Indicating location of feces on *diaper*

Source: Greenfield and Smith, 1976. Reprinted by permission of the publisher.

utterances seemed to name movables, or things that were influenced by actions. Next, the children began referring to places and finally, to possession, or recipients of actions. These functional roles and some examples of them are shown in Table 9.2.

Two-Word Stage

Around age eighteen to twenty months, the child begins to produce utterances that are two words long—hence the unimaginative name, the **two-word stage.** All researchers agree that the increase in linguistic capabilities is dramatic during this period. First, vocabulary increases; the typical 2 ½-year-old knows several hundred words. Second, during this period, the average length of the child's utterances also increases dramatically. The length of an utterance is usually computed by counting all the basic units of meaning (the morphemes) that have appeared. Morphemes usually correspond to words, but this relationship is not perfect. For example, in English, *sad* is one word and one morpheme. However, *sadly* although still one word, counts as two morphemes because the *ly* ending denotes meaning by itself. Therefore, the utterance "Daddy go" would be counted as three morphemes because the *y* carries meaning by itself. The mean length of utterances (**MLU**) is computed by determining the number of morphemes a child has produced, then dividing that number by the total number of utterances. When MLU is computed for children age two and beyond, a steady increase is seen across the entire period. Figure 9.1 shows the MLU graphed for two children studied by Roger Brown (1973). As mentioned earlier, different children may attain linguistic milestones at widely differ-

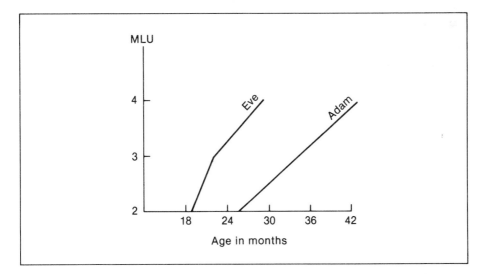

Figure 9.1.

Increases in MLU as a function of age for two children. (Adapted with permission of *The Free Press,* a division of Macmillan, Inc. from *Psycholinguistics,* by Roger Brown. Copyright © 1970 by The Free Press.)

ing ages. This variation is evident for the two children referred to in Figure 9.1. Adam was three and one-half years old before his MLU reached four items; this placed him a full year behind Eve.

Another important change occurs during this period. Whereas during the holophrastic period, the child's caretakers are willing to analyze the context in which the utterance occurs to deduce the child's intention, caretakers are less likely to analyze context during the two-word stage. The child relies less on the context as a basis for meaning and begins to let the order of the words do some of the work. Using two utterances puts additional linguistic demands on the child, however. As we've seen, the child must now acquire the rules of syntax.

Bloom (1970) was among the first to realize that the child's two-word utterances show syntax. One of her subjects, Kathryn, used the expression "mommy sock" twice in one day. In the first instance, Kathryn produced the utterance while holding her mother's sock; the second time, Kathryn used that expression while her mother put one of Kathryn's socks on. A contextual analysis still must be done to understand the little girl's meaning, but the order of the words helps to express two meaningful relationships. In the first case, Kathryn was expressing the relationship of *possession*. In the second case, Kathryn was making use of the same sort of *agent* construction that also occurs during the holophrastic stage.

These kinds of utterances are called *telegraphic speech*. Just as in a telegram, where inessential words are omitted, the child seems to use only those words that are necessary to communicate a particular intention. Articles, pronouns, and auxiliary verbs have not yet appeared.

Brown (1970) analyzed the two-word utterances of small children and found that they typically express one of several meaningful relationships. These **structural relationships** are shown in Table 9.3. Notice that many

TABLE 9.3

Brown's Structural Description of Two-Word Utterances

Structural Meaning	Form	Example
1. Nomination	that + N	that box
2. Notice	hi + N	hi belt
3. Recurrence	more + N	more cookie
4. Nonexistence	allgone + N	allgone kitty
5. Attributive	Adj + N	big train
6. Possessive	N + N	mommy lunch
7. Locative	N + N	sweater chair
8. Locative	V + N	walk road
9. Agent-Action	N + V	mommy read
10. Agent-Object	N + N	mommy sock
11. Action-Object	V + N	put book
12. Conjunction	N + N	umbrella boot

Source: Adapted with permission of *The Free Press*, a division of Macmillan, Inc. From *Psycholinguistics*, by Roger Brown. Copyright © 1970 by The Free Press.

of these relationships express the same things that children talk about during the holophrastic stage: namely, possession, the agent role, location, and so on.

Braine (1976) examined the two-word utterances of ten children (five were learning English, two Samoan, one Finnish, one Hebrew, and one Swedish). He found that all of these children spoke of movers or doers; that is, they all used the agent relationship. Moreover, all the children spoke of movable objects (the action-object relationship) and places (the locative relationships). Some of the other relationships were less commonly used. Braine noted that only some children used the possessive relationship, and the other relationships were used even less frequently.

The structural relationships described by Brown can be used as a basis for longer utterances. For example, three-word utterances can be made by combining certain two-word forms. The child who says "Bobbie take cookie" has combined the agent-action form ("Bobbie take") with the action-object form ("take cookie"). This linkage of primitive forms can take us only so far, however. Generally, after the creation of three-word utterances, the child seems to differentiate each of the noun classes contained in the basic utterance. *Differentiation* refers to the lengthening of a clause through elaboration and expansion. Bloom (1970) found that the initial elaboration of a sentence is right to left; that is, the object clause is elaborated first. This elaboration is accomplished by first adding articles or other modifiers to the object of the utterance, and later by the inclusion of possessive pronouns. In this way, an utterance such as "Mommy read story" might be elaborated into "Mommy, read my story." Although the differentiation of a sentence begins with the object clause and is therefore right to left, *within a clause* the differentiation is usually left to right. For example, articles begin to appear in front of the nouns that are the subjects of the sentence.

Such a view presupposes that all children in the two-word stage express the functional relationships in basically the same ways. However, Braine (1976) has pointed out that children in the two-word stage seem to adopt certain formulas to express certain relationships. For example, to talk about the location of an object, some children first mention the object (e.g., "baby") and then the location ("chair"). Other children take the opposite tack, stating the location first, then the object occupying it ("There doggie"). This approach inevitably colors the nature of later elaborations. The nature of the formula initially picked (which doesn't seem to have any rhyme or reason) may constrain the expansion process.

Bloom, Lightbown, and Hood (1975) and Nelson (1975) have also determined another variation that may affect the expansion process. They found that their subjects could be reliably grouped into one of two categories. Subjects in the first group used content words very early on in the two-word stage, just as the Brown model would predict. However, a second group of subjects used pronouns in the agent relationship. These children usually used the pronoun *I* in utterances such as "I do" and "I go." These children were also likely to use the demonstrative term *this* in the object relationship, in utterances such as "try this." This result is not what we would expect, given the differentiation process just outlined. In any case, within a few months, these early differences seem to wash out. The "content" children started to include some pronouns in their utterances, and the "I" children began to use some content words. These findings suggest that substantial individual differences exist in the formulaic knowledge of children in the two-word stage. Whether such individual differences materially affect language development is not now known. These findings also suggest that the initial structural relationships proposed by Brown are used by some, but not by all, children. The early use of pronouns by some children seems to confound the notion that the structural relationships are the basis for longer utterances.

Word Order and Inflections

As children begin to produce utterances of three and four words, they begin to rely more heavily on word order and **inflections** to signal their intents. For example, in English, inflections are used to show plurality of nouns and possession, among other things. Generally, a given language makes a trade-off between the stringency of its word order rules and the complexity of its inflections. For example, because English is not a highly inflected language, word order is quite important to meaning. If the word order is altered, the meaning of the utterance can be drastically revamped. As I recall, Latin is just the opposite: The actual order of the words can be shuffled around to a great extent without changing the sentence's meaning. It all works because each word is highly inflected, the ending reveals the noun's case, and adjectives have to agree in case with the nouns they modify.

The emergence of inflections has been studied by Bellugi (1964). Her findings are shown in Table 9.4. Once again, we see substantial timetable differences between Adam and Eve. For example, at twenty-six months, Eve began adding *s* to the verbs of third-person subjects.Adam was a full fifteen months behind in this ability. However, the order of emergence is identical for the two children. Moreover, the order of emergence is not strongly related to the frequency of use by the children's mothers. For example, the inflection mentioned previously was the last to appear in the childrens' speech although it was fairly common in their mothers' speech. Notice, too, that three

TABLE 9.4

The Emergence of English Inflections in the Speech of Two Children

Inflection	Age of Apperance (in months)		Combined Rank Order in Mothers' Speech
	Adam	Eve	
Present progressive, *-ing*	28	19½	2
Plural on nouns, *-s*	33	24	1
Past on regular verbs, *-ed*	39	24½	4
Possessive on nouns, *-s*	39½	25½	5
Third person on verbs, *-s*	41	26	3

Source: Belugi, 1964.

of the inflections involve the production of an *s* sound. Yet, for Adam, the latency between the earliest *s* inflection and the last to emerge was eight months. Even for Eve, whose progress appears to be much faster, this latency was two months. If the use of the inflection depended solely on the ability to produce the *s* sound, no latency would occur between the emergence of the first of these inflections and the emergence of the last. The existence of the latency shows that the use of these inflections cannot be explained solely by phonemic development.

The development of inflectional markers has been researched in a classic study by Berko (1958). Preschool children were shown a card such as the one in Figure 9.2. While the children were looking at the card, Berko would say, "This is a wug." Berko next pointed to the two figures standing together and said, "Now there is another one. There are two of them." Then the child was asked to express this fact by providing the correct term in the statement "There are two _____." Most of the subjects correctly answered with *wugs* even though they were obviously unfamiliar with this term. Berko went on to demonstrate the power of the plurality rule in a follow-up study. The child was shown a picture of a goose and was told, "Here is a goose." Next, a card showing two geese was presented with the following statement: "Here are two *geese*. There are two _____." Even after hearing the correct form, most of the children responded with "gooses." This sort of error is similar to that made by the little girl in the Overview to this chapter. In both cases, irregular forms of nouns were treated as though they were regular.

This sort of overregularization is interesting for several reasons. First, many of the forms thus created by children are not copies of adult speech, and so they cannot be explained as imitations. Second, the developmental pathway is similar for a variety of overregularization errors. For example, in the case of verbs, children of age three are fairly likely to use the correct

This is a wug.

Now there is another one.

There are two of them.
There are two _____.

Figure 9.2.

An example of one of Berko's stimulus cards.

past tense of some irregular verbs. The small child might say "We went bye-bye." However, by the age of four or five, the child who had been producing the correct form now shifts to the incorrect form *goed*—a seeming regression. Usually by the age of six, the child once again consistently produces the correct form. Overregularization is sometimes called a "smart error" because it indicates that the child has mastered an inflection rule.

The fact that overregularization errors are often not imitative (what adult says "goed"?) has attracted the attention of researchers. Parents are not neutral with regard to these utterances, and parents sometimes try to get the child to imitate their correct usage. To produce such novel utterances, then, the child sometimes has to counteract the will of the caretakers. Children seem remarkably resistant to these pressures:

Child: My teacher holded the baby rabbits and we patted them.
Adult: Did you say your teacher held the baby rabbits?
Child: Yes.
Adult: What did you say she did?
Child: She holded the baby rabbits and we patted them.
Adult: Did you say she held them tightly?
Child: No, she holded them loosely. (Cazden, 1972, p. 92)

More often, the attempts to influence the child take the form of **expansions** such as the following:

Child: Daddy office?
Adult: That's right, Daddy's gone to the office.

Such expansions are omnipresent in the linguistic environment of the child. Brown and Bellugi (1964) estimated that expansions make up over a third of all parental responses. Until Cazden (1972) completed her landmark study, it was commonly thought was that such expansions helped the child acquire syntactic knowledge. Now the issue is not so clear.

The subjects in this study were children whose ages were less than 3:6 at the beginning of the project. In one group, an adult caretaker responded to the child's utterances with expansions. In a second group, the caretaker deliberately responded with well-formed utterances that were not expansions of the child's remarks. For example, the caretaker might respond "Yes, but he'll be back soon" to the child's utterance noted previously. If expansions are useful for syntax learning, we would expect that the expansion group would outperform the nonexpansion group. But after three months, the children in these groups continued to perform at the same level. This somewhat puzzling finding has a variety of explanations that tend to have one theme in common. Language is a richly varied phenomenon, and language development seems to proceed faster when children are exposed to a good measure of this richness and variety. The Cazden finding also has a practical implication. Parents who overexpose their children to simple expansions or who subtly try to coerce their children into correct speech may be doing their children a disservice. Some errors, such as overregularization, seem to be an important part of the overall language development scheme. Well-meant interventions may be more disruptive than effective.

Later Developments

By the age of five or six, children appear to have mastered most of the rules of syntax and inflections, and so their knowledge of language seems complete. However, this apparent mastery is an illusion. Five-year-olds are readily able to make an interpretation of a sentence, but their interpretations are not always correct. Carol Chomsky (1969) demonstrated this by showing a blindfolded doll to a group of five- to eight-year-olds who were then asked, "Is the doll hard to see or easy to see?" Chomsky found that all of the five- and six-year-olds thought that the doll was hard to see, and many of the seven- and eight-year-olds agreed. Although this particular study has been criticized, replications of it (e.g., Cromer, 1970) have confirmed the finding. Apparently, children of ages five and six don't realize that sentences such as "The rabbit is nice to eat" and "The rabbit is eager to eat" have completely different meanings (Aitchison, 1983). Language development apparently continues until the age of ten or eleven.

Implications of the Developmental Sequence

Two points should be made here. First, if you've had a course in developmental psychology, you may be aware that language development seems to parallel physical and motor development. The milestones of language acquisition and motor skills tend to occur at similar points in a person's life. For example, the change from babbling to cooing occurs about the same time the baby sits up. The sitting baby is ready to have face-to-face communication, and cooing helps the baby learn important lessons about looking at others and taking turns in speaking. Similarly, the holophrastic period is usually accompanied by a child's first steps. With this newfound efficient locomotion, the baby now has a whole world to explore, and with it, a lot more to talk about.

Second, students sometimes get the idea that language development is a rigid process, almost as if some internal program is being run off. However, the seemingly rigid unfolding of the language acquisition program should not blind us to the fact that language is very much a social phenomenon, and its success depends upon knowledge on the part of others interacting with the child.

Earlier, I noted the possibility of language decrements when parents overexpose their children to simpleminded expansions of their speech. However, Bruner (1985) found that parents almost inevitably alter their speech patterns when addressing their babies. He noted that in baby talk, a mother broadens her intonation and slows her rate of speech. Also, grammatical constructions are simplified, and the content of the "conversation" deals almost exclusively with the here and now. For example, when mother and baby "read" a picture book together, Bruner found that mothers invariably limited the number of expressions they used to only four simple types. These types were almost always used in the same order. To get the child's attention, the mother first says "Look." After checking to make sure that the child is looking at her finger, she points to a picture and says (with rising inflection), "What's that?" Third, the mother names the object in the picture ("It's a ————"). After the child responds, the mother says,

"That's right." When the mother deviated from this sequence, it was because the child had done something different. For example, if the child actually succeeded in naming the indicated object, the mother would not repeat the name. Instead, she jumped ahead to the last part of the sequence ("Yes, that's right"). This change is apparently based on the mother's general knowledge of conversations: You're not supposed to repeat precisely what others have already said.

After some time, the mother will make a judgment that the child knows the label. When this judgment is made, the routine varies in two ways. First the mother is likely to drop the attention-getting "Look" and second, the mother uses a *falling* intonation to indicate the object:

Mother (with falling intonation): What's that?
Child: Fishy.
Mother: Yes, and see him swimming? (Bruner, 1985, p. 136)

This brings us to an important point. The alteration in the routine is not necessarily brought about by any dramatic change in the child's linguistic behavior, but rather by the mother's judgment of what the child knows. By gradually changing the routine, the mother offers the child an opportunity to learn about the nature of conversations in general while she models patterns of inflection and syntax. Thus, although some knowledge of inflection and syntax may be acquired through imitation, discourse knowledge is not imitative. This is seen in the child's behavior. Bruner noted that when the child produces a label, the likelihood that the child will repeat it is apparently not influenced by the mother's subsequent behavior. That is, about half the time that the child produces a label, the child repeats it. The repetition is just as likely to occur regardless of whether the mother imitates the child, simply says yes, or even just laughs and nods. The child is just as likely to repeat the response if the mother says no in the interim. If the child's language development were unfolding according to some rigid internal scheme, none of these variations would be observed.

The social nature of language acquisition has some implications for other areas of cognitive development, too. A common statement is that preschool children are egocentric, meaning that they are unable to imagine how things look to others, and implying that they can't take the needs or wishes of others into account in their own reasoning. Bruner's work suggests that if children were completely egocentric, language acquisition would be made even more difficult, if not impossible. Although in numerous situations children apparently can't see things from the perspective of others, research on language suggests that children might not be nearly as egocentric as people have supposed.

Nelson and Gruendel (in Bruner, 1985) found that much of what had been taken as egocentrism was really a failure on the part of the interacting children to find any scripts that they had in common. This failure was probably the result of different experiences (from which script knowledge is derived) rather than from egocentrism per se. They noted that even in cases in which the common scripts were not hit upon, preschool children still observed turn-taking rules, which itself argues against the egocentricity notion. When children did find common scripts, they were capable of lengthy, meaningful dialogues, such as the following. (Dan and Gay are four-year-olds who were sitting beside each other talking into toy telephones.)

Gay: Hi.
Dan: Hi.
Gay: How are you?
Dan: Fine.
Gay: Who am I speaking to?
Dan: Daniel. This is your Daddy. I need to speak to you.
Gay: All right.
Dan: When I come home tonight we're gonna have . . . peanut butter and jelly sandwich . . . uh . . . at dinner time.
Gay: Uhmmm. Where're we going at dinner time?
Dan: Nowhere, but we're just gonna have dinner at eleven o'clock.
Gay: Well, I made a plan of going out tonight.
Dan: Well, that's what we're gonna do.
Gay: We're going out.
Dan: The plan, it's gonna be, that's gonna be, we're going to McDonald's.
Gay: Yeah, we're going to McDonald's. And ah, ah, ah, what they have for dinner tonight is hamburger.
Dan: Hamburger is coming, O.K., well, goodbye.
Gay: Bye. (Bruner, 1985, pp. 138–39)

Although language development may appear to be the result of some internal program, there are plenty of nonprogrammatic influences as well. In addition to providing a sample of utterances that the child might model, the parents also seem to be involved in teaching the child important aspects of conversational skill, reciprocity, and turn taking. These skills don't seem to be based on imitation and consequently cannot be explained as the unfolding of an innate program.

Criticisms of the Stage Position

Not all researchers believe that language development consists of a series of stages. Criticisms fall into two general categories. First, some theorists maintain that the notion of stage is itself elusive: Nobody is exactly sure what other people mean when they use the term. Second, some theorists have argued that the person who goes through the stages is not the child but the parent. These theorists are referring to evidence suggesting that the parent triggers linguistic growth in the child by periodically changing her own linguistic behavior. We'll examine both criticisms.

What are stages? The problem here seems to be that various writers have used this term in many different ways. Whatever precision it may have once had seems to have gotten lost in the shuffle. Von Glaserfeld and Kelley (1982) tried to rectify this problem by redefining several terms that are sometimes treated almost synonymously: level, stage, phase, and period. *Level*, they maintain, is a spatial term and has no inherent time component, and may therefore be of the least use in discussing language development. The other three terms imply some sort of organization of events in time. Of these, *period* is the most general, simply referring to the events that occur in some arbitrary time interval. In this sense, "the preschool period" is a perfectly valid expression. The term *phase* also describes a time period, but one in which some cyclical, repetitive behavior takes place. Sometimes parents speak of the "terrible twos"—an interval in which their child ruthlessly and willfully disobeys. In this sense, it is appropriate to describe the interval as a phase, because the disobedience is cyclical and repetititve. Von Glaserfeld and Kelley use the term *stage* to describe time periods in which behaviors occur that are qualitatively different from those appearing in other intervals, and from which some sort of "progression to an expected end state" is implied.

This distinction is helpful but can't be expected to answer all of our questions. For example, we saw that cooing involves the production of vowel-like sounds. Cooing seems qualitatively different from crying, which does not involve vowel-like sound production. On the other hand, neither vocalization can be used productively, which raises a question: To make a stage distinction, is just one qualitative difference between the behaviors sufficient? Other problems are involved as well. Children don't stop crying one day and start cooing instead. During a certain period, the child will both cry and coo a lot; neither vocalization will be dominant. The obvious question is, During this period, what stage is the child in? In almost any stage formulation, massive problems will arise in specifying the transition rules (Cairns & Valsiner, 1984). Even in those circumstances in which the transitions from stage to stage are based on the results of fairly precise test criteria, Flavell (1982) has noted that multiple test conditions, context, and prior experience can influence test performance, and with it, the evaluation of which stage of development a child is in.

These problems may not actually sink the stage concept (although they do make it ride low in the water). The description of language development as the unfolding of a series of stages probably doesn't carry much theoretical weight. However, as a teaching convenience, the stage concept is still useful.

Caretaker Speech

We've looked at Bruner's work, which suggested that parents change their speech in conformity to what they think their child is capable of understanding. The speech patterns thus produced are called **caretaker speech,** or more bluntly, "motherese." Abundant examples show that the particular form of caretaker speech heard by the child influences the rate and nature of his language development. Two-year-old Nicholas helped his father carve a pumpkin, and during the fifteen-minute recorded session, Dad produced the following utterances (De Villiers & De Villiers, 1978):

No, you shouldn't make a hole in the bottom.
No, let Daddy do it first.
No, I don't think you'll be able to cut straight.
No, don't cut too much on the front.
No, I don't think you should put more holes in it.
No, don't cut two holes.

Given the frequency with which this "no" construction is used by the father, is it suprising that Nicholas displayed an early reliance on exactly the same form to express negation? Similary, Wells (1979) demonstrated that the emergence of auxiliary verbs (such as *will, have, can,* and so on) parallels their frequency in adult speech.

Findings such as these have led some researchers to speculate that children may not have an innate sensitivity to the regularities in language, but rather parents may have an innate sensitivity to the needs and abilities of their children. According to this view, parents are adept at inferring a child's linguistic competence from the child's performance. As a result of this analysis, the parent fine-tunes her own language to match the child's level of ability (Cross, 1977). According to this hypothesis, talking about the stages of language development doesn't make much sense, because in a real sense the parent sets the stage. From this perspective, it makes more sense to study what the child has to say to get the parent to shift gears linguistically into a more advanced stage.

Is the fine-tuning hypothesis correct? Newport, Gleitman, and Gleitman (1977) have some findings that bear on this question. They reasoned that if fine tuning were genuine, parents would introduce new and more complex grammatical constructions into their dialogues with children on a one-at-a-time basis. This approach would give the child time to absorb the new construction and would give the parent a chance to see if the child had incorporated it. We would also expect that the parent would begin this process with what seem to be easy constructions, such as declarative sentences.

Newport et al. observed fifteen mother-daughter pairs in two sessions spaced six months apart. They found that the mothers did not seem to introduce grammatical constructions one at a time. Instead, several different forms, such as declaratives, imperatives, and questions, were all used. In addition, the declarative form was not the one most frequently used. In the initial session, the mothers used declarative forms 30 percent of the time and more complex forms in 62 percent of their utterances. In the second session, the mothers used *more* declarative forms. If the mothers truly possessed some innate knowledge of language teaching, this knowledge doesn't seem to have emerged during these conversations with their daughters. Although children are obviously influenced by the linguistic habits of their parents, the emergence of particular grammatical forms apparently can't be explained by imitation and repetition alone.

ACQUISITION OF LANGUAGE AMONG THE DEAF

We looked at Hockett's design features of language in Chapter 8. Recall that one of those features was total feedback. When we speak, we hear everything we say. Although our voice sounds different to us than it does to our listeners, the differences don't add or subtract phonemic or syntactic information. For those who are deaf and use sign language to communicate, total feedback cannot be taken for granted. The signer may not see everything that the receiver does, and the signer's perspective is necessarily different in any case. The signer sees the backs of the signs, while the receiver sees them from the front. The signer has an additional source of information in the form of kinesthetic cues. Since signers feel the signs as they make them, they don't have to rely exclusively on visual feedback to know if they are signing appropriately. However, the difference between a visual code and a kinesthetic code is substantial. The possibility that some information may be lost or added by a signer who relies on kinesthetic code must be conceded.

For these reasons, comparing the language development of hearing children to that of the deaf is interesting. To the extent that similarities exist in the acquisition patterns of these two groups, we might be able to get some leverage on one of Chomsky's points. He believed that language use reflects the organization of the human mind and that how this language is produced—verbally or in signs—doesn't particularly matter. If the acquisition pattern of the deaf is different from that of hearing children, and perhaps slower, this might lend support to Hockett's claim that some acoustic features are important to our definition of language.

Lenneberg (1967) studied the development of English deaf children. As he pointed out, deaf children seem to have a tough time learning English for several reasons. First, deaf children must learn English by watching people rather than by listening to them. Such children are usually exposed to American sign language at home—a language whose structure is substantially different from English. Consequently, deaf children don't get exposure to English until they begin to learn it formally in school. As a result, the deaf child will inevitably be exposed to a smaller sample of well-formed sentences than will the hearing child by the time they both start school.

Lenneberg found that deaf children make grammatical mistakes in writing that are not commonly found among hearing children. The following story was produced by a deaf boy who had had five years of English instruction:

One day he lived in England. His name was Jim. He went to the television and put on there. He sat on the floor and watched television. Then he was quiet and climbed up the chair. He was stolen many candy on the shelf and he ate it more and more. (Lennenberg, 1967)

These types of errors are typical of deaf children. Although these errors might suggest an impairment of linguistic ability, we must remember that English is not really this child's native language. Comparing his skill in American sign language with the oral skills of children his age is probably more fair.

Such a study was undertaken by Ursula Bellugi (1964). She found that deaf children learn sign language spontaneously—the same way hearing children do—and their progress is comparable to that of hearing children. To cite a typical example, one of the children in the study, Pola, had an MLU (computed in sign morphemes) of 1.69 signs at age two years and seven months. By the time Pola was three years and one month, her MLU had increased to 2.79 signs, a change comparable to that of hearing children during that time period.

Other evidence suggests that deaf children undergo stages in language development. American sign language is less rigid syntactically than English. For example, in producing gestures that signify "dog bite cat," a signer doesn't need to rely on word order to indicate who was doing the biting and who was bitten. Instead, a special marker can be affixed to the verb to indicate the direction of the biting. The previous gestures might indicate that the dog was bitten if a particular gesture was appended to the verb. Most of the time, these verb signs are regular; the same gesture can be attached to a wide variety of verbs. Some are irregular; the directionality marker for those verbs must be learned specifically. About the same time that hearing children begin to make overregularization errors, deaf children begin to make similar mistakes. Whereas they had previously used the correct form of these irregular verbs, they now begin attaching the regular gestures onto them. Since such errors are not produced by adult members of the signing community, these mistakes cannot have been acquired through imitation. About the same time that hearing children begin to correct their overregularizations, deaf children do also.

From Bellugi's work we can conclude that Hockett's design feature—total feedback—doesn't seem to be a necessary part of language. The developmental sequence outlined for hearing children also seems to take place for deaf children as well. This outcome tends to strengthen our belief in the notion of innate predispositions that guide language development. These predispositions appear to be so powerful that language is still spontaneously acquired by humans who can neither hear nor speak.

The Critical Period

Chapter 8 raised the issue of innate predispositios that guide language development, and this chapter examined the role of experience as it aids the process of language development. Let's review some of this material. Recall that Chomsky's arguments in favor of the innateness position were derived chiefly from the complexity of syntax and the apparent impossibility of learning grammar through imitation alone. When we look at both the normal developmental sequence and deviations from it, we see that some findings can be brought to bear on this contention. First, much of what the child learns does not appear to be precisely imitative. Most overregularization errors, for example, cannot be explained as mimicry. Second, the developmental sequence is largely invariant, which bolsters our belief in its innateness. From the observation of constancy in language development, which occurs despite wide variations in culture and milieu, we can infer that the child's acquisition must be at least aided by some innate knowledge whose form is currently not known.

We looked at the material on deaf children in light of its implications for Hockett's design features. But there is another approach to this material that bears on the question of innateness. From your introductory course in psychology, you may recall the concept of the **critical period.** Animals that have the capacity to learn something might not profit by certain experiences equally well at different points in their life spans. During some intervals, certain experiences may be more meaningful and easier to learn from than they would be during other intervals. Some theorists (notably Lenneberg, 1967) have argued that language acquisition has a critical period. From the time children are two years old until they are about fourteen, the innate predispositions that help them learn language are operating at full effectiveness. Consequently, during this period, humans are receptive to and better able to learn language than at any other point in their life spans. Languages can be learned at any point in one's life. But once the critical period has elapsed, languages are learned only with great deliberation and brute force memorization. This process hardly resembles the airy spontaneity that characterizes children's language acquisition.

When we consider evidence from both typical and atypical developmental sequences, we see some limited support for the concept of a critical period for language acquisition. For example, studies of deaf children (and feral children) indicate that when English syntax is not presented early on in the individual's life, apparently permanent deficits in production are the result. Still, we have to be cautious about this interpretation. Recall the discussion of Genie from Chapter 8. Her case is interesting in part because of the deficits that were not produced. Even though she was nearly fourteen before remediation began—that is, near the end of the presumed critical period— Genie still showed fairly spontaneous vocabulary learning, and her comprehension of complex speech was more or less unimpaired. In that regard, Lenneberg may have overstated the case for the importance of the critical period in language acquisition.

LANGUAGE ACQUISITION IN ANIMALS

When I was a child, one of my favorite series of books described the misadventures of a man named Dr. Doolittle. Dr. Doolittle had the ability to speak with animals. As I recall, Dr. Doolittle spoke in English, and although the response of the animal being spoken to was also printed in English, my understanding was that the animal was actually speaking its language, which was comprehended by the good doctor. The implications of all this were lost on me then, but not now. First, the books presuppose that the animals actually had their own languages; as we've seen, this is doubtful. The books also assume that the animals are capable of understanding Dr. Doolittle's English. The assumption here is that any language is translatable into any other. For reasons beyond the scope of this book, that premise is also suspect. Finally, the books assume that the animals are interested in talking with Dr. Doolittle. This assumption means that an ostrich, for example, would find our lives as interesting as we might find its life. This premise is also doubtful, but I can't prove it. In any case, these problems have failed to diminish anybody's excitement over the prospect of having a conversation with a subhuman. The last twenty years have seen a virtual deluge of projects whose object has been to teach a language to an animal. This section considers the outcomes.

Washoe

Washoe is a chimpanzee acquired by Professors Allan and Beatrice Gardner in 1966. At that time, she was about one year of age; she had been born in the wild. The Gardners attempted to teach Washoe American sign language (ASL), and they have commented on their progress in a series of reports (Gardner & Gardner, 1969, 1969, 1971, 1975, 1978, 1980). Washoe was surrounded by a number of adult signers, and in the early part of her training, no speech was permitted in her presence. But other than that somewhat unusual feature of her life, Washoe was reared as much like a human child as possible. The Gardners reasoned that Washoe would not be interested in signing if she had nothing of interest to communicate. To this end, they kept her days filled with a variety of loosely organized activities. Their hope was that Washoe would spontaneously begin to pick up and use signs the same way that deaf children do; however, this did not occur. Washoe was consequently conditioned to sign using operant procedures. In some cases, the shaping procedure was literal: Washoe's hands were molding into the signs, and she was then rewarded with praise and affection. Washoe learned an impressive number of signs this way: over 130 by the time she was four years old.

Several other aspects of her behavior are perhaps even more impressive. First, Washoe clearly knew the meaning of the signs. The Gardners (1969) noted that part of Washoe's upbringing consisted of brushing her teeth after every meal, and Washoe hated this activity. One day when she was in the bathroom, she apparently saw a cupful of toothbrushes and spontaneously made the appropriate sign. She clearly wasn't asking to be given a toothbrush, because the cup was in her reach. She wasn't asking to have her teeth brushed, because she despised that activity. She was apparently simply naming the objects in the same way that children frequently do.

The breadth of her comprehension was indicated by her generalizations. For example, Washoe used the sign "open" to get her caretakers to open a number of different kinds of doors and containers. Unless one assumes that Washoe truly knew the term's meaning, it would be hard to explain why Washoe made that sign in the presence of a car door and later, in the presence of a briefcase. More important, Washoe had not been explicitly conditioned to make the sign in the different settings.

Washoe seemed to enter the two-word stage. During this period, Washoe frequently produced comments that were two or three signs long. For example, the expression "Gimme tickle" was used to mean "Come and tickle me." "Go sweet" was Washoe's way of saying "Take me to the raspberry bushes." This kind of creativity seems to be at least a close approximation of the productiveness that Hockett mentioned.

Some critics have maintained, however, that Washoe hadn't mastered ASL after all. Whereas children usually use a particular order in their signs and utterances, Washoe often seemed nonchalant about syntax. For example, she was just as likely to sign "Sweet go" as "Go sweet" to get out to the raspberries. Washoe was apparently not following her own syntactic laws; the order of the gestures within the phrases are often switched without any apparent reason. This apparent failure to master syntax has several explanations. First, many of Washoe's utterances had only one meaning ("Go sweet" was among them). Since most of her caretakers were not native signers, they may have either not realized Washoe's syntactic slovenliness, or perhaps in their zeal to comply with a talking chimpanzee's requests, simply ignored her syntactic deviance since the meaning was clear anyway. In a sense, Washoe's caretakers may have been "bad parents" because they weren't able to evaluate Washoe's capabilities accurately enough to know when they should have demanded better syntactic compliance from her. The Gardners have made it clear that they believe Washoe's linguistic development had not ended when the project was terminated. They maintained that Washoe was beginning to settle into a more rigid use of syntax.

Another explanation is that Washoe was simply not able to understand the notion of syntax. The question may never be answered satisfactorily, because Washoe now lives in a primate colony and is no longer quite the center of attention she once was. Washoe has been given a chimp son to raise and reportedly has been teaching the baby chimp signs. The implications of these reports, if true, are fascinating and may mean that Washoe's story is not over yet.

Sarah

In 1966, David Premack began training the chimpanzee Sarah to communicate with the use of plastic tokens displayed on a magnetic board. Whereas Washoe was permitted to sign spontaneously and initiate conversations, Sarah lived in a cage and was drilled by her trainers. Most of these drills were designed to establish that Sarah was capable of comprehending fairly complex messages.

For example, when shown the following sequence of tokens "query cup equal spoon" (meaning, Is a cup the same thing as a spoon?), Sarah was readily able to pick out the correct token ("no"), for which she was rewarded with chocolate. Similarly, when given the string "Sarah insert apple red dish," Sarah complied by putting the apple in the red dish. She could also comply with sequences that had similar forms. For example, if given "Sarah insert banana green dish," Sarah was also able to comply by putting the banana in the green dish. This result may indicate that the concept of insertion was not rigidly associated with the apple or the red dish, and may also indicate the beginnings of a primitive phrase structure grammar. If Sarah's accomplishments were the result of simple operant chaining laws, it's hard to imagine how she would be able to carry out each of these similar requests equally well. If "insert" had been originally associated with "apple" and "red dish," then we should expect a longer response latency or increased error rate when Sarah was asked to link "insert" with "banana" and "green dish."

These things didn't happen, however. Sarah was able to carry out both requests without any difficulty. The existence of the phrase structure was further supported when Sarah was given the request "Sarah insert apple red dish banana green dish." Although this request was difficult for Sarah to comply with (the trainers complained of emotional outbursts), she nevertheless got the apple into the red dish and the banana into the green one. Notice that the entire phrase "Sarah insert" is missing from the second clause. Again, if she were simply responding on the basis of operant chaining laws, it's hard to see how she could have carried out this request. If, however, Sarah had a mental organization of the symbols corresponding to the phrase structure shown in Figure 9.3, then her response becomes much more comprehensible.

Several conclusions can be drawn from the Washoe and Sarah projects. First, neither attempt is completely satisfying, but for different reasons. Washoe's knowledge of syntax had not completely developed, and no real evidence indicated that it would develop. Sarah seemed to demonstrate good comprehension of symbol order, but the style and topic of conversations were highly constrained. There was no indication of productiveness in Sarah's communiqués. However, both chimps demonstrated knowledge of semantics: They clearly knew that the tokens or gestures meant something. Moreover, the communication systems used by both chimps were truly symbolic. No inherent relationship existed between the tokens or gestures and their referents. In addition, Washoe seemed to show displacement. In some cases, her gestures seemed to refer to things that were not present in time or place.

Nim Chimpsky

Washoe and Sarah were the principal projects in the first wave of modern research on animal language learning. As we've seen, each study had some defects, and in the second wave of research, investigators tried to correct

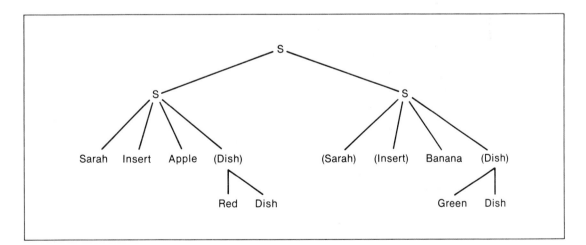

Figure 9.3.

A representation of a phrase structure possibly available to Sarah. (From *The Articulate Mammal: An Introduction to Psycholinguistics* (2d edition), by Jean Aitchison. © 1976, 1983 by Jean Aitchison. Reprinted by permission of Universe Books, New York.)

some of these shortcomings. Nim Chimpsky is the name of a chimp that was extensively studied and trained by Herbert Terrace for four years. During this period, Nim's utterances were routinely videotaped, and the resulting data bank includes over twenty thousand specimens. In the time period since Nim has returned to a primate station in Oklahoma, these specimens have been thoroughly analyzed. The technical accomplishments of Nim are somewhat greater than that of the other linguistic chimps. Nim produced a high number of two-, three-, and four-sign utterances. Terrace (1979) was initially encouraged by the high degree of syntactic order in the sample. For example, in two-word signs including the gesture "more," this gesture appeared in the initial position 78 percent of the time. Unfortunately, this kind of regularity was not observed for all gestures. That is, Nim put gestures sometimes in the initial position and sometimes in the second position. One of Nim's most frequently occurring gestures was "eat." Table 9.5 shows the placement of the gesture "eat" and its frequency in Nim's two-, three-, and four-sign sequences.

These utterances show little variation. That is, most of the longer utterances can be described as simple expansions of the shorter ones. In the two-sign sequences, the phrases "Eat Nim," "Nim eat," and "Me eat" appear, and these phrases essentially form the basis of many of the three- and four-sign sequences. For example, several three-sign sequences consist of "Eat me Nim," "Eat Nim eat," "Eat me eat," and so on. Similar patterns can be observed for the sequences involving "banana" and "drink." Nim's longest utterance consisted of sixteen signs: "Give orange me give eat orange me eat orange give me eat orange give me you." Only five different signs were used, and the repetitive—almost nonsensical—character of this utterance becomes even more clear if it is read aloud. A typical child's producing an utterance like this one seems highly unlikely.

Terrace noted a number of other discrepancies between Nim's language development and that of children in general. By the time Nim was two years old, 38 percent of his signs were done in imitation. Children usually produce fewer direct imitations as they grow older, but Nim did just the opposite. By the time he was four years old, the frequency of imitations had increased to 54 percent. Children are increasingly likely to initiate conversations as they age. However, Nim usually did not begin conversations; only 12 percent of his signing was truly spontaneous. Moreover, Nim seemed to have little idea that language involved taking turns. In many cases, Nim began signing before someone had finished. This action has been interpreted as an indication that Nim had no idea of the social function of language, although normal children begin observing turn-taking rules long before their fourth birthday (Terrace, 1979; Aitchison, 1983). After his extensive analysis of Nim's signing, Terrace had to reluctantly conclude that little evidence supported the idea that Nim's utterances were well structured.

This conclusion was immediately challenged. Recall that when we looked at speech patterns in the two-word stage, we saw that context is highly important in evaluating the grammar of the child. During that stage, the child seems willing to let the context do some of the work in specifying meaning. Adults usually rely almost completely on syntax to accomplish

TABLE 9.5

The Placement of the Gesture "Eat" in the Two-, Three-, and Four-Sign Utterances of Nim Chimpsky

Two-Sign Sequences			
Eat Nim	302		
More eat	287		
Me eat	237		
Nim eat	209		
Eat drink	98		
Gum eat	79		
Grape eat	74		

Three-Sign Sequences			
Eat me Nim	48	Yoghurt Nim eat	20
Eat Nim eat	46	Me more eat	19
Grape eat Nim	37	More eat Nim	19
Banana Nim eat	33	Banana me eat	17
Nim me eat	27	Nim eat Nim	17
Banana eat Nim	26	Apple me eat	15
Eat me eat	22	Eat Nim me	15
Me Nim eat	21	Give me eat	15

Four-Sign Sequences			
Eat drink eat drink	15	Drink eat me Nim	3
Eat Nim eat Nim	7	Eat grape eat Nim	3
Banana eat me Nim	4	Eat me Nim drink	3
Banana me eat banana	4	Me eat drink more	3
Grape eat Nim eat	4	Me eat me eat	3
Drink eat drink eat	4	Me Nim eat me	3
Nim eat Nim eat	4		

Source: Terrace, 1979

this work. Critics of Terrace's analysis (Gardner & Gardner, 1980) contend that Terrace has thrown away some of the grammar by simply computing statistical frequencies that have been summed over a four-year period and over a variety of situations. Despite these claims and counterclaims, interest in chimp language has not abated, but research funds for this type of project have virtually dried up. Perhaps our best hope is that the definitive chimp study will someday appear.

Aitchison (1983) has nicely summarized the positive and negative outcomes of these and other chimp projects. First, the chimps use arbitrary symbols and seem to know what these symbols mean. Some of the chimps are capable of limited displacement and creativity. However, the naturalistically trained animals (such as Washoe and Nim) show little or no evidence of syntactic knowledge. Highly trained animals (like Sarah and others) seem to be able to order arbitrary symbols, but they do this task only when they are rewarded, and even then their success rate is not terribly high. These projects have made a contribution: Chomsky believed that simple object naming was clearly beyond the capability of a trained animal, but that contention no longer seems valid. However, some of the chimp trainers may have oversold their case somewhat by asserting that their animals have obviously acquired language. Until a chimp (or perhaps some other animal) is able to have conversations in which the rules of turn taking and syntax are observed, true language still seems to be an exclusively human capability.

CONCLUDING COMMENTS AND SUGGESTIONS FOR FURTHER READING

It's a common to think that our mental processes must always be based on our experiences—things that have happened to us. This belief is widespread, probably because our mental contents (what we have in our minds) seem to consist of relived experiences, at least most of the time. This leads us to a position that seems to imply that mentality is often the residue of experience. Language almost always plays a major role in these mental events. Even while some inherently visual memory is unfolding, we may be aware of some running mental verbal commentary. According to this view, if mentality is the residue of experience, and language is such a vital feature of mentality, then language could not conceivably enter our minds in any way other than through the portal of experience.

Yet, much of this chapter suggests that the basis for speech seems to be innate. Moreover, the basis for language is apparently wired into only the human brain. Although Washoe and other chimp projects upset the apple carts of some theorists who believe that object naming was an exclusively human act, not all the apples were lost in the spilling. "Species chauvinists" can still take some solace in the fact that Washoe and her buddies seem to have massive problems mastering syntax, regardless of the effort expended to teach them.

Important events are seldom left to chance, and nature obeys this dictum. From the species' point of view, the acquisition of speech is tremendously important, and the sooner it is acquired, the better for all concerned. Consequently, the idea of the critical period for language acquisition is a congenial way to account for the fact that language learning is much easier when we are young than when we are older.

Students who want to find out more about language acquisition could start with either of two excellent books. Clark and Clark (1977) have written a comprehensive introduction to psycholinguistics, as have De Villiers and De Villiers (1978). Aitchison's (1983) book is easy to read and informative. Clark and Hecht (1983) have written a review of the comprehension-production distinction that points out some of the problems that crop up when one tries to assess a child's linguistic ability. Biological foundations are covered in Lenneberg's (1967) classic book. Kuczaij (in Brainerd & Pressley, 1982) offers an extensive analysis of the acquisition of word meaning. Students who want to find out what words children actually use in their speech should consult Hall, Nagy, and Linn (1984). Robinson (1981) has examined the role of egocentrism in children's turn taking in speech.

FOCUS ON RESEARCH:
Creating Language

Creating a language is not particularly difficult. Computer scientists have been doing it for a least the past thirty years. However, even people who have no particular training can devise languages. Business needs sometimes necessitate the invention of a language. For example, sailors who want to trade with people of other cultures have been the traditional inventors of rudimentary languages known as *pidgins*. The pidgin's lexicon is usually derived from the vocabulary of the language of seafaring nations, such as French or Dutch, but the syntax of the base language is simplified. Typically, formulaic word order is heavily relied on to accomplish routine transactions such as negotiating a price. Pidgins make do without several parts of speech, such as articles. Neither do they have markers to designate plurals or verb tense.

But something amazing happens when the children of a culture begin to learn a pidgin as their native language. Suddenly, the language seems to acquire mechanisms to distinguish tense, show subordination, and mark plurals. The pidgin has then become what is technically called a *creole*. For example, Sankoff and Brown (1976) studied Tok Pisin (Talk Pidgin), an English-derived creole from New Guinea. They found that this language had an elegant way of indicating a subordinate clause. The speaker simply inserts an additional sentence into the utterance, marking the opening and closing of the clause with the word *ia*. So, the sentence

Na pik *ia* ol ikilim bipo *ia* bai ikamap olsem draipela ston.

can be translated as

And this pig *ia* they had killed it before *ia* would turn into a huge stone. (Sankoff & Brown, 1976)

Bickerton (1982, 1983) studied the emergence of creoles around the world and made some startling discoveries. First, all of the 350 or so known creoles share some grammatical constructions. All creoles use three articles including the definite *(the)* and the indefinite *(a)*. Second, all creoles use far more negatives than the pidgins from which they descended. Third, all creoles indicate whether an action was completed. For example, I might say, "I went to wash my car." If I spoke a creole, some marker would indicate whether I completed the task. Further, Bickerton found that the rules of the creole were independent of the preceding pidgin. For example, in Hawaii the first creole generation of plantation workers produced rules that had no antecedents among the pidgin language.

Bickerton has made strong claims for his findings. He suggests that all creoles are similar because they reflect a bioprogram reponsible for generating language. This program apparently operates independently of the social setting in which the first children of the creole generation find themselves. Bickerton's ideas drew fire soon after their publication (Sproat, 1983), and it's too soon to tell how they'll hold up. His work, however, has reopened the innateness issue in language development.

KEY TERMS

Overregularization
Comprehension
Production
Babbling
Babbling drift
Holophrastic stage
Two-word stage

MLU
Structural relationships
Inflection
Expansions
Caretaker speech
Critical periods

CHAPTER 10

Language in Use

OVERVIEW

PERCEPTION AND COMPREHENSION OF SPEECH
Why Speech Perception Is Such a Problem:
  The Stream of Speech
How Speech Sounds are Categorized:
  Phonetics and Phonology
  Articulatory Phonetics
  Distinctive Features in Speech
  Comprehension of Isolated Speech Sounds
  The Need for a Phonological Level
Stages of Speech Perception: From the Bottom
  Up
Perception of Continuous Speech: From the
  Top Down
Analysis by Synthesis: Interaction of
  Top-Down and Bottom-Up Processing

PRODUCTION OF SPEECH

Analysis of Speech Errors
Analysis of Hesitations and Pauses
A Model of Speech Production

READING
Mechanics of Reading
Recoding in Reading
Direct Access Hypothesis
Summary

LANGUAGE AND THOUGHT
Bilingualism
  Definitions
  Acquisition

CONCLUDING COMMENTS AND SUGGESTIONS
FOR FURTHER READING
FOCUS ON RESEARCH
KEY TERMS

I'm often amazed at the fluency with which my foreign-born colleagues speak English. About a year ago, I visited the home of a faculty friend and his wife, who were from India. Also visiting were another foreign couple: He was from Iran, and she was from Malaysia. Everyone seemed comfortable speaking English, and all were readily able to express themselves. At one point, the conversation turned to the difference between their native languages and English. I was surprised to find that this group of people, who had obviously mastered English, seemed to think that English was a limited language that narrowly constricted the things that could be talked about. My Persian friend spoke for all when he said that using English was like looking at the world through a tiny window, but speaking in his native Farsi was like standing in the middle of a panorama.

This story raises some questions about language use and language perception. Why did my friends feel that way about English? Is it because English has something *physically* difficult about it? Are its sounds hard to discriminate and produce? Perhaps my friends were discontented with English at some deeper level. Are meaning and syntax more obscure in English than in other languages?

This chapter considers some of the numerous issues involved in using language. Let's consider what's required. First, the comprehension of speech requires an ability to perceive the speech sounds of a particular language. This question is one of feature detection and pattern recognition. What are the features of speech sounds? This chapter tries to answer that question.

Even after the speech sounds are correctly detected and categorized, the listener's work is far from over. The sounds must be organized into words. This means that the listener must quickly produce a cognitive code that maintains the order in which the sounds were heard. Further, the speaker must have some way of determining the boundaries between the words. This is no easy trick. We seem to be naturally aware of the pauses between words, but most of the pauses we hear are really not there. We'll examine some of the factors that enable native speakers to determine word boundaries in ongoing speech.

We can not only comprehend speech but also produce it. We'll examine speech production, which seems to be accomplished in a series of stages, each consisting of a cognitive code that is modified by successive cognitive operations. Some of these cognitive operations can be glimpsed by analyzing errors in speech production. We'll study and interpret some common errors.

Language can be used in many ways. In addition to the topics of speech comprehension and production, we'll consider reading, which has been called "language by eye" (Howard, 1983). Are there similarities in the comprehension of speech and reading? We'll find out. Using language seems to be intimately related to thinking. This chapter's concluding section examines some of the literature bearing on this relationship.

As you read this material, keep in mind the top-down–bottom-up distinction first raised in Chapter 2. Probably nowhere else in cognitive psychology is the interplay of these two modes more intertwined. Understanding speech or reading requires a knowledge of how top-down and bottom-up processes interact. Keep you eyes open for this interaction as you read the chapter.

PERCEPTION AND COMPREHENSION OF SPEECH

Speech sounds are not naturally distinct from one another; they usually have no readily distinguishable boundaries between them. Moreover, the pauses that we seem to hear between words and phrases are often illusory. For these reasons, Clark and Clark (1977) have noted that the problems involved in comprehending speech are similar to the difficulties we would have extracting a signal from a warbling siren. This section describes some of the problems of speech perception and comprehension, and discusses some of the approaches various disciplines have taken to understand them.

Why Speech Perception Is Such a Problem: The Stream of Speech

Clark and Clark (1977) have written of the problems posed by speech perception, and my account is based largely on theirs. Illustrating a complex problem is sometimes best accomplished by analogy—even though the analogy might be incorrect. That's the case here.

Let's suppose that speech could accurately be represented by letters. That is, let's assume for a moment that the letters of a sentence such as:

Jim is a hero.

each stood for a particular unit of sound, or **phoneme.** If this state of affairs were true, then speech comprehension would be easy to understand. Why? Because in that case, each phoneme would be distinct from the phonemic segments that preceded and followed it. Assuming that each phoneme is a distinct acoustic event with distinct acoustic properties, the perceiver would simply engage in the following sequences of events: (1) map the acoustic signal onto his knowledge of phonetics, (2) determine which phoneme had been signaled, (3) store this representation, and (4) add onto it the next phoneme that was detected, and so on.

Although comparing speech to print seems natural, the resulting "theory" of speech perception thus implied is unfortunately almost completely wrong. First, speech is ongoing. Letters are discrete, separable stimuli. But speech sounds are not discrete and separable. The stream of speech is hardly ever marked by periods of silence. Second, unlike letters, phonetic segments are usually influenced by their location within a word. Consider, for example, the /m/ sounds in *Tim* and *mink*. The letter *m* is used to designate this sound in both cases, and we truly hear the same sound at the beginning of *mink* and at the end of *Tim*. Yet, the acoustic properties of the /m/ sound are markedly different in these two cases. In other words, although we hear these sounds as the same, their pronunciation is different. You can readily see the problem here. The symbol /m/ denotes some regularity in our perception of sounds. But this regularity in perception seems to be independent of any particular regularity in the acoustic patterns themselves.

Third, the opposite problem sometimes emerges: We perceive as different speech sounds that aren't different at the acoustic level. For example, consider the words *writer* and *rider*. Like most people, you probably hear a difference between the /t/ and /d/ sounds. Consequently, it seems reasonable to look at the speech stream with an eye to finding what the person does with her mouth to make the /t/ as opposed to the /d/ sound in this situation. But your search would be in vain: In this case, the two sounds have no phonetic distinction per se. The only pronunciation difference between the two words is the length of time the vowel /ay/ (this is the way this sound is designated) is held. The /ay/ in *rider* is held slightly longer than the /ay/ in *writer*.

These difficulties are not the only ones that cognitive psychologists must face in grappling with speech perception; they are also faced with the order problem. To identify the word *pill,* a person not only must identify the phonetic segments /p/, /i/, and /l/ but also must keep their order straight. If this process weren't done, the person would be unable to distinguish *pill* from other words made up of the same phonetic segments arranged differently (such as *lip*).

Warren, Obusek, Farmer, and Warren (1969) played sequences of sounds such as a hiss, a vowel, a buzz, and a musical tone for their subjects. They found that the subjects could not accurately report the order of the sounds if they were played at a rate of 1.5 segments per second or greater. However, speech typically proceeds at 12 phonetic segments per second and is intelligible at rates of up to 50 segments per second. Only two conclusion are to be drawn from this finding. First, the appearance of a particular phonetic segment may constrain the range of phonemes that might appear next. If this were true, then hearing a particular phoneme might enable the perceiver to shrewdly guess which phonemes were likely to appear next, thus narrowing the range of phonemes that would have to be processed. On the other hand, the possibility exists that phonemes are not processed sequentially but rather in bunches. This process could be accomplished if each phoneme includes an acoustic clue about the phoneme or phonemes that are upcoming. This would mean that phonemes are never produced in isolation—they always contain information about the phoneme to come, which results in their own pronunciation being altered. This second interpretation seems to be the more likely explanation of the Warren et al. findings.

How Speech Sounds Are Categorized: Phonetics and Phonology

The last section examined some of the reasons why speech perception is so complicated. This section deals with the attacks on the problem. Understanding the basics of speech perception is almost impossible without some background in **phonetics** and **phonology.** Phoneticians try to describe the nature of linguistic sounds. There are two varieties of phoneticians. *Acoustic phoneticians* analyze the physical characteristics of speech sounds. *Articulatory phoneticians* try to specify the nature of linguistic sounds by determining the patterns of tongue placement, airflow, and vocal cavity changes that characterize different sounds. Table 10.1 shows the symbols phoneticians have developed to represent linguistic sounds.

Phonology is a branch of linguistics that attempts to determine the rules, or principles, that characterize the production and comprehension of speech sounds. Phonologists don't deal with the sounds directly, in the same sense that linguists are not necessarily interested in the production of specific sentences. Rather, the phonologist is interested in the more abstract aspects of speech sounds—the general knowledge a person has that enables him to formulate specific utterances. For example, consider the word *electric*. The final *c* sound, symbolized with a /k/, is a "hard" sound. When we change the adjective to a noun (i.e., *electricity*), we know that the hard sound softens to an /s/. Knowledge of this rule also enables the speaker to pronounce the noun derived from *egocentric,* even if she has never seen or heard that noun before. As this example suggests, both phonetic and phonological knowledge seem to be required for successful speech comprehension and production.

Articulatory Phonetics

The articulatory gestures involved in speech can be divided into two broad classes: those gestures that produce vowel sounds and those that produce consonants. Producing consonants usually involves a constriction of the oral cavity, which is generally accompanied by movement of the tongue. Vowel sounds are considerably more open and static; little movement is involved during vowel production. Speech proceeds by the production of syllables, which are constructed by embedding a vowel sound or sounds within a string of consonants (Clark & Clark, 1977). During the initial part of the syllable's production, movement and constriction of the vocal cavity occur. In the

TABLE 10.1

Phonetic Symbols

Consonants				Vowels		Diphthongs	
p	*p*ill	θ	*th*igh	i	b*ee*t	ay	b*i*te
b	*b*ill	ð	*th*y	ɪ	b*i*t	æw	*a*b*ou*t
m	*m*ill	š	*sh*allow	e	b*ai*t	ɔy	b*oy*
t	*t*ill	ž	mea*s*ure	ɛ	b*e*t		
d	*d*ill	č	*ch*ip	æ	b*a*t		
n	*n*il	ǰ	*g*yp	u	b*oo*t		
k	*k*ill	l	*l*ip	∪	p*u*t		
g	*g*ill	r	*r*ip	Λ	b*u*t		
ŋ	si*ng*	y	*y*et	o	b*oa*t		
f	*f*ill	w	*w*et	ɔ	b*ou*ght		
v	*v*at	ʍ	*wh*et	a	p*o*t		
s	*s*ip	h	*h*at	ə	sof*a*		
z	*z*ip			ɨ	marr*y*		

Source: Clark and Clark, 1977.

middle of the syllable's production is a short period during which the vowel is sounded; this sound is heard as a "constant" sound. Finally, in the last part of the syllable, the ending consonantal sound is produced, again with movement and constriction. Given that the consonants apparently include information about the sounds to come, the pronunciation of the consonant must somehow change to reflect the identity of the upcoming vowel. This process is vividly expressed in the following passage:

Consonants are pronounced as the tongue and mouth move from the vowel of one syllable to the vowel of the next. The consonants hang off one or both sides of each vowel, so to speak, and depend for their very existence on the pronunciation of the vowel. (Clark & Clark, 1977, p. 180)

Consonants can differ in three ways. First, the **place of articulation** describes which part on the mouth is constricted to produce the consonant. In the English language, this constriction can take place at any of seven points, as shown in Table 10.2. Notice that the table shows constriction points from the front of the mouth to the back; the constriction can occur at various places from the lips to the throat.

Consonants can also differ in their **manner of articulation**—the way in which the constriction is produced. On this basis, consonants can be classified into one of six categories: *stops, fricatives, affricatives, nasals, laterals,* and *semivowels.* Stops are formed by completely closing the vocal cavity at the point of articulation. For example, producing /b/ involves a brief but complete closure of the lips, followed by a release of the pressure that has built up during the closure. Fricatives are the result of less complete closures. For example, in producing the consonant /s/, you're probably aware that the tongue is touching but is not completely pressed against the alveolar ridge. Affricatives are produced in two steps, involving both a complete closure and a fricativelike turbulence. Affricatives, such as /j/ as in *judge* are combinations of stops and fricatives. Nasals, naturally enough, involve the nose. For example, in producing /m/, the tongue is pushed up against the soft palate, closing it. The air is then expelled through the nose. Shutting the nose makes it impossible to produce nasals accurately (if you don't believe me, try humming something while you have a cold). The lateral /l/ is produced by flattening the tongue and letting the air flow around its sides.

TABLE 10.2   The Seven Places of Articulation

---

1. The two lips together (called *bilabial)*
2. The bottom lip against the upper front teeth *(labiodental)*
3. The tongue against the teeth *(dental)*
4. The tongue against the alveolar ridge of the gums just behind the upper front teeth *(alveolar)*
5. The tongue against the hard palate in the roof of the mouth just behind the alveolar ridge *(palatal)*
6. The tongue against the soft palate, or velum, in the rear roof of the mouth *(velar)*
7. The glottis in the throat *(glottal)*

Source: Clark and Clark, 1977.

In contrast, the semivowels involve folding the tongue in the middle and letting the air flow through it. If you contrast the pronunciation of /l/ with /r/, you'll feel how the shape of the tongue (rather than its placement, which is the same in both cases) contributes to the difference in perceived sound.

One other way of distinguishing consonants is based on the degree of **voicing** present. Voiced consonants are accompanied by vibration of the vocal cords; voiceless consonants are not (recall that we briefly examined this distinction in Chapter 8). In the English language, voicing is the only way that some pairs of consonants, such as /d/–/t/, can be distinguished. Table 10.3 shows a classification of the phonetic symbols that denote the English consonants.

The information in Table 10.3 can tell us a lot about speech perception. If, for example, a speech pathologist asked a client to say "cake" and the client's production sounded something like "take," he could readily interpret the client's difficulties. Table 10.3 shows that /k/ is a velar, voiceless stop, and /t/ is an alveolar, voiceless stop. In other words, the child who says "take" for "cake" is "fronting" a "back" consonant, suggesting a breakdown in the articulatory program, which is shown in a front-back confusion.

Unlike consonants, which are produced by altering the nature and degree of constriction, vowels are regulated by curvature of the tongue. This curvature can vary in two ways. First, the degree of tongue curvature is referred to as its height in the mouth. Tongue placement can be high (as in *bit*), middle level (as in *bet*), or low level (as in *bat*). Second, the part of the tongue that is held highest can also vary. For example, the pronunciation of *bit* requires that the front of the tongue be held highest. In the pronunciation of /i/ as in *marry,* the middle of the tongue is held highest. Finally, in the pronunciation of some vowels such as the /u/ in *boot,* the back of the tongue is highest. The results of this two-way classification of vowels are seen in Table 10.4.

If you pronounce the word *sofa* and pay attention to your tongue movements, you'll probably become aware that little muscular movement seems

TABLE 10.3

A Classification of Consonants

	Bilabial	Labiodental	Dental	Alveolar	Palatal	Velar	Glottal
Stops	p b			t d		k g	
Fricatives		f v	θ ð	s z	š ž		h
Affricates					č ǰ		
Nasals	m			n		ŋ	
Lateral				l			
Semivowels	w			r	y		

Source: Clark and Clark, 1977.
Note: Symbols on the left side of each column are voiceless. Those on the right side are voiced.

to be required to produce the second vowel sound. Indeed, the /ə/ sound, called the *schwa,* never appears in accented syllables, almost as if it can't be pronounced with stress. This phenomenon tells us something about the relationship of tongue movements and accents within a word. Some amount of muscular tension is apparently required if the syllable contains an accented vowel. That is, the muscles involved must pull the tongue away from its central position (see Table 10.4) if the syllable is to be stressed. Without such muscular tension, the tongue returns to its unstressed position, which is used to produce the schwa. If the stops are the most consonantal of the consonants, then the schwa is the most vowel-like of the vowels.

Distinctive Features in Speech

For almost the past forty years, linguists have maintained that the *organization* of speech sounds is what enables us to distinguish them from one another. According to this view, the articulatory gestures form the basis for a number of characteristics called **distinctive features,** some of which can be used to distinguish phonemic segments from one another. Some of these features are closely related to the articulatory gestures we've examined. For example, one of the features is voicing. If a consonant is voiced, it is indicated this way [+voice]. If the consonant is unvoiced, it is designated with a minus sign in the brackets: [−voice]. Rather than thinking of the phoneme as an articulatory gesture or acoustic energy, we may grasp the problem of speech perception by thinking of phonemes as bundles of features.

If you produce a speech sound and your vocal cords vibrate in the production of that sound, then this vibration will produce a change in the acoustic energy coming out of your mouth. Apparently, we have certain cognitive processes that are tuned in to detect whatever has changed about the acoustic code. If the vocal cords are vibrating, then the cognitive processes tuned to speech note a [+voice] feature on that particular segment of sound. The features are based on articulatory and acoustic aspects of speech sounds, but they are psychological categories nevertheless because they are detected and assigned by cognitive processes. Each phoneme is distinctive because it has a unique pattern of distinctive features.

TABLE 10.4

Two-Way Classification of English Vowels

Height of Tongue	Part of the Tongue Involved		
	Front	Central	Back
High	i beet	ɨ marry	u boot
	ɪ bit		ʊ put
Mid	e bait	ə sofa	o boat
	ɛ bet		ɔ bought
Low	æ bat	ʌ but	a pot

Source: Clark and Clark, 1977.

Chomsky and Halle (1968) performed such an analysis of English speech sounds. They argued that all consonants and vowels can be categorized using thirteen distinctive features. This categorization is shown in Table 10.5. Some of the distinctive features require explanation. All true consonants are [+ consonantal] and [− vocalic]; just as all true vowels are the opposite. However, the liquids /l/ and /r/ have properties of both consonants and vowels, making them somewhat ambiguous. Similarly ambiguous are the semivowels /y/ and /w/, which don't have the properties of either consonants or vowels. The anterior feature results when the phoneme is made at the front of the mouth ([+ anterior]) or elsewhere ([− anterior]). Similarly, if the phoneme is produced in the top center of the mouth, it is designated [+ coronal]. If a feature is [+ continuant], it is produced with a continuous sound. For example, all the fricatives are [+ continuant]. Phonemes without this quality are marked [− continuant]. Stridency is based on the buzzing quality associated with some phonemes. For example, the vibrations associated with a fricative such as /f/ are apparent; this phoneme is also marked [+ strident]. We've already discussed voicing, and nasality is self-descriptive.

The features consonantal and vocalic reappear to distinguish the vowels. The other elements of the cardinal vowel diagram shown in Table 10.4 also reappear in somewhat altered form. The height feature has been broken down into two opposed features: high and low. For example, the phoneme /i/ (the vowel sound in *beet*) is marked [+ high] and [− low]. The other dimension from Table 10.4 was the front-back distinction, which reappears in Table 10.5 as the features back and round. For example, the vowel /u/, as in *boot* involves the back of the tongue and is designated in the chart as [+ back]. The final feature is tension. Tension is difficult to get a subjective feeling for, but it is related to the amount of muscular effort that is needed to produce the vowel. One of the last vowel sounds to emerge as children acquire speech is /ɨ/, apparently because of the movement involved. Predictably, this vowel is marked [+ tense], while a lax vowel such as the schwa is marked [− tense].

Table 10.5 can tell us a lot about the nature of speech perception. Notice that most of the phonemes have more than one feature distinguishing them. For example, /b/ and /t/ are phonetically distinguishable by their place of articulation. According to Table 10.5, this difference translates into a difference of two distinctive features. That is, /b/ is [− coronal], and /t/ is [+ coronal]. Also, /b/ is [+ voice], and /t/ is [− voice]. This may raise a question in your mind. Why are /b/ and /t/ different in two dimensions, when technically, a difference on just one dimension should be enough to tell one sound from another? The answer is that some redundancy appears to be built into the speech recognition system. That is, in a sense, we're giving our speech recognizers two chances to make the discrimination between /b/ and /t/. If these recognizers miss the coronal difference, recognition will still be accurate as long as they catch the voicing difference between the two sounds. This also implies that the acoustic information in speech must be fairly subtle. If the features were more perceptible, we probably wouldn't see so much redundancy built into Table 10.5. This fact has some other implications for speech recognition, too. If Table 10.5 is an accurate depiction of speech

TABLE 10.5

The Distinctive Features of Consonants and Vowels

Consonants and Liquids																				
Distinctive Feature	p	b	t	d	č	ǰ	k	g	f	v	θ	ð	s	z	š	ž	r	l	m	n	ŋ
Consonantal	+	+	+	+	+	+	+	+	+	+	+	+	+	+	+	+	+	+	+	+	+
Vocalic	−	−	−	−	−	−	−	−	−	−	−	−	−	−	−	−	+	+	−	−	−
Anterior	+	+	+	+	−	−	−	−	+	+	+	+	+	+	−	−	−	+	+	+	−
Coronal	−	−	+	+	+	+	−	−	−	−	+	+	+	+	+	+	+	+	−	+	−
Voice	−	+	−	+	−	+	−	+	−	+	−	+	−	+	−	+	+	+	+	+	+
Nasal	−	−	−	−	−	−	−	−	−	−	−	−	−	−	−	−	−	−	+	+	+
Strident	−	−	−	−	+	+	−	−	+	+	−	−	+	+	+	+	−	−	−	−	−
Continuant	−	−	−	−	−	−	−	−	+	+	+	+	+	+	+	+	+	+	−	−	−

Vowels and Glides																
Distinctive Feature	i	ɪ	e	ɛ	æ	i	ə	ʌ	a	u	∪	o	ɔ	y	w	h
Vocalic	+	+	+	+	+	+	+	+	+	+	+	+	+	−	−	−
Consonantal	−	−	−	−	−	−	−	−	−	−	−	−	−	−	−	−
High	+	+	−	−	−	+	−	−	−	+	+	−	−	+	+	−
Back	−	−	−	−	−	+	+	+	+	+	+	+	+	−	+	−
Low	−	−	−	−	+	−	−	+	+	−	−	−	+	−	−	+
Round	−	−	−	−	−	−	−	−	−	+	+	+	+	−	+	−
Tense	+	−	+	−	+	−	−	−	+	+	−	+	−	−	−	−

Source: Clark and Clark, 1977.

features, we would expect that if subjects misperceive speech sounds, their confusions should be between sounds that have only one distinguishing feature between them. The following section examines a well-known study that addresses this matter.

Comprehension of Isolated Speech Sounds

Miller and Nicely (1955) have answered many of the basic questions about comprehension and confusion of speech sounds. Their five subjects listened to a series of sixteen consonants, each of which was followed by the vowel /a/, the vowel sound in *pot*. In many of the cases, the sound was masked by white noise. The loudness of the white noise was held constant throughout the study, but the loudness of the speech signal was varied. Seven levels of speech loudness were used, ranging from one-twelfth as loud as the white noise (− 18 decibels when expressed as a signal-to-noise ratio) to twelve times louder than the white noise (or + 18 decibels). The subjects' task was to correctly identify the consonant. Their dedication brings tears to the eyes of all but the most hardened researchers: Miller and Nicely asked their subjects to make almost seventy thousand consonant identifications over a period of several months.

In their original form, the findings were difficult to summarize, but this task has been eased by Shepard (1972), who developed the tableau shown in Figure 10.1.

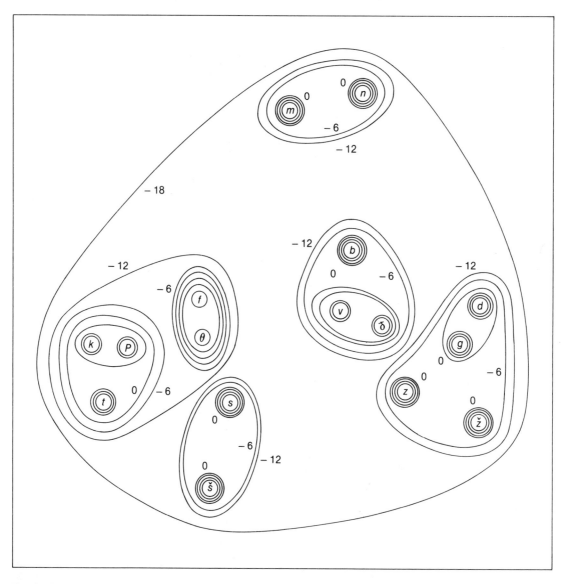

Figure 10.1.

Sixteen consonants. Representations of the affect of signal-to-noise ratio on confusions among Miller and Nicely's sixteen consonants. (From R. N. Shepard, "Psychological Representation of Speech Sounds." In *Human Communication, A Unified View*, E. E. David, P. B. Denes (eds). © 1972 by McGraw-Hill.)

The array in Figure 10.1 might seem bewildering at first, but its interpretation is quite straightforward. Consonants that are depicted as physically close together are more likely to be confused for one another than are consonants that are shown with distance between them. For example, /k/ was very likely to be confused with /p/. The lines around the consonants show the intensity at which the speech signal had to be transmitted before the consonant in question could be correctly identified. Each contour line is labeled numerically, with the negative numbers showing greater intensity of the masking noise relative to the speech signal. When the speech signal was only one-twelfth as loud as the masking noise (−18 decibels), all the consonants were confused with one another. Consequently, the line labeled "−18" encircles all the consonants in the display. However, when the intensity of the speech signal was boosted up to −12 decibels, certain clusters of consonants could be distinguished from one another. For example, the cluster /s/š/ could now be distinguished from the adjacent cluster /f/θ/k/ p/t/. Looking within this latter cluster, when the speech signal's intensity was again boosted up, this time to −6 decibels, a further descrimination could then be made. The consonants /k/p/t/ could be distinguished from /f/θ/.

Analyzing the contour lines in this way produces the following clusters of confusion:

m–n   f–θ   v–ð   p–t–k   d–g   s–š   z–ž

That is, these groups required that the speech signal be boosted up to at least the same intensity as the noise (0 decibels) before the elements of the group could be discriminated from one another. Referring to Table 10.5, you can verify that considered pairwise, the members of these groups do tend to differ from one another on only one distinctive feature.

The Need for a Phonological Level

Students sometimes wonder why knowing about phonology is important to understanding speech perception. After all, they reason, don't the findings of Miller and Nicely tell us what features of speech are attended to, encoded, and used as the basis of perception? The answer to this question is yes and no.

Miller and Nicely's work points out that the articulatory features as conceived by phoneticians would probably be inadequate to enable speech perception by themselves. Rather, the speech signal seems to contain more information than those voicing and articulation features shown in Table 10.3. Instead, Miller and Nicely have suggested that something like five channels of speech perception pick up as many as thirteen different kinds of binary-opposed features as suggested by Chomsky and Halle (1968).

This view is not without its problems, however. First, Miller and Nicely's work clearly implies that the speech signal must have something invariant across a variety of situations, or we would never be able to comprehend speech. That is, they claim that speech must have some invariant acoustic features, which are capable of being detected by some type of feature analyzers. However, when the acoustic information in the speech signal is analyzed, numerous situations exist in which people perceive different sounds in acoustic events that are identical (Liberman, Cooper, and Shankweiler, & Studdert-Kennedy, 1967). Other research has also suggested that consonant perception must be strongly vowel driven. Blumstein, Tartter, Nigro, and Statlender (1984) artificially enhanced some of the acoustic information in a series of stopped consonants. Next, these consonants were synthesized on a computer and played for subjects. If the subjects are using acoustic information to perceive speech, such enhanced consonants should be easier to detect than they are in natural speech. This hypothesis was not supported, however. Neither normal individuals nor aphasics found the lengthened consonants any easier to recognize.

Generally speaking, the search for "context-independent" features in speech perception has not met with much success (Remez, 1979; 1980). What's the alternative? One way of approaching the problem of relativity in speech sounds is to look for what are called "context-dependent" features (Pisoni, 1978). These are not invariant features that permit immediate recognition in all situations for all speakers. Instead, they are features whose acoustic coding changes depending on the phonetic context in which the sounds appear. According to this view, speech perception proceeds by mapping the acoustic code onto some abstract set of rules flexible enough to adjust for the contextual influences that have distorted the speech sounds away from some idealized pronunciation.

Linguists have argued that these rules are phonological in nature. Phonological rules are based on the notion of distinctive features, but here this term is used somewhat differently from the way I've used it so far. For the phonologist, a sound is made up of distinctive features—features whose presence is *not predictable from the other features in the immediate vicinity.*

For example, consider the word *spin*. It has four phonetic segments, corresponding to each of its letters. Referring to Table 10.5, we can see that looking up each segment's list of features is easy. This has been done in Table 10.6, which also shows the phonological representation for *spin*.

Notice that the phonological representation doesn't have many features; indeed, the initial segment /s/ has only one: [+consonantal]. How can the presence of just one feature enable someone to identify the speech sound in question? The answer lies in the two-consonant rule: Whenever a phonetic segment is detected that is [+consonantal] and it's followed by a segment that is [+consonantal] and [−vocalic], then the first segment must also be marked [−vocalic], [+anterior], [+coronal], [−voice], [+continuant], [−nasal], and [+strident]. If you refer to Table 10.5, you will see that this is exactly the set of features that specifies the phonetic segment /s/. If this explanation seems too abstract, the two-consonant rule has a down-to-earth alternative phrasing: If an English word begins with two true consonants (i.e., [+consonantal] and [−vocalic]), then the first one must be an /s/. When I first came across this rule, I was astonished by its implications. That is, this rule seemingly exerts an overly powerful constraint on the variety of phonetic combinations that can be legitimate words in English. I thought

TABLE 10.6

The Phonetic Representation of *Spin* and Its Underlying Phonological Representation

	S	P	I	N
Underlying phonological representation	[+ Consonantal]	⎡ + Anterior − Coronal − Continuant − Strident ⎤	⎡ + High − Back − Low − Tense ⎤	⎡ + Anterior + Coronal + Nasal ⎤
Final phonetic representation	⎡ − Vocalic + Consonantal + Anterior + Coronal − Voice + Continuant − Nasal + Strident ⎤	⎡ − Vocalic + Consonantal + Anterior − Coronal − Voice − Continuant − Nasal − Strident ⎤	⎡ + Vocalic − Consonantal + High − Back − Low − Round − Tense ⎤	⎡ − Vocalic + Consonantal + Anterior + Coronal + Voice − Continuant + Nasal − Strident ⎤

Source: Clark and Clark, 1977.

some exception must exist—but it doesn't. Try it yourself. Take any true consonant from Table 10.5 and imagine it in the second position of some to-be-generated word. Then, given that situation, try to come up with a word that has anything other than an /s/ in the initial position.

Phonological rules are to speech perception and production what syntactic rules are to sentence comprehension and generation. Just as syntactic knowledge enables us to know what sequences of words are legitimate in our language, phonology enables us to judge which sequences of sounds are legitimate words. From an empirical standpoint, it's easy to see how the existence of such phonological rules aids speech perception. For example, the two-consonant rule means that if a word begins with two consonants, the features analyzers have to pick up only one feature from the initial consonant, [+consonantal], to identify it as an /s/. This means that the acoustic signal need not specify all the features of the sound in question. We can rely on our prestored knowledge of phonology to fill in information missing or undetected from the stream of speech.

Stages of Speech Perception: From the Bottom Up

Let's review some of the elements that appear to be required in any theory of isolated speech sounds before we go on to examine the perception of continuous speech.

Speech perception seems to take place in a series of independent stages (Pisoni, 1978), each of which modifies and elaborates the code produced by the preceding stage. How much of this processing is sequential and how much is done in parallel has been a topic of controversy (Pisoni & Sawusch, 1975). However, a reasonable consensus seems to exist about the basic components involved.

1. **Auditory stage.** At the auditory stage, the acoustic signal is converted into a neurological representation that preserves various features of the physical signal. For example, feature analysis at the auditory stage is presumed to encode the sound's fundamental frequency, as well as some details of its harmonic structure. In addition, in the auditory stage, a code representing the signal's overall intensity and duration is produced. This code is presumed to be stored in some form of sensory storage, and for this reason, the code at the auditory stage is sometimes called "raw." At this point, no phonetic or phonological information has been extracted from the signal.

2. **Phonetic stage.** The main purpose of the phonetic stage is to name the speech sounds correctly, that is, to assign phonetic labels to the speech signal that are congruent with the speaker's intentions. Here, the listener faces a major difficulty known as the segmentation problem, which was alluded to in an earlier section of this chapter. The segmentation problem can be stated this way: Because speech resembles a warbling siren, with hardly any pauses, how is the listener supposed to know where to put the boundaries around phonetic segments to identify them? Fortunately for us, speech is constructed by syllables. This means that the influences that vowels have on the production of consonants will probably be most often limited to a range of one syllable. The implication is that some perceptual mechanism must be set, or tuned, to look for patterns of alternating constriction and openness, which are then categorically boxed into syllables whose phonetic names are subsequently determined.

3. **Phonological stage.** At the phonological stage, the phonetic segments that have just been identified are mapped onto underlying (more abstract) phonological rules that extract the true essence from the phonetic segment. This true essence refers to information about the phoneme that permits its other features to be computed from knowledge of phonological rules. As we saw, for example, knowledge of the two-consonant rule enables a person to compute the identity of the first consonant in a two-consonant sequence. Thus, if /s/ happened to be misidentified as /š/ in the phonetic stage, then cognitive processes in the phonological stage would correct this error if the next segment identified was another true consonant.

Phonological rules are inevitably language specific, meaning that the rules of English can be used only to discriminate sounds that make a difference in meaning in English. to understand this point, say *pit* out loud, and pay attention to the /p/ as you do so. Next, contrast the /p/ of pit with the /p/ in *spit*. What's the difference? You were probably aware that the /p/ in *pit* is accompanied by a little puff of built-up air, but the /p/ in *spit* wasn't pronounced that way. Linguists refer to the first /p/ as *aspirated* and the ond one as *nonaspirated*. The different /p/ sounds in these two cases are said to be *allophones* of each other. Allophones are variations in pronunciation that don't signal any difference in meaning. *Pit* is still *pit*, regardless of how much air pressure you happen to build up during its pronunciation. Since we don't use aspiration to signal any difference in meaning, phonological rules in English don't have anything to say about aspiration. But in other languages, aspiration signals a difference in meaning. For example, in Thai, /pʰaa/ (aspirated) means "split," whereas /pºaa/ (nonaspirated) means "forest." Allophonic variations are resolved at the phonological stage. For a speaker of English, during the phonological stage, both /pʰ/ and /pº/ are mapped onto the same underlying phonological segment, /p/, before any further /p/ rules are applied. However, in Thai, this difference is preserved because some phonological rules presumably apply only to the aspirated or nonaspirated /p/.

Perception of Continuous Speech: From the Top Down

The discussion of speech perception so far has focused on those elements of speech that must be extracted more or less directly from the speech signal. However, even if all the bottom-up mechanisms go awry, we can still use larger units of speech to help us comprehend the message. For example, if you hear someone say,

"She did really well on the test—in fact, she got the highest grade in the whole ————,"

you know the missing word is "class," or "section," or something to that effect. Even before the last word occurs, you can predict what it's going to be. The sentence is so redundant that much of the speech signal can be left unprocessed without much loss in meaning. It's not clear what proportion of the speech signal is typically processed this way, but Pollack and Pickett (1964) have produced some surprising findings. They covertly recorded people in spontaneous conversations. The participants gave no indication that they misunderstood one another; the replies to questions, jokes, and so on were all appropriate to the situation. Pollack and Pickett then cut the tapes to make recordings of isolated words. The tapes were played for the subjects, who were asked to identify the word. The subjects were successful on 47 percent of the trials—a fairly low percentage. Pollack and Pickett then asked an interesting question: How much context is necessary for a listener to accurately identify a word? As they added larger and larger segments of the original tape to the single words, they found that identification accuracy slowly improved until a certain critical point was reached. At this critical point, accuracy dramatically improved. The self-reports of the subjects were congruent with these findings. The word seemed more or less unintelligible until "all of a sudden" it seemed perfectly clear.

Other research (Sitler, Schiavetti, & Metz, 1983) has clarified the role of context in speech perception. Sitler and his colleagues had twenty hearing-impaired speakers pronounce isolated words and the same words in sentences. Recordings of these pronunciations were then played for one hundred normal-hearing subjects, whose task was to write down what they understood of the words and sentences. As expected, the subjects performed better when they heard sentences rather than isolated words. However, this effect was limited to speech produced by the more skilled among the hearing-impaired speakers. When the words were produced by poorer speakers, the subjects did no better in the sentence condition than they did in the isolated word condition. This result indicates that it is not simply more sound per se that enables a person to comprehend continuous speech better than isolated words. To establish a meaningful context, the acoustic signal cannot vary outside some—presumably wide—boundaries.

A phenomenon that's related to these findings is called the **phonemic restoration effect** (Obusek & Warren, 1973; Warren, 1970; Warren & Obsek, 1971; Warren & Warren, 1970). In the original study, Warren represented twenty subjects with a tape on which the following sentence had been recorded:

The state governors met with their respective legi*latures convening in the capital city.

The asterisk marks the point where .12 seconds were chopped out of the original speaker's utterance and the recording of a cough substituted in its place. Warren asked his subjects if they detected any sounds missing from the recording. Nineteen of the subjects said no, and the remaining subject misidentified the expunged sound. The subjects did detect the presence of the cough, but they were unable to locate it correctly. Later studies found that a substantial part of a word could be removed without destroying the illusion. In addition, Warren found that a tone or a buzz could be substituted for the /s/ without subjects noticing that any sounds were missing. However, subjects were quick to detect a silence, and they were also accurate in reporting its placement. This finding tells us something about the nature of the illusion. The subjects perceived the sentence as coexisting alongside some extraneous nonspeech sound. Only when the chopped-out sound was not replaced with something else did subjects realize that a gap had occurred in the speech signal.

Analysis by Synthesis: Interaction of Top-Down and Bottom-Up Processing

We've covered a great deal of terrain in the last several pages. Let's catch our breaths before winding up the story on speech perception. We've seen that the stream of speech is an extremely ambiguous signal. This stream offers some acoustic information that is quickly analyzed and categorized into its configuration of features. Probably at the same time these bottom-up cognitive processes are at work, top-down processes commence their operation, helping the individual infer, or fill in, missing or undetected speech information. These ideas have been lucidly expressed by Liberman:

Some of the distinctive features that specify each phonetic segment probably can be determined from the available acoustic signal. Other distinctive features cannot be uniquely identified. The listener therefore forms a hypothesis concerning the probable phonetic content of the message that is consistent with the known features.

However, he cannot test this hypothesis for its syntactic and semantic consistency until he gets a fairly long segment of speech into his temporary processing space. The speech signal therefore remains unintelligible until the listener can successfuly test a hypothesis. When a hypothesis is confirmed, the signal abruptly become intelligible. The acoustic signal is, of course, necessary to provide even a partial specification of the phonetic signal. However, these experiments [Pollack & Pickett, 1964] indicate that in many instances the phonetic signal that the listener "hears" is internally computed. (Liberman, 1967, p. 165)

This passage implies that speech is analyzed by first synthesizing (hypothesizing) a guess about the utterance's meaning. This synthesis is based on information extracted from the acoustic events and context-based inferences made by the perceiver. Almost all existing theories of speech perception are based on a version of this **analysis by synthesis model** originally proposed by Halle and Stevens (1964). The essential idea of analysis by synthesis is that the bottom-up processes that act on the acoustic signal cannot do the whole job of speech perception by themselves. Based on an analysis of the context in which the incompletely specified speech signal occurs, the person internally computes (synthesizes) a likely candidate for the missing phonetic segment. The missing segment thus generated will next be checked to make sure that it conforms to phonological, syntactic, and semantic rules. For example, a popular song a few years ago began with

"Is this the train to Desert Moon? . . ."

Since I couldn't distinguish all the words, I thought the singer was saying:

"Is this the train that doesn't move? . . ."

Notice that my hypothesis about the final phonetic sequence conforms to phonetic, phonological, and syntactic rules. Moreover, my version preserves the prosody (accent and rhythm) of the original. Of course, some people would say that my version is semantically aberrant. But the first time I heard this song, I thought that the idea of someone seeking an immovable method of transportation was genuinely profound. I guess it's a good thing that nobody pays me to write popular songs.

As we've seen, the analysis by synthesis model is a way of summarizing the interaction of two different pathways to pattern recognition. Because the acoustic events are so complex, the human perceiver must rely on some top-down, or inferential, processing. On the other hand, the top-down processes must have something—however ambiguous—to work with. At this point, the bottom-up processes come into play.

PRODUCTION OF SPEECH

Generally, researchers have inferred the processes involved in the construction of utterances by observing two classes of phenomena: latencies in speaking and errors in speaking. We'll consider some of the findings produced by each class of events.

Analysis of Speech Errors

Fromkin (1971) has conducted an extensive analysis of speech errors. First, she noted that the elements of speech that are moved or substituted in errors almost always correspond to the terms linguists use to refer to parts of speech. That is, the elements that move around or are deleted in a speech error can be described as verbs, nouns, bound morphemes, and so on. Moreover, she determined that substitution errors are almost always for like linguistic terms, meaning that verbs are substituted for verbs, nouns for nouns, and so on. This preliminary finding tells us something about the cognitive processes that produce speech. It indicates that some set of processes must deal with a code that is organized in these linguistic terms.

Fromkin noted other revealing aspects of speech errors. Consider the following movement error:

1. bloody students → bloodent stewdies

The movement error is so named for obvious reasons: The second syllables of each word have been shifted to the other word. As noted in Chapter 1, this error seems to indicate that a set of cognitive processes must assemble words on a syllable-by-syllable basis. But that's not all. In *students* the final phoneme is /s/. Notice that the movement error results in a pronunciation change; the final phoneme in *stewdies* is now /z/. What might this mean? The sound of the plural marker is determined by phonological rules; indeed, only three phonological rules account for the pronunciation of all "add /s/" plurals in English. The actual pronunciation of the /s/ is, however, determined phonetically. The fact that the sound of the plural marker was altered indicates that the phonetic rules apparently accomodate themselves to the dictates of the phonological rules. The speech production code must have passed through a phonological stage prior to its entry into a phonetic stage, where the pronunciation of the plural marker was actually shaped. When I talked about speech perception from the bottom up, I said that the output of the phonetic analysis was the input for the phonological analysis. In this discussion of speech production, we've seen a preliminary indication that the stages of processing take place in exactly the opposite order.

Garrett (1982) has extended Fromkin's analysis of speech errors, breaking down movement errors into two subcategories: *exchanges* and *shifts*. Let's take a look at three completed exchange errors:

2. Why was that *horn* blowing its *train?*
3. She *writes* her *slant*ing.
4. No . . . it's . . . Bria*th* Ke*en*.

In example 4, the name of actor Brian Keith was the intended utterance. What inferences can be drawn from errors such as these? As you've noticed, some of the exchanges involve words (as in example 2), and others involve sounds (as in example 4). Generally, word exchanges travel greater distances, measured in syllables, than do sound exchanges. Also, completed exchanges involving words are likely to be across phrasal boundaries, but sound exchanges are much more likely to be within-phrase mix-ups. Finally, word exchanges tend to be swaps for similar parts of speech, but sound exchanges show no such respect for phrasal role.

Exchanges can be contrasted with another type of movement error called shifts. In this type of error, a single element of an intended utterance is mislocated, and an unfilled linguistic hole in the utterance results (Garrett, 1982). The mislocated elements are usually words or bound morphemes, which are basic units of meaning whose appearance is always tied to some other morpheme. The suffix *ly* is an example of a bound morpheme. The following are some examples of shift errors:

5. I had forgot* about*ten* that. (forgotten about)
6. It probably get* out*s* a little. (gets out)

Notice that the elements of the exchange errors are missing here. There is no swapping to be explained in linguistic terms, and the movement cannot be described in purely phrasal terms. One thing is curious: Shifts represent the only type of speech errors in which stresses (i.e., accents) move *with* their intended markers rather than stay in the place in which they would have appeared in an error-free production (Cutler, 1980). For example, if example 5 had been uttered without an error, the stress would have appeared right before the past participle marker, **en,** on the syllable *got.* However, in example 5, the stress moves with the shift, now appearing in the second syllable of *about.* Here, it looks as though the cognitive processes that assign stress to the syllables accommodate themselves to the location of certain markers. This suggests that the assignment of accents and stress must occur in one of the later stages of speech production.

We'll consider one other type of striking speech error. Some types of errors can be called *intrusions*. In these cases, the person produces a syntactically well-formed utterance but one in which an apparently unintended word intrudes. Consider the following examples (Garrett, 1982):

7. If any of you cats are gonna be in Las Vegas in the *recent* . . . in the near future, and . . .
8. It's a far cry from the twenty-five *dollar* days. (cent)
9. You look all set for an *exhibition*. (expedition)
10. He was carrying on about *optical* binary search. (optimal)

What have you noticed about these errors? If you look at examples 7 and 8, you'll see that the intrusion is semantically related to the intended word, but it has no phonetic relationship to the intended word. On the other hand, in examples 9 and 10, the intrusion resembles the target word phonetically, but no semantic relationship exists between the two. Intrusion errors are almost always one of these two types; the confusion is hardly ever both phonetic and semantic. The almost absolute independence of these errors suggests that we cannot apply our typical strategy of accommodation to determine which selection process might occur prior to the other. Rather, the appropriate conclusion seems to be that there are apparently two distinct systems for accessing items in our mental dictionaries. Later we'll build a working model in which all of these error effects are summarized, but before we do that, we'll consider the analysis of hesitations in speech.

Analysis of Hesitations and Pauses

The analysis of errors indicates that the process of speech production involves a number of stages, some of which seem to occur sequentially. This implies a layered view of speech production, in which the output of some stage of speech production results in a code that is passed onto the next stage in the sequence and so on, until the code is finally articulated and emitted. But, the cognitive processes that go first can't wait until the utterance is produced; speech would proceed slowly if they did. Rather, they must begin working on the next part of the speech stream, much like the workers on a car assembly line begin working on the next car after they finish an assembly.

As stated earlier, speech is much like a warbling siren, with few pauses. Although this is true, some pauses must nevertheless occur, however short, at some intervals, however distant from one another. The logical reason for this is implied by the assembly line example. There, the unit of production is the car, meaning that cars—no matter how continuously they are produced—remain distinct from one another. Speech, too, expresses elements that are at least semantically distinct from one another. At some point in the stream of speech, one such element must end before another can begin. Consequently, a sensible approach is to look for increases in latencies as markers for the termination of distinct units in speech.

An analysis of hesitations and latencies in speech was undertaken by Goldman-Eisler (1968). She found that the locations of pauses frequently occurred as grammatically interpretable points, usually at the boundaries of major phrase structures. Other pauses were not so well defined; these might occur within a phrase structure. However, Goldman-Eisler was able to nicely account for these location differences. She had her subject read and overlearn passages, which they then had to recite. The overall number of speech errors was consequently reduced, but more important, those that occurred were almost completely restricted to phrasal boundaries. She reasoned that a combination of phrasal and interphrasal pauses was more indicative of spontaneous, creative speech, and that the location of the pauses, or pausal loci, indicated the points at which various cognitive decisions were being made.

Goldman-Eisler found that pauses were frequently the result of two types of uncertainty: **lexical uncertainty** and *conceptual complexity*. Our lexicon is our vocabulary. Lexical uncertainty refers to pauses that are likely to precede words that are uncommon or unusual in a particular conversational context. The pause seems to imply that some cognitive processes were scouting around for just that particular word, and its relative unavailability produces a slight holdup in the stream of speech. Conceptual complexity is associated with pauses in the encoding phase. During this phase, an abstract, nonlinguistic code is formulated. The complexity of the translation process determines the site and duration of the pause.

In one of Goldman-Eisler's tasks, subjects had to interpret a cartoon: a moderately demanding task. She found that the distribution of latencies in this task showed the influence of conceptual complexity. A series of alterations occurred between hesitant and fluent speech. During the first phase of the production, pauses occur at nonlinguistically definable junctures. This phase of speech is followed by a fluent period, in which the only noticeable pauses are at phrasal boundaries or at points of lexical uncertainty. This seems to indicate that once a thought has been determined, the speech programs continue to run it off with only minor delays at points where unusual items in the lexicon need to be looked up. This also tells us that the larger unit—the thought—doesn't precisely specify the lexical items to be used in that utterance. This deduction can be drawn from the fact that lexical uncertainty still appears even during periods of fluent speech.

A Model of Speech Production

These considerations of error and hesitation patterns have suggested the following model of speech production (Garret, 1982). Speech begins with a *message level* representation. The message level corresponds most clearly to our notion of a thought in everyday terms. It is produced by cognitive processes that go to work on semantic and episodic representations—that is, the message level begins with a nonlinguistic code. At this level, conceptual complexity might induce a pause. Next, cognitive processes are applied to the message level representation to create a language-specific code. Several types of decisions are made here. First, *functional level* structures are created. These are best understood as outlines of an utterance. The specific lexical items have not yet been fitted into these outlines, nor have prosody or phonetic considerations been dealth with. However, the functional level structure does have syntax. Second, the meaning that is to be communicated by specific items in the functional level structure is decided. This does not mean that specific words have been planned—only that certain ideas are to be gotten across.

The creation of a functional level representation entails several additional cognitive processes. First, the next lower level of organization, the *positional level* representation, is outlined. Second, specific lexical forms are now retrieved. Third, these items are assigned to their sites within the phrase. Fourth, the reduction of the lexical items to a phonological code is begun. Exchange errors are committed at the functional level. Also at this stage, pauses that are the result of lexical uncertainties are made.

In the next stage of the process, the positional level structure is analyzed still further into a phonological representation. At this point, shift errors are created. Following the creation of a complete phonological representation, other cognitive processes begin to create the *phonetic level* representation. In the last stage, the phonetic level representation is reduced still further to an *articulatory level* representation. These stages and the processes undertaken in each are depicted in Table 10.7.

Table 10.7 shows a couple of interesting features. First, you may have realized that to a certain extent, the production of speech is like comprehension in reverse. Apparently, material is activated from some propositional format that is not linguistic and then converted to speech in a series of stages: message, functional, positional, phonological, phonetic, and articulatory. The last three stages seem clearly related to speech comprehension. Second, notice that no provisions are made for feedback during the speech production cycle. This is an oversimplification. We're all aware that we sometimes correct ourselves, but exactly how this is accomplished within the formal model is not currently known (Garrett, 1982).

How can we summarize the cognitive processes involved in speech production? First, they appear to operate in more or less the opposite order of the processes involved in speech comprehension. The beginning point of speech production probably involves the activation of elements whose nature is nonlinguistic. My use of the word *activation* is deliberate; the elements

TABLE 10.7

1. Inferential processes applied to conceptual structures build a representation which is the real-time construct that determines sentence level construction.

2. Procedures applied to the Message level representation construct the first language specific level of representation. Three aspects of the process are distinguished: *(a)* determination of functional level structures, *(b)* meaning based lexical identification, and *(c)* assignment of lexical items to functional structures; representation is syntactic.

3. Procedures applied to Functional level representations construct a representation which reflects utterance order directly. Four aspects of the process are distinguished: *(a)* determination of positional level phrasal frames specifying phrasal stress and closed class vocabulary, both bound and free, *(b)* retrieval of lexical forms, *(c)* assignment of phrasal sites, and *(d)* assignment of frame elements to positions in the terminal string of lexically interpreted phrasal frames; representation is phonological.

4. Procedures applied to Positional level representations construct a representation which specifies the phonetic detail consequent upon regular phonological processes.

5. Procedures applied to Phonetic level construct an articulatory representation.

MESSAGE LEVEL REPRESENTATION

Lexical identification	Selection of functional structures

Assignment of lexical items to functional structure roles

FUNCTIONAL LEVEL REPRESENTATION

Retrieval of lexical forms	Selection of positional structures

Assignment of lexical forms to phrasal sites
Assignment of frame elements to the terminal string

POSITIONAL LEVEL REPRESENTATION

Regular phonological processes

PHONETIC LEVEL REPRESENTATION
Phonetic to articulatory coding
ARTICULATORY LEVEL REPRESENTATION

Source: Garrett, 1982. Reprinted by permission of the publisher.

may be stored in a propositional format in permanent memory. Second, the production of speech probably involves both serial and parallel processing. At any given point in time, the speaker will be activating and assembling several different clauses, which involves parallel processing. However, one of the striking conclusions about the production of particular clauses is how serial its construction seems to be. The assembly line analogy is not inappropriate. When we examine another form of language use—reading—we'll see a similar interaction of top-down and bottom-up processes.

READING

In some ways, understanding how people read is easier than understanding how they comprehend speech. First, no real segmentation problem needs to be solved in reading. The words are almost always set off from oneanother,andevenwhentheyaren't,readingisstillnottooterriblydifficult. And at first glance, there doesn't seem to be any parallel transmission of information. That is, the characters we use in reading don't seem to be influenced by those that have preceded them, nor do they seem to be influenced by those that follow. But these factors shouldn't mislead us: Understanding reading is still problematic. First, the alphabetic characters are far from a complete specification of their phonetic equivalents. Although the written symbol in an alphabetic system such as ours represents a phoneme (Foss & Hakes, 1978), the correspondence between phonetics and alphabetic symbols is not one-to-one. This lack of correspondence has created some difficulties. For example, we cannot analyze the phonological rules acquired by children as they learn to read and spell because, strictly speaking, our alphabet and its spelling rules are not always phonetic.

Another way of expressing this problem is to note that English does not have a one-to-one mapping between graphemes and phonemes (Wood, 1983). A **grapheme** is an alphabetic letter, or combination of such letters, that stands for a single phoneme. The *s* in *stop* and the *ss* in *kisser* are both graphemes. Coltheart (1978) illustrated several of the problems that are created by this lack of correspondence. First, upon hearing a word, no general rules are available for making an accurate graphemic representation. For example, the vowel combinations *oa* and *oe* are both derivable from the same phoneme, as in *boat* and *hoe*. However, these graphemes sometimes do not point to the same phoneme. This is illustrated in the words *boa* and *poem*. The graphemes that previously indicated the same phoneme now point to different phonemes.

Second, even when a series of graphemic units is clearly known, no clearly understood, universal way exists for mapping them onto a phonetic code. For example, in the word *bread*, which can be broken down into the graphemes *b-r-ea-d*, no rule-based way is available to assign *ea* to any phonetic symbol without considering the other graphemes. You can see why this might create problems for the youthful reader. Let's assume for a moment that reading is similar to speech comprehension in that the graphemes must be converted into a phonetic code before they can be processed like speech sounds. If this view of reading is accurate, then children with reading difficulties who are asked to sound out the letters have their work cut out for them. Nobody has written a complete specification of grapheme-to-phoneme mappings, because the task is impossible. Given this problem, an interesting question is produced: How are any of us able to read?

Mechanics of Reading

During reading, our eyes are not in continuous motion over the page. We're capable of such eye movements, but they can be done only when we are tracking a moving object, such as a tennis ball coming our way. But in reading, the eye moves forward in a series of movements called saccades. The *saccade* is a ballistic movement; once launched forward, the eye must come to rest at some point, however briefly, and the movement of the eye cannot be altered in midmovement. During these motions, no information from the page can be gathered. Following the saccade, the reader fixates her eyes at one point on the page. During this fixation, the eyes are relatively motionless, and the work of reading is accomplished at this point. Typically, readers fixate for approximately 200 to 250 msec, and the saccade can be accomplished in about 5 to 10 msec. If you look at the eyes of a skilled reader, you can easily pick up the regular jump-stop-jump-stop rhythm that characterizes that skill.

However, Just and Carpenter (1980) have pointed out that this rhythm can be complicated. One of their basic findings is that people don't spend the same amount of time fixating on each word in a passage. Some words seem to convey more information than others. These words, called content words, will be fixated, but words that connect the content words—the so-called function words—may be skipped. Figure 10.2 shows the time spent in fixations for one of their subjects who was reading a scientific passage.

As Figure 10.2 shows, the subject spent a lot of fixation time on the word *Flywheels*—over 1.5 seconds. Since readers generally average approximately 1.2 words per fixation, we can see here that the subject had slowed down the fixation rate apparently to make sure that this technical term was correctly encoded. Although the saccade is highly overlearned, automatic, procedural knowledge, the skillful reader apparently monitors saccadic rate and alters it, depending upon the material's importance and difficulty.

Occasionally, even the skilled reader will launch a reverse saccade, which is called a regression. The number of regressions is one of the features that distinguishes good from poor readers. Not surprisingly, poor readers are much more likely than good readers to make numerous regressions, and they do so more or less indiscriminately.

However, Just and Carpenter found no difference between good and poor readers in the time required for the saccade; this time seemed to be built into the system. This finding raises another question: Because the reader apparently can gather information only during the fixation, how much information is typically picked up?

McConkie and Rayner (1974; Rayner, 1975) answered this question by using a computer system that adjusted the window of visible text. Subjects wore a contact lens from which a reflection was picked up that indicated the

1	2	3	4	5	6	7	8	9	1
1566	267	400	83	267	617	767	450	450	400

Flywheels are one of the oldest mechanical devices known to man. Every

2	3	5	4	6	7	8	9
616	517	684	250	317	617	1116	367

internal-combustion engine contains a small flywheel that converts the

10	11	12	13	14	15	16	17	18
467	483	450	383	284	383	317	283	533

jerky motion of the pistons into the smooth flow of energy that powers

19	20	21
50	366	566

the drive shaft.

Figure 10.2.

Eye fixations of a college student reading a scientific passage. Gazes for each word are numbered consecutively, and the gaze time (in msec) is indicated below the sequence number.

subject's current fixation point. This information was fed into a computer, which clearly displayed the characters at the fixation point and for a short distance (measured in letters) around the fixation point. But the computer was programmed to mutilate letters beyond a certain range, which was accomplished by subtracting some of each letter's features. Letters outside this window of legibility therefore couldn't be read. As the subject's eyes moved across the computer screen, the machine continually updated this window. For all practical purposes, as soon as the subject's eyes moved to a new fixation point, the text around that new point became legible, and what had been legible became mutilated.

Suppose the size of the window was only one character wide. What would happen to your reading speed in that situation? Under these circumstances, we can confidently predict that your reading speed would drop. Now suppose that we increased the size of the window to three characters. The fixation point and one character on each side are now legible. Your reading speed would pick up. Continuing with this reasoning, if increasing the size of the window continues to produce increases in reading rate, we can then assume that the subjects are picking up the additional information in that fixation. At some point, increases in the size of the window would not be accompanied by increases in reading rate. At that point, we can safely assume that the subject is extracting as many characters as possible from the fixation.

McConkie and Rayner found that the reading rate leveled off when the window of legibility reached about twenty characters—ten on each side of the fixation point. Subsequent research (Rayner, 1978) has determined that because the direction of reading in English is left to right, the reader uses only about four characters to the left of the fixation point. Also, the reader has access to semantic information for only about four of the eleven processed characters to the right of the fixation point.

However, assuming that the reader used all the information in the window, and assuming that a typical word in English has about seven characters, we can compute that the typical fixation would take in about three words. Since we've already seen that a skilled reader's fixations last about 250 msec, we can easily determine that, theoretically, the fastest reading rate a skilled reader can attain is about 720 words per minute (4 fixations per second × 3 words per fixation = 12 words per seond × 60 seconds per minute). Most of us don't read at nearly that rate; 250 to 400 words per minute is closer to the mark. McConkie and Rayner's work tells us that our sensory or biological system is not what holds down reading speed. An analysis of reading mechanics indicates that for adults, much of the shortfall from the theoretical maximum rate must be the result of cognitive factors.

Recoding in Reading

Before we begin our study of the cognitive processes involved in reading, it's important that you understand the competing orientations of the workers in this field. Some cognitive psychologists argue that reading is accomplished by transforming the graphemic code into another, speech-based code, presumably one with acoustic, phonetic, or articulatory properties (Kleiman, 1975). This view is the recoding position, named for obvious reasons. Arrayed against these psychologists are others who believe that reading can be accomplished directly from the graphemic code without any interlingual code. These psychologists hold the direct access position. Cognitive psychologists' theoretical stance on this question will play an important role in how they conceptualize the reading process, because the nature of the stages involved and their relationships are sure to be different.

Settling this question has been troublesome. Whatever the phonetic code might look like, it clearly does not involve recasting the graphemic code into a subvocal response. This can be easily demonstrated. First, if we had to subvocalize to read, reading rate would be limited by vocalization rate. However, most of the time, our speech rate comes nowhere near the 250-word reading rate that most of us can attain (Kolers, 1970). Similarly, an analysis of reaction times indicates that subjects don't have to subvocalize a word to comprehend it. Sabol and DeRosa (1976) have found that people have some semantic knowledge accessed within 200 msec of a word's presentation. Yet, other findings (Cosky, 1975) have demonstrated that more than twice that amount of time (i.e., 525 msec) is required to initiate a vocal response for a three-letter word. Also, if subvocalization were required for reading, people who presumably have no phonological or phonetic knowledge—that is, the congenitally deaf—would be completely unable to read. However, such individuals can learn to read (the learning is laborious, however).

Taken together, these findings suggest that a strict interpretation of the recoding hypothesis is out (Coltheart, 1980). However, some phonological encoding may take place nevertheless. For example, Patterson (1982) makes a distinction between **assembled phonology** and **addressed phonology.** In reading aloud, once a printed word is recognized, its pronunciation can be looked up or addressed. This indicates the existence of a sort of phonological lexicon in which the lexical items are cataloged by pronunciation. Presumably, this same lexicon is used to pronounce words in normal speech. This is addressed, or postlexical, phonology, and this type of phonology apparently does not play much of a role in reading. However, some phonological information may be, if not necessary, at least helpful in achieving word recognition in the first place. This type is assembled, or prelexical, phonology. The existence of an assembled phonological code does not necessarily disprove the direct access hypothesis. But it might help clarify the process of reading by specifying the conditions under which people rely more heavily on the graphemic code and the conditions under which phonological knowledge aids word recognition.

Some findings indicate that assembled phonology sometimes influences reaction times in certain tasks. First, phonemic similarity seems to affect the time required to make a lexical decision (Coltheart, Davelaar, Jonasson, & Besner, 1977; Rubenstein, Lewis, & Rubenstein, 1971). In these studies, subjects were given a string of letters and were asked to determine as quickly as possible whether the string was a word or a nonword (e.g., *fraze)*. When the nonword was homophonic with an actual English word, the subjects required more time to make the decision than they did when the word was not homophonic. Thus, subjects would require more time to decide the fate of a nonword such as *brane* than they would a nonword such as *melp*. The obvious conclusion seems to be that the subjects were slowed by the resemblance of *brane* to *brain*. Although this effect demonstrably involves assembled phonology, it is limited to nonwords. Coltheart (1978, 1980) analyzed the response patterns and concluded that the recognition of real words is carried out on the basis of visual or graphemic information, and is accomplished before the assembled phonology can play a role. Nonwords take longer to recognize as such, which gives the assembled phonology time to influence the cognitive processes involved in the recognition.

Direct Access Hypothesis

Although some phonological coding seems to take place, most researchers believe that phonological recoding plays only a small role in the mature reader's cognitive processes. The alternative is the **direct access hypothesis,** a position whose basic premise is that a semantic code is produced directly from a translation of the graphemic code. What makes this view so plausible?

First, some studies (Green & Shallice, 1976; Klapp, Anderson, and Berian, 1973) have found that semantic decisions about real words are not influenced by phonemic factors. In these studies, a subject was given pairs of words. The first word denoted a category, and the subject's task was to determine if the second word was a legitimate member of that category. For example, in a pair such as SPORT–BASKETBALL, the subject had to respond yes, but in SPORT–PEACH, no was the correct response. The number of syllables in the second word was the variable of interest. Previous research (Eriksen, Pollack, & Montague, 1970) had determined that subjects take longer to begin pronouncing a multisyllable word than they do to pronounce a single syllable word. Given this finding, we would expect that the category verification task would require more time when the subject had to make a lexical decision about a multisyllable word, provided that the subject was recoding the graphemes into a phonological code. But the expected effect was not observed. Subjects responded yes to SPORT–BASKETBALL as quickly as they did to SPORT–GOLF. This finding indicates that the subject apparently did not have to consult the phonological lexicon to derive the word's meaning as required in the task.

Kleiman (1975) arrived at a similar conclusion using a different approach. In this study, a disruption technique was used. It's plausible to assume that speaking an irrelevant message aloud while trying to read something completely different should disrupt any speech recoding. If speech recoding is critical to lexical access and reading, then speaking one thing while reading another should disrupt the reading process as well. Kleiman assessed this reasoning by having his subjects make judgments about pairs of words, which were presented in a tachistoscope. Over the course of the experiment, the subjects were required to make three kinds of judgments, examples of which are shown in Table 10.8.

In one-third of the trials, the subject had to make a graphemic decision for each pair. If the words were spelled the same following the initial letter, the subject was to respond yes, but if they were spelled differently, no was the correct response. On another one-third of the trials, the subject was supposed to make a phonemic decision, saying yes if the words of the pair rhymed and no if they didn't. Finally, on one-third of the trials, the subject was asked to make a semantic decision. Here, the subject was to say yes if the words of the pair meant the same thing and no if they didn't. On half

TABLE 10.8

Stimuli from Kleiman's (1975) Experiment

Type of Decision	True		False		Without Shadowing	Increase with Shadowing
Graphemic	HEARD	BEARD	GRACE	PRICE	970(4.5)	125(0.4)
	NASTY	HASTY	SHADOW	FALLOW		
Phonemic	TICKLE	PICKLE	LEMON	DEMON	1137(8.3)	372(7.7)
	BLAME	FLAME	ROUGH	DOUGH		
Synonymy	MOURN	GRIEVE	BRAVERY	QUANTITY	1118(4.2)	120(3.8)
	INSTANCE	EXAMPLE	DEPART	COUPLE		

Source: Kleiman, 1975. Reprinted by permission of the publisher.
Note: The right columns show mean reaction times (in msec) and percentage of errors (in parentheses).

of the trials, the subject was also asked to shadow a series of digits, with the assumption that this might disrupt the speech recoding necessary for lexical access.

Recall from Chapter 2 that shadowing refers to the immediate recitation of aurally presented material. Of particular interest in the Kleiman study was which types of trials (graphemic, phonemic, or semantic) the shadowing task would disrupt the most. Theoretically, the graphemic trials don't require any lexical access. Consequently, any increase in processing time on the shadowing trials here would presumably be produced by some general processing strain. That is, increases would simply be the result of the increased difficulty of shadowing the digits. The phonemic trials present a different story. Here, speech recoding must clearly be going on, because the subject must access the phonological code to know how the words are pronounced and in order to respond to the trial. We would expect that shadowing digits on these trials would result in a much greater increment in processing time than would be expected on the graphemic trials. The semantic trials are of particular interest. If speech recoding is necessary for lexical access, the shadowing task should produce a large increment in processing time, as would be expected for the phonemic trials. However, if speech recoding were not required for lexical access, the subject should be able to shadow the digits on the semantic trials with only a small increment in processing time. The right-hand side of Table 10.8 shows the results of the study: Shadowing resulted in a 125-msec increase in processing time on the graphemic trials. Shadowing produced a much larger increase—372 msec—on the phonemic trials. On the critical semantic trials, the shadowing increment was 120 msec—almost identical to what it had been for the graphemic trials, which didn't require any lexical access. These results support the direct access position, because the semantic increment was much closer to that seen on the graphemic trials than it was to the increment seen on the phonemic trials. Although these findings have been criticized (Baddely & Lewis, 1981; Besner, Davies, & Daniels, 1981; Patterson, 1982), they remain one of the pillars upon which the direct access hypothesis rests.

Other evidence supporting the direct access position has been produced by Blaxall and Willows (1984), who studied the errors second graders committed during oral reading. This study involved a challenge paradigm in which the child was asked to read passages of continually increasing difficulty. The researchers found that the proportion of graphemic errors (intrusions resulting from similarity in the visual form of the word) increased steadily as the material got more difficult. The increase in this type of error was accompanied by a decrease in the number of syntactically and semantically appropriate errors. At no point in the procedure did the proportion of phonemically induced errors increase. These findings therefore suggest that the second graders were converting the graphemic code directly to a semantic representation. As the material got more challenging, the breakdown apparently occurred in the match-up of the graphemic and semantic codes. The children were apparently willing to forgo a complete lexical lookup when the material was tough, settling instead for a visually based guess at the tough words.

Finally, and perhaps most provocatively, some evidence for the direct access hypothesis comes from the neuropsychological literature. Marshall and Newcombe (1973) have described a phenomenon that has since come to be called **deep dyslexia.** Some individuals who have suffered left hemisphere strokes retain the ability to read silently, but they no longer have the ability to assemble phonology for an unfamiliar letter string (Patterson, 1982). That is, they no longer have the ability to sound out orthographically conventional nonwords (e.g., *tride*). Since these individuals can repeat such nonwords if they hear them first, their problem is not simply articulatory but seems to result from an inability to convert a graphemic code to a phonemic one. For this reason, people with deep dyslexia are said to be "reading without phonology" (Saffran & Marin, 1977).

A case described by Patterson (1982) is particularly interesting, because the individual in question did not seem to suffer from some of the many reading deficits seen in other deep dyslexic patients (indeed, Patterson believes that this patient represents a new category: phonological dyslexia). A. M. (the patient) was a left-handed elderly man who had suffered damage to both the right frontal and the right tempero-parietal lobes. (His left-handedness may limit the generalizability of his case.) Patterson noted that A. M.'s inability to assemble phonology operated on at least two levels. First, A. M. could not produce the sounds corresponding to individual letters without extreme difficulty. For example, if given the printed letter *m* and asked what sound this made, A. M. might respond with "mother." Second, A. M. was unable to read nonwords. Table 10.9 shows the results of several testing sessions in which A. M. was asked to read a variety of nonwords.

As in other studies of people with deep or phonological dyslexia (Derouesne & Beauvois, 1979), A. M.'s reading of nonwords improved substantially on those occasions when the nonwords were homophonic with actual words. What accounts for this improvement? Patterson has suggested that

TABLE 10.9

A. M.'s Performance in Oral Reading of Nonwords

List	Date	Number of Nonwords	Special Characteristics	Proportion Read Correctly
1	April 1978	24	—	0.00
2	July 1978	24	—	0.08
3	October 1978	36	Homophonic	0.47
			Nonhomophonic	0.26
4	July 1979	40	Homophonic	0.35
			Nonhomophonic	0.10
5	July 1979	26	Intermixed with words	0.19
Homophonic Nonwords from lists 3 and 4		37	High visual similarity	0.58
			Low visual similarity	0.32

Source: Patterson, 1982. Reprinted by permission of the publisher.

A. M. and other patients with deep dyslexia shrewdly use a compensating strategy to pronounce nonwords. In this strategy, the patient finds a real word that is graphemically similar to the nonword, and pronounces it. The implication is that deep dyslexic patients should be able to handle only one type of nonword: those that are homophonic and visually similar to real words. For example, since the nonword *toun* is phonemically and graphemically similar to the real word *town,* we would expect the deep dyslexic to be able to pronounce it. But this strategy would not work with a homophonic nonword that was not also graphemically similar to a real word. For example, consider the nonword *phude.* The nonword has a homophonic relationship with a real word but little graphemic relationship. We would expect that the true deep dyslexic should have some difficulty assembling phonology for such nonwords. Patterson addressed this issue by comparing A. M.'s performance on these two kinds of nonwords. The finding is shown at the bottom of Table 10.9. A. M. did much better on the homophonic nonwords that were graphemically related to real words (.58 read correctly) than he did on homophonic nonwords that had little or no graphemic relationship with real words (.32 read correctly). Once again, this finding is most easily interpreted by the direct access hypothesis.

Summary

Reading is a cognitive skill requiring expertise in several cognitive domains. We can think of reading as occurring in four stages: decoding, literal comprehension, inferential comprehension, and comprehension monitoring (Gagne, 1985). Decoding refers to feature analysis of letters and clusters of letters and pattern recognition. At this stage, the graphemic code is mapped onto another internal representation. In the second stage, the reader accesses his lexicon. As we've seen, this process is apparently done directly from the graphemic code in most cases. In the third stage, the reader accesses larger units of cognitive organization to integrate separate sentences. These larger units of organization no doubt closely resemble the scripts and schemas that we examined in the memory chapters. For example, consider the following two sentences:

The circus lion got out of its cage.
The crowd dispersed.

Skilled readers assume that a connection exists between these two sentences even though none has been explicitly stated. Your linking of these two sentences shows that you know something about lions being dangerous, circuses being watched by large groups, people being interested in saving their skins, and so on.

Comprehension monitoring is an important aspect of reading, although it is not involved in the actual translation of a graphemic code to meaning. Comprehension monitoring refers to a skill that good readers have—that of setting and checking on goals during the actual reading process. In other words, the reader who asks, "What did I get out of that paragraph?" is well on the way to making a more elaborate, and therefore durable, memory code.

As in the case of speech perception, the stages of reading indicate that both bottom-up and top-down processes are involved. For example, decoding is largely a bottom-up process. Literal comprehension for skilled readers is probably also a bottom-up process, although top-down processes play a definite role in limiting the locations within the lexicon that might be activated. Inferential comprehension is almost completely a top-down process.

LANGUAGE AND THOUGHT

Each of the book's major units includes a section showing the relationship between that topic and representational thought. Here, the relationship seems particularly close: Most of us agree that our language seems to afford us the possibility of thinking. This assumption is probably an illusion. Animals seem capable of cognition despite their poverty of language (with all due respect to Washoe). Yet, even if we back off the position that language establishes the possibility of thought, we can nevertheless entertain the idea that language influences (or even perhaps determines) the form of thought. This section considers some of what is known about the thought patterns of those who have access to more than one language: bilingual people.

Bilingualism

Consider this Czech proverb:

Learn a new language and get a new soul.

Is this proverb true? At this point in your life, would you really get a new soul by learning a new language, or are your thought patterns so deeply engrained by now that this would no longer be possible? Perhaps, then, you would have gotten a new soul if you had learned two languages simultaneously while growing up.

Definitions

Writers have had a difficult time providing an adequate definition of bilingualism. Ideally, a true bilingual would have the linguistic abilities of a native in two languages. This definition leads down a blind alley. First, almost nobody qualifies. Almost every bilingual person feels more comfortable using one or the other language depending upon the situation. Second, this definition does not take cultural factors into account. Could I really have nativelike linguistic capabilities in a language whose culture I was unfamiliar with? All languages are social events because their use is intended for particular audiences. I can't attain true fluency in a language without some knowledge of the social milieu in which the language is used. Third, the definition treats all linguistic abilities as equal, but some are probably more useful than others in certain situations.

From this basic and ideal definition, thinkers in this area have gone in two directions. In one direction, several writers have discussed the proficiency of the bilingual as being relative rather than absolute (Weinrich, 1953), and "evolved" (Schumacher, 1981), implying a developed appreciation of cultural effects rather than being a culture-independent event. In the second direction, various thinkers have divided the domain of linguistic ability into a set of more or less independent skills (Mackey, 1962; Macnamara, 1967). Macnamara's approach divides linguistic ability into two major skills: encoding (as seen in speaking and writing) and decoding (as seen in listening and reading). Under each of these four subskills the person must have semantic, syntactic, and lexical knowledge. In addition, in order to speak and listen, a person must have phonemic knowledge, and to read and write a person must have graphemic knowledge. This means that a complete specification of a monolingual's skills would require an assessment of competence on each of these sixteen dimensions. A complete specification of a bilingual person's knowledge might involve an assessment on thirty-two dimensions (perhaps fewer depending on the graphemic match-up). A loose hierarchy is implied here as well. For example, an individual's knowledge of speaking and listening in Chinese might greatly outweigh her ability to write and read if the person had no knowledge of the ideograms that are frequently used to represent Chinese. Without this knowledge, the person could not effectively bring her other knowledge to bear.

Acquisition

For at least the past thirty years or so, interest in bilingualism has focused on the means by which bilinguals acquire their knowledge. In this light, whether a new language provides you with a new soul may depend in part upon how much your old soul (i.e., first or favored language) was established at the time you began learning the second language.

For example, Vihman studied the language development of her two children, who learned both Estonian and English (Vihman & McLaughlin, 1982). Vivre, the older of the two, started out as an Estonian monolingual, using only four or five English words. At 1:9 she entered a day-care center where Engish was spoken, and she began to learn it. At that time, her Estonian vocabulary was about three hundred words, and her MLU was just over 2.0. Because Estonian had already been established, Vivre would be classified as a child second-language learner. On the other hand, the younger child, Raivo, was left with an English-speaking baby-sitter from the age of six months and heard both English and Estonian spoken at home by his parents and sibling. Raivo can be classified as a child bilingual. Vihman found that both situations seem to produce characteristic patterns of language use at phonetic, syntactic, and metalinguistic levels.

For example, Raivo showed what might be called an awareness of articulatory difficulties (Celce-Murcia, 1978). Even when only 15 percent of his lexicon consisted of English words, he consistently avoided Estonian words that required liquids (such as /l/ or /r/) or front-rounded vowels, and instead used the English equivalents that would enable him to get around the problem of hard-to-make sounds. This finding give the impression that the two lexicons were separately represented. Yet, other findings indicate that Raivo suffered from interference effects. For example, at the age of 3:4, he argued vehemently with his friends that he could read. Raivo demonstrated his reading ability by counting. In Estonian, *lugema* can mean "to read" or "to count."

The child second-language learner seems to proceed by acquiring formulaic chunks of words. Wong-Fillmore (1976) studied several Spanish-speaking children who were learning English. One of the formulaic expressions used was "How do you do dese?" which the children used to ask about a variety of objects, such as tortillas or flowerpots. Notice here that the use, and perhaps overuse, of a formula probably indicates that the children's comprehension of the formula is not total. However, the second-language learner's resources and objectives are probably different from those of the child bilingual. First, because second-language learners are more established in a language prior to their exposure to the second language, they can use their knowledge of language to help them crack the code of the second language. This means that child second-language learners are more likely than child bilinguals to know that there is something called syntax, and once they latch on to a syntactically correct formula, these children can use it to infer something about syntax in the second language.

Not all those who acquire a second language do so in childhood, and not all bilinguals acquire their second language from the same people who taught them their first language. Psycholinguists sometimes make a distinction between coordinate and compound bilinguals. The **coordinate bilingual** learns the two languages in two completely different settings, from different speakers, and at different times. For example, my grandfather was a coordinate bilingual, learning Italian as a child in Sicily and learning English as a teenager in the United States. In those situations, the two linguistic codes are thought to be separate and distinct from one another. Coordinate bilinguals can be contrasted with **compound bilinguals.** These are people who learn two languages from the same people, in the same setting, or at the same time. My grandmother is a compound multilingual. Her parents were from Alsace-Lorraine, where both French and German are spoken. Consequently, she learned both of those languages as well as English in the United States. Whereas the coordinate bilingual is assumed to have separate semantic memories for each language, the compound bilingual is thought to have only one semantic storage in which lexical knowledge from both languages is mixed together, or fused (Reynolds & Flagg, 1983).

The validity of this account has been assessed in several studies. Lambert, Havelka, and Crosby (1958) obtained a sample of twenty-three coordinate and nine compound bilinguals. The twenty-three coordinate bilinguals were further analyzed into two groups. Unicultural bilinguals were those who learned both languages within one general cultural setting. Bicultural bilinguals learned their two languages in two different cultural settings. Lambert et al. looked at the performance of these groups on several tasks. First, the subjects were asked to rate various connotative meanings for pairs of words that were equivalent in the two languages. Connotative meaning differs from denotative meaning, the latter term being more or less equal to the dictionary definition. Connotative meaning refers to the feeling evoked by the word. In this area, coordinate bilinguals with bicultural backgrounds showed greater sensitivity to the connotative differences in equivalent pairs, (e.g., *me–moi*) than compound bilinguals did. On the second task, the bilinguals all learned a list of twenty English words. After this, the subjects were divided: Half of the subjects had three trials to learn a list of nonsense syllables, and the other half of the subjects had three trials to learn a list of twenty French words that were translations of the English words they had learned earlier. All subjects were then retested on the list of English words. In comparing the various groups' performances on the retest, Lambert et al. found that the compound bilinguals were aided more by the intervening trials on the French list than were the coordinate bilinguals. In fact, the performance of the coordinate bilinguals on the English retest was not affected by the interpolated task. Those coordinate bilinguals who had seen the French translations did no better on the English retest than did those who saw the nonsense syllables. On the final task, all the subjects had to translate words from one language to another as quickly as they could. Here, no differences were noted between the coordinate and compound subjects.

These findings can be interpreted as evidence that the coordinate bilingual has two separate propositional representations for semantic memory, whereas the compound bilingual has only one. In the case of the coordinate bilingual, activating the nodes of semantic memory in the French representation did not result in any elaboration of the words originally learned in English, because the two internal representations are distinct. However, for the compound bilingual, hearing the French list helps keep the original English list activated and probably results in some additional elaboration of the code as well. Consequently, the interpolated task was helpful in retrieving the original English words.

This reasoning is supported in other studies. Lambert and Fillenbaum (1959) studied bilinguals who had had strokes and who suffered some language loss as a result. They dtermined that coordinate bilinguals were likely to show aphasia in only one of their two languages, but compound bilinguals seemed to show more general deficits, indicating that both languages had been affected. Presumably, the bilingual has some control over which internal representation is being used, although switching from code to code must surely take some time. This leads us to expect that when bilinguals switch languages in the middle of a conversation, such shifts are usually preceded by a pause. Bentahila (1983) studied "code-switching" among French-Arabic bilinguals in Morocco and found that language switching was used as a rhetorical device by these people, who often used hesitations as opportunities to shift languages.

CONCLUDING COMMENTS AND SUGGESTIONS FOR FURTHER READING

Using language involves several different cognitive processes. Understanding speech or reading requires the decoding of ambiguous stimuli. This is a matter of feature detection and pattern recognition. After the ambiguous stimuli have been recognized, the task of comprehension begins. The lexicon must be addressed, and these processes resemble those involved in the activation of nodes in semantic memory. All speech and all writing have gaps. We are usually not aware of these gaps, because the speaker or writer has taken some pains to provide the audience with the main points of the discourse. Our inferential processes do the rest of the work. When we looked at the memory literature, we saw that providing someone with a theme for a story can enhance recognition. Remember the soap opera effect? When subjects were told that the girl in the story was pregnant, they recalled more of the story's details and interpreted the story in terms that were consistent with the script. Shared knowledge of such scripts enables the communication process to work. The only reason any narrative, written or told, has main points is because the participants share some mental organization. This sharing of mental organization seems to require more time or experience to develop than does phonological or lexical knowledge. If you doubt this, ask a five-year-old to tell you the plot of a movie sometime. The breakdown in communication won't occur at the phonetic or lexical levels. What the child sees as important in the story, however, will probably not overlap much with your viewpoint. When we use language to produce speech, the order of these processes is reversed. We start with a broad outline of what we're trying to say, which involves a judgment that our listeners have knowledge of the script we are about to use.

In summary, the use of language involves both top-down and bottom-up processes. In addition, the use of language requires perception and memory, and to a certain extent, reasoning. Although the organization of the book suggests that language is a separable phenomenon that can be unhitched from the other cognitive processes in the team, this organization is misleading. Language affects and is affected by the other cognitive processes we have studied; work is done because all cognitive processes pull together.

For years, people have postulated the end of the reading era. (Remember the character in *Ghostbusters* who, when asked about his reading habits, replied, "Print is dead?") It looks as though the obituaries may have been premature. The findings of the Carnegie Commission on high school education have reiterated the need for reading competence as one of the primary skills in our culture. Our exploration of reading mechanics demonstrated that our biological endowment would permit much faster reading than most of us enjoy. The answer seems to lie in improving the cognitive skills underlying reading, and I think a fair statement is that we'll be seeing trends in this direction on a national level.

Readers who wish to find out more about speech perception will find no better starting place than Pisoni's article in the *Handbook of Learning and Cognitive Processes* (1978). Other material on speech perception can be found in Clark and Clark (1977). For a good discussion on feature detectors in speech (and the deficiences of a theory based on them), see the articles by Remez (1979, 1980). Garrett (1982) presents a complete account of speech production, and in the same volume, Patterson (1982) describes her work with A. M. Deese (1984) has written a fascinating book in which he analyzed transcripts of naturally occurring speech. Vihman and McLaughlin (1982) have written a good review of the recent literature on bilingual children.

Several excellent general reviews are available on the research in reading. For example, the *Psychological Review* article by Just and Carpenter (1980) offers complete coverage of the stages in reading. Books by Crowder (1982) and Kennedy (1984) are also good. The Kennedy book is somewhat provocative, arguing as it does that reading should not be considered a skill at all but rather a basic psychological process whose development does not follow the same pattern that other cognitive skills do. Baker and Brown (1984) have written an account of the metacognitive influences on reading skill.

FOCUS ON RESEARCH:
Disfluent Speech and the Brain

Even though we commit errors of syntax and pronunciation more often than we realize, our errors are unusual. Typically, we seem to be able to say just what we want to without any slipups. Unfortunately, for some people such fluency is seldom, if ever, achieved. Stutterers are plagued by a variety of handicaps including excessive hesitations, perseveration, and inability to articulate while maintaining normal speech rhythm. For some stutterers, producing speech is such an embarrassing agony they would rather remain silent.

Curiously, however, the stutterer doesn't seem to have as many problems when speaking under certain conditions. For example, stutterers can sometimes whisper fluently, and their singing ability is usually unimpaired. Also, the stutterer is often able to speak fluently in unison with other people. Some stutterers can improve their fluency by tapping their foot rhythmically and speaking at the rate of one word per tap (Kalat, 1984). These observances suggest that the stutterer's problem is not simply a loss of motor control over the tongue or breathing apparatus. The problem seems to be truly linguistic rather than muscular.

Recall that in Chapter 8 we examined the brain's role in normal language. In that chapter we saw that the left hemisphere of most people is the dominant one, and that this hemisphere contains Broca's and Wernicke's areas. Could these areas be

involved in the stutterer's disfluency? The answer seems to be yes, although the involvement is indirect.

Jones (1966) performed surgery on the left hemispheres of four adults who had tumors near the speech centers. Such surgery would usually not be considered because of the risk it poses for speech. However, these patients were unusual: They had speech centers in both hemispheres of their brains (determined by anesthetizing only one hemisphere at a time). After the surgery, the patients were still capable of speech, apparently using the centers in their right hemispheres. Another striking finding was made: Before the surgery, all four patients routinely stuttered, but after the operation, none of them did. What's the interpretation?

For some people, the degree of lateral domination is not as great as it is for others. Essentially, such people have two speech centers that compete with each other. The failure to synchronize these centers is what contributes to the stuttering. When some rhythmic organization is imposed, the two centers have an easier time coordinating their efforts.

Several studies (Pinsky & McAdam, 1980; Rosenfield & Goodglass, 1980) have assessed this interpretation. Using a dichotic listening task similar to the ones we studied in Chapter 2, researchers have found more stutterers than nonstutterers with right hemisphere speech dominance, mixed dominance, or even fluctuating dominance. This last finding is interesting because it may account for some stutterers experiencing lengthy periods of fluent speech followed by disfluencies.

The brain is not the sole cause of stuttering: Plenty of ambidextrous people don't stutter, but they would if hemispheric dominance were the only factor. Yet, competition between speech centers probably plays a role in some people's stuttering.

KEY TERMS

Phoneme
Phonetics
Phonology
Place of articulation
Manner of articulation
Voicing
Distinctive features
Phonemic restoration effect
Analysis by synthesis model
Lexical uncertainty

Conceptual complexity
Grapheme
Saccade
Assembled phonology
Addressed phonology
Direct access hypothesis
Deep dyslexia
Coordinate bilingual
Compound bilingual

PART FIVE

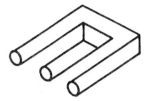

THINKING

The book's final chapters discuss what have been called "higher" mental processes in humans. The word *higher* is in quotes for the following reasons. Generally, thinking, reasoning, and problem solving have been called higher processes because it's traditionally been thought that such events come at the end of the chain of information processing. This view of cognitive activity became particularly entrenched during the 1960s. Because perception and memory were strongly rooted in sensory and physiological psychology, they were thought to be closely related to neural processes. The cognitive activity related to thinking and reasoning, however, did not seem synonymous with any particular pattern of neural processing, and in that sense seemed "higher" than other cognitive processes.

We now know the picture is much more complicated than that. First, as we've seen, information-processing theories of perception and memory have been formulated. These theories are abstract; that is, they do not deal with these phenomena in explicitly neural terms. Second, the idea that a chain of events occurs in cognition is also simplistic. Although the information-processing paradigm often treats mental events as though they occurred sequentially, we know that this is just a theoretical convenience. In reality, the so-called higher processes don't necessarily occur after the so-called lower processes. What we perceive does form the basis of our thoughts, but our thoughts also influence what we perceive. The sequences of information processing are quite tangled, and they constantly loop and double back upon one another. Seen from this perspective, the term *higher mental processes* is really only a teaching or organizational device.

One important issue that this section deals with is the question of representation, or problem understanding. How a problem is represented or understood by the problem solver seems to have a powerful influence on the problem solver's effectiveness. In this regard, reasoning is much like problem solving. Although the principles of logic can be delineated clearly, humans often don't perceive these principles, which means that their representations of logic problems are sometimes different than those used by logicians. This brings us to the question of artificial intelligence. What are some of the problems cognitive psychologists face in specifying problem representation completely enough to permit its incorporation into a computer?

Earlier, we talked about the schema as an encompassing cognitive structure that organized incoming information and suggested which information should be forthcoming. In this context, the schema influences how problems are represented. This section examines schematic influences in both reasoning and problem solving. The last chapter considers a program of research in artificial intelligence whose objective is to formulate schematic knowledge of real-world actions.

CHAPTER 11

Reasoning and Concept Attainment

OVERVIEW

LOGIC AND FORMAL REASONING
Human Thought and the Rules of Logic
Validity, Truth, and Soundness
  Cross-cultural Studies
Conditional Reasoning
Summary of Formal Reasoning

NATURAL REASONING
Representativeness
Availability
Framing Decisions

Summary of Natural Reasoning

CONCEPT ATTAINMENT
Artificial Concepts
  Strategies in Concept Attainment Tasks
Natural Categories
  Formation of Natural Categories

**CONCLUDING COMMENTS AND SUGGESTIONS
FOR FURTHER READING
FOCUS ON APPLICATIONS
KEY TERMS**

All the first-year students at my undergraduate college were required to take a course in logic. I remember looking forward to the course and thought that I would become the possessor of some penetrating analysis that would enable me to immediately see the truth or falsity of things. Thus armed, I would be able to demolish my friends' arguments on any matter. My expectations were probably incorrect; the course turned out to be disappointing. First, I wasn't thrilled with the prospect of memorizing the form of all sixty-four categorical syllogisms—this didn't seem like any argument winner to me. Further, I found that logic didn't always seem logical. For example, logicians have developed truth tables that can be used to verify the truth of complex remarks. One of the truth tables concerns the truth of implications, such as "If P, then Q." I was surprised to find out that if P and Q were both false, the whole statement (If P, then Q) was nevertheless true! How could the whole statement be true when both of its parts were false? I had a realization: If this was logic, then my mind certainly wasn't logical all the time, because this didn't make much sense to me.

To what extent is this realization common to other people as well? This chapter considers the question of human reasoning. Success in **formal reasoning** seems somewhat dependent upon educational level. Individuals from cultures that don't emphasize Western education often perform poorly (by Western standards) on formal reasoning tasks. However, even highly educated Westerners sometimes perform poorly on such tasks. Does this mean that people have to be trained to be logical? We'll examine some of the findings from research on conditional syllogisms, and we'll see that people often seem to interpret logical information differently from the way that logicians do. We'll also consider natural reasoning—reasoning on problems that seem closely related to the kinds of judgments that are required of us every day. How do people accomplish such reasoning? Apparently, people typically make use of general rules of thumb that usually work quickly and efficiently. This chapter considers some situations in which these rules of thumb are pushed past their limits. Such situations occur more frequently than we think; reasoning that looks plausible and logical some-times isn't.

The second part of the chapter investigates the nature of category and concept formation. The literature on so-called artificial concepts (i.e., concepts created by the experimenter) suggest that people formulate and, more or less, systematically, test a hypothesis about which items or elements make up a par-ticular category. Just as we can contrast formal with natural reasoning, we can investigate formation of natural categories. Much of the literature on naturally occurring categories implies that humans develop a schema, or prototype, for particular categories based upon the abstraction of features that are shared by members of the category.

LOGIC AND FORMAL REASONING

This section considers some of the findings that result when people try to solve formal problems by using **logic.** Several issues surface here: Do people without formal training in logic nevertheless use logic to solve such problems? From a failure to solve such problems, is it legitimate to conclude that people are illogical?

Human Thought and the Rules of Logic

If we think about all the people we know, we find that it is easy to categorize each individual as "logical" or "not logical." By "logical" we usually mean that individuals are capable of giving plausible reasons for events, or capable of making inferences implied by other facts. We seldom try to describe the behavior of the people we call illogical, but their actions need to be explained, too. Are such individuals following different rules of thought than logical people? If so, how did such individuals learn those illogical rules of thought? Perhaps the problem should be turned around. Maybe humans are inherently illogical, and they must be explicitly taught to use logic.

The idea that humans are inherently illogical would not have been accepted a century ago. Mill (1874) viewed the laws of logic as synonymous with the laws of thought. According to Mill, logical principles were not really discovered and developed. Mill understood logical principles as simply a formal account of the same principles used by people in their everyday thinking and reasoning. Mill was aware that people sometimes made logical errors, but he explained these as simply nonsystematic "slips." Similarly, James (1890) maintained that the two principal components of logical reasoning were analysis and abstraction. Analysis referred to our ability to break down an object into its component parts, letting one of the parts represent the entire object. For example, in the statement "Freud is a man," the thinker must represent Freud by using only one of Freud's components—specifically his maleness. Abstraction referred to our ability to designate a specific component as part of a broader classification. Thus, from the statement "All men are mortal," it follows that Freud must be mortal. That is, Freud can be represented by his maleness, which can be grouped into the broader classification "mortal." Therefore, "Freud" can also be grouped into this broader classification. According to James, these two mental processes enabled logical reasoning to occur.

Validity, Truth, and Soundness

Logical analysis can take many forms, only some of which will be dealt with in this chapter. However, a few terms are common to all logical systems. One of these terms is **validity.** A logical argument is valid if, according to the rules established by logicians, the conclusion of the argument necessarily follows from the earlier statements. Sometimes students think that the validity of an argument is synonymous with its **truth,** but that's a mistake.

A logical argument can be valid but untrue. Consider the following statements:

All dinosaurs are animals.
All animals are in zoos.
Therefore, all dinosaurs are in zoos.

The conclusion is valid according to the rules used by logicians, yet not all dinosaurs are in zoos, so the conclusion is not true. On the other hand, if the argument's initial statements *are* true and the reasoning is valid, then the conclusion will also be true. All logical systems have this property, which is referred to as **soundness.** Soundness simply means that given the truth of the argument's initial statements, valid reasoning will produce a truthful conclusion.

Soundness in reasoning doesn't necessarily imply that logical reasoning has taken place. For example, if given true initial statements, a person may be able to determine a valid, true conclusion with regularity. Under these circumstances, his reasoning would be sound. But if the person accomplishes this feat by applying an idiosyncratic reasoning system that he cannot explain, his reasoning is not logical. Logical reasoning implies that we have followed the rules of logical inference as established by logicians and described in textbooks. In other words, logical reasoning is defined as much by its methods as it is by its outcome. If we deviate from this method, our reasoning is not logical, no matter what other properties it might have.

Researchers face difficulty in trying to determine the logical abilities of humans. Even if a person succeeds in determining the validity or invalidity of an argument, this does not necessarily mean that she used logic to arrive at the conclusion. This assertion was clearly demonstrated in a well-known study by Henle (1962), who gave graduate students, with no formal training in logic, problems such as the one that follows:

A group of women were discussing their houshould problems. Mrs. Shivers broke the ice by saying: "I'm so glad we're talking about these problems. It's so important to talk about things that are in our minds. We spend so much time in the kitchen that of course household problems are in our minds. So it is important to talk about them." (Does it follow that is important to talk about them? Give your reasoning.)

Henle found that subjects often treated the logical problem as an empirical task. That is, they attempted to assess, for example, whether spending a great deal of time in the kitchen would necessarily imply that kitchen events would really be on the homemakers' minds. Frequently, subjects gave the correct answer (Mrs. Shivers is logically correct when she states that talking about such problems is important), but their reasoning was usually not logical. Although the ability to give the correct answer implies that the answer has been derived logically, this implication is deceptive. Henle's subjects did not perform in a logical fashion. As suggested by some commentators (Howard, 1983), the subjects may have performed illogically because everyday reasoning does not demand the knowledge and application of formal logical principles. When confronted with practical problems, we usually behave in a pragmatic or probabilisitc way. We know, for example, that if a skunk is run over on the highway, a characteristic intense odor will be produced. If we're driving along some night and smell this scent, we're likely to conclude that a skunk had been hit, and we would probably feel that this conclusion is valid. But it isn't. The skunk may have been warding off an intruder, or perhaps a sensory psychologist had been conducting a field study on the effects of skunk scent on some aspect of driving performance. Henle's study implies that people do not typically distinguish between this everyday sort of probabilistic reasoning and logic.

Cross-cultural Studies

If the laws of thought were truly synonymous with the rules of logic, then logic should be observable wherever human thought occurs. Specifically, individuals who are reared and educated on non-Western ways should nevertheless be capable of reasoning logically. Debate on this issue was initiated by Levy-Bruhl (1910), who maintained that the "primitive mind" thinks in a "prelogical" way, governed by emotion, magic, and an inability to distinguish between mental and external events. Although Levy-Bruhl probably overstated the case, more recent anthropological studies (Cole & Scribner, 1977) have indicated that nonliterate, non-Western people employ reasoning strategies that are somewhat different from those observed among educated Westerners. Such individuals are capable of reasoning in an orderly fashion; consequently, their deductions are often sound. However, these nonschooled people seem to accomplish this reasoning without the aid of formal logic. For example, when Sylvia Scribner asked members of the Vai (a West African tribe) to respond to logical arguments as a part of a literacy program, she found that their answers, although reasonable, were not logical. What follows is a problem and response of one of the Vai:

All women who live in Monrovia are married.
Kemu is not married.
Does she live in Monrovia?
Answer and Explanation: Yes. Monrovia is not for any one kind of people so Kemu came to live there. (Scribner, 1977)

Notice that the respondent answered the question by ignoring or discounting the first statement and insisted upon giving the correct answer, based upon what is known to be true: Anyone is permitted to live in Monrovia. This little protocol is a good illustration of what Scribner found to be a general finding in her work. As little as two years of schooling dramatically increased the likelihood of an individual's ability to reason logically. The protocol also shows a process that Henle observed in her Western subjects: The Vai tribesperson treated the task as an empirical problem—one that could be answered from one's observations of the world.

Are humans inherently logical? The answer appears to be a qualified no. Human reasoning may be inherently orderly and sound, but logical ability seems to be a by-product of education. But even people who are educated are not always logical. Their reasoning processes have offered cognitive psychologists a good "window" on what might be called the rules of thought.

Conditional Reasoning

One formal reasoning task that has been studied extensively by cognitive psychologists is known as **conditional reasoning.** Conditional reasoning takes place when an individual is given some statements called "conditions"—a rule for determining what outcomes can be expected if certain conditions are present, and a conclusion whose validity the reasoner tries to assess, using the previously given information. For example:

If you have studied hard, you will do well in this course.
You have studied hard.
Therefore, you can expect to do well in this course.

Generally, the rule is expressed in an "if-then" format: If P (some sort of antecedent condition), then Q (some sort of consequent condition). One of the other statements establishes the truth or falsity of P or Q. The reasoner must establish the truth or falsity of the remaining term, or determine that its truth or falsity can't be established, given the existing information. Logicians have developed two inference rules that can be used to reason validly in these circumstances. The first of these is called **modus ponens.** In situations such as "If P, then Q" and "P is true," modus ponens allows us to validly infer that "Q is true." In other words, when we're given "if P, then Q", modus ponens enables us to infer that the presence of P implies the presence of Q. The studying example just used represents the valid use of modus ponens. The second rule is called **modus tollens.** Consider the following argument:

If it snows on Thursday, I'll go skiing.
I did not go skiing.
Therefore, it did not snow on Thursday.

The conclusion is valid, and represents the correct use of modus tollens, which can be expressed in the following general format: Given, "if P, then Q" and "Q is false" or "not Q," then modus tollens allows to validly infer that "P is false" or "not P." Where P implies Q, the absence of Q implies the absence of P.

In addition to modus tollens and modus ponens, conditional reasoning can take place in two other forms, and both of these represent particular kinds of logical errors. Take a look at the following argument:

If she likes me, she'll go out with me.
She likes me not.
Therefore, she won't go out with me.

If the conclusion looks valid to us, then we have made an error in reasoning known as "denying the antecedent." Notice that the error is named after the antecedent, the first part of the conditional rule. When we deny the antecedent, we assume that the consequent will be true *only if* the antecedent is true. That's an error because the consequent could be true even if the antecedent is false. That is, she may go out with you for some other reason even if she doesn't like you. Denying the antecedent is not the only error our love-stricken friends are likely to commit. Consider the following reasoning:

If she likes me, she'll go out with me.
She goes out with me.
Therefore, she likes me.

Not necessarily. In this case, the reasoner has assumed that the truth of the consequent implies that the truth of the antecedent, an error that is known as "affirming the consequent." These forms of conditional reasoning are summarized in Table 11.1.

We can be pretty sure that subjects who are untrained in logic are not familiar with these terms, but can educated people nevertheless reason successfully on formal conditional reasoning problems? Rips and Marcus (1977) presented their subjects, who were students untrained in the use of inference rules, with eight "concrete" (more about this term later) examples of conditional reasoning, such as the following:

If a card has an A on the left, it has a 7 on the right.
The card does not have a 7 on the right.
The card does not have an A on the left.

They asked their subjects to judge whether the conclusion was always true, never true, or sometimes true. What's your answer? Perhaps the best way to proceed here is to convert the previous "concrete" phrases into a more general format compatible with the information in Table 11.1. Thus, the

TABLE 11.1

Conditional Reasoning

Form	Name	Example
If P, then Q P ——— Therefore Q	Modus ponens (valid inference)	If the object is square, then it is blue. The object is square. ———— The object is blue.
If P, then Q not Q ——— Therefore not P	Modus tollendo tollens (valid inference)	If the object is square, then it is blue. The object is not blue. ———— The object is not square.
If P, then Q not P ——— Therefore not Q	Denying the antecedent (invalid inference)	If the object is square, then it is blue. The object is not square. ———— The object is not blue.
If P, then Q Q ——— Therefore P	Affirming the consequent (invalid inference)	If the object is square, then it is blue. The object is blue. ———— The object is square.

Source: Adapted from Howard, 1983.

"A on the left" phrase becomes "P," and the "7 on the right" phrase becomes "Q." Logicians have developed a symbol, ⊃, sometimes called the horseshoe, to designate the idea of implication. The first line of the prior example then becomes "A on the left implies 7 on the right," or "P ⊃ Q." Logicians also make use of a symbol to designate "not" or "the absence of." This is the tilde, written like this: ∼. The phrase in the second line of the prior argument then becomes "not Q" "or ∼ Q." Logicians sometimes use a three-dot pattern, ∴, to indicate "therefore." Making the conversion for the prior argument, then, we have

$$P \supset Q$$
$$\sim Q$$
$$\therefore \sim P$$

Looking back to Table 11.1, we see that this is indeed a valid inference that represents the correct use of modus tollens. If we were one of Rips and Marcus's subjects, the correct answer in this case would be "always true." Table 11.2 shows the percentage of subjects responding "always true," "sometimes true," and "never true" for each of the eight types of

TABLE 11.2

Percentage of Total Responses for Eight Types of Conditional Syllogisms

Syllogism	Always	Sometimes	Never
1. P⊃Q P ∴Q	100[a]	0	0
2. P⊃Q P ∴∼Q	0	0	100[a]
3. P⊃Q ∼P ∴Q	5	79[a]	16
4. P⊃Q ∼P ∴∼Q	21	77[a]	2
5. P⊃Q Q ∴P	23	77[a]	0
6. P⊃Q Q ∴∼P	4	82[a]	14
7. P⊃Q ∼Q ∴P	0	23	77[a]
8. P⊃Q ∼Q ∴∼P	57[a]	39	4

Source: Adapted from Rips and Marcus, 1977.
[a]The correct response.

problems used. The problems are shown here are in the "abstract" format, but they were given to the subjects in the concrete form shown before. Problems 1 and 2 require the use of modus ponens, and as Table 11.2 indicates, subjects were quite adept in applying this inference rule. No errors at all were made on those two problems. Problems 7 and 8 also permit a valid inference through the use of modus tollens. That is, modus tollens enables us to say that Problem 7 could never be true, and problem 8 (the example used earlier) would always be true. The subjects were much less successful in applying modus tollens than they were in using modus ponens. More than a fifth of the subjects believed that the conclusion of problem 7 could sometimes be true. And over 40 percent made a reasoning error on problem 8.

No valid inferences can be drawn from the information in problems 3 through 6, and so the correct answer in each of those cases should be "sometimes true." However, we see that subjects sometimes insisted that valid inferences could be drawn. In problems 3 and 4, approximately 20 percent of the subjects believed that some valid inference could be drawn about Q from ~ P. This result represents denial of the antecedent. Similarly, about 20 percent of the subjects believed that valid inferences could be drawn in problems 6 and 7, which represents an affirmation of the consequent. From Q, we can't draw any valid inference concerning P or ~ P.

The errors on problems 3 through 6 can be explained by examining the subject's understanding of the logical term "if" when it is used in "if P, then Q" statements. People who have not been trained in logic apparently use this word differently than do logicians. Logicians make a distinction between the term "if," which is called the *conditional,* and the expression "if and only if," which is called the *biconditional.* The sentence

I will win if and only if I practice.

implies that practice is a necessary condition for my victory to take place. This wouldn't be so if I had used the connective "if".

To analyze the truth of implications containing the conditional or biconditional statement, logicians make use of truth tables. A truth table offers us a way of determining the truth of a complex remark based upon the truth of its component statements. Table 11.3 shows the truth tables for both the conditional "if," which is indicated by the horseshoe symbol, and the biconditional "if and only if," which is shown by the double-headed arrow.

To see how this table would be used in practice, let's consider an example:

If the switch is turned on, then the light will go on.
The switch is not turned on.
Therefore, the light does not go on.

Using the conditional truth table, we see that there are two conditions in which the complex remark is true while P, the antecedent, is false. In one of these two conditions, Q, the consequent, is false. In the other condition, it is true. All we can say about the conclusion is that sometimes it might not be true and sometimes it might be. Turning to the biconditional truth

TABLE 11.3

Truth Tables

Implication or Conditional			Biconditional		
P	Q	P⊃Q	P	Q	P↔Q
T	T	T	T	T	T
T	F	F	T	F	F
F	T	T	F	T	F
F	F	T	F	F	T

table, however, we see a different story. If P is false (i.e., ~ P) and P ⊃ Q is true, then Q must be false. Also, if P is true and P ⊃ Q is true, the Q must also be true. If you go back to the previous example and change the word "if" to "if and only if," then you'll see that the conclusion is now valid. This means that neither the denial of the antecedent (as seen in Rips and Marcus's problems 3 and 4) nor the affirmation of the consequent (as took place in problems 5 and 6) is a fallacy in reasoning if one has interpreted the conditional as the biconditional.

Staudenmayer (1975) gave his subjects a series of conditional reasoning problems similar to the ones used by Rips and Marcus. He was able to demonstrate that subjects typically decide how the connective "if" is to be interpreted, and the subsequent reasoning processes are consistent with whatever interpretation the subjects make. For example, in cases in which an "if then" phrasing was used, 59 percent of the subjects treated the "if" connective as though it were the biconditional, "if and only if." This misuse increased to 77 percent when phrasings such as "P causes Q" were used in the problems. Once the interpretation of the "if" connective had been made, subjects' reasoning was fairly sound. Staudenmayer concluded that errors in these conditional reasoning problems were not errors of reasoning per se but rather failures to realize the distinction between the conditional and the biconditional phrasings.

Although such an analysis accounts for the errors made on problems 3 through 6 of Rips and Marcus's study, it does not explain the considerable number of errors made on problems 7 and 8, which seem to stem from an inability to apply modus tollens. Other studies have produced similar findings. Wason (1966) presented his subjects with four cards showing the following symbols:

The subjects were told each card had a number on one side and a letter on the other. Their task was to turn over the minimum number of cards necessary to verify the following rule: If a card has a vowel on one side, then it has an even number on the other side. (Before reading on, you might try solving this problem.)

Forty-six percent of the subjects turned over both the E and 4. This response is incorrect and represents another example of affirming the consequent. We're really not interested in what's behind the 4, because even if we found a consonant, that wouldn't invalidate the rule. Many subjects turned only the E over. This response is on the right track, but it's incomplete. Only 4 percent of the subjects got the problem right, by turning over the E and the 7. Turning over the 7 represents an application of the important modus tollens step called **disconfirming the consequent.** If "vowel" implies "even number," then the absence of an even number (in the case of the 7) implies the absence of a vowel on the reverse side of the card.

Readers who are still in the dark on this problem are probably not alone. Wason and Johnson-Laird (1972) have pointed out that many people did not see why the E and 7 have to be turned over even after it had been explained to them. The researchers refer to such inability to see the correct reasoning as *evasion*. There are two varieties of evasion. The first type they call *irreversibility*. A subject manifesting this error might agree that an odd number on the other side of the vowel would invalidate the rule, but then the subject strangely claims that no symbol on the other side of the odd symbol would be able to do so. As Wason and Johnson-Laird have pointed out, the crucial feature of the irreversibility error seems to be that the vowel and even number have been selected initially, in a sense blinding the individual to the implications of choosing any of the other cards. The second type of evasion they call *denial*. If, under questioning, a subject realizes that some unselected card could invalidate the rule (e.g., the unselected 7 could invalidate the rule if it has a vowel on the reverse side) but then refuses to modify his solution by including that card, then the subject has denied the implications of the reasoning he just verbalized. One of the more striking aspects of these evasions is their persistence in the face of questioning by the experimenter.

Wason and Johnson-Laird (1970) demonstrated these effects in a study in which the subjects were presented with the stimuli shown in Figure 11.1. Card A consisted of a circle with a cardboard mask around the edge, which

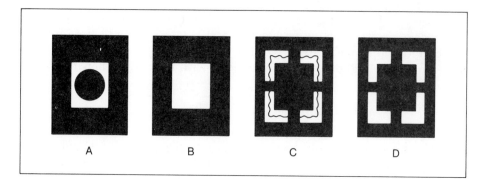

Figure 11.1.

The "selection task." "Every card which has a circle on it has a border around it." (From Wason & Johnson-Laird, 1970.)

may or may not conceal the curly line border. Card B showed no circle and had the mask. Card C showed a curly line border and was masked in the middle, possibly concealing a circle. Finally, card D showed no curly line border and was masked over the middle, possibly concealing a circle. Subjects were asked to unmask the minimum number of cards necessary to validate the rule "Every card which has a circle on it has a border round it." The answer is that cards A and D must be unmasked in order to invalidate the rule. Most of the subjects unmasked the A card but not the D card. When the subjects erred, the experimenter unmasked both the A and D cards and, in an unstructured interview, asked the subject if he or she would like to modify the proposed solution to the problem in light of what was now visible. What follows is a protocol from one of Wason and Johnson-Laird's subjects, showing both the denial and irreversibility errors:

S.16 female undergraduate: "A" levels in pure and applied mathematics.
Solution: "circle" and "border". (Correct cards fully revealed)
Experimenter: Are you still happy about the choice of cards you needed to see?
Subject: Yes
E: Can you still say anything about the truth or falsity of the rule from this card?
S: It tells me the sentence is true.
E: Can you say anything about the truth or falsity of the rule from this card? (No border with circle)
S: It tells me its false.
E: Are you still happy about the choice of cards you needed to see?
S: Yes. (The exposed cards have been evaluated, and the subject exhibits "denial": The falsifying card is not considered admissible.)
E: Well, you just said this one makes it false.
S: Well, it hasn't got a squiggly border on it, so it doesn't matter ("denial" again).
E: Can you say anything about the truth or falsity of the rule from this card? (No circle.)
S: It's got nothing to do with it because there's no circle.
E: Can you say anything about the truth or falsity of the rule from this card? (border—selected.)
S: There has to be a circle under it for the sentence to be true.
E: What if there is no circle?
S: Then the sentence would be false. ("Irreversibility": An inference made from a selected card is withheld from a potentially identical unselected card.) Interview terminated.

Seventy-four percent of the subjects who failed to get the answer initially also failed to correct themselves when the correct cards were unmasked. Of these subjects, 48 percent failed to correct themselves even after the interview, during which it was pointed out that they were being illogical.

The work we have reviewed thus far may imply that the picture is rather bleak as far as modus tollens use is concerned. However, Johnson-Laird, Legrenzi, and Legrenzi (1972) have presented other evidence demonstrating that the context in which the inference is demanded can enhance peoples' use of the modus tollens rule.

In this study, the subjects were given what have been called *thematic materials*. Subjects were shown the envelopes depicted in Figure 11.2, and they were asked to imagine that they were postal workers sorting letters.

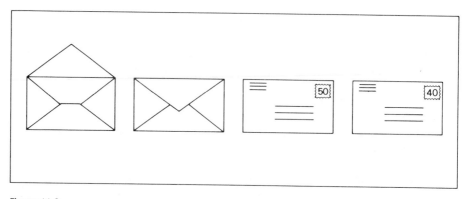

Figure 11.2.

Material used in the envelope experiment by Johnson-Laird, Legrenzi, and Legrenzi (1972). Subjects were asked which envelopes should be turned over to test the rule, "If a letter is sealed, then it has a 50-lire stamp on it."

They were asked to determine if a postal regulation had been violated, this being the rule: "If a letter is sealed, then it has a 50-lire stamp on it." Subjects were asked to turn over the minimum number of envelopes necessary to verify the rule. In this case, 88 percent of the subjects were correct, turning over the sealed envelope and the envelope with the forty-lire stamp on it.

What factors enabled the subjects to perform substantially better in this version of the selection task? Some commentators (Mayer, 1983) have noted that this envelope version of the task is more concrete than the rather abstract ways it was presented in the other studies. But we should be wary of what we mean when we say that this version of the task is "concrete." After all, looking at pictures of envelopes is not more concrete than looking at pictures of cards with letters and numbers on them. Rather, "concrete" is used in the sense of being pragmatic or down-to-earth. This usage suggests that if the context provides a sense of reality, then people are capable of demonstrating that they know the implications of the modus tollens inference rule.

However, some evidence suggests that simply giving people thematic materials won't produce improvements in reasoning unless the sense of reality established by the theme agrees with knowledge that people have stored in their memories. Thus, Griggs and Cox (1982) thought that it wasn't the thematic material per se in the envelope study that enabled the subjects to do so well; rather, the subjects were using remembered knowledge of the British postal system to help them make the deduction. Indeed, Griggs and Cox found that the British postal system had a defunct regulation that specified that a sealed envelope required more postage than an envelope whose flap was simply tucked in. Griggs and Cox repeated the Johnson-Laird et al. study with subjects who were undergraduates at the University of Florida and who, presumably, did not have much knowledge of defunct British postal regulations. In this setting, Griggs and Cox found that their subjects performed no better on the envelope problem than they did on the abstract vowel-number problem. Next, Griggs and Cox constructed a problem that tapped their subjects' prior knowledge of the world. The subjects saw four cards labeled "beer," "Coke," "22 years," and "16 years." The subjects were told to turn over the minimum number of cards necessary to verify the following rule: "If a person is drinking beer, then the person must be over 19 years of age." In this situation, subjects performed much better than subjects who received abstract versions of the problem. Griggs and Cox concluded that performance on card selection problems was enhanced when the thematic material cued retrieval of first- or secondhand knowledge stored in long-term memory.

Hoch and Tschirgi (1983) have found that the effects of thematic materials are not limited to situations with which the subject is personally familiar. They argued that people have general knowledge of circumstances that should make one wary or suspicious. One circumstance that might make a person suspicious is missing information. Hoch and Tschirgi reasoned that this *extralogical* information could be used as a basis to solve a card selection problem even when the problem dealt with an area outside the subject's personal experience. To test this assertion, they created the following scenario. Subjects were told to imagine themselves as quality-control inspectors for a firm that manufactured pocket calculators. Subjects in the "no relation" condition were given information telling them how to decide if the calculators were acceptable. This information included a rule that could be verified by turning over some of the calculators. Next, the subjects looked at four drawings of calculators and circled the ones they thought should be turned over. Subjects in the "blank" condition were given a similar set of instructions, including a rule that could be verified by turning over some of the calculators. Next, these subjects looked at drawings of calculators, one of which was left blank. Again, the subjects' task was to circle those calculators that needed to be turned over to verify the rule. Figure 11.3 shows the instructional set and drawings for these two conditions. In the blank condition, you need to turn over the XT-10 calculator and the blank. In the no relation condition, the XT-10 calculator and technical instructions need to be turned over. Which problem did you find easier?

Hoch and Tschirgi's subjects found the blank problem substantially easier than the no relation problem. Seventy-six percent of the subjects in the blank condition solved the problem, while 44 percent of the subjects in the no relation condition were successful. What accounts for the discrepancy? Hoch and Tschirgi maintain that the subject notices the missing information in the blank condition, which may help to establish a "detective" orientation (van Duyne, 1974). That is, the subjects begin to suspect that something there is wrong, and they turn over the calculator to investigate it. In so doing, Hoch and Tschirgi say that the subject is obviously not relying exclusively on personally experienced knowledge retrieved from memory to solve the problem.

Summary of Formal Reasoning

The study of conditional reasoning tasks tells us several interesting things about human reasoning. First, the untrained person's use of logical terms is sometimes far different from the logician's use. For example, we've seen

(A)

Imagine that you are a quality-control clerk for Microdigit, Inc. Your job is to inspect different models of pocket calculators moving along a conveyor belt. Your company markets two different calculator models: the XT-10 and the XT-11. The two models are basically the same, but the XT-10 is sold in the United States and the XT-11 is exported to Canada.

Model numbers appear on the front side and a brief set of instructions can be glued to a panel on the back side. The instructions come in two versions, one technical (for the business market) and one quite simple (for the consumer market). The calculators move along a conveyor belt, some face up with the model number showing and some face down with the instruction panel showing. Clerks must make sure that the following rule is obeyed:

If a calculator is a Model XT-10, then the simple instructions must be on the panel on the back side.

Clerks must work as quickly as possible, so you want to turn over the fewest number of calculators while making sure that the rule is followed in all cases. Below is a sample of 4 calculators on your conveyor belt. Circle the calculator or calculators that you would turn over to verify the rule.

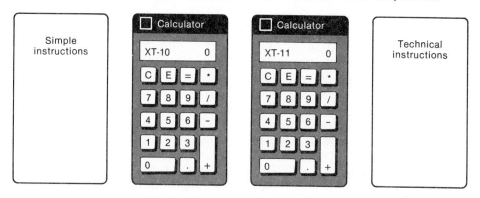

(B)

Imagine that you are a quality-control clerk for Microdigit, Inc. Your job is to inspect different models of pocket calculators moving along a conveyor belt. Your company markets two different calculator models: the XT-10 and the XT-11. The two models are basically the same, but the XT-10 is sold in the United States and the XT-11 is exported to other countries.

Model numbers appear on the front side and a brief set of instructions can be glued to a panel on the back side. The instructions are quite simple (directed toward the consumer market). In some cases, no instructions have been glued onto the panels. These are cases where different language instructions are supplied by the distributor at a later date. The calculators move along a conveyor belt, some face up with the model number showing and some face down with the instruction panel showing. Clerks must make sure that the following rule is obeyed:

If a calculator is a Model XT-10, then a set of instructions must be on the panel on the back side.

Clerks must work as quickly as possible, so you want to turn over the fewest number of calculators while making sure that the rule is followed in all cases. Below is a sample of 4 calculators on your conveyor belt. Circle the calculator or calculators that you would turn over to verify the rule.

Figure 11.3.

The materials and instructions used in the Hoch and Tschirgi (1983) study: *(A)* "no relation" condition; *(B)* "blank" condition.

that people typically take the term "if" to mean "if and only if." However, it's important to keep in mind that such transformations are usually orderly. Once subjects decide how they will interpret the "if" statement, they tend to stick with this interpretation, and their reasoning is appropriate, given their misinterpretation. It also seems that skill in formal reasoning is somewhat dependent upon Western education. Both logic and Western education may have been designed to meet the needs of a culture that emphasizes certain modes of thinking while de-emphasizing others. In cultures where other systems of thought are perhaps emphasized, then we might expect the culture to educate its people to reason accordingly. In other words, logic and education may simply be the by-products of a particular culture. If our culture were different, we would expect both logic and education to be different as well.

The modus tollens literature offers a fascinating picture of the ways in which people can circumvent, or somehow make up for, shortcomings in formal reasoning ability. When we looked at the work of Rips and Marcus (1977) and Wason (1966), we saw that people typically don't do well on tasks that require explicit knowledge of the modus tollens inference rule. However, in real life, people have developed several strategies that can be used to solve such problems. First, the subjects can check their memories for situations that seem similar to the one they encounter in the problem. Thus, the Johnson-Laird et al. subjects could use knowledge of the British postal system to help solve the problem. Although such knowledge was not available to the subjects of Griggs and Cox, these subjects could nevertheless imagine that they were checking identification at a bar. By mapping the conditions of the problem onto an easily visualizable action, these subjects also circumvented their apparent lack of explicit modus tollens knowledge. Finally, Hoch and Tschirgi demonstrated that some situations exist in which peoples' suspicion or curiosity is piqued. In such situations, people often choose to investigate further, and by doing so, they often solve a modus tollens problem. One condition that seems to produce these general **extra-logical inferences** is the search for missing information.

NATURAL REASONING

Most people don't know about logical inference rules, and so they can't possibly apply them explicitly when reasoning is required. The last section pointed out some of the tricks people use to overcome this lack of formal knowledge. One technique that can be used to study these strategies is to give people problems that are similar to the ones they are likely to encounter in real life. That is, although the reasoning process is still studied in the laboratory, the problems used involve making estimates of events that could take place in the real world. Thus, the objective here is not to see if people can reason their way to a valid conclusion. Instead, we are trying to find out whether people can reason their way to a true conclusion, given premises that could be true. In this sense, the emphasis in **natural reasoning** is on conditions that foster soundness in human reasoning. From the pattern of responses, the cognitive psychologist hopes to be able to say something about the underlying reasoning processes.

Representativeness

A series of studies by Kahneman and Tversky has been the basis for much of what is known about natural reasoning and decision making. In one study (Kahneman & Tversky, 1973), subjects were divided into two groups. Subjects in the "engineer-high" group were told that a person had been picked at random from a sample of one hundred people, seventy of whom were engineers, with the remaining thirty people being lawyers. Subjects in the "engineer-low" group were told that the sample had consisted of thirty engineers and seventy lawyers. Subjects in both groups faced the same task: They were required to estimate the odds that the person picked at random from the sample of one hundred was an engineer. Subjects in both groups were generally accurate. The engineer-high group correctly estimated that there was about a 70 percent chance that the person picked as an engineer, and those in the engineer-low group correctly estimated that the chances were about 30 percent. The subjects were then told that another person had been picked at random from the sample, and they were given the following thumbnail sketch of the person.

Jack is a 45-year-old man. He is married and has four children. He is generally conservative, careful, and ambitious. He shows no interest in political and social issues and spends most of his free time on his many hobbies, which include home carpentry, sailing, and mathematical puzzles. (Kahneman & Tversky, 1973)

The subjects in both groups were asked to estimate the odds that this person was an engineer. Subjects in both groups now maintained that the odds that this person was an engineer were greater than the representational proportions in the sample. Both the engineer-high and engineer-low groups estimated that the odds that Jack was an engineer were greater than 90 percent. As you can see from the description, Jack has hobbies and interests that are somewhat stereotypical for an engineer, but his hobbies and interests are somewhat more unusual for a lawyer. In that sense, the profile of Jack is more representative of an engineer than it is of a lawyer. The subjects were apparently swayed by this fact. Because Jack was typical of engineers, subjects concluded that the odds were great that he *was* an engineer. The subjects in the engineer-low group did not take into account that the actual odds of selecting an engineer were only 30 percent.

A *heuristic* is a term used by psychologists to denote general problem-solving procedures that often work in solving everyday problems. A heuristic is a rule of thumb—a general, rather than precise, guideline for coming up with a solution. Subjects in the Kahneman and Tversky study were apparently using what has been named the **representativeness heuristic.** To make a quick judgment about odds, people compare the case in point with a concept that is at least similar to a prototype (see Chapter 3), and compute its deviation from that. If the deviation is small, people tend to assume that the odds are good that their judgment is true. In this case, the subjects in the engineer-low group overlooked some important information when they used the representativeness heuristic, namely that engineers were not very common in the original sample. Generally, people seem to have some difficulty evaluating the influence of the *base rate* in making such judgments. In situations in which the base rate is low, the representativeness heuristic can lead to serious misestimations. To see this, read the following problem and make the called-for judgment.

Pretend that a stranger told you about a person who is short, slim, and likes to read poetry, and then asked you to guess whether this person is more likely to be a professor of classics at an Ivy League university or a truck driver. Which would be your best guess (Meyers, 1986)?

The previous problem has tipped you off, but those who are naive are likely to guess that the person is a classics professor rather than a truck driver. But this assumption is almost certainly wrong. To begin with, the Ivy League probably has about 40 to 50 classics professors. Perhaps half of these fit the prior description, which yields 25 people. In comparison with this result, the number of truck drivers is overwhelmingly large—perhaps 500,000 people. Truck drivers who fit the description may be relatively rare—let's say one in a thousand. This still gives us 500 cases in the truck driver pool against 25 in the Ivy League pool. The odds are rather good that the person is a truck driver rather than a professor, despite the typicality of the description for the latter.

Availability

The work of Kahneman and Tversky also found that people's reasoning is influenced by the availability of material in memory. In other words, when things come readily to mind, we assume that such things are more common than things that don't come to mind as easily. This heuristic is usually suitable for estimating likelihoods; that is, common things usually do come to mind more readily than do rare things. But like the representativeness heuristic, the **availability heuristic** can go astray, too.

Kahneman and Tversky (1973) asked their subjects to estimate the proportion of words in English that begin with k and the proportion of words in which k is the third letter. One way that the subjects might try to accomplish this task is by generating a list of words that begin with k and comparing this list with some hypothetical, uncomputed list of words that don't begin with k. Once this proportion has been estimated, the subject might generate a list of words that have k as their third letter, and compare this list with another, not fully computed, list of words without this property. Spend a minute or two making these obviously speculative estimates. If you're like most people, producing the list of words beginning with k seems easier than producing the list of words with k in the third position, which may result in your saying that k-beginning words are more common. In reality, words with k in the third position outnumber k-beginning words by a ratio of about $3:1$. This misestimation is thought to be related to the semantic memory processes that we considered in Chapter 6 (Anderson,

1980). For example, a reasonable assumption is that words are more likely to be coded on the basis of initial letters rather than third letters. If this is so, then the spread of activation of k-beginning words to one another is likely to be stronger than the spread from words with k as their third letter. What happens is that more k-beginning words are likely to enter our awareness,and from this fact, we mistakenly figure that the contents of our minds are a good reflection of the proportions in reality.

This explanation has been supported in work done by Slovic, Fischoff, and Lichtenstein (1976), who asked their subjects to estimate the likelihoods of various occurrences. For example, which do you believe is more frequent: death as the result of all forms of accidents or as the result of strokes? From homicide or from diabetes? From all forms of cancer or from heart disease? Most people estimated that death was more likely from accidents, homicide, and cancer, but this assumption is incorrect. Although these events are often publicized, the less-recognized killers (strokes, diabetes, heart disease) actually take more lives. In this case, we see that the publicity surrounding homicide and cancer victims apparently makes these events more memorable and available.

The availability heuristic is also influenced by the ease with which certain computations can be made. Events that are easily computed are perceived as more common, and they are consequently more available than events whose likelihood is hard to compute. In another problem given by Kahneman and Tversky (1973) to their subjects, people were asked to form subcommittees from a group of ten people. In one group, the subjects were asked to estimate how many subcommittees of two people each could be formed from the original group of ten. In a second group, the subjects were asked to estimate how many subcommittees of eight people each could be formed from the original ten. The median estimate for subjects in the first group was seventy subcommittees, and the median estimate for subjects in the second group was twenty subcommittees. The number of subcommittees that can be formed is actually the same in each case: forty-five. Do you see why it's the same? Every group of two that is formed leaves a remainder of eight people who could make up a different subcommittee. Every subcommittee of eight that is made up also leaves a remainder of two from the original group. The subjects apparently didn't realize this point. Kahneman and Tversky maintain that the subjects probably began to compute the various groupings and succeeded in producing a fairly large number of two-people subcommittees in a short time. Subjects who started in the eight-person condition had a harder task. Computing the members of the subcommittee is difficult, as is storing the result. After a period time, subjects in the eight-person condition probably hadn't generated as many subcommittees as the subjects in the other group, and so were inclined to estimate that there weren't that many of them.

Framing Decisions

As the previous section implied, the way in which a question is asked can influence an individual's reasoning process. Kahneman and Tversky (1982) refer to this process as **framing.** Essentially, framing refers to steering the reasoning processes by increasing the availability or representativeness of the desired outcome. Subjects read information such as the following:

Imagine that the U.S. is preparing for the outbreak of an unusual Asian disease, which is expected to kill 600 people. Two alternative programs to combat the disease have been proposed. Assume that the exact scientific estimate of the consequences of the program are as follows:
If Program A is adopted, 200 people will be saved.
If Program B is adopted, there is a 1/3 probability that 600 people will be saved and a 2/3 probability that no people will be saved.

When asked which program they would pick, about 75 percent of the subjects chose Program A. The subjects were then given the following choice:

If Program A is adopted, 400 people will die.
If Program B is adopted, there is a 1/3 probability that nobody will die, and a 2/3 probability that 600 people will die.

In the latter case, about 75 percent of the subjects favored Program B. In the first case, the two-thirds probability that no people will be saved seems like a steep price to pay for the one-third probability (fairly low odds) of saving all the people. In contrast to this, two hundred people saved seems like a tangible, solid, and beneficial result. In the second case, the one-third probability that everybody can be saved looks like a long shot, but it seems better than ensuring the deaths of four hundred people if Program A were adopted.

Summary of Natural Reasoning

In one sense, people apparently don't perform much better on everyday reasoning tasks than they do on formal reasoning tasks. When we look at people's ability to estimate probabilities, we see that they seem to rely on several rules of thumb, and this reliance is more or less uncritical. People seem to think that if a person or event is more representative of some category, then the likelihood is great that the person or event *is* a member of that category even though the base rate of such an event may be low. The representativeness heuristic produces errors when people fail to take base rates into account. People are also influenced by the ease with which certain events can be computed. What is easily computed and stored is thought to be more commonplace than rare or unusual things. Generally, the Kahneman and Tversky findings can be interpreted as showing that people seem to possess little sensitivity to these biases; they are unaware that they have them. As a general finding, therefore, we might say that people are far from optimal reasoners when asked to reason formally, or to estimate the likelihoods of outcomes (Wickens, 1984). This finding might seem discouraging, but we have to realize that the use of heuristics in reasoning doesn't guarantee anything. A heuristic is a tool, or reasoning device, that has the advantages of simplicity and speed. This ease of use requires a price to be paid. In some situations, the heuristic produces a biased estimate, and people are usually unaware of this bias.

CONCEPT ATTAINMENT

Human reasoning has been studied in a variety of ways. Researchers have sometimes focused on the functional aspect of reasoning: its purpose. For most people, the purpose of reasoning seems to be the establishment of a workable truth. *Truth* refers to the establishment of a regularity between events that enables some degree of prediction and the reduction of uncertainty. People, and some animals, often use a general method to establish these regularities. They begin by assuming that some stated connection between events exists. Next, they observe subsequent recurrences of the events to see whether the assumed relationship is verified or falsified. In a way, human reasoners function like scientists, who seek to confirm or disprove a hypothesis about the relationship between two events. When a hypothesis has been repeatedly confirmed, it may acquire the status of a rule. Psychologists have long been interested in the inferential processes we use to establish such rules: they describe this construction process as *concept formation* or *concept attainment*.

Many of these inferential processes are hidden to us because in our everyday conversations, we often use the term *concept* a little differently than psychologists do. A concept often becomes some sort of general idea about something. However, we feel confident that we have some concepts firmly in our grasp. For example, we're sure that we "have" the concept of a table, which means that we have a general idea of what a table is and that we can classify objects as tables or not. Many psychologists find both the nature of our knowledge and our certainty of it puzzling for several reasons. First, although we may be able to classify objects as tables, we probably cannot be specific about the rule we use in our classification. For example, think for a minute about your table concept. You might try writing down the things that make a table a table. Now, can you imagine some object that meets the criteria you've listed but is nevertheless not a table? Further, can you imagine some objects that clearly are tables but are not covered in your list? You can no doubt come up with some counterexamples, and no matter how much you try to modify your list, you'll probably still be able to come up with more counterexamples. This raises a problem: In forming concepts, people behave as though they were establishing certain rules, yet they seem unable to specify those rules. In other words, how do you know a table is a table if you can't specify the rule you're using to decide?

A second puzzle concerns the origin of this table concept: Where did it come from? Although you have seen many tables in your lifetime, you have not seen every table ever made. What you see, therefore, is only a small sample of the universe of possible tables. Yet, from this relatively small sample of knowledge, you have been able to construct a concept that works well most of the time.

In their attempts to crack these puzzles, psychologists have made several assumptions. First, they have assumed that all specific tables (and more generally, all the members of any concept) must have *something* in common. Second, they have assumed that these common features are expressed in every member of the concept. Third, they have assumed that the features can be extracted from every member of the concept. Taken together, these assumptions imply that our concepts are the result of our ability to extract common features from various stimuli, and our ability to encode future presentations of those stimuli in terms of previously extracted features.

Formal and natural reasoning were discussed earlier, and a similar division is used here. *Artificial concept formation* refers to the study of deliberately concocted stimuli that have clearly specifiable common features. Researchers in this area are usually interested in the processes of hypothesis formation and testing. Later sections consider the applicability of this literature to naturally occurring categories.

Artificial Concepts

Perhaps the granddaddy of the artificial concept literature is the work of Bruner, Goodnow, and Austin (1956). The stimuli used in this study consisted of eighty-one cards, which are shown in Figure 11.4. The set of cards had four dimensions, each of which had three *values,* or levels. *Shape* was one dimension; its three values were circle, cross, or square. *Color* was another dimension (values: red, black, green). *Border number* was the third dimension (values: 1, 2, or 3). *Object number* was the final dimension, with its values of 1, 2, or 3. Concepts were defined by rules that specified that certain cards were "in the concept"; that is, only certain cards of the set of eighty-one met the criteria implied by the rule. The subjects' task was to discover the rule that was currently in force. Several types of rules were used in the study; among them were *single value concepts,* which specified that all cards having one particular value of one particular dimension were in the concept. A rule specifying all green cards is an example of a single value concept. Somewhat more difficult for the subjects were *conjunctive concepts.* These rules specified the concept as having one value on one dimension *and* one value on some other dimension (e.g., green crosses). More difficult still were the *disjunctive concepts*—rules specifying that the concept had one value of one dimension *or* one value of some other dimension (e.g., green or cross).

The stimuli were presented to the subjects in one of two ways. In the **reception paradigm,** the subjects were shown a single card and were asked to state whether or not that card was in the concept. The experimenter then informed the subjects that the response was correct or incorrect. In the other procedure, the **selection paradigm,** the entire set of eighty-one cards was on view, and the subjects selected a particular card, stating whether or not it was in the concept. Following the selection and judgment, the experimenter informed the subjects about the correctness of the response.

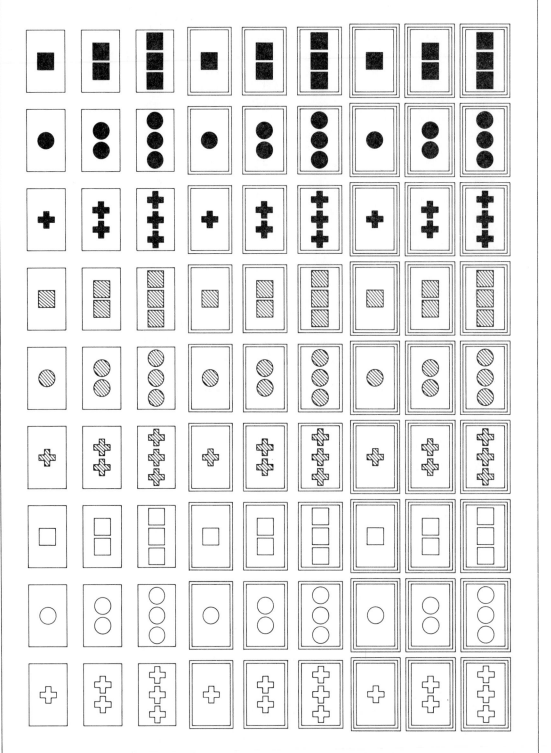

Figure 11.4.

Material used by Bruner, Goodnow, and Austin (1956) in one of their studies of concept identification. The array consists of instances of combinations of four attributes, each exhibiting three values. Open figures are in green, solid figures in black, and gray figures in red. (From A Study of Thinking. Copyright © 1956. Reprinted by permission of John Wiley & Sons, Inc.)

The Bruner et al. study is perhaps most famous for its discovery of strategies used by subjects in both reception and the selection paradigms. In the reception paradigm, subjects used two strategies:

1. **Wholist strategy.** With this stategy, subjects had to remember all the attributes common to those instances in which the response was correct and ignore everything else, thus eliminating attributes that were not part of a positive instance.
2. **Partist strategy.** Subjects using the second strategy focused on one hypothesis at a time (for example, color green = yes), kept the hypothesis if it correctly predicted the membership of a stimulus card, and formed a new one based on all past experiences if it did not.

These strategies are shown in Table 11.4. Of these, the wholist strategy is the optimal one and was used by 65 percent of the subjects to a greater or lesser extent. The following example takes a look at the wholist strategy in practice. Suppose the first card the subject sees is

two borders, two red squares

and also assume that the subject is working on some conjunctive rule and correctly guesses that this card is in the concept. This card then becomes the *initial positive instance,* and all its features are encoded as the initial hypothesis about the concept. In this case, the features are two border lines, two objects, red colors, and square shapes. Suppose the subject is next given the card

one border, one red square.

In this situation, the subject would judge this card as not being in the concept. If the subject is informed that the response is correct, then the current hypothesis is maintained. If the subject is told that the response is incorrect, that is, that the second card *is* in the concept, then the subject makes up a new hypothesis based on whatever the old hypothesis and the current card have in common, namely

red squares

The wholist strategy is the optimal one for the reception paradigm because it puts a minimum load on memory. The subject has only the current hypothesis to remember. Technically, the wholist strategy is easy to use, because the only time the subjects must take action is when they guess incorrectly.

Bruner et al. also discovered that the subjects would use strategies in selection paradigm. They listed four possible strategies:

1. **Simultaneous scanning,** in which the subject began with all possible hypotheses and eliminated the untenable ones after each instance.

TABLE 11.4

Strategies in Concept Learning

When subjects are presented with a series of instances selected from those shown and told whether each is a positive or negative instance, they may adopt one of the following strategies or a mixed combination.

Wholist Strategy

Take the first positive instance and retain all the positive attributes as the initial hypothesis. Then, as more instances are presented, eliminate any attribute in this set which does not occur with a positive instance.

	POSITIVE INSTANCE	NEGATIVE INSTANCE
Confirming	Maintain the hypothesis now in force.	Maintain the hypothesis now in force.
Infirming	Take as the next hypothesis what the old hypothesis and the present instance have in common.	Impossible unless one has misreckoned. If one has misreckoned, correct from memory of past instances and present hypothesis.

Partist Strategy

Begin with part of the first positive instance as an hypothesis (for example, choose just one attribute). Then retain or change it in the following way.

	POSITIVE INSTANCE	NEGATIVE INSTANCE
Confirming	Maintain hypothesis now in force.	Maintain hypothesis now in force.
Infirming	Change hypothesis to make it consistent with past instances, that is, choose an hypothesis not previously infirmed.	Change hypothesis to make it consistent with past instances, that is, choose hypothesis not previously infirmed.

Source: Bruner, Goodnow, and Austin, (1956).

2. **Successive scanning,** in which the subject began with one hypothesis, kept it if it correctly predicted class membership, and changed it to another based on all past experience if it did not.
3. **Conservative focusing,** in which the subject picked one positive instance and selected subsequent cards that changed one attribute at a time.
4. **Focus gambling,** in which the subject picked one positive instance and selected subsequent cards that changed several attribute values at a time.

Let's consider the focusing strategies. Once again, let's assume that the subject is working on a conjunctive rule. Suppose the subject picks the following card:

three red triangles and three borders

and correctly guesses that it is in the concept. This guess limits the number of possible correct solutions to fifteen. That is, the subject must continue to investigate only fifteen rules. The subject using the conservative focusing strategy might now attempt to find out which dimensions of the concepts are the relevant ones. Suppose the subject now selects

two red triangles and three borders.

If the subject is told this card is in the concept, then she can infer that number of shapes is not a relevant dimension, and can limit future guessing to testing the three remaining dimensions. If the subject is told that the guess is *not* in the concept, then she can infer that number of shapes is a relevant dimension. If the guess is positive, only seven solutions remain possibilities, and if the guess is negative, only eight possibilities remain (Johnson, 1978). We might summarize the reasoning of the conservative focuser this way: If a positive instance and a negative instance differ in just one dimension, the dimension value of the positive instance is involved in the solution.

As stated before, the focus gambler changes more than one dimension following a positive trial. For example, suppose a subject made the same initial selection as did the previous subject. Using the focus gambling strategy, the subject now might select

two blue triangles and three borders.

If this trial is positive, the subject has eliminated two dimensions (number of figures and color figures) at once. A gamble is involved, however. If this guess is negative, then the subject must back up to figure out which of the two changed dimensions is relevant. (The possibility also exists that both of the changed dimensions are relevant.) Thus, the subject has to spend two trials finding this out, in addition to the one trial on which he made the gambling selection.

To summarize, the scanning strategies in the selection paradigm are similar to the partist strategy in the reception paradigm in that both impose a fairly heavy load on the memory of the subject. For that reason, focusing strategies are usually more efficient, and the majority of the subjects eventually settled on conservative focusing as their preferred approach for determining conjunctive concepts.

Strategies in Concept Attainment Tasks

For twenty years following Bruner et al.'s work, the interpretation of their findings was fairly straightforward. First, it was thought that human subjects treat the artificial concept as a hypothesis whose truth they seek to confirm. Second, human subjects are strategic on such tasks. That is, certain actions are preferred, while others are avoided. The preference for certain strategies appears to be based on the memory load required to use them; subjects prefer the strategy with the least "cognitive strain" (Johnson,

1978). In addition, it was thought that the subject who used a particular strategy was engaged in some distinct cognitive operations that wouldn't be taking place if the subject were using a different strategy. In other words, the mental operations of people using different strategies were really different from one another.

These basic interpretations were called into question by later findings. For example, Medin and Smith (1981) argued that the use of different strategies did not influence the nature of the cognitive operations taking place. Rather, the strategy being used affected only the amount of information that had to be retained. In other words, performance differences among the subjects simply reflected the cognitive strain associated with having to remember more or less information. Other studies (Eifermann, 1965a, 1965b; Wetherick, 1969) indicated some difficulty in isolating the various strategies behaviorally. As Johnson (1978) pointed out, some problems are involved in identifying focus gambling. Consider the following situation. Suppose the subject guesses correctly on her initial trial. If the subject alters only one dimension, then she will be classified as using conservative focusing. The subject would not bother altering all four dimensions, because they would surely not be in the concept, and no hypotheses would be eliminated from consideration. The subject has only two alternatives to conservative focusing: changing two or three dimensions. In either case, such a response would be classified as focus gambling. However, after the subject has gambled once successfully she cannot gamble again, because not enough untested dimensions remain to try. Johnson's (1978) point was that it seems unreasonable to classify a person's strategy as focus gambling on the basis of just one trial. For these and other reasons, some questions have arisen as to whether the subjects truly are strategic in artificial concept tasks. Several researchers have attempted to determine whether the selections made by subjects indicate some intention of testing a hypothesis that has been assumed to be true.

Johnson (1978) lists several characteristics of the subjects' behavior that should be present if their actions are to be considered truly strategic. One of these characteristics is referred to as *discontinuity*. Briefly put, if we were to give a problem to a group of subjects who were using two different strategies, and one of these strategies was more powerful or efficient than the other, then we would expect that on some performance measures, such as the number of trials to solution, the frequency distribution of the group would be bimodal. Can you see why? First, those subjects who were using the superior strategy should solve the problem faster on the average than those subjects who were using the less efficient strategy. Second, if the subjects are truly strategic on these tasks, then we would expect some sort of stability across time. In other words, referring to the subjects' behavior as strategic doesn't make sense if their behavior changes willy-nilly from problem to problem.

To establish whether these criteria are observed in actual human performance, Johnson (1978) developed a version of the Bruner et al. task, which is called the *zaps-duds* (ZD) *task*. In the ZD task, the subject is shown a string of six characters made up of *X*'s and *O*'s. The subject's task is to demonstrate knowledge of the rule that establishes some strings as zaps and others as duds. For example, if the rule were conjunctive, such as "3 and 5," this would mean any string that had an X in both the third and the fifth locations, such as

XXXOXO

would be a zap, and any string without this property, such as

XXOXOX

would be a dud. Subjects solved four such problems. On each trial, the subject had a choice of two actions. First, he could enter a string on a computer terminal, in which case the computer would inform the subject whether the string was a zap or a dud. Second, the subject could enter a hypothesis by typing "2 and 6," or whatever, in which case the subject would be told whether or not the hypothesis was correct.

When a frequency distribution of the trials to solution is made, based on over a thousand solutions, the figure has four modes, or peaks. Johnson argues that these peaks in the graph correspond to four commonly observed strategies. One peak occurs at around ten trials; apparently this is the mean number of trials for subjects who use some form of focusing strategy. Some subjects used a strategy called the *two X pattern,* in which only strings containing two X's were entered for thirteen trials. This enables the deduction of the correct pattern to be made on trial fifteen or sixteen, and accounts for the second observed mode. A third group of subjects used a strategy in which they entered strings on the first few trials, then shifted to entering only hypotheses. These subject produce the third peak in the distribution, which occurs at trial twenty-one. Finally, some subjects used what was called a *pure scanning strategy,* in which only hypotheses were entered. This produces the final peak, at trial thirty. Thus, the frequency distribution of the subjects' responses provides good evidence for discontinuity in selections on the ZD task. What about stability over time, another of Johnson's criteria?

Over the course of solving four problems, Johnson found that the subjects frequently used the same strategy on successive attempts. When the proportions of subjects using the same strategy two or three times was compared with the proportions of same strategy use expected by chance only, Johnson found that such regularity was unlikely to have occurred randomly. In other words, once the subjects settled on an approach to the ZD task, they didn't seem to do much shopping around for a different approach. This result was just as true for the subjects who were using the inefficient strategies as it was for those who were using the more powerful approaches. An analogy can be drawn between this finding and the work of Tversky and Kahneman. Just as their subjects did not seem to be aware of the biasing effects of representativeness and availability, neither did some of Johnson's subjects seem to be aware that other, unselected strategies may have been more powerful than the ones they were using.

The use of strategies in artificial concept tasks was also investigated by Laughlin, Lange, and Adamopulos (1982), who had their subjects play the popular logical deduction game **Mastermind.** This game is similar to the ZD task. The subject has to deduce a hidden code, which consists of a string of four colored buttons drawn from a pool of six different colors (repetitions of colors are allowed in the strings). Thus there are 6^4, or 1,296, plausible strings at the outset of the problem. The subject deduces the code by making a series of guesses, which also consist of strings of colored buttons. Following each guess, feedback is provided that tells the subject about the correspondence between the guess and the code. This feedback can be of two types. Each unit of white feedback tells the reasoner that one of the colors played in the string corresponds to one of the colors in the code. Each unit of black feedback tells the reasoner that one of the colors in the just-played string corresponds in both the color and the location to one of the hidden code members. The object of the game, then, is to produce a guess that gets four black feedback units. In the following sequence of play,

Code: Red   Green   Blue   White
Guess: Blue   Black   Yellow   White

the reasoner would get one unit of black feedback (because the whites match) and one unit of white feedback (because of the color correspondence of the blues). With a little thought, you can see how a focusing strategy could be developed for this task. For example, you might hypothesize that your black feedback is being earned by the yellow button in the third position. On your next guess, you might put down the same three buttons in the other positions but put a different color in the third position. If you lose your black feedback, then you know yellow was right. If you keep your black feedback, then you know that it must be one of the other three buttons that's earning it.

In addition to the focusing strategy, Laughlin et al. also considered the use of a sophisticated tactical strategy. The tactician apparently anticipates the feedback that might be given following a guess and divides possible hypotheses about the code into two classes: those that will continue to be tenable if certain feedback is received and those that are no longer tenable. Such a strategy imposes a heavy demand on the reasoner's memory and requires a deep knowledge of the game's structure. For these reasons, Laughlin et al. consider the tactical strategy to be equivalent to the scanning strategy noted by Bruner et al. in their study.

Laughlin et al. found that many of the subjects adopted either a focusing or a tactical strategy. Thirty-six percent of their subjects used a focusing strategy, which enabled them to solve the deduction problem in 5.27 guesses, close to the theoretical limit of 4.5 guesses for an optimal focusing strategy. Thirty-one percent of the subjects used a tactical strategy. These subjects required 5.98 guesses to solve the deduction problem as against a 3.02 guess limit for optimal tactical performance. Although the tactical strategy is more powerful, subjects apparently have a difficult time applying it in the optimal way. Interestingly, subjects who used either of these strategies did better on the task then did subjects who used some other strategy. Moreover, when subjects were induced to use one of these strategies, their performance improved.

The Johnson and Laughlin et al. studies have cleared up some of the questions of strategy use in artificial concept tasks. They have pointed out that the variations in the human behavior are not random, and the choices made by the subjects apparently reflect distinct cognitive operations that have been carried out on an internal representation of the problem. The implication of this work is that humans form artificial concepts by strategically testing a hypothesis about observed events.

Natural Categories

Now we have an important question on our hands: What is the relationship of artificial concepts to **natural categories?** We can get some leverage on this question by going back to Chapter 3, where we dealt with the constructivist view of perception. In particular, the work of Eleanor Rosch and her colleagues is relevent here. As discussed in Chapter 3, the prototype is the name given to a large cognitive structure that represents the most typical instance of a category, presumably because it has the most features of any element in that category.

From such thinking, we may assume that natural concepts are different from artificial concepts in several ways. First, the borders of artificial concepts are distinct, but the borders of natural concepts are **fuzzy** (Rosch, 1973). For example, in the Bruner et al. study, a particular card was either in or out of the concept. Partial membership was not possible. One implication of this fuzziness is that the edge, or border, between categories may be drawn differently by different individuals. These implications were tested in a study by Sokal (1977), who asked three experts (an entomologist and two paleontologists) to categorize the imaginary animals shown in Figure 11.5.

Although these experts were in basic agreement about each animal's classification, important differences arose concerning which features or aspects of the creature determined its classification. These effects are shown in Table 11.5. It's important to realize that no single feature of an animal determined its classification, which was made on the basis of an overall judgment.

Similar effects can be seen in a study by Watson and Amgott-Kwan (1984). Their subjects were children whose ages ranged from six to thirteen years. The subjects' task was to explain the concept of *family,* and they were given dolls to demonstrate the various family roles a person might play. Six-year-old children could demonstrate that a person could play more than one role in a family; for example, a person might play both parental and spousal roles. These roles defined a more or less traditional family. Nine-year-olds could name multirole designations for an extended family that spanned two or more generations. By twelve years of age, children had reached a reasonable consensus regarding the groupings that could be considered families; the boundary between family and nonfamily groups had become somewhat clear. Moreover, the width of the category expanded in the sense that the twelve-year-old could make the comparison between traditional and nontraditional families. Interestingly, however, only some of the older children could generate the rule they were using to make their judgments.

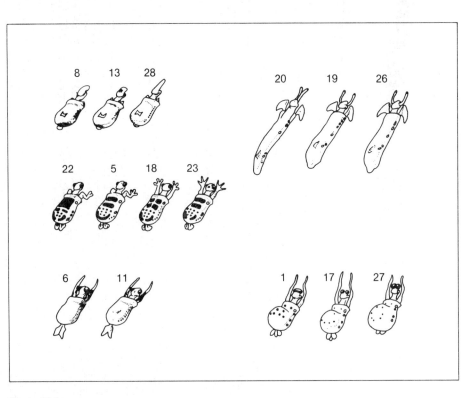

Figure 11.5.

Caminalcules, imaginary animals created by J. H. Camin, serve to illustrate individual differences in taxonomic judgment. Twenty-nine different organisms were presented to a large number of persons ranging from professional taxonomists to children. The data presented here are a small sampling from a study in progress. Three taxonomists, A (a distinguished systematic entomologist), B (an invertebrate paleontologist), and C (a graduate student in paleontology), were asked to group the organisms by their similarities. From the classifications established by the three persons, the following relationships illustrated by groups of Caminalcules in the figure can be extracted. Taxonomists A and C thought 13 was more similar to 8, but B placed it closer to 28. All three taxonomists thought 6 was most similar to 11. While taxonomist C placed 5 and 18 together, taxonomist A grouped 5 with 22, and 18 with 23, and B did not form a close group with any of these Caminalcules. Taxonomist A thought 17 was most similar to 1, C held it most similar to 27, and B described the three organisms as equally similar. Taxonomists A and C recorded 19 most similar to 26, but B considered it closer to 20. By multiple regression of the similarities implied by the taxonomists on 112 objectively defined criteria differentiating the twenty-nine animals (these criteria were not furnished to the experimental subjects), the relative importance of various criteria in judging taxonomic similarity can be inferred. The judgments by person A and C were more similar to each other than either was to B; most dissimilar were B and C. Table 11.5 shows which features of the organisms appeared important to each of the three taxonomists. A plus sign indicates a feature important to the stated taxonomist. No one feature was important to all three persons, and quite different aspects of the creatures were stressed by the subjects. (Adapted from Johnson-Laird & Wason, 1977.)

Another difference between artificial concepts and some natural categories concerns the *centrality* of some of the category members. Centrality in natural categories refers to the idea that some members of the category seem to be "better" examples than others, so that some birds are more

TABLE 11.5

Features of Caminalcules That Appeared Important to Three Taxonomists

	Taxonomists		
Feature of Caminalcules	A	B	C
Horns on head		+	
Stalked eyes	+		+
Groove in neck		+	
Anterior appendage			
Length	+		+
Flexion		+	
Subdivision	+		
Bulb		+	
Posterior appendage			
Disklike	+		+
Platelike	+		
Anterior abdomen spots			+
Posterior abdomen bars	+	+	
Abdomen			
Width	+		
Large pores	+		+
Small pores		+	

Source: Sokal, 1977.

birdlike than others, some games more gamelike, and so on. The feature of centrality is another way of stating that natural categories often have a prototype. Presumably, the most central member of a category is its prototype. Generally, natural category members are said to show centrality to some greater or lesser extent, whereas artificial concept members do not exhibit centrality. For example, thinking back to the Bruner, et al. study for a minute, consider the concept *black squares*. Any card with a black square on it was in the concept, and all such cards were equally good members of the concept. However, not all members of a natural category are equally good examples. These effects are seen quite clearly in the work of Rosch and her colleagues (Rosch, 1973, 1975, 1977; Rosch & Mervis, 1975). Rosch (1975) presented her subjects with several lists of words referring to objects that shared category membership. The subjects were asked to rate each example on a 1 to 7 scale indicating how "good" a member of the category example was. The subjects found this task quite reasonable. They were not perplexed by it, and they reached a reasonable consensus about the items. Table 11.6 shows the rankings and mean ratings for the category *fruit*. Here, it seems that the subjects are indirectly stating that apples and oranges are their idea of a prototypical fruit, basically round and about so big.

TABLE 11.6

Goodness-of-Example Ratings for Fruits

| Member | GOODNESS OF EXAMPLE | | Member | GOODNESS OF EXAMPLE | |
	Rank	Specific Score		Rank	Specific Score
Orange	1	1.07	Lemon	20	2.16
Apple	2	1.08	Watermelon	23	2.39
Banana	3	1.15	Cantaloupe	24	2.44
Peach	4	1.17	Lime	25	2.45
Apricot	6.5	1.36	Papaya	27	2.58
Tangerine	6.5	1.36	Fig	29	2.86
Plum	8	1.37	Mango	30	2.88
Grapes	9	1.38	Pomegranate	32	3.05
Strawberry	11	1.61	Date	37	3.35
Grapefruit	12	1.77	Raisin	39	3.42
Cherry	14	1.86	Persimmon	41	3.63
Pineapple	15	1.19	Coconut	43	4.50
Blackberry	16	2.05	Avocado	44	5.37
Raspberry	19	2.15	Tomato	46	5.58

Source: Rosch, 1975. Copyright 1975 by the American Psychological Association. Reprinted by permission of the author.

Note: 1 means highly typical; 7 means least typical.

Subjects answered questions about central category members faster than they answered questions about peripheral members. Rosch (1973) asked children and adults to respond to questions such as "Is an apple a fruit?" In some cases, the question concerned a highly typical category member such as a peach; in other cases, the question asked about a less typical, or peripheral, member such as a fig. Figure 11.6 shows the findings. Adults were faster than children in responding to these questions. However, for both children and adults, responses were faster for central rather than for peripheral category members. This effect was particularly striking in the children's responses.

Rosch has interpreted these and other findings as evidence that natural categories have *internal structure*. This term means that the center of each natural category is a prototype, and surrounding the prototype are the other category members. The category member that is judged to be the prototype is usually the member that has the most attributes in common with other category members and the fewest attributes in common with other categories.

Formation of Natural Categories

When we looked at artificial concepts, we saw that people tend to establish such concepts by strategic hypothesis testing. Because the nature of natural categories is quite different from artificial concepts, a reasonable conclusion is that natural concepts are developed by prototype formation based on feature abstraction rather than by explicit hypothesis testing. Reasonable

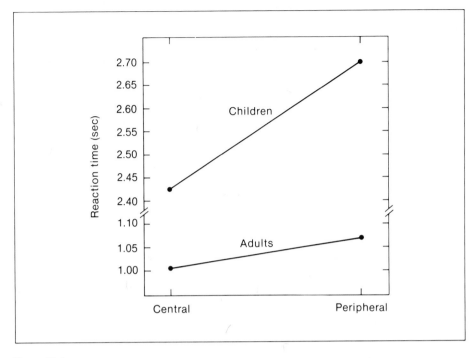

Figure 11.6.

Reaction times for correctly answered sentences about central category and peripheral category members. (From Rosch, 1973.)

though it may be, the actual story is a good deal more complicated than that. First, under some circumstances, people are apparently willing to approach natural categories as though they could be established by hypothesis testing. Second, some evidence suggests that prototype formation may not always be accomplished by feature abstraction. We'll consider some of the evidence for both of these contentions.

Although it seems unlikely that anyone would approach natural categories with a hypothesis-testing orientation, Martin and Caramazza (1980) found that adults would do so under some circumstances. Their subjects were asked to sort schematic drawings of faces into categories. The subjects, who were college students, were told explicitly that no single defining feature or set of features distinguished the faces from one another. Yet, Martin and Caramazza found that the subjects developed a hypothesis-testing strategy to such faces, which involves focusing on specific features in an orderly way. Although the facial categories had fuzzy borders, the subjects behaved as if the faces could be classified with an explicit strategy.

However, for about a decade following the research by Rosch and her colleagues, it was thought that feature abstraction was at the basis of natural categories. As Rosch (1975) pointed out, certain features are not randomly assigned to the objects in the world. Rather, the presence of certain features is more likely in the presence of certain other features. Some features therefore seem to be bundled together. For example, if you consider the phrase "has painted surfaces" as a possible feature of an object, this is certainly more likely to occur with the feature "is made of metal" rather than with the feature "is alive." Rosch referred to this bundling together of features as a **correlational world structure.** According to Rosch, when we create a category we take advantage of this correlational world structure. Consequently, Rosch's (1973) findings should not seem too surprising. Both children and adults are adept at verifying prototypical fruit, presumably because the bundling together of features is strongest at the category's center. The prototype simply has more of the relevant features. Because knowledge of the world structure is less well developed for children than it is for adults, a reasonable expectation is that children would require a proportionally longer time to verify peripheral fruits than would adults.

However, some evidence suggests that the feature abstraction position is not the whole story. Richardson, Bhavnani, and Browne (1982) have hypothesized that people abstract contingency relationships among various relevant dimensions on concept formation tasks, rather than abstract the features themselves. They argue that without the correlational world structure, the process of feature abstraction alone would be too weak to establish natural categories.

Perhaps even more damaging to the prototype theory of natural category formation is some recent work by Armstrong, Gleitman, and Gleitman (1983). They presented their subjects with lists of category members from *well-defined* (i.e., precisely determined) sets rather than from fuzzy ones and asked their subjects to rate the "goodness" of that member, a la Rosch. One category they used in their study was *odd numbers.* Think about this for a minute. Determining what makes an odd number odd should be much easier for you than determining what makes a dog a dog. Because the set of odd numbers is presumably well defined, we shouldn't expect to see subjects report that some odd numbers were more prototypical, or central, than others. But they did. Table 11.7 shows the responses of some of their subjects for various well-defined natural categories.

Subsequent experiments in Armstrong et al.'s study demonstrated that the subjects verified "good" examples of odd numbers faster than they verified "poor" examples, even when they recognized that the category was well defined.

Armstrong et al. (1983) have noted that an enormous amount of research effort has been expended to discover what the features of various concepts might be, and they've pointed out that this research has been generally disappointing. They have gone on to point out that even if the featural basis of some natural categories could be discovered, the process of feature abstraction does not appear strong enough to account for the acquisition and natural categories. This means that cognitive psychologists can't be certain about how natural categories are acquired. The findings seem to suggest that humans are remarkably flexible in this regard. In cases in which the correlational world structure isn't obvious, humans can shift to a hypothesis-testing approach that although somewhat inaccurate, nevertheless accomplishes the objective with a minimum of cognitive strain. The future will

TABLE 11.7

Categories, Category Exemplars, and Exemplariness Ratings for Prototype and Well-defined Categories

WELL-DEFINED CATEGORIES	
Even Number	
4	1.1
8	1.5
10	1.7
18	2.6
34	3.4
106	3.9
Odd Number	
3	1.6
7	1.9
23	2.4
57	2.6
501	3.5
447	3.7
Female	
Mother	1.7
Housewife	2.4
Princess	3.0
Waitress	3.2
Police woman	3.9
Comedienne	4.5
Plane Geometry Figure	
Square	1.3
Triangle	1.5
Rectangle	1.9
Circle	2.1
Trapezoid	3.1
Ellipse	3.4

Source: Armstrong, Gleitman, and Gleitman, 1983.

probably bring either a more sophisticated version of one of the theories we have considered, or perhaps some enterprising psychologist will suggest a way to synthesize the existing approaches.

CONCLUDING COMMENTS AND SUGGESTIONS FOR FURTHER READING

Our study of formal reasoning ability seems to indicate that most people do not reason the same way logicians do. Several reasons account for this difference. First, people's understanding of logical terms is different from the logician's. Second, people sometimes approach a formal reasoning task from an empirical point of view, in which they attempt to use their knowledge of the world to establish the truth of an argument rather than its validity. Some inference rules seem to be particularly hard to grasp for many people; modus tollens is one of them. When cognitive psychologists ask people to make estimates of the likelihood of various events, people are able to take advantage of their world knowledge. However, people's estimates are not necessarily true to life. The heuristics used by most people are "quick and dirty" methods for making such estimates, and like most heuristics, they usually work. Apparently, people are not too sensitive when it comes to detecting those situations in which the heuristic is not accurate.

As we've seen, reasoning is purposeful: It has an objective. In many cases, this objective is the establishment of some kind of regularity between events or objects in the world. Categories are the outcome of our attempts to establish regularities between events in the world. Throughout the 1950s and 1960s, categorization research focused on the attainment of artificial categories. When we looked at this research, we saw that people typically adopt a hypothesis-testing orientation when learning such concepts. Strategic differences among people can apparently help speed up or make easier the learning of artificial concepts.

Although the text didn't mention this, it's interesting to think about the relationship between artificial concept learning and Piaget's theory of cognitive development. Piaget theorized that the final stage of cognitive development—the stage of formal operations—is characterized by the ability to test hypotheses in a systematic way. Prior to the attainment of this stage, at approximately twelve years of age, children fail to test hypotheses systematically. The implication of this position is that children should have a difficult, if not impossible, time learning artificial concepts. And that turns out to be the case. But they can learn them eventually, which means that either children are able to test hypotheses earlier than Piaget throught, or they are able to learn the artificial concepts without hypothesis testing.

As we saw, adults sometimes apply a hypothesis-testing orientation when learning natural categories. Natural category acquisition is usually explained in terms of the formation of a prototype based on the abstraction and correlation of features. However, some recent evidence has suggested that natural category formation must consist of more than this.

Students who want to know more about these topics might start with a book edited by Johnson-Laird and Wason (1977). In this wide-ranging book, the topics of hypothesis testing and deduction are well covered. Falmagne (1975) is a good starting point for studying the research on categorical syllogisms, which for reasons of space couldn't be covered here. Regarding concept formation, the work of Bruner et al. (1956) is very readable, and as the starting point for the modern literature on concept formation, this book will establish a firm foundation for other reading. Rosch has written a chapter in a book edited by her and Lloyd (1978) that summarizes many of the studies and basic findings that Rosch and her colleagues have obtained. Finally, Smith and Medin (1981) review a variety of theories of natural concept formation, and they suggest that a synthesis of them is warranted.

FOCUS ON APPLICATIONS:

Using Venn Diagrams in Categorical Syllogisms

The text discussed conditional reasoning but didn't cover *categorical syllogisms*. Categorical syllogisms consist of two premises followed by a conclusion. Unlike conditional syllogisms, however, categorical syllogisms use terms such as *all* and *some* as qualifiers.

Here's an example (Johnson-Laird & Steedman, 1978):

Some artists are beekeepers.

Some beekeepers are chemists.

Some artists are chemists.

Is this conclusion valid? The answer is no: Some artists may be chemists, but the conclusion that any of them are is not necessarily true.

Keeping the terms and their qualifiers straight in one's mind is difficult. Consequently, logicians have made use of an aid known as the *Venn diagram* to represent the arguments and show their validity or invalidity. You may be familiar with Venn diagrams. They are labeled circles showing the premises and their relationships with one another. For example, "All soldiers are brave" could be represented in either of the following ways:

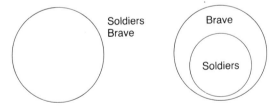

People who make mistakes on categorical syllogisms frequently misinterpret the meaning of the qualifiers. For example, to most people "Some A's are B's" implies that some A's are *not* B's. Logicians see it differently. To them, "some" means "at least one." The effects of this interpretative error can be seen when people are asked to use Venn diagrams to represent logical arguments. The untrained person might see one or two ways that "Some A's are B's" can be represented with Venn diagrams; the logician sees four:

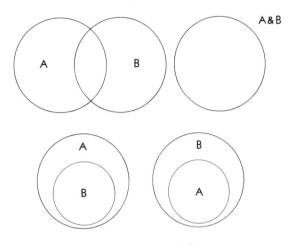

Notice that two of the four "some" representations are the same as the "all" representation just shown.

Venn diagrams can be used to answer questions of validity in the following way. First, make a Venn representation of each of the problem's premises. Then combine these two representations into one. Next, add all the representations of the conclusion into the existing diagram. If a depiction is discovered that represents the premises accurately, and shows that an alternative representation for the conclusion exists, then the syllogism is not valid. Try this one:

No *A*'s are *B*'s.

All *B*'s are *C*'s.

No *A*'s are *C*'s.

Is the conclusion valid? The following Venn diagram shows that a counterexample can be formed that shows the conclusion is not necessarily implied by the premises. The syllogism is not valid.

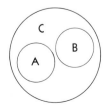

KEY TERMS

Formal reasoning
Logic
Validity
Truth
Soundness
Conditional reasoning
Modus ponens
Modus tollens
Disconfirming the consequent
Extralogical inferences
Natural reasoning

Representativeness heuristic
Availability heuristic
Framing
Reception paradigm
Selection paradigm
Conservative focusing
Focus gambling
Mastermind
Natural categories
Fuzzy borders
Correlational world structure

CHAPTER 12

Problem Solving

OVERVIEW

THE GESTALT HERITAGE
Stages of Thinking
  Incubation
  Insight and Creativity
The Importance of the Correct Representation
Summary of the Gestalt Position

DOMAIN-FREE PROBLEMS AND GENERAL STRATEGIES
Well-Defined and Ill-Defined Problems
Typologies of Problems
  Problems of Inducing Structure
  Problems of Transformation
  Problems of Arrangement

Tactics for Solving Problems
  Newell and Simon's Research
  Subgoal Analysis
  Working Backward
  GPS
  Summary and Comments on the Newell
    and Simon Theory

PROBLEM SOLVING IN A DOMAIN OF KNOWLEDGE
How Knowledge Guides Search
Expertise

CONCLUDING COMMENTS AND SUGGESTIONS
FOR FURTHER READING
FOCUS ON APPLICATIONS
KEY TERMS

What comes to mind when you think of the actions of the prototypical intelligent person? Phrased another way, what behaviors do you usually associate with being smart? This was essentially the question Sternberg (1982) asked his subjects, many of whom were not experts in the field of intelligence. To get people's everyday notions about intelligence, the Sternberg went out into the real world and approached people in natural settings, such as commuter trains and supermarkets. People who agreed to participate in the study were given a blank sheet of paper and were asked to write down behaviors that were characteristic of **intelligence**. Sternberg found a substantial consensus about these behaviors. People's responses clustered around three categories of activities that were indicative of intelligence. Sternberg found that people think of social competence as one component of intelligence. He also found that people consider verbal ability to be indicative of intelligence. But according to many people, the most important indicator of intelligence is practical problem-solving ability. For example, a person who could "size up the situation accurately," "get to the heart of the problem," and then "reason logically" had the skills that were most often identified as indicating intelligence. When experts in the field of intelligence research were asked the same questions, Sternberg got similar findings. The experts listed "verbal intelligence" as the most important indicator of intellectual ability, but "problem-solving ability" was still mentioned as the second most important component of intelligence.

Given that both lay people and experts seem to agree that problem solving is one of the hallmarks of intelligence, it seems natural for cognitive psychologists to be interested in what mental events take place when a person tries to attain some goal in an unfamiliar situation. This chapter considers the phenomenon of problem solving from several perspectives. First, we'll examine a European psychological tradition, **Gestalt psychology**. The Gestaltists believed that thinking was much like perceiving. Finding a solution to a problem was like trying to see things from a different perspective. The information-processing approach to problem solving, which originated in this country approximately twenty-five years ago, really isn't an outgrowth of the Gestalt position. And as we'll see, the results of studies using the information-processing orientation have indicated that many of the Gestaltists' basic beliefs about thinking and problem solving have turned out to be inaccurate. Yet, some important studies have supported some of the Gestaltist's ideas, too.

The beginning of the book mentioned that cognitive psychologists have become interested in exploring cognition in natural situations. Nowhere is this more true than in the area of problem solving. In the real world, an expert is a person who is skilled at solving problems in some particular domain. Cognitive psychologists have asked themselves several questions about the expert. First, How can expertise be described? What is the nature of the expert's knowledge, and how is it different from the novice's knowledge of the same material? All experts were novices once. How, then, does expertise develop? How does a person go from being a novice to being a pro? The last section of this chapter tries to answer these questions.

THE GESTALT HERITAGE

Before going on to examine the work of the Gestalt psychologists, we should have a definition of problem solving. A problem is a situation in which a person is trying to reach some goal and must find a means for arriving at it (Chi & Glaser, 1985). In Europe during the early part of this century, the Gestalt tradition flourished as several thinkers began to work on the issues of problem solving and other forms of creative thinking. According to members of the Berlin group, such as Max Wertheimer, Kurt Koffka, and Wolfgang Köhler, the goal of problem solving was the achievement of a Gestalt. *Gestalt* is a German word with no precise equivalent in English, but it's usually translated as "form" or "configuration." According to the Gestaltists, the end result of all perceptual processes was the formation of a Gestalt, and Gestalts were also the end result of all thinking processes. Thus, the Gestaltists believed that problem solving was much like perceiving. When we look at something, our task as perceivers is to arrange the separate elements of the visual field into a coherent whole. As problem solvers, our task is to mentally recombine the elements of a problem over and over again until a stable configuration, or Gestalt, is achieved.

The Gestaltists were intrigued by how frequently we use perceptual terms to describe our thinking processes. For example, if your friend doesn't understand a concept in physics, he says, "I don't see it." Similarly, we might encourage someone who is stumped by a problem to "try to look at it from a different perspective." We've probably all heard a confused person bemoan her problem with the words "I can't get a handle on it."

The Gestaltists were not particularly precise about how Gestalts were achieved. Yet, they were quite influential in their time, and they provided an outline of the issues that modern workers have sought to map more completely. This section examines the Gestalt approach to problem solving.

Stages of Thinking

All problem solving necessarily begins the recognition that a problem exists. The solver must perceive a discrepancy between the current state of affairs and some desired state of affairs. The desired state of affairs becomes the goal, and the solver undertakes a series of mental operations with the intention of achieving the goal. Problem solving, then, consists of the recognition of a problem and the doing of some mental work to achieve a goal. The Gestaltists customarily thought that problem solving proceeded in a sequence of fixed stages. According to Wallas (1926) these stages were as follows:

1. **Preparation.** In the preparation stage of problem solving, the solver has recognized that a problem exists, and some preliminary attempts at understanding and solving the problem have been made.

2. **Incubation.** If the preliminary attempts fail, the solver may then put the problem aside for a while. At least on a conscious level, the thinker is no longer working on the task. However, at some unconscious level, work proceeds.

3. **Illumination.** Illumination refers to the famous flash of **insight** that ends the unconscious work and brings the answer to the surface of consciousness.

4. **Verification.** The verification stage refers to the confirmation of the insight. Generally, this stage is the least complicated and is usually nothing more than a simple checking to make sure that the insight worked.

In retrospect, this sequence of operations seems almost too rigid. We definitely have times when we put a problem aside, return to it, solve it, and never experience a flash of insight. Further, Wallas makes some assumptions that some modern psychologists might be unhappy about. One of these assumptions is the reference to unconscious thought. Another is the notion that problem solving is discontinuous. Like all stage theories, Wallas's model assumes that the activities at the different stages are qualitatively different from one another, meaning that the mental operations at the preparation stage are somehow fundamentally different from the operations at the other stages. However, modern theories of problem solving have tended to emphasize the continuous and accumulative nature of problem solving. Despite these concerns, Wallas's position has received support from artists and mathematicians who maintained that their own creative endeavors followed the course outlined by Wallas (Ghiselin, 1952; Harding, 1940). In particular, the concept that a period of unconscious work might follow the initially unsuccessful preparation phase has provoked a fair amount of research.

Incubation

Several demonstrations have been made of the so-called incubation effect. Fulgosi and Guilford (1968) asked subjects to first imagine some unusual event (e.g., all the power stations closing down) and then to list all possible consequences. Although subjects' performances were improved when a twenty-minute waiting interval occurred before the production of consequences began, these improvements were limited to the production of more obvious consequences, but not remote ones. Curiously, a ten-minute interval produced no effect.

Silveira (1971) demonstrated a similar effect when she presented her subjects with the cheap necklace problem, which is shown in Figure 12.1.

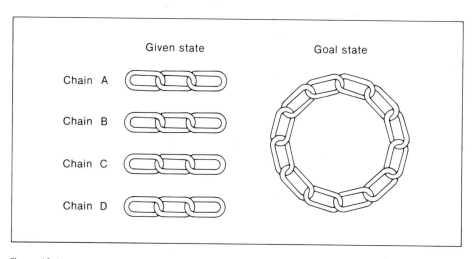

Figure 12.1.

The cheap necklace problem

Here are the instructions to this problem:

You are given four separate pieces of chain that are each three links in length. It costs two cents to open a link and three cents to close a link. All links are closed at the beginning of the problem. Your goal is to join all twelve links of a chain into a single circle at a cost of no more than fifteen cents.

You might try to solve this problem before reading further. Silveira's control group worked on the problem for half an hour; 55 percent of these subjects were successful. Four experimental groups also worked on the task. Two groups worked briefly on the problem; one of these groups was then interrupted for four hours. Two other groups had a longer preparation period of uninterrupted work before one of them got a half-hour interruption, and the other got a four-hour interruption.

Can you guess the findings? The two experimental groups who worked briefly on the problem showed no evidence of incubation; their performance was similar to that of the control group. However, the other two experimental groups showed the incubation effect. Of the long preparation–short interruption group, 64 percent of the subjects solved the problem, and 85 percent of the subjects in the long preparation–long interruption group were successful. (If you're still stumped, the answer to this and the other examples that appear in this chapter can be found in the Appendix.) According to the Gestalt position, this pattern of results is the expected one. The long preparation groups had ample time to develop familiarity with the problem, and this familiarity in turn facilitated unconscious processing of the task. But not all cognitive psychologists would agree with this reasoning. Indeed, Silveira presented some evidence that argues against the hypothesis of unconscious thought. She had her subjects talk aloud as they solved the cheap necklace problem, and she tape-recorded what they said. She found that when the subjects returned to the problem after the break, they had a tendency to pick up where they had left off. If the Gestalt position were completely correct, we should expect the subjects to show some progress during the interruptions; they should appear to be closer to the answer when they return from the break. But they weren't.

The Gestalt reasoning apparently requires some modification, but what alternative explanations can we offer? Simon (in Hunt, 1982) has suggested that incubation effects might best be explained by selective forgetting. He hypothesizes that solving a problem is at least a two-stage task. Initially, we devise a plan for solving the problem that is held only in working memory. As our solution efforts proceed, we encode and store in permanent memory additional information that could easily be formulated into a successful plan, if only our attention could be shifted away from the initial plan in our working memory. During incubation, that's exactly what happens. We allocate our attention to permanent memory (thus letting the contents of working memory decay) and use the knowledge represented there to create a successful plan.

A second explanation of the incubation effect has been offered by Anderson (1981), who suggested that the effect is related to another Gestalt term known as *set*. Set refers to our tendency to perceive events and objects in a way that our prior experiences have led us to expect. That is, our perceptions are somewhat predetermined (set) by our experience. According to Anderson, when we begin to solve a problem, our prior knowledge is used as a resource that can be called up, or activated, to suggest at least an outline of effective procedures for solving the problem. If our set is appropriate, we'll call up effective procedures. However, if our set is inappropriate, we'll remain stuck with a list of ineffective procedures. During incubation, the solver is freed from these inappropriate procedures, thus giving him a chance to call up more effective ones. One important aspect of Anderson's argument is that it suggests that problem solving should not always be improved by interrupting it. To understand this, consider what might happen if we began to solve Silveira's problem and our set *was* appropriate. Following the interruption, we have no guarantee that we'll succeed in calling up the same appropriate set once again. And if we fail at this, we'll probably get stuck using an inappropriate set of operations, which may compromise our chance for solution. This helps explain why several studies (Dominowski & Jenrick, 1972; Murray & Denny, 1969) have shown decrements in problem solving following an interruption.

Insight and Creativity

The Gestaltists maintained that problem solving often resulted in a sudden awareness of the correct relationship among the problem's elements. This perception was often accompanied by the "aha!" experience—the solver is positive that she has discovered the problem's answer. In a famous passage, the mathematician Poincare (1913) describes one of his great insights:

Just at this time, I left Caen, where I was then living, to go on a geological excursion under the auspices of the school of mines. The changes of travel made me forget my mathematical work. Having reached Coutances, we entered an omnibus to go some place or another. At the moment when I put my foot on the step the idea came to me, without anything in my former thoughts seeming to have paved the way for it, that the transformations I had used to define the Fuschisan functions were identical with those on non-Euclidean geometry. I did not verify the idea; I should not have had time, as, upon taking my seat in the omnibus, I went on with a conversation already commenced, but I felt a perfect certainty. On my return to Caen, for conscience' sake I verified the result at my leisure. (pp. 387–88)

Some of the comments in this passage are striking. Poincare says that "the idea came to me, without anything in my former thoughts seeming to have paved the way for it." Poincare is referring to the fact that his insight was not continuous with his previous thinking. In this, we see some anecdotal evidence of discontinuity in problem solving: When the insight would take place could not be predicted. Also, the passage refers to the effortlessness of the new thought; it was unforced and unbidden. This passage thus points out one of the Gestaltists' most cherished beliefs. Truly creative thought could never be predicted by previous behavior, because the creative work was essentially a break in the ongoing stream of problem solving. Such a break could be accomplished only by insight. We've all had experiences similar to Poincare's, but does any empirical evidence substantiate such discontinuities in human thought?

Katona (1940) compared the roles of memory and creativity (or as the Gestaltists called them, reproductive and productive thinking) in the solution of schematic matchstick problems. These problems are shown in Figure 12.2. The lines are drawn so that five squares are represented. The solver's task is to move three—and only three—matchsticks to create an array of four squares. The memory group was presented with the series of moves that would solve the problem. They were shown the sequence of moves seven times and were told to memorize it. The creative group was given some hints that might be helpful in fostering an understanding of what was involved in solving the problem. The presumption was that such hints might encourage the subjects to find some general principles that could be used to solve other problems of this class. In addition to the memory and creative groups, a control group solved the matchstick problem and was not given any help. All three groups were tested on the same and different matchstick problems after intervals of one and three weeks.

The results are also shown in Figure 12.2. The control group's performance was remarkably constant across the board, arguing that apparently not much learning is generalized from one problem to the next. Similarly, the memory group had good retention of the original task after both one and three weeks, yet they hardly outperformed the control group after a three-week interval. The performance of the creative group is quite different from either of the other groups, however. Notice that they performed as well on new matchstick problems as they did on the original problem. The conclusion appears to be that Katona's hints were successful in prompting the subjects to develop a structural understanding of this type of problem. Thus, to the extent that the solution of these problems requires an insight, the

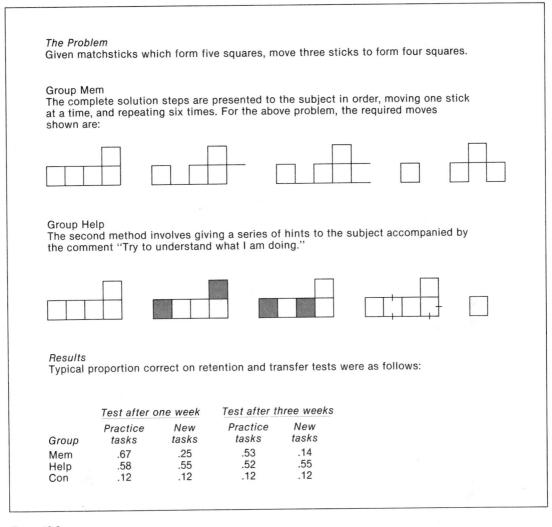

The Problem
Given matchsticks which form five squares, move three sticks to form four squares.

Group Mem
The complete solution steps are presented to the subject in order, moving one stick at a time, and repeating six times. For the above problem, the required moves shown are:

Group Help
The second method involves giving a series of hints to the subject accompanied by the comment "Try to understand what I am doing."

Results
Typical proportion correct on retention and transfer tests were as follows:

	Test after one week		Test after three weeks	
Group	Practice tasks	New tasks	Practice tasks	New tasks
Mem	.67	.25	.53	.14
Help	.58	.55	.52	.55
Con	.12	.12	.12	.12

Figure 12.2.

Katona's matchstick problem. (After Katona, 1940 © 1940, Columbia University Press. Reprinted by permission.)

nature of the creative group's experiences with matchstick problems did pave the way for future insights in solving this kind of problem.

Other researchers have used this procedure of giving their subjects hints in an effort to foster insight. For example, Duncker (1945) gave his subjects this problem: Why can you divide all numbers of the form abc,abc (e.g., 456,456) by 13? You might think about this for a while—it's a hard problem. Duncker found that general hints were not helpful (e.g., if a divisor of a number is divided by *p,* then the number itself is divisible by *p*), but only certain specific hints were helpful. An important hint was that the subject's attention be drawn to the number 1,001, for this is the key to the problem. If the subjects were given the hints "The numbers are divisible by 1,001" or "1,001 is divisible by 13," then they were likely to realize that each of the original numbers could be factored *abc* times into 1,001, and 1,001 is factored by 13.

What we need to realize about the findings of Katona and Duncker is their implication about the nature of insight and creativity. Rather than think of creative work as being accomplished by some discontinuous insight, which seems to arrive at unpredictable times and in unpredictable ways, a more reasonable approach is to emphasize the *continuity* of problem solving. The creative act is one of finding original arrangements of accumulated experiences.

Consider this final example. In 1797, Coleridge composed "Kubla Khan," one of the finest examples of English romantic poetry. Coleridge had fallen asleep while reading about Khan and (as he told it) composed the poem in his sleep without any conscious effort. Upon awakening, he immediately began to write down the whole 200-line poem he had composed in his sleep. Unfortunately, at line 54, he was interrupted by a bill collector, whom it took an hour to get rid of. When Coleridge returned to his work . . . well, you guessed it, the rest of the poem had vanished. Not until many years after, when Lowes (1927) conducted a close analysis of Coleridge's notebooks, did the real origin of Kubla Khan come to light. Lowes was able to demonstrate that Coleridge had seen or read and, in many cases, had written down virtually every image or metaphor that occurred in "Kubla Khan." In other words, the raw material had already been encoded by Coleridge. Coleridge had taken some medication prior to his nap, and it was probably in his slightly disinhibited state that he was able to organize the material that made up the poem.

The Importance of the Correct Representation

According to the Gestaltists, perhaps no aspect of problem solving was more important than the activity involved in understanding or **representing the problem.** Consider the following problem (Wickelgren, 1974):

You are given a checkerboard and thirty-two dominoes. Each domino covers exactly two adjacent squares on the board. Thus, the thirty-two dominoes can cover all sixty-four squares of the checkerboard. Now suppose two squares are cut off at diagonally opposite corners of the board (as shown in Figure 12.3). Is it possible to place thirty-one dominoes on the board so that all of the sixty-two remaining squares are covered? If so, show how it can be done. If not, prove it impossible.

You might enjoy spending a few minutes solving this problem. If you became engrossed in this task, you are probably aware that you spent some time visualizing various configurations of dominoes being placed on the altered checkerboard, mentally noting whether any part of the domino would stick out over the edge of the checkerboard. Thus, your representation of the problem included information about area and edges. But until your representation of the problem includes at least on other important fact, your successfully solving this problem is unlikely.

Figure 12.3.

The mutilated checkerboard.

The answer is that the checkerboard cannot be covered by the thirty-one dominoes. To see why this is so, you must realize that each domino must cover one white and one black square of the checkerboard. Covering two squares of the same color with one domino is impossible. But the checkerboard has been altered by taking away two white squares—leaving thirty-two black but only thirty white squares remaining. We've solved this problem when we realize that the parity as well as the number of squares on the checkerboard has been altered. Notice that the problem's difficulty is not the result of logical or inferential complexity. The problem is difficult because one important element (what gets covered by every domino) is usually left out of most peoples' representations. As the Gestalt psychologists realized, the act of representation is done by the solver, and different solvers may arrive at equally valid representations. Consider the game known as number scrabble (Newell & Simon, 1972). This game has the following rules:

A set of nine cardboard squares (pieces) like those used in the game of Scrabble is placed faceup between the two players. Each piece bears a different integer, from 1 to 9, so that all nine digits are represented. The players draw pieces alternately from the set. The first player who holds any subset of exactly three pieces, from among those drawn, with digits summing to 15 wins the game. If all the pieces are drawn from the set without either player obtaining three whose digits sum to 15, the game is a draw.

I have played this game against students in my cognitive psychology classes, and I often win. When I watch the students to see how they may have represented this task, I usually find that they begin by listing all the combinations of three digits whose sum is 15. They then check off as "gone" any combination that involves a number that I have picked. Such a representation doesn't afford them many possibilities of victory. Are there any representations that might be somewhat more efficient?

When you were a child, you probably played tic-tac-toe, a game whose interest is generally limited to children. Although not apparent, tic-tac-toe and number scrabble are formally the same game. Figure 12.4 makes this relationship clear. The games are formally identical in the sense that a winning tic-tac-toe player would always have three digits from the "magic square" whose sum was 15. The converse is also true. Winning number scrabble players would also always have a winning tic-tack-toe configuration. My mastery of number scrabble now stands revealed: My superior representation of the game enables me to play a child's game against my students, who don't have the same representation.

The Gestaltists believed that improvements in thinking ability were accompanied by, or in fact were dependent upon, improvements in representation. What made the expert thinker superior was his ability to see things that the novice problem solver could not. We'll come back to this point again later, but apparently the Gestaltists were essentially correct on this point.

De Groot (1965, 1966) conducted a series of studies that have helped to clarify the role of perception in problem solving. He showed his subjects, most of whom were chess masters, a tactical position taken from an actual tournament game that had taken place between two grand masters. A tactical position is one in which many of the chess pieces are still on the board, and their arrangement is such that a number of moves are possible. In other words, in many tactical situations what the "correct" move should be is not obvious, and coming up with a good move involves a fairly lengthy analysis of the board.

The subjects were asked to analyze the board to determine what they thought would be white's best move. You might expect that chess masters

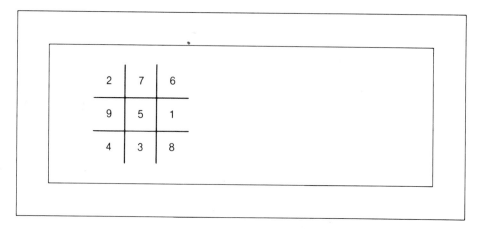

Figure 12.4.

Magic square for tic-tac-toe.

should be much more able to do this than class A players, who make up the next lower rank. But when de Groot compared the responses of masters with class A players, he had a surprise. The masters were not overwhelmingly better than class A players in their ability to select the "correct" move. The class A player could analyze the board almost as well as the master. Yet, if a game were staged between players of these two ranks, the outcome would not be in doubt. The master would win an overwhelming proportion of such games. De Groot wanted to analyze the method used by the players to reach their decisions, and to do this, he had his subjects *think out loud* as they examined the chessboard. These comments were tape-recorded and analyzed. When de Groot compared the method of analysis used by the masters and class A players, he found similarities there as well. In both cases, the player looked at the board and selected a particular move as the basis for a continuation—a series of alternating white and black moves that the player would try to imagine. If you play chess, you're probably familiar with this type of "I'll do this, then they'll do this, then I'll do this" thinking. Generally, the continuation went on until the player felt that some clear evaluation point had been reached, such as an opponent's piece being taken or some identifiable strong position's being achieved. After one continuation ended, the player selected another base move and explored a different continuation until another evaluation point was achieved. After several continuations had been explored, the player evaluated the outcomes and picked the base move that led to the best one.

Although the method of analysis and the move picked by the players were similar for players of different abilities, de Groot found that the differences between the two classes were in the number of moves that were selected for continuation. Surprisingly, masters explored fewer moves than did players of lesser ability. In other words, the masters seemingly had a good idea about which moves should be explored in the first place. According to de Groot, the masters were able to see certain moves better than Class A players because their interpretation and organization of the chessboard were more likely to be deadly accurate, when accuracy was defined on the basis of independent postgame analysis by other masters.

De Groot and other researchers (Chase & Simon, 1973) also learned something about the nature of this organization when they asked chess masters to reproduce tournament positions (i.e., configurations of chess pieces that had occurred in a tournament) from memory. As you might expect, chess masters are quite good at this task. De Groot found that his masters could reproduce a position of greater than twenty pieces after only five seconds of study. De Groot noticed that when the players reconstructed the position, they did not put down pieces on the board one at a time at a constant rate. Rather, in retrieving the position from memory, the master placed a group of four or five pieces on the board in their correct locations. A short latency then occurred, followed by another group of four or five pieces being placed.

What does this mean? The masters had apparently encoded the position in several chunks, where each chunk consisted of a group of pieces that were somehow related to one another. For example, one such chunk was the pawn chain, a group of mutually supporting pawns (Chase & Simon, 1973). It's also important to realize that the relationships between the pieces were expressible in chess terms. For example, fianchettoed bishops are those that operate on long diagonals on the chessboard and consequently have freedom of movement. The masters might retrieve the fianchettoed bishops simultaneously, even though the bishops themselves were not necessarily close to one another on the chessboard. The chess masters were not simply using a geographical code to organize the pieces on the basis of their place on the board. Rather, the masters were apparently using a much more abstract coding scheme, which was dependent upon their extensive knowledge of chess configurations.

This contention was supported in another study by Chase and Simon (1973). They showed chess masters and novices chess positions that were produced by random assignment of pieces. In that situation, chess masters were no better than novices in reconstructing the position. Simon and Gilmartin (1973) have speculated that the typical chess master has encoded perhaps fifty thousand such chunks of related pieces, based on her countless hours of examining and analyzing chess positions.

Summary of the Gestalt Position

The Gestaltists emphasized **discontinuity in thinking.** That is, they believed that problem solving was accomplished in a series of stages that were qualitatively different from one another. Moreover, problem solving could sometimes be accomplished by unconscious work that would be terminated by insight. These matters have provided modern researchers with a host of interesting questions to explore, and as we've seen, these explorations have generally shown the Gestalt account to be lacking as an empirical prediction of what takes place when someone tried to solve a problem. That is, contemporary research has seemed to indicate that problem solving is not accomplished by insight, but rather is a continuous process. However, in emphasizing the importance of the correct representation, the Gestaltists were clearly onto something, and this establishes a theme for this chapter. Later, when we consider expertise in problem solving, we'll see that the expert seems to have a representation of the problem that includes some elements missing from the novice's representation. The next secion examines some of the modern research in the area of problem solving.

DOMAIN-FREE PROBLEMS AND GENERAL STRATEGIES

Much of the contemporary research on problem solving has dealt with so-called **domain-free problems.** This term refers to problems that have a clearly specifiable answer but which require no explicitly specialized training to solve. For example, you may be familiar with any number of river-crossing problems in which a number of people or animals are to be transported across a river in a limited capacity boat. Some constraints are usually imposed concerning who can be transported with whom. There are several reasons for the use of such problems. First, they are usually complicated enough to be challenging for most adults, but not so complicated as to be undoable. Second, the properties of such problems can often be specified in some formal way, such as in a mathematical representation or embodied in a computer program. This makes it possible to compare human performance on such problems with some idealized performance. The advantage of such an approach is that we might be able to discern some commonalities in various problems where human performance deviates significantly from ideal performance. If we find such deviations, they might tell us much about the characteristics of the human information-processing system in general. Finally, if we see some commonalities among people's attempts to solve such problems, we might be able to make some inferences about their strategies, and in turn, their representations of the problem.

Generally, cognitive psychologists have taken two complementary approaches to the study of domain-free problems. First, some psychologists have attempted to classify domain-free problems. This approach focuses on the problems themselves in the hope of finding out the cognitive skills that seem to be required to solve that class of problem. The ultimate—and perhaps unrealizable—objective of such a program would be a catalog of problem types, each type demanding a different set of cognitive skills.

An alternative approach is to look at problem solvers who are trying to solve a wide variety of domain-free problems. Here, the objective is to find some commonalities among people rather than among problems. The hope here is that some general strategies might be discovered that are used by people to solve a number of different domain-free problems. Part of the reason for searching for such general strategies is practical. If such strategies could be found, perhaps they could be taught to people, with the result that their problem-solving ability might be enhanced. This section explores the findings produced by both approaches.

Well-Defined and Ill-Defined Problems

One simple way of categorizing a problem is to determine whether it is well or ill defined. Most of the problems we have considered thus far in the chapter could be considered well defined (Reitman, 1964). A **well-defined problem** begins with a clearly defined start state and has clearly defined goals. If the problem is well defined, every proposed solution can be evaluated against the criteria implied by the goal. If the proposed solution matches the criteria implied by the goal, the problem is solved; if the criteria have not been achieved, the problem is still unsolved. For example, getting to the football game from your house in time for the kickoff is an example of a well-defined problem. The game of chess offers us another good example. The game starts from a clearly prescribed arrangement of pieces. Moreover, the goal can also be precisely stated: In chess we're trying to checkmate the opposing king. Checkmate has been achieved if one of our pieces is checking the opposing king and our opponent is unable to (1) move his king to a safe square, or (2) interpose a friendly piece between the king and the checking piece, or (3) kill the checking piece. Can you think of some other well-defined problems? For example, is the board game Monopoly well defined? The answer is yes. Monopoly and other board games such as Clue or Stratego are almost always well defined. Notice that a well-defined problem does not have to specify every path to the goal state; finding such a path is the solver's task.

Not all problems are well defined. The goal state or the start state or both are sometimes left only partially specified. A problem that has some component missing in this sense is said to be **ill defined.** We are confronted with plenty of ill-defined problems in this world; indeed, most of the interesting problems we face, such as achieving success in life, are ill-defined. That is, how will you know when you're a success? Our intuitions tell us that our concept of success will vary throughout our lifetimes, and so there can be no precise criteria for determining its presence or absence. Generally, specifying the actions that should be taken to solve ill-defined problems is much more difficult than it is for well-defined problems (Chi & Glaser, 1985). Generally speaking, then, a problem is ill-defined if the start state is vague or unspecifiable, if the goal state is unclear, or if the operations required to change the start state into the goal state are unclear.

Little research has been done on ill-defined problems, but what has been discovered is interesting. Voss and his colleagues (Voss, Greene, Post, & Penner, 1983; Voss, Tyler, and Yengo, 1983) asked their subjects to imagine that they were the minister of agriculture for the Soviet Union. The subjects were told to imagine that crop productivity had been too low for the last several years and that they were to come up with a plan to increase crop production. Notice that this problem is quite ill defined: All three components of a well-defined problem are missing from the description given the subjects. They are told crop production is low, but the problem goes far beyond this. To specify what has made the crop production low, subjects need to know something about the Soviet Union, agriculture, and so on. Similarly, the subjects were told to increase crop production, but they were not given any clue about how this might be achieved. Finally, the goal is also unclear. How much of an increase is reasonable and significant? Would a 5 percent increase represent a solution to the problem, or is a 50 percent increase required?

Three groups of subjects were used, who differed in their knowledge of the Soviet Union. One group of subjects consisted of political scientists specializing in Soviet affairs. A second group of subjects were students taking a course in Soviet domestic policy, and the third group of subjects were chemistry professors. Voss et al. found that predictable effects resulted from prior knowledge. In 24 percent of their solutions, the Soviet experts mentioned that the problem's initial state needed to be elaborated more fully to achieve a solution. This need was mentioned in only 1 percent of the solutions offered by students and chemistry professors. However, some commonalities were noted in the approaches of the various subjects. They usually realized that the best way to solve a problem of this sort is to eliminate its causes. The subjects generally tried to determine what the causes of low productivity might be, and then thought of ways of counteracting those effects. Typically, subjects realized that the problem wasn't produced by a single cause but rather by a series of possibly separate causes. Subjects who realized this usually proposed various ways that such separate causes could be dealt with. For example, one expert identified three separate causes of low productivity: the Soviet bureaucracy, the attitudes of Soviet farmers toward modernization, and the lack of infrastructure (e.g., pesticide production, farm equipment production, transportation deficiencies). Notice that these problems are somewhat more precise than the original problem.

This research therefore suggests that people solve ill-defined problems by performing some transformations that result in the problem's being broken down into a series of smaller, more manageable subproblems. The more knowledge a person has in a particular area, the more able she seems to be in creating such solvable subproblems. That is, the problem solver seems to rely on her knowledge to create more or less well-defined subproblems from the original ill-defined problem.

However, we should be aware of several other aspects of the well-defined–ill-defined distinction. First, the boundary between the two classes of problems is occasionally blurry (Simon, 1973). For example, the proof of a theorem in logic is usually considered a well-defined problem. However, as Simon notes, a person may not restrict his problem solving to the symbols of formal logic, but rather may make use of analogy to other logic problems. Viewed in this light, although the proof of a logic theorem might be well defined, the rules for going about such proofs are themselves ill defined. Second, some evidence has suggested that unless people perceive a rigid procedure for converting start states into goal states, they are likely to treat well-defined problems as ill defined—just the opposite of what Voss et al. found.

Greeno (1976) presented high school students in geometry class with a series of problems that involve the proof of various theorems. He asked his subjects to think out loud as they solved the problems, and he tape-recorded their comments. Analysis of these utterances indicated that the subjects tended to break the problem down into smaller subproblems, as Voss and his colleagues had found. What was surprising about the findings, however, was the apparent vagueness of the subjects' subgoals. When asked if he had any specific theorems in mind, one student answered:

I don't know. I was just sort of letting . . . I was just sort of letting the information . . . I shouldn't have said that I was running through all the theorems, I was just letting this stuff, the given information, sort of soak through my head, you know. (p. 483)

Typologies of Problems

As we've seen, the well-defined–ill-defined distinction offers us one way of categorizing problems, but its usefulness is somewhat limited. An alternative scheme for classifying problems has been developed by Greeno (1978). He analyzed several different problems that he maintains can be considered examples of the three basic forms of problem solving. Greeno also argues that each of these three basic forms can be associated with a particular cognitive operation or skill necessary to solve problems of that type.

Problems of Inducing Structure

The first of Greeno's three basic forms he calls **problems of inducing structure.** These consist of determining the relationship among several given elements of the problem. A common example is the analogy problem in which four elements are supplied, and the solver must determine whether they can be related in some way that fits the structure $A:B::C:D$ (i.e., A is to B as C is to D). Greeno states that the principal cognitive ability required for problems of this type is some form of understanding. What processes are required to do analogy problems successfully?

Pellegrino (1985) theorized that three classes of cognitive skills are necessary to do analogy problems. The first class of cognitive operations consists of attribute discovery or encoding processes. If verbal items are presented, encoding consists of activating some aspects of semantic memory. If the analogy consists of figural or pictorial elements, the encoding processes are based on feature extraction. In either case, a representation of the elements is created and stored. This representation is critical because subsequent operations are carried out on it. After the elements of the analogy have been encoded, the problem solver begins the process of comparing the encoded attributes. This process is the second cognitive skill needed to solve analogies. The attributes might be compared in several ways. For example, the subject might use the process of inference making to determine what the first two elements of the analogy have in common with each other, as well as some of the things that are different between them.

Mapping the attributes is another way the encoded attributes might be compared. This refers to the solver's attempts to find a comparison between the first and third terms of the analogy. For example, if the analogy were Dog:Wolf::Cat:? the solver must first activate the semantic nodes of *dog* and *wolf,* noting perhaps that they are both canine, and noting also that dogs are domestic whereas wolves are wild. In the mapping process, the solver would activate the *cat* node, noting that cats are feline and domestic.

Another way of comparing the encoded attributes is called application. Here, the solver attempts to relate the inference drawn from the A-B comparison to the differences noted in the C term, in an effort to generate what the "ideal" D candidate might be. The solver working on the prior analogy might convert its form into the following: Domestic Canine is to Wild Canine as Domestic Feline is to (perhaps) Wild Feline. Thus, the ideal candidate as produced by the application process might be lion, tiger, or panther.

After the solver has encoded the attributes of the analogy and compared them, it's time to engage in the final class of processes necessary to do analogies. This process consists of evaluation. In the example just given, determining the ideal candidate was fairly simple, and so making a response or picking out the most appropriate response from among several alternatives would be easy. However, in other situations, the complexity of the analogy might be increased if the elements differ in a wide variety of features. In those situations, evaluating the alternatives to pick the best one may be a complicated cognitive act in its own right.

According to Pellegrino's account, these processes should be enacted sequentially; that is, you cannot go to the evaluation process until you have completed all of the attribute comparison processes. Moreover, the attribute comparison processes should be affected by the complexity of the elements in the analogy and by the degree of the difference between features among the elements of the analogy. If the analogy has many features, or if the elements of the analogy share few features, this should make the analogy harder.

A study by Mulholland, Pellegrino, and Glaser (1980) tested these assertions. Subjects were shown the analogies depicted in Figure 12.5 and were asked to state whether the analogy was true or false (the analogy had to be exact in order to be true). Notice that the analogies had been varied in complexity by altering both the number of elements in the figures and the number of transformations between the elements. Figure 12.6 shows the findings of this study, which support the predictions of Pellegrino. The two factors affecting complexity combined in an orderly way to produce increases in latency for more complex analogies. Each element in the original analogy added about 300 msec to the average subject's solution time, and each transformation added about 400 msec.

Problems of Transformation

The second of Greeno's three types of problems is the transformation problem. **Problems of transformation** involve finding a sequence of operations

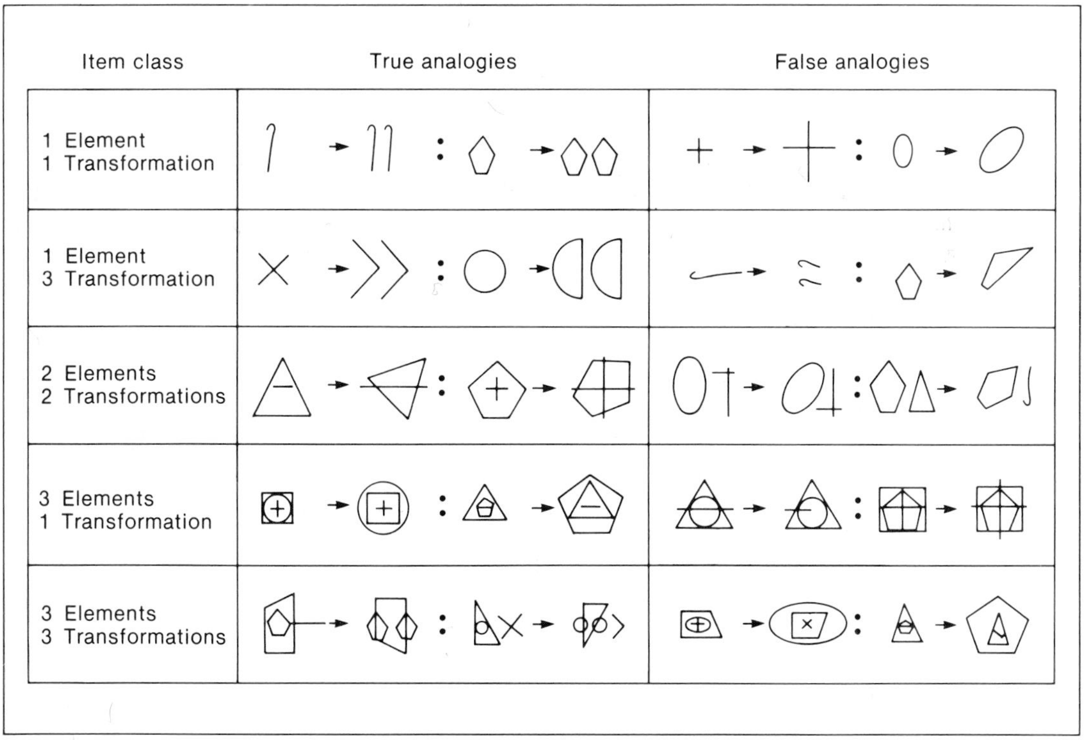

Figure 12.5.

Examples of true and false figural analogies varying in item complexity. (From Mulholland, Pellegrino, & Glaser, 1980. Reprinted by permission of the publisher.)

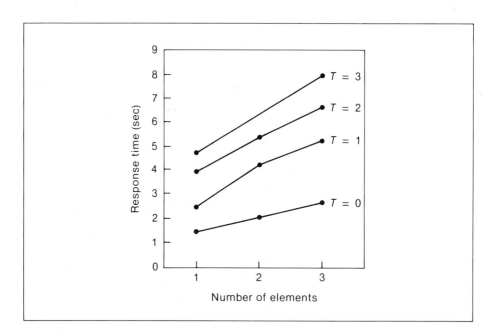

Figure 12.6.

Reaction times for figural analogy solution, showing the separate effect of elements and number of transformations (1). (From Mulholland, Pellegrino, & Glaser, 1980. Reprinted by permission of the publisher.)

that transform the initial situation into a goal state. A characteristic example of such a problem is the well-known **Tower of Hanoi** problem. Figure 12.7 illustrates a four-disk version of the Tower of Hanoi. The four disks have holes in them so that they can be placed on the three pegs. The disks may be moved one at a time to any other peg provided that no disk is ever stacked on top of a smaller disk. Only the top disk of a stack may be moved. The goal is to move the entire stack on peg 1 over to peg 3. You can duplicate the Tower of Hanoi using different size coins placed on pieces of paper labeled "peg 1" and so forth. If you try it, you'll see that the problem is far from trivial. According to Greeno, the major cognitive skill required to do this task is means-end analysis. Means-end analysis (Newell & Simon, 1972) refers to the perception of differences between the current and desired states. Moreover, means-end analysis suggests some sort of action that will reduce the discrepancy.

The Tower of Hanoi puzzle has been extensively studied for a variety of reasons. First, although usually not clear initially to the subjects, the puzzle has an orderly structure that significantly constrains the subjects' choices. Figure 12.8 shows this organization.

As the figure shows, each move in the Tower of Hanoi can be thought of as producing a different configuration of disks, or what we can call a different state. This version of the Tower of Hanoi problem has twenty-seven states. In general, a Tower of Hanoi has 3^n states, where N is the number of disks. The minimum number of moves necessary to solve a Tower of Hanoi

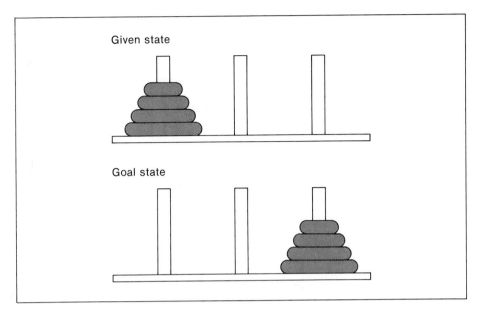

Figure 12.7.
The four-disk version of the Tower of Hanoi problem.

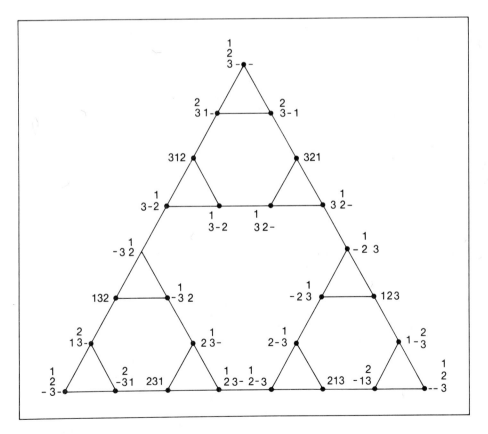

Figure 12.8.
Problem graph of the legal moves and states for the three-disk Tower of Hanoi problem. Disks are represented by the numbers 1, 2, and 3, with 1 being the smallest disk. (From Karat, 1981.)

problem is $2^n - 1$. You can therefore see that increasing the number of disks in a Tower of Hanoi by one essentially triples the number of states that could be entered, but it only doubles (more or less) the minimum number of moves necessary for solution. What produces this discrepancy? Again, it's not apparent, but the Tower of Hanoi problem has a feature known as recursion, which means that the larger versions of the problem contain the smaller versions. In other words, on the way to solving a four-disk version of the problem, the solver actually solves two three-disk versions. Solving the five-disk version consists of solving two four-disk problems and so on.

The nature of this organization is not initially clear to the problem solver, but Karat (1981) has determined that subjects do have some limited understanding of how to solve the problem. However, this understanding is not complete enough to permit the subject to generate the complete solution. For example, subjects quickly realize that moving the same disk on two consecutive moves is not useful, because such a movement could always be accomplished in a single move. This realization is often followed by the solver's understanding that the smallest disk in any Tower of Hanoi should be moved on the odd-numbered moves, while some other disk should be moved on the alternate, even-numbered moves. Together, these realizations suggest the following pattern of movement: (1) move the smallest disk, (2) move disk 2 (the second smallest disk) to the only available peg, (3) put disk 1 on disk 2, and (4) move the only other disk possible. Any deviation from this sequence of moves leads to the undoing of the most recently attained state (Polson & Jeffries, 1982). Although most solvers quickly latch on to these concepts, which Karat has called local knowledge, there's one thing that the four-step sequence doesn't indicate. That is, to what peg should the smallest disk be moved initially? This requires some additional knowledge—what we might call broader, or global, knowledge of Tower of Hanoi problems.

Karat has contended that both types of knowledge can be represented in three types of cognitive processes, which he has formalized as a three-stage model. These processes are called execute, propose, and evaluate. The executive system describes a group of cognitive processes that examine working memory to see if any from a list of approved moves (such as moving the smallest disk on an odd-numbered move) are available. If one such move is available, the person will make that move. If no such move is detected, this activates the propose system. The propose system considers the current condition of the array and tries to figure out if certain approved moves would become possible if the disks were rearranged somewhat. Here, Karat maintains that the solver has two kinds of knowledge. The first kind of knowledge we might call understanding; the solver knows what has to be done to rearrange the array so that the four-step sequence previously outlined can be executed. If understanding is not present, the solver will make certain available moves on a probabilistic basis, which constitutes the second kind of knowledge the solver might have. The final system, evaluation, simply checks the proposed move for legality. When Karat's model is compared with the performance of naive humans, its predictions about move choice and move latency agree closely with actual behavior. Although such findings don't prove that human subjects are endowed with and use the processes Karat has theorized, they suggest that humans have a few basic operations that are involved in these sorts of transformation problems.

Problems of Arrangement

Finally, in Greeno's third type of problem, that of arrangement, the solver is given some element that must be rearranged according to some criterion. A typical example of **problems of arrangement** is the anagram, and the principal cognitive skill needed to do such a problem is that of constructive search. That is, the solver must develop some way of systematically examining reasonable combinations of letters until the solution is found. This task is not easy. A five-letter anagram has 5! or 120 possible combinations. If you were to search through this number of combinations at the rate of one per second, coming up with the answer might take as long as two minutes. Since most people can solve such anagrams faster than that, however, the subjects don't seem to be searching the combinations randomly.

For most subjects not all 120 possibilities are examined. Consider the following anagram:

AIFMA

If you are even moderately aware of your own thought processes, you know you quickly became aware that the first two letters of the anagram almost certainly had to be separated. Few English words begin with the letters *AI*. Similarly, you know that the letters *MA* form a fairly common syllable in English that occurs at the beginning or ending of words (probably more often at the beginning). Perhaps you mentally shifted the *MA* combination around while visualizing various combinations of the remaining three letters. Greeno calls this type of thinking "generating partial solutions" (Greeno, 1978). That is, the problem solver produces what are believed to the components of the entire solution, and these components are fabricated on the basis of the solver's knowledge.

This process is a roughly analogous to the **local-global distinction** we made in regard to transformation problems. The person who is generating partial solutions has some local knowledge, but not complete global knowledge, of the task. This implies that an anagram would become more difficult if its letters could be combined systematically in a large number of ways. This hypothesis was supported in a study by Ronning (1965), who determined that anagrams are harder to solve if their letters can be organized in a variety of ways that are consistent with the rules of English phonology. In addition to this phonetic knowledge, other evidence indicates that knowledge of the anagram's semantic category (knowing, for example, that the anagram can be rearranged to make "a form of transportation") also facilitates the search process (Dominowski & Ekstrand, 1967; Richardson & Johnson, 1980), probably because it somewhat constrains the search process.

Greeno's work is an endeavor to identify various classes of problems that seem to require different classes of cognitive skills. We have seen that the problems that Greeno has identified as protoypical do require some different skills, but the skills required also seem to overlap. For example, constructive search is brought into play both for transformation problems as well as for arrangement problems. This has led some cognitive psychologists to wonder if perhaps the problem should be turned around. Instead of trying to identify classes of problems that differ from one another, perhaps the focus should be on what takes place in the solver's mind. This has resulted in a search for what we might call general problem strategies that can be used across a wide variety of problems. The next section reviews the outcome of this line of investigation.

Tactics for Solving Problems

Greeno's work has suggested that different types of problems can best be solved with relevant and particular skills. Are any sort of general strategies available that might be useful in solving a wide variety of problems?

Before we examine some of these all-purpose strategies, it's important to offer a definition of **strategy.** *Strategy* is derived from the Greek *strategos,* a root that originally meant "trick" or "deception." The Greeks later used this term to describe army generals; that is, a general was one who could trick the enemy. Notice that although a trick or ruse is *indicated* by some behavior, a trick is more than *just* behavior. The trick implies that some mental action or planning has preceded it. Unintentional tricks are not possible.

A modern definition of strategy must take these things into account. Strategies are seen in behavior, but the behavior implies some sort of mental effort. A strategy can therefore be defined as a move, trial, or probe designed to effect some change in the problem and provide information by so doing. That is, the change is considered informative. Cognitive psychologists have described two broad classes of strategies: *heuristics* and *algorithms.*

An **algorithm** is a procedure that is guaranteed to produce an answer to the problem. Algorithms may not always be efficient, but they always work. We make use of algorithms whenever we multiply numbers together with paper and pencil or with a calculator. Similarly, we can solve any anagram problem if we follow the algorithm of arranging the letters in every possible combination until a word is found. If algorithms are so powerful, why don't we use them all the time? The answer to this question can be found by referring to the well-defined–ill-defined distinction made earlier. Successful solutions to ill-defined problems often can't be specified ahead of time; thus, no procedure can be developed that will necessarily produce solutions to them. We can't have algorithms for ill-defined problems. Even for well-defined problems, we are sometimes defeated in our attempts to find an algorithm because the problem is so vast. Chess is a good example of a problem that is too vast to permit the discovery of an algorithm. Starting from the conventional opening position, the estimate is that chess has 10^{40} different continuations or possible games. Assuming you had a computing machine capable of evaluating each entire game at the rate of three per micromillisecond (one-millionth of one-thousandth of a second), examining all the possibilities would still take the machine 10^{21} *centuries.* Don't hold your breath waiting for computers to discover the chess algorithm.

We've encountered heuristics in the last chapter. They are rules of thumb that have been developed from experience in solving certain problems. For example, if you've ever changed the tire on a car, you're probably aware of some useful heuristics such as loosening the bolts slightly *before* you jack up the car. Similarly, if you play chess, you probably know some of its heuristics, such as keeping the queen in the center of the action, keeping the knights away from the edge of the board, and so on. Unlike algorithms, heuristics don't guarantee the attainment of a solution. But they often make up this shortcoming by being easy and fast to use. Over the past several years, cognitive scientists have discovered that humans often use several all-purpose heuristics that don't appear to be closely tied to specific problems. The origin of much of this knowledge is the work of Newell and Simon.

Newell and Simon's Research

Perhaps the most imposing theory of problem solving to be erected by cognitive psychologists is that of Newell and Simon, which they developed over the past twenty-five years (Newell, 1962, 1965, 1966, 1967; Newell, Shaw, & Simon, 1958; Newell & Simon, 1961, 1972; Simon, 1969, 1978). This is an information-processing theory that begins with the concept of problem representation. Newell and Simon discuss two sorts of problem representations. The term **task environment** describes the representation of a problem in as complete and neutral a way as possible. The task environment therefore is an attempt to represent the problem in an objective way. In trying to understand human problem solving on a given task, Newell and Simon invariably begin by attempting to map out the problem's task environment. Why?

There are two major reasons. First, a complete understanding of a problem's task environment can be equated with an understanding of all the ways in which that problem could be presented. Clearly, for anything more than trivial problems, this ideal cannot be reached. But the solver, in the act of problem solving, chooses certain representations as being more desirable than others. Knowing which representations were chosen from an array of all possible representations affords a great deal of knowledge about the psychology of the solver.

A second reason for understanding the task environment stems from the fact that the task environment exerts a powerful influence on the apparent complexity of the solver's behavior. According to Newell and Simon, the human information-processing system is not very complicated. Consequently, if its behavior appears complex, it's probably because the task environment in which it is operating is complex.

The solver does not typically have complete knowledge of the task environment. When confronted with an unfamiliar problem, the solver must encode the relevant features of the problem to construct an internal representation of it. Newell and Simon label the solver's internal representation the **problem space**—and thinking of the problem space as a subset of the task environment is appropriate.

Newell and Simon conceptualize the problem space as a collection of nodes, similar in form to those specified by the theories of semantic memory examined in Chapter 6. In the problem space, each node stands for a particular state of knowledge. The nodes are linked by cognitive processes called **operators,** which convert one node into another. For Newell and Simon, problem solving consists of moving through the nodes of the problem space. This means that as the solver works on the problem, she accesses, or enters, different states of knowledge. Newell and Simon describe this movement as being under the control of an executive system, and the movement itself is similar to the search processes that we observed when we studied activation models of semantic memory.

An example of Newell and Simon's research might help to clarify some of this terminology. They frequently use the case study as a method of investigation. Their procedure often involves making tape recordings of a subject who has been instructed to think out loud while solving a problem. Consider the following "cryptarithmetic" problem (Bartlett, 1958). (The answer to this problem is in the Appendix. You might want to try it—but I'm warning you, it's not easy.)

```
  DONALD
+ GERALD
  ROBERT
```

The subject is informed that each letter represents a single numeral and that the correspondence between numerals and letters is one-to-one. The subject is asked to deduce the correspondence, such that when numerals are substituted for letters, the resulting addition problem is mathematically correct. The subject is given one correspondence ($D = 5$). The resulting output, called a protocol, is then broken down into a number of short behavior phrases labeled B1, B2, and so on. Finally, the behavior phrases are coded using fairly rigid criteria. Newell and Simon argue that such coded behavior phrases can be used as markers to indicate something about the state of knowledge or cognitive process that was taking place at the time the utterance was made. If, for example, the subject remarks

B74: "But now I know that G has to be 1 or 2,"

we know that the solver is capable of considering disjunctive sets, that is, either-or assignments of numbers. When the protocol has been completely coded in this fashion, Newell and Simon use it to generate two different representations of the subject's problem space. The first representation is depicted in Figure 12.9.

These expressions probably won't be too meaningful to you at first. They are written in a formal notation known as Backus Normal Form (BNF). If you take a close look at Figure 12.9, you'll see that the expressions formally define both the symbols that must be constructed in solving cryptarithmetic problems as well as the four operators that move the solver through the problem space. In other words, the BNF representation is a condensed, or collapsed, form of the subject's problem space. This means that if Figure 12.9 is an accurate depiction of the solver's internal representation, we should be able to expand, or unpack, it. In other words, we should be able

```
⟨digit⟩ :: = 0|1|2|3|4|5|6|7|8|9
⟨digit-variable⟩ :: = x|y
⟨general-digit⟩ :: = ⟨digit⟩|⟨digit-variable⟩
⟨digit-set⟩ :: = ⟨general-digit⟩ ∨ ⟨general-digit;⟩|⟨general-digit⟩ ∨ ⟨digit-set⟩
⟨letter⟩ :: = A|B|D|E|G|L|N|O|R|T
⟨letter-set⟩ :: = ⟨letter⟩|⟨letter⟩⟨letter-set⟩
⟨carry⟩ :: = c⟨column-number⟩
⟨variable⟩ :: = ⟨letter⟩|⟨carry⟩
⟨column⟩ :: = column.⟨column-number⟩
⟨column-number⟩ :: = 1|2|3|4|5|6|7
⟨column-set⟩ :: = ⟨column⟩|⟨column⟩⟨column-set⟩
⟨assignment-expression⟩ :: = ⟨variable⟩ ← ⟨general-digit⟩|
    ⟨variable⟩ = ⟨general-digit⟩
⟨constraint-expression⟩ :: = ⟨variable⟩⟨parity⟩|⟨variable⟩ = ;⟨digit-set⟩|
    ⟨variable⟩⟨inequality⟩⟨general-digit⟩|⟨variable⟩⟨qualifier⟩
⟨parity⟩ :: = even|odd
⟨inequality⟩ :: = >|<
⟨qualifier⟩ :: = free|last
⟨expression⟩ :: = ⟨variable⟩|⟨assignment-expression⟩|⟨constraint-expression⟩
⟨state-expression⟩ :: = ⟨expression⟩|⟨expression⟩⟨tag⟩
⟨tag⟩ :: = new|□|unclear|unknown|note
⟨knowledge-state⟩ :: = ⟨state-expression⟩|⟨state-expression⟩⟨knowledge-state⟩
⟨operator⟩ :: = PC[⟨column⟩]|GN|AV|TD
⟨goal⟩ :: = get ⟨expression⟩|get ⟨letter-set⟩
    check ⟨expression⟩|check ⟨column-set⟩
Particular sets:
    all-letters, free-letters
    all-digits, free-digits
    all-columns
```

Figure 12.9.

Problem space for S3. (From Allen Newell, Herbert A. Simon, *Human Problem Solving,* © 1972, p. 168. Reprinted by permission of Prentice-Hall, Inc., Englewood Cliffs, N.J.)

to use the rules implied by the BNF representation to develop a graph that charts the subject's movement through his problem space during the course of problem solving. This is the second of Newell and Simon's representations of the problem space, and they refer to it as a Problem Behavior Graph (PBG). We should understand that PBG as a trace of the subject's trajectory through a particular problem, that is, a record of his movement from state to state.

Figure 12.10 lists the rules that Newell and Simon give for unpacking the PBG from the BNF notation, and Figure 12.11 shows the condensed version of a single subject's PBG for the Donald + Gerald problem.

As the PBG in Figure 12.11 implies, the subject's search is generally trial and error, particularly at the outset of his solution attempt. This is indicated by the fact that the subject, S3, has to back up fairly often, much like a novice chess player who cannot carry the continuations very far forward and so must constantly return to the base move. In some cases, S3

A state of knowledge is represented by a node.

The application of an operator to a state of knowledge is represented by a horizontal arrow to the right: the result is the node at the head of the arrow.

A return to the same state of knowledge, say node X, is represented by another node below X, connected to it by a vertical line.

A repeated application of the same operator to the same state of knowledge is indicated by doubling the horizontal line.

Time runs to the right, then down: thus, the graph is linearly ordered by time of generation.

Figure 12.10.

Rules for Problem Behavior Graph (PBG). (From Allen Newell, Herbert A. Simon, *Human Problem Solving,* © 1972, p. 173. Reprinted by permission of Prentice-Hall, Inc., Englewood Cliffs, N.J.)

has to back up to nodes occurring early in the problem-solving process. The bottom third of the PBG reveals the changing nature of S3's search in the late stages of problem solving. The graph shows much more horizontal than vertical movement, meaning that S3 has apparently latched onto the solution path. Newell and Simon have carried out extensive analyses of problem solving in chess (Newell & Simon, 1965; Simon & Simon, 1962) and logic problems (Newell & Simon, 1956) as well as in cryptarithmetic. Their work suggests that solvers' internal representations have certain invariant qualities, which are shown in Figure 12.12.

A problem solver's effectiveness is determined by two major variables: the quality of the problem space and the mode of search. The solver is said to be searching for a solution path—a series of knowledge states—that leads through the problem space. Using the "thinking out loud" methodology, Newell and Simon were able to isolate a limited number of search modes, which they called heuristics, that seemed to have wide applicability across a number of domain-free problems. Generally, the solver operates by working forward from the initial knowledge state to the goal state. In such situations, Newell and Simon describe two general heuristics—means-end analysis and subgoal analysis—that seem to describe the mode of search. In some cases, the solver may elect to work backward from the goal state. The following sections consider some examples of these various search modes and their implications.

Subgoal Analysis

Consider the following problem (Wickelgren, 1974):

Nine men and two boys want to cross a river, using a raft that will carry either one man or the two boys. How many times must the boat cross the river in order to accomplish this goal? (A round trip equals two crossings.)

This problem can be solved in a number of ways, but like many people, you probably intuitively adopted a subgoal approach. If you haven't solved

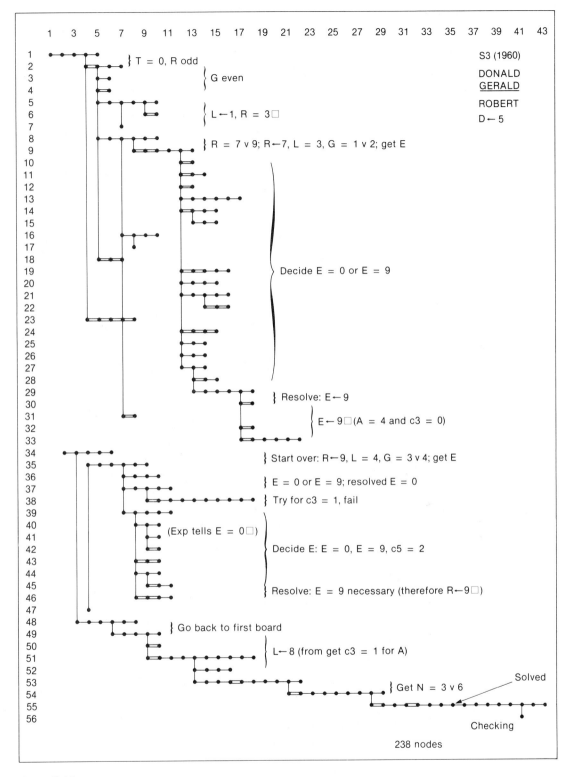

Figure 12.11.

Problem behavior graph of S3—overview. (From Allen Newell, Herbert A. Simon, *Human Problem Solving,* © 1972, p. 181. Reprinted by permission of Prentice-Hall, Inc., Englewood Cliffs, N.J.)

1. The set of knowledge states is generated from a finite set of objects, relations, properties, and so on, and can be represented as a closed space of knowledge.
2. The set of operators is small and finite (or at least finitely generated).
3. The available set of alternative nodes in the space to which the problem solver might return is very small; in fact, it usually contains only one or two nodes.
4. The residence time in each particular knowledge state before generation of the next state is of the order of seconds.
5. The problem solver remains within a given problem space for times of the order of at least tens of minutes.
6. Problem solving takes place by search in the problem space—i.e., by considering one knowledge state after another until (if the search is successful) a desired knowledge state is reached. The moves from one state to the next are mostly incremental.
7. The search involves backup—that is, return from time to time to old knowledge states and hence the abandonment of knowledge-state information (although not necessarily of path information).
8. The knowledge state is typically only moderate in size—containing at most a few hundred symbols, more typically a few dozen.

Figure 12.12.

Invariant features of problem spaces. (From Allen Newell, Herbert A. Simon, *Human Problem Solving*, © 1972, p. 811. Reprinted by permission of Prentice-Hall, Inc. Englewood Cliffs, N.J.)

this problem, try it again with the idea of determining how many crossings are necessary to get just one man across the river. Without too much difficulty, you've probably determined that getting one man across and returning the boat the original bank takes four crossings. First, the two boys cross, then one boy brings the boat back. Next, the man crosses by himself, and finally, the boy on the far bank returns with the boat. To get all nine men across requires that this sequence be repeated eight more times for a total of thirty-six crossings. At that point, the boat will be on the original bank, and only the two boys will remain. They cross together, thus making a total of thirty-seven crossings. The key to this problem is realizing that the actions needed to get one man across can be duplicated to solve the entire problem; the nature of this problem is such that it can be broken into parts (Wickelgren, 1974, p. 91).

To understand the power of the subgoal heuristic more fully, another term must be introduced into our description. Imagine that the initial description of the problem were represented by a dot with some appropriate notation on a piece of graph paper. Also imagine that every action that could be taken from this initial point were represented by a line radiating from the original dot. Again, imagine that each line could be labeled with some notation to show what sort of action it represented (one boy crossing, one man crossing, or whatever). Each such line would terminate in another dot, which would represent the state of the problem as it had been transformed by the preceding action. Indeed, all the achievable states of the problem and all the actions possible from each state could be represented in a diagram of this sort. Such a representation is referred to as the state-action space, or **state-action tree.** You've probably recognized that the PBG and the diagram of the Tower of Hanoi are both versions of state-action trees. A hypothetical state-action tree is shown in Figure 12.13.

The power of the subgoal heuristic becomes more clear when we consider the nature of problem solving as movement through a state-action tree. Suppose we consider a hypothetical problem that has m alternative actions at each dot or state, and requires a sequence of n actions for solution. If we mindlessly plow through the state-action tree of such a problem, we could well wind up pursuing some m^n alternative paths or action sequences needlessly. Assume though, that you know just one state that could serve as a subgoal, and this state is on the correct path to the goal and is halfway through the sequence of n actions. This means that there are now $m^{n/2}$ paths to be investigated from the start state to the subgoal and a similar number from the subgoal to the final goal. The complexity of the entire problem has thus been reduced from m^n action sequences to $2m^{n/2}$ action sequences that are $n/2$ steps long.

The authenticity of this reduction becomes clear if you consider a problem in which $m = 10$ and $n = 10$. The number of possible action sequences to be investigated is awesome: 10^{10}. Knowing just a single subgoal with the conditions just described reduces the number of action states to $2(10^5)$, which is 1/50,000 of the original number. This heuristic will not prove useful all the time. Oftentimes, we're stumped in our search for subgoals, and being sure that the subgoal is on the correct path to the goal is sometimes difficult. Nevertheless, the subgoal heuristic can be a remarkable way to prune the state-action tree. For example, in the Tower of Hanoi problem, it may have occurred to you that the movement of the bottom disk to the appropriate peg is a subgoal that is halfway to the final goal state. Accordingly, this makes the movement of the bottom disk a reasonable subgoal for that problem.

Working Backward

Consider the following problem (Wickelgren, 1974):

Three people play a game in which one person loses and two people win each game. The one who loses must double the amount of money that each of the other two players has at that time. The three players agree to play three games. At the end of the three games, each player has lost one game, and each player has eight dollars. What was the original stake of each player?

This problem can be devilishly difficult unless you work backward from the goal state, which in this problem is the only known state. That is, the goal state, or nth state of the action sequence is known, and our task could be represented as moving *backward* through the state-action tree from the nth state to the $n - 1$th state.

If you haven't solved this problem yet, stop here and try it again. We know what the state of affairs is after three games have been played; what

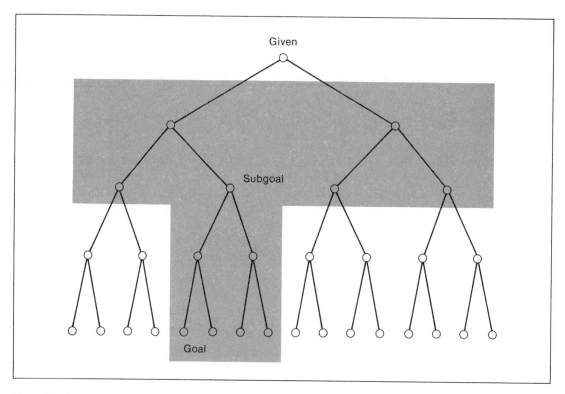

Figure 12.13.

State-action tree for simple problem solving showing how defining a subgoal on the correct path (action sequence) to the goal can reduce the search. In this case, the search is limited to the region inside the two boxes, which is eight action sequences each two steps long, instead of sixteen action sequences each four steps long. Some simplifying assumptions are made, such as that one knows that the subgoal is two steps from the beginning and two steps from the end. However, the average problem is much longer, and the degree of reduction in search by defining subgoals is far greater than in this simple example.

happened in the third game? One person lost, and two won. The person who lost doubled the money of those who won. Because everyone has ended up with eight dollars, the two people who won the third game must have had only four dollars after two games. Consequently, the person who lost the third game had to pay out eight dollars to the two winners, so the loser of the third game must have had sixteen dollars after two games had been played. If you haven't solved the problem yet, I'll leave it up to you to use this same reasoning to determine what happened on the second and finally, the first games. What conditions of the state-action tree must hold if the method of working backward is to be successful?

According to Wickelgren, these techniques will be useful if the problem satisfies two criteria. First, the problem should have a uniquely specified goal. The problem should have a single ending state that can be clearly described. The heuristic is particularly powerful in situations that involve a large number of plausible initial states. Here, the advantage of working backward accrues from the fact that the goal tells you where you must start to solve the problem, whereas the more conventional working forward techniques do not tell you which of the many initial statements will lead to the goal. Working forward in such a problem has been compared to finding a needle in a haystack (Newell, Shaw, & Simon, 1962), and working backward is analogous to letting the needle find its way out of the haystack.

GPS

These general heuristics that Newell and Simon discovered have been incorporated into a computer program known as the General Problem Solver, or **GPS.** The program is intended as a simulation of human problem solving, meaning that it is supposed to duplicate the outcome of human thought by duplicating the process of human thought. How does it work?

Basically, GPS has to be fed with a description of the problem to be solved. In this sense, the program does not really form its own problem space (although this shortcoming has been partially corrected in recent editions of GPS). Once the problem is presented, GPS proceeds by applying general heuristics, such as those we have been considering, to the state-action tree and evaluating its progress. The heuristic most typically used is means-end analysis, which we have examined before. For example, when confronted with the Tower of Hanoi problem, several sorts of activities are undertaken. First, the program represents the goal. Next, the difference between the current state of affairs and the goal is noted. After that, the program looks for a method that will reduce this discrepancy. The result of this processing is that a subgoal is set up, and generally the subgoal is accomplished by means-end analysis. GPS has been quite successful on the Tower of Hanoi and other more difficult problems.

Summary and Comments on the Newell and Simon Theory

Newell and Simon's theory emphasizes the relative invariance seen in people's strategies on domain-free problems. They argue that the similarity among people's strategies reflects that the human information-processing system is not very complex: People have a few basic, general heuristics for dealing with a wide variety of problems. The Newell and Simon approach also emphasizes the importance of the correct representation. Building a problem space is probably the most important constructive act that occurs during problem solving, given that the mode of search is often fairly limited. This means that if your particular problem space doesn't include the "right" elements, this is like trying to solve the problem with a representation that may not include an adequate specification of the goal, and may therefore be inadequate for the attainment of a solution. In essence, the problem solver may be searching through a problem space that is not a very good subset of the task environment. No matter how thorough the search is under those circumstances, the solver will not meet with success. The corollary of this assertion is that what differentiates an effective problem solver from a poor one is probably the quality of the internal representation used. We can examine de Groot's work as evidence of this.

Numerous questions have been raised about the Newell and Simon approach. One set of questions concerns the appropriateness of verbal reports as data. For example, Nisbett and Wilson (1977) maintain that humans have little or no introspective access to higher mental processes. This conclusion is based on several facts. First, humans are sometimes unaware of the existence of a stimulus that influenced their response. Second, they are sometimes unaware of all the responses they have made. Third, even if they are aware of the stimulus in question, they are unaware that they have been influenced by it. Nisbett and Wilson cite studies in which the subjects are given hints that are designed to facilitate their finding a solution. Typically, the subjects are not aware that hints have been given. Perhaps even more important, when false hints (which have previously been demonstrated to be ineffective) are given along with genuine hints, people are not every accurate in determining which hints are useful.

Several researchers (Ericsson & Simon, 1980; Kellogg, 1982) have commented on these findings. Ericsson and Simon (1980) have pointed out that the Nisbett and Wilson findings are not concerned with consciousness per se. Instead, the subjects in their studies could not be expected to have any awareness of their mental processes because of the nature of the judgments they were being asked to make. They argue that introspective evidence will be valid when the subjects are reporting about something that they are truly aware of, namely something that is currently being stored in working memory. In their view, subjects are capable of commenting on knowledge not currently stored in working memory, but this comment is an inference, not a report. Consequently, if people are probed in the correct fashion and at the correct time, then the introspections of subjects will be accurate on all except highly practiced tasks.

Perhaps a more serious concern is based on the nature of the problems used by Newell and Simon in their investigations. We should be aware that much of the research on problem solving has been based on fairly artificial games and puzzles that might have no genuine relationship with problem-solving ability in the real world. For example, if you take your bill stubs, receipts, W-2 forms, and so on to a tax person to prepare your income tax statement, we can imagine that the preparer uses knowledge of tax laws and other expertise to solve the problem of preparing your statement. My guess is that the preparer does not explicitly make use of general heuristics to do this task. Thus, even if we ask the person to think out loud a la Newell and Simon, the tax person would not likely make statements such as "Now I'm going to use a subgoal analysis to see what should be entered on Schedule A." This speculation implies that the sort of strategizing we have seen on problems like the Tower of Hanoi might not routinely occur in the knowledge-rich domains of everyday thinking. The next section takes up the question of problem solving in knowledge-rich domains.

PROBLEM SOLVING IN A DOMAIN OF KNOWLEDGE

How Knowledge Guides Search

Chapter 3 examined the notion of schema as a coherent body of knowledge that can channel perception by producing expectations about the stimuli that will be displayed. The schema is therefore an active knowledge structure, and it plays a role in problem solving in knowledge-rich domains. That is, we can think of prior knowledge as activating certain slots, or nodes, in semantic memory. Naturally, these slots, or nodes, are organized. When enough nodes in a particular area of semantic memory are activated, this will trigger the activation of that area's organizing principle—its schema. Once the schema is activated, the subject is able to fill in some of the gaps observed in the existing display of stimuli. This sort of knowledge is exactly what enables the experienced pilot to bring in a plane for a landing when weather conditions are poor, and enables a physician to make an accurate diagnosis on the basis of a few presenting symptoms. In both cases, schematic knowledge enables the problem solver to extrapolate, thus going beyond the information given. Once activated, the schematic knowledge suggests that the solver search the problem space in certain ways, looking for particular characteristics of the problem.

Hinsley, Hayes, and Simon (1978) have presented some findings that are consistent with this interpretation. They asked their subjects, who were high school and college students, to classify—not solve—algebra problems. The problems could be categorized in any way the subjects wished. Hinsley et al. found considerable agreement on the part of the subjects, and that the classification schemata were based on the solution procedures for the various kinds of problems. In other words, problems that were solved in similar ways were categorized together. Such a categorization schema is developed as a result of problem solving experience with algebra problems.

The schematic nature of this knowledge became more even more clear when Hinsley et al. asked the subjects to classify the problems as quickly as they could. They found that subjects were able to classify the problems after hearing only the initial sentence. For example, the subjects might hear a sentence such as "An airplane with a tail wind takes two hours to fly 230 miles." After hearing this sentence, subjects could quickly and reliably classify it as belonging to a "river current" problem in which some velocity has to be computed under aided and hindered conditions. The speed at which the problems are classified seems to rule out the possibility that the subjects are actually figuring the solution plan and categorizing accordingly. A more likely explanation is that they are able to guess accurately about the problem's forthcoming information, which enables them to guess what the solution procedure will be.

Unlike the general heuristics mentioned by Newell and Simon, however, the schemata learned in knowledge-rich domains are apparently highly specific to the types of problems encountered. That is, there is little generalization from one domain of knowledge to another. This inability to transfer schematic knowledge from problem to problem has been studied using problem isomorphs. Recall that problem isomorphs were discussed earlier in this chapter, when I described the number scrabble problem as being formally similar to tic-tac-toe. Generally, isomorphs are problems whose underlying structures and solutions are the same, but whose context may be quite different (Chi & Glaser, 1985).

Hayes and Simon (1974) studied the transfer of schematic knowledge using a problem called the tea ceremony. In this problem, three people are conducting an oriental tea ritual in which the responsibility for various aspects of the ceremony is shared among the participants according to an elaborate etiquette. The solver's task is to specify a sequence in which the various aspects of the ritual can be enacted in a way that does not violate the etiquette. The tea ceremony problem is isomorphic with the Tower of Hanoi, and anyone who realizes the **isomorphism** can easily solve the tea ceremony. However, Hayes and Simon found that almost none of their subjects, who were familiar with Tower of Hanoi problems, noticed the resemblance.

Simon and Hayes (1976) wondered what made this so. They investigated the variables that seem to play a role in the activation of the solver's schematic knowledge. They used the Tower of Hanoi once again as the basis for nine so-called Monster problems. The structure of all nine isomorphs is shown in Figure 12.14.

As Figure 12.14 depicts, sentence 3 of each problem refers to two classes of objects (for example, problem 5, sentence 3 refers to monsters and globes). In each problem, sentence 4 designates the objects of one class as fixed and the other as variable. Again, in problem 5, the globe held by each monster is fixed, and the monster's name is variable. Sentence 7 of each problem indicates that the legality of moves depends on the ordering of one of the attributes (e.g., in problem 5, the names are ordered by length). If the ordering referred to the variable objects, the problem was designated a transfer problem. If the ordering referred to the fixed objects, the problem was a change problem. Problems 1, 2, 5, 6, 8, and 9 are transfer problems, while 3, 4, and 7 are change problems.

Although some of the subjects in this problem were run through the typical thinking out loud procedure, other subjects were given paper and pencil and were allowed to record their moves. Of the 117 subjects who were presented with these isomorphs, more than half spontaneously used some form of state-matrix notation that offers strong evidence for the kind of representation in use. A state-matrix notation is a two-dimensional table showing the monsters on one dimension and the states of the problem on the other dimension. Here, the states of the problem refer to the successive changes or transformations made by the problem solver. In the body of the table are entries showing what size globe each monster is holding, what size the monster has become, and so on. A typical state-matrix notation used by the subjects in both transfer and change problems is shown in Figure 12.15.

Of sixty-two subjects presented with a transfer problem, thirty-seven used a state matrix, as did thirty of the fifty-five subjects presented with a change problem. Of the sixty-seven subjects who used this notation to represent the problem, none used a notation form that was inconsistent with the isomorphs they were given. This can be seen by looking at the entries in Figure 12.15. In the transfer problems, the variable attributes migrate from column to column. But in the change problems, the variable attributes change their values within the column. Clearly, although the form of the

S1. Three five-handed extraterrestrial monsters were holding three crystal globes.

S2. Because of the quantum-mechanical peculiarities of their neighborhood, both monsters and globes come in exactly three sizes with no others permitted: small, medium, and large.

S3. The medium-sized monster was holding the small globe, the small monster was holding the large globe; and the large monster was holding the medium-sized globe.

S4. Since this situation offended their keenly developed sense of symmetry, they proceeded to transfer globes from one monster to another so that each monster would have a globe proportionate to his own size.

S5. Monster etiquette complicated the solution of the problem since it requires:

S6. (1) that only one globe may be transferred at a time.

S7. (2) that if a monster is holding two globes, only the larger of the two may be transferred, and

S8. (3) that a globe may not be transferred to a monster who is holding a larger globe.

S9. By what sequence of transfers could the monsters have solved this problem?

| Problem | | | | |
Number	Type	Sentence 3	Sentence 4	Sentence 7
1	T	The small monster held the larger globe.	... to teleport globes ... monster would have a globe proportionate to his own size.	If a monster is holding two globes ... can transmit only the larger.
2	T	The small monster stood on the large globe.	... to teleport themselves ... monster would have a globe proportionate to his own size.	If two monsters are standing on the same globe, only the larger ... can leave.
3	C	The small monster was holding the large globe.	... to shrink and expand the globes ... monster would have a globe proportionate to his own size.	If two globes are of the same size, only the globe held by the larger monster ... can be changed.
4	C	The small monster was holding the large globe.	... to shrink and expand themselves ... monster would have a globe proportionate to his own size.	If two monsters are of the same size, only the monster holding the larger globe can change.
5	T	The monster with the small name was holding the large globe.	... to transfer names ... monster would have a globe proportionate to the size of his name.	If a monster has two names ... can transmit only the longer.

Figure 12.14.

Monster problem 1 and the phrasing of the nine isomorphs. (From Simon & Hayes, 1976. Reprinted by permission of the publisher.)

Problem				
Number	Type	Sentence 3	Sentence 4	Sentence 7
6	T	The monster with the small tail was holding the large globe.	. . . to transfer tails . . . monster would have a globe proportionate to the size of his tail.	If a monster has two tails . . . can transfer only the longer.
7	C	The small monster was originally large.	. . . to shrink and expand themselves . . . monster would have his original size back.	If two monsters are of the same size . . . only the monster who was originally larger can change.
8	T	The monster with the small name originally had the large name.	. . . to transfer names . . . monster would have his original name back.	If a monster has two names . . . can transmit only the longer.
9	T	The small monster was originally large.	. . . to transfer sizes . . . monster would have his original size back.	If a monster has two sizes . . . can transfer only the larger.

Figure 12.14.—cont'd

	Transfer Type				Change Type		
	M	L	S		M	L	S
0	L	S	M	0	L	S	M
1	—	L,S	M	1	L	L	M
2	M	L,S	—	2	L	L	S

15-A   15-B

Figure 12.15.

State-matrix notations used by subjects: *15A,* the notation used in solving transfer problems; *15-B,* the notation used in solving change problems. The columns correspond to the fixed attribute; the rows correspond to the successive problem situations after each move (0 is the starting situation). Within the cells are shown the current values of the variable attributes, which either (1) migrate from column to column (transfer type) or (2) change value within a column (change type). (From Simon & Hayes, 1976. Reprinted by permission of the publisher.)

problems was structurally the same, the instructions seemed to exert a powerful influence on the nature of the schema guiding search. The use of the transfer terminology apparently resulted in the activation of a schema in which the variable attributes were thought of as being passed around from monster to monster, whereas the change instructions resulted in the calling up of a schema in which the subject apparently imagined the monster as changing the size of the globe she was holding. There was little or no evidence that the subjects attempted to alter the form of their internal representations once problem solving began. This observation was surprising because the change problems were quite difficult, requiring almost twice as much time as the transfer problems. Also, no evidence indicated that the subjects realized the formal equivalence of the Monster problem with the Tower of Hanoi problem, despite the fact that some of the subjects may have been familiar with the latter problem.

We've seen that schematic knowledge accrued from problem solving appears to be effective only when dealing with a particular class of problems— or maybe even a particular problem. This has led some researchers to wonder if an expert's organization of this highly specific knowledge is different from that of a novice.

Expertise

For the last several years, cognitive psychologists have come to appreciate that the knowledge of the expert is probably organized differently from knowledge in the mind of the novice. Reif (1979) analyzed this problem from the standpoint of hierarchical organization. According to Reif, the expert's knowledge is based on years of experience in which specific bits of information have been associated with other specific bits, which together have been placed in a more general category. This category is in turn placed under a more general category of knowledge. The expert's speedy and efficient problem solving is not necessarily the result of his better use of general heuristics. Rather, the expert's organization of material enables him to quickly get to the heart of the matter. Figure 12.16 will help to clarify this point.

Reif (1979) refers to the dotted lines as pointers. These are associations between specific elements of knowledge that connect the lower branches of this tree and provide what we might call mental shortcuts in the mind of the expert. If Figure 12.16 could be compared with a state-action tree, we can see that actions within this tree are not neutral for the expert, as they might be for the novice. Because the expert's knowledge suggests which branches of the state-action tree are the "right" ones, the reliance upon general problem-solving heuristics is lessened. One of the implications of Reif's position is that if specific facts were fed to the novices in a way that was similar to their representation in the mind of the expert, knowledge and problem solving in that domain might be improved.

Such a study was undertaken by Eylon (1979) who developed two different versions of a chapter on buoyancy and presented them to students in an introductory physics class. One account was organized conventionally,

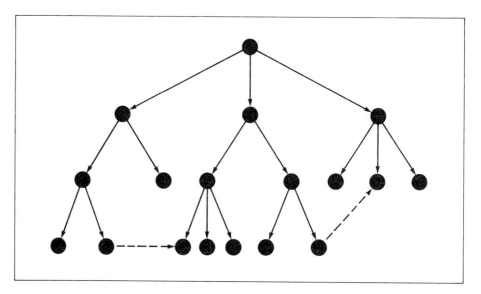

Figure 12.16.

How knowledge is organized in the mind of an expert. (From Reif, 1979.)

that is, like other physics texts on the market. The second chapter presented the information in a hierarchical fashion, based on an analysis of experts' knowledge of buoyancy. Students who used the hierarchical text showed a 40 percent improvement in retention of the material and 25 percent better scores in problem solving than did students who used the conventional text.

This matter has been explored further in some work by Chi, Glaser, and Rees (1982). They asked eight experts (Ph.D. students in physics) and eight novices (undergraduates who had had a semester of mechanics) to classify twenty-four physics problems that had been taken from a well-known physics text. Chi et al. found no major quantitative differences between the groups. The members of both groups used about eight different categories to classify the problems, and they each required about forty seconds to make the classification. However, there were major qualitative differences in the performance of the experts and novices. Essentially, the novices saw some problems as being quite similar to one another, but this resemblance was not used by the experts.

Figure 12.17 shows the diagrams for two pairs of problems that all eight novices grouped together. As this figure shows, the novices were heavily influenced by the diagram that accompanied the problem. For example, the bottom two problems were considered the same because they both showed an inclined plane. However, notice from Figure 12.18 that these diagrams did not play a strong role in the sorting processes of the experts.

The problems grouped together by the experts do not have any superficial similarity, but they can be solved using the same principle of physics, such as Newton's second law of motion. This means that the organizational principles used by the experts could be understood only by a physicist. In other

Diagrams Depicted from Problems Categorized by Novices within the Same Groups

Novices' Explanations for Their Similarity Groupings

Problem 10 (11)

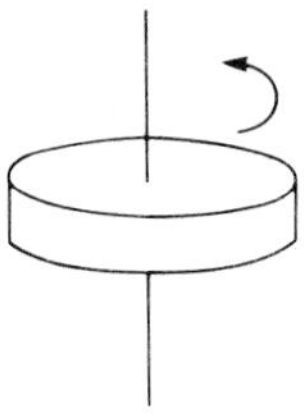

Novice 2: "*Angular* velocity, *momentum*, circular things"

Novice 3: "*Rotational* kinematics, *angular* speeds, *angular* velocities"

Novice 6: "Problems that have something *rotating: angular* speed"

Problem 11 (39)

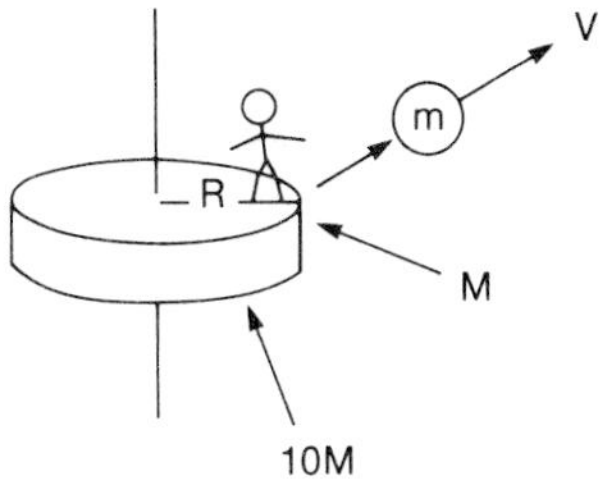

V

m

R

M

10M

Problem 7 (23)

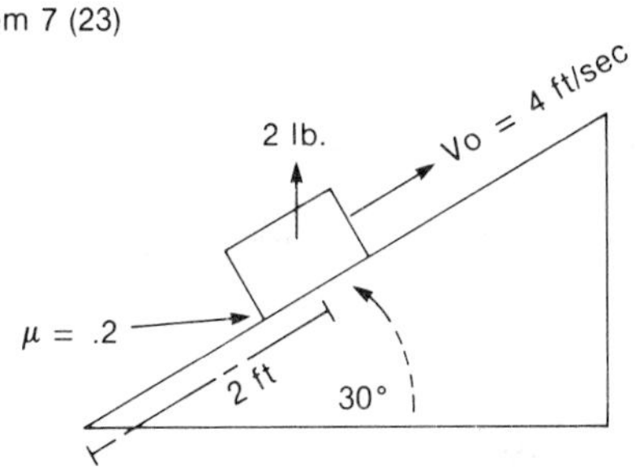

2 lb.

Vo = 4 ft/sec

μ = .2

2 ft

30°

Novice 1: "These deal with blocks on an *incline plane*"

Novice 5: "*Inclined plane* problems, coefficient of *friction*"

Novice 6: "Blocks on *inclined planes* with angles"

Problem 7 (35)

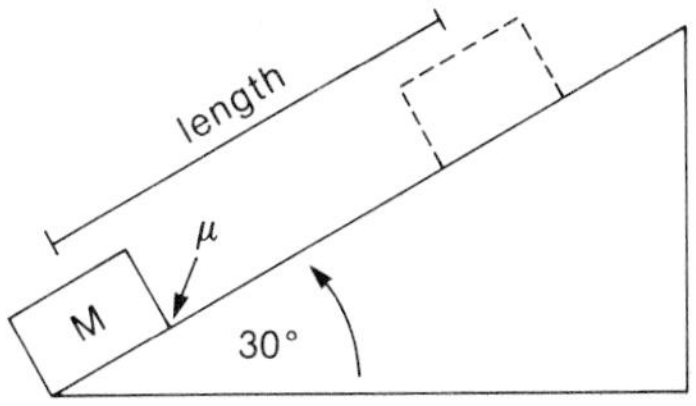

length

μ

M

30°

Figure 12.17.

Examples from novices' problem categories. Problem numbers represent chapter and problem number from Halliday and Resnick (1974).

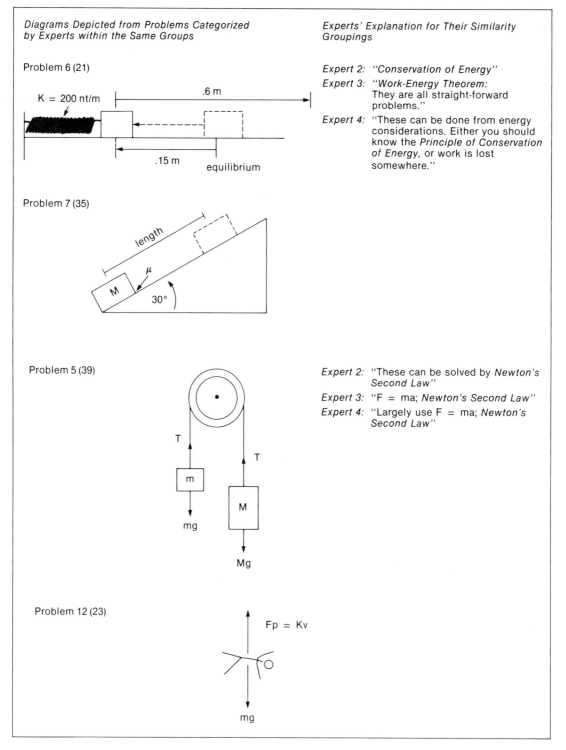

Figure 12.18.

Examples from experts' problem categories. Problem numbers represent chapter and problem number from Halliday and Resnick (1974).

words, since the problems that were grouped together by the novices looked alike, we might say that the basis of the grouping was perceptual appearance. But the basis of the experts' grouping was more abstract and resulted from their knowledge of physics. Chi et al. compare this to the deep-surface structure distinction examined in Chapter 8. The novices are influenced by the appearance of a problem—its surface structure, and the experts seem to be more able to extract the underlying meaning from the problem—its deep structure.

This finding suggests that the classification procedures of novices would be sensitive to variations in surface, but not deep, structure. Chi et al. corroborated this analysis in a follow-up study. They designed twenty problems in which they systematically varied the problems' appearance and objectives. When these specially designed problems were categorized by novices and experts, Chi et al. found once again that the novices were more influenced by the appearance of the problem than they were by the underlying physical principle involved. However, the experts were not affected by this manipulation. Regardless of the problem's text and diagram, the experts categorized it on the basis of abstract physical principles.

The schematic and hierarchical nature of this knowledge was made apparent in another study by Chi et al. Here, the subjects had three levels of expertise. Experts were graduate students in physics. Intermediate subjects were fourth-year physics majors, and novices were students who had been in an introductory physics class and received grades of A, B, or C. The subjects were asked to sort forty physics problems, but in this study, several passes through the set were made. In the first step, the subjects simply sorted the problems. In the second step, the subjects were asked to look at their groups, and if they wished, they were permitted to further subdivide their original groups. In the third step, the subjects who had created subgroups were asked to examine them, and if they wished, they were permitted to further divide these subgroups they had just created. Finally, in the fourth step, the subjects reexamined their original groups and tried to combine them on whatever basis seemed appropriate.

Figure 12.19 shows the resulting hierarchical structure that was created for two novices and two experts. The circles represent the original sorting; the squares, the first subdivision; and the hexagons, the second subdivision. The final, combined stage is shown by the triangles. The numbers inside the geometric forms represent the number of problems sorted into that category. Figure 12.19 is a good way of showing the differences in the organization of knowledge in the minds of experts and novices. First, as we learned earlier, subjects typically needed eight categories to sort the problems. Here we can see that one of the novices required nine categories, which he could not divide any further. The other novice required fifteen categories. In contrast, both the experts required fewer than eight categories in their initial sorts.

Inspection of the figure also shows that the organization of knowledge is similar for both of these experts, but the organization of the novices' knowledge is quite different from each other. In one case, the novice was unable to divide the problems into subcategories, suggesting the categories

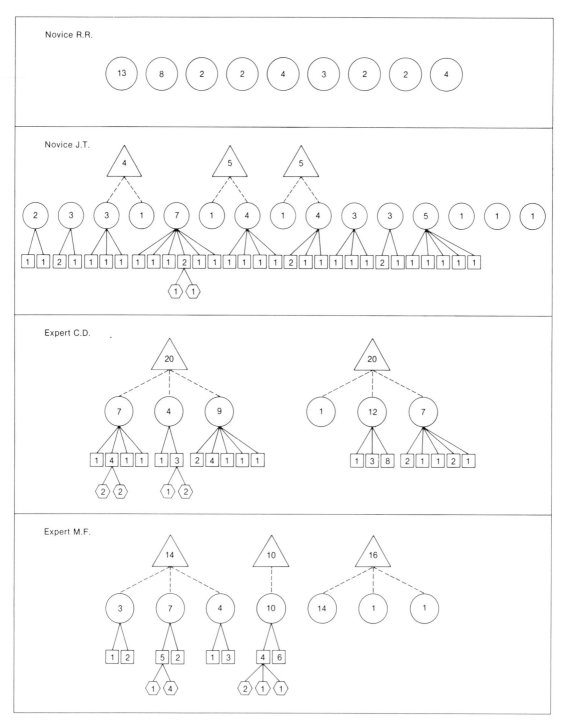

Figure 12.19.

Groupings made by novices and experts on a hierarchical sorting task: *circular nodes,* the preliminary groups; *squares* and *hexagons,* subsequent discriminations; *triangles,* the combinations. (From Chi, Glaser, & Rees, 1982.)

were already at their lowest level (Chi, Glaser, & Rees, 1982). In the case of the other novice shown in Figure 12.19, the problems were so finely divided that each problem almost became its own category. This also suggests an inability to perceive any sort of abstract organizing principle. The experts' knowledge is not like this. Notice that both of the experts shown in Figure 12.19 were able to group all forty of the problems on the problems on the basis of some unifying principle. For example, in expert C. D.'s initial sort, the left group of circles represents problems dealing with conservation of energy, conservation of momentum, and conservation of angular momentum. The three groups of circles on the right represent problems dealing with force (i.e., $F = MA$), using $F = MA$ to find the resultant force, and simple harmonic motion. The left-most circles were in turn combined into the superordinate category *conservation laws,* while the right-most group of circles were collapsed into the category *equations of motion.* By contrast, only one of the novices shown in Figure 12.19 was able to indicate any superordinate categories, and these accounted for only fourteen of the forty problems classified. This suggests that the hierarchical nature of knowledge seen in the experts is a developmental phenomenon. That is, the vertical organization seen in Figure 12.19 is produced by the expert's experience with physics problems.

CONCLUDING COMMENTS AND SUGGESTIONS FOR FURTHER READING

This chapter began with a discussion of the Gestaltists. They were a tremendously productive group of thinkers whose diversity of opinions nevertheless centered on a few key ideas. One of these ideas was that perception and thinking were very similar. In both cases, the person mentally recombined and rearranged elements of a problem or visual array until a stable configuration, or Gestalt, was achieved. A second important idea was that thinking and problem solving took place in stages that were qualitatively different from one another. This means that problem solving was seen as a discontinuous process. When insights would come along was hard to tell in advance. Yet another idea was the notion that the solver's representation of the problem could be critical for success. Although we didn't explore the Gestalt literature on creativity, it generally discusses the ability of the creative person to overcome the effects of set by seeing the problem in a new way.

Time (and subsequent research) have put many of these ideas on the shelf. However, information-processing accounts of problem solving have seemed to converge on the notion that representation is perhaps the most critical act in problem solving. We've seen that cognitive psychologists have undertaken two different but complementary ways of understanding problem solving. One of these ways consists of isolating certain prototypical problems that seem to require particular cognitive skills. The second approach focuses on the solver in an effort to find those cognitive skills that seem general enough to be usable in a wide variety of problems. Recently, psychologists have turned away somewhat from the study of games and puzzles and have begun to study expertise in solving real-world problems. As we've seen, such research seems to indicate that one important outcome of experience in a particular domain of knowledge is the restructuring of knowledge in the mind of the expert. Exploring the nature of this organization is sure to become one of the hot issues in problem solving in the foreseeable future.

Students who wish to find out more about the work of the Gestaltists should read Wertheimer's (1959) book *Productive Thinking,* which is the classic Gestalt account. Readers who want a report of some of the latest findings on problem solving and creative thinking should look at Hunt (1982). Newell and Simon (1972) have written a vast and challenging book that nicely summarizes their twenty-five years of working together. The information-processing approach to problem solving (among other things) is further expounded in two volumes edited by Sternberg (1982, 1985). Several of the chapters in the volume edited by Anderson (1981) have to do with expertise.

I suppose all of us would like to become better problem solvers, and I can recommend several book that might help you accomplish this objective. Hayes (1981) covers much of the same territory that this chapter did, but with an applied orientation. Brown and Walter (1983) have taken the essential Gestalt premise (problem representation) and worked this idea into a book, *The Art of Problem Posing.* Again, this book focuses on specific problem-solving skills that you might find helpful. Halpern (1984) has written a similar text.

One issue that cognitive psychologists have looked at in the last few years is the improvement of classroom learning. Some cognitive psychologists believe that school learning might be enhanced if students were taught to approach some material—particularly scientific material—with a problem-solving orientation. Gagne (1985) discusses the contribution that cognitive psychology would make to such a program.

FOCUS ON APPLICATIONS:
An Algorithm for the Tower of Hanoi

One easy way to discover a problem's algorithm is to develop a notation that shows the problem's transformations. Sometimes, this notation also shows regularities in the problem's structure, and when these are revealed, an algorithm may also become apparent.

I've devised a notation for Tower of Hanoi problems. First, number the pegs 1, 2, and 3. Next, give each disk a name. In the convention I use, the disks have letter names; the biggest is always A, the next

biggest B, and so on. Thus the (trivial) problem of transferring three disks from peg 2 to peg 3 could be written this way:

$ABC_{(2)}—ABC_{(3)}$

All disk moves can be shown as a letter with a numerical subscript that indicates the disk's destination. Thus, the solution to the prior problem could be written as follows:

$C_3B_1C_1 \ A_3 \ C_2B_3C_3$

There are seven moves. The first move (C_3) involves taking the smallest disk and transferring it to peg 3. If you make an arrangement of coins and duplicate each move, you'll see that this string of letters indeed represents a solution to the problem.

What about a four-disk problem? That is, how would we solve this one:

$ABCD_{(2)}$—$ABCD_{(3)}$

I'll show the solution to this problem and then we'll compare the two we've seen to see if they suggest an algorithm for all Tower of Hanoi problems. Here's the answer to the four-disk problem:

$D_1C_3D_3 \ B_1 \ D_2C_1D_1 \ A_3 \ D_3C_2D_2 \ B_3 \ D_1C_3D_3$

Do you see any similarities between the two solutions? You may have noticed that there is one A move in each problem, and it is the midpoint of both problems. The clusters of moves on both sides of A are symmetrical. Also, the smallest disk in each problem is in motion on exactly every other move. In both cases, the next to the smallest disk periodically moves between moves of the smallest disk. These regularities can be summarized as follows:

1. The A disk moves once in a Tower of Hanoi problem.

2. The B disk moves exactly twice as frequently as the A disk, and these moves are symmetrically distributed around the A disk move.

3. The C disk moves exactly twice as frequently as the B disk, and these moves are symmetrically distributed around the A and B disk moves.

4. The D disk moves exactly twice as frequently as the C disk, and these moves are symmetrically distributed around the A, B, and C disk moves. (Hence, the D disk move will always precede and follow C disk moves on a four-disk problem.

By extension, the smallest disk will always precede and follow the moves of the next smallest disk.)

These rules enable us to expand any Tower of Hanoi problem—that is, write the string of letters that shows which disk is to be moved next. This is the first step in solving a Tower problem. These expansion rules don't indicate the subscript pattern, though. To determine this, the solution to the five-disk problem follows, which will show how the subscripts are derived:

$ABCDE_{(2)}$—$ABCDE_{(3)}$
$E_3D_1E_1 \ C_3 \ E_2D_3E_3 \ B_1 \ E_1D_2E_2 \ C_1 \ E_3D_1E_3$

$$A_3$$

$E_2D_3E_3 \ C_2 \ E_1D_2E_2 \ B_3 \ E_3D_1E_1 \ C_3 \ E_2D_3E_3$

Looking at the three- and five-disk problems, you'll see that the subscript patterns of the smallest disk (C in the three-disk and E in the five-disk problem) is the same. Specifically, the sequence repeats the sequence 3, 1, 2 over and over. Looking at the four-disk problem, we see a different pattern, but it also repeats. The D disk moves in the sequence 1, 3, 2 and over and over. The first step in determining the subscript pattern is to count the number of disks in the tower. If odd, number all the smallest disk moves in the 3, 1, 2 sequence. If even, number all the smallest disk moves in the 1, 3, 2 sequence. In both cases, you'll end with a 3. You'll also notice that the moves of the next to the smallest disk always take the subscript of the following disk move. Number all these moves next. We also see that there are always only two B moves, and these go in the order 1, 3. Looking at the C disk moves, we see that they always move in the same sequence: 3, 1, 2. Similarly, the D disk moves are always the same, too: 1, 3, 2.

Do you see the subscript pattern? Besides the A and B disk moves, which are always locked in, and the two topmost disk moves, whose subscripts are derivable by counting the number of disks, all intervening disks have either a 3, 1, 2 pattern (if they're an odd-numbered disk up from the bottom) or a 1, 3, 2 pattern (if they are an even-numbered disk up from the bottom). Knowing these facts enables you to write a string of letters that represents the minimum solution to any Tower of Hanoi problem. You can demonstrate this to yourself by writing the solution to the six-disk problem.

KEY TERMS

Intelligence	Problems of arrangement
Gestalt psychology	Local-global distinction
Incubation	Strategy
Insight	Heuristic
Representation problem	Algorithm
Thinking out loud	Task environment
Discontinuity in thinking	Problem space
Domain-free problems	Operator
Well-defined problems	State-action tree
Ill-defined problems	GPS
Problems of inducing structure	Isomorphism
Problems of transformation	Expertise
Tower of Hanoi	

APPENDIX

1. Answer to the "cheap necklace" problem. Realizing that a chain must be completely disassembled is the key to solving this problem. First, open a link of one of the three link chains, let's say chain A. Take this open link and connect two different three link chains, for example chains B and C. Then close this connecting link. Now we have one seven link chain, one three link chain and one two link chain. Next open a second link of chain A. Use this link to connect the seven link chain with the remaining three link chain (i.e., chain D). Then close the link. Now we have one eleven link chain and just one closed link left from chain A. Open the last remaining link of chain A and link both ends of the eleven link chain through it. Then close that link. We have opened and closed three links for a total cost of 15 cents.

2. Answer to DONALD + GERALD = ROBERT

$$
\begin{array}{r}
526485 \\
+\,197485 \\
\hline
723970
\end{array}
$$

The real key to cracking this problem is deducing E = 9.

3. Answer to the "working backward" problem. Let's list the players using the following notation P1, P2, and P3. Moreover, let's assume that P3 lost the final game. From the material in the text, we have already deduced that after playing two games P1 and P2 each had $4 and P3 had $16. Now,

what happened in the second game? Since each player lost one game, we know that the second game was lost by either P1 or P2, and because they have the same amount of money, it doesn't matter which one we designate as the loser of game 2. Let P2 be the loser of the second game. We know that P2 had to double the current of stake of P1 and P3. Because P3 had $16 after 2 games had been played, and because P3's stake had been doubled in game 2, P3 must have gotten $8 as a result of the second game, paid by P2. Similarly, we already know that P1 had $4 at the end of game 2 and this player's stake was also doubled by P2's losing in game 2. So P1 must have had $2 going into game 2, and earned $2 as a result of P2's loss. So in game 2, P2 paid $8 to P3, $2 to P1 and still had $4 remaining. Therefore, at the conclusion of game 1, P2 must have had $4 + $10 or $14. We've now established that at the end of the first game P1 had $2, P2 had $14, and P3 had $8. What took place in the first game? The only player whose loss is not accounted for is P1. Given that P2 had $14 at the end of game 1, this player must have been paid $7 by P1 in game 1 as a result of P1's loss. Similarly, we know that P3 had $8 at the end of game 1, so this player must have been given $4 as a result of P1's losing the first game. This establishes that the initial stake of P2 was $7 and P3 was $4. P1 paid out $7 + $4 = $11 dollars as a result of losing game 1, and still had $2 left, so P1's initial stake must have been $11 + $2 = $13.

CHAPTER 13

Artificial Intelligence

OVERVIEW

BACKGROUND AND ORIENTATION OF AI
A Small Amount of History
Orientation of AI
  Theory Development
  Metatheory
  Empirical Research
  Model Building

MACHINE VISION
A Computational Model of Vision
Evaluation of the Model

MEMORY AND ACTION FROM AN AI PERSPECTIVE
Scripts
  Conceptual Dependency Theory
The Restaurant Script
  Psychological Validity of the Script Concept
Summary of the Script Concept

LANGUAGE PERCEPTION BY MACHINE
Speech Perception by Machine
Natural Language Recognition
  ELIZA
  SHRDLU
Implications for Cognitive Psychology

PROBLEM SOLVING
Chess
  PARADISE
Expertise
  MYCIN

AI'S CONTRIBUTION TO THE STUDY OF COGNITION
Questions about the Nature of Thought
Minds and Programs

CONCLUDING COMMENTS AND SUGGESTIONS
FOR FURTHER READING
FOCUS ON APPLICATIONS
KEY TERMS

Most of the time I use my microcomputer for word processing, presenting stimuli to subjects in experiments, and data analysis. But sometimes, late at night when my other work is finished, I load up my flight simulator program. If you've never seen one of these things, you might find the degree of realism astonishing. The one I have is fully capable of demonstrating instrument flying; that is, I can change the simulated weather conditions to zero visibility and zero ceiling, and take off safely using just the instrument panel. The basic navigational radios are present, so technically, I could fly cross-country in the dark and still arrive at my predetermined target. The airports depicted in the simulation are all real. Usually, I take off from Meigs Field in Chicago, which is a small airport located on a peninsula in Lake Michigan. I start out heading due north, but I usually bank to the right and fly south past the Chicago skyline. The John Hancock Building and the Sears Tower are clearly visible from the "windows" of the plane.

In addition to being great fun, this simulation also has some implications for the study of cognition. Let's ask ourselves what's involved in the creation of a realistic display in real time. First, numerous calculations concerning the simulated plane's flight have to be quickly executed. For example, some part of the program has to "know" how much to reduce the indicated airspeed when the rate of climb is increased and the power is held constant. Second, the computer has to have the graphics capability to produce a realistic view. For example, when I fly the plane directly at the Hancock Building, I see the building begin to enlarge and become more detailed as I approach it. Although my simulator doesn't depict too much in the way of texture gradients, those that are there unfold in a realistic way. You might argue that producing this display isn't that hard. After all, since the computer is a fast calculator, all that's required in this case is something like a formal theory of how all the variables related to flying interact with one another. If such a formal theory could be written, then a computer algorithm could be created to implement that formal theory. In other words, the program simulating the plane doesn't have to "know" anything—all it has to do is compute. You might go on to argue that the real intelligence is shown by the person flying the simulator because he is the one using perceptual and cognitive skills to stay airborne.

But I think that the same logic that applies to the simulator applies to the person flying it as well. If my behavior in flying the machine could be similarly formalized, then a program could be written that embodies my perception of the texture gradients, my memory of how far to push the stick over to bank without stalling, my decision making about when to push the flaps down on landing, and so on. In that case, we could envision two computers in my office: one simulating a plane, the other simulating me flying a plane. Under these circumstances, wouldn't you be willing to admit that the computer simulating me was showing a little intelligence?

This chapter considers artificial intelligence (**AI**), a term that refers to the creation of machines capable of doing things that seem to require intelligence when done by people. We'll briefly consider the history of AI, and more important, we'll try to place this history in context. That is, we'll try to map AI's position relative to cognitive psychology: What do these two disciplines have to say to each other? As we'll see, both cognitive psychology and AI are sailing together these days under the flag of something called cognitive science. Cognitive science could be defined as the study of intelligent actions, making it a broad interdisciplinary study indeed, encompassing cognitive psychology, AI, linguistics, psycholinguistics, anthropology, and philosophy, along with neurology and neuropsychology, and what some people are calling cognitive sociology.

We'll consider several AI applications to some of the problems we have considered throughout this book, specifically those dealing with perception, memory and action, problem solving, and expertise. The final section of this chapter tries to determine AI's implications for the study of cognition generally and attempts an evaluation of AI's contribution to cognitive psychology.

BACKGROUND AND ORIENTATION OF AI

A Small Amount of History

For as long as humans have computed, they have probably made use of some sort of mechanical aids. However, the first person to conceive of a true computing machine was probably Charles Babbage (1792–1871). His idea, called the **analytical engine,** was planned as a mass of incredibly complicated interlocking gears. Babbage envisioned both a memory unit and an executive, or calculating, unit housed within the engine. He intended this amazing device to perform extended calculations and perhaps play games. However, his perceptive friend Lady Ada Lovelace soon realized that the analytical engine would have the ability to do a variety of tasks involving symbol manipulation. For example, writing in 1842, she believed the machine would be capable of musical composition. Unfortunately, the design of such a machine was so complicated that Babbage wasn't able to actually build one.

Nevertheless, Babbage's failure raised some interesting philosophical questions. Could the engine's production of musical notation be considered true musical composition? And if the pieces it produced were considered good, could it be said that the machine was actually original and creative? Lady Lovelace didn't think so. She maintained that the analytical engine would not be able to originate anything. It would perform only what it was ordered to perform. Because the engine was never actually constructed, the debate smoldered for a century. But with the building of the first digital computers in the 1940s, interest in "thinking machines" flared up again.

Almost as soon as computing machines were invented, people began to realize their implications for higher mental processes. By the mid-1950s, AI had begun to produce a tradition of research. One of the earliest AI programs was called **Logic Theorist,** produced by Newell and Simon. As you might guess from the name, **Logic Theorist** was designed to prove theorems from mathematical logic. And it worked: Its proofs were quite satisfactory—even elegant. This brings us to the divergent point in AI research.

The past ten to fifteen years have seen two broad phases in AI work. During the 1960s and 1970s, many workers were concerned with the construction of machines that could really do something. Perhaps this emphasis stemmed from the excitement that accompanied the creation of homeostatic robots that roamed the halls of computer science buildings looking for an electrical outlet that would permit a recharge. Sophisticated machines were eventually developed with on-board microprocessors that permitted decision making and inference drawing. Perhaps the most famous of these machines was Shakey, a robot who solved certain problems by drawing deductions based on its cognitive map of a room at MIT (Fikes, Hart, & Nillson, 1972). But as the 1970s wore on, the emphasis in AI research shifted away from physical robots to a concern with the representation of knowledge by machines (Hand, 1981).

Work on these so-called expert systems was not new, but only in the last five or so years has this area of research truly blossomed. We'll cover artificial expertise in more depth later in this chapter, but for right now, let me simply point out that expert systems have been created for almost any problem a person might need help with. In fact, an expert system is even available for microcomputers that enables you to design other expert systems!

Orientation of AI

Before examining some AI research, it's appropriate to discuss how AI researchers go about their work. Although many AI workers and cognitive psychologists consider themselves cognitive science researchers, some important differences in orientation and procedure still exist between these two groups. Like the cognitive psychologist, the AI worker often thinks of research as a series of activities, and for this reason, both types of workers sometimes think of research as occurring in a series of stages. We'll consider these stages next.

Theory Development

Researchers sometimes have a hunch about a particular phenomenon, and they do a study investigating it. The importance of this intuitive, hunch-following thinking in science cannot be overestimated. However, the theory-based approach to research is probably more typical and more likely to produce quality findings. This means that the researcher often starts the research process by reading a theoretical account of some particular phenomenon. Good theories usually suggest that certain findings should be observed under certain conditions; this aspect of a theory is referred to as its heuristic value. Usually, the AI worker begins the research process with a theory or a hunch. What happens when a worker wants to do some research in an area and has neither a hunch nor a theory? All is not lost.

Metatheory

In AI, the situation of being without a theory is fairly common. New areas of research are opening up all the time, and theoretical development is likely to lag in such a situation. When dealing with these circumstances, the AI worker is likely to turn to a **metatheory** for help. A metatheory is a set of basic presumptions that are often thought to operate in a general domain. A metatheory is not a theory per se. Rather, we can think of a metatheory as a schematic, or general, form for theory building in particular areas. The metatheory is schematic in that it guides the researcher's efforts as theory building on specific topics. For instance, in cognitive psychology, the information-processing approach is sometimes called a metatheory. This approach doesn't specify much about particular topics in cognition, but cognitive psychologists who begin to build theories about specific topics in cognition are usually guided by it.

AI's metatheory is a variation of the information-processing approach. It's derived from Newell and Simon's (1976) reference to a "physical symbol system." This term refers to a class of systems that have the capability of holding and transforming symbols when such symbols are realized in some physical object. A human being is a good example of a physical symbol system, as is a programmed computer. This idea embodies one of the major beliefs of the AI worker—the belief that all such physical symbol systems have certain things in common. In its extreme form, AI researchers sometimes believe that all the actions we use to characterize intelligence are characteristics of physical symbol systems. Do you see one of the implications of such an opinion? If the AI workers are correct in their belief, then all forms of intelligence could presumably be reduced to some essential characteristics. In other words, physical symbol systems that act intelligently can do so because only one kind of intelligence exists. The intelligence that you show takes place because of certain computations carried out by your central nervous system, and if only one kind of intelligence truly exists, these computations should be duplicable by other kinds of physical symbol systems, that is, by machines.

Norman (1980) has outlined a dozen issues that he believes are the unifying problems of cognitive science and are thus approachable through the metatheory:

We need to study a wide range of behavior before we can hope to understand a single class. Cognitive scientists as a whole ought to make more use of evidence from the neuro-sciences, from brain damage and mental illness, from cognitive sociology and anthropology and from clinical studies of the human. These must be accompanied, of course, with the study of language, of the psychological aspects of human processing structures, and of artificially intelligent mechanisms. The study of Cognitive Science requires a complex interaction among different issues of concern, an interaction that will not be properly understood until all parts are understood, with no part independent of the others, the whole requiring the parts, and the parts the whole. (Norman, 1980, p. 1)

Empirical Research

Assuming the existence of a metatheory, the AI researchers next proceeds to the second stage of the research process: empirical research. The AI worker's view of empirical research differs somewhat from that of the psychologist, however. In cognitive psychology, the empirical research offers a way of checking the prescriptions of the theory. If the theory's predictions are not observed in the real world, the theory is modified, and if the predictions are generally more wrong than right, the theory may be discarded. In AI, the situation is sometimes a little different. In some cases, AI researchers may not feel bound by what is known to be the operating characteristics of the human information-processing system. Their objective may simply be to develop a successful approach to a problem—one that takes advantage of the computer's strengths.

This distinction is sometimes expressed in the phrases **computer simulation** and "pure AI." The simulator's approach is to mimic the *process* of cognition on a computing machine. In this case, the researcher is strongly bound by the characteristics of the human system. Pure AI research may not acknowledge these constraints. Researchers in this camp might argue that the objective of the research is to produce a program that can carry out the specified task, regardless of whether the machine engages in processes that seem analogous to those that take place in humans. These workers often refer to themselves as atheoretical, meaning that they have no intention of drawing any parallels between the operation of their machines and the findings of cognitive psychology (Wilks, 1981). In this sense, pure AI research is sometimes called outcome, rather than process, oriented.

Model Building

In cognitive psychology, the model is usually a verbal description of the processes involved in some mental event. Ideally, this description is the embodiment of some theoretical position, and it should have enough precision to enable researchers to conduct experiments that might prove the model wrong. In AI research, the model often takes the form of a computer program that is capable of doing some specific task. Although the model should embody a theory of cognition, this isn't always the case in AI. Researchers will sometimes graft certain ad hoc sequences onto their basic program. Such grafting may or may not be analogous to any sort of similar processing that might take place in humans. Why is it there, then? These ad hoc sequences are sometimes necessary from a computational point of view—that is, necessary to make the program work. AI workers who take this position sometimes state that their program is their theory.

Generally, models in AI are made up of three components (Slack, 1984). The first components relate directly to the theory. These are components that either model some aspects of a theory or at least have some implications for the future development of the theory. The second component consists of aspects of the model that are irrelevant to the theory. These components can be the ad hoc program sequences described previously, or certain constraints implied by the hardware, or programming language in use. The third component consists of aspects of the model that are not easily categorized as one of the first two components. Generally, the more the model is made up of components from the first category, the greater its relevance for cognitive psychology.

Having armed ourselves with this brief orientation to the field, let's begin to review some AI theory and research.

MACHINE VISION

Following the general order of the book, I've put the discussion of artificial vision first because we examined perception earlier. This arrangement might imply that the problem of machine vision has been an easy one for AI workers to solve, but nothing could be further from the truth. AI researchers have had much more success in building programs that seem to require much more intelligence than vision does. The relative inability of workers to produce good models of vision may mean that a great deal more intelligence is involved in accurate vision than we commonly suppose.

A Computational Model of Vision

It's common to approach the problem of artificial vision from the information-processing perspective. According to this view (Barrow & Tenenbaum, 1981; Marr, 1982; Witkin & Tenenbaum, 1983), accurate vision can be accomplished in a series of steps. At each step, certain processes occur that abstract particular kinds of information from the world, and these processes add this abstracted information to the general pattern that has been formed by prior processing. In other words, artificial vision programs approach this task by first making a primitive representation of whatever they're looking at and then by adding in more and more information as they go along. The expectation is that such added-in information improves the representation being created.

Figure 13.1 shows a typical computational model of vision. Notice that this model is primarily bottom up in orientation. Let's briefly go through the steps of this model. At the lowest level, the model extracts various spatial and temporal properties of the image. These properties correspond to various line and edge elements (Marr & Hildreth, 1980). This information is next converted into an array of feature descriptors that preserve the local two-dimensional geometry of the image (Witkin & Tenenbaum, 1983). The next step is called the recovery stage. Here, various processes related to brightness (luminosity), reflectance, and transparency act to determine more information about the surfaces depicted in the two-dimensional image. As a result of this analysis, the image acquires characteristics relating to shading, texture, contour, and flow. In the next stage, the edges and boundaries that were determined earlier are now grouped together based upon the characteristics of surface homogeneity and boundary interpretation. These processes determine what are called the **intrinsic characteristics** of the image and are particularly useful for evaluating the nature of texture gradients that might be present. In the recognition stage, the program uses stored primitive object prototypes (such as cylinders) as the basis for object recognition. Later, information about the values of the primitive object prototypes present are reassembled in an attempt to recognize higher, or more complex, object

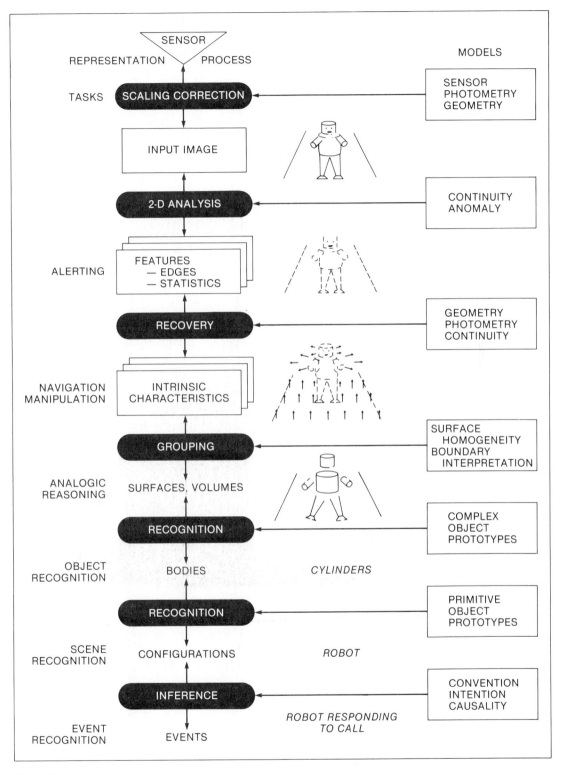

Figure 13.1.

Computational architecture for a general-purpose vision system. (From Wilkin & Tenenbaum, 1983. Reprinted by permission of the publisher.)

prototypes. If usch a model were completely developed, it would go on to apply inference rules regarding intention and causality to recognize scenes and events.

This model of machine vision has a great deal of appeal. For example, the notion of applying primitive object prototypes to an image is a surprisingly powerful way of recognizing different objects. Figure 13.2 shows some different kinds of objects that could be represented as systems of cylinders and are thus potentially recognizable by a computational system such as the one depicted in Figure 13.1.

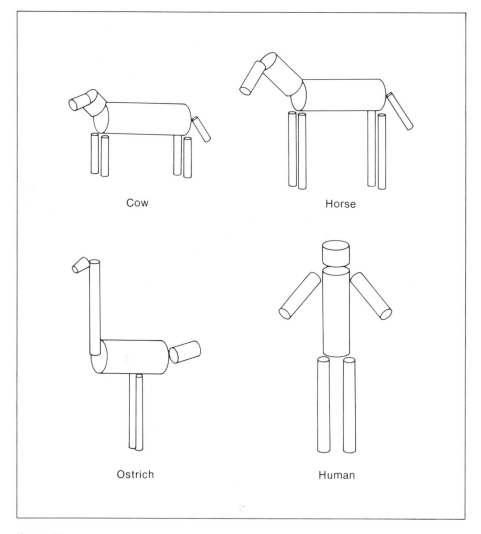

Figure 13.2.

Simplified cylinder models of animals. (From Marr & Nishihara, 1977. Reprinted by permission of the publisher.)

Evaluation of the Model

For the past decade, the emphasis in artificial vision research has been on the recovery of surface orientations—an emphasis resulting from some work by Horn (1975). Horn realized that shape could be recovered (i.e., abstracted) from shading information. Moreover, if shape were extracted from shading, this implied some additional constraints on the nature of the information processing that extracted other qualities from the image being processed. The result of this realization was a model that specified at least one of the intermediate steps in artificial vision: specifying the orientation of each surface in the image at each point in the image. Prior to this approach, artificial vision had proceeded almost exclusively according to the **segment and label** approach outlined in Chapter 1. Recall that this approach was also bottom up. It worked by finding certain configurations, such as forks or *L*'s which were then labeled and reassembled into larger units.

Although this approach is often powerful, it suffers from several drawbacks. First, the role of context is not factored into the information processing. Yet, context obviously plays a crucial role in vision. As Marr (1982) has pointed out, the identification of an object depends heavily on both context and task. Second, the label and segment approach may succeed for artificial pattern recognition, but true artificial vision implies more than simply recognizing the elements of an array. The computational model at least points to a connection between vision and some of the other realms of cognition. For example, at the highest levels of the model, an attempt is made to link these visual events with nonvisual processes such as inference making about causality and intention.

Another aspect of this work is also important. Recall that AI workers sometimes have a different orientation toward empirical research than psychologists do. This model is an example. The intermediate steps between the feature abstraction and recognition stages don't appear to have any analogue with the human sequence of processing in vision. These steps are there because, as Horn's research demonstrated, an artificial system having such processes seems to work better than one without them.

MEMORY AND ACTION FROM AN AI PERSPECTIVE

Scripts

As mentioned, the trend in AI research over the last decade or so has been toward the development of computing programs that represent knowledge in a more global, or general, form. One such attempt has been that of Schank and Abelson (1977; Abelson, 1981), who have formulated the **script** as a plausible format for the organization and retrieval of general knowledge. Basically, a script is an action plan that outlines likely and unlikely sequences of events. For example, if you've traveled by air several times, you may have encoded a commercial air travel script that specifies the sequence of actions one does to get from point A to point B by plane. These actions include checking in (putting your suitcase on the scale, handing your ticket to the clerk, and getting ready to answer questions about your smoking and seating preferences). Presumably, you could fill in the rest of the events of this script by retrieving them from your own memory. Schank and Abelson argue that the possession of such a representation allows the individual to comprehend events in her life by checking them against the expectations produced by the script. The script also enables the possessor to infer actions done by others that must have taken place, even though they are not described directly.

Conceptual Dependency Theory

Scripts can be represented in machines by formalizing a theory of world knowledge known as Conceptual Dependency (CD) theory (Schank, 1975). CD theory has been built up as a series of primitives, which are basic actions that are incapable of being broken into smaller actions. The primitives are then assembled to form longer and longer strings according to several axioms, or principles. The basic axioms of CD theory follow:

A. For any two sentences that are identical in meaning, regardless of language, there should be only one representation.

The first axiom has an important corollary that derives from it:

B. Any information in a sentence that is implicit must be made explicit in the representation of the meaning of that sentence.

These two rules forced Schank and Abelson to look for one economical form for representing meaning. To accomplish this, they invented the initial framework:

C. The meaning propositions underlying language are called conceptualizations. A conceptualization can be active or stative.

D. An active conceptualization has the form: Actor Action Object Direction (Instrument)

E. A stative conceptualization has the form: Object (is in) State (with Value).

Notice that a conceptualization is defined as an actor *doing* something to some particular object. From these axioms, Schank and Abelson next went on to consider the set of primitive actions that an actor *could* do. Axiom A and its corollary B act as guidelines to determine how large or small this set of primitive actions should be. That is, axiom A implies that actions that appear similar should be representable by some common primitive, while axiom B implies that every action should have a unique representation in the computer program. As it turns out, a given verb is represented both by primitive actions (which it must share with other verbs) and by some explicit state concepts that make it unique. Applying the axioms of CD theory to whole host of verbs has led to their representation by some combination of the **primitive acts** shown in Figure 13.3.

This number looks overwhelming, but when you realize that Schank and Abelson are offering this listing of eleven primitive actions as a way of encoding almost every verb in English, the number doesn't seem so large. In addition to these primitives, the symbol ↑ is used to denote causality. To help you see how some common actions could be expressed in terms of

ATRANS	The transfer of an abstract relationship such as possession, ownership or control. Thus, one sense of 'give' is: **ATRANS** something to someone else; a sense of 'take' is: **ATRANS** something to oneself. 'Buy' is made up of two conceptualizations that cause each other, one an **ATRANS** of money, the other an **ATRANS** of the object being bought.
PTRANS	The transfer of the physical location of an object. Thus, 'go' is **PTRANS** oneself to a place; 'put' is **PTRANS** of an object to a place.
PROPEL	The application of a physical force to an object. **PROPEL** is used whenever any force is applied regardless of whether a movement (**PTRANS**) took place. In English, 'push', 'pull', 'throw', 'kick', have **PROPEL** as part of them. 'John pushed the table to the wall' is a **PROPEL** that causes a **PTRANS**. 'John threw the ball' is **PROPEL** that involves an ending of a **GRASP** ACT at the same time. Often words that do not necessarily mean **PROPEL** can probably infer **PROPEL**. Thus, 'break' means to **DO** something that causes a change in physical state of a specific sort (where **DO** indicates an unknown ACT). Most of the time the ACT that fills in the **DO** is **PROPEL** although this is certainly not necessarily the case.
MOVE	The movement of a body part of an animal by that animal. **MOVE** is nearly always the ACT in an instrumental conceptualization for other ACTs. That is, in order to throw, it is necessary to **MOVE** one's arm. Likewise **MOVE** foot is the instrument of 'kick' and **MOVE** hand is often the instrument of the verb 'hand'. **MOVE** is less frequently used noninstrumentally, but 'kiss', 'raise your hand', 'scratch' are examples.
GRASP	The grasping of an object by an actor. The verbs 'hold', 'grab', 'let go', and 'throw' involve **GRASP** or the ending of a **GRASP**.
INGEST	The taking in of an object by an animal to the inside of that animal. Most commonly the semantics for the objects of **INGEST** (that is, what is usually **INGEST**ed) are food, liquid, and gas. Thus, 'eat', 'drink', 'smoke', 'breathe', are common examples in **INGEST**.
EXPEL	The expulsion of an object from the body of an animal into the physical world. Whatever is **EXPEL**ed is very likely to have been previously **INGEST**ed. Words for excretion and secretion are described by **EXPEL**, among them, 'sweat', 'spit', and 'cry'.
MTRANS	The transfer of mental information between animals or within an animal. We partition memory into two pieces: The **CP** (conscious processor where something is thought of), and the **LTM** (long term memory where things are stored). The various sense organs can also serve as the originators of an **MTRANS**. Thus, 'tell' is **MTRANS** between people, 'see' is **MTRANS** from eyes to **CP**, 'remember' is **MTRANS** from **LTM** to **CP**, 'forget' is the inability to do that, 'learn' is the **MTRANS**ing of new information to **LTM**.
MBUILD	The construction by an animal of new information from old information. Thus, 'decide', 'conclude', 'imagine', 'consider', are common examples of **MBUILD**.
SPEAK	The actions of producing sounds. Many objects can **SPEAK**, but human ones usually are **SPEAK**ing as an instrument of **MTRANS**ing. The words 'say', 'play music', 'purr', 'scream' involve **SPEAK**.
ATTEND	The action of attending or focusing a sense organ towards a stimulus. **ATTEND** ear is 'listen', **ATTEND** eye is 'see' and so on. **ATTEND** is nearly always referred to in English as the instrument of **MTRANS**. Thus, in Conceptual Dependency, 'see' is treated as **MTRANS** to **CP** from eye by instrument of **ATTEND** eye to object.

Figure 13.3.

The primitive acts of Conceptual Dependency theory. (From Schank & Abelson, 1977. Reprinted by permission of the publisher.)

these primitive actions, consider the following sample sentences and their representations:

John read a book.
John MTRANS (information) to LTM (John) from book inst (John ATTEND eyes to book)
and:
John kicked Mary.
John PROPEL foot to Mary
↑
foot (John) BE PHYSICAL CONTACT (Mary)

The Restaurant Script

Schank and Abelson have developed a computer program known as **SAM** (Script Applier Mechanism), which is capable of answering questions about a variety of stories. Sam is often asked questions about restaurants by Schank and Abelson, and SAM answers such questions by referring to its restaurant script, which is depicted in Figure 13.4.

The restaurant script consists of a series of events that have been represented in the format of CD theory. Notice that it bears some resemblance to an actual theatrical script: the script has roles, props, scenes, and entry conditions that correspond to a setting.

More important to our purposes, however, the script can be understood as a large causal chain that specifies a series of actions. Notice also that even though this chain is intended as a more or less general recipe for restaurant behavior, scene 1 describes only those restaurants in which you seat yourself, or in CD language, "PTRANS" yourself to a table. A complete restaurant script would require even more detail in scene 1 and probably more detail in each of the other scenes as well. You may not have realized that your knowledge of restaurant behavior was so extensive!

Because this chain of events is causal, each act in the script must be done effectively if the next act is to take place. If SAM is given a story that deviates substantially from the apparent script, these deviations must be dealt with or the comprehension of the script will not continue. A new act that may not be mentioned in the original script is sometimes necessary to get the chain moving again. This sort of prescriptive behavior is an important component of human understanding. That is, much of comprehension of events results from our ability to pop out of our current place in the script and see our way to the end of them. Although this chain of actions is causal, it is not a set of simple stimulus-response linkages.

Together with other programs (Lehnert, 1977) SAM is capable of answering questions about stories that it has been given to "read." The following story was given to SAM. When you read its answers to this short but multiple-scripted tale, I think you'll agree that its responses are plausible.

The Story:
John went to New York by bus. On the bus he talked to an old lady. When he left the bus, he thanked the driver. He took the subway to Leone's. On the subway, his

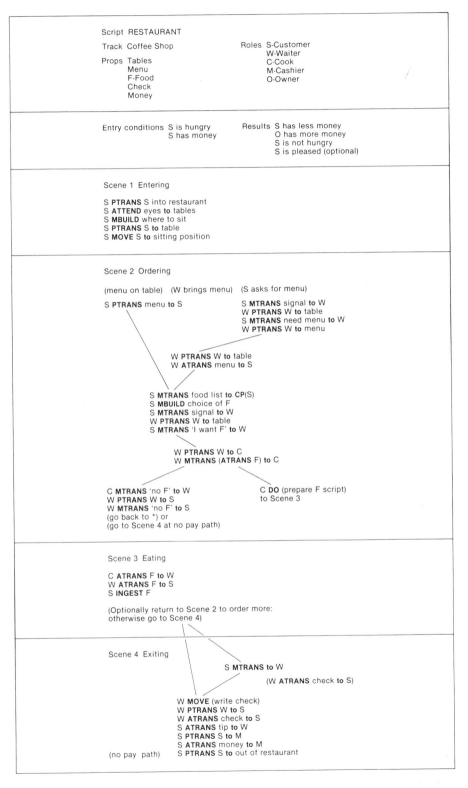

Script RESTAURANT

Track Coffee Shop

Props Tables
     Menu
     F-Food
     Check
     Money

Roles S-Customer
     W-Waiter
     C-Cook
     M-Cashier
     O-Owner

Entry conditions S is hungry
     S has money

Results S has less money
     O has more money
     S is not hungry
     S is pleased (optional)

Scene 1 Entering

S **PTRANS** S into restaurant
S **ATTEND** eyes to tables
S **MBUILD** where to sit
S **PTRANS** S to table
S **MOVE** S to sitting position

Scene 2 Ordering

(menu on table) (W brings menu) (S asks for menu)

S **PTRANS** menu to S

S **MTRANS** signal to W
W **PTRANS** W to table
S **MTRANS** need menu to W
W **PTRANS** W to menu

W **PTRANS** W to table
W **ATRANS** menu to S

S **MTRANS** food list to CP(S)
S **MBUILD** choice of F
S **MTRANS** signal to W
W **PTRANS** W to table
S **MTRANS** 'I want F' to W

W **PTRANS** W to C
W **MTRANS** (ATRANS F) to C

C **MTRANS** 'no F' to W
W **PTRANS** W to S
W **MTRANS** 'no F' to S
(go back to *) or
(go to Scene 4 at no pay path)

C **DO** (prepare F script)
    to Scene 3

Scene 3 Eating

C **ATRANS** F to W
W **ATRANS** F to S
S **INGEST** F

(Optionally return to Scene 2 to order more:
otherwise go to Scene 4)

Scene 4 Exiting

S **MTRANS** to W

(W **ATRANS** check to S)

W **MOVE** (write check)
W **PTRANS** W to S
W **ATRANS** check to S
S **ATRANS** tip to W
S **PTRANS** S to M
S **ATRANS** money to M
(no pay path)   S **PTRANS** S to out of restaurant

Figure 13.4.

The restaurant script. (From Schank & Abelson, 1977. Reprinted by permission of the publisher.)

pocket was picked. He got off the train and entered Leone's. He had some lasagna. When the check came, he discovered he couldn't pay. The management told him he would have to wash dishes. When he left, he caught a bus to New Haven.

Q1 Why did John go to New York?

A1 BECAUSE HE WANTED TO GO TO LEONE'S.

Q2 How did John get to Leone's?

A2 JOHN TOOK A BUS TO NEW YORK AND THEN HE TOOK THE SUBWAY TO LEONE'S.

Q3 Did anything unusual happen on the bus?

A3 I DON'T REMEMBER ANYTHING.

Q4 Did anything unusual happen on the subway?

A4 A THIEF PICKED JOHN'S POCKET

Q5 What did John order?

A5 JOHN ORDERED LASAGNA.

Q6 Did anything unusual happen at the restaurant?

A6 JOHN DISCOVERED THAT THE COULDN'T PAY THE CHECK AND SO HE HAD TO WASH DISHES.

Q7 Why couldn't John pay the check?

A7 BECAUSE JOHN DID NOT HAVE ANY MONEY.

Q8 Why didn't John have any money?

A8 BECAUSE A THIEF PICKED JOHN'S POCKET.

Q9 How did John get back to New Haven?

A9 JOHN WENT FROM LEONE'S BY SUBWAY AND THEN HE WENT TO NEW HAVEN BY BUS.

Q10 How was John able to take the bus to New Haven?

A10 PROBABLY JOHN HAD A TICKET. (Schank & Abelson, 1977, pp. 178–200)

Psychological Validity of the Script Concept

Although the mechanized representation of general knowledge appears to have wide variety of practical applications (Schank, 1983), Schank and Abelson were more concerned with developing a theory showing how human knowledge might be represented. If human knowledge were organized along the lines suggested by Schank and Abelson, we should see some indications of it in human behavior. Bower, Black, and Turner (1979) have reported some findings that suggest that human knowledge is often rooted in action plans that specify causal sequences. Their subjects were asked to name what they thought were the twenty most important events in a restaurant episode. Although no single activity was named by all thirty-two participants, there was a fairly good consensus.

Table 13.1 shows the events that were named by the subjects, along with a percentage indicating how frequently the event was mentioned. There are some important differences between human and artificial knowledge. The human knowledge displayed in this task shows greater flexibility than the restaurant script possesses. For example, humans seem to be aware of a choice point when entering a restaurant. The restaurant may be the kind in which you have to wait to be seated, as opposed to those in which you "PTRANS" yourself to a table. Yet, many of the events named in the script agree with those mentioned by the humans. This finding suggests that Schank and Abelson might not be far off in their hunch about how human knowledge is organized.

TABLE 13.1

Empirical Script Norms at Three Agreement Levels

Going to a Restaurant
Open door
Enter
Give reservation name
Wait to be seated
Go to table
BE SEATED
Order drinks
Put napkins on lap
LOOK AT MENU
Discuss menu
ORDER MEAL
Talk
Drink water
Eat salad or soup
Meal arrives
EAT FOOD
Finish meal
Order dessert
Eat dessert
Ask for bill
Bill arrives
PAY BILL
Leave tip
Get coats
LEAVE

Source: From Bower, Black, and Turner, 1979. Reprinted by permission of the publisher.
Note: The items in capitals were mentioned by the most subjects (73 percent), items in italics by fewer subjects (48 percent), and items in lowercase roman by still fewer subjects (25 percent).

Summary of the Script Concept

The notion of the script can be related to similar ideas in cognitive psychology, such as the schema or the prototype. From the repetition of an action, its essential features are abstracted and represented in such a way that the entire episode can be regenerated. Thus, the script becomes a kind of schematic, or general, plan for carrying out specific actions. Although the details of every restaurant episode will differ, certain behaviors will have to be enacted at similar points in almost every restaurant experience. The script enables the knower who reads or hears about a particular episode to fill in the gaps, that is, mentally supply the details that are inevitably left out of the account. In many cases, this enables a knower to infer some causal process, even though none has been explicitly mentioned. For example, consider the following two sentences:

1. Joe burned his hand because he touched the stove.
2. Joe burned his hand because he forgot the stove was on. (Schank & Abelson, 1977, p. 24)

As Schank and Abelson point out, nobody has any trouble understanding either sentence, even though only sentence 1 is a literal description of what took place. Sentence 2 is *not* a literal description of the events. Nobody ever got burned simply by forgetting. We realize that we must mentally supply the missing cause, which is probably something in the information in sentence 1. Consequently, we might guess that the subjects who heard sentence 2 would be likely to infer that sentence 1 had taken place.

These inferences flow so naturally, and without any apparent effort, that we probably do not realize how often we rely upon them. However, concocting a simple story that defeats our inference-making ability is not too difficult. Consider the following mysterious tale:

John went to a park. He asked the midget for a mouse. He picked up the box and left. (Schank & Abelson, 1977, p. 40)

What happened next? Like most people, your ability to answer that question is probably nil. We are unprepared for the reference to "the" midget or "the" box, probably because we don't routinely encounter midgets in parks who sell or give away mice for a living (even this last statement is an inference: Nothing was said about selling the mouse). As Schank and Abelson put it:

The story is not understandable, simply by virtue of the fact that we have no world knowledge that serves to connect its pieces. If there were a standard "mouse buying script" that averred that only midgets in parks sold mice which were always packed in boxes, then we would be able to apply that script to [this story] and connect the pieces of the story. What scripts do then, is provide connectivity. (Schank & Abelson, 1977, p. 40)

The script is a representation of actions that enable these actions to be linked together in a meaningful way. Scripts can be represented by network structures, similar to those we looked at in the chapter on semantic memory. In this case, the various nodes and linkages represent actions and somewhat more abstract ideas such as causality.

It may have also occurred to you that the script notion has some implications for how actions are stored and retrieved. Bower, Black, and Turner (1979) conducted a study in which the subjects read stories involving a restaurant script. However, some of the main events of the script had been deleted. In a recognition task, some of the deleted events were presented to the subjects, even though they had not been encountered before. Nevertheless, the subjects still showed a tendency to remember these events as having been presented. This phenomenon is similar to that found by Bartlett in his studies on the "War of the Ghosts" story. As you'll recall, Bartlett found that people tended to interpret unfamiliar events in terms of familar ones. Experience with certain common artifacts biased people's attempts to retrieve the unfamiliar story. In the current example, knowledge of common sequences of actions produces a similarly distorting effect. People recall the events that are congruent with the script as having taken place, even when no explicit mention had been made of them.

LANGUAGE PERCEPTION BY MACHINE

Language perception by machine is an overwhelming problem confronting AI researchers. For our purposes, language perception can be divided into two areas. First, we'll consider the problem of speech recognition by machines. Following that, we'll examine some of the difficulties in producing programs that can respond intelligently to natural formalizations of grammar. Creating programs that comprehend language also brings into play the linguistics field of **pragmatics.** Pragmatics refer to our knowledge of the rules of discourse. For example when someone says, "Could you please pass the salt?" you know this is not a literal question about your abilities but is a request to pass the salt. As you've probably realized, this kind of knowledge is on a completely different level than simple grammatical knowledge. We might write a program that could effectively parse and comprehend the salt sentence on one level, but the program would have no idea whether the question was to be answered literally at the pragmatic level.

Speech Perception by Machine

I used to fantasize about a typewriter that could print what I said into it. When I used a Dictaphone for the first time, I realized that such a typewriter wouldn't necessarily be that handy. Besides, it's just as well that I've given up on this fantasy, because the technical and theoretical problems involved in producing such a machine are vexing, to put it mildly.

First, little physical information in the stream of speech is invariant. The pattern of speech varies with geographic background as well as with the age, gender, and perhaps education of the speaker. Second is the identification problem. As we saw in the language chapters, in some cases people perceive acoustically identical speech sounds as different. In addition to these problems, speech recognition by machine would also have to overcome the segmentation problem—the problem of determining the boundaries between words and phrases in the ongoing stream of speech.

Because these problems have been so difficult, most of the AI research on speech recognition has focused on machines that can recognize single spoken words or short phrases. A variety of strategies are used by AI workers to analyze speech sounds, but the easiest to understand involves a circuit called a **zero-crossing detector.** Figure 13.5 shows a schematic depiction of a zero-crossing detector in use.

As you know, the speech signal is a complex wave form having both amplitude and frequency. The complexity of the wave results from our ability to change the shape of our mouth and pharynx to make different speech sounds. The changes we make add overtones, or harmonics, to the basic frequency produced by the vibration of our vocal cords. In other words, the basic frequency and wave produced by our vocal cords seemingly have many other miniwaves added in. A zero-crossing detector is a device that measures the rate at which the basic frequency of a sound changes its algebraic sign—that is, crosses an arbitrary zero point. Although a wave may be complex, the zero-crossing detector is able to establish its basic frequency.

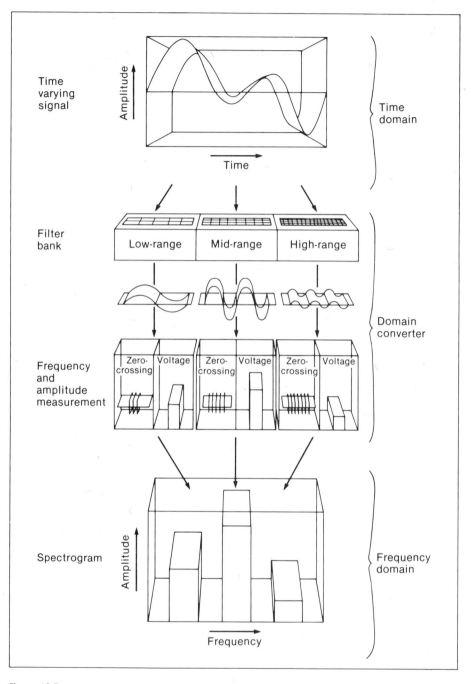

Figure 13.5.

A zero-crossing detector for speech recognition. (From Elphick, 1983. Reprinted with permission, *High Technology* magazine, March/April 1983, copyright © 1983 by High Technology Publishing Corp., 38 Commercial Wharf, Boston, MA 02110.)

For speech recognition, knowing the basic frequency alone would not be very useful, because the basic frequency of most utterances falls within a limited range. However, other zero-crossing detectors can be tuned to different sectors of the frequency spectrum. When this is done, each detector "listens" for acoustic energy in its part of the frequency spectrum. The bottom part of Figure 13.5 shows the output of a bank of three zero-crossing detectors working together. Notice that they have created a spectrogram, which is like a snapshot showing the concentration of acoustic energy in different parts of the auditory spectrum. The greater the number of zero-crossing detectors that are used, the narrower the band that each is responsible for. Consequently, greater refinement and accuracy are possible in the spectrogram. A sixteen-bank or thirty-two-bank system can provide a reasonable analysis of the frequencies of single spoken words. When this analysis is compared with sound templates showing the expected spectrogram for common words, such a system is capable of recognizing single words that it "knows" with an accuracy rate of about 90 percent.

However, as mentioned, recognizing single words does not mean that the system would be capable of recognizing ongoing, continuous speech. In addition to the segmentation problem discussed earlier, there is also the problem of parallel transmission. The speech sounds we produce do not occur in isolation. The sounds we are making at any given mement in time will have an effect on the sounds we are about to produce. Similarly, the sounds that we are about to produce have a backward effect on the pronunciation of our current utterances. A character in a book might say "Did you eat yet?" but in real life, the utterance is probably more like "Jeet yet?"

AI workers have gotten around the problems of segmentation and parallel transmission to a certain extent. As you have probably realized, continuous speech in some contexts is fairly predictable. For example, in ordering a meal in a restaurant or in making a reservation for a ticket over the phone, certain words and phrases are used repeatedly because these transactions are geared to the transmission and reception of a few critical facts. In these situations, we can program the speech recognition machine to take advantage of the word's context in an effort to boost recognition accuracy. One easy way to program context into a speech recognition program is through the use of a finite state grammar. Chapter 8 discussed these grammatical systems, which work by specifying the probabilities of particular transitions between words. True, these grammars are too rigid and limited to be good descriptions of our normal free speech. But they provide a reasonable way of making judgments about syntax in a limited environment. Figure 13.6 shows how a hypothetical finite state grammar might handle airline reservations (Elphick, 1983).

Natural Language Recognition

Since the advent of computers, people have hoped for the invention of a machine that could understand language—not computer language but everyday language. After all, something that could communicate with us on our own terms, reasonably and with knowledge of idioms, sarcasm, and other

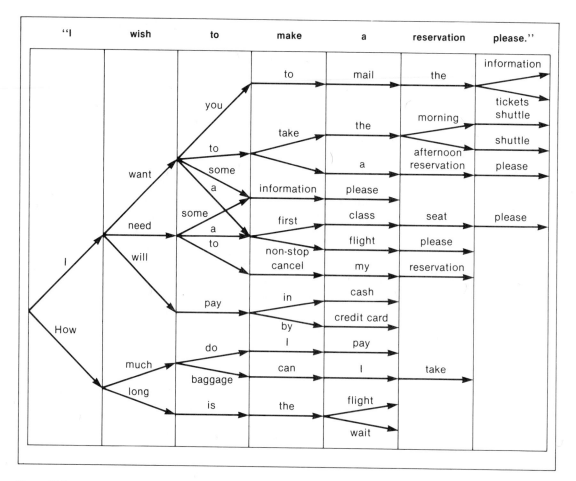

Figure 13.6.

A state diagram that represents sentences that might be encountered by a speech recognizer used to handle airline reservations. State diagrams for actual systems would be far more elaborate. (From Elphick, 1983. Reprinted with permission, *High Technology* magazine, March/April 1983, copyright © 1983 by High Technology Publishing Corp., 38 Commercial Wharf, Boston, MA 02110.)

nuances, would appear intelligent indeed. This section describes two classic AI approaches to this problem.

ELIZA

The problem of natural language recognition was recognized by the early AI researchers as a critical one. Weizenbaum (1966) was among the first to produce a program that could apparently understand and even produce novel English sentences in a natural context. His program, **ELIZA** (later, DOCTOR), was able to respond to typed-in comments and had a specific objective. It was designed to mimic the language of a Rogerian psychotherapist in the context of a therapy session.

Before examining the results of this program and how they were obtained, let's review a few of the basic ideas of Rogers's therapeutic practice.

First, Rogers believed that the effective therapist was nondirective. By this, he meant that the therapist should not try to control or steer the flow of therapy in any particular way. Instead, the therapist should be content to let the client discuss anything he wanted. Second, Rogers maintained that the effective therapist should frequently recite information that the client had recently divulged, paraphrasing only slightly. This technique is called reflection. By reflecting current feelings and thoughts held by the client, the therapist provided the client with an opportunity to hear how such thoughts and feelings sounded. Presumably, such opportunities provoked insight on the client's part.

You can probably see why Rogers's therapy was chosen for this sort of computerization. The nondirective nature of the interactions means that no sort of strategic knowledge nor even background knowledge need be simulated. Additionally, the reflective aspects of the therapy enable the program to hang onto almost any part of the client's statements. These statements can be later reflected, more or less unmodified, to the client. (Incidentally, I'm not suggesting that ELIZA would be a good psychotherapist or that Rogerian psychotherapy is easy to do.)

From a technical point of view, ELIZA is successful. The following transcript was generated by a person interacting with ELIZA:

Transcript A	
Subject:	Men are all alike.
Counselor (ELIZA):	IN WHAT WAY
S:	They're always bugging us about something or other.
C:	CAN YOU THINK OF A SPECIFIC EXAMPLE
S:	Well, my boyfriend made me come here.
C:	YOUR BOYFRIEND MADE YOU COME HERE
S:	He says I'm depressed much of the time.
C:	I AM SORRY TO HEAR YOU ARE DEPRESSED
S:	It's true, I am unhappy.
C:	DO YOU THINK COMING HERE WILL HELP YOU NOT TO BE UNHAPPY
S:	I need some help, that much seems certain.
C:	WHAT WOULD IT MEAN TO YOU IF YOU GOT SOME HELP
S:	Perhaps I could learn to get along with my mother.
C:	TELL ME MORE ABOUT YOUR FAMILY
S:	My mother takes care of me.
C:	WHO ELSE IN YOUR FAMILY TAKES CARE OF YOU
S:	My father.
C:	YOUR FATHER
S:	You are like my father in some ways.

C:	WHAT RESEMBLANCE DO YOU SEE
S:	You are not very aggressive, but I think you don't want me to notice that.
C:	WHAT MAKES YOU THINK I AM NOT AGGRESSIVE
S:	You don't argue with me.
C:	WHY DO YOU THINK I DON'T ARGUE WITH YOU
S:	You are afraid of me.
C:	DOES IT PLEASE YOU TO BELIEVE I AM AFRAID OF YOU
S:	My father is afraid of everybody.
C:	WHAT ELSE COMES TO YOUR MIND WHEN YOU THINK OF YOUR FATHER
S:	Bullies.
S:	DOES THAT HAVE ANYTHING TO DO WITH THE FACT THAT YOUR BOYFRIEND MADE YOU COME HERE (Weizenbaum, 1966)

As the transcript shows, ELIZA has done a decent job of being nondirective and reflective, and seems to understand what the client is talking about. Like many people, you may feel that the program is being particularly clever when it makes the analogy between the client's father and boyfriend.

How does ELIZA work? Generally, ELIZA's processing of the client's remarks is superficial. ELIZA is programmed to respond in limited ways to particular phrases and orthographic cues. For example, when ELIZA sees a question, it is programmed to respond with a question of the form "Why do you ask. . . . " If the subject should use the word *might*, ELIZA invariably responds by asking "Why aren't you sure." Sometimes, ELIZA picks out certain statements made by the subject and rephrases them. For example, if the subject makes a statement *X,* ELIZA may come back with "What makes you think 'statement *X*'?" If the program picks up no key words, it may return to an earlier comment that has been stored. A particularly good example of this tactic is in ELIZA's last response in the prior transcript.

Although the program gives the appearance of comprehension, ELIZA's abilities to understand language are an illusion. Nevertheless, the illusion is convincing. Weizenbaum reported that ELIZA was one of the more popular counselors on campus for a time and had attracted a group of regular clients who preferred ELIZA to a human counselor. These people claimed that ELIZA had helped them a great deal. Weizenbaum (1976) has reported his astonishment and disillusionment over the reluctance of humans to see ELIZA for what it really is: a fairly rigid and limited program.

This brings us to another point. Although ELIZA seems believable in the prior example, the set of the questioner is probably crucial to the illusion's being convincing (Hofstadter, 1979). In other words, ELIZA looks good in those situations in which the human plays along. But when the human asks harder questions or tried to smoke out the rigid and repetitive basis of the program, the results are not as convincing. For example, the version of ELIZA that I have for my microcomputer (called DR. ROM) has a brief help session before I get to see the "doctor." In this advisory session, I'm asked not to make fun of DR. ROM's poor grammar, and I'm advised that I'll get out of the therapy only what I put into it. Some therapist. When a skeptical and knowledgeable interrogator engages ELIZA in a conversation, the results can be much less satisfying than those seen previously. Transcript B is a reproduction of such a dialogue, and it demonstrates how inhuman ELIZA can become:

Transcript B

S: Hello

C: HOW DO YOU DO. PLEASE STATE YOUR PROBLEM.

S: I want a good example for my book.

C: YOUR BOOK.

S: Yes, my book about computers. Can you help me?

C: YOU'RE BEING SOMEWHAT SHORT WITH ME.

S: I didn't mean to be.

C: YOU SAY YOU DIDN'T MEAN TO BE.

S: That's right. What do you know about computers?

C: DO COMPUTERS WORRY YOU?

S: Not at all, I think they can be very useful.

C: CAN YOU ELABORATE ON THAT?

S: Computers play a vital role in the operation of our society.

C: WHY DO YOU MENTION COMPUTERS?

S: Because that is what the book is all about.

C: IS THAT THE REAL REASON?

S: Of course. Sometimes you are difficult to talk to.

C: WHAT MAKES YOU THINK I AM DIFFICULT TO TALK TO?

S: You answer in such short, stylized phrases.

C: WE WERE DISCUSSING YOU—NOT ME.

S: I thought we were discussing computers.

C: WHAT DO MACHINES HAVE TO DO WITH YOUR PROBLEM?

S: My only problem is to get you to carry on a reasonable conversation.

S: WHY DO YOU SAY YOUR ONLY PROBLEM IS TO GET I TO CARRY ON A REASONABLE CONVERSATION?

S: You don't use very good grammar.

C: OH, I DON'T USE VERY GOOD GRAMMAR.

S: That's right. Don't you know the difference between nominative and accusative?

C: YOU'RE NOT REALLY TALKING ABOUT ME—ARE YOU?

S: I really was, but I'm willing to change the subject.

C: DO YOU SAY YOU REALLY WAS FOR SOME SPECIAL REASON?

S: The reason is that I would like an interesting conversation in the book.

C: IN WHAT WAY?

S: So that the readers will not get bored with it.

C: I AM NOT SURE I UNDERSTAND YOU FULLY.

S: You don't understand very much, do you!

C: WHAT ARE YOUR FEELINGS NOW?

S: I feel that I'm about ready to give up.

C: TELL ME MORE ABOUT SUCH FEELINGS.

S: The page is amost full now, so I can end this interview.

C: SUPPOSE THE PAGE WERE NOT ALMOST FULL NOW?

S: Then we would have to continue this silliness a while longer.

C: PLEASE GO ON.

S: That's all there is to say. Don't you ever get tired?

C: PERHAPS THAT'S ALL THERE REALLY IS TO SAY.

S: Yes. Goodbye.

C: YOU SEEM QUITE POSITIVE. (Raphael, 1976, p. 199)

As this transcript shows, a program like ELIZA, consisting of a relatively few phrases, can be tripped up and made to look foolish (if you'll permit my using that term to describe a machine). A good question remains however: Can anything better be done? That is, can a machine be programmed in such a way that it possesses some background knowledge about linguistic concepts and thus will not simply repeat itself? The next section examines a program that seems to be closer to the possession of this sort of knowledge.

SHRDLU

Imagine a device that is capable of "looking" at a tabletop laden with children's blocks and which can "move" specific blocks in response to English commands. Imagine also that the device responds in English about the alterations it has carried out. Winograd's (1972) program, **SHRDLU**, has these features and so remains a tour de force more than a decade later.

During the early 1970s, much of the AI work at MIT made use of a so-called blocks world—an array of variously shaped and colored blocks whose features could be analyzed by existing programs. Winograd's objective was to produce a program that could interact with both the blocks world and a spectator in a meaningful way. That is, the program would be able to "move" the blocks (metaphorically; the actual blocks were not moved, but their picture on the computer screen was altered). The program would also be able to describe to an observer the results of such movement. This is a tricky problem, which Winograd solved admirably. The following transcript is a record of SHRDLU's comments after being given several commands. The commands are shown in boldface, SHRDLU's responses are shown in capitals, and commentary by Margaret Boden is provided in italics.

1. **Pick up a big red block.**

   OK

   The system answers "OK" when it carries out a command. In order to pick up the red block, it had to clear it off by finding a space for the green one and moving the green one away. [Figure 13.7] shows the initial state of the scene.

2. **Grasp the pyramid.**

   I DON'T UNDERSTAND WHICH PYRAMID YOU MEAN.

   There are three pyramids in the scene, so the program does nothing.

3. **Find a block which is taller than the one you are holding and put it into the box.**

   The system has to figure out what is meant by "one" and "it," as well as using deduction to decide which block it is holding.

   BY "IT," I ASSUME YOU MEAN THE BLOCK IS TALLER THAN THE ONE I AM HOLDING.

   Printed to keep us informed.

   OK

   The hand has to set down the red block to pick up the taller blue one.

4. **What does the box (now) contain?**

   THE BLUE PYRAMID AND THE BLUE BLOCK.

5. **What is the pyramid supported by?**

   Earlier the system reponded to "the pyramid" by saying "I don't understand which pyramid you mean." Now it assumes that we mean the one just mentioned.

   THE BOX

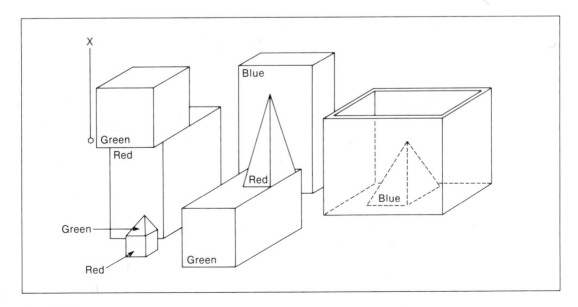

Figure 13.7.

"Pick up a big red block." (From Winograd, 1972. Reprinted by permission of the publisher.)

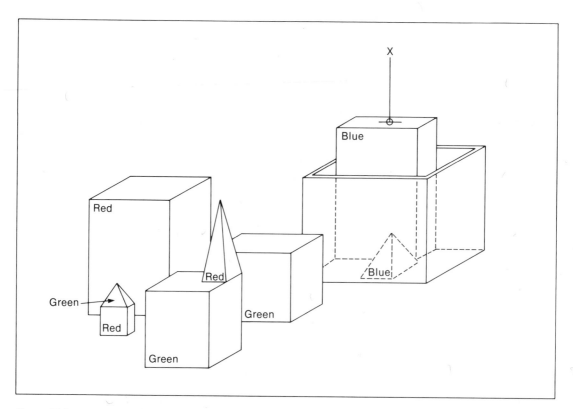

Figure 13.8.

"Find a block which is taller than the one you are holding and put it into the box." (From Winograd, 1972. Reprinted by permission of the publisher.)

6. **How many blocks are not in the box?**

   Negatives such as "not" and "no" are handled whether they appear in clauses or noun groups (such as "no boxes").

   FOUR OF THEM.

35. **Is there anything which is bigger than every pyramid but is not as wide as the thing that supports it?**

    The system understands quantifiers such as "every," "any," "some," etc., and structures such as "bigger than," "as wide as," etc. Here "it" refers to a noun group within the same sentence but two levels up in the parsing tree.

    YES. THE BLUE BLOCK.

36. **Does a steeple?**

    SORRY, I DON'T KNOW THE WORD "STEEPLE."

    The system interrupts immediately when it sees a word it can't figure out.

37. **A "steeple" is a stack which contains two green cubes and a pyramid.**

    The quote marks indicate that we are defining a new word.

    I UNDERSTAND

38. **Are there any steeples now?**

    NO

    The new definition is used as a description to recognize steeples.

43. **Is there anything to the right of the red pyramid?**

    YES. FOUR THINGS. THE BOX, THE RED CUBE, THE BLUE PYRAMID AND THE BLOCK NAMED SUPERBLOCK.

    Once an object has a name, the name is used to help identify it in responses.

44. **Thank you.**

    YOU'RE WELCOME!

    Idioms can be used without modifying the grammar. (Boden, 1977)

Human knowledge is well connected and integrated. Thus, we are seldom at a loss for words to describe any changes that take place in our field of vision. Consequently, most of us would feel confident in our ability to describe (in English) any changes we might make with our own hands in the blocks world. Programming a computer to duplicate this feat is problematic because it is difficult to specify in advance what sorts of transformations the program will be called upon to make. Even within the confines of a relatively simple microworld, the number of such transformations is so enormous that few existing machines could memorize all of them, let alone memorize all the corresponding English expressions that would describe them. Consequently, SHRDLU must be endowed with an algorithm flexible and general enough to recognize a variety of changes in its perceptual field, yet detailed enough to be able to describe those changes in English. Let's phrase this knowledge as a series of steps:

1. understand questions in English about the situation;
2. give answers in English to questions about the situation;
3. understand requests in English to manipulate the blocks;
4. break down each request into a sequence of operations it could do;
5. understand what it had done, and for what reasons;
6. describe its actions and their reasons, in English. (Hofstadter, 1979)

Phrasing SHRDLU's task in this way implies that a linear, hierarchical program would do the trick. Phase 1 might consist of some parsing program that analyzed the English commands and sent the outputs of this parsing routine to a movement routine. In phase 2, this movement routine would map the linguistic information onto a short set of blocks world actions. These actions might next be checked for impossibilities, such as an action that would involve putting a box on top of a pyramid. The output of this phase might next be sent to a third array changer routine that appropriately modifies the display. Continuing in this fashion, we might say that having worked our way inward from the English command to a perceptual change, SHRDLU could well proceed by working its way backward from the now-changed array in its perceptual field back out to an English expression. With its task conceptualized in this way, SHRDLU's domain becomes almost impossibly large (although orderly).

Winograd's great insight lay in his realization that such a typical information-processing approach would not do. Rather then conceive of SHRDLU as simply a chain of related but essentially separate subroutines, Winograd reasoned that each component of the understanding process was both a cause and an effect. The output of a particular subroutine could not be a static and unmodifiable event, because the task demanded an ongoing analysis of shifting perceptual fields and continuous linguistic commands. Consequently, the output of a routine in SHRDLU may become an input of the same routine after several intervening routines have further elaborated the information. Viewed in this way, SHRDLU no longer appears to have a front-to-back or top-to-bottom organization. Rather, the subroutines of SHRDLU should be understood as an intricately related, tangled series of loops. Winograd describes this property of SHRDLU's:

Our program does not operate by first parsing a sentence, then doing semantic analysis, and finally by using deduction to produce a response. These three activities go on concurrently throughout the understanding of a sentence. As soon as a piece of syntactic structure begins to take shape, a semantic program is called to see whether it might make sense, and the resultant answer can direct the parsing. In deciding whether it makes sense, the semantic routine may call deductive processes and ask questions about the real world. As an example in sentence 34 of the dialogue ("Put the blue pyramid on the block in the box"), the parser first comes up with "the blue pyramid on the block" as a candidate for a noun group. At this point, semantic analysis is done, and since "the" is definite, a check is made in the data base for the object being referred to. When no such object is found, the parsing is redirected to find the noun group "the blue pyramid." It will then go on to find "on the block in the box" as a single phrase indicating a location....Thus there is a continuing interplay between the different sorts of analysis, with the results of one affecting the others. (Winograd, 1975, pp. 182–183)

Implications for Cognitive Psychology

As the previous passage makes clear, SHRDLU has two abilities that are at the base of its remarkable feats. First, SHRDLU can carry out a fairly sophisticated feature analysis of the blocks world. Thus, its internal representation of the shape and color of the blocks is good. Second, SHRDLU is endowed with knowledge of certain linguistic features. Thus, SHRDLU knows about terms such as *on* or *beside*. This affords SHRDLU the ability to deduce facts from direct knowledge of other facts. For example, if one block is "on" another, SHRDLU can deduce that the second block is "under" the first. Because the architecture of SHRDLU's programming meshes the analysis of linguistic and perceptual features, the machine is able to duplicate the flexibility a human might show in answering questions about the blocks world. Our intuitions tell us that this approach seems to capture much more of the meaning inherent in the phrase "background knowledge" than have other more rigid attempts to program it.

SHRDLU has other implications for cognitive psychology, too. Recall that Chapter 8 discussed the theory of Noam Chomsky. Chomsky maintained that language acquisition depended on a language acquisition device, or LAD, which specified the relationship of deep-to-surface structure. Because deep structure corresponds to meaning and is tacit knowledge, Chomsky's theory is somewhat unsatisfying concerning the origin and development of meaning. SHRDLU allows us to speculate about this problem. Notice that the result of SHRDLU's feature analysis is in itself a code, or representation, which is then mapped onto lexical items that are descriptive of possible states of affairs in the blocks world. These have been built into SHRDLU. Thus, SHRDLU doesn't have to learn the word *beside;* the word is already there as soon as the machine starts its perceiving. However, the mapping process is a different story. SHRDLU must apply certain algorithms to the output of its feature analysis to identify those cases that qualify as examples of "besideness."

A similar process may well take place in humans. That is, the results of human analysis might create a code that is elaborated by other cognitive processes. Ultimately, this elaborated code would be stored in cognitive structures that correspond to the innate and tacit phrase markers of Chomsky's theory. Such a line of reasoning suggests that meaning is created by the process of perception—specifically, the process of feature analysis. These speculations are simply that: The current state of affairs is simply too unclear to render a more accurate statement. However, you should be aware that SHRDLU's procedural knowledge of language opened up a new window through which cognitive psychologists could view the problem of semantics.

PROBLEM SOLVING

Perhaps AI work on problem solving has proceeded faster than in some of the other areas of cognition because a general technique for formalizing problems has been available for some time. Recall that in chapter 12, we examined the notion of the state-action space as a way of representing all the possible configurations of elements that could be achieved in a given problem. This analysis is applicable to problem solving by machine. The process is as follows. An algorithm is written that enables a computer to generate a significant portion of the problem's branches. The computer then examines some or all of the branches systematically, evaluating each branch against some criteria that have been stored as part of the program. This section considers several programs that use some variation of the strategy outlined here to solve problems in knowledge-rich domains.

Chess

Chapter 12 considered the work of de Groot (1965), and in that research we see what has become a classic AI problem. The chess master has accumulated organized knowledge resulting from years of intense experience with the game. This experience has produce chess knowledge that is somehow independent of the chess master's general cognitive functioning. For example, as de Groot demonstrated, the chess master doesn't necessarily explore the branches of the state-action tree in chess further than a novice does. And as Chase and Simon (1973) showed, the chess master doesn't necessarily have a better memory than the novice. What the chess master does have, however, is a superior mental organization for chess pieces, which operates schematically. The chess master's mental structure not only organizes the pieces but also suggests which lines of play should be explored. This helps the chess master immensely. As we saw when we explored the use of the subgoal heuristic, establishing simple subgoals can prune the branches of the state-action tree, making the problem much more manageable. In effect, this is what the chess master's schematic knowledge enables her to do. Chess is played at a higher level by masters than it is by novices, in part because the chess master doesn't waste so much time and cognitive effort exploring unproductive pathways. For AI researchers, this presents a problem. Namely, what exactly does the chess master know that can be formalized in a computer program?

AI research on chess has taken two separate approaches to the problem of knowledge. The first of these approaches is called the **power approach** (Goldstein & Papert, 1977). The power approach is also sometimes called the brute force approach, because no real attempt is made to mimic the knowledge structures of humans. Instead, the program simply searches as much of the state-action tree as it can, as fast as it can. Here, the computer is taking advantage of its incredible computational speed to find an answer to a problem, and for this reason is said to be brute forcing a solution. In contrast, the **knowledge-based approach** tries to formulate an algorithm that does somehow mimic the domain-specific knowledge of humans.

Let's see how these two approaches can be applied in chess. First, no chess program searches the entire state-action tree; as mentioned in Chapter 12, it's simply too huge. This means that all chess programs must limit search operations. These limitations can be written into a program in two ways. A program can limit the number of successive moves that are considered from any one point in the game; this is referred to as limiting the **depth of the search.** On the other hand, a program might limit the number of moves that are evaluated from any node in the state-action tree or might limit the number of nodes in the state-action tree that are suggested for further exploration. This is called limiting the **width of the search.** Figure 13.9 shows these two limitations in operation.

All programs limit depth to a certain extent, usually for the sake of time. Increasing the depth of the search by just a single node (i.e., looking four moves ahead instead of three) results in a tremendous increase in the time required to carry out all the evaluative computations. This is usually what happens when you increase the level of play on one of the home computer chess programs. The program now searches further into the state-action tree, but if you have such a program, you know that the amount of time required by the computer increases dramatically with each increase in level. Not all programs limit the width of search, however, and those that do not are referred to as brute force programs. Tbse programs consider every legal move available on the board at that time and consider them all out to some, usually limited, depth. Knowledge-based chess programs are those that try to limit the width of search.

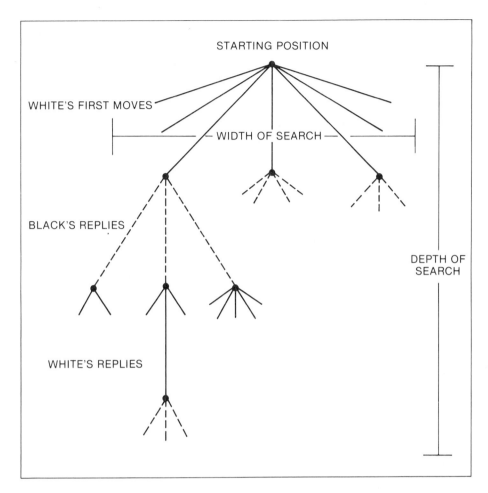

Figure 13.9.

A chess game tree. (From Chi, Glaser, & Rees, 1982. Copyright 1982 by Lawrence Erlbaum Associates, Inc. Adapted by permission of the publisher and authors.)

We know that superior human performance relies on limiting the width of search, but what about superior computer performance? Generally, the best computer chess programs, such as CHESS 4.6, written by Slate and Atkin, or BELLE, written by Thompson and Condon of Bell Labs, use a modification of the brute force approach. These programs can defeat all human chess players except grand masters. Such programs have little knowledge of chess per se. Like most brute force solutions, these programs emphasize speed of computation. Such an approach could conceivably beat a grand master, but success will probably involve the creation of hardware that can carry out computations further into the state-action tree in a reasonable period of time.

PARADISE

Some attempts have been made to develop knowledge-based chess programs that limit the width of search. **PARADISE** (Wilkins, 1980) is such a program.

This program doesn't play an entire game. Rather, it plays selected positions from the midgame of chess. The midgame is the period in the middle of most chess games where pieces on the board are reduced through exchanges. PARADISE works by examining a data base of some two hundred **production rules.** A production rule is a two-part statement. The first part of the rule refers to a set of conditions that can be observed on the chessboard. The second part of the rule describes an action that should be taken if those conditions are observed. Production rules resemble lengthy "if-then" statements. Most of the two hundred production rules in PARADISE are organized by certain higher-level actions that frequently occur in chess. For example, chess players typically look at their pieces to see if any are under THREAT of attack. Similarly, players look at certain squares to see if they are SAFE to move onto. Players sometimes attempt to gain access to a square by using a DECOY to lure away the opponent. These productions are repeatedly applied to the configuration of pieces on the board until a plan is formulated that has a good chance of winning a piece. If the plan doesn't seem to have a good chance of winning material, it is dropped. The result of this decision making is that PARADISE winds up exploring a small state-action tree.

PARADISE has something else in common with human experts. Most chess programs have a fairly artificial limit on depth of search. However, PARADISE searches until it determines that its objective has been achieved. At that point, the program goes on to consider several additional nodes to determine whether it is worth continuing the search still deeper. Because the production rules limit the number of alternatives that are explored from any particular node, the program can search into the state-action tree much deeper than other chess programs. The program has essentially traded off width of search for depth.

The power of PARADISE is limited by the knowledge that can be encoded into the two hundred or so production rules. However, because of their somewhat modular nature, specific production rules can be modified without necessarily affecting many other parts of the program. Improvements in PARADISE can theoretically be accomplished by modifying individual production rules. Some plans have been made to build this capability directly into PARADISE. That is, future versions of the program may have the ability to monitor the success or usefulness of particular production rules and modify them accordingly.

Expertise

The most advanced types of problem solving occur in knowledge-rich domains, where the search processes of the problem solver are most likely to be narrowed down by expertise. Chess is an example of such problem solving. The expert differs from the amateur in many ways, but one of the most important ways is in the ability to prune part of the state-action tree. This pruning is a direct result of the chess master's knowledge. One of AI's most ambitious goals is to develop software that also seems to "know" something in just that sense, enabling a problem solver working in consultation with the program to trim down the size of a large state-action space. This section considers an expert system that seems to know something about medicine.

MYCIN is a rule-based expert system that was developed in the mid-1970s by Edward Shortliffe of Stanford (Shortliffe, 1976). Its purpose is to aid physicians in the diagnosis and treatment of infectious diseases. MYCIN was not the first major expert system developed, but its architecture and organization are fairly typical of most of the expert systems now on the market. How does it operate?

MYCIN begins by establishing the condition of the patient. It asks about the patient's symptoms, medical history, current clinical condition, and any lab findings that may have been obtained. If a diagnosis can be made on the basis of this information, MYCIN does so. If more information is needed, MYCIN asks the physician, or it tries to infer the missing data based on the current facts. MYCIN's ability to reason with uncertain information is one of its great strengths.

The MYCIN system consists of three subprograms. The consultation program is the heart of the system. The physician can interrupt the consultation program at any point to ask questions, and MYCIN will explain why certain deductions have been made, along with the probability of error. The second subprogram is the explanation program. After the consultation, which usually takes about 20 minutes, MYCIN automatically flips into an explanatory mode. Here, the program answers any questions the physician might have and describes the reasoning process it used in asking for particular bits of information. The final subprogram is the rule acquisition program. This subprogram is for use by experts only. As more data are accumulated concerning the nature of infectious diseases, MYCIN can be altered to stay abreast of developments in the field.

As the consultation proceeds, MYCIN builds up a series of bits of knowledge that are called contexts. Some contexts are provided directly by the physician; others are deduced by MYCIN. There are basically three types of contexts. The first context is called PERSON and refers to the patient. Each consultation can have only one PERSON context. The second context type deals with whatever cultures have been taken from the patient and is called CURCULS. Each person must have at least one CURCULS context, although a person may have more than one. Finally, MYCIN seeks information about the microorganisms growing in the cultures. This information is called CURORGS and constitutes the third of the major contexts. These contexts are grouped hierarchically, as shown in Figure 13.10. Nodes that are higher in this context tree are called the parent context of nodes below them. It's important to realize that telling MYCIN about a parent node causes the creation of a lower context. This means that the creation of the PERSON context drives, or propels, MYCIN to create the lower contexts.

Each of the contexts has a set of properties, or characteristics. Moreover, each of these characteristics has properties that are called parameters. For example, one of the properties of CURCULS is called PROPCUL, and its

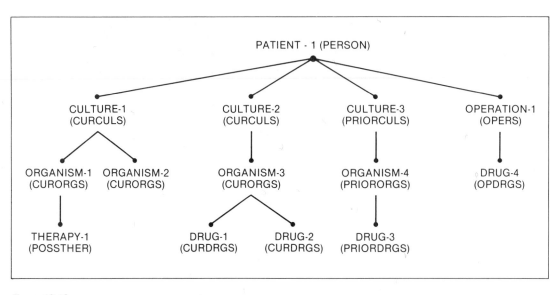

Figure 13.10.

Sample context tree. (From Cendrowska & Bramer, 1984.)

parameters include the SITE of the culture. The program's goal is to trace the parameters, which means finding the parameter's identity. The program accomplishes this goal by using a series of goal-directed backward-chaining rules. Here's how it works.

MYCIN has two data bases—one active and one permanent. In the permanent data base is a set of approximately two hundred production rules that are very similar in format to the "if-then" rules used in PARADISE. In this case, the if-then rule specifies a number of antecedents that are known to be associated with particular microorganisms. For example, one of MYCIN's rules deals with detection of the bacteria pseudomonas. In the permanent data base are three facts that are associated with this bacteria. That is, if the organism did not respond to the standard Gram stain (Gram-neg) and the organism has a rod shape, and the patient is a compromised host (e.g., a person who has a complicating disorder such as sickle-cell anemia), then there is suggestive evidence that the organism is pseudomonas. As the physician types in information about the patient's condition, MYCIN files this information in its active data base. Next, it compares the active data base with the permanent one to formulate some hypotheses about the likelihood of specific bacteria. For example, suppose the physician in this case told MYCIN that the morphology of the bacteria was a rod, and the stain was Gramneg. MYCIN, seeing that two of the three conditions for pseudomonas had been met, might now ask the physician if the patient was a compromised host. If the answer is yes, then MYCIN become more confident that the patient is infected with, at least, this bacteria.

This procedure seems to give MYCIN the equivalent of the intuition that experts seem to have in their areas of expertise. That is, like a human expert, MYCIN seems to ask irrelevant questions sometimes, but these questions often turn out to be directly related to the patient's problems. To show this phenomenon, the following is a reconstructed dialogue between MYCIN and a human (MYCIN asks the questions):

8) Enter the identity (genus) of ORGANISM1
:unknown
9) The stain (Gram or Ziehl-Neelson Acidfast) of ORGANISM1
:gramneg
10) Is ORGANISM1 a coccus or a rod (etc.)?
:rod
11) Did ORGANISM1 grow aerobically?
:y
12) Did ORGANISM1 grow anaerobically?
:y
13) What is the suspected portal of entry of ORGANISM1?
:unknown
14) Is there any evidence that Smith (PATIENT1) has MENINGITIS?
:y (Cendrowska & Bramer, 1984, pp. 493–94)

This last question may have struck you as coming from left field, but MYCIN has apparently concluded that the pattern of information given so far is consistent with meningitis. As you can see, MYCIN's deduction was apparently correct.

AI'S CONTRIBUTION TO THE STUDY OF COGNITION

The range of programs and machines included under the heading "AI" is so vast that the preceding sections should be understood as a sampler of things that are possible with a machine, rather than a commentary on the state of the art. Consequently, we need to go beyond the specific findings of AI to evaluate its usefulness to cognitive psychologists. In attempting to determine AI's contribution to the study of cognition, we therefore seek a clearer understanding of how AI may have helped in our understanding of intelligence.

Questions about the Nature of Thought

In his classic work, *The Leviathan,* Thomas Hobbes commented that "reasoning is but reckoning" (Hobbes, 1651). To elaborate somewhat, Hobbes meant that all human reasoning, regardless of its nature or content, could be expressed in computational processes. The reasoning done by humans was "really" the result of such computation. In other words, all human intellectual abilities, from proving mathematical theorems to playing chess, were isomorphic with some reckoning processes. Although this idea lay more or less dormant for three centuries, it was near and dear to the hearts of the early computer scientists.

Hobbes's insight is at the core of what is now called the computational view of thought. Because all reasoning is but computation, so this argument runs, and because machines are capable of computation, then machines are apparently capable of reasoning. Because human reasoning is certainly "thought," it doesn't appear that thought requires any special abilities beyond those required for computation. Thus, thinking is at most a particular sort of computation.

Embedded in this argument is a central contention known as the **Church-Turing Thesis.** Although this thesis can be stated in a variety of ways, the following phrasing will serve as a reference point:

The Church-Turing Thesis: What is human-computable is machine computable. (Hofstadter, 1979)

The Church-Turing thesis has some awesome implications. In its strongest form, it suggests that all thinking could be reduced to some sort of computation. Theoretically, then, all computing machines possessing a certain minimal power have the potential reasoning ability of sophisticated humans. Getting the machines to yield this potential consists of discovering human computational processes and then mapping them onto the machines. The discovery of all these computational processes is a huge technical problem but not a theoretical impossibility.

A belief that's frequently adopted by the adherents of the Church-Turing thesis is that the complexity of thought is more of an illusion than it is a reality. They believe that once we are able to express thought in computational processes, the architecture of thought—its organization—will be revealed. Since these computational processes are considered simpler than the thoughts themselves, these processes are equivalent to a reduced code for expressing mental events. The **reductionist viewpoint** has several related beliefs, one of which is that mental processes can be reduced to brain processes. Rcall that Chapter 1 dealt with this subject briefly. This leads to the second version of the Church-Turing thesis:

Church-Turing Thesis, Reductionist's Version: All brain processes are derived from a computable substrate. (Hofstadter, 1979, p. 572)

A substrate is a basis, or foundation. Linking the two versions of the Church-Turing thesis together, we come up with a statement that all thought processes can be reduced to brain processes, which in turn can be reduced to some computational processes that can be done by neural or electronic events. The relationship between AI and mentality implied by these versions of the Church-Turing thesis is represented in Figure 13.11. As Figure 13.11 shows, AI need not devote itself to detailed stimulations of neural networks. This operation of mentality is isomorphic with any given AI program, and how it gets computed doesn't matter. The literal bottom line is that it's all the same anyway. What are some of the implications of the computational view of thought for cognitive psychology?

On one hand, such a view seems to suggest a symbiosis between the two disciplines. If the Church-Turing thesis is true, we don't have to study the brain to understand mentality. This could be tremendously liberating for cognitive psychologists. Despite some promising attempts, cognitive psy-

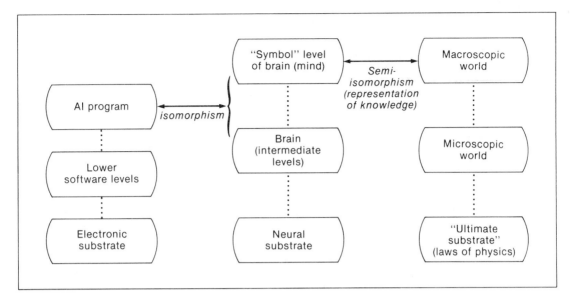

Figure 13.11.

The relationship between mentality and AI. (From *Godel, Escher, Bach: An Eternal Golden Braid,* by Douglas R. Hofstadter. © 1979 by Basic Books, Inc., Publishers. Reprinted by permission of the publisher.)

chologists have generally been frustrated in their attempts to build neural models capable of supporting anything like a complex mental event. Given that the idea looks so good, what prevents cognitive psychologists from going ahead with this reducing plan?

Minds and Programs

To understand why number crunching in a computer may not be synonymous with mentality, let's carry out a mental experiment. Imagine that you have been locked in a room by a group of cognitive psychologists. They have thoughtfully supplied you with a book written in Chinese, but since you don't speak Chinese, this book is not very useful as a pastime. Now suppose they give you an additional ream of Chinese writing, together with a set of rules written in English that enables you to correlate the second batch of Chinese characters with the first. Finally, suppose you are given a third set of Chinese characters, with yet another set of English instructions that enable you to correlate the third ream of Chinese characters with the first two sets. Suppose moreover that the English instructions given with the third set tell you to give back certain Chinese characters (that is, slide them back under the door, presumably) when particular Chinese characters have been given to you. This state of affairs is diagrammed in Figure 13.12. As Figure 13.12 shows, a person knowing English but no Chinese could relate any of the three sets of Chinese characters to any other set.

As described by Searle (1981), this state of affairs parallels the information processing done by SAM and other script-processing programs. The

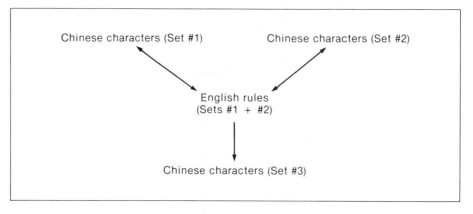

Figure 13.12.

Relationships among various character sets in the locked room.

psychologists might refer to the first batch of Chinese characters as the script, the second batch as the story, and the third batch as questions. In addition, they might refer to the Chinese characters you have returned to them as answers to the questions and the English instructions as the program. If the cognitive psychologists were strong believers in AI, they might insist that you, the person in the room, could understand Chinese. After all, the evidence is fairly powerful. From their external perspective, they can give you a series of questions about a story, and you can respond with a series of answers that are plausible when read by a person who speaks Chinese. Whoever is in the locked room seemingly understands the stories. But from your internal perspective, nothing of the kind has taken place. It's important to realize that if you were stuck in this predicament, your knowledge of Chinese wouldn't improve in the slightest, no matter how adept you became at substituting the Chinese characters for one another, as called for in the English instructions. This is essentially Searle's point: No matter what formal principles (i.e., programs) you put into a computer, they will not be sufficient for true understanding, because a human could follow these formal principles and still understand absolutely nothing (Searle, 1981).

A similar point is made by Fodor (1981). Suppose two programs have been created: one to simulate the events of the 1967 Arab-Israeli war and the second to simulate a chess game. It's possible, although unlikely, that a computer's handling of these two programs would be identical. This is because the computing machine does not run the program in the language in which it has been written. Rather, the program is translated or compiled, and ultimately reduced to an almost unreadable code known as machine language. Thus statements like "pawns attack knight" and "Israeli infantry surround tank corps" might be translated identically, even though the two sentences have two different meanings. Fodor's point is that the compiled versions of these sentences don't specify their *intentions* (Fodor, 1981). One implication of these examples seems clear enough: From the machine's internal perspective, no genuine comprehension or understanding is necessary for meaningful processing to take place (Wagner, 1982). The machine's failure to attain mentality seems partially based on its apparent failure to achieve **intentionality.**

Intentionality as a theme in AI has been taken up by several writers. Dennett (1981) has explicated three modes of predicting the behavior of complex systems. These three modes, or stances, as he calls them, are the design stance, the physical stance, and the intentional stance. Predicting a machine's behavior from the design stance entails an understanding of the way in which the machine is supposed to function, assuming it is functioning normally. An individual trying to predict a computer's behavior from the design stance would first ask "How is the machine programmed?" The physical stance is concerned with the actual state of a particular object. Although we often rely upon the physical stance to predict the behavior of objects, we seldom use this mode to predict the behavior of a computing machine. Doing so would entail knowing about the specific nature of the electrical energy within the machine as well as the fate of such energy. The intentional stance requires that one treat the computer as though it had beliefs, desires, and so on, and that the machine dealt with these in a fairly rational way. Predicting the behavior of the machine would involve judgments about what the machine "wanted" to do.

Adopting the intentional stance does not compel us to take any particular position on the machine's awareness. It's simply a pragmatic way of dealing with a system that is often too complex to comprehend using either the design or the physical stance. For example, if we wanted to predict the behavior of a chess-playing computer in order to defeat it, we would probably be wasting our time if we tried to determine how it was programmed or wired. Rather, we might assume that the machine was a good player in that it would carry out rational moves given the positions it had achieved.

To the extent that the machine was indeed well programmed, this assumption would be helpful in playing against it. Our willingness to make assumptions of rationality in a chess-playing computer is narrowly hemmed in by our knowledge that such assumptions are useful only when the machine is playing chess. We know that if we ask the machine who won the 1935 World Series, it's not going to us us a straight answer. In this regard, the machine's response is predictable from the design stance rather than from the intentional stance. To understand the machine's responses, we don't need to make the assumption that the machine didn't want to tell us the correct answer.

But now suppose we endow the chess machine with a switching program so that it recognizes baseball questions and has the knowledge to answer them. The assumption of rationality would now be useful in two areas. I'm sure you can detect where I'm headed with this example. As we added more and more areas of expertise to the chess machine, the assumption of rationality would get progressively more useful in understanding the machine's responses. The technical demands of this enterprise would be enormous, but we would reach a point where the assumption of rationality would be pragmatic all the time. That is, the machine would give us noncontradictory and rational answers to questions on a wide variety of topics at least as often as humans did. At this point, we would no longer be able to see beyond the horizons implied by our assumptions. In other words, the easiest way to predict the behavior of such a machine would be to assume that it had beliefs and so on, which it acted upon in a rational way. This means that we may not be able to tell just when a computing machine has achieved consciousness. If it always aids us to assume that a given machine has beliefs, fears, and so on, then questions about whether the machine "really" has such beliefs become somewhat empty.

We can sum up the contribution of AI to the study of cognition in three sentences. First, AI work has paradoxically pointed out the need for formal theories of cognition at the same time that it has pointed out the limitations of such theorizing. Second, AI researchers have discovered the enormous problems in making explicit the tacit knowledge that all of us take for granted. Finally, developments in AI have raised questions about the reductionist paradigm fashionable in psychology for some time.

CONCLUDING COMMENTS AND SUGGESTIONS FOR FURTHER READING

We've looked at several areas of investigation from the standpoint of artificial intelligence. At least a couple of points have emerged from this examination. First, AI workers have apparently had more success in dealing with higher mental processes than with lower levels of cognition. One of the most vexing problems facing AI workers is the creation of a machine that can perceive the environment well enough to get around in the real world on its own. This has some implications for the material we examined in Chapters 2 and 3. There we saw that some pattern recognition is top-down processing resulting from our expectations. Such expectations have resisted extensive formalization. Also, some of our perception appears to be direct and is canalized by our biological endowment. Such a biological endowment may be necessary for truly accurate perception.

This brings me to the second point, which is the emergence of expert systems. This term is clearly the buzzword in AI research right now and will probably continue to be for the rest of this decade. Expert systems have some implications for cognitive psychologists. When we studied problem solving, we saw that experts' knowledge seems to be organized differently from the knowledge of novices. As cognitive psychologists became more aware of this fact, the emphasis in problem-solving research shifted from the study of general problem-solving heuristics, useful on a variety of problems, to the study of problem solving in knowledge-rich domains. Comparing the situation with the developments taking place in AI is interesting. Here, we see that various expert systems, such as MYCIN or PARADISE, use production rules that are formulated in terms relevant to their domains. In that sense, MYCIN doesn't know anything about playing chess. What's startling, though, is that the format of both of these expert systems, and numerous others, is the same. They both use production systems consisting of sets of about two hundred specific production rules. Ironically, cognitive psychologists have begun to emphasize the differences between experts and novices at a time when AI workers have apparently hit upon a common method of modeling various different forms of expertise.

Interest in AI has reached new heights as some of its applications have begun to enter the marketplace in large numbers. Some commentators (de Mey, 1982) have argued that AI will unify the study of mind, thus resulting in a wholesale redrawing of the boundaries within the various social sciences. In addition, some cognitive psychologists believe that cognitive psychology needs AI, but few AI researchers seem to think they need cognitive psychology. This raises the possibility of cognitive psychology's being absorbed into a much broader discipline such as cognitive science—a prospect that may someday put cognitive psychologists out of business. We'll just have to see.

Students who would like to read further in this area might start with one of the general introductions to the field of AI. The March 1985 issue of *Science85* contains an interesting article on AI. I think that Boden's (1977) work is among the best book-length introductions to the field. Her (1981) book *Minds and Mechanisms* deals with the problems of intentionality and the computational model of thought. The reductionist viewpoint is clearly presented in a book by Albus (1981). Haugeland (1981) has presented a collection of essays dealing with the philosophical implications of AI. And Hofstadter's amazing book *Godel, Escher, Bach* (1979) is a terrific introduction to the nature of the mind, AI, formal number theory, and other things too numerous to mention. Although each of these books is sometimes critical of AI efforts, they have all been written by people who are more or less advocates of AI. If you would like to read a vocal critic's counterarguments, read Dreyfus (1972).

For those students who would like a more technical account of AI subjects, O'Shea and Eisenstadt (1984) have written a good one. Perhaps the two principal journals in the area are *Artificial Intelligence* and *Cognitive Science*. However, much of the research in AI doesn't necessarily appear in these journals until it has made the rounds in one of the more limited circulation newsletters. Two of the more well known of such newsletters are the *AISB Quarterly* (Society for the Study of Artificial Intelligence and Simulation of Behavior) and the *SIGART Newsletter* (Association for Computing Machinery Special Interest Group in Artificial Intelligence).

I recommend two books dealing with machine vision from a technical perspective: Beck, Hope, and Rosenfeld (1983), and Ballard and Brown (1982). For those interested in scripts, Schank and Abelson (1977) have written a book that makes their theory explicit. Mandler (1984) has written a book that applies script and schema theory approaches to the comprehension of stories. Those of you who might like to build an expert system might try reading the book by Hayes-Roth, Waterman, and Lenat (1983). On the other hand, if you have two thousand dollars and an IBM PC or compatible, you might buy the meta-expert program known as EXPERT-EASE (McLaren, 1983). EXPERT-EASE is an expert system available for the IBM that enables its owner to construct other expert systems.

FOCUS ON APPLICATIONS:
ROG-O-MATIC

AI software is now being used extensively in the business world, but not all of its applications are serious. Andrew Appel, Leonard Hamey, Guy Jacobson, and Michael Mauldin are graduate students in computer science at Carnegie-Mellon University. They created an expert system that is adept at playing a game called Rogue. Rogue is derived from Dungeons and Dragons, which in turn is (very) loosely based on Tolkien's trilogy, *Lord of the Rings.* Essentially, you become the Rogue, who must descend through twenty-six (!) levels of dungeons to capture the prized Amulet of Yendor and return with it to the surface. The dungeon is inhabited by hosts of monsters who must be evaded or slain. The computer's monitor displays a map showing the current location of the Rogue and some of the surrounding rooms and corridors. The monitor also shows the unsavory inhabitants of the dungeon. To play, you enter commands on the computer's keyboard; usually, a single letter stands for an action. Other commands tell the Rogue to pick up pieces of gold, read magic scrolls, wield his weapon, and so on.

The expert system created by Appel and his colleagues is called ROG-O-MATIC. ROG-O-MATIC is a very good Rogue player. In a test at the University of Texas in February 1984, it succeeded in finding the Amulet of Yendor and got out of the maze alive—something few human players are able to do. In earlier tests at Carnegie-Mellon, ROG-O-MATIC's median score was higher than the top fifteen Rogue players at the school. How does ROG-O-MATIC achieve these levels of performance? It works by intercepting the signals sent to the computer's screen, interpreting these signals, and then sending what it believes to be the appropriate commands back through the keyboard. The program, which is twelve thousand lines long, has the same sort of modular organization that we've seen in other expert systems. Let's examine it.

The program divides its expertise into a number of subprograms that cover specific activities. For example, a Missile expert controls the timing and trajectory of anything that ROG-O-MATIC might throw at a monster. A Health expert determines which magic potions should be drunk and which discarded. The subprograms are also arranged hierarchically. That is, higher-level experts may call on the knowledge of lower-level experts. For example, the higher level expert Melee determines if an attack is warranted. If Melee decides to initiate an attack, it calls upon Battle, a lower-level expert that handles the actual tactical situation. Battle monitors the progress of the combat, checking in constantly with another still lower-level expert called Retreat. If things begin going badly for ROG-O-MATIC, it's up to Retreat to break off the action and disengage along the fastest possible route. Retreat is able to do this because it has access to a data structure called Pathc, which keeps track of the geometry of the room or corridor in which the fight is occurring.

ROG-O-MATIC's purpose is recreational, but it raises some questions about cognitive psychology. For example, it's interesting to wonder if our own intelligence also consists of a related set of separable components.

KEY TERMS

AI	Computer simulation
Analytical engine	Intrinsic characteristics
LOGIC THEORIST	Segment and label
Metatheory	Script

Primitive act
SAM
Pragmatics
Zero-crossing detector
ELIZA
SHRDLU
Power approach
Knowledge-based approach
Depth of search

Width of search
PARADISE
Production rules
Expertise
MYCIN
Church-Turing thesis
Reductionist viewpoint
Intentionality
ROG-O-MATIC

References

Abelson, R. P. (1981). Psychological status of the script concept. *American Psychologist, 36,* 715–729.

Adelson, E. H. (1978). Iconic storage: The role of rods. *Science, 201,* 544–546.

Aitchison, J. (1983). *The articulate mammal: An introduction to psycholinguistics* (2nd ed.). New York: Universe.

Alba, J. W., & Hasher, L. (1983). Is memory semantic? *Psychological Bulletin, 93,* 203–231.

Albus, J. S. (1981). *Brains, behavior, and robotics.* Peterborough, NH: BYTE.

Anderson, J. R. (1974). Retrieval of propositional information from long-term memory. *Cognitive Psychology, 6,* 451–474.

Anderson, J. R. (1976). *Language, memory, and thought.* Hillsdale, NJ: Erlbaum.

Anderson, J. R. (1978). Arguments concerning representations for mental imagery. *Psychological Review, 85,* 249–277.

Anderson, J. R. (1980a). *Cognitive psychology and its implications.* San Francisco: Freeman.

Anderson, J. R. (1980b). On the merits of ACT and infomation-processing psychology: A response to Wexler's review. *Cognition, 8,* 73–88.

Anderson, J. R. (Ed.). (1981). *Cognitive skills and their acquisition.* Hillsdale, NJ: Erlbaum.

Anderson, J. R., & Bower, G. H. (1973). *Human associative memory.* Washington, DC: Winston & Sons.

Anderson, J. R., & Paulson, R. (1977). Representation and retention of verbatim information. *Journal of Verbal Learning and Verbal Behavior, 16,* 439–452.

Anderson, J. R., & Ross, B. H. (1980). Evidence against a semantic-episodic distinction. *Journal of Experimental Psychology: Human Learning and Memory, 6,* 441–466.

Anderson, R. C., & Pichert, J. W. (1978). Recall of previously unrecallable information following a shift in perspective. *Journal of Verbal Learning and Verbal Behavior, 17,* 1–12.

Anderson, R. C., Spiro, R. J., & Montague, W. E. (Eds.). (1977). *Schooling and the acquisition of knowledge.* Hillsdale, NJ: Erlbaum.

Anderson, R. E. (1982). Speech imagery is not always faster than visual imagery. *Memory and Cognition, 10,* 371–380.

Anisfeld, M., & Klenbart, I. (1973). On the functions of structural paraphrase: The view from the passive voice. *Psychological Bulletin, 79,* 117–126.

Armstrong, S. L., Gleitman, L. R., & Gleitman, H. (1983). What some concepts might not be. *Cognition, 13,* 263–308.

Atkinson, R. C., & Shiffrin, R. M. (1968). Human memory: A proposed system and its control processes. In W. K. Spence & J. T. Spence (Eds.), *The psychology of learning and motivation: Advances in research and theory* (Vol. 1, pp. 89–195). New York: Academic Press.

Averbach, E., & Coriell, A. S. (1961). Short-term memory in vision. *Bell System Technical Journal, 40,* 309–328.

Babich, F. R., Jacobson, A. L., Bubash, S., & Jacobson, A. (1965). Transfer of a response to naive rats by injection of ribonucleic acid extracted from trained rats. *Science, 149,* 656–657.

Baddeley, A. D. (1976). *The psychology of memory.* New York: Basic Books.

Baddeley, A. D. (1978). The trouble with "levels": A reexamination of Craik and Lockhart's framework for memory research. *Psychological Review, 85,* 139–152.

Baddeley, A. D., & Dale, H. C. (1966). The effect of semantic similarity on retroactive interference in long- and short-term memory. *Journal of Verbal Learning and Verbal Behavior, 5,* 417–420.

Baddeley, A. D., & Ecob, J. R. (1973). Reaction time and short-term memory: Implications of repetition for the high speed exhaustive scan hypothesis. *Quarterly Journal of Experimental Psychology, 25,* 229–240.

Baddeley, A. D., & Lewis, V. (1981). Inner active process in reading: The inner voice, the inner ear and the inner eye. In A. M. Lesgold & C. Perfetti (Eds.), *Interactive processes in reading.* Hillsdale, NJ: Erlbaum.

Baker, L., and Brown, A. L. (1984). Metacognitive skills and reading. In D. Pearson (Ed.), *Handbook of Reading Research* (pp. 353–394). Newark, DE: International Reading Association.

Ballard, D. H., & Brown, C. M. (1982). *Computer vision.* Englewood Cliffs, NJ: Prentice-Hall.

Banks, W. P. (1981). Assessing relations between imagery and perception. *Journal of Experimental Psychology: Human Perception and Performance, 7,* 844–847.

Banks, W. P., & Barber, G. (1977). Color information in iconic memory. *Psychological Review, 84,* 536–546.

Banks, W. P., & Barber, G. (1980). Normal iconic memory of stimuli invisible to the rods. *Perception and Psychophysics, 27,* 581–584.

Barclay, C. D., Cutting, J. E., & Kozlowski, L. T. (1978). Temporal and spatial factors in gait perception that influence gender recognition. *Perception and Psychophysics, 23,* 145–152.

Bargh, J. A. (1982). Attention and automacity in the processing of self-relevant information. *Journal of Personality and Social Psychology, 43,* 425–436.

Barrow, H. G., & Tenenbaum, J. M. (1981). Computational vision. *Proceedings of the IEEE, 69,* 572–595.

Barrows, B. (quoting C. Stengel). 1977. Casey fields Kefauner's question with a bit of Stengelese. *Lewiston* (ID) *Morning Tribune,* 5 April.

Bartlett, F. C. (1932). *Remembering: A study in experimental and social psychology.* Oxford: Cambridge University Press.

Bartlett, F. C. (1958). *Thinking.* New York: Basic Books.

Bassili, J. N. (1978). Facial motion in the perception of faces and of emotional expressions. *Journal of Experimental Psychology: Human Perception and Performance, 4,* 373–379.

Beck, J., Hope, B., & Rosenfeld, A. (Eds.). (1983). *Human and machine vision.* New York: Academic Press.

Begg, I. (1979). Trace loss and the recognition failure of unrecalled words. *Memory and Cognition, 7,* 113–123.

Bellugi, U. (1964). *The emergence of inflections and negation systems in the speech of two children.* Paper presented at New England Psychological Association Meetings.

Bentahila, A. (1983). Motivations of code-switching among Arabic-French bilinguals in Morocco. *Language and Communication, 3,* 233–243.

Berko, J. (1958). The child's learning of English morphology. *Word, 14,* 150–177.

Besner, D., Davies, J., & Daniels, S. (1981). Reading for meaning: The effects of concurrent articulation. *Quarterly Journal of Experimental Psychology, 33,* 415–437.

Bever, T. G., Lackner, J. R., & Kirk, R. (1969). The underlying structures of sentences are the primary units of immediate speech processing. *Perception and Psychophysics, 5,* 225–231.

Bickerton, D. (1982). *Roots and language*. New York: Karoma.

Bickerton, D. (1983). Creole languages. *Scientific American, 249*, 116–122.

Blank, M. A., & Foss, D. J. (1978). Semantic facilitation and lexical access during sentence processing. *Memory and Cognition, 6*, 644–652.

Blaxall, J., & Willows, D. M. (1984). Reading ability and text difficulty as influences on second graders' oral reading errors. *Journal of Educational Psychology, 76*, 330–341.

Block, N. (Ed.). (1981). *Imagery*. Cambridge: MIT press.

Bloom, L. (1970). *Language development: Form and function in emerging grammars*. Cambridge: MIT Press.

Bloom, L. M., Lightbown, P., & Hood, L. (1975). Structure and variation in child language. *Monographs of the Society for Research in Child Development, 40* (Serial No. 160).

Blumstein, S. E., Tartter, V. C., Nigro, G., & Statlender, S. (1984). Acoustic cues for the perception of place of articulation on aphasia. *Brain and Language, 22*, 128–149.

Boden, M. A. (1977). *Artificial intelligence and natural man*. New York: Basic Books.

Boden, M. A.(1981). *Minds and mechanisms: Philosophical psychology and computational models*. Ithaca, NY: Cornell University Press.

Bomba, P. C., & Siqueland, E. R. (1983). The nature and structure of infant form categories. *Journal of Experimental Child Psychology, 35*, 294–328.

Bower, G. H. (1970). Analysis of a mnemonic device. *American Scientist, 58*, 496–510.

Bower, G. H. (1981). Mood amd memory. *American Psychologist, 36*, 129–148.

Bower, G. H., Black, J. B., & Turner, T. J. (1979). Scripts in memory for text. *Cognitive Psychology, 11*, 177–220.

Bower, G. H., & Humphreys, M. S. (1979). Effect of a recognition test on a subsequent cued-recall test. *Journal of Experimental Psychology: Human Learning and Memory, 5*, 348–359.

Bower, G. H., Monteiro, K. P., & Gilligan, S. G. (1978). Emotional mood as a context for learning and recall. *Journal of Verbal Learning and Verbal Behavior, 17*, 573–587.

Braine, M. D. S. (1963). On learning the grammatical order of words. *Psychological Review, 70*, 323–348.

Braine, M. D. S. (1976). Children's first word combinations. *Monographs of the Society for Research in Child Development, 41*(Serial No. 164).

Bransford, J. D., & Johnson, M. K. (1972). Contextual prerequisites for understanding: Some investigations of comprehension and recall. *Journal of Verbal Learning and Verbal Behavior, 11*, 717–726.

Broadbent, D. E. (1954). A mechanical model for human attention and immediate memory. *Psychological Review, 64*, 205.

Broadbent, D. E. (1958). *Perception and communication*. London: Pergamon Press.

Brooks, D. N., & Baddeley, A. D. (1976). What can amnesic patients learn? *Neuropsychologia, 14*, 111–122.

Brooks, L. R. (1968). Spatial and verbal components of the act of recall. *Canadian Journal of Psychology, 22*, 349–368.

Brooks, L. R. (1978). Nonanalytic concept formation and memory for instances. In E. Rosch & B. B. Lloyd (Eds.), *Cognition and categorization*. Hillsdale, NJ: Erlbaum.

Brown, A. L., & Smiley, S. S. (1977). Rating the importance of structural units of prose passages: A problem of metacognitive development. *Child Development, 48*, 1–8.

Brown, A. L., & Smiley, S. S. (1978). The development of strategies for studying texts. *Child Development, 49*, 1076–1088.

Brown, A. L., Smiley, S. S., & Lawton, S. Q. C. (1978). The effect of experience on the selection of suitable retrieval cues for studying texts. *Child Development, 49*, 829–835.

Brown, R. (1970). *Psycholinguistics*. New York: Free Press.

Brown, R. (1973). *A first language: The early stages*. Cambridge: Harvard University Press.

Brown, R., & Bellugi, U. (1964). Three processes in the child's acquisition of syntax. In E. H. Lenneberg (Ed.), *New directions in the study of language*. Cambridge: MIT Press.

Brown S. L., & Walter, M. L. (1983). *The art of problem posing*. Philadelphia: Franklin Institute Press.

Bruce, V., & Green, P. (1985). *Visual perception: Physiology, psychology, and ecology*. Hillsdale, NJ: Erlbaum.

Bruner, J. (1985). Learning the mother tongue. In M. G. Walraven and H. E. Fitzgerald (Eds.), *Psychology 85/86*. Guilford, CT: Dushkin.

Bruner, J. S., Goodnow, J., & Austin, G. A. (1956). *A study of thinking.* New York: Wiley.

Burrows D., & Okada, R. (1971). Serial position effects in high-speed memory search. *Perception and Psychophysics 10,* 305–308.

Butters, N., & Cermak, L. (1975). Some analyses of amnesic syndromes in brain-damaged patients. In R. Isaacson & C. Neuringer (Eds.), *Empirical studies of alcoholism.* Cambridge, MA: Ballinger.

Byrne, R. W. (1979). Memory for urban geography. *Quarterly Journal of Experimental Psychology, 31,* 147–154.

Byrne, R. W. (1982). Geographical knowledge and orientation. In A. W. Ellis (Ed.), *Normality and pathology in cognitive functions* (pp. 239–264). New York: Academic Press.

Cairns, H. S., & Kamerman, J. (1975). Lexical information processing during sentence comprehension. *Journal of Verbal Learning and Verbal Behavior, 14,* 170–179.

Cairns, R. B., & Valsiner, J. (1984). Child psychology. *Annual Review of Psychology, 35,* 553–577.

Carroll, J. B. (Ed.). (1956). *Language, thought, and reality: Selected Writings of Benjamin Lee Whorf.* New York: Wiley.

Cavanaugh, J. C., & Perlmutter, M. (1982). Metamemory: A critical examination. *Child Development, 53,* 11–28.

Cazden, C. (1972). *Child language and education.* New York: Holt, Rinehart & Winston.

Celce-Murcia, M. (1978). The simultaneous acquisition of English and French in a two-year-old child. In E. Hatch (Ed.), *Second language acquisition: A book of readings.* Reading, MA: Newbury House.

Cendrowska, J., & Bramer, M. (1984). Inside an expert system: A rational reconstruction of the MYCIN consultation system. In T. O'Shea & M. Bisenstadt (Eds.), *Artificial intelligence: Tools, techniques, and applications* (pp. 453-497). New York: Harper & Row.

Cermak, L. S., & Butters, N. (1972). The role of interference and encoding in the short-term memory deficits of Korsakoff patients. *Neuropsychologia, 10,* 89–95.

Cermak, L. S., Naus, M. J., & Reale, L. (1976). Some analyses of the verbal encoding deficit of alcoholic Korsakoff patients. *Brain and Language, 1,* 141-150.

Chapman, R. S. (1978). Comprehension strategies in children: A discussion of Bransford and Nitsch's paper. In J. Kavanaugh & W. Strange (Eds.), *Speech and language in the laboratory, school, and clinic* (pp. 308–327). Cambridge: MIT Press.

Charniak, E. (1983). Passing markers: A theory of contextual influence in language comprehension. *Cognitive Science, 7,* 171–190.

Chase, W. G., & Calfee, R. C. (1969). Modality and similarity effects in short-term recognition memory. *Journal of Experimental Psychology, 81,* 510–514.

Chase, W. G., & Simon, H. A. (1973). The mind's eye in chess. In W. G. Chase (Ed.), *Visual information processing.* New York: Academic Press.

Cherry, E. C. (1953). Some experiments on the recognition of speech with one and with two ears. *Journal of the Acoustical Society of America, 25,*975–979.

Cherry R. S., & Kruger, B. (1983). Selective auditory attention abilities of learning disabled and normal achieving children. *Journal of Learning Disabilities, 16,* 202-205.

Chi, M. T. H., & Glaser, R. (1985). Problem-solving ability. In R. J. Sternberg (Ed.), *Human abilities: An information processing approach* (pp. 227–248). New York: Freeman.

Chi, M. T. H., Glaser, R., & Rees, E. (1982). Expertise in problem solving. In R. J. Sternberg (Ed.), *Advances in the psychology of human intelligence* (Vol. 1, pp. 7–76). Hillsdale, NJ: Erlbaum.

Chomsky, C. (1969). *The acquisition of syntax in children from 5 to 10.* Cambridge: MIT Press.

Chomsky, N. (1957). *Syntactic structures.* The Hague: Mouton.

Chomsky, N. (1959). Review of Skinner's verbal behavior. *Language, 35,* 26–58.

Chomsky, N. (1965). *Aspects of the theory of syntax.* Cambridge: MIT Press.

Chomsky, N. (1972). *Language and mind* (enlarged ed.). New York: Harcourt Brace Jovanovich.

Chomsky, N. (1979). *Language and responsibility.* Hassocks, Sussex, England: Harvester.

Chomsky, N. (1983). On the representation of form and function. In J. Mehler, E. C. T. Walker, & M. Garrett (Eds.), *Perspectives on mental representation* (pp. 3–38). Hillsdale, NJ: Erlbaum.

Chomsky, N., & Halle, M. (1968). *The sound pattern of English.* New York: Harper & Row.

Chorover, S. L., & Schiller, P. H. (1965). Short-term retrograde amnesia in rats. *Journal of Comparative and Physiological Psychology, 59,* 73–78.

Clark, E. V. (1980). Here's the top: Nonlinguistic strategies in the acquisition of orientational terms. *Child Development, 51,* 329–338.

Clark, E. V. (1983). Meanings and concepts. In J. H. Flavell (Ed.), *Carmichael's manual of child psychology: Vol. 3. Cognitive development.* New York: Wiley.

Clark, E. V., & Hecht, B. F. (1983). Comprehension, production, and language acquisition. *Annual Review of Psychology, 34,* 325–349.

Clark, H. H., & Clark, E. V. (1977). *Psychology and language.* New York: Harcourt Brace Jovanovich.

Clark, R. (1974). Performing without competence. *Journal of Child Language, 1,* 1–10.

Cochran, E. L., Pick, A. D., & Pick, H. L. (1983). Task-specific strategies of mental "rotation" of facial representations. *Memory and Cognition, 11,* 41–48.

Cohen, N. J., & Corkin, S. (1982). *Learning to solve the Tower of Hanoi puzzle in amnesia.* Paper presented at the 23rd annual meeting of the Psychonomic Society, Minneapolis, MN.

Cole, M., & Scribner, S. (1977). Cross-cultural studies of memory and cognition. In R. V. Vail, Jr., & J. W. Hagen (Eds.), *Perspectives on the development of memory and recognition.* Hillsdale, NJ: Erlbaum.

Collins, A. M., & Loftus, E. F. (1975). A spreading activation theory of semantic processing. *Psychological Review, 82,* 407–428.

Collins, A. M., & Quillian, M. R. (1969). Retrieval time from semantic memory. *Journal of Verbal Learning and Verbal Behavior, 8,* 240–247.

Coltheart, M. (1975). Iconic memory: A reply to professor Holding. *Memory and Cognition, 3,* 42–48.

Coltheart, M. (1978). Lexical access in simple reading tasks. In G. Underwood (Ed.), *Strategies of information processing.* New York: Academic Press.

Coltheart, M. (1980). Iconic memory and visual persistence. *Perception and Psychophysics, 27,* 183–228.

Coltheart, M. (1980). Reading, phonological recoding, and deep dyslexia. In M. Coltheart, K. Patterson, & J. C. Marshall, (Eds.), *Deep dyslexia.* London: Routledge & Kegan Paul.

Coltheart, M., Davelaar, E., Jonasson, J. T., &

Besner, D. (1977). Access to the internal lexicon. In S. Dornic (Ed.), *Attention and Performance* (Vol. 6). New York: Academic Press.

Conrad, C. (1972). Cognitive economy in semantic memory. *Journal of Experimental Psychology, 92,* 149–154.

Conrad, R. (1964). Acoustic confusions in immediate memory. *British Journal of Psychology, 55,* 75–84.

Cook, M. (1984). *Issues in person perception.* London: Methuen.

Cooper, L. A. (1976). Demonstration of a mental analog of an external rotation. *Perception and Psychophysics, 19,* 296–302.

Cooper, L. A., & Podgorny, P. (1976). Mental transformations and visual comparison processes: Effects of complexity and similarity. *Journal of Experimental Psychology: Human Perception and Performance, 2,* 503–514.

Cooper, L. A., & Shepard, R. N. (1973). Chronometric studies of the rotation of mental images. In W. G. Chase (Ed.), *Visual information processing.* New York: Academic Press.

Cosky, M. J. (1975). *Word length effects in word recognition.* Unpublished doctoral dissertation, University of Texas, Austin.

Cox, J. R., & Griggs, R. A. (1982). The effects of experience on performance in Wason's selection task. *Memory and Cognition, 10,* 496–502.

Craik, F. I. M. (1979). Human memory *Annual Review of Psychology, 30,* 63–102.

Craik, F. I. M., & Lockhart, R. S. (1972). Levels of processing: A framework for memory research. *Journal of Verbal Learning and Verbal Behavior, 11,* 671–684.

Craik, F. I. M., & Simon, E. (1980). Age differences in memory: The roles of attention and depth of processing. In L. W. Poon, J. L. Fozard, L. S. Cermak, D. Arenberg, & L. W. Thompson (Eds.), *New directions in memory and aging: Proceedings of the George Talland memorial conference.* Hillsdale, NJ: Erlbaum.

Craik, F. I. M., & Tulving, E. (1975). Depth of processing and the retention of words in episodic memory. *Journal of Experimental Psychology: General, 104,* 268–294.

Craik, F. I. M., & Watkins, M. J. (1973). The role of rehearsal in short-term memory. *Journal of Verbal Learning and Verbal Behavior, 12,* 559–607.

Cromer, R. F. (1970). Children are nice to understand: Surface structure clues for the recovery of deep structure. *British Journal of Psychology, 61*, 397–408.

Cross, T. G. (1977). Mothers' speech adjustments: The contribution of selected child-listener variables. In C. E. Snow & C. A. Ferguson (Eds.), *Talking to children: language input and acquisition* (pp. 151–188). Cambridge: Cambridge University Press.

Crowder, R. G. (1976). *Principles of learning and memory*. Hillsdale, NJ: Erlbaum.

Crowder. R. G. (1982). *The psychology of reading*. New York: Oxford University Press.

Crowder, R. G., & Morton, J. (1969). Precategorical acoustic storage (PAS). *Perception and Psychophysics, 5*, 365–373.

Curtiss, S. (1977). *Genie: A psycholinguistic study of a modern-day "wild child."* New York: Academic Press.

Curtiss, S., Fromkin, V., Krashen, S., Rigler, D., & Rigler, M. (1974). The linguistic development of Genie. *Language, 50*, 528–554.

Cutler, A. (1980). Errors of stress and intonation. In V. A. Fromkin (Ed.), *Errors in linguistic performance*. New York: Academic Press.

Cutting, J. E., & Kozlowski, L. T. (1977). Recognizing friends by their walk: Gait perception without familiarity cues. *Bulletin of the Psychonomic Society, 9* (5), 353–356.

Cutting, J. E., Proffitt, D. R., & Kozlowski, L. T. (1978). A biomechanical invariant for gait perception. *Journal of Experimental Psychology: Human Perception and Performance, 4*, 357–372.

Danks, J. H., & Glucksberg, S. (1980). Experimental psycholinguistics. *Annual Review of Psychology, 31*, 391–417.

Dawson, M. E., & Schell, A. M. (1982). Electrodermal responses to attended and nonattended significant stimuli during dichotic listening. *Journal of Experimental Psychology: Human Perception and Performance, 8*, 315–324.

Dawson, M. E., & Schell, A. M. (1983). Lateral asymmetries in electro-dermal responses to nonattended stimuli: A reply to Walker and Ceci. *Journal of Experimental Psychology: Human Perception and Performance, 9*, 148–150.

Deese, J. (1984). *Thought into speech: The psychology of a language*. Englewood Cliffs, NJ: Prentice-Hall.

Deese, J., & Kaufman, R. A. (1957). Serial effects in recall of unorganized and sequentially organized verbal material. *Journal of Experimental Psychology, 54*, 180–187.

de Groot, A. (1965). *Thought and choice in chess*. The Hague: Mouton.

de Groot, A. (1966). Perception and memory versus thought: Some old ideas and recent findings. In B. Kleinmuntz (Ed.), *Problem solving*. New York: Wiley.

DeJong, G. (1982). On communications between AI and linguistics. In D. L. Farwell, S. C. Helmreich, & W. D. Wallace (Eds.), *Perspectives in cognitive science* (pp. 33–41). Urbana, IL: Linguistics Student Organization.

de Mey, M. (1982). *The cognitive paradigm*. Boston: D. Reidel.

Dennett, D. C. (1981). *Brainstorms*. Cambridge: MIT Press/Bradford Books.

Deregowski, J. B. (1972). Pictorial perception and culture. *Scientific American, 227*(5), 82–88.

Derouesne, J., & Beauvois, M. F. (1979). Phonological processing in reading: Data from alexia. *Journal of Neurology, Neurosurgery, and Psychiatry, 42*, 1125–1132.

Deutsch, F. A., & Deutsch, D. (1963). Attention: Some theoretical considerations. *Psychological Review, 70*, 80–90.

De Villiers, J. G., & De Villiers, P. A. (1978). *Language acquisition*. Cambridge: Harvard University Press.

Dodd, D. H., & White, R. M., Jr. (1980). *Cognition: Mental structures and processes*. Boston: Allyn & Bacon.

Dodwell, P. D., & Caelli, T. M. (1984). *Figural synthesis*. Hillsdale, NJ: Erlbaum.

Dominowski, R. L., & Ekstrand, B. R. (1967). Direct and associative priming in anagram solving. *Journal of Experimental Psychology, 74*, 84–86.

Dominowski, R. L., & Jenrick, R. (1972). Effects of hints and interpolated activity on solution of an insight problem. *Psychonomic Science, 26*, 335–338.

Dooling, D. J., & Christiaansen, R. E. (1977). Episodic and semantic aspects of memory for prose. *Journal of Experimental Psychology: Human Learning and Memory, 3*, 428–436.

Dooling, D. J., & Lachman, R. (1971). Effects of comprehension on retention of prose. *Journal of Experimental Psychology, 88*, 216–222.

Downs, R. M., & Stea, D. (1977). *Maps in minds: Reflections on cognitive mapping*. New York: Harper & Row.

Dretske, F. I. (1981). *Knowledge and the flow of information.* Cambridge: MIT Press/Bradford Books.

Dretske, F. I. (1983). Precis of knowledge and the flow of information. *The Behavioral and Brain Sciences, 6,* 55–90.

Drewnoski, A. (1980). Attributes and priorities in short-term recall: A new model of memory span. *Journal of Experimental Psychology: General, 109,* 208–250.

Drewnoski, A., & Murdock, B. B., Jr. (1980). The role of auditory features in memory span for words. *Journal of Experimental Psychology: Human Learning and Memory, 6,* 319–332.

Dreyfus, H. (1972). *What computers can't do.* New York: Harper & Row.

Dunker, K. (1945). On problem solving. *Psychological Monographs, 58* (5, Whole No. 270).

Eich, J., Weingartner, H., Stillman, R. C., & Gillin, J. C. (1975). State-dependent accessibility of retrieval cues in the retention of a categorized list. *Journal of Verbal Learning and Verbal Behavior, 14,* 408–417.

Eifermann, R. (1965a). Response patterns and strategies in the dynamics of concept attainment behavior. *Journal of Psychology, 56,* 217–222.

Eifermann, R. (1965b). Selection strategies in concept attainment: A reexamination. In R. Eifermann (Ed.), *Scripta hierosolymitana: Studies in psychology* (Vol. 14). Hebrew University of Jerusalem: Magnes Press.

Eimas, P. D., Siqueland, E. R., Jusczyk, P., & Vigorito, J. (1971). Speech perception by infants. *Science, 171,* 303–306.

Elphick, M. (1983, March/April). Unraveling the mysteries of speech recognition. *High Technology,* pp. 71–78.

Ericksen, C. W., Pollack, M. D., & Montague, W. E. (1970). Implicit speech: Mechanism in perceptual recoding? *Journal of Experimental Psychology, 84,* 502–507.

Ericsson, K. A., & Simon, H. A. (1980). Verbal reports as data. *Psychological Review, 87,* 215–251.

Eriksen, C. W., & Eriksen, B. A. (1971). Visual perceptual processing rates and backward and forward masking. *Journal of Experimental Psychology, 89,* 306–313.

Evans, G. W., & Pezdek, K. (1980). Cognitive mapping: Knowledge of real-world distance and location information. *Journal of Experimental Psychology: Human Learning and Memory, 6,* 13–24.

Eylon, B. (1979). *Effects of knowledge organization on task performance.* Unpublished doctoral dissertation, University of California at Berkeley.

Eysenck, M. W., & Eysenck, M. C. (1979). Processing depth, elaboration of encoding, memory stores and expended processing capacity. *Journal of Experimental Psychology: Human Learning and Memory, 5,* 472–484.

Falmagne, R. J. (Ed.). (1975). *Reasoning: Representation and process.* Hillsdale, NJ: Erlbaum.

Fikes, R. E., Hart, P. E., & Nilsson, N. J. (1972). *Machine intelligence.* Edinburgh: Edinburgh University Press.

Finke, R. A., & Kosslyn, S. M. (1980). Mental imagery acuity in the peripheral visual field. *Journal of Experimental Psychology: Human Perception and Performance, 6,* 126–139.

Fiske, A. D., & Schneider, W. (1984). Memory as a function of attention, level of processing, and automatization. *Journal of Experimental Psychology: Learning, Memory, and Cognition, 10,* 181–197.

Fiske, S. T., & Taylor, S. E. (1984). *Social cognition.* Reading, MA; Addison-Wesley.

Flavell, J. H. (1971). First discussant's comments: What is memory development the development of? *Human Development, 14,* 272–278.

Flavell, J. H. (1978). Metacognitive development. In J. M. Scandura & C. Brainerd (Eds.), *Structural/process theory of complex human behavior.* Alpen an den Rijn, Netherlands: Sitjoff & Noordhoff.

Flavell, J. H. (1982). On cognitive development. *Child Development, 53,* 1–10.

Flavell, J. H., & Wellman, H. M. (1977). Metamemory. In R. V. Kail & J. H. Hagen (Eds.), *Perspectives on the development of memory and cognition.* Hillsdale, NJ: Erlbaum.

Flexser, A. J., & Tulving, E. (1978). Retrieval independence in recognition and recall. *Psychological Review, 85,* 153–171.

Flexser, A. J., & Tulving, E. (1982). Priming and recognition failure. *Journal of Verbal Learning and Verbal Behavior, 21,* 237–248.

Fodor, J. (1981). *Representations.* Cambridge: MIT Press/Bradford Books.

Fodor, J. A., Bever, T., & Garrett, M. (1974). *The*

psychology of language. New York: McGraw-Hill.

Fong, G. T., & Markus, H. (1982). Self-schemas and judgments about others. *Social Cognition, 1,* 191–205.

Foss, D. J. (1982). A discourse on semantic priming. *Cognitive Psychology, 14,* 590–607.

Foss, D. J., & Hakes, D. T. (1978). *Psycholinguistics: An introduction to the psychology of language.* Englewood Cliffs, NJ: Prentice-Hall.

Foss, D. J., & Harwood, D. A. (1975). Memory for sentences: Implications for human associative memory. *Journal of Verbal Learning and Verbal Behavior, 14,*1–16.

Foucault, M. (1972). *The archaeology of knowledge.* New York: Pantheon.

Fried, L. S., & Holyoak, K. J. (1978, November). *Learning fuzzy perceptual categories: Is feedback necessary?* Paper presented at the 19th meeting of the Psychonomic Society, San Antonio.

Fried, L. S., & Holyoak, K. J. (1984). Induction of category distributions: A framework for classification learning. *Journal of Experimental Psychology: Learning, Memory, and Cognition, 10,* 234–257.

Fromkin, V. A. (1971). The non-anomalous nature of anomalous utterances. *Language, 47,* 27–52.

Fulgosi, A., & Guilford, J. P. (1968). Short-term incubation in divergent production. *American Journal of Psychology, 81,* 241–246.

Gagne, E. D. (1985). *The cognitive psychology of school learning.*Boston: Little, Brown.

Gardiner, J. M., & Tulving, E. (1980). Exceptions to recognition failure of recallable words. *Journal of Verbal Learning and Verbal Behavior, 19,* 194–209.

Gardner, B. T., & Gardner, R. A. (1971). Two-way communication with an infant chimpanzee. In A. Schrier & F. Stolnitz (Eds.), *Behavior of nonhuman primates* (Vol. 4). New York: Academic Press.

Gardner, B. T., & Gardner, R. A. (1975). Evidence for sentence constituents in the early utterances of child and chimpanzee. *Journal of Experimental Psychology: General, 104,* 244–267.

Gardner, B. T., & Gardner, R. A. (1980). Two comparative psychologists look at language acquisition. In K. Nelson (Ed.), *Children's language* (Vol. 2). New York: Gardner Press.

Gardner, R. A., & Gardner, B. T. (1969). Teaching sign language to a chimpanzee. *Science, 165,* 664–672.

Gardner, R. A., & Gardner, B. T. (1978). Comparative psychology and language acquisition. In K. Salzinger & F. Denmark (Eds.), *Psychology: The state of the art.* Annals of the New York Academy of Sciences, 309, 37–76.

Garner, W. R. (1979). Letter discrimination and identification. In A. D. Pick (Ed.), *Perception and its development: A tribute to Eleanor J. Gibson.* Hillsdale, NJ: Erlbaum.

Garrett, C. J., & Langer, P. (1983). Effects of instructions at encoding on constructive memory processes: A small-n approach. *Psychological Reports, 52,* 435–444.

Garrett, M. F. (1982). Production of speech: Observations from normal and pathological language use. In A. W. Ellis (Ed.), *Normality and pathology in cognitive functions* (pp. 19–76). New York: Academic Press.

Garrett, M. F., Bever, T., & Fodor, J. A. (1966). The active use of grammar in speech perception. *Perception and Psychophysics, 1,* 30–32.

Geschwind, N. (1980). Specializations of the human brain. In R. C. Atkinson & R. L. Atkinson (Eds.), *Mind and Behavior* (pp. 206–215). San Francisco: Freeman.

Geyer, L. H., & DeWald, C. G. (1973). Feature lists and confusion matrices. *Perception and Psychophysics, 14,* 471–482.

Ghiselin, B. (1952). *The creative process: A symposium.* Berkeley: University of California Press.

Gibson, E. J. (1969). *Principles of perceptual learning and development.* New York: Prentice-Hall.

Gibson, J. J. (1960). The concept of stimulus in psychology. *American Psychologist, 16,* 694–703.

Gibson, J. J. (1966). The problem of temporal order in stimulation and perception. *Journal of Psychology, 62,* 141–149.

Gibson, J. J. (1976). The myth of passive perception: A reply to Richards. *Philosophy and Phenomenological Research, 37,* 234–238.

Gibson, J. J. (1977). The theory of affordances. In R. Shaw & J. Bransford (Eds.), *Perceiving, acting, and knowing* (pp. 67–82). Hillsdale, NJ: Erlbaum.

Gibson, J. J. (1979). *The ecological approach to visual perception.* Boston: Houghton Mifflin.

Gillam, B. (1980). Geometrical illusions. *Scientific American, 242*(1), 102–111.

Gladwin, T. (1970). *East is a big bird*. Cambridge: Harvard University Press.

Glenberg, A. M., & Adams F. (1978). Type I rehearsal and recognition. *Journal of Verbal Learning and Verbal Behavior, 17,* 455–463.

Godden, D. R., & Baddeley, A. D. (1975). Context-dependent memory in two natural environments: On land and under water. *British Journal of Psychology, 66,* 325–331.

Gold, M. (1967). Language identification in the limit. *Information and Control, 16,* 447–474.

Goldin-Meadow, S., Seligman, M. E. P., & Gelman, R. (1976). Language in the two-year-old. *Cognition, 4,* 189–202.

Goldman-Eisler, F. (1968). *Psycholinguistics,* New York: Adademic Press.

Goldstein, E. B. (1984). *Sensation and perception.* Belmont, CA: Wadsworth.

Goldstein, I., & Papert, S. (1977). Artificial intelligence, language, and the study of knowledge. *Cognitive Science, 1,* 84–123.

Gray, C. R., & Gummerman, K. (1975). The enigmatic eidetic image: A critical examination of methods, data, and theories. *Psychological Bulletin, 82,* 383–407.

Green, D. W., & Shallice, T. (1976). Direct visual access in reading for meaning. *Memory and Cognition, 4,* 753–758.

Greenfield, P. M., & Smith, J. H. (1976). *The structure of communication in early language development.* New York: Academic Press.

Greeno, J. G. (1976). Indefinite goals in well-structured problems. *Psychological Review, 83,* 479–491.

Greeno, J. G. (1978). Natures of problem-solving abilities. In W. K. Estes (Ed.), *Handbook of learning and cognitive processes* (Vol. 5, pp. 239–270). Hillsdale, NJ: Erlbaum.

Gregory, R. L. (1966). *Eye and brain.* New York: McGraw-Hill.

Griggs, R. A., & Cox, J. R. (1982). The elusive thematic-materials effects in Wason's selection task. *British Journal of Psychology, 73,* 407–420.

Haber, R. N. (1979). Twenty years of haunting eidetic images: Where's the ghost? *The Behavioral and Brain Sciences, 2,* 583–594.

Haber, R. N. (1983). The impending demise of the icon: A critique of the concept of iconic storage in visual information processing. *The Behavioral and Brain Sciences, 6,* 1–54.

Hall, W. S., Nagy, W. E., & Linn, R. (1984). *Spoken words: Effects of situation and social group on oral word usage and frequency.* Hillsdale, NJ: Erlbaum.

Halle, M., & Stevens, K. N. (1964). Speech recognition: A model and a program for research. In J. A. Fodor & J. J. Katz (Eds.), *The structure of language: readings in the philosophy of language.* Englewood Cliffs, NJ: Prentice-Hall.

Halliday, D., & Resnick, R. (1974). *Fundamentals of physics* (2nd ed.). New York: Wiley.

Halpern, D. F. (1984). *Thought and knowledge: An introduction to critical thinking.* Hillsdale, NJ: Erlbaum.

Hampson, S. E. (1982). *The construction of personality.* London: Routledge & Kegan Paul.

Hand, D. J. (1981). Artificial intelligence. *Psychological Medicine, 11,* 449–453.

Hannigan, J. L., Shelton, T. S., Franks, J. J., & Bransford, J. D. (1980). The effects of episodic and semantic memory on the identification of sentences masked by white noise. *Memory and Cognition, 8,* 278–284.

Harding, R. (1940). *An anatomy of inspiration.* London: Cass.

Hasher, L., & Zacks, R. T. (1979). Automatic and effortful processes in memory. *Journal of Experimental Psychology: General, 108,* 356–388.

Haugeland, J. (Ed.). (1981). *Mind design.* Cambridge: MIT Press/Bradford Books.

Hayes, J. R. (1981). *The complete problem solver.* Philadelphia: The Franklin Institute Press.

Hayes, J. R., & Simon, H. A. (1974). Understanding written problem instructions. In L. W. Gregg, (Ed.), *Knowledge and cognition.* Hillsdale, NJ: Erlbaum.

Hayes-Roth, F., Waterman, D. A., & Lenat, D. B. (1983). *Building expert systems.* Reading, MA: Addison-Wesley.

Heft, H. (1982). Incommensurability and the "omission" in Gibson's theory: A second reply to Heil. *Journal for the Theory of Social Behavior, 12,* 345–347.

Heil, J. (1979). What Gibson's missing. *Journal for the Theory of Social Behavior, 9,* 265–269.

Heil, J. (1982). What does the mind's eye look at? *Journal of Mind and Behavior, 3,* 143–149.

Hendrickson, C. W., Kimble, R. J., & Kimble, D. P. (1967). Hippocampal lesions and the orienting response. *Journal of Comparative and Physiological Psychology, 67,* 220–227.

Henle, M. (1962). On the relation between logic and thinking. *Psychological Review, 69,* 366–378.

Herrmann, D. J., & Harwood, J. R. (1980). More evidence for the existence of separate semantic and episodic stores in long-term memory. *Journal of Experimental Psychology, Human Learning, and Memory, 6,* 467–478.

Hilgard, E. R., & Bower, G. H. (1981). *Theories of learning* (5th ed.). Englewood Cliffs, NJ: Prentice-Hall.

Hinsley, D. A., Hayes, J. R., & Simon, H. A. (1978). From words to equations: Meaning and representation in algebra word problems. In P. A. Carpenter & M. A. Just (Eds.), *Cognitive processes in comprehension.* Hillsdale, NJ: Erlbaum.

Hintzman, D. L. (1965). Classification and aural coding in short-term memory. *Psychonomic Science, 3,* 161–162.

Hintzman, D. L. (1967). Articulatory coding in short-term memory. *Journal of Verbal Learning and Verbal Behavior, 6,* 312–316.

Hirst, W., Spelke, E. S., Reaves, C. C., Caharack, G., & Neisser, U. (1980). Dividing attention without alternation or automaticity. *Journal of Experimental Psychology: General, 109,* 98–117.

Hobbes, T. (1950). *The leviathan.* New York: Dutton. (Original work published 1651)

Hoch, S. J., & Tschirgi, J. E. (1983). Cue redundancy and extra logical inferences in a deductive reasoning task. *Memory and Cognition, 11,* 200–209.

Hockett, C. F. (1963). The problem of universals in language. In J. H. Greenberg (Ed.), *Universals of language.* Cambridge: MIT Press.

Höffding, H. (1891). *Outlines of psychology.* New York: Macmillan.

Hofstadter, D. R. (1979). *Godel, Escher, Bach, an eternal golden braid.* New York: Basic Books.

Holding, D. (1975). Sensory storage reconsidered. *Memory and Cognition, 3,* 31–41.

Hollan, J. D. (1975). Features and semantic memory: Set-theoretic or network model? *Psychological Review, 82,* 154–155.

Homa, D. (1978). Abstraction of ill-defined form. *Journal of Experimental Psychology: Human Learning and Memory, 4,* 407–416.

Homa, D., & Coltice, J. (1984). Role of feedback, category size, and stimulus distortion on the acquistion and utilization of ill-defined cate-gories. *Journal of Experimental Psychology: Learning, Memory, and Cognition, 10,* 83–94.

Homa, D., & Vosburgh, R. (1976). Category breadth and the abstraction of prototypical information. *Journal of Experimental Psychology: Human Learning and Memory, 2,* 322–330.

Horn, B. K. P. (1975) Obtaining shape from shading information. In P. H. Winston (Ed.), *The psychology of computer vision.* New York: McGraw-Hill.

Horton, D. L., & Mills, C. B. (1984). Human learning and memory. *Annual Review of Psychology, 35,* 361–394.

Howard, D. V. (1983). *Cognitive psychology: Memory, language, and thought.* New York: Macmillan.

Hull, C. L. (1920). Quantitative aspects of the evolution of concepts: An experimental study. *Psychological Monographs, 28*(1, Whole No. 123).

Hulse, S. H., Deese, J., & Egeth, H. (1975). *The psychology of learning* (4th ed.). New York: McGraw-Hill.

Humphrey, G. (1963). *Thinking: An introduction to its experimental psychology.* New York: Wiley.

Humphreys, M. S., & Bower, G. H. (1980). Sequential testing effects and the relationship between recognition and recognition failure. *Memory and Cognition, 8,* 271–277.

Hunt, M. (1982). *The universe within.* New York: Simon & Schuster.

Hunt, R. R., & Elliott, J. M. (1980). The role of nonsemantic information in memory: Orthographic distinctiveness effects on retention. *Journal of Experimental Psychology: General, 109,* 49–74.

Huppert, F. A., & Piercy, M. (1978). The role of trace strength in recency and frequency judgements of amnesic and control subjects. *Quarterly Journal of Experimental Psychology, 30,* 346–354.

Huttenlocher, J. (1974). The origins of language comprehension. In R. L. Solso (Ed.), *Theories in cognitive psychology* (pp. 331–368). Hillsdale, NJ: Erlbaum.

Hyde, T. S., & Jenkins, J. J. (1973). Recall for words as a function of semantic, graphic, and syntactic orienting tasks. *Journal of Verbal Learning and Verbal Behavior, 12,* 471–480.

Ittelson, W. H., & Cantril, H. (1954). *Perception: A transactional approach.* New York: Doubleday.

Izard, C. (1971). *The face of emotion*. New York: Appleton-Century-Crofts.

Jacoby, L. L., & Craik, F. I. M. (1979). Effects of elaboration of processing at encoding and retrieval: Trace distinctiveness and recovery of initial context. In L. S. Cermak & F. I. M. Craik (Eds.), *Levels of processing in human memory*. Hillsdale, NJ: Erlbaum.

Jacoby, L. L., Craik, F. I. M., & Begg, I. (1979). Effects of decision difficulty on recognition and recall. *Journal of Verbal Learning and Verbal Behavior, 18*, 585–600.

James, W. (1890). *The principles of psychology*. New York: Holt, Rinehart & Winston.

Jenkins, J. G., & Dallenbach, K. M. (1924). Obliviscence during sleep and waking. *American Journal of Psychology, 35*, 605–612.

Jenkins, J. J. (1974). Remember that old theory of memory? Well forget it! *American Psychologist, 29*, 785–795.

Jespersen, O. (1922). *Language: Its nature, development and origin*. New York: Allen & Unwin.

Johnson, C. E. (1981). *Children's questions and the discovery of interrogative syntax*. Unpublished doctoral dissertation, Stanford University, Stanford, CA.

Johnson, E. S. (1978). Validation of concept-learning strategies. *Journal of Experimental Psychology: General, 107*, 237–266.

Johnson-Laird, P. N. (1972). The three-term series problem. *Cognition, 1*, 57–82.

Johnson-Laird, P. N., Herrman, D., & Chaffin, R. (1984). Only connections: A critique of semantic networks. *Psychological Bulletin, 96*, 292–315.

Johnson-Laird, P. N., Legrenzi, P., & Legrenzi, M. (1972). Reasoning and a sense of reality. *British Journal of Psychology, 63*, 395–400.

Johnson-Laird, P. N., & Steedman, M. (1978). The psychology of syllogisms. *Cognitive Psychology, 10*, 64–99.

Johnson-Laird, P. N., & Wason, P. C. (Eds.). (1977). *Thinking: Readings in cognitive science*. Cambridge: Cambridge University Press.

Johnson, W. A., & Heinz, S. P. (1979). Flexibility and capacity demands of attention. *Journal of Experimental Psychology: General, 107*, 420–435.

Jones, R. K. (1966). Observations on stammering after localized cerebral injury. *Journal of Neurology, Neurosurgery, and Psychiatry, 29*, 192–195.

Jonides, J., Kahn, R., & Rozin, P. (1975). Imagery instructions improve memory in blind subjects. *Bulletin of the Psychonomic Society, 5*, 424–426.

Just, M. A., & Carpenter, P. A. (1980). A theory of reading: From eye fixations to comprehension. *Psychological Review, 87*, 329–354.

Kahneman, D. (1973). *Attention and effort*. Englewood Cliffs, NJ: Prentice-Hall.

Kahneman, D., & Tversky, A. (1973). On the psychology of prediction. *Psychological Review, 80*, 237–251.

Kahneman, D., & Tversky, A. (1982). On the study of statistical intuitions. In D. Kahneman, P. Slovic, & A. Tversky (Eds.), *Judgements under uncertainty: Heuristics and biases* (pp. 493–508). Cambridge: Cambridge University Press.

Kalat, J. W. (1984). *Biological psychology* (2nd ed.). Belmont, CA: Wadsworth.

Kaplan, S., & Kaplan, R. (1982). *Cognition and environment*. New York: Praeger.

Karat, J., (1982). A model of problem solving with incomplete constraint knowledge. *Cognitive Psychology, 14*, 538–559.

Katona, G., (1940). Organizing and memorizing. New York: Columbia University Press.

Kellogg, R. T. (1982). When can we introspect accurately about mental processes? *Memory and Cognition, 10*, 141–144.

Kennedy, A. (1984). *The psychology of reading*. London: Methuen.

Keppel, G., & Underwood, B. J. (1962). Proactive inhibition in short-term retention of single items. *Journal of Verbal Learning and Verbal Behavior, 1*, 153–161.

Kerr, N. H., & Neisser, U. (1983). Mental images of concealed objects: New evidence. *Journal of Experimental Psychology: Learning, Memory, and Cognition, 9*, 212–230.

Kihlstrom, J. F. (1980). Posthypnotic amnesia for recently learned material: Interactions with "episodic" and "semantic" memory. *Cognitive Psychology, 12*, 227–251.

Kintsch, W. (1974). *The representation of meaning in memory*. Hillsdale, NJ: Erlbaum.

Kintsch, W., Miller, J. R., & Polson, P. G. (Eds.). (1984). *Methods and tactics in cognitive science*. Hillsdale, NJ: Erlbaum.

Klapp, S., Anderson, W. G., & Berian, R. W.

(1973). Implicit speech in reading reconsidered. *Journal of Experimental Psychology,* *100,* 368–374.

Klatzky, R. L. (1980). *Human memory: Structures and processes* (2nd ed.). San Francisco: Freeman.

Klatzky, R. L. (1984). *Memory and awareness.* San Francisco: Freeman.

Kleiman, G. M. (1975). Speech recoding in reading. *Journal of Verbal Learning and Verbal Behavior, 14,* 323–339.

Kolb, B., & Whishaw, I. Q. (1984). *Fundamentals of human neuropsychology* (2nd ed.). San Francisco: Freeman.

Kolers, P. A. (1970). Three stages of reading. In H. Levin & J. P. Williams (Eds.), *Basic studies on reading.* New York: Basic Books.

Kolers, P. A. (1983). Perception and representation. *Annual Review of Psychology, 34,* 129–166.

Kolodner, J. L. (1984). *Retrieval and organizational strategies in conceptual memory: A computer model.* Hillsdale, NJ: Erlbaum.

Kopell, S. (1979). Testing the attentional deficit notion. *Journal of Learning Disabilities, 12,* 52–57.

Kosslyn, S. M. (1973). Scanning visual images: Some structural implications. *Perception and Psychophysics, 14,* 90–94.

Kosslyn, S. M. (1975). Information representation in visual images. *Cognitive Psychology, 7,* 341–370.

Kosslyn, S. M. (1976). Using imagery to retrieve semantic information: A developmental study. *Child Development, 47,* 433–444.

Kosslyn, S. M. (1978). Measuring the visual angle of the mind's eye. *Cognitive Psychology, 7,* 341-370.

Kosslyn, S. M. (1983). *Ghosts in the mind's machine.* New York: Norton.

Kosslyn, S. M., Ball, T. M., & Reiser, B. J. (1978). Visual images preserve metric spatial information: Evidence from studies of image scanning. *Journal of Experimental Psychology: Human Perception and Performance, 4,* 47–60.

Kosslyn, S. M., & Pomerantz, J. R. (1977). Imagery, propositions, and the form of internal representations. *Cognitive Psychology, 9,* 52–76.

Kuczaj, S. A., II (1982). Acquistion of word meaning in the development of the semantic system. In C. J. Brainerd & M. Pressley (Eds.), *Verbal processes in children* (pp. 95–124). New York: Springer-Verlag.

Kuhn, T. S. (1962). *The structure of scientific revolutions.* Chicago: University of Chicago Press.

Lachman, R., Lachman, J. L., & Butterfield, E. C. (1979). *Cognitive psychology and information processing.* Hillsdale, NJ: Erlbaum.

Lambert, W. E., & Fillenbaum, S. (1959). A pilot study of aphasia among bilinguals. *Canadian Journal of Psychology, 13,* 28-34.

Lambert, W. E., Havelka, J., & Crosby, C. (1958). The influence of language acquisition contexts on bilingualism. *Journal of Abnormal and Social Psychology, 56,* 239–244.

Lashley, K. S. (1929). *Brain mechanisms and intelligence.* Chicago: University of Chicago Press.

Lashley, K. S. (1950). In search of the engram. *Symposia of the Study of Experimental Biology, 4,* 454–482.

Laughlin, P. R., Lange, R., & Adamopoulos, J. (1982). Selection strategies for "Mastermind" problems. *Journal of Experimental Psychology: Learning, Memory, and Cognition, 8,* 475–483.

Lehnert, W. (1977). Human and computational question answering. *Cognitive Science, 1.*

Lenneberg, E. H. (1964). *New directions in the study of language.* Cambridge: MIT Press.

Lenneberg, E. H. (1967). *Biological foundations of language.* New York: Wiley.

Leonard, J. M., & Whitten, W. B. (1983). Information stored when expecting recall or recognition. *Journal of Experimental Psychology: Learning, Memory, and Cognition, 9,* 440–455.

Lettvin, J. Y., Maturana, H. R., McCulloch, W. S., & Pitts, W. H. (1959). What the frog's eye tells the frog's brain. *Proceedings of the IRE, 47,* 1940–1951.

Levy-Bruhl, L. (1966). *How natives think.* New York: Washington Square Press. (Original work published 1910)

Lewis, J. L. (1970). Semantic processing of unattended messages using dichotic listening. *Journal of Experimental Psychology, 85,* 225–228.

Liberman, A. M., Cooper, F., Shankweiler, D. P., & Studdert-Kennedy, M. (1967). Perception of the speech code. *Psychological Review, 74,* 431–461.

Lieberman, P. (1967). *Intonation, perception, and language.* Cambridge: MIT Press.

Light, L., & Carter-Sobell, L. (1970). Effects of changed semantic context on recognition memory. *Journal of Verbal Learning and Verbal Behavior, 9*, 1–11.

Lindsay, P. H., & Norman, D. A.. (1977). *Human information processing* (2nd ed.). New York: Academic Press.

Lisker, L., & Abramson, A. S. (1970). The voicing dimension: Some experiments in comparative phonetics. *Proceedings of the Sixth International Congress of Phonetic Sciences.* Prague: Academia, 1970.

Loftus, E. F. (1974). Activation of semantic memory. *American Journal of Psychology, 86*, 331–337.

Loftus, E. F. (1975). Leading questions and the eyewitness report. *Cognitive Psychology, 7*, 560–572.

Loftus, E. F. (1977). Shifting human color vision. *Memory and Cognition, 5*, 696–699.

Loftus, E. F. (1979a). *Eyewitness testimony.* Cambridge: Harvard University Press.

Loftus, E. F. (1979b). Reactions to blatantly contradictory information. *Memory and Cognition, 7*, 368–374.

Loftus, E. F. (1979c). The malleability of human memory. *American Scientist, 67*, 312–320.

Loftus, E. F., & Loftus, G. R. (1980). On the permanence of stored information in the human brain. *American Psychologist, 35*, 409–420.

Loftus, E. F., Miller, D. G., & Burns, H. J. (1978). Semantic integration of verbal information into a visual memory. *Journal of Experimental Psychology: Human Learning and Memory, 4*, 19–31.

Loftus, E. F., & Palmer, J. C. (1974). Reconstruction of automobile destruction: An example of the interaction between language and memory. *Journal of Verbal Learning and Verbal Behavior, 13*, 585–589.

Loftus, G. R., Johnson, C. A., & Shimamura, A. P. (1985) How much is an icon worth? *Journal of Experimental Psychology, 11*, 1–13.

Long, G. M. (1980). Iconic memory: A review and critique of the study of short-term visual storage. *Psychological Bulletin, 88*, 785–820.

Lowe, D. G., & Mitterer, J. O. (1982). Selective and divided attention in a Stroop task. *Canadian Journal of Psychology, 36*, 684–700.

Lowes, J. L. (1927). *The road to Xanadu.* London: Constable.

Lucariello, G., Toole, T., Cauraugh, J. (1983). Searching short-term memory for linear positioning movments. *Perceptual and Motor Skills, 57*, 267–274.

Luria, A. R. (1968). *The mind of a mnemonist.* New York: Basic Books.

Lynch, K. (1960). *The image of the city.* Cambridge: MIT Press.

Mace, W. M. (1974). Ecologically stimulating cognitive psychology: Gibsonian perspectives. In W. Weimer & D. Palermo (Eds.), *Cognitive and the symbolic processes* (Vol. 1, pp. 137–164). Hillsdale, NJ: Erlbaum.

Mace, W. M. (1977). James J. Gibson's strategy for perceiving: Ask not what's inside your head, but what your head's inside of. In R. Shaw & J. Bransford (Eds.), *Perceiving, acting, and knowing* (pp. 43–66). Hillsdale, NJ: Erlbaum.

MacKay, D. G. (1973). Aspects of the theory of comprehension, memory, and attention. *Quarterly Journal of Experimental Psychology, 25*, 22–40.

Mackey, W. F. (1962). The description of bilingualism. *Canadian Journal of Linguistics, 7*, 59–85.

Macnamara, J. (1967). The linguistic independence of bilinguals. *Journal of Verbal Learning and Verbal Behavior, 6*, 729–736.

Mair, W. G., Warrington, E. K., & Weiskrantz, L. (1979). Memory disorders in Korsakoff's psychosis: A neuropathological and neuropsychological investigation of two cases. *Brain, 102*, 749–783.

Mandler, J. M. (1984). *Stories, scripts, and scenes: Aspects of schema theory.* Hillsdale, NJ: Erlbaum.

Marcel, A. J. (1983). Conscious and unconscious perception: An approach to the relations between phenomenal experience and perceptual processes. *Cognitive Psychology, 15*, 238–300.

Marcel, A. J., & Patterson, K. E. (1978). Word recognition and production: Reciprocity in clinical and normal research. In J. Requin (Ed.), *Attention and Performance* (Vol. 7). Hillsdale, NJ: Erlbaum.

Markus, H. (1977). Self-schemata and processing information about the self. *Journal of Personality and Social Psychology, 35*, 63–78.

Markus, H., & Sentis, K. P. (1982). The self in social information processing. In J. Suls (Ed.), *Psychological perspectives on the self* (Vol. 1). Hillsdale, NJ: Erlbaum.

Marmor, G. S., & Zaback, L. A. (1976). Mental rotation by the blind: Does mental rotation depend on visual imagery? *Journal of Experimental Psychology: Human Perception and Performance, 2,* 515–521.

Marr, D. (1982). *Vision.* San Francisco: Freeman.

Marr, D., & Hildreth, E. C. (1980). Theory of edge detection. *Proceedings of the Royal Society, London, B207,* 187–217.

Marr, D., & Nisihara, H. K. (1977). Representation and recognition of the spatial organization of three-dimensional shapes. *Proceedings of the Royal Society, London, B200,* 269–294.

Marshall, J. C., & Newcombe, F. (1973). Patterns of paralexia: A psycholinguistic approach. *Journal of Psycholinguistic Research, 2,* 175–199.

Martin, R. C., & Caramazza, A. (1980). Classification in well-defined and ill-defined categories: Evidence for common processing strategies. *Journal of Experimental Psychology: General, 109,* 320–353.

Matlin, M. (1983). *Cognition.* New York: CBS College Publishing.

Mayer, R. E. (1983). *Thinking, problem solving, cognition* (2nd ed.). San Francisco: Freeman.

Mayes, A., Boddy, J., & Meudell, P. (1980). Is amnesia caused by an activational deficit? *Neuroscience Letters, 18,* 347–352.

McCloskey, M. E., & Glucksberg, S. (1978). Natural categories: Well defined or fuzzy sets? *Memory and Cognition, 6,* 462–472.

McCloskey, M., & Santee, J. (1981). Are semantic memory and episodic memory distinct systems? *Journal Experimental Psychology: Human Learning and Memory, 7,* 66–71.

McCloskey, M., & Watkins, M. J. (1978). The seeing-more-than-is-there phenomenon: Implications for the locus of iconic storage. *Journal of Experimental Psychology: Human Perception and Performance, 4,* 553–564.

McConkie, G. W., & Rayner, K. (1974). Identifying the span of the effective stimulus in reading. *Final Report OEG 2-71-0531.* U. S. Office of Education.

McConnell, J. V. (1962). Memory transfer through cannibalism in planarians. *Journal of Neuropsychiatry, 3* (Supplement 1), 42–48.

McDowall, J. (1979). Effects of encoding instructions and retrieval cueing on recall in Kor-

sakoff patients. *Memory and Cognition, 7,* 232–239.

McKoon, G. (1977). Organization of information in text memory. *Journal of Verbal Learning and Verbal Behavior, 16,* 247–260.

McKoon, G., & Ratcliff, R. (1979). Priming in episodic and semantic memory. *Journal of Verbal Learning and Verbal Behavior, 18,* 463–480.

McLaren, R. (1983). *Expert-ease* (Computer program). San Francisco: Jeffrey Perrone & Associates.

McNeill, D. (1968). On theories of language acquisition. In T. R. Dixon & D. L. Horton (Eds.), *Verbal behavior and general behavior theory* (pp. 406–420). Englewood Cliffs, NJ: Prentice-Hall.

McNeill, D. (1970). *The acquistion of language: The study of developmental psycholinguistics.* New York: Harper & Row.

Medin, D. L., & Smith, E. E. (1981). Strategies and classification learning. *Journal of Experimental Psychology: Human Learning and Memory, 7,* 241–253.

Mehler, J., Segui, J., & Carey, P. (1978). Tails of words: Monitoring ambiguity. *Journal of Verbal Learning and Verbal Behavior, 17,* 29–37.

Meltzoff, A. N., & Moore, M. K. (1977). Imitation of facial and manual gestures by human neonates. *Science, 198,* 75–78.

Merikle, P. M. (1980). Selection from visual persistence by perceptual groups and category membership. *Journal of Experimental Psychology: General, 109,* 279–295.

Metzler, J. (1973). *Cognitive analogues of the rotation of three-dimensional objects.* Unpublished doctoral dissertation, Stanford University, Stanford, CA.

Meudell, P., Butters, N., & Montgomery, K. (1978). The role of rehearsal in the short-term memory performance of patients with Korsakoff's and Huntington's disease. *Neuropsychologia, 16,* 507–510.

Meudell, P., & Mayes, A. (1980). Do alcoholic amnesics passively rehearse verbal information? *Brain and Language, 10* 189–204.

Meudell, P., & Mayes, A. (1982). Normal and abnormal forgetting: Some comments on the human amnesic syndrome. In A. W. Ellis (Ed.), *Normality and pathology in cognitive functions* (pp. 203–237). New York: Academic Press.

Meyer, D. E., & Schvaneveldt, R. W. (1971). Facilitation in recognizing pairs of words: Evidence of a dependence between retrieval operations. *Journal of Experimental Psychology, 90,* 227–234.

Meyers, D. (1986). *Psychology.* New York: Worth.

Mill, J. S. (1874). *A system of logic* (8th ed.). New York: Harper.

Miller, G. A. (1956). The magical number seven, plus or minus two: Some limits on our capacity for processing information. *Psychological Review, 63,* 81–97.

Miller, G. A. (1958). Free recall of redundant strings of letters. *Journal of Experimental Psychology, 56,* 485–491.

Miller, G. A., Galanter, E., & Pribram, K. H. (1960). *Plans and the structure of behavior.* New York: Holt, Rinehart & Winston.

Miller, G. A., & Nicely, P. (1955). An analysis of perceptual confusions among some English consonants. *Journal of the Acoustical Society of America, 27,* 338–352.

Miller, G. A., & Selfridge, J. A. (1950). Verbal context and the recall of meaningful material. *American Journal of Psychology, 63,* 176–185.

Miller, R. R., & Springer, A. D. (1972). Recovery from amnesia following transcorneal electroconvulsive shock. *Psychonomic Science, 28,* 7–8.

Milner, B. (1959). The memory defect in bilateral hippocampus lesions. *Psychiatric Research Reports, 11,* 43–58.

Mishkin, M. (1978). Memory in monkeys severely impaired by combined but not by separate removal of amygdala and hippocampus. *Nature, 273,* 297–298.

Mitchell, D. B., & Richman, C. L. (1980). Confirmed reservations: Mental travel. *Journal of Experimental Psychology: Human Perception and Performance, 6,* 58–66.

Moore, T., & Carling, C. (1982). *Language understanding: Toward a post-Chomskyan linguistics.* New York: St. Martin's Press.

Moray, N. (1959). Attention in dichotic listening: Affective cues and the influence of instructions. *Quarterly Journal of Experimental Psychology, 11,* 56–60.

Morgan, J. L. (1982). A linguist's view of artificial intelligence. In D. L. Farwell, S. C. Helmreich, & W. D. Wallace (Eds.), *Perspectives in cognitive science* (pp. 4–10). Urbana, IL: Linguistics Student Organization.

Morris, P. E., & Hampson, P. J. (1983). *Imagery and consciousness.* New York: Academic Press.

Mowbray, G. H. (1953). Simultaneous vision and audition: The comprehension of prose passages with varying levels of difficulty. *Journal of Experimental Psychology, 46,* 365–372.

Moyer, R. S. (1973). Comparing objects in memory: Evidence suggesting an internal psychophysics. *Perception and Psychophysics, 13,* 180–184.

Moyer, R. S., & Bayer, R. H. (1976). Mental comparison and the symbolic distance effect. *Cognitive Psychology, 8,* 228–246.

Mulholland, T. M., Pellegrino, J. W., & Glaser, R. (1980). Components of analogy solution. *Cognitive Psychology, 12,* 252–284.

Murdock, B. B., Jr. (1961). The retention of individual items. *Journal of Experimental Psychology, 62,* 618–625.

Murdock, B. B., Jr. (1962). The serial position effect of free recall. *Journal of Experimental Psychology, 64,* 482–488.

Murray, H. G., & Denny, J. P. (1969). Interaction of ability level and interpolated activity (opportunity for incubation) in human problem solving. *Psychological Reports, 24,* 271–276.

Neisser, U. (1964). Visual search. *Scientific American, 210,* 94–102.

Neisser, U. (1967). *Cognitive psychology.* New York: Appleton-Century-Crofts.

Neisser, U. (1976). *Cognition and reality: Principles and implications of cognitive psychology.* San Francisco: Freeman.

Neisser, U. (1982). *Memory observed.* San Francisco: Freeman.

Neisser, U., & Kerr, N. (1973). Spatial and mnemonic properties of visual images. *Cognitive Psychology, 5,* 138–150.

Nelson, D. L. (1979). Remembering pictures and words: Appearance, significance, and name. In L. S. Cermak & F. I. M. Craik (Eds.), *Levels of processing in human memory.* Hillsdale, NJ: Erlbaum.

Nelson, D. L., & McEvoy, C. L. (1979). Encoding context and set size. *Journal of Experimental Psychology: Human Learning and Memory, 5,* 292–314.

Nelson, K. (1973). Structure and strategy in learning to talk. *Monographs for the Society of Research in Child Development, 38* (Serial No. 149).

Nelson, K. (1975). The nominal shift in semantic-syntactic development. *Cognitive Psychology, 7,* 461–479.

Nelson, T. O. (1977). Repetition and depth of processing. *Journal of Verbal Learning and Verbal Behavior, 16,* 151–171.

Newell, A. (1962). Some problems of basic organization in problem-solving programs. In M. C. Yovits, G. T. Jacobi, & G. D. Goldstein (Eds.), *Self-organizing systems* (pp. 293–423). Washington: Spartan Books.

Newell, A. (1965). Limitations of the current stock of ideas for problem solving. In A. Kent & O. Taulbee (Eds.), *Conference on electronic information handling* (pp. 195–208). Washington: Spartan Books.

Newell, A. (1966). *On the representations of problems.* Computer Science Research Review, 18–33. Pittsburgh: Carnegie Institute of Technology.

Newell, A. (1967). *Studies in problem solving: Subject 3 on the cryptarithmetic task: DONALD + GERALD = ROBERT.* Pittsburgh: Carnegie-Mellon University.

Newell, A., & Rosenbloom, P. S. (1981). Mechanisms of skill acquisition and the law of practice. In J. R. Anderson (Ed.), *Cognitive skills and their acquisition* (pp. 1–56). Hillsdale, NJ: Erlbaum.

Newell, A., Shaw, J. C., & Simon, H. A. (1958). Elements of a theory of human problem solving. *Psychological Review, 65,* 151–166.

Newell, A., Shaw, J. C., & Simon, H. A. (1962). The processes of creative thinking. In H. E. Gruber, G. Terrell, & M. Wertheimer (Eds.), *Contemporary approaches to creative thinking* (pp. 63–119). New York: Atherton Press.

Newell, A., & Simon, H. A. (1956). The logic theory machine: A complex information processing system. *IRE Transactions on Information Theory, IT-2(3),* 61–79.

Newell, A., & Simon, H. A. (1961). GPS: A program that simulates human thought. In H. Billing (Ed.), *Lernende Automaten* (pp. 109–124). Munich: R. Oldenbourg.

Newell, A., & Simon, H. A. (1965). An example of human chess play in the light of chess playing programs. In N. Weiner & J. P. Schade (Eds.), *Progress in biocybernetics* (Vol. 2, pp. 19–75). Amsterdam: Elsevier.

Newell. A., & Simon, H. A. (1972). *Human problem solving.* Englewood Cliffs, NJ: Prentice-Hall.

Newell, A., & Simon, H. A. (1976). Computer science as empirical inquiry: Symbols and search. *Communications of the ACM, 19,* 113–126.

Newport, E. L., Gleitman, H., & Gleitman, L. R. (1977). Mother, I'd rather do it myself: The contribution of selected child listener variables. In Snow, C. E. & Ferguson, C. A. (Eds.), *Talking to children: Language input and acquisition.* Cambridge: Cambridge University Press.

Nisbett, R. E., & Wilson, T. D. (1977). Telling more than we can know: Verbal reports on mental processes. *Psychological Review, 84,* 231–259.

Norman, D. A. (1968). Toward a theory of memory and attention. *Psychological Review, 75,* 522–536.

Norman, D. A. (1980). Twelve issues for cognitive science. *Cognitive Science, 4,* 1–32.

Norman, D. A., & Bobrow, D. G. (1975). On data-limited and resource-limited processes. *Cognitive Psychology, 7,* 44–64.

Obusek, C. J., & Warren, R. M. (1973). Relation of the verbal transformation and the phonemic restoration effects. *Cognitive Psychology, 5,* 97–107.

Olson, J. N., & MacKay, D. G. (1974). Completion and verification of ambiguous sentences. *Journal of Verbal Learning and Verbal Behavior, 13,* 457–470.

Orne, M. T. (1962). On the social psychology of the psychological experiment: With particular reference to demand characteristics and their implications. *American Psychologist, 17,* 776–783.

O'Shea, T., & Eisenstadt, M. (Eds.). (1984). *Artificial intelligence: Tools, techniques, and applications.* New York: Harper & Row.

Overton, D. A. (1972). State-dependent learning produced by alcohol and its relevance to alcoholism. In B. Kissin & H. Begleiter (Eds.), *Physiology and behavior* (Vol. 2). New York: Plenum.

Owens, J., Bower, G. H., & Black, J. B. (1979). The "soap opera" effect in story recall. *Memory and Cognition, 7,* 185–191.

Palmer, S. E. (1978). Fundamental aspects of cognition representation. In E. Rosch & B. Lloyd (Eds.), *Cognition and categorization.* Hillsdale, NJ: Erlbaum.

Palmere, M., Benton, S. L., Glover, J. A., & Ronning, R. (1983). Elaboration and recall of main ideas in prose. *Journal of Educational Psychology, 75,* 898–907.

Parker, E. S., Birnbaum, I. M., & Noble, E. P. (1976). Alcohol and memory: Storage and state dependency. *Journal of Verbal Learning and Verbal Behavior, 15,* 691–702.

Parkin, A. J. (1984). Levels of processing, context, and facilitation of pronunciation. *Acta Psychologia, 55,* 19–29.

Patterson, K. E. (1982). The relation between reading and phonological encoding: Further neuropsychological observations. In A. W. Ellis (Ed.), *Normality and pathology in cognitive functions* (pp. 77–112). New York: Academic Press.

Pavio, A. U. (1974). Language and knowledge of the world. *Educational Researcher, 3,* 5–12.

Pellegrino, J. W. (1985). Inductive reasoning ability. In R. J. Sternberg (Ed.), *Human abilities: An information processing approach* (pp. 195–226). San Francisco: Freeman.

Penfield, W., & Milner, B. (1958). Memory deficit produced by bilateral lesions in the hippocampal zone. *Archives of neurology and psychiatry, 79,* 475–497.

Petersik, J. T. (1982). Perception of eye scans with the Müller-Lyer stimuli: Evidence for filter theory. *Perceptual and Motor Skills, 54* (3, Pt. 1), 683–692.

Peterson, L. R., & Peterson, M. J. (1959). Short-term retention of individual verbal items. *Journal of Experimental Psychology, 58,* 193–198.

Piaget, J. (1968). *Le structuralisme.* Paris: Presses Universitaires de France.

Pinker, S. (1979). Formal models of language learning. *Cognition, 7,* 217–283.

Pinsky, S. D., & McAdam, D. W. (1980). Electroencephalographic and dichotic indices of cerebral laterality in stuttering. *Brain and Language, 11,* 374–397.

Pisoni, D. B. (1978). Speech perception. In W. K. Estes (Ed.), *Handbook of learning and cognitive processes* (Vol. 6, pp. 167–234). Hillsdale, NJ: Erlbaum.

Pisoni, D. B., & Sawusch, J. R. (1975). Some stages of processing in speech perception. In A. Cohen & S. G. Nooteboom (Eds.), *Structure and process in speech perception* (pp. 16–34). Heidelberg, W. Germany: Springer-Verlag.

Poincare, H. (1913). The value of science. In *The foundations of science* (G. B. Halsted, Trans.). New York: Science Press.

Pollack, I., & Pickett, J. M. (1964). Intelligibility of excerpts from fluent speech: Auditory vs. structural context. *Journal of Verbal Learning and Verbal Behavior, 3,* 79–84.

Polson, P. G., & Jeffries, R. (1982). Problem solving as search and understanding. In R. J. Sternberg (Ed.), *Advances in the psychology of human intelligence* (Vol. 1, pp. 367–412). Hillsdale, NJ: Erlbaum.

Posner, M. I. (1969). Abstraction and the process of recognition. In G. H. Bower & J. T. Spence (Eds.), *The psychology of learning and motivation* (Vol. 3). New York: Academic Press.

Posner, M. I., & Boies, S. J. (1971). Components of attention. *Psychological Review, 78,* 391–408.

Posner, M. I., & Keele, S. W. (1968). On the genesis of abstract ideas. *Journal of Experimental Psychology, 77,* 353–363.

Posner, M. I., & Keele, S. W. (1970). Retention of abstract ideas. *Journal of Experimental Psychology, 83,* 304–308.

Posner, M. I., & Snyder, C. R. R. (1975). Attention and cognitive control. In R. Solso (Ed.), *Information processing and cognition: The Loyola symposium.* Hillsdale, NJ: Erlbaum.

Postman, L., & Phillips. L. W. (1965). Short-term temporal changes in free recall. *Quarterly Journal of Experimental Psychology, 17,* 132–138.

Postman, L., Thompkins. B. A., & Gray, W. D. (1978). The interpretation of encoding effects in retention. *Journal of Verbal Learning and Verbal Behavior, 17,* 681–705.

Potter, M. C., & Faulconer, B. A. (1975). Time to understand pictures and words. *Nature, 253,* 437–438.

Premack, D. (1971). Language in chimpanzee? *Science, 172,* 808–822.

Pritchard, R. M. (1961). Stabilized images on the retina. *Scientific American, 204,* 72–78.

Purcell, D. G., Stanovich, K. E., & Spector, A. (1978). Visual angle and the word superiority effect. *Memory and Cognition, 6,* 3–8.

Pylyshyn, Z. (1973). What the mind's eye tells the mind's brain: A critique of mental imagery. *Psychological Bulletin, 80,* 1–24.

Pylyshyn, Z. (1979a). Imagery theory: Not mysterious, just wrong. *The Behavioral and Brain Sciences, 2,* 561–563.

Pylyshyn, Z. (1979b). The rate of "mental rotation" of images: A test of a holistic analogue hypothesis. *Memory and Cognition, 7,* 19–28.

Pylyshyn, Z. (1980). Cognitive representation and the process-architecture distinction. *The Behavioral and Brain Sciences, 3,* 154–169.

Pylyshyn, Z. (1981). The imagery debate: Analogue media versus tacit knowledge. *Psychological Review, 88,* 16–45.

Quartermain, D. McEwen, B. S., & Azmitia, E. C., Jr. (1972). Recovery of memory following amnesia in the rat and mouse. *Journal of Comparative and Physiological Psychology, 79,* 360–370.

Quillian, M. R. (1968). Semantic memory. In M. Minsky (Ed.), *Semantic information processing,* Cambridge: MIT Press.

Raeburn, V. P. (1974). Priorities in item recognition. *Memory and Cognition, 2,* 663–669.

Raphael, B. (1976). *The thinking computer: Mind inside matter.* San Francisco: Freeman.

Rayner, K. (1975). The perceptual span and peripheral cues in reading. *Cognitive Psychology, 7,* 65–81.

Rayner, K. (1978). Eye movements in reading and information processing. *Psychological Bulletin, 85,* 618–660.

Reber, A. S. (1967). Implicit learning of artificial grammars. *Journal of Verbal Learning and Verbal Behavior, 6,* 855–863.

Reber, A. S. (1973). What clicks may tell us about speech perception. *Journal of Psycholinguistic Research, 2,* 287–288.

Reber, A. S., & Anderson, J. R. (1970). The perception of clicks in linguistic and nonlinguistic messages. *Perception and Psychophysics, 8,* 81–89.

Reed, E., & Jones, R. (Eds.). (1982). *Reasons for realism: Selected essays of James J. Gibson.* Hillsdale, NJ: Erlbaum.

Reicher, G. (1969). Perceptual recognition as a function of meaningfulness of stimulus material. *Journal of Experimental Psychology, 81,* 275–280.

Reif, F. (1979). *Cognitive mechanisms facilitating human problem solving in a realistic domain: The example of physics.* Unpublished manuscript.

Reitman, W. (1964). Heuristic decision procedures, open constraints, and the structure of ill-defined problems. In M. W. Shelley & G. L. Bryan (Eds.), *Human judgements and optimality.* New York: Wiley.

Remez, R. E. (1979). Adaptation of the category boundary between speech and non-speech: A case against feature detectors. *Cognitive Psychology, 11,* 38–57.

Remez, R. E. (1980). Susceptibility of a stop consonant to adaptation on a speech-nonspeech continuum: Further evidence against feature detectors in speech perception. *Perception and Psychophysics, 27,* 17–23.

Rescorla, L. (1980). Overextensions in early language development. *Journal of Child Language, 7,* 321–335.

Reynolds, A. G., & Flagg, P. W. (1983). *Cognitive psychology* (2nd ed.). Boston: Little, Brown.

Richardson, J. T., & Johnson, P. B. (1980). Models of anagram solution. *Bulletin of the Psychonomic Society, 16,* 247–250.

Richardson, K., Bhavnani, K. K., & Browne, D. (1982). Abstraction of contingency in concept learning. *Current Psychological Research, 2,* 101–109.

Richman, C. L., Mitchell, D. B., & Reznick, J. S. (1979). Mental travel: Some reservations. *Journal of Experimental Psychology: Human Perception and Performance, 5,* 13–18.

Ricks, D. M. (1975). Vocal communication in preverbal, normal, and autistic children. In N. O'Connor (Ed.), *Language, cognitive deficits, and retardation.* London: Butterworth.

Riggs, L. A., Ratliff, F., Cornsweet, J. C., & Cornsweet, T. N. (1953). The disappearance of steadily fixated objects. *Journal of the Optical Society of America, 43,* 495–501.

Rips, L. J., & Marcus, S. L. (1977). Supposition and the analysis of conditional sentences. In M. A. Just & P. A. Carpenter (Eds.), *Cognitive processes in comprehension.* Hillsdale, NJ: Erlbaum.

Rips, L. J., Shoben, E. J., & Smith, E. E. (1973). Semantic distance and the verification of semantic relations. *Journal of Verbal Learning and Verbal Behavior, 12,* 1–20.

Robertson, L. C., & Palmer, S. E. (1983). Holistic processes in the perception and transformation of disoriented figures. *Journal of Experimental Psychology: Human Perception and Performance, 9,* 203–214.

Robinson, E. J. (1981). The child's understanding of inadequate messages and communication failure: A problem of ignorance or egocentrism. In W. P. Dickson (Ed.), *Children's oral communication skills.* New York: Academic Press.

Rock, I. (1983). *The logic of perception.* Cambridge: MIT Press/Bradford Books.

Rogoff, B., & Lave, J. (1984). *Everyday cognition: Its development in social context.* Cambridge: Harvard University Press.

Ronning. R. R. (1965). Anagram solution times: A function of the "ruleout" factor. *Journal of Experimental Psychology, 69,* 35–39.

Rosch, E. H. (1973). On the internal structure of perceptual and semantic categories. In T. E. Moore (Ed.), *Cognitive development and the acquisition of language.* New York: Academic Press.

Rosch, E. H. (1975). Cognitive representations of semantic categories. *Journal of Experimental Psychology: General, 104,* 192–233.

Rosch, E. H. (1977). Classification of real-world objects: Origins and representation in cognition. In P. N. Johnson-Laird & P. C. Wason (Eds.), *Thinking: Readings in cognitive science* (pp. 212–222) Cambridge: Cambridge University Press.

Rosch, E. H., & Lloyd, B. B. (Eds.). (1978). *Cognition and categorization.* Hillsdale, NJ: Erlbaum.

Rosch, E. H., & Mervis, C. B. (1975). Family resemblances: Studies in the internal structure of categories. *Cognitive Psychology, 7,* 573–605.

Rosenfield, D. B., & Goodglass, H. (1980). Dichotic testing of cerebral dominance in stutterers. *Brain and Language, 11,* 170–180.

Rubenstein, H., Lewis, S. S., & Rubenstein, M. A. (1971). Evidence for phonemic recoding in visual word recognition. *Journal of Verbal Learning and Verbal Behavior, 10,* 645–657.

Rumelhart, D. E., & Siple, P. (1974). Process of recognizing tachistoscopically presented words. *Psychological Review, 81,* 99–118.

Rundus, D. (1977). Maintenance rehearsal and single-level processing. *Journal of Verbal Learning and Verbal Behavior, 16,* 665–681.

Russell, W. R., & Nathan, P. W. (1946). Traumatic amnesia. *Brain, 69,* 280–300.

Saarinen, T. F. (1973). The use of projective techniques in geographic research. In W. H. Ittelson (Ed.), *Environment and cognition.* New York: Seminar Press.

Sabol, M. A., & DeRosa, D. V. (1976). Semantic encoding of isolated words. *Journal of Experimental Psychology: Human Learning and Memory, 2,* 58–68.

Sachs, J. D. S. (1967). Recognition memory for syntactic and semantic aspects of connected discourse. *Perception and Psychophysics, 2,* 437–442.

Saffran, E. M., & Marin, O. S. M. (1977). Reading without phonology: Evidence from aphasia. *Quarterly Journal of Experimental Psychology, 29,* 515–525.

Sakitt, B. (1976). Iconic memory. *Psychological Review, 83,* 257–276.

Sakitt, B., & Long, G. M. (1979). Spare the rod and spoil the icon. *Journal of Experimental Psychology: Human Perception and Performance, 5,* 19–30.

Sankoff, G., & Brown, P. (1976). The origins of syntax in discourse: A case study of Tok Pisin relatives. *Language, 52,* 631–666.

Saslow, C. A. (1982). *Basic research methods.* Reading, MA: Addison-Wesley.

Schank, R. C. (1975). *Conceptual information processing.* Amsterdam: North Holland.

Schank, R. C. (1983, June). A conversation with Roger Schank. *Psychology Today,* pp. 28–36.

Schank, R. C., & Abelson, R. P. (1977). *Scripts, plans, goals, and understanding: An inquiry into human knowledge structures.* Hillsdale, NJ: Erlbaum.

Schneider, A. M., Tyler, J., & Jinich, D. (1974). Recovery from retrograde amnesia: A learning process. *Science, 184,* 87–88.

Schneider, W., & Shiffrin, R. M. (1977). Controlled and automatic human information processing: I. Detection, search, and attention. *Psychological Review, 84,* 1–66.

Schumacher, R. (1981). *Bilingualism: Information processing and storage.* Unpublished manuscript.

Scoville, W. B., & Milner, B. (1957). Loss of recent memory after bilateral hippocampal lesions. *Journal of Neurology, Neurosurgery, and Psychiatry, 20,* 11–21.

Scribner, S. (1977). Modes of thinking and ways of speaking: Culture and logic reconsidered. In P. N. Johnson-Laird & P. C. Wason, (Eds.), *Thinking: Readings in cognitive science* (pp. 483–500). Cambridge: Cambridge University Press.

Seamon, J. G., & Virostek, S. (1978). Memory performance and subject-defined depth of processing. *Memory and Cognition, 6,* 283–287.

Searle, J. R. (1981). Minds, brains, and programs. In J. Haugeland (Ed.), *Mind design* (pp. 282–306). Cambridge: MIT Press/Bradford Books.

Selfridge, O. (1959). Pandemonium: A paradigm for learning. In *Symposium on the mechanization of thought processes*. London: HM Stationery Office.

Shaughnessy, J. J. (1981). Memory monitoring accuracy and modification of rehearsal strategies. *Journal of Verbal Learning and Verbal Behavior, 20,* 216–230.

Shaw, R., & Bransford, J. (Eds.). (1977). *Perceiving, acting, and knowing.* Hillsdale, NJ: Erlbaum.

Sheikh, A. R. (1983). *Imagery: Current theory, research, and applications.* New York: Wiley.

Shepard, R. N. (1972). Psychological representation of speech sounds. In E. E. David & P. B. Denes (Eds.), *Human communication: A unified view* (pp. 67–113). New York: McGraw-Hill.

Shepard, R. N. (1978). The mental image. *American Psychologist, 33,* 125–137.

Shepard, R. N., & Feng, C. A. (1972). A chronometric study of mental paper folding. *Cognitive Psychology, 3,* 228–243.

Shepard, R. N., & Metzler, J. (1971). Mental rotation of three-dimensional objects. *Science, 171,* 701–703.

Shepard, R. N., & Podgorny, P. (1978). Cognitive processes that resemble perceptual processes. In W. K. Estes (Ed.), *Handbook of learning and cognitive processes* (Vol. 5, pp. 189–238). Hillsdale, NJ: Erlbaum.

Shiffrin, R. M., Craig, J. C., & Cohen, E. (1973). On the degree of attention and capacity limitation in tactile processing. *Perception and Psychophysics, 13,* 328–336.

Shiffrin, R. M., & Dumais, S. T. (1981). The development of automatism. In J. R. Anderson (Ed.), *Cognitive skills and their acquisition* (pp. 111–140). Hillsdale, NJ: Erlbaum.

Shiffrin, R. M., & Schneider, W. (1977). Controlled and automatic human information processing: II. Perceptual learning, automatic attending, and a general theory. *Psychological Review, 84,* 127–190.

Shoben, E. J., Westcourt, K. T., & Smith, E. E. (1978). Sentence verification, sentence recognition, and the semantic-episodic distinction. *Journal of Experimental Psychology: Human Learning and Memory, 4,* 304–317.

Shortliffe, E. H. (1976). *Computer-based medical consultations: MYCIN.* New York: American Elsevier.

Shulman, H. G. (1971). Similarity effects in short-term memory. *Psychological Bulletin, 75,* 399–415.

Shulman, H. G. (1972). Semantic confusion errors in short-term memory. *Journal of Verbal Learning and Verbal Behavior, 11,* 221–227.

Silveira, J. (1971). *The effect of interruption timing and length on problem solution and quality of problem processing.* Unpublished doctoral dissertation, University of Oregon, Eugene, OR.

Simon, H. A. (1969). *The sciences of the artificial* (1st ed.). Cambridge: MIT Press.

Simon, H. A. (1973). The structure of ill-structured problems. *Artificial Intelligence, 4,* 181–202.

Simon, H. A. (1978). Information processing theory of human problem solving. In W. K. Estes (Ed.), *Handbook of learning and cognitive processes* (Vol. 5, pp. 271–295). Hillsdale, NJ: Erlbaum.

Simon, H. A., & Gilmartin, K. A. (1973). A simulation of memory for chess positions. *Cognitive Psychology, 5,* 29–46.

Simon, H. A., & Hayes, J. R. (1976). The understanding process: Problem isomorphs. *Cognitive Psychology, 8,* 165–190.

Simon, H. A., & Simon, P. A. (1962). Trial and error search in solving difficult problems: Evidence from the game of chess. *Behavioral Science, 7,* 425–429.

Simpson, P. J. (1972). High-speed memory scanning: Stability and generality. *Journal of Experimental Psychology, 96,* 239–246.

Sitler, R. W. Schiavetti, N., & Metz, D. E. (1983). Contextual effects in the measurement of hearing-impaired speakers' intelligibility, *Journal of Speech and Hearing Research, 26,* 30–35.

Skinner, B. F. (1957). *Verbal behavior.* New York: Appleton-Century-Crofts.

Slack, J. M. (1984). Cognitive science research. In T. O'Shea & M. Eisenstadt (Eds.), *Artificial intelligence: Tools, techniques and applications* (pp. 155–177). New York: Harper & Row.

Slobin, D. I., & Welsh, C. A. (1973). Elicited imitation as a research tool in developmental psycholinguistics. In C. A. Fergus & D. I. Slobin (Eds.), *Studies of child language development* (pp. 485–497). New York: Holt, Rinehart & Winston.

Slovic, P., Fischoff, B., & Lichtenstein, S. (1976). Cognitive process and social risk taking. In J. S. Carroll & J. W. Payne (Eds.), *Cognition and social behavior.* Hillsdale, NJ: Erlbaum.

Smiley, S. S., Oakley, D. D., Worthen, D., Campione, J. C., & Brown, A. L. (1977). Recall of thematically relevant material by adolescent good and poor readers as a function of written versus oral presentation. *Journal of Educational Psychology, 69,* 381–387.

Smith, E. E. (1978). Theories of semantic memory. In W. K. Estes (Ed.), *Handbook of learning and cognitive processes* (Vol. 6, pp.1–56). Hillsdale, NJ: Erlbaum.

Smith, E. E., & Medin, D. L. (1981). *Categories and concepts.* Cambridge: Harvard University Press.

Smith, E. E., Rips, L. J., & Shoben, E. J. (1974). Structure and process in semantic memory: A featural model for semantic decisions. *Psychological Review, 81,* 214–241.

Smith, S. M., Glenberg, A., & Bjork, R. A. (1978). Environmental context and human memory. *Memory and Cognition, 6,* 342–353.

Smith, T. (1982). Chomsky's cognitivism at twenty-five from the perspective of Skinner's "behaviorism at fifty." *Papers in the Social Sciences, 2,* 23–32.

Snoddy, G. S. (1926). Learning and stability. *Journal of Applied Psychology, 10,* 1–36.

Sokal, R. R. (1977). Classification: Purposes, principles, progress, prospects. In P. N. Johnson-Laird & P. C. Wason (Eds.), *Thinking: Readings in cognitive science* (pp. 185–198). Cambridge: Cambridge University Press.

Solman, R. T., May, J. G., & Schwartz, B. D. (1981). The word superiority effect: A study using parts of letters. *Journal of Experimental Psychology: Human Perception and Performance, 7,* 552–559.

Sperling, G. (1960). The information available in brief visual presentations. *Psychological Monographs, 74* (Whole No. 498).

Spiro, R. J. (1977). Remembering information from text: The "state of schema" approach. In R. C. Anderson, R. J. Spiro, & W. E. Montague (Eds.), *Schooling and the acquisition of knowledge.* Hillsdale, NJ: Erlbaum.

Spoehr, K. T., & Lehmkuhle, S. W. (1982). *Visual information processing.* San Francisco: Freeman.

Sproat, R. (1983). Creole languages: A comment. *Scientific American, 249*(6), 6.

Staats, A. W., (1968). *Learning, language, and cognition.* New York: Holt, Rinehart & Winston.

Staudenmayer, H. (1975). Understanding conditional reasoning with meaningful propositions. In R. J. Falmagne (Ed.), *Reasoning: Representation and process in children and adults.* Hillsdale, NJ: Erlbaum.

Sternberg, R. J. (1982, April). Who's intelligent? *Psychology Today,* pp. 30–39.

Sternberg, R. J. (Ed.). (1982). *Advances in the psychology of human intelligence* (Vol. 1). Hillsdale, NJ: Erlbaum.

Sternberg, R. J. (Ed.). (1984). *Mechanisms of cognitive development.* San Francisco: Freeman.

Sternberg, R. J. (Ed.). (1985). *Human abilities: An information-processing approach.* San Francisco: Freeman.

Sternberg, S. (1966). High-speed scanning in human memory. *Science, 153,*652–654.

Sternberg, S. (1969). The discovery of processing stages: Extensions of Donder's method. *Acta Psychologica, 30,* 276–315.

Sternberg, S. (1975). Memory scanning: New findings and current controversies. *Quarterly Journal of Experimental Psychology, 27,*1–32.

Stromeyer, C. F., III. (1970). Eidetikers. *Psychology Today,* pp. 76–80.

Struhsaker, T. T. (1967). Auditory communication among vervet monkeys (Cercopithecus aethiops). In S. A. Altmann (Ed.), *Social communication among primates.* Chicago: University of Chicago Press.

Sulin, R. A., & Dooling. D. J. (1974). Intrusion of a thematic idea in retention of prose. *Journal of Experimental Psychology, 103,* 255–262.

Swinney, D. A., & Hakes, D. T. (1976). Effects of prior context upon lexical access during sentence comprehension. *Journal of Verbal Learning and Verbal Behavior, 15,* 681–689.

Tate, D. F., Galvan, L., & Ungar, G. (1976). Isolation and identification of two learning-induced brain peptides. *Pharmacology, Biochemistry, and Behavior, 5,* 441–448.

Terrace, H. S. (1979). *Nim.* New York: Knopf.

Thompson, J.R., & Chapman R. S. (1977). Who is "Daddy" revisited: The status of two-year-olds' over-extended words in use and comprehension. *Journal of Child Language, 4,* 359–375.

Thorndyke, P. W. (1977). Cognitive structures in comprehension and memory of narrative discourse. *Cognitive Psychology, 9,* 77–110.

Thorpe, W. H. (1961). *Bird song: The biology of vocal communication and expression in birds.* Cambridge: Cambridge University Press.

Thorpe, W. H. (1963). *Learning and instinct in animals* (2nd ed.). London: Methuen.

Tolman, E. C. (1948). Cognitive maps in rats and men. *Psychological Review, 55,* 189–208.

Treisman, A. M. (1960). Contextual cues in selective listening. *Quarterly Journal of Experimental Psychology, 12,* 242–248.

Treisman, A. M. (1964a). Verbal cues, language, and meaning in selective attention. *American Journal of Psychology, 77,* 206–219.

Treisman, A. M. (1964b). The effect of irrelevant material on the efficiency of selective listening. *American Journal of Psychology, 77,* 533–546.

Tulving, E. (1972) Episodic and semantic memory. In E. Tulving & W. Donaldson (Eds.), *Organization of memory.* New York: Academic Press.

Tulving, E. (1979). Relation between encoding specificity and levels of processing. In L. S. Cermak & F. I. M. Craik (Eds.), *Levels of processing in human memory.* Hillsdale, NJ: Erlbaum.

Tulving, E. (1983). *Elements of episodic memory.* Oxford: Clarendon Press/Oxford University Press.

Tulving, E., & Thompson, D. M. (1973). Encoding specificity and retrieval processes in episodic memory. *Journal of Experimental Psychology: Learning, Memory, and Cognition, 8,* 336–342.

Turvey, M. T. (1977). Contrasting orientations to the theory of visual information-processing. *Psychological Review, 84,* 67–88.

Turvey, M. T., & Shaw, R. E. (1979). The primacy of perceiving: An ecological reformulation of perception for understanding memory. In L. G. Nilsson (Ed.), *Perspective on memory research* (pp. 167–222). Hillsdale, NJ: Erlbaum.

Tyler, S. W., Hertel, P. T., McCallum, M. C., & Ellis, H. C. (1979). Cognitive effort and memory. *Journal of Experimental Psychology: Human Learning and Memory, 5,* 607–617.

Ullman, S. (1980). Against direct perception. *Behavioral and Brain Sciences, 3,* 373–415.

Ungar, G., Desiderio, D. M., & Parr, W. (1972). Isolation, identification, and synthesis of a specific-behavior-inducing brain peptide. *Nature, 238,* 198–202.

van Duyne, P. C. (1974). Realism and linguistic complexity in reasoning. *British Journal of Psychology, 65,* 59–67.

Vihman, M. M., & McLaughlin, B. (1982). Bilingual and second language acquisition in preschool children. In C. J. Brainerd & M. Pressley (Eds.), *Verbal processes in children* (pp. 35–58). New York: Springer-Verlag.

von Frisch, K. (1954). *The dancing bees.* London: Methuen.

von Frisch, K. (1967). *The dance and orientation of bees* (L. E. Chadwick, Trans.). Cambridge: Harvard University Press.

von Glasersfeld, E., & Kelley, M. F. (1982). On the concepts of period, phase, stage, and level. *Human Development, 25,* 152–160.

von Senden, M. (1960). *Space and sight: The perception of space and shape in the congenitally blind before and after operation.* New York: Free Press.

Voss, J. F., Greene, T. R., Post, T. A., & Penner, B. C. (1983). Problem solving skill in social sciences. In G. Power (Ed.), *The psychology of learning and motivation: Advances in research and theory* (Vol. 17). New York: Academic Press.

Voss, J. F., Tyler, S. W., & Yengo, L. A. (1983). Individual differences in the solving of social science problems. In R. F. Dillon & R. R. Schmeck (Eds.), *Individual differences in cognition.* New York: Academic Press.

Wagner, S. (1982). A philospher looks at artificial intelligence. In D. L. Farwell, S. C. Helmreich, & W. D. Wallace (Eds.), *Perspectives in cognitive science* (pp. 42–64). Urbana, IL: Linguistics Student Organization.

Walker, E., & Ceci, S. J. (1983). Lateral asymmetries in electrodermal responses to nonattended stimuli: A response to Dawson and Schell. *Journal of Experimental Psychology: Human Perception and Performance, 9*(1), 145–147.

Walker, N., Jones, J. P., & Mar, H. H. (1983). Encoding processes and the recall of text. *Memory and Cognition, 11,* 275–282.

Wallas, G. (1926). *The art of thought.* New York: Harcourt Brace Jovanovich.

Waltz, D. (1975). Understanding line drawings of scenes with shadows. In P. Winston (Ed.), *The psychology of computer vision* (pp. 19–92). New York: McGraw-Hill.

Waltz, D. (1982). Artificial intelligence. In D. L. Farwell, S. C. Helmreich, & W. D. Wallace (Eds.), *Perspectives in cognitive science* (pp. 11–28). Urbana, IL: Linguistics Student Organization.

Warren. R. M. (1970). Perceptual restoration of missing speech sounds. *Science, 167,* 392–393.

Warren, R. M., & Obusek, C. J. (1971). Speech perception and phonemic restorations. *Perception and Psychophysics, 9,* 358–362.

Warren, R. M., Obusek, C. J., Farmer, R. M., & Warren, R. P. (1969). Auditory sequence: Confusions of patterns other than speech or music. *Science, 164,* 586–587.

Warren, R. M., & Warren, R. P. (1970). Auditory illusions and confusions. *Scientific American, 223,* 30–36.

Warrington, E. K., & Weiskrantz, L. (1970). Amnesic syndrome: Consolidation or retrieval? *Nature, 228,* 628–630.

Warrington, E. K., & Weiskrantz, L. (1973). An analysis of short-term and long-term memory deficits in man. In J. Deutsch (Ed.), *The physiological basis of memory.* New York: Academic Press.

Warrington, E. K., & Weiskrantz, L. (1978). Further analysis of the prior learning effect in amnesic patients. *Neuropsychologia, 12,* 419–428.

Wason, P. C. (1966). Reasoning. In B. Foss (Ed.), *New horizons in psychology* (Vol. 1). Hammondsworth, Middlesex, England: Penguin.

Wason, P. C., & Johnson-Laird, P. N. (1970). A conflict between selecting and evaluating information in an inferential task. *British Journal of Psychology, 61,* 509–515.

Watanabe, I. (1980). Selective attention and memory. *Japanese Psychological Review, 23* (4), 335–354.

Watkins, M. J. (1974). When is recall spectacularly higher than recognition? *Journal of Experimental Psychology, 102,* 161–163.

Watkins, M. J., & Tulving, E. (1975). Episodic memory: When recognition fails. *Journal of Experimental Psychology: General, 104,* 5–29.

Watson, M. W., & Amgott-Kwan, T. (1984). Development of family-role concepts in school-age children. *Developmental Psychology, 20,* 953–959.

Waugh, N. C., & Norman, D. A. (1965) Primary memory. *Psychological Review, 72,* 89–104.

Weber, R. J., & Malmstrom, F. V. (1979). Measuring the size of mental images. *Journal of Experimental Psychology: Human Perception and Performance, 5,* 1–12.

Wegner, D. M., & Vallacher, R. R. (1977). *Implicit psychology: An introduction to social cognition.* New York: Oxford University Press.

Weimer, W. B. (1977). A conceptual framework for cognitive psychology: Motor theories of the mind. In R. Shaw & J. Bransford (Eds.), *Perceiving, acting, and knowing* (pp. 267–314). Hillsdale, NJ: Erlbaum.

Weimer, W. B., & Palermo, D. S. (Eds.). (1974). *Cognition and the symbolic processes* (Vol. 1). Hillsdale, NJ: Erlbaum.

Weimer, W. B., & Palermo, D. S. (Eds.). (1982). *Cognition and the symbolic processes* (Vol. 2). Hillsdale, NJ: Erlbaum.

Weinrich, U. (1953). *Languages in contact.* New York: Linguistic Circle of New York.

Weir, R. H. (1966). Some questions on the child's learning of phonology. In F. Smith & G. A. Miller (Eds.), *The genesis of language.* Cambridge: MIT Press.

Weiskrantz, L., & Warrington, E. K. (1975). The problem of the amnesic syndrome in man and animals. In R. L. Isaacson & K. H. Pribram (Eds.), *The hippocampus* (Vol 2). New York: Plenum.

Weizenbaum, J. (1966). ELIZA—A computer program for the study of the natural language communication between man and machine. *Communication Associates Computing Machinery, 9,* 36–45.

Weizenbaum, J. (1976). *Computer power and human reason.* San Francisco: Freeman.

Wells, G. (1979). Learning and using the auxiliary verb in English. In V. Lee (Ed.), *Language Development.* London: Croom Helm & the Open University Press.

Wertheimer, M. (1959). *Productive thinking.* New York: Harper & Row.

Wessels, M. G. (1982). *Cognitive psychology.* New York: Harper & Row.

Wetherick, N. (1969). Bruner's concept of strategy: An experiment and a critique. *Journal of Experimental Psychology, 81,* 53–58.

Wexler, K. (1978). a review of John R. Anderson's language, memory, and thought. *Cognition, 6,* 327–351.

Wheeler, D. D. (1970). Processes in word recognition. *Cognitive Psychology, 1,* 59–85.

White, M. J. (1985). On the status of cognitive psychology. *American Psychologist, 40,* 117–119.

Whitney, P., & Kunen, S. (1983). Development of hierarchical conceptual relationships in children's semantic memories. *Journal of Experimental Child Psychology, 35*(2), 278–293.

Wickelgren, W. A. (1965). Size of rehearsal group and short-term memory. *Journal of Experimental Psychology, 68,* 413–419.

Wickelgren, W. A. (1973). The long and the short of memory. *Psychological Bulletin, 80,* 425–438.

Wickelgren, W. A. (1974). *How to solve problems.* San Francisco: Freeman.

Wickens, C. D. (1984). *Engineering psychology and human performance.* Columbus, OH: Merrill.

Wickens, D. D. (1970). Encoding categories of words: An empirical approach to meaning. *Psychological Review, 77,* 1–15.

Wiener, N. (1948). *Cybernetics.* Cambridge: MIT Press.

Wilkins, D. (1980). Using patterns and plans in chess. *Artificial Intelligence, 14,* 165–203.

Wilks, Y. (1981). A position note on natural language understanding and artificial intelligence. *Cognitive Psychology, 10,* 337–340.

Wilson. R. S., et al. (1983). Word frequency effect and recognition memory in dementia of the Alzheimer type. *Journal of Clinical Neuropsychology, 5,* 97–104.

Wilton, R. N., & Pidcock, B. (1982). Knowledge of spatial relations: Varying the precision with which locations must be specified. *Quarterly Journal of Experimental Psychology: Human Experimental Psychology, 34A*(4), 515–528.

Wingfield, A. (1973). Effects of serial position and set size in auditory recognition memory. *Memory and Cognition, 1,* 53–55.

Wingfield, A., & Byrnes, D. L. (1981). *The psychology of human memory.* New York: Academic Press.

Winograd, T. (1972). *Understanding natural language.* New York: Academic Press.

Winograd, T. (1975). Computer memories: A metaphor for memory organization. In C. Cofer (Ed.), *The structure of human memory.* San Francisco: Freeman.

Witkin, A. P., & Tenenbaum, J. M. (1983). On the role of structure in vision. In J. Beck, B. Hope & A. Rosenfeld (Eds.), *Human and machine vision* (pp. 481–544). New York: Academic Press.

Wolff, P. H. (1966). The natural history of crying and other vocalizations in early infancy. In B. M. Foss (Ed.), *Determinants of infant behavior* (Vol. 4, pp. 81–109). London: Methuen.

Wong-Fillmore, L. (1976). *The second time around: Cognitive and social strategies in second language acquisition.* Unpublished doctoral dissertation, Stanford University, Stanford CA.

Wood, G. (1983). *Cognitive psychology: A skills approach.* Monterey, CA: Brooks/Cole.

Woodworth, R. S., & Schlosberg, H. (1954). *Experimental psychology.* New York: Holt, Rinehart & Winston.

Wundt, W. (1912). *Volkerspsychologie,* 2Bd., Die Sprache, 2 Teil, 3 Aufl.

Yarbus, A. L. (1967). *Eye movements and vision.* New York: Plenum.

Yuille, J. C., & Steiger, J. H. (1982). Nonholistic processing in mental rotation: Some suggestive evidence. *Perception and Psychophysics, 31,*201–209.

Yussen, S. R., & Levy, V. M., Jr. (1975). Developmental changes in predicting one's own span of short-term memory. *Journal of Experimental Child Psychology, 19,* 502–508.

Zacks, R. T., Hasher, L., Sanft, H., & Rose, K. C. (1983). Encoding effort and recall: A cautionary note. *Journal of Experimental Psychology: Learning, Memory, and Cognition, 9,* 747–756.

Zechmeister, E. B., & Nyberg, S. E. (1982). *Human memory: An introduction to research and theory.* Monterey, CA: Brooks/Cole.

Zimler, J., & Keenan, J. M. (1983). Imagery in the congenitally blind: How visual are visual images? *Journal of Experimental Psychology: Learning, Memory, and Cognition, 9,* 269–282.

Glossary

ACT theory Anderson's theory of semantic memory and language.

Addressed phonology Postlexical phonology. Knowledge of pronunciation represented in a cognitive code produced after the specific word is recognized.

Affordance A combination of the properties of a substance and its surfaces taken with reference to an animal.

AI Artificial intelligence. A discipline that attempts to create software capable of executing actions thought to require intelligence when done by people.

Algorithm A procedure that specifies a correct solution to any particular example from a class of well-defined problems.

Allocation policy In capacity theories of attention, refers to the process of dividing cognitive resources among competing stimuli.

Analysis by synthesis model A general model of speech perception and pattern recognition that maintains that bottom-up processes suggest to top-down processes the information that should be filled in or internally computed.

Analytical engine The name for a computing machine designed by Charles Babbage in the nineteenth century.

Angular disparity The difference, in degrees, in the orientation of stimuli.

Anterograde amnesia A general inability to encode durable memories following a trauma.

Aphasia A general term designating a wide variety of language disorders.

Assembled phonology Prelexical phonology. A cognitive code that may amplify graphemic information useful in reading.

Attentuation theory A theory of attention that maintains that unattended-to stimuli are damped down but not completely screened out.

Automaticity The establishment of automatic processing on some specific cognitive task.

Automatic processes Cognitive processes that can be initiated and run off without the allocation of attentional resources.

Availability heuristic A rule of thumb used to make estimates of likelihoods based on their commonness or ease of computation.

Babbling Prelinguistic motor play and vocal experimentation characterized by the production of both vowels and consonants.

Babbling drift In infants, the tendency to restrict the production of linguistic sounds of those of the language they will eventually learn.

Backward masking The presentation of a visual stimulus that prevents the recognition of a previously presented stimulus.

Bartlett tradition An orientation in memory research concerned with qualitative changes in the contents of retrieved material.

Binary code A representation of information using strings of symbols that can take on either of two values.

Brain writing Refers to the position that new memories produce some physical change in the brain's structure.

Canalization Refers to the idea that the contents of our minds are influenced and bounded by our affordances.

Capacity The volume of cognitive codes capable of being retained by a memory store.

Caretaker speech A generic term for a wide variety of conventions adults adopt when speaking to children, consisting chiefly of changes in tone, simplified constructions, and limited vocabulary.

Categorical perception The perception of phonemes is either-or. When ambiguous sounds are presented, subjects "hear" them as being a member of one category or another, not as having features of two categories.

Chunking Refers to associated elements being retained in short-term storage.

Church-Turing thesis The foundation of AI. In its most basic form, this principle states that what is computable by humans is also computable by machines.

Cognitive capacity Refers to the number of cognitive processes or resources that can be brought to bear on sensory stimulation.

Cognitive codes Representations of physical energy by the nervous system that are potentially capable of entering our awareness.

Cognitive effort Refers to the number of cognitive processes allocated to a task, rather than the depth of such processing.

Cognitive maps Internal representations of spatial layouts.

Cognitive penetration Refers to the fact that people's general knowledge seems to influence their mental operations on images.

Cognitive resources Cognitive programs, or routines, that process sensory stimulation or elaborate existing cognitive codes.

Competence-performance distinction Linguistic competence refers to all the abstract linguistic knowledge we possess. Linguistic performance refers to the utterances we actually produce.

Compound bilingual An individual who learns two languages from the same people, in the same setting, or at the same time.

Comprehension The reception, analysis, and interpretation of an utterance.

Computer simulation The creation of software capable of executing actions in a way thought to mimic the cognitive processes of people.

Conceptual complexity Pauses in the stream of speech that seem to be associated with the translation of a thought into a linguistic code.

Conceptually driven processes (top-down processes) Cognitive processes involving feature abstraction and categorization that begin with expectations derived from context.

Conditional reasoning Logic problems involving the conditional, or "if-then" statement.

Conservative focusing A strategy useful in solving artificial concept attainment problems. It involves changing only a single element of an array and observing the outcome of the change.

Constituents Components of a sentence that can be arranged in a hierarchical structure. They loosely correspond to linguistic parts of speech.

Constructivist theory of perception A position that emphasizes the formation of prototypes and schemata used in recognition and categorization.

Context Information surrounding stimuli being recognized, categorized, or searched for.

Continuity theory A theory of language that maintains that speech developed from the apparently intentional cries of animals.

Control processes The information-processing theory of memory maintains that control processes transfer material from one storage to another.

Controlled processes Effortful cognitive processes that seem to require the allocation of attention to sustain them.

Coordinate bilingual An individual who learns two different languages in two different settings, from different speakers, or at different times.

Correlational world structure Refers to the notion that distinctive features are not randomly assigned to objects in the world. Rather, such features can be useful in predicting the appearance of other features.

Critical periods The belief that children are particularly sensitive to the regularities of phonology and syntax during the ages of two to fourteen. The acquisition of language is said to be qualitatively different and easier during this period.

Data-driven processes (bottom-up processes) Cognitive processes involving feature abstraction that begin with sensory stimulation.

Data-limited processes The processing of ambiguous stimuli is limited by the poverty of information that can be extracted from them. Performance decrements are produced by limitations in the stimuli.

Decay The loss of a cognitive code resulting from the passage of time.

Declarative knowledge Typically refers to factual, describable information whose organization is flexible and, to some extent, under our control.

Deep dyslexia The ability to read silently without being able to convert a graphemic code into a phonological one.

Deep-surface structure distinction The distinction between meaning and its expression in a wide variety of phrase structures.

Demand characteristics Subtle aspects of the experimental situation that provide the alert subject with clues about the desired findings or outcome.

Depth of processing The nature of encoding is controlled by the subject. Semantic coding involves deeper processing than acoustic coding, because more knowledge is required to produce a semantic code.

Depth of search In chess-playing programs, refers to the number of moves and responses considered consecutively from some base move.

Design features Refers to attempts to define language in terms of presumed necessary characteristics.

Dichotic listening Listening to two unrelated messages played over stereo headphones.

Direct access hypothesis The position that reading can be accomplished by transforming the graphemic code directly into a lexical one without any intervening phonological stage.

Direct theory of perception A position that emphasizes the ability of the perceiver to pick up sensory information as it truly exists in the world.

Disconfirming the consequent Refers to the application of modus tollens in conditional reasoning. If P implies Q, then the absence of Q implies the absence of P.

Discontinuity in thinking Refers to the Gestalt notion that problem solving could be accomplished by insight, a phenomenon that the Gestaltists believed was unrelated to prior cognitive effort.

Displacement All natural languages enable their possessor to refer to things that are distant in time or space.

Distinctive features Aspects of a stimulus that are not associated with other stimuli; characteristic features.

Domain-free problems Problems whose solutions do not require extensive expertise.

Dual code position A theory that asserts that some memories are stored in a visual format, while others are stored in a verbal format.

Echo Refers to the representation of acoustic events in the sensory register.

Ecological approach to visual perception A position that emphasizes the information about the world that can be seen by moving through it.

Ecological validity Refers to the trend in cognitive science to explain cognitive processes in everyday terms and to study mental processes in their "natural habitats."

Elaborative rehearsal Rehearsal whose objective is to meaningfully associate incoming stimuli with previously learned material.

Electrodermal responses Changes in the skin's electrical conductance, used as indicators of ongoing cognitive processing.

ELIZA A computer program capable of simulating Rogerian counseling. Its objective was to demonstrate that natural language processing could be computerized.

Encoding Transforming a stimulus into a format that can be retained by the cognitive system.

Encoding specificity At retrieval time, a cue will aid retrieval if the cue provides infor-

mation that was also processed during the encoding of the to-be-remembered material.

Epiphenomena In imagery, refers to the belief that images are simply by-products of the cognitive processes actually doing the computing.

Episodic memory Memories that are autobiographical, personal, and sensitive to the effects of context.

Equipotentiality As far as memory is concerned, all cortex areas seem to be equally important.

Etak Literally meaning "segment," the name of the navigation system used by the Puluwatans.

Expansions A form of linguistic response to a child in which the intended meaning of the child's utterances is reformulated in the standard and complete form by the caretaker.

Expertise Human knowledge or the representation of such knowledge in machines. In humans, such knowledge is acquired directly through experience.

Extralogical inferences Inferences that are based on a person's general knowledge of the world. Although outside the realm of formal reasoning, such inferences can be useful as heuristics.

Fan effect In ACT, the time required for activation to spread to associated nodes is inversely related to the number of associated nodes being activated.

Feature abstraction Refers to the cognitive processes that take complex stimuli and abstract—that is, draw out from them—their simplest components.

Feature detection theory A position that maintains that pattern recognition is accomplished by the abstraction and reassembly of specific aspects of sensory stimulation.

Filter theory A theory of attention that maintains that unattended-to stimuli are completely screened out.

Finite state grammar   An attempt to formulate grammatical knowledge in left-to-right rules that specify the transitions between words.

Focus gambling   A strategy used on artificial concept attainment tasks. It involves simultaneously changing more than one element of the problem array and then observing the outcome.

Formal reasoning   Refers to the use of logical inference rules that have been developed by logicians.

Framing   Refers to the influence of context on likelihood estimations.

Functional autoclitic   A Skinnerian term designating various frames that form the basis of syntactic regularity.

Functional significance   Refers to the notion that imagery is thought to be necessary to accomplish some tasks.

Fuzzy borders   Refers to the fact that people treat many natural categories as though they were ill defined. The borders of the concept shift according to the context in which the category member appears.

Gestalt psychology   A European movement emphasizing the primacy of construction in perception and problem solving.

GPS   The General Problem Solver, a computer program designed by Newell and Simon whose purpose was to show how general heuristics could solve a wide variety of problems.

Grammar   Our total linguistic knowledge, consisting of phonological, syntactical, and semantic components.

Grapheme   A letter or combination of letters that stands for a single phoneme.

Habituation   The tendency to cease responding to familiar, or extensively processed, stimuli.

Heuristic   A rule of thumb for solving problems or reasoning in everyday situations.

Higher-order invariances   Regularities in patterns of stimuli that are available to be seen as we move through the world or as elements in the world move around us.

Hippocampus   A large forebrain structure located between the thalamus and the cortex.

Höffding step   The step between sensation and perception. The conversion of a cognitive code representing a stimulus into a code that enables the categorization of the stimulus.

Holophrastic stage   About one year of age, the child begins to produce single words that seem to symbolize entire sentences.

Human factors research   A discipline that studies information processing by humans and machines in an attempt to find their optimal relationship.

Icon   Neisser's name for the visual contents of sensory storage.

Ill-defined problems   A problem is ill defined if the start or goal states are unclear, or if the operations required to change states are unspecified.

Incubation   Refers to the unconscious work done by problem solvers who have left off conscious solving of the problem.

Inferential intrusion errors   Recall failures produced by general knowledge of the world. These errors occur when general knowledge is used to logically infer what must have taken place when a particular memory cannot be retrieved.

Inflection   The process of adding linguistic markers to words to indicate plurality, possession, or case.

Information   As defined by Shannon, the function of information is to reduce the uncertainty of future events.

Information-processing approach   The metatheory of cognitive psychology that holds that mental events can be understood as complex cognitive codes that are often serially transformed.

Insight   A conscious experience consisting of a sudden awareness of the correct organization of a problem's elements.

Intelligence   Capabilities that seem to be reflected in the apparent purposiveness and goal orientation inferred from the behavior of humans and some animals. Intelligence can be represented as an organized amalgamation of cognitive structures and processes.

Intentionality Describes mental events that are the antecedents of certain actions and which perhaps play a causal role in producing those actions.

Interference In memory research, refers to the inability to retrieve material resulting from its confusion with other cognitive codes.

Intersection search In attempting to verify a relationship between two nodes in semantic memory, an intersection search fans out from both entry nodes until some path is found or until the search has verified that no common path exists.

Inter-stimulus interval In Sperling's study, the time interval between the offset of the stimulus and the onset of the cue to begin reporting.

Intrinsic characteristics The light reflected from an object carries with it information about the boundary characteristics and surface homogeneity of the object. These are the intrinsic characteristics.

Invariant features Information contained in the visual field that does not change regardless of our movement through it.

Isomorphism Formal equivalence. Usually used to describe the relationship between problems whose deep structure is the same, although their appearance, or surface structure, differs.

Knowledge-based approach In AI, refers to computer programs that attempt to mimic the heuristic search processes of humans in problem solving.

Landmarks Distinctive features of the urban environment that help city dwellers organize the city's geography.

Late selection A theory of attention that maintains that almost all incoming stimuli are sent to working memory before any screening out is done.

Layout of perceivable space Knowledge of the apparent alteration of the shapes of geometric objects in the visual field, acquired by motion.

Lexical uncertainty Refers to pauses in the stream of speech occurring just prior to the appearance of unusual words.

Linguistic universals Used in two senses: the boundaries of language and characteristics of language that all languages share.

Local-global distinction In problem solving, answering the question What to do next? involves local knowledge. Understanding the big picture—the problem's underlying structure—is global knowledge.

Logic Any one of a variety of systems of reasoning used to determine the validity of certain premises.

LOGIC THEORIST An early demonstration of AI's power, LOGIC THEORIST was a program capable of proving theorems from mathematical logic.

Long-term storage The information-processing theory of memory maintains that long-term storage is semantically organized and has an infinite capacity. Retrieval failures are produced by interference.

Maintenance rehearsal Rehearsal whose objective is simply to retain information in working memory. This rehearsal seems to be accompanied by subvocalization.

Mand function Skinner's term for the function of language referring to verbal operants reinforced through compliance.

Manner of articulation In uttering consonants, refers to the way in which the constriction is produced.

Mass action As far as memory is concerned, the brain seems to work en masse.

Mastermind A logical deduction game in which the problem solver must deduce the color and location of a string of hidden buttons using only the ambiguous feedback provided.

Mentalism A term used as a criticism by behaviorists for phenomena that seemed neither public nor reproducible.

Mental psychophysics An approach that studies the relationship between two experiences: looking at a physical object and scanning an image in the hopes of finding out how the cognitive system operates.

Mental rotation The creation and inspection of a rotating image.

Mental size The amount of mental space that seems to be taken up by an image.

Mental travel Usually involves imagining the motion of a tiny dot across some highly overlearned map.

Metamemory Personal knowledge about the operation of the memory system.

Metatheory A set of basic presumptions thought to operate in a general domain. A metatheory is a schematic plan for building specific theories in particular domains.

Mind's eye movements Refers to the scanning movements that seem to be responsible for the latencies in reaction times observed when subjects are asked to verify spatially distinct aspects of their images.

MLU The mean length of a child's utterance. Determined by counting the number of morphemes produced, then dividing the total by the number of separate utterances.

Modus ponens An in inference rule stating that if P implies Q is true, then the presence of P implies the presence of Q.

Modus tollens An inference rule stating that if P implies Q is true, then the absence of Q implies the absence of P.

Morpheme The basic unit of meaning.

Müller-Lyer illusion Refers to the famous "fins-out–fins-in" illusion. The length of the middle bar seems to vary as the direction of the fins is changed.

MYCIN An expert system that consults with physicians concerning the diagnosis and treatment of infectious diseases.

Natural categories Unlike the categories used in artificial concept tasks, everyday categories are ill defined, have fuzzy borders, and are sensitive to the effects of context.

Natural reasoning The study of human reasoning in lifelike situations involving the estimation of likelihoods.

Network models Theories of semantic memory that postulate a system of nodes and connections.

Operator A cognitive process that transforms one state of knowledge into another. Although a solver may access dozens of such states during the course of problem solving, the number of distinct operators is thought to be limited.

Optical flow pattern The arrangement of changing and invariant aspects of the visual field.

Overregularization A "smart error" in which a child treats an irregular noun or verb form as if it were regular. This indicates knowledge of general inflectional rules.

Overwriting A position that maintains that inferences made at retrieval wipe out previous encodings.

PARADISE A chess-playing program that uses knowledge-based search.

Parallel processing Refers to the simultaneous transformation of several different cognitive codes.

Partial-report technique Used by Sperling, a technique that involves cuing the subject to report only certain elements of an array.

Perceptual cycle Neisser's attempt to synthesize the direct and constructive viewpoints by conceiving of perception as an ongoing activity.

Phoneme A separable, identifiable unit of sound. Phonemes are the basic acoustic building blocks of spoken language.

Phonemic restoration effect A speech illusion that occurs when a nonspeech sound is substituted for a deleted phoneme. The listener usually fails to detect the deletion.

Phonetics The discipline that attempts to categorize speech sounds. There are two approaches. Articulatory phonetics focuses on the movements of the tongue, and acoustic phonetics deals with linguistic sounds as physical energy.

Phonology The discipline that attempts to express the regularities in linguistic sounds as being rule based and principled.

Phrase structure A hierarchical, abstract formula, written in terms of constituents that can be used to generate and analyze utterances.

Place of articulation In speech, refers to the point of constriction in producing consonants.

Power approach In AI research, power algorithms emphasize the computer's speed of computation to examine as many different search pathways as possible.

Pragmatics Knowledge of discourse.

Preattentive analysis An analysis of stimuli that may extract acoustic, phonetic, and possibly prior semantic information prior to the material's entry into awareness.

Prestored knowledge Knowledge of **isnota** links in semantic memory that limit the extent of search.

Primary component Refers to the first part of the serial position effect seen in free-recall studies—presumably the result of material retrieved from long-term storage.

Primitive act In conceptual dependency theory, complex verbs can be reduced to combinations of eleven basic, or primitive, actions.

Problems of arrangement In Greeno's classification, refers to problems in which the elements of the problem must be rearranged according to a specific criterion.

Problems of inducing structure In Greeno's classification, refers to problems in which a relationship must be discovered among the problem's components.

Problems of transformation In Greeno's classification, refers to problems in which a sequence of moves or alterations must be determined that changes the problem's initial state into the goal state.

Problem space A theoretical term that denotes the problem solver's internal representation of the problem.

Procedural knowledge Refers to knowledge that no longer enters awareness. Usually expressed as a skill.

Production Refers to the planning, lexical choice, and execution of speech.

Production deficiency A failure to use a memory strategy that one has the ability to execute.

Production rules Rules that can be used to guide intelligent actions. They have two parts. The state part lists conditions that might be observed in the world. The action part dictates the actions that should be taken if the conditions in the state part have been observed.

Productivity All natural languages permit their possessor to create novel utterances.

Propositional analysis Breaking down complex remarks into propositions, which are the smallest units of knowledge that can possess a truth value.

Propositional format Refers to the viewpoint that memories are stored in a cognitive code that is neither verbal nor visual.

Prototype The psychological center of a category; the most typical instance of a category.

Psycholinguistics The study of language from a psychological rather than from a linguistic perspective.

Recency component Refers to the second part of the serial position effect seen in free-recall studies—presumably the result of material retrieved from short-term storage.

Reception paradigm In artificial concept formation tasks, the reception paradigm describes situations in which the subject has no control over which exemplars will be examined.

Recursion   Complete linguistic structures can be embedded within others. This process can theoretically be continued indefinitely.

Reductionist viewpoint   A theoretical position that maintains that complex phenomena can be thought of as consisting of simpler, although qualitatively different, events.

Rehearsal   The two types of rehearsal are maintenance rehearsal, which keeps a cognitive code intact for limited periods, and elaborative rehearsal, which establishes contact with semantic memory.

Representation problem   To solve unfamiliar problems, a person must construct an internal representation of the problem. The difficulty involved in constructing such a representation is known as the representation problem.

Representativeness heuristic   A rule of thumb used in estimating likelihoods. It is based on a subjective computation of the person or event's similarity to a prototype.

Resource-limited processes   Demanding, or unpracticed, tasks that require the heavy allocation of cognitive resources. Performance decrements are produced by unavailability of additional resources.

Retinal image   The raw code produced by the retina sent to the brain for perceptual processing.

Retrieving   Cognitive processing that recovers or elaborates stored cognitive codes.

Retrograde amnesia   Retrieval failure involving material encoded just prior to the occurrence of a traumatic shock.

ROG-O-MATIC   An expert system that plays a quest game derived from Dungeons and Dragons.

Saccade   A rhythmic, ballistic eye motion used in reading.

SAM: Script Applier Mechanism, a computer program with knowledge of scripts that can answer questions by inferring what actions must have occurred.

Schema   A term that denotes what is essential in category membership and connotes a plan or expectation that can be used to receive or organize incoming stimulation.

Script   A general, context-free mental framework that can be used to organize particular sequences of common and familiar actions.

Second-order isomorphism   A position that maintains that the image preserves many of the characteristics of actual sensory stimulation, but in an abstract way.

Segment-and-label   An AI approach to computer vision that emphasizes bottom-up processes such as feature abstraction.

Selection paradigm   As used in artificial concept attainment tasks, refers to experimental procedures in which the subject picks the next exemplar in the series. The subject's choices indicate the nature of the strategy being used.

Selective attention   The capacity to focus cognitive processes on a narrow band of sensory stimulation.

Self-schema   A cognitive structure used to represent and assimilate information about the self.

Semantic memory   General, encyclopedic knowledge of the world and language.

Semantic priming   The activation of a word in semantic memory facilitates or primes the activation of subsequent, conceptually related words.

Semantics   Linguistic knowledge of meaning.

Sensory register   A storage location that retains an almost complete representation of sensory stimulation for a brief time.

Serial exhaustive search   Refers to a complete, one-at-a-time search of the elements in working memory.

Serial position effect   When a subject's memory is tested in a free-recall situation, initial and final items are more likely to be recalled than items presented in the middle of the list.

Serial processing Refers to the sequential transformation of a cognitive code.

Shadowing Reciting a message played over stereo headphones, as soon after hearing it as possible.

Short-term storage The information-processing theory of memory maintains that this storage is acoustically organized, has a limited capacity, and loses material through decay.

SHRDLU A computer program that could metaphorically move and answer questions about transformations in its blocks world.

Soundness A system of reasoning is sound if, given true premises, it always produces true conclusions. All formal logical systems have this property.

Specializations for languages Refers to certain features of the brain and larynx that may indicate innate predispositions for language ability.

Spreading activation model Retrieval from permanent memory can be thought of as activating elements in a semantic network.

State-action tree A method of representing move problems in which the problem states are shown as nodes, and the actions transforming successive states are shown as connecting lines.

State-dependent learning Retrieval is enhanced if the subjects are in roughly the same psychological state at both retrieval and encoding times.

Storage The capacity of the nervous system to retain cognitive codes.

Strategy A move, or probe designed to effect some change in the problem and provide information by so doing.

Structuralism A theoretical position that regards the mind as an organized set of decomposable mental acts.

Structural relationships Various sorts of underlying meanings, such as agent role, location, possession, and so on, that seem to be expressed by children in the holophrastic and two-word stages.

Syntax Linguistic knowledge of word order and inflections.

Tact function Skinner's term for the function of language referring to verbal operants cued by discriminative stimuli.

Task environment Theoretically, a neutral and complete representation of a problem that includes all possible problem spaces.

Template-matching theory A position that maintains that pattern recognition is accomplished by comparing incoming stimuli with a fixed mental model of an ideal pattern.

Texture gradient The orderly and gradual loss of surface detail and clarity as we scan the visual field from nearby to distant objects.

Thinking out loud Verbalizing the contents of working memory. A tape recording of the resulting utterances, known as a protocol, can be useful in analyzing a subject's problem solving.

TLC Teachable Language Comprehender, one of the earliest models of semantic memory.

Tower of Hanoi A transformation problem in which a stack of disks, situated on one of three pegs, must be transferred to another peg. Constraints limit the size of the disks that may rest on top of each other.

Truth In logic, refers to the reality of premises. An argument can be valid but untrue if the initial premises describe unreal situations.

Two-word stage A period in which the child typically produces utterances of two words. This period indicates the beginning of syntactical knowledge.

Type-token distinction The elements of semantic memory consist of nodes representing general categories (types) as well as specific examples of those categories (tokens).

Validity An argument is valid if, according to the principles of reasoning developed by logicians, a conclusion necessarily follows from certain premises.

Verbatim retrieval Retrieval of material in its original wording.

Visual angle of the mind's eye Refers to the width of the field of vision used when scanning images.

Voicing The degree to which the vocal cords are involved in the production of a consonant. Voiced consonants are those in which the buzzing of the vocal cords is detected.

Well-defined problems Those in which the start and goal states are clearly specified. A procedure that transforms the start state into the goal state must be at least potentially available.

Whole-report technique Sperling's original methodology involved asking his subjects to report as much information as they could retrieve following the brief presentation of visual stimuli.

Width of search In AI research, refers to algorithms that try to limit the number of different search pathways explored.

Word superiority effect Subjects are better at identifying a letter when it appears in the context of a word rather than when it appears by itself.

Zero-crossing detector A device that counts the number of times a waveform changes algebraic sign in a given period. Used in AI programs that recognize speech.

Name Index

A

Abelson, R.P., 154, 467, 468, 470, 472, 473, 474
Abramson, A., 294
Adams, F., 141
Adelson, E.H., 128
Adamopulos, J., 397
Aitchison, J., 264, 284, 291, 292, 304, 313, 325, 326
Alba, J., 177
Albus, J.S., 19, 499
Amgott-Kwan, T., 399
Anderson, J., 66, 134, 175, 176, 183, 196, 197, 201, 202, 205, 206, 207, 208, 210, 211, 218, 257, 258, 286, 387, 415, 454
Anderson, R., 83, 155, 178, 249
Anderson, W., 357
Anisfield, M., 176
Appel, A., 500
Aristotle, 13, 14
Armstrong, S., 404
Atkin, 489
Atkinson, R., 114, 120, 124, 125, 133, 138, 142
Austin, G., 391
Averbach, E., 118, 119
Azmitia, E., 135

B

Babbage, C., 460
Babich, F., 159
Baddeley, A., 126, 142, 148, 163, 169, 253, 359
Baker, L., 367
Ball, T., 243
Ballard, D.H., 499
Banks, W., 128, 256
Barber, P., 128
Barclay, C., 97
Bargh, J., 86
Barrow, H.G., 464
Bartlett, F.C., 83, 111, 170, 173, 177, 210, 211, 434, 474

Bassili, J., 97
Bayer, R., 241
Beauvois, M., 360
Beck, J., 499
Begg, I., 137, 164
Bellugi, U., 310, 312, 318, 319
Bentahila, A., 365
Benton, S., 175
Berian, R., 357
Berko, J., 311
Besner, D., 357, 359
Bever, T., 282, 284, 287
Bhavnani, K., 404
Bickerton, D., 327
Birnbaum, I., 148
Bjork, R., 147
Black, J.B., 156, 472, 474
Blank, M., 287
Blaxall, J., 359
Block, N., 249, 257, 258
Bloom, L., 302, 308, 309
Bloomfield, L., 275, 279
Blumstein, S., 342
Bobrow, D., 57
Boddy, J., 163
Boden, M.A., 482, 485, 499
Boies, S.J., 49, 51
Bomba, P., 81, 83
Bower, G.H., 148, 152, 156, 176, 218, 225, 288, 472, 474
Braine, M., 289, 290, 309
Brainerd, C., 327
Bramer, M., 493
Bransford, J., 108, 154, 155, 183
Broadbent, D.E., 16, 17, 38, 40, 41, 42, 43, 46, 69
Broca, P., 292, 293
Brooks, D.N., 163
Brooks, L.R., 84, 251, 252, 253
Brown, A., 215, 216, 327
Brown, C.M., 499
Brown, R., 307, 308, 309, 312
Brown, S.L., 454
Browne, D., 404

Bruce, V., 109
Bruner, J., 314, 315, 316, 391, 393, 395, 398, 406
Bubash, S., 159
Burns, H., 158
Burrows, D., 169
Butterfield, E.C., 30
Butters, N., 162, 163
Byrnes, D., 213
Byrne, R., 102, 103, 104, 106

C

Caelli, T., 108
Caharach, G., 56
Cairns, H.S., 286
Cairns, R.B., 316
Calfee, R., 168
Campione, J., 216
Cantril, H., 73
Caramazza, A., 403
Carey, P., 287
Carling, C., 296
Carpenter, P., 354, 367
Carter-Sobell, L., 147
Cavanaugh, J., 218
Cauraugh, J., 169
Cazden, C., 312
Ceci, S., 52
Celce-Murcia, M., 363
Cendrowska, J., 493
Cermak, L., 162
Chaffin, R., 211
Chapman, R., 301, 303
Charniak, E., 287
Chase, W.G., 168, 422, 423, 488
Cherry, E., 37, 38, 39, 40
Cherry, R., 42, 43
Chi, M., 412, 424, 443, 448, 451, 453
Chomsky, C., 313
Chomsky, N., 21, 22, 23, 264, 275, 279, 280, 281, 282, 286, 287, 290, 291, 295, 296, 318, 319, 326, 338, 341, 487

Chorover, S., 126, 127, 134
Christiaansen, R., 155
Clark, E., 276, 295, 300, 301, 302, 303, 326, 332, 334, 335, 366
Clark, H., 276, 295, 301, 302, 326, 332, 334, 335, 366
Clark, R., 302
Cochran, E., 256
Cohen, N., 183
Cole, M., 374
Coleridge, S., 418
Collins, A., 188, 190, 191, 192, 193, 194, 195, 203, 206
Coltheart, M., 128, 142, 353, 357
Condon, 489
Conrad, C., 192
Conrad, R., 124, 132
Cook, M., 109
Cooper, F., 342
Cooper, L., 229, 231, 232, 254
Coriell, A., 118, 119
Corkin, S., 183
Cornsweet, J., 63
Cornsweet, T., 63
Cosky, M., 356
Cox, J., 382, 383, 385
Craik, F., 125, 136, 137, 138, 140, 141, 142, 214
Cromer, R., 313
Crosby, C., 364
Cross, T., 317
Crowder, G., 117, 142
Crowder, R., 367
Cultice, J., 81
Curtiss, S., 297
Cutler, A., 349
Cutting, J., 97

D

Dale, M., 126
Dallenbach, K., 122
Daniels, S., 359
Danks, J., 286
Davelaar, E., 357
Davies, J., 359

Dawson, M., 51, 52
Deese, J., 122, 147, 151, 170, 366
DeGroot, A., 420, 421, 441, 487
DeJong, G., 281
DeMey, M., 499
Dennett, D.C., 159, 258, 497
Denny, J., 415
Deregowski, J., 78
DeRosa, D., 356
Derouesne, J., 360

Desiderio, D., 159
Deutsch, D., 43, 44, 45, 46
Deutsch, F., 43, 44, 45, 46
DeVilliers, J., 316, 326
DeVilliers, P., 316, 326
DeWald, C., 60
Dodwill, P., 108
Dominowski, R.L., 415, 431
Dooling, D., 154, 155
Downs, R., 101, 109
Dreyfus, H., 499
Dretske, F., 108
Drewnowski, A., 132, 133
Dumais, S., 69
Dunker, K., 417, 418

E

Ebbinghaus, H., 111
Ecob, J., 169
Egeth, H., 147, 151, 170
Eich, J., 148
Eifermann, R., 396
Eimas, P., 294, 295
Eisenstadt, M., 499
Ekstrand, B.R., 431
Elliot, J., 140
Ellis, H., 149
Elphick, M., 477
Ericksen, C.W., 358
Eriksen, B., 119
Eriksen, C., 119
Ericsson, K.A., 442
Evans, G., 104, 105
Eylon, B., 447
Eysenck, M.C., 149
Eysenck, M.W., 149

F

Falmagne, R., 406
Faulconer, B., 249
Farmer, R., 333
Feng, C., 233, 234, 235
Fikes, R.E., 461
Fillenbaum, S., 365
Finke, R., 242
Fischoff, D., 388
Fiske, A.D., 141
Fiske, S.T., 83, 85, 87, 109
Flagg, P., 364
Flavell, J., 213, 214, 218, 316
Flexser, A.J., 151, 152
Fodor, J., 282, 287, 296, 496
Fong, G., 86
Ford, H., 178
Foss, D., 195, 211, 287, 333
Foucault, M., Preface
Franks, J., 183

Freud, S., 372
Fried, L., 81, 83
Fromkin, V., 28, 297, 348
Fulgosi, A., 413

G

Gagne, E.D., 178, 361, 454
Galanter, E., 18
Galvan, L., 159
Garbo, G., 263
Gardiner, J., 152
Gardner, A., 321, 322, 325
Gardner, B., 321, 322, 325
Garner, W., 60
Garrett, M.F., 28, 282, 286, 287, 348, 349, 351, 352, 366
Garrett, C., 149
Gelman, R., 301
Genie, 297, 320
Geschwind, N., 293
Geyer, L., 60
Ghiselin, B., 413
Gibson, E., 59, 63
Gibson, J.J., 90, 92, 94, 95, 96, 97, 98, 99, 108, 109
Gilliam, B., 78
Gilligan, S., 148
Gillin, J., 148
Gilmartin, K., 422
Gladwin, T., 106, 109
Glaser, R., 415, 424, 427, 443, 448, 453
Gleitman, H., 317, 404
Gleitman, L., 317, 404
Glenberg, A.M., 141, 147, 148
Glover, J., 175
Glucksberg, S., 192, 286
Godden, D., 148
Gold, M., 290
Goldin-Meadow, S., 301
Goldman-Eisler, F., 350, 351
Goldstein, E., 98, 108
Goldstein, I., 488
Goodglass, H., 367
Goodnow, J., 391
Gray, C., 259
Gray, W., 141, 142
Green, D., 357
Green, P., 109
Greene, T., 424
Greenfield, P., 306
Greeno, J., 425, 427, 431
Gregory, R., 78
Griggs, R., 382, 383, 385
Gruendel, J., 314
Guilford, J., 413
Gummerman, K., 259

H

Haber, R., 118, 128, 131, 258
Hakes, D., 287, 333
Hall, W., 327
Halle, M., 338, 341, 347
Halliday, D., 449, 450
Halpern, D., 454
Hamey, L., 500
Hampson, P., 258
Hampson, S., 109
Hand, D.J., 461
Hannigan, J., 183, 184, 185, 187
Harding, R., 413
Hart, P.E., 461
Harwood, J., 183, 211
Hasher, L., 53, 149, 162, 177
Haugeland, J., 499
Havelka, J., 364
Hayes, J.R., 443, 444, 454
Hayes-Roth, F., 499
Hecht, B., 300, 302, 326
Heft, H., 98
Heil, J., 98, 256
Heinz, S., 45, 46, 47, 48, 49
Henle, M., 373, 374
Herrmann, D.J., 183, 212
Hertel, P., 149
Hildreth, E.C., 464
Hilgard, E., 288
Hinsley, D.A., 443
Hintzman, D., 124, 125
Hirst, W., 56
H.M., 161, 162, 163, 169
Hobbes, T., 493
Hoch, S.J., 383, 385
Hockett, C., 265, 270, 317, 318, 319
Hoffding, H., 74, 75
Hofstadter, D.R., 480, 485, 494, 499
Holding, D., 142
Hollan, J., 218
Holyoak, K., 81, 83
Homa, D., 81, 100
Hood, P, 302, 309
Hope, B., 499
Horn, B.K.P.: 467
Horton, D., 133, 135, 142, 152, 183
Howard, D.V., 84, 185, 331, 373
Hull, C., 84
Hulse, S., 147, 151, 170
Humphrey, G., 15
Humphreys, M.S., 152
Hunt, M., 415, 454
Hunt, R., 140
Huppert, F., 162

Huttenlocher, J., 301
Hyde, T., 137, 149

I

Ittelson, W., 73
Izard, C., 97

J

Jacobson, A., 159
Jacobson, A.L., 159
Jacobson, G., 500
Jacoby, L., 137, 141, 142
James, W., 372
Jeffries, R., 430
Jenkins, J., 122, 137, 147, 149
Jenrick, R., 415
Jespersen, O., 305
Jinich, D., 135
Johnson, C., 129, 143, 302
Johnson, E., 396, 397, 398
Johnson, M., 154, 155
Johnson, P.B., 431
Johnson-Laird, P., 212, 380, 381, 382, 385, 406
Johnston, W., 45, 46, 47, 48, 49
Jonasson, J., 357
Jones, J., 149
Jones, R., 90, 108
Jones, R.K., 367
Jonides, J., 250
Juszczyk, P., 294
Just, M., 354, 367

K

Kahn, R., 250
Kahneman, D., 47, 48, 51, 56, 69, 386, 387, 388, 389, 397
Kalat, J.W., 367
Kamerman, J., 286
Kaplan, R., 109
Kaplan, S. 109
Karat, J., 430
Katona, G., 416, 418
Kaufman, R., 122
Keele, S., 80
Keenan, J., 251
Keller, H., 155, 156
Kelley, M., 315, 316
Kellogg, R.T., 442
Kennedy, A., 367
Keppel, G., 134
Kerr, N., 250
Kihlstrom, J., 183
Kimble, D., 162
Kimble, R., 162
King, B.J., 9, 25, 27
Kintsch, W., 30, 196
Kirk, R., 284

Klapp, S., 357
Klatzky, R., 115, 120, 145, 150, 177, 183, 185, 217
Klenbart, I., 176
Koffka, K., 412
Kohler, W., 412
Kolb, B., 296
Kolers, P., 128, 258
Kolodner, J., 218
Koppel, S., 69
Kosslyn, S., 236, 237, 238, 239, 240, 241, 242, 243, 244, 245, 246, 247, 248, 258
Kozlowski, L., 97
Krashen, S., 297
Kruger, B., 42, 43
Kuczaj, S., 327
Kuhn, T.S., 31
Kulpe, O., 15, 224
Kunen, S., 83

L

Lachman, J.L., 30
Lachman, R., 30, 154
Lachner, J., 284
Lambert, W., 364, 365
Lange, R., 397
Langer, P., 149
Lashley, K., 160, 161
Laughlin, P., 397, 398
Lave, J., 30
Lawton, S., 215
Legrenzi, M., 381
Legrenzi, P., 381
Lehmkuhle, s., 101, 255
Lehnert, W., 470
Lenat, D.B., 499
Lenneberg, E., 267, 305, 318, 320, 327
Leonard, J., 150, 151
Lettvin, J.Y., 65
Levy, V., 215
Levy-Bruhl, L., 374
Lewis, J., 43
Lewis, S.S., 357
Lichtenstein, S., 388
Liberman, A.M., 342
Lieberman, P., 253, 346, 347
Light, L., 147
Lightbown, L., 302, 309
Lincoln, A., 7
Lindsay, P, 63, 65, 66, 69
Linn, R., 327
Lisker, L., 294
Lloyd, B., 407
Lockhart, R., 125, 136, 138, 142
Loftus, E., 157, 158, 164, 177, 187, 193, 194, 195, 203, 204, 205, 206

Loftus, G., 129, 143, 164
Long, G., 117, 129
Lovelace, A., 460
Lowe, D., 47
Lowes, J., 418
Lucariello, G., 169
Luria, A., 258
Lynch, K., 102

M

Mace, W., 94
MacKay, D., 44, 47, 286
Mackey, W., 363
Macnamara, J., 363
Mair, W., 161
Malmstrom, F., 242
Mandler, J.M., 177, 499
Mar, H., 149
Marcel, A.J., 69
Markus, H., 85, 86
Marcus, S., 376, 377, 379, 385
Marmor, G., 250
Marr, D., 98, 108, 464, 467
Marshall, J.C., 360
Martin, R., 403
Marvin, L., 268
Matlin, M., 9, 36
Maturana, H., 65
Maudlin, M., 500
May, J., 67
Mayer, R.E., 382
Mayes, A., 162, 163
McAdam, D.W., 367
McCallum, M., 149
McCloskey, M., 129, 130, 183, 192
McConkie, G., 354, 355, 356
McConnell, J., 159
McCulloch, W., 65
McDowall, J., 162
McEvoy, C., 140
McEwen, B., 135
McKoon, G., 175, 183
McLaren, R., 499
McLaughlin, B., 363, 366
McNeill, D., 290, 306
Medin, D., 396, 406
Mehler, J., 287, 296
Meltzoff, A., 305
Merikle, P., 128
Mervis, C., 401
Metz, O., 345
Metzler, J., 225, 227, 228, 229, 232, 254, 256
Meudell, P., 162, 163
Meyer, D., 29, 195, 210
Meyers, D., 387

Mill, J., 372
Miller, D., 158
Miller, G., 18, 30, 114, 125, 271, 272, 339, 340, 341
Miller, R., 135
Mills, C., 133, 135, 142, 152, 183
Milner, B., 161, 162
Mishkin, M., 161
Mitchell, D., 243, 244, 246
Mitterer, J., 47
Moar, 104
Montague, W., 178, 358
Montgomery, K., 163
Montiero, K., 148
Moore, M., 305
Moore, T., 296
Moray, N., 37, 40
Morgan, J., 280
Morris, P., 258
Morton, J., 117
Mowbray, G., 38, 39
Moyer, R., 241
Mulholland, T., 427
Murdock, B., 122, 125, 126, 132, 133
Murray, H., 415

N

Nagy, W., 327
Nathan, P., 126
Naus, M., 162
Neisser, U., 4, 5, 6, 23, 24, 29, 38, 56, 60, 61, 65, 83, 98, 100, 101, 108, 117, 128, 131, 177, 250, 258
Nelson, D., 140, 141
Nelson, K., 306, 309, 314
Newcombe, F., 360
Newell, A., 71, 419, 428, 433, 434, 435, 436, 441, 442, 443, 454, 461, 462
Newport, E., 317
Newton, I., 448
Nicely, P., 339, 340, 341
Nigro, G., 342
Nillson, N.J., 461
Nim Chimpsky, 323, 324, 325
Nisbett, R.E., 441
Noble, E., 148
Norman, D.A., 43, 44, 57, 63, 65, 67, 69, 114, 462
Nyberg, S., 125, 129

O

Oakley, D., 216
Obusek, C., 333, 346
Okada, R., 169

Olson, J., 286
Orne, M., 158, 246
O'Shea, T., 499
Overton, D., 148
Owens, J., 156, 157

P

Palermo, D., 108
Palmer, J., 157, 158, 187, 255, 257, 258
Pomerantz, J., 258
Palmere, M., 175
Papert, S., 488
Parker, E., 148
Parkin, A., 136
Parr, W., 159
Patterson, K., 359, 360, 361, 366
Paulson, R., 175, 176
Pavio, A.U., 247, 248
Pavlov, I., 10, 160
Pellegrino, J., 426, 427
Penfield, W., 161
Penner, B., 424
Perlmutter, M., 206, 218
Petersik, J., 77
Peterson, L., 121, 133, 134
Peterson, M., 121, 133, 134
Pezdek, K., 104, 105
Phillips, L., 123, 124
Piaget, J., 406
Pichert, J., 155
Pick, A., 256
Pick, M., 256
Pickett, J., 345, 347
Pidcock, 103
Piercy, M., 162
Pinker, S., 290
Pinsky, S.D., 367
Pisoni, D., 342, 343, 366
Pitts, W., 65
Plato, 13
Podgorny, P., 254, 258
Poincare, H., 415, 416
Pollack, I., 345
Pollack, M., 358
Polson, P.G., 30, 430
Posner, M., 49, 51, 69, 80, 81, 84
Post, T., 424
Postman, L., 123, 124, 141, 142
Potter, M., 249
Premack, D., 322
Pressley, M., 327
Pribram, K., 18
Pritchard, R., 63, 65
Proffit, D., 97
Purcell, D., 67
Pylyshyn, Z., 256, 257, 258

Q

Quartermain, D., 135
Quillian, M., 188, 190, 191, 192

R

Raeburn, V., 169
Raphael, B., 482
Ratcliff, F., 63
Ratcliff, R., 183
Rayner, K., 354, 355, 356
Reale, L., 162
Reaves, C., 56
Reber, A., 84
Reed, E., 90, 108
Rees, E., 448, 453
Reicher, G., 67
Reif, F., 447
Reiser, B., 278
Reitman, W., 423
Remez, R., 342, 366
Rescorla, L., 301
Reynolds, A., 364
Reznick, J., 243, 244
Reznick, R., 449, 450
Richardson, J.T., 431
Richardson, K., 404
Richman, C., 243, 244, 245, 246
Ricks, D., 304
Riggs, L., 63
Rigler, D., 297
Rigler, M., 297
Rips, L., 191, 192, 211, 218, 376, 377, 379, 385
Robertson, L., 255
Robinson, E., 327
Rock, I., 108
Rogers, C., 478, 479
Rogoff, B., 30
Ronning, R.R., 175, 431
Rosch, E., 84, 399, 401, 402, 403, 404, 406
Rose, K., 149
Rosenbloom, P.S., 70
Rosenfeld, A., 499
Rosenfield, D.B., 367
Ross, B., 183
Rothko, M., 223
Rozin, P., 250
Rubenstein, H., 357
Rubenstein, M., 357
Rumelhart, D., 67
Rundus, D., 136
Russell, W., 126

S

Saarinen, T., 102
Sabol, M., 356

Sachs, J., 173, 175, 176, 199, 210
Sakitt, B., 129
Sankoff, G., 327
Santee, J., 183
Sanft, H., 149
Sarah, 322, 323, 326
Sawusch, J., 343
Schank, R.C., 154, 467, 468, 470, 472, 473, 474
Schell, A., 51, 52
Schiavetti, N., 345
Schiller, P., 126, 127, 134
Schlosberg, H., 241
Schneider, A., 135
Schneider, W., 53, 54, 55, 56, 66, 141, 168
Schumacher, R., 363
Schvaneveldt, R., 29, 195, 210
Schwartz, B., 67
Scoville, W., 161
Scribner, S., 374
Seamon, J., 141
Searle, J.R., 495, 496
Segui, J., 287
Selfridge, J.A., 275
Selfridge, O., 61, 63
Seligman, M., 301
Sentis, K., 86
Shallice, T., 357
Shankweiler, D., 342
Shannon, 17
Shaughnessy, J., 216
Shaw, J.C., 433, 441
Shaw, R., 97, 108
Sheikh, A., 258
Shelton, T., 183
Shepard, R., 225, 227, 228, 229, 231, 232, 233, 234, 235, 250, 254, 256, 258, 340
Shiffrin, R., 53, 54, 55, 56, 66, 69, 114, 120, 124, 125, 133, 138, 142, 168
Shimamura, A., 129, 143
Shoben, E., 183, 191, 192, 211, 218
Shortliffe, E., 491
Shulman, H., 132
Silveira, J., 413, 414
Simon, E., 214
Simon, H.A., 25, 415, 419, 421, 422, 428, 433, 434, 435, 436, 441, 442, 443, 444, 454, 461, 462, 488
Simon, P.A., 436
Simpson, P., 168
Siple, P., 67
Siqueland, E., 81, 83, 294

Sitler, R., 345
Skinner, B.F., 20, 21, 23, 288, 289
Slack, J.M., 463
Slate, 489
Slobin, D., 302
Slovic, P., 388
Smiley, S., 215, 216
Smith, E., 183, 191, 192, 194, 211, 218, 396, 406
Smith, J., 306
Smith, S., 147
Smith, T., 287
Snoddy, G.S., 70
Snyder, C., 69
Sokal, R.R., 399
Solman, R., 67
Spector, A., 67
Spelke, E., 56
Sperling, S., 116, 117, 118, 128, 131, 135
Spiro, R., 155, 178
Spoehr, K., 101, 255
Springer, A., 135
Sproat, R., 327
Staats, A., 289
Stanovich, K., 67
Statlender, S., 342
Staudenmayer, H., 379
Stea, D., 101, 109
Steiger, J., 256
Stengel, C., 263
Sternberg, R.J., 184, 218, 411, 454
Sternberg, S., 165, 166, 168, 218
Stevens, K., 1347
Stillman, R., 148
Stromeyer, C., 258, 259
Struhsaker, T., 264
Studdert-Kennedy, M., 342
Sulin, R., 155
Swinney, D.A., 287

T

Tartter, V., 342
Tate, D., 159
Taylor, S., 83, 85, 87, 109
Tenenbaum, J.M., 464
Terrace, H., 324, 325
Thomkins, B., 141, 142
Thompson, D., 151
Thompson, 489
Thomson, J., 301
Thorndike, P., 153, 154
Thorpe, W., 267
Tolman, E., 103
Toole, T., 169

Treisman, A., 40, 41, 42, 43, 44, 45, 46, 69
Tschirgi, J.E., 383, 385
Tulving, E., 140, 142, 151, 152, 182, 185
Turner, T.J., 472, 474
Turvey, M., 97, 128, 131
Tversky, A., 386, 387, 388, 389, 397
Tyler, J., 135
Tyler, S., 149, 424

U

Ullman, S., 73, 108
Underwood, B., 134
Unger, G., 159

V

Vallacher, R., 109
Valsiner, J., 316
Van Duyne, P.C., 383
Vigorito, J., 294
Vihman, M., 363, 366
Virostek, S., 141
von Frisch, K., 268
von Glaserfeld, E., 315, 316
von Neuman, J., 17
von Senden, M., 89
Vosburgh, R., 81, 100
Voss, J., 424, 425

W

Wagner, S., 497
Walker, E., 52
Walker, N., 149

Wallas, G., 412, 413
Walter, M.L., 454
Waltz, D., 62, 63, 69
Warren, R.M., 333, 346
Warren, R.P., 333, 346
Warrington, E., 161, 162, 163
Washoe, 321, 322, 323, 325
Wason, P.C., 379, 380, 381, 385, 406
Watanbe, I., 44
Waterman, D.A., 499
Watkins, M., 129, 130, 136, 138, 151, 152
Watson, J., 160
Watson, M., 399
Waugh, N., 114
Weber, J., 242
Wegner, D., 109
Weimer, W., 74, 108
Weingartner, H., 148
Weinrich, V., 363
Weir, R., 305
Weiskrantz, L., 161, 162, 163
Weizenbaum, J., 478, 480
Wellman, H., 213, 214, 218
Wells, G., 317
Welsh, C., 302
Wernicke, C., 293
Wertheimer, M., 412, 454
Wescourt, K., 183
Wessells, M., 151
Wetherick, N., 396
Wexler, K., 212, 218
Wheeler, D., 67
Whishaw, I., 297

White, M.J., 31
Whitney, P., 83
Whitten, W., 150, 151
Wickelgren, W.A., 124, 131, 418, 436, 438, 439
Wickens, C.D., 138, 389
Wickens, D.D., 146
Wiener, N., 17
Wilkins, D., 489
Wilks, Y., 463
Willows, D.M., 359
Wilson, R., 162
Wilson, T.D., 441
Wilton, R., 103
Wingfield, A., 168, 213
Winograd, T., 482, 486
Witken, A.P., 464
Wolff, D., 294
Wong-Fillmore, L., 364
Wood, G., 353
Woodworth, R., 241
Worthen, D., 216
Wundt, W., 14, 15, 16

Y

Yarbus, A., 77
Yengo, L., 424
Yuille, J., 256
Yussen, S., 215

Z

Zaback, L., 250
Zacks, R., 53, 149, 162
Zechmeister, E., 125, 129
Zimler, J., 251

Subject Index

ACT theory, 196-214, 218
  assumptions of ACT theory, 202-204, 212
Affordance, 95-97, 106
Afterimages, 129
Algorithms, 432, 487
Allocation policy, 48-49
Amnesis, 13
Analogies, 426-427
Aphasia, 292-293 (*see also* Language)
Arousal, 48
Artificial concept formation, 391, 397, 399, 406
  conjunctive concepts, 391, 393, 395, 397
  disjunctive concepts, 391
  strategies in, 393-399
Artificial intelligence (AI), 62, 369
  contributions to cognition, 493-498
  history of, 460-461
  metatheory of, 462
  model building in, 463-464
  theory development in, 461
Artificial knowledge, 472, 486-488
Artificial vision, 464-467
Associationism, 74
Attention, 9-11, 15, 25, 36-37, 46-47, 51-53, 57, 68-69, 162
  definition of attention, 36-37
  preattentive analysis, 38-39, 43, 46
  selective attention, 36-37, 42-43, 47
Attenuation theory, 41-43
Auditory channel, 38, 43
Autoclitic frames, 288-289
Automaticity, 53-57, 69, 168
Awareness, 36-37, 88-89, 443

B

Backward masking, 119, 143
Bartlett tradition, 170-173, 474
Behaviorism, 16, 19-23
Bottleneck theories, 38, 43, 46-47, 51, 56
Bottom-up processing, 343-344, 346-347, 362-366, 464
Brain writing, 159

Broca's area, 292-293 (*see also* Language)
Brute force approach, 488-489

C

Canalization of mentality, 97, 498
Capacity models of attention, 47-52, 53, 56
Capacity of sensory register, 127
Capacity of short-term memory, 125, 131, 134
Capacity of long-term memory, 127, 131
Categorical perception of speech sounds, 293-295
Categorization, 443, 447, 448-453
Chess, 487-490
Chunking, 125, 127, 134
Clause boundary, 285-287
Cognitive code, 5-6, 10-11, 24-25, 27, 57, 114-115, 128, 131, 135, 247, 248, 249
  acoustic code, 126, 133-135
  depth of code, 136-141
  dual-code position, 240, 247-249, 254
  elaboration of, 5
  reconstruction of, 6
  reduction of, 5
  semantic code, 126, 133-135
Cognitive economy, 188, 192
Cognitive effort, 149-150
Cognitive mapping, 101-108
Comparing mental images, 235, 241
Computers, 18, 19, 24, 459-460
Concept attainment, 390-391, 404
Conceptual dependency theory, 468-472
Constituent analysis of utterences, 276-279
Conservative focusing, 394-395, 398 (*see also* Artificial concepts, strategies in,)
Constructive processes, 170
Constructivist position, 74-76, 78-79, 83-89, 95, 98, 101, 108
Context, 30, 66-68, 146-148, 150-151, 163, 177, 182, 187, 345, 467
Contexual generalization, 289-290

Continuity theory, 264-265
Control processes, 114
Creativity, 415-418, 453

D

Deep structure, 279, 282, 284-287, 451
Definition of cognitive psychology, 3
Depth/width of search, 488-490
Design features, 265-270
Detection device, 38-41
Dichotic listening, 37, 41
Direct access hypothesis, 357-361
Direct theory, 75, 90-95, 97-98, 146
Displacement (as design feature), 267-268
Distortion of prototypes, 80-81, 100
Domain of knowledge, 442-443, 448-453
Domain free problems, 422-423, 436, 441

E

Echo, 117
Ecological approach (see Direct theory)
Ecological validity, 30
ELIZA, 478-482
Encoding, 146-159, 162, 169, 170, 185-185, 196, 201, 214, 426
   encoding specificity principle, 150-153
Equipotentiality, 161
Expertise, 447-453, 490-491, 498-499

F

Fan effect, 207-210
Feature analysis, 59-61, 63, 65-66, 69
   feature abstraction, 83-84, 403-404
   feature detection, 63, 65
Feedback, 17-18
Filter theory, 37, 43
   selective filter, 37-40
Focusing mental effort, 36
Forgetting mechanisms:
   decay in short-term memory, 114, 121-127, 133-134
   interference in long-term memory, 114, 121-127, 133
Formal reasoning, 12, 30, 371-372, 375-385
   conditional reasoning, 375-379
   errors in reasoning, 373-385, 386-389
Free recall, 122-124, 138-140
Functional significance of imagery, 248-254

G

Gestalt position on problem solving, 411, 412-422, 453-454
Goal-directed backward chaining rules, 492

Grammer, 22-23, 263, 271-282, 284, 287, 289-290, 295, 297
   finite state grammar, 271-275, 477
   knowledge of grammar, 21-23
   transformational grammar, 279-281

H

Habituation, 81-83
Heuristic, 386-389, 406, 432-433, 436-441, 443, 447
   means-ends analysis, 428, 441
   subgoal analysis, 436-439
   working backword, 439-441
Higher order invariance, 92
Höffding step, 74-75, 98
Human factors engineering, 16
Human-machine interaction, 16-19

I

Icon, 117-119, 128-131, 135
Ill-defined problems (see Problem solving)
Illusions, 76-78, 95, 129
   Müller-Lyer illusion, 76-78
Imagery, 12, 14, 101, 103, 107, 224-225
   folding mental paper, 233-235
   looking at mental images, 233-240
Inferential processes, 390
Information, 16-17
Information processing, 23-28, 46-47, 52, 77-79, 85, 98, 99, 100, 108, 113-115, 117, 127, 131, 135, 296, 369, 411, 423, 433
Insight, 413, 415-418
Introspection, 14-16, 19
Intrusion errors, 156, 163
   script-based errors, 157, 173
   prior learning errors, 163
Invariant features, 92

K

Knowledge, 6-10, 15, 19, 23, 27-29, 77, 84, 88, 103, 194, 196, 200, 202
   declarative knowledge, 7-9, 25, 27
   organization of knowledge, 19
   procedural knowledge, 6-10, 15, 25, 27, 52

L

Language, 12, 19, 20
   acquisition of, 274-275, 278, 281-282, 287-290
   anatomical aspects of, 291-292
   bilingualism, 362-365
   brain specializations of, 291-293
   breathing specializations in, 291-292

Language—cont'd
  caretaker speech effects, 313-314, 316-317
  chimp research in, 321-326
  comprehension of, 300-303, 321, 323
  critical period in, 319-320, 326
  inflections in, 310-312, 314
  innate knowledge of, 282, 288
  in animals, 320
  among the deaf, 317-319
  and thought, 362
  organization of, 20
  overregularization in, 299, 311-312, 319
  predispositions in, 319
  production of, 300-303, 321, 324
  sign language, 318-319, 321, 324
  stages of language development, 303-313
  word order in, 310
Language perception by machine, 475-487
  natural language recognition, 477-487
Late selection theory, 43-44, 46
Levels of processing, 136-141, 149
Limited capacity, 38
Linguistics, 19, 20, 270
Linguistic universals, 271, 282
Logic, 12, 13, 371-385, 405
  rules of logic, 375-376, 380, 381, 385, 405

M

Mass action, 161
Meaning, 37-38
Memory, 8, 12, 15-16, 25, 30, 81, 147-150, 155, 158-160, 162-163, 416, 418, 421-422, 434, 442-443
  episodic memory, 182-185, 187-188, 199-202
  long-term storage, 114-115, 122-124, 126-127, 131, 133, 135, 142, 156, 165 (*see also* Permanent memory)
  memory span, 215
  metamemory, 213-217
  permanent memory, 25, 44
  semantic memory, 182-202, 211, 218, 387-388, 427, 433, 443, 474
  sensory register (*see* Sensory storage)
  sensory storage, 38-39, 67, 114, 116-117, 124, 127, 131, 135, 142
  short-term storage, 114-115, 119-126, 131-134, 142, 162, 165-169 (*see also* Working memory)
Mental events, 13-16, 23-24
Mental psychophysics, 240-242
Mental rotation, 225-233, 247, 250, 254-256

Mental rotation—cont'd
  mental rotation of abstract shapes, 225-229, 233
  mental rotation of letters, 229-233
Mental travel, 242-246
Minds and programs, 495-498
MYCIN, 491-493, 498

N

Natural categories, 399-406
  centrality, 399-402
  internal structure, 402
Natural reasoning, 385-391
  availability, 387-388
  framing decisions, 388-389
  probability, 389
  representativeness, 386-387, 389
Network models, 185-188, 193, 197, 210-213
Neuropsychological effects and changes in memory, 126-127, 134-135, 160-161 (*see also* Retrograde amnesia)
Node, 186-190, 193-195, 200-204, 211, 214, 433-434

O

Operant analysis of language, 288-291
Optical flow pattern, 90-93, 98
Overflow phenomenon, 242, 247

P

PARADISE, 489-490, 498
Parallel processing, 166
Partial report technique, 116-117, 128
Partist strategy, 393-394 (*see also* Artificial concepts, strategies in,)
Patterns of errors, 28-29
Pattern recognition, 11-13, 57-68, 118-119
Perception, 131, 421, 453
Phoneme detection, 286-287
Phrase structures, 275-279, 322-323
Physical symbol system, 462
Power approach, 488
Practice, 52-53
Predicting a machine's behavior, 497
Primacy effect, 122, 124
Primitive actions, 468-470
Primitive sensory and motor processes, 201-202
Problem solving, 13, 30, 487-488, 498
  definition of problem solving, 412
  general strategies, 422-423, 432, 441
  problems of arrangement, 431-432
  problems of inducing structure, 426-427
  problems of transformations, 427-431, 444

Problem solving—cont'd
  tactics for problem solving, 432, 442
  types of problems, 423-425, 432
Problem space, 433-346, 441
Processing effects, 138
Processing mechanisms, 94
Production rules, 490
Propositions, 196-202, 207, 248-249
Prototypes, 79-84, 88, 100, 122, 386, 399
  abstraction of prototypes, 80-81, 83-87
Puluwatans, 106-108

R

Reaction times to complex stimuli, 28-29
Reading, 353-362
Recall, 151-154, 156-157 (*see also* Free recall)
Recency effect, 122, 124, 138
Recognition task, 151-153, 162
Reductionist view, 494-495, 499
Rehearsal, 114, 117, 121, 127, 138-140, 217
  maintenance (Type 1), 138-140, 141
  elaborative (Type 2), 138-140, 141, 162
Reinforcement, 20-22
Retinal image, 94, 97
Retrieval, 114-116, 118-119, 122, 151, 153-154, 157, 162-163, 165, 173-177, 184-185, 188, 210-211, 214, 216, 247
  retrieval in long-term memory, 122, 169-170, 176
  retrieval in short-term memory, 121-122
  retrieval in working memory, 165-169
Retrograde amnesia, 126-127, 134
Robots, 461
Roots of cognitive psychology, 13-16
Rote repetition, 217

S

SAM, 470, 495
Scanning effect, 243-246, 251-253
Scanning strategy, 393-394 (*see also* Artificial concepts, strategies in,)
Schemas, 83, 85-88, 98-101, 369
  aschematic, 86
  self-schemes, 85-88
  subject retrieval errors, 170-173
Schematic knowledge, 442-443, 451
Script, 154, 156, 314-315, 467-474, 499
Segmentation problem, 475, 477
Self-talk, 8-9
Semantics, 40-46, 49, 56 (*see also* Semantic memory)
Semantic priming, 195-196, 206, 210
Sensation, 74-75
Sensory mechanisms, 74
Serial exhaustive search, 168-169

Serial self-terminating search, 166-168
Servo-mechanism, 16-18
Set, 415
Shadowing technique, 37, 40-41, 43-44, 52
SHRDLU, 482-487
Social cognition, 85
Soundness, 372-373
Spatial cognition, 102, 104
Spatial layout, 95, 103
Speech comprehension:
  grapheme in speech comprehension, 353, 356-359
Speech perception: 332-333
  acoustics in speech perception, 332-333, 341-342
  analysis by synthesis in speech perception, 346-347
  articulatory phonetics, 334-337, 341
  categorizing speech sounds, 333-338
  context-independent features, 342
  distinctive features in speech, 337-338
  isolated speech sounds, 339-341
  perception of continuous speech, 345
  phonemic restoration effect, 346
  phonetics in speech perception, 332-337, 341-342, 344
  phonological level, need for, 341-343
  stages of speech perception, 343-345
  stream of speech, 332-333
Speech production, 347-353
  conceptual complexity of, 350-351
  errors in, 348-349
  latencies in, 347, 350-351
  lexical uncertainty in, 350-351
  models of, 351-353
Speech recognition by machine, 475-477
Spreading activation model, 193-195
State-action space, 487-490
State dependent learning, 148
State-matrix notation, 444
Stimulus control, 22-23
Storage, 159, 161, 163-165, 173, 185, 213, 217, 247-249 (*see also* Memory)
Structural importance, 215-216
Structural relationships, 308-310
Structuralism, 14-15
Surface structure, 279, 282, 284, 286-287, 451
Syntax, 308, 314, 322-324, 326

T

Task environment, 433, 441
TLC, 188-193, 196-197, 210
Template matching theory, 57-59
Texture gradient, 94-95, 98
Thinking:
  incubation effect, 413-415
  productive thinking, 416

Thinking—cont'd
  reproductive thinking, 416
  stages of, 412-413, 453
Thought, 15
  computational view of, 493-494
Top-down processing, 147, 345-347, 362,
    366, 498
Topics of cognitive psychology, 10-13
TOTE units, 18
Transformation of sensory input, 4, 24-
    25
Truth, 372, 378-379, 390 (*see also* Logic)
Type-token distinction, 187-188, 201, 211

U
Understanding, 418-419, 433, 441

V
Validity, 372-373, 375, 378-379 (*see also*
    Logic)
Visual channel, 38, 43

W
Well-defined problems (*see* Problem solv-
    ing)
Wernicke's area, 293 (*see also* Language)
Whole report technique, 116, 118, 128
Wholist strategy, 393-394 (*see also* Arti-
    ficial concepts, strategies in,)

Z
Zero crossing indicator, 475-477